SILENCE, CONFESSIONS AND IMPROPERLY OBTAINED EVIDENCE

Silence, Confessions and Improperly Obtained Evidence

PETER MIRFIELD

CLARENDON PRESS · OXFORD

This book has been printed digitally and produced in a standard specification in order to ensure its continuing availability

OXFORD
UNIVERSITY PRESS

Great Clarendon Street, Oxford OX2 6DP

Oxford University Press is a department of the University of Oxford.
It furthers the University's objective of excellence in research, scholarship,
and education by publishing worldwide in

Oxford New York

Auckland Bangkok Buenos Aires Cape Town Chennai
Dar es Salaam Delhi Hong Kong Istanbul Karachi Kolkata
Kuala Lumpur Madrid Melbourne Mexico City Mumbai Nairobi
São Paulo Shanghai Taipei Tokyo Toronto

Oxford is a registered trade mark of Oxford University Press
in the UK and in certain other countries

Published in the United States
by Oxford University Press Inc., New York

Reprinted 2003

ISBN 0-19- 826269-8

Cover illustration: ' And when did you last see your Father ? ', 1878 by
W. F. Yeames , Board of Trustees of the National Museums and Galleries on Merseyside
(Walker Art gallery, Liverpool).

General Editor's Introduction

This book explores the effects of pre-trial interactions between police and suspects on the admissibility of evidence at trial. To what extent does admissibility depend on the way in which real evidence or a confession was obtained, or on the suspect's approach to answering or not answering the investigator's questions? To what extent, if at all, should the admissibility of evidence at trial be affected by those earlier events? These questions of criminal justice are of considerable constitutional significance, and in this study Peter Mirfield presents a detailed analysis of the relevant English law, examined in the context of the various rationales for excluding evidence, of the European Convention of Human Rights and its jurisprudence, and of the approaches adopted in other jurisdictions. This scholarly monograph should serve as a fine resource for appellate court arguments and law reform initiatives, as well as a treasury for teachers and students.

Andrew Ashworth

Preface

When my book *Confessions* was published in 1985, it was, I believe, the first monograph concerned with that topic in English law since Joy's *The Admissibility of Confessions and the Challenge of Jurors* (1842). Things have moved on at a great pace since 1985. Indeed, a major work for practitioners, *Confession Evidence*, by Wolchover and Heaton-Armstrong, was published in 1996.

Since 1985, a vast amount of case law has added flesh to the bare bones of sections 76 and 78 of the Police and Criminal Evidence Act 1984. However, in the case of section 78, a great deal of the authority concerns the exclusion of non-confessional evidence. Twelve years ago, it seemed rational to divide off confessions from the rest, but, in my view, that no longer holds. So this new book is concerned no less with real and other non-confessional evidence than with confessions. The reader will find that the two chapters dealing with the exclusionary discretion, Chapters 6 and 7, do not attempt to divide that matter according to whether or not the evidence is confessional. Of course, where there is a need to draw the distinction for purposes of explanation or elucidation, I have acted accordingly.

I deliberately left out of my earlier work the law relating to the effect of maintaining silence in the face of police questioning. The important recent changes to that law effected by sections 34, 36 and 37 of the Criminal Justice and Public Order Act 1994 have convinced me that one should now think of the suspect's possible responses to police interrogation as all of a piece, so Chapter 9 is principally concerned with silence in the police station.

As in 1985, I have included a significant amount of comparative material, this time in my final chapter, Chapter 12. No comparativist myself, I offer here my apology for the errors which I have no doubt made. The matters which are the concern of this work have agitated lawyers and judges throughout the common law world. The questions which they have posed and the solutions which they have offered ought to provide the English lawyer with food for thought. In addition, the jurisprudence of the European Convention on Human Rights has already had a very significant effect upon the way English lawyers think about self-incrimination. Should the present Government get its way, the Convention will soon be made part of English domestic law. It seems certain that there will then be a need for even more detailed attention to Article 6 and the cases about it, especially given that there is a very real tension between the direction in which the Court and Commission are taking the Article and the direction in which our law of police interrogation has been going in recent years.

Many people have assisted me with the preparation of this work, some more directly than others. My colleagues teaching Evidence here in Oxford, Professor

Colin Tapper, Dr Katharine Grevling and Mr Roderick Bagshaw, have all contributed to my thoughts about the subject-matter. My pupils, over many years, doing the B.C.L. course have been a great source of fresh intellectual interest. More specifically, Professor Andrew Ashworth has been, as so often in the past, a great encouragement to me, willingly offering his helpful comments whenever asked. Dr Michael Byers, of my own College, helped me greatly with Chapter 11. There may well be others too, for my own memory has considerable limitations. My thanks to all of them are accompanied by the usual absolution from blame for my remaining errors.

From the Oxford University Press, I had unstinting support throughout, but I would particularly like to single out Richard Hart and John Whelan, both of whom have now moved on to other things, for their enthusiasm for my project. As in 1985, the book is considerably longer than I had initially proposed, and I am grateful to the Press for their tolerance of my "breach" of contract.

I have attempted to state the law as at May 31, 1997, though I have been able to add some material at page proof stage. My gratefulness for receipt of a copy of the opinions of the House of Lords in *Myers* the day after they had been handed down (on July 24, 1997) was somewhat tinged by my regret at being unable to do justice to this important case.

Peter Mirfield
Jesus College
Oxford

July 31, 1997

Contents

Table of Cases

Table of Statutes

STATUTORY INSTRUMENTS

CONVENTIONS

1

Introduction

Scope of the Book

In what follows are gathered together three topics in the law of evidence which might once have been considered separately but which are now so interwoven that such an approach seems no longer eligible. They are the law relating to confessions, the law concerned with unlawfully or unfairly obtained evidence, and that concerned with the evidential effects of the accused's silence when questioned by the police.

It was by reason of a comparatively recent set of events that the first two topics became interrelated. Before the decision of the House of Lords in *Sang*,[1] there already existed a well-established exclusionary rule for confessions obtained by threats, promises, or oppression, together with an exclusionary discretion for cases where rules laid down by the judges and others to govern police questioning had been breached.[2] As regards non-confession evidence, by contrast, there were but a collection of post-Second World War *dicta* recognizing, in principle, a judicial discretion to exclude such evidence where obtained unfairly and two briefly-reported Court of Criminal Appeal cases in which the trial judge's decision not to exercise that discretion in favour of exclusion had been overturned.[3] Then, in *Sang* itself, Lord Diplock offered an explanation of these various judicial statements which tied the judicial discretion firmly to the law relating to confessions. In his words, the discretion is one to exclude 'evidence tantamount to a self-incriminatory admission which was obtained from the defendant after the offence had been committed, by means which would justify a judge in excluding an actual confession which had the like self-incriminating effect.'[4]

Though there were doubts whether or not the rest of their Lordships accepted that the discretion was available only in cases where the analogy with confessions was present,[5] the enactment of section 78(1) of the Police and Criminal Evidence Act 1984 ('the 1984 Act') has proved to have had the effect of welding firmly together the discretions for confession and non-confession cases. This result was

[1] [1980] AC 402.

[2] See, finally, the Judges' Rules and Administrative Directions 1964, as detailed in H.O. Circular No 31/1964.

[3] *Court* [1962] Crim.LR687; *Payne* [1963] 1 WLR 637.

[4] [1980] AC 402, at 436.

[5] This point is considered, at Ch. 6, text to nn. 51–67 below.

brought about rather by accident. The subsection was introduced into the Bill by the Government at a very late stage of the parliamentary process in order to head off the much more radical amendment which had been moved by Lord Scarman at both the committee and report stages in the House of Lords.[6] The Scarman amendment had the form of a reverse onus exclusionary rule for evidence which had been obtained improperly, but it explicitly excluded confessions from its ambit. Section 78(1) contains no such exclusion, but simply allows the court to exclude evidence where its admission would have such an adverse effect on the fairness of the proceedings that it ought not to be admitted. As we shall see, the subsection has been interpreted by the courts as being no less applicable to confessions than to non-confession evidence.[7] It follows, of course, that the same test for exclusion applies to both kinds of evidence. Though the application of that test has proved to have rather different effects according to the nature of the evidence in question, the case law relating to section 78(1) provides a necessarily unifying feature.

More recently, the enactment of sections 34, 36, and 37 of the Criminal Justice and Public Order Act 1994, by altering the evidential significance properly to be attached to the suspect's failure to respond to or deal with incriminating questions or facts put to him by police officers, has added a further dimension to the process of interrogation in the police station. So, the failure of the accused to mention, at that stage, facts which he later relies upon at the trial has a potentially incriminating effect under section 34. It would seem artificial to deal in this work with the law relating to the evidential consequences of one kind of response to police questioning but not with that relating to another kind of (non-)response. Once again, the section 78(1) discretion provides a formally unifying feature, in that it is quite clear that an incriminatory 'silence' may be excluded thereunder.[8]

The Issues

Though we may properly emphasize the inter-connections between the three topics with which this book is concerned, it is no less important to be aware of the differences between the legal régimes applicable to the three. Only in the case of confessions does an exclusionary *rule* apply. That rule has two branches to it. Under section 76(2) of the 1984 Act, an incriminating statement is to be excluded where either obtained by oppression or obtained in consequence of something said or done which was, in the circumstances existing at the time, likely to render it unreliable.[9] But a statement which escapes exclusion under section 76(2) may still be excluded as a matter of discretion, either under section 78(1) or under the

[6] See HL Debs., vol. 454, cols. 931–2 (11 July 1984) and HL Debs., vol. 455, cols. 427 and 653 (26 July 1984).

[7] See Ch. 6, text to nn. 69 and 70 below.

[8] See Ch. 9, text to nn. 190–7 below.

[9] The formulation in the text is merely intended as a guide. For a definitive treatment of the rule, see Ch. 5, below.

common law as preserved by section 82(3) of the same Act. Just as the rule contains what may broadly be described as a misconduct head and an unreliability head, so do the two discretionary powers seem, in practice, to allow both for exclusion on the basis of the improper or unfair treatment of the accused by the police and for exclusion of unreliable evidence.

It is quite common for the defence to argue, in the same case, both for exclusion of the incriminating statement under the rule and for its exclusion as a matter of discretion. However, it is very important to realize, at the outset, that the rule and the discretion differ in their juridical nature, as well as in their specific content. From the point of view of the trial judge, the exercise in which he engages is of the same kind whether it be the rule or the discretion which has been invoked. Was the confession brought about by oppression? Would its admission in evidence jeopardize the fairness of the proceedings? Though these are complex, value-loaded questions, the judge can no more say that he finds that fairness would be jeopardized yet will, as a matter of discretion, allow that jeopardy to be created than that he finds the confession to have been produced by oppression yet fail to exclude it. It is at appeal level that the juridical difference can be appreciated. Whilst allowing an appropriate degree of sovereignty to the trial judge over issues of fact, the appeal court retains the ultimate responsibility of deciding whether or not the conduct which led the accused to confess was oppressive. It cannot say that, though it would, for its own part, have found that conduct to be oppressive, it refuses to overturn the trial judge's assessment. It is quite different with exclusion as a matter of discretion. The appeal court may, perfectly properly, disagree with the judge on, say, the issue of the effect on fairness of the proceedings, but go on to uphold him on the basis that his assessment was not wholly unreasonable or perverse and did take account of all relevant factors.

A third possible issue, with regard to confessions, is limited to cases involving accused who are mentally handicapped. Under section 77 of the 1984 Act, the issue is one not of exclusion but of whether or not an appropriate warning to the jury of a special need for caution is required, or, in the case of summary trial, in effect an appropriate self-direction. The mentally handicapped are but one kind of vulnerable suspect, and section 77 addresses but one aspect of the special problems associated with the questioning of members of that group. A separate chapter is devoted to the broader issues concerning vulnerable suspects who are in custody—the mentally ill and juveniles, as well as the mentally handicapped.

In the case of non-confession evidence, there is neither an exclusionary rule nor any special warning requirement to be invoked. The sole potential issue for judicial consideration is whether or not to exclude the evidence as a matter of discretion. Therefore, the element of first-instance sovereignty over the decision is emphasized, though, as has already been pointed out, that sovereignty is not one to decide perversely.

The straightforward picture of exclusion of non-confession evidence just presented is complicated somewhat by a recent development as a matter of judicial legislation. In *Latif and Shahzad*,[10] the House of Lords extended the burgeoning power of the judge to stay criminal proceedings as an abuse of the process of the court to cases of alleged entrapment of the accused to which the section 78(1) discretion also applies. The exact limits of that decision remain to be worked out, but there are *dicta* of Lord Steyn[11] which seem to be quite capable of comprehending use of the power in cases other than ones involving entrapment. That said, it is important to stress the difference between the exclusion of an *item of evidence* under section 78(1) and the staying of a *cause of action* for abuse of process. The latter is, in principle, a much more extreme step, though the practical effect of excluding evidence may quite often be to deny the prosecution the whole of its case against the accused.

As will appear in the course of this book, there is no shortage of authority on sections 76 to 78 of the 1984 Act. Cases concerned with adverse inferences from silence in the police station began to emerge only towards the end of 1996, so treatment of sections 34, 36, and 37 of the 1994 Act will necessarily be more skeletal at this stage. However, it may be remarked now that there seem to be, essentially, three major issues. First, are the facts of the case such that an adverse inference may, under the terms of one of those three sections, permissibly be drawn? Secondly, if so, what is the proper nature and strength of that inference? Thirdly, were the circumstances in which the accused was relevantly silent such as to render the proceedings unfair, in terms of section 78(1) of the 1984 Act, if that silence were to be used against him?

Though much of what has been said so far has assumed that the relevant issues arise in the context of the jury trial, it must not be forgotten that the evidential principles with which we are concerned apply, as a matter of substance, equally to trials in the magistrates' court. Where the principles in question require or permit exclusion of evidence by the court, there are, inevitably, special problems attached to the situation in which the same body must both rule on the exclusion issue and weigh the evidence, should it decide to admit it. The problem is, of course, a general one, not restricted to the subject-matter of this book. However, detailed consideration of the procedural issues arising for magistrates in our area of interest is to be found in Chapter 2.

Broader Considerations

Though the principal focus will be upon the domestic law of England relating to the three topics, there is much else to be said. The jurisprudence of the European Convention on Human Rights, in as far as it recognizes a right to silence under Article 6(1), is of direct significance for domestic law because the English courts seem to be increasingly willing to have regard to treaty obligations in interpreting that law and, in particular, to have regard to Convention jurisprudence.

[10] [1996] 1 WLR 104. [11] *Ibid*. 112–13.

However, in addition, the domestic criminal trial of Mr Ernest Saunders in relation to matters arising from the takeover of Distillers Plc by Guiness Plc has had repercussions of a highly significant kind for the European Commission of Human Rights and the European Court of Human Rights.[12] It is, at the very least, a source of embarrassment, and perhaps more than that, when English rules, made by Parliament, allowing for the compulsory questioning of suspects and others are found not to pass muster under the Convention. It remains possible that the more general provisions of sections 34, 36, and 37 of the 1994 Act will, at least in respect of their effects in some cases, be found equally wanting. Therefore, the Convention jurisprudence will be given brief consideration in its own right, as well as for its actual and potential influence upon domestic law. One should, of course, note that the Labour Government which was elected in May 1997 has announced plans to make the Convention itself part of domestic law.

During the last thirty-odd years, the treatment of confessions and unlawfully or unfairly obtained evidence have been matters of anxious concern no less in other common law jurisdictions than in England itself. Approaches to those basic issues have been strikingly different in the United States, as well as in some of the various countries of the Commonwealth. This is not a comparative treatise, but one may hope to learn more about one's own system from exactly how similar matters are dealt with elsewhere. Not of least interest is the question whether or not, at least in some circumstances, a warning to the jury of the dangers of unreliability attached to confession evidence ought to be required.

However, before attempting to survey the detail at home and the differences elsewhere, one must first ask what principle or principles underlie or, at least, inform the exclusionary authority. It is to that task that attention must now be turned.

[12] (1994) 18 EHRR CD 23 (Commission); (1997) 23 EHRR 313 (Court).

2

The Principles Behind Exclusion

Introduction

English courts, at least in criminal cases, and probably more widely, are inclined to reason pragmatically, rather than by reference to theory or principle.[1] So it is hardly surprising that the judges have been reluctant to articulate what principle or principles lie behind the various rules and discretionary powers governing confessions, unlawfully or unfairly obtained evidence, or the right to silence in the police station. A good example of this reluctance is *DPP* v. *Ping Lin*.[2] The House of Lords was called upon to stake out the limits of the mature exclusionary rule at common law for confessions, yet the four Law Lords who delivered speeches refused to disclose whether, in their view, the rule was based upon what is described as the 'reliability principle' or upon what is known as the 'disciplinary principle'. Indeed, Lord Scarman specifically stated that this 'is possibly an important philosophical question but for present purposes it is only of academic interest'.[3] There is, then, some irony in the fact that the House's decision in that case entailed implicit rejection of the disciplinary principle.[4]

This is not, of course, a necessary feature of the authorities. There are cases in which courts have been prepared to indicate what principle lies or principles lie behind the law. A good example is the speech of Lord Diplock in *Sang*,[5] which contains a very clear, express endorsement of the principle *nemo debet prodere se ipsum* as governing exclusion of confession evidence and exclusion of unlawfully or unfairly obtained evidence, and an equally clear and express rejection of the disciplinary principle.[6] In several other cases, courts have gone out of their way to reject the disciplinary principle.[7] Furthermore, it must not be supposed that, because no explicit statement of underlying principle is to be found in the case, there is equally no implicit assumption of what is or are the appropriate governing principle or principles. Judges may prefer not to box themselves in for future cases by articulating principle in the present one.

[1] Professor P. S. Atiyah delivered his Hamlyn lectures in 1987 on this very point—see *Pragmatism and Theory in English Law* (1987), *passim*.

[2] [1976] AC 574. [3] *Ibid*. 607. [4] See P. Mirfield, *Confessions* (1985), 119–20.

[5] [1980] AC 402. [6] *Ibid*. 436.

[7] See, e.g., *Mason* [1988] 1 WLR 139; *Oliphant* [1992] Crim.LR 40; *Christou and Wright* [1992] QB 979; *Hughes* [1994] 1 WLR 876. See Ch. 6, text to nn. 128–32 below.

The Reliability Principle

It was in *Warickshall*[8] that a reason for the exclusionary rule for confessions was first articulated. Confessions forced from the suspect by the flattery of hope or the torture of fear were to be excluded because they came in a questionable shape and were undeserving of credit. Such a 'reliability principle' would inevitably appeal to evidence specialists, for it is a central concern of the law of evidence to ensure that, at the least, the trier of fact is made aware of factors indicating that a given item of evidence may be unreliable and, sometimes, that such evidence is not adduced at all.

Confessions, Unlawfully or Unfairly Obtained Evidence, Silence—and Reliability

We should, at once, be aware of an important difference between testimonial evidence and real evidence, so far as reliability is concerned. The question for the decision of the court in *Warickshall* was whether or not the stolen goods which had been found in Jane Warickshall's bed were to be excluded as evidence. They clearly were incapable of suffering from the same infirmity as did the confession which led to their discovery. As it was put in *Warickshall* itself, 'a fact, if it exist at all, must exist invariably in the same manner whether the confession from which it derived be in other respects true or false'.[9] In other words, the reliability of real evidence is unaffected by the manner of its acquisition; it speaks for itself. A confession from the accused or, for that matter, testimonial evidence from any other person is subject to all the potential inaccuracies which flow from the human capacity for error and dissimulation. As regards documents, the crucial question, for these purposes, would seem to be whether or not a human being has played a part in their composition such that that capacity may have been exercised.

One should beware of making too much of the distinction so clearly drawn in *Warickshall*. Thus, there may be occasions where, though a human being has been involved in the relevant way, the circumstances are such as to satisfy us that there is no real, as opposed to fanciful, danger of unreliability. Say that documents recording the numbers stamped into the cylinder blocks of cars by particular employees were to be, in some way or other, obtained unlawfully by the police.[10] Putting to one side any hearsay objections, were there to be cogent evidence of the accuracy of the system, it is difficult to see how one could be doubtful about the reliability of those documents, for there would be no reason for the employee to make misleading records and the evidence of system would relieve us of our fear of error.

More surprisingly, perhaps, it is not always the case that there can properly be sufficient confidence in the reliability of real evidence. For example, in

[8] (1783) 1 Leach CC 263, 168 ER 234. [9] *Ibid.* 264.
[10] The example is suggested by *Myers* v. *DPP* [1965] AC 1001.

Sokialious,[11] the prosecution sought to rebut the accused's statement to the police that he was not a drug dealer, nor even someone who took drugs, by evidence of the discovery of a quantity of cocaine inside a holdall in his hotel room. Though the drugs certainly spoke for themselves, it was argued that they were not reliable as rebuttal evidence, in that the accused alleged that one of his co-accused had 'planted' them. This was dealt with as a matter of judicial direction in the particular case, but the important point which remains is that the probative force or reliability of real evidence is always a function of what it is being used to prove.

However, the more specific point of *Warickshall* may seem to have more complete force. The stolen goods were not made unreliable *by* any impropriety in the way Jane Warickshall had been led to reveal their whereabouts. Even if she had been tortured, their cogency would have been the same. Yet, not even this point about causation is absolute. Though it went unacknowledged in the case itself, *Kuruma*[12] provides us with a good example. Under Kenyan emergency legislation, the police were granted certain powers to stop and search persons, but only where the officers involved were of the rank of assistant inspector or above. The search of Kuruma had been illegal because the officers involved were both below that rank. The prosecution alleged that two rounds of ammunition had been found in Kuruma's possessions, but he flatly denied that allegation. Whether he said so expressly or not, he must have been saying, in effect, that the ammunition had been 'planted'. It seems highly likely that the requirement of rank was designed to ensure that evidence would not be 'planted' on suspects. Hence, there would seem to have been a strong argument, in terms of unreliability, for exclusion of the evidence. Any such unreliability would indeed have followed from the illegality of the search.[13]

More difficult still may seem to be the question of applicability of the reliability principle in respect of the adverse inference from silence in the face of police questioning which sections 34, 36, and 37 of the Criminal Justice and Public Order Act 1994 ('the 1994 Act') now allow, in certain circumstances, to be drawn. If one accepts the oft-repeated argument that only the guilty take advantage of the possibility of refusing to answer police questions,[14] it might be thought to follow that no silence could be unreliable. In fact, very few, if any, advocates of that kind of argument would adopt such an all-embracing position. The Criminal Law Revision Committee, which first recommended in 1972 the changes eventually made in 1994, took no such position and expressly acknowledged that '[o]bviously there may be reasons for silence consistent with innocence'.[15] This

[11] [1993] Crim.LR 872.

[12] [1955] AC 197. See also *King* v. *The Queen* [1969] 1 AC 304.

[13] The argument related in the text seems first to have been put forward by Franck (1955) 33 *Can.Bar.Rev.* 721, at 730. See also Heydon [1973] Crim.LR 603, at 607 and Morisette (1983–4) 29 *McGill LJ* 521, at 549–50.

[14] This argument is considered in detail, at Ch. 9, text to nn 73–7 below.

[15] *Eleventh Report*, Cmnd. 4991, June 1972, para. 35.

possibility may be catered for by the fact that the 1994 Act provisions permit only *proper* adverse inferences, so that no inference should be drawn in such a case. However, it can certainly be argued that some kinds of police (mis)behaviour are capable of leading to the suspect's silence being used against him unreliably in a way which ought to result in its exclusion, as a matter of discretion, under section 78(1) of the 1984 Act. For example, an accused might claim that he did not, in fact, maintain silence, but that he told the police his side of the story during the course of an interview which they improperly failed to record. Were there to be such a breach of the rules, that breach might well be thought to render it unfair to draw any adverse inference from the 'unreliable silence'.[16] Other examples may be imagined. If a mentally disordered or handicapped suspect were to be denied access to a solicitor and not to be provided with an 'appropriate adult' at his interview, his failure to mention something later relied on at trial might, because unadvised, be entirely unreliable as adverse evidence. This is, of course, separate and apart from the question whether or not other elements of trial unfairness, quite unrelated to issues of reliability, might flow from adverse use of silence as evidence in the particular case.

Reliability Principle as Paramount or Exclusive?

Some writers on evidence have seen the reliability principle as not merely the central concern of the law of evidence in this area, but as its *exclusive* concern. Bentham is often regarded as having considered what he described as 'rectitude of decision' to be of overriding importance throughout the law of evidence, so that other policies extraneous to accuracy of decision-making were to be eschewed.[17] In fact, this is an over-simplified view of Bentham's approach, which allowed for exclusion because of delay, vexation, or expense in some limited contexts,[18] but he was certainly no friend of the principles, other than the reliability principle, to which reference will be made later in this Chapter. Wigmore certainly did insist that the sole proper basis for exclusion of confessions was their unreliability. Thus, he stated positively: '[t]he principle upon which a confession is treated as sometimes inadmissible is that *under certain conditions it becomes untrustworthy as testimony*.'[19] A couple of pages later, in a section headed 'Other Theories not sanctioned', he went on to dismiss the ideas that a confession might be excluded because of any breach of confidence or good faith which might thereby be involved, or because of any illegality in the method of obtaining it or the speaker's situation at the time of making it, or because of any connection with the privilege against self-incrimination.[20]

[16] See Dennis [1995] Crim.LR 4, at 14. And see Fenwick [1995] Crim.LR 132.

[17] See *A Treatise on Judicial Evidence* (ed. Dumont, 1825), *passim*.

[18] For a stimulating view of the complexity of what Bentham really thought about these matters, see Lewis [1990] *CLP* 135. See also Twining, *Theories of Evidence: Bentham and Wigmore* (1985), 88–100.

[19] *Evidence* (3rd. edn. 1940), iii, § 822, 246 (emphasis in original).

[20] *Ibid.* 248–9.

Wigmore was even more dismissive of concerns other than reliability as regards illegally obtained evidence. In his words: 'it has long been established that the *admissibility of evidence is not affected by the illegality of the means through which the party has been enabled to obtain the evidence*'.[21] He went on to condemn *Weeks* v. *US*,[22] the precursor of the exclusionary rule for evidence obtained in breach of the Fourth Amendment right not to be subjected to unreasonable search or seizure,[23] as having had an 'heretical influence' in spreading and evoking 'a contagion of sentimentality'.[24]

The greater strength of the condemnation offered by Wigmore here should not be found surprising, for, though, as we have seen, there *are* cases, like *Kuruma*, where the reliability of real evidence is adversely affected by the unlawfulness of its obtaining, such cases are unusual. In the most typical case, the real or other evidence in question will be wholly reliable, so that the cost of excluding it for some reason extrinsic to rectitude of decision-making will, other things being equal, be obvious and significant. Of course, if the conduct which led to its being obtained was particularly egregious, such that one of those extrinsic reasons applied with very great force, not all would accept the soundness of the result of Wigmore's unbending approach. In the case of confessions, rectitude of decision-making and extrinsic reasons are very much less likely to be in opposition. So, if we imagine that the egregious conduct in question were to be the torturing of a suspect and that he confessed in consequence, the two factors would very probably march together, for that which gave us extrinsic reason to exclude might well also cast the gravest of doubt upon reliability.[25]

Sources of Unreliability

We must now focus our attention on the possible sources of unreliability for confessions and other evidence subject to a real risk of human error or dissimulation. At least for the lawyer steeped in the common law treatment of confessions, the most obvious source of unreliability is the presence of a threat or promise held out to the accused. If the police threatened the accused with violence or promised him a pardon, we may suppose that even a person of ordinary fortitude might succumb to the temptation to confess untruthfully. As the apparent level of temptation involved becomes less, the character of the particular suspect seems to bear more largely on the question. Other circumstances become relevant or more significant. Was the suspect in familiar surroundings or at the police station? Did he have a lawyer present to advise and support him? Was he surrounded by family and friends, or only by police officers?

[21] N. 19 above, viii, § 2183, 5 (emphasis in original). A good example of an English commentator with views similar to those of Wigmore is Andrews—see [1963] Crim.LR 15 and 77.

[22] 232 US 383 (1914).

[23] That rule was later announced in *Mapp* v. *Ohio*, 367 US 643 (1961).

[24] N. 19 above, § 2184, 32.

[25] For a recent judicial acknowledgement of this point, see *Cooke* [1995] 1 Cr.App.R 318, at 328G.

Of course, a confession may be rendered unreliable by police conduct which does not involve the making of a threat or giving of a promise. A suspect kept without rest or refreshment for substantial periods of time and questioned persistently throughout those periods may well, we may tend to assume, attempt to escape from his predicament by giving the police what they want. He may persuade himself that the untruthfulness of his confession will be manifest to all in the end. The oppression head of the English exclusionary rule is capable of being seen as some recognition of the reality of his dilemma.

Furthermore, the interrogation techniques employed by the police in order to persuade a reluctant suspect to confess may themselves be such as to cast a cloud over the reliability of any confession eventually made, whether or not they constitute oppression in law. This is not the place for a detailed treatment of these techniques,[26] many of which are proposed and promoted by a number of interrogation manuals published in the United States. It suffices to refer briefly to the leading such manual, that of Inbau, Reid, and Buckley,[27] in order to get the flavour of the recommended techniques. If and when the interrogator feels reasonably sure of the suspect's guilt, he should begin by expressing confidence in that guilt, stressing that the evidence, even if in fact there is little or none, points unequivocally at him. Where he concludes that the suspect has an emotional personality, he should play upon it, perhaps by suggesting that anyone else faced with the same situation might equally have committed the offence, or by playing down the moral seriousness of the offence. He should praise and flatter the suspect in order to manipulate him. If he categorizes the suspect as non-emotional, a rather more analytical approach is advised. He should seek to catch him out in an incidental lie or persuade him to associate himself with the crime by, for example, placing himself at or near the scene. Whatever the perceived personality of the suspect, if other tactics have proved fruitless, the officer or officers should consider using the friendly/unfriendly or 'Mutt and Jeff' tactic, at one moment appearing to be sympathetic, at the next condemnatory.

A survey carried out by Irving in 1979 for the Royal Commission on Criminal Procedure suggested that a number of the tactics advocated by the manuals were being employed by officers of the Brighton CID, though almost certainly without any knowledge of or reference to those manuals.[28] Further empirical research, carried out after enactment of the Police and Criminal Evidence Act 1984 ('the 1984 Act') and the introduction of Code of Practice C (dealing, *inter alia*, with interviews at the police station), suggested that the use of these kinds of 'manipulative and persuasive tactics'[29] had declined.[30]

[26] The most thorough English survey thereof is to be found in Gudjonsson, *The Psychology of Interrogations, Confessions and Testimony* (1992), ch. 3.

[27] *Criminal Interrogation and Confessions* (3rd. edn. 1986). An English manual is Walkley, *Police Interrogations. A Handbook for Investigators* (1987).

[28] *Royal Commission on Criminal Procedure*, Research Study No 2 (1980), particularly ch. 8. See also Softley, *Police Interrogation*, Home Office Research Study No 61 (1980), at 32–4.

[29] The phrase is Gudjonsson's—see n. 26 above, 44.

[30] See Irving and McKenzie, *Police Interrogation: The Effects of the Police and Criminal Evidence Act 1984* (i) and *Custodial Interviewing Revisited* (ii) (1989), and, in particular, ii, 172–8.

There does now seem to be an emerging consensus in official circles, not least in the Home Office and within the police service, that the kind of technique or tactic advocated by Inbau, Reid, and Buckley, as well as being arguably unethical, is also inimical to the gathering of reliable confession evidence. Though the Royal Commission on Criminal Justice did not refer specifically to such tactics, it did express concern at the research evidence of 'an over-ready assumption on the part of some interviewing officers of the suspect's guilt and on occasion the exertion of undue pressure amounting to bullying or harassment'.[31] It went on to commend Home Office Circular 22/1992 as putting forward a new and better approach to investigative interviewing.[32] That circular was followed, later in 1992, by the issue of a package of materials concerned with interviewing skills. This package,[33] now known by the acronym PEACE, is as much directed at the effectiveness and efficiency of interviewing as at the need to eschew the manipulation of the suspect. We may note, for present purposes, that it, like the earlier circular, indicates that the officer should keep an open mind, rather than taking the suspect's guilt as read. It tells the officer to be alert to and to respond appropriately to contradictory evidence. One commentator, who was involved in the development of the package, adds:[34]

> In the interview the officer should explain the reason for arrest, and then obtain an account from the suspect which should be listened to without interruption. The officer should proceed to probing, either immediately or after obtaining a second or more accounts. When probing the officer should avoid using closed, leading and other suggestive questions. The officer should be mindful not to interrupt when the suspect is replying.

Of course, no matter how careful the officer is to avoid seeking to manipulate the suspect towards a confession, there are elements of the interrogation process which may increase the likelihood of a confession being made, yet be indifferent as regards its truth or falsity. A police station is likely to be, for most people, a strange and hostile place. Feelings of strangeness and fear are likely to be accentuated if neither family nor friends are present. The status and authority of the police officer is obvious to everyone, thus creating a psychological advantage, no matter how reasonably the actual interview may be conducted. Furthermore, there may be something in the character or mental condition of the particular suspect which makes him more likely to confess and may make that confession likely to be unreliable. Equally, the state of the suspect at the time, for example, because he is drunk or drugged, may provoke concerns about reliability.

Three Modes of Responding to Unreliability

The most obvious way of dealing with concerns about the unreliability of

[31] See *Royal Commission on Criminal Justice*, Cm 2263, July 1993, ch. 2, para. 18.

[32] *Ibid.*, para. 21.

[33] Its availability was announced by HO Circular 7/1993.

[34] Mortimer (1994) 10 *Policing* 111, at 112. Two other articles concerned with the need for a change of emphasis meriting attention are Williamson (1992) 8 *Policing* 286 and McKenzie (1993) 9 *Policing* 17.

evidence, whether confessional or non-confessional, might seem to be to leave the jury to decide what weight should be given to it, perhaps with the help of an appropriate direction from the judge referring to its possible infirmities.[35] Though this was rejected long ago by the English common law as the exclusive line of approach for confessions, it remains an entirely appropriate response where no, more drastic, step needs to be taken. Indeed, as we shall see in Chapter 10, section 77 of the 1984 Act *requires* a particular kind of direction in the case of some confessions of mentally handicapped accused.

Alternatively, one might permit the judge to form his own view of the reliability of any given item of evidence acquired by the police during the course of their investigations. So, with confessions, the question he might be required to answer might be, 'was this confession made in circumstances such that it is unlikely to be reliable?'. An affirmative answer would demand exclusion of the confession, the fear being that the jury might be insufficiently assiduous in taking account of factors pointing to unreliability. We shall see, later in this work, that both the common law and the 1984 Act apply a test of more or less that kind as a matter of discretionary power. The second line of approach shares in common with the first that it addresses directly the reliability of the particular item of evidence in the case at hand.

Differing from the first two approaches in the last-mentioned respect is a third one. Rather than concerning ourselves only with the case at hand, we may have the future in mind. For example, it is perfectly possible that a torturer will have chosen the right person. So a guilty suspect may confess that guilt under torture. He may go on, say, to reveal the whereabouts of the murder weapon. We can be confident that his confession is truthful, yet we might, very properly, exclude it. Torture is indifferent as between the guilty and the innocent, and we may fear that, next time, the wrong person will be chosen. Though there are, of course, other good reasons for excluding the confession, it seems entirely justifiable to exclude it to discourage the obtaining of unreliable confessions in the future. The immediate exclusionary purpose here may properly be called a disciplinary one, though the ultimate goal is clearly dictated by the reliability principle. So the common law exclusionary rule for confessions might be regarded as defensible on the basis that, though some specific examples of threats or promises might be most unlikely to generate unreliability, the clarity of the message to the police that they should eschew *all* threats and promises might have the overall effect of promoting rectitude of decisions.

THE *NEMO DEBET* PRINCIPLE

Another principle which, it might be argued, either does or should mould the law is the principle that nobody ought to be compelled or required to betray himself.

[35] As suggested, for confessions, in *Baldry* (1852) 2 Den. 430, at 445 (*per* Parke B) and at 446–7 (*per* Lord Campbell CJ).

This will be referred to as the *nemo debet* principle, following the maxim *nemo debet prodere se ipsum*.[36] Thus, in *Sang*, Lord Diplock claimed, of the law relating to confessions and to evidence obtained from the accused after commission of the offence that is tantamount to a confession, that:[37]

> [t]he underlying rationale of this branch of the criminal law, though it may originally have been based upon ensuring the reliability of confessions is . . . now to be found in the maxim nemo debet prodere se ipsum, no one can be required to be his own betrayer or in its popular English mistranslation 'the right to silence'.

Nemo Debet, the Right to Silence, and the Privilege against Self-incrimination

It is important to consider how the *nemo debet* principle relates to the right to silence and the privilege against self-incrimination, not least because there is no general agreement on this. Confining ourselves here to present-day opinion,[38] Lord Diplock, as we have just seen, regarded the *nemo debet* principle and the right to silence as synonymous. Galligan argues that the apparently equivalent Latin maxim, *nemo tenebatur prodere seipsum* refers to the privilege against self-incrimination, which, though related to, is different from the right to silence.[39] For him, the right to silence is potentially at issue both when the accused has maintained silence in the face of police questioning and when he has waived it by confessing.[40] Zuckerman too regards that privilege and that right as different, but, for him, it is the right to silence which has nothing to do with the suspect who either refuses to speak or utters incriminatory words. The right to silence is apt to describe the general right of a citizen, *qua* citizen, to withhold information from the police.[41] Sir John Smith adds yet a fourth view, for, though he agrees with Zuckerman that the right to silence properly describes the ordinary citizen's general right to withhold information, he regards the suspect as no less a beneficiary of that right, with the result that the issue of what use can be made at trial of an accused's silence when questioned does pertain to that right.[42] But he does not seem to agree with Galligan that where a confession was made under questioning, that right may equally be at issue.

One notable feature of the 'right to silence' as understood by Lord Diplock has recently been controverted by Lord Mustill. In *R.* v. *Director of Serious Fraud Office ex p. Smith*,[43] his Lordship said that he regarded that term as referring to a disparate group of immunities, six of which he went on to name. He indicated that these various immunities differed in their nature, origin, incidence, and

[36] There are several other versions of the Latin maxim available for use here. Others are *nemo tenetur seipsum prodere* and *nemo tenetur seipsum accusare*. The writer follows Lord Diplock in *Sang* [1980] AC 402, at 436, in using the version in the text.

[37] [1980] AC 402, at 436.

[38] For historical treatment, see works at Ch. 9, n. 7 below.

[39] [1988] *CLP* 69, at 69.

[40] *Ibid*. 77.

[41] See, e.g., (1986) 102 *LQR* 43, at 48; *The Principles of Criminal Evidence* (1989), 305–6.

[42] See *Criminal Evidence* (1995), 169–70.

[43] [1993] AC 1.

importance, though he acknowledged that, because all were concerned with protection of the citizen from abuse of power by those investigating crimes and because each was of great importance, it tended to be assumed that all were different ways of expressing the same principle. They comprehended the privilege of the witness in court not to incriminate himself no less than the right of the suspect not to be made to answer questions or the right of the accused not to testify or that of the ordinary citizen not to co-operate by providing information to the police.[44] What all share in common is that they relate to the freedom to be silent in the face of *questioning*.[45] No such constraint is placed upon the right to silence, or, more properly, the *nemo debet* principle, by Lord Diplock.

Having regard to this welter of dispute, it is not surprising that there is a tendency for lawyers to look for other principles than any from this cluster of three as lying behind the law about confessions and unfairly obtained evidence. However, Lord Diplock's statement could hardly be clearer, and it is not difficult to see that it may be considered objectionable for the police or other agency to be permitted to use certain methods in order to wrest self-incriminatory material from the suspect.

If, with Lord Diplock, we focus attention upon the Latin maxim itself, we may regard it as capable of providing the rationale for a family of lower-order rules.[46] It explains the privilege against self-incrimination, understood as the privilege of a witness who is not an accused to refuse to answer any question which has a tendency to incriminate him.[47] If this privilege did not exist, a refusal to answer questions of an incriminatory kind would presumably amount to a contempt. The rule rendering an accused competent but not compellable can be explained by the *nemo debet* principle. Were he compellable, a refusal to testify would, in the same way, constitute a contempt. In both cases, the threat of contempt proceedings would have an obvious tendency to make the accused speak. Furthermore, the principle was capable of justifying the common law rules which limited what a judge might say about an accused's silence when charged with an offence or about an accused's failure to give evidence at trial. By contrast, a rule allowing the judge to encourage the jury to draw adverse inferences directly from the accused's silence clearly makes less eligible the option of not speaking.[48] There is no difficulty in describing such a rule as requiring the suspect to be his own betrayer. The *nemo debet* principle even seems to be capable of comprehending cases where a person who is not a suspect is persuaded to provide evidence against himself, though certainly not to cases where he provides evidence against others.

[44] See, *ibid.* 30–2. [45] A point made by Dennis [1995] *Camb. LJ* 342, at 345.

[46] Dennis argues that, as a matter of principle, what he refers to as the privilege against self-incrimination is capable of explaining a group of ancillary or derivative applications—see *ibid.* 346. His position seems to be akin to that argued for in the text. See also Jackson (1994) 57 *MLR* 270, at 274.

[47] This is obviously a very simplified statement of the privilege. For detailed treatment, see, e.g., Cross and Tapper, *Evidence* (8th. edn., 1995), 453–69.

[48] See, now, Criminal Justice and Public Order Act 1994, ss. 34–8, considered in Ch. 9, below.

THE CONTENT OF THE *NEMO DEBET* PRINCIPLE

All that the *nemo debet* principle tells us is that a person must not be 'required' or 'made' or 'compelled' or 'bound' to provide evidence against himself. In the context of police interrogation, plainly no police officer can operate for a suspect the muscles which enable him to speak or otherwise to produce evidence against himself. One might regard only violence, oppression, and similar strong tactics as sufficiently compelling. One might go further, and include trickery and bluffing assertion. One might permit the suspect to be asked questions but not to be cross-examined. It is to be noted that Channell J considered any questioning of a suspect, once taken into police custody, to be improper, his reason being that '[a] magistrate or judge cannot do it, and a police officer certainly has no more right to do so'.[49] So, until we fill out this open-textured *nemo debet* principle with content, defining what we mean by requiring a person to be his own betrayer, we will not be able to say what evidence it requires to be excluded. Having put it like that, one should add that, once it has been decided what constitutes conduct which is deemed to have made a person betray himself, it does not *necessarily* follow that exclusion of that evidence is mandated. So, one could regard breach of the principle as a reason for exclusion, but not one requiring it in every case. In other words, one could argue for discretionary exclusion. It might even be argued that some extraneous remedy, perhaps an action in damages, would be more appropriate, though it will be contended shortly that this is rather a weak argument.

The open texture of the *nemo debet* principle is certainly problematical, yet it is worth remarking that there does seem to be one feature of the principle that aids clear definition. When we say that nobody can be required to be his own betrayer or that nobody can be made to provide evidence against himself, a key element of the objection to self-incrimination of this kind is that the person's *will has been engaged*. So, if the police threaten the suspect with violence unless he turns out his jacket pockets and he does then turn them out, revealing them to contain illegal drugs, he has been persuaded by the threat to bring forth evidence of crime. If, on the other hand, the police forcibly remove the jacket and discover the drugs for themselves, no element of persuasion arises—the suspect's will has not been engaged. Likewise, when the police require a motorist, under pain of penalty, to provide a sample of breath, the *nemo debet* principle is at issue, though in this situation statute overrides it. But were the police to take blood from an unconscious person suspected to be over the prescribed limit, they might well assault him, but they would certainly not engage his will.[50] Of course, it does not at all follow that the use of actual force against a suspect is morally preferable to the use of persuasion by threat, whether of force or of something else.

[49] *Knight and Thayre* (1905) 20 Cox CC 711, at 713.

[50] Though the contrary seems to have been held by the Supreme Court of Canada in *Pohoretsky* (1987) 39 DLR (4th.) 699.

The Validity or Value of the *Nemo Debet* Principle

Though this is not the place for an extended debate about the validity or value of the *nemo debet* principle, a brief description of two conflicting views will be offered. For Zuckerman, what he describes as the privilege (or right) against self-incrimination is the *bête noire* of the law relating to police interrogation.[51] Because it confers upon the guilty a freedom to refrain from providing information which could establish their guilt, it acts to frustrate another purpose of criminal justice, namely the conviction of those guilty persons. Therefore, it is particularly hard for judges to bring themselves to apply it. If we were to take it seriously, we would back it up by ensuring proper protection for the suspect in the police station such that he was, in practice, and not just in theory, free to exercise the privilege. Yet, by paying it lip service, we divert ourselves from protecting the suspect from other risks of harm which flow from custodial interrogation, namely 'the risk of abuse of his person or dignity and the risk of distortion or manipulation of his statements so as to implicate him in crime'.[52] For him, it would be better to ditch the privilege altogether and to concentrate on these important and more achievable goals.

A much more sympathetic view is that of Galligan.[53] Though, as has been mentioned already, he prefers to talk in terms of the right to silence rather than the *nemo debet* principle, which he takes to refer to the privilege against self-incrimination (considered only as the privilege of a witness), he does regard that right as significant and important, so far as the existing law is concerned, both as regards the maintaining of silence and as regards the making of a confession while under interrogation. However, he does not stop with the present law, but supports the right to silence as valuable in principle. In his view, '[t]he argument from privacy provides a sound case for the right to silence'.[54] Privacy protects personal identity and autonomy, and, although the stakes in terms of frustration of the valuable purpose of controlling crime are high, so also is the value of privacy in the context of police interrogation of a suspect. It is clear, then, that, for Galligan, the idea of the right to silence has more than merely instrumental value.

In any event, there can be no doubt that the *nemo debet* principle is *capable* of explaining much, or even all, of the common law relating to confessions and, perhaps, that relating to discretionary exclusion of non-confession evidence. As we have seen, Lord Diplock thought it the sole principle behind both of those common law doctrines. And, whether particular commentators like it or not, it is quite capable of explaining a great deal of the equivalent law under the 1984 Act.

[51] Reliance will be placed here upon *The Principles of Criminal Evidence* (1989), but he has made similar points in a number of articles published in legal periodicals. See, e.g., (1986) 102 *LQR* 43; [1989] Crim.LR 855; (1994) 144 *NLJ* 1104.

[52] See *The Principles of Criminal Evidence*, n. 51 above, 302.

[53] See n. 39 above. [54] *Ibid*. 89–90.

The Protective Principle

The *nemo debet* principle is a substantive one, and no less so because of the uncertainty of its content. The protective principle, on the other hand, is remedial in nature. It supports whatever minimum standards for the treatment of suspects are chosen by demanding that, once a legal system declares that they should be met, that system should take seriously what it says. According to Ashworth,[55] who coined the phrase 'protective principle', it demands that, where a suspect has not been treated in accordance with a particular minimum standard, he should not suffer any disadvantage thereby.

Three points should be made about the protective principle. First, it clearly invokes the causative efficacy of the breach of the minimum standard in question as a necessary element. Only where the breach *results* in prejudice will there be a call for remedial action. It follows that, if the breach took place after the evidence was procured, no question of the principle applying could arise. Secondly, one may add further elements to the calculation by saying that the breach in question must be more than merely technical and/or that the prejudice to the accused must be significant.[56] Thirdly, though the appropriate way of preventing the relevant disadvantage or prejudice may well be to exclude the evidence obtained, this is not necessarily the only way of responding. As Ashworth himself puts it, '[i]deally, the strength of the response should be in some way proportionate to the degree of disadvantage to the defendant'.[57] So, where the degree of disadvantage is particularly high, it may be appropriate to go as far as staying the proceedings or providing a substantive criminal defence. At the other end of the scale, mitigation of sentence may be all that is required.[58] And, even where exclusion of evidence is to be considered, this may be either as a matter of rule or of discretion. Ashworth himself seems to favour the latter, though with clear principles established to guide or structure its exercise.[59]

It will be evident that the protective principle is capable of providing remedial support not only for the *nemo debet* principle. The substantive rights accorded to citizens who find themselves bound up in the criminal process, and, in particular, to citizens suspected of crime, are certainly not all capable of being brought under the umbrella of the *nemo debet* principle. Limitations placed by law upon powers of arrest, search, or seizure are clearly outside its cover, for they are dictated by concern for the interest of the person in question in bodily security or privacy. The same must be said of powers of detention enjoyed by the police, whether with or without judicial approval. Where the suspect is in police custody, rules requiring cells to be aired and cleaned, and reasonable washing and toilet facilities to be provided, are concerned with the suspect's dignity and comfort. The rule requiring the police to ensure that medical treatment is

[55] [1977] Crim.LR 723. See also his work *The Criminal Process* (1994), at 122–3 and 302–3.
[56] Ashworth, *The Criminal Process*, n. 55 above, 302–3. [57] *Ibid.* 303.
[58] See the article at n. 55 above, at 725. [59] *Ibid.* 733.

provided for an ill or injured suspect flows from straightforward humanitarian considerations.

Nonetheless, it is submitted that the *nemo debet* principle has a special call for remedial support through exclusion of evidence, a call which the other rights or interests of the suspect do not share. This is because the *nemo debet* principle is specifically concerned, and concerned only, with the procuring of incriminating material from the suspect himself. Thus, it is inevitably concerned, in the present context, with adverse *evidence*. So, where the police apply oppressive tactics to persuade the accused to confess and a confession results, that entails achievement of their purpose. Of course, an illegal arrest or search may be part of a process designed to obtain adverse evidence, but there is no necessity of that. For example, a search may be carried out to harrass individuals seen by the police as troublemakers, or the police may already have sufficient evidence to charge the person arrested. It is entirely consistent with the point being made that, where some coercive power is employed for the purpose of obtaining evidence for potential use at a later trial, the argument for exclusion draws extra force from the protective principle, but that is because of the analogy with the core case of compelled self-incrimination.

There is another feature of the *nemo debet* principle which marks it out from at least some of the other rights of the suspect. The right not to be arrested, searched, or detained or have one's property seized are free-standing aspects of personal liberty. If one of those rights is trampled upon, there is a whole gamut of potential criminal and civil remedies against the transgressor. This is not the case with the right not to be required to be one's own betrayer. Though there may certainly be situations in which, for example, the oppressive behaviour of the police does amount to a crime or tort, this is certainly not necessarily so and would seem to be rather unlikely. One response to this argument is that the law *should* provide a separate remedy in support of the *nemo debet* principle. This usually seems to be simply an argument against exclusion of evidence, rather than a sincere call to provide a more appropriate remedy for a clear breach of one's rights. Even where it can be shown by extraneous evidence that the suspect betrayed himself untruthfully and is innocent of the offence in question, the law provides no remedy extraneous to the trial process, yet the law has no difficulty in providing a tort remedy for someone unlawfully but successfully searched. Perhaps, then, there is no extraneous remedy for the person compelled to betray himself precisely because the obvious one is already available.

The Disciplinary Principle

The Nature of the Disciplinary Principle

While the protective principle is concerned with what happened to the particular accused and with providing him with an adequate remedy where improperly treated, the disciplinary principle has wider concerns. It looks to cases which have not yet arisen. If the police are denied the use of evidence in the present case because of their failure to achieve acceptable standards of conduct, they will be more likely to achieve acceptable standards in future cases.[60] In the short term, both the police officer involved in the present case and other police officers who get to know about the decision of the court to exclude the evidence will be deterred. In the long term, perhaps, the court will, by defining the boundaries of proper conduct in such a concrete fashion, educate police officers to respect those boundaries.[61]

We have seen already that the reliability principle may have a disciplinary aspect.[62] Thus, we may exclude this confession, though itself reliable, because the conduct which led to it being made is likely to lead in future cases to unreliable confessions. But the disciplinary principle proper concerns itself with the unacceptability of the relevant conduct *as such*, and not with its tendency to promote the unreliability of evidence.[63] For example, there is a good disciplinary reason of this kind for excluding a confession where a threat of violence was made, such reason deriving simply from a concern that the police should not abuse their position of authority by threatening unlawful (and here criminal) action.

The disciplinary principle differs in two important respects from the protective principle. To repeat, it is forward-looking, its concern being the interests of future suspects. If evidence against the present accused is excluded for a disciplinary reason, he is the fortunate recipient of a collateral benefit. The consequence of this is that the disciplinary principle need take no account of causation in fact. It is not necessary that the conduct sought to be deterred caused the evidence in question to be obtained. It is not even necessary that it preceded the obtaining. However, it would seem that the conduct must be *capable* of resulting in the obtaining of incriminating evidence. The other difference is that the disciplinary principle is preventive, not remedial, in nature. We can tell very easily whether or not the present accused was accorded protection; was the evidence used against him? It is far more difficult to assess the deterrent efficacy of exclusion. But if we are satisfied that the exclusion of evidence will have no deterrent effect at all, exclusion serves no disciplinary purpose, and we must think of some better way of carrying out that purpose. Thus, the nature and concerns of the disciplinary principle are significantly different from those of the protective principle.[64]

This should not lead us to the conclusion that the protective and disciplinary principles are in opposition. We may very well conclude that police conduct which ought to be discouraged is also conduct which, in the particular case, breached some right of the accused deserving of remedial support. One might even pursue both principles at the same time, excluding evidence if either principle so dictated.

[60] For a helpful recent exposition of the difference between the protective and disciplinary principles, see Stuntz [1989] Crim.LR 117, at 123.

[61] For these two points, see Oaks (1970) 37 *U Chi.. L Rev.* 665, at 668.

[62] See p. 13 above.

[63] See Kamisar (1963) 17 *Rutgers L Rev.* 728, at 753.

[64] Cf. Williams (1983) 3 *OJLS* 222, at 226.

Predicting Disciplinary Efficacy of Exclusion

The disciplinary principle is, then, purely instrumental in its nature. It is always relevant to ask, where it is proposed to exclude evidence in order to deter police misconduct, whether or not exclusion would be likely to have that effect. There are various reasons why there may be doubt about the efficacy of exclusion in this respect. As to one important general reason, we should note the findings of an exhaustive study, carried out by Oaks, of cases in which the evidence sought to be acquired by the police through unlawful action was real evidence.[65] He pointed out that there are many goals or motivations other than obtaining convictions which may prompt an arrest followed by search and seizure. So, for example, search may be for the purpose of recovering stolen property from someone not involved in the crime. He concluded that:[66]

> [t]here is no reason to expect the rule to have any direct effect on the overwhelming majority of police conduct that is not meant to result in prosecutions, and there is hardly any evidence that the rule exerts any deterrent effect on the small fraction of law enforcement activity that is aimed at prosecution. What is known about the deterrent effect of sanctions suggests that the exclusionary rule operates under conditions that are extremely unfavorable for deterring the police. The harshest criticism of the rule is that it is ineffective.

Confessions cases, as Oaks himself had earlier pointed out,[67] differ significantly from search and seizure cases. Once suspicion has focused on a particular person, the predominant motive for questioning him is to obtain evidence for use in court. In Oaks's own words, 'police conduct in this area is likely to be responsive to judicial rules governing the admissibility of that evidence'.[68] But, even here, it has to be borne in mind that most prosecutions result, in any event, in guilty pleas, with the result that any improper conduct does not come to light.

There are three particularly important elements of the disciplinary message which undoubtedly affect its likely efficacy. First, where the substantive rules with which the officer is to be encouraged to comply are vague or complex, or both, the potential for success is thereby reduced. So it may be supposed that it is easier for an officer to carry out a direction not to threaten suspects or promise them things than to comply with one not to be oppressive towards them. Secondly, the judge must make it clear what rule has been broken and that he has excluded the evidence because of that breach. If his reasoning is shrouded in uncertainty, the officer will find it difficult to work out how he is meant to react. Most important of all, perhaps, is the third point. The direct recipients of the message, if the evidence is excluded, will be solely the officers involved in the case, while, if a judge's decision not to exclude is overturned on appeal, even they may

[65] N. 61 above.

[66] *Ibid.* 755. A less negative view of the deterrent effect of the exclusionary rule in search and seizure cases is taken by Canon (1974) 62 *Kentucky LJ* 681. Like Oaks, Canon considers a considerable amount of empirical evidence.

[67] N. 61 above, 722. [68] *Ibid.*

not receive it. Presumably, more general dissemination is required, and this will have to entail some internal police procedure designed to achieve that purpose.

It has to be said that the prospects of all three elements of the message being present, to a reasonable degree, at the same time, are not very high. However, the American experience indicates that, if the message is clear enough and important enough, it will get through. There can hardly be a police officer in the whole of the United States who is unaware that, before he embarks upon custodial interrogation of a suspect, he must inform that suspect of his right to be silent, his right to a lawyer, and his right to have a lawyer provided free of charge if he cannot afford one.[69] Furthermore, it may be argued that it is wrong to concentrate exclusively upon the particular case. As we shall see, the chapters of this book which deal with the exclusionary rule and discretion show that there is a large, and ever-increasing, number of cases in which appeal courts have overturned trial court decisions to admit evidence acquired in breach of some provision of the 1984 Act or one of the codes of practice made thereunder. A message which could hardly fail to get through is the admittedly unspecific one that breach may well lead to exclusion. That represents a ground for compliance whether or not it is acted upon. In other words, the decisions may be having a general disciplinary *effect*, though this is certainly not to say that they had a disciplinary *purpose*.

The Wrong Vehicle or Wrong Place for Discipline?

Those who argue against the disciplinary principle usually do so, not for pragmatic reasons concerned with the likely inefficacy of the disciplinary message, but rather because they regard exclusion as the wrong vehicle for discipline, or the judges as the wrong people to make themselves responsible for discipline, or both. For judicial opinion, it suffices to quote the words of Lord Diplock in *Sang*, for they embrace both points:[70]

> It is no part of a judge's function to exercise disciplinary powers over the police or prosecution as respects the way in which evidence to be used at the trial is obtained by them. If it was obtained illegally there will be a remedy in civil law; if it was obtained legally but in breach of the rules of conduct for the police, this is a matter for the appropriate disciplinary authority to deal with.

The distinction between the argument from function and that from the existence of other remedies is of some importance. The latter argument may always be met by a suggestion that the other remedies are not, in practice, effective. Thus, the Royal Commission on Criminal Procedure put its faith in police supervisory and disciplinary procedures,[71] involving, as they must, 'contemporaneous controls' rather than 'review long after the event'.[72] It did go on to recommend certain ways

[69] Following *Miranda* v. *Arizona*, 384 US 436 (1966)

[70] See [1980] AC 402, at 436. Expressions of similar judicial opinion in post-Act cases are to be found, at Ch. 6, text to nn. 129–32 below.

[71] *Report*, Cmnd. 8092, Jan. 1981, paras. 4.118 and 4.127.

[72] *Ibid.*, para. 4.118.

in which the likelihood of such procedures being effective might be increased,[73] yet there remained and remains a considerable amount of room for scepticism about their efficacy. So far as the possibility of a civil remedy is concerned, it is relatively easy to argue that the victims of overreaching police behaviour are, in the generality of cases, unlikely to have either the inclination or the resources to pursue their remedy. The functional argument is not vulnerable to these kinds of pragmatic consideration, for it represents a value judgement about the proper role of the criminal judge. However, it is worth pointing out that the US Supreme Court has no such qualms about using its powers of exclusion for disciplinary purposes. Both the *Miranda* requirements for confessions and the exclusionary rule in cases of search and seizure in contravention of the Fourth Amendment are now explained by a majority of the court entirely in disciplinary or deterrent terms.[74]

The Judicial Integrity Principle

We may now turn to a principle, or, more properly, a clutch of principles, which focus attention not upon reliability, or upon the rights and interests of the particular accused or citizens more generally, but rather upon the administration of justice itself. The idea that judicial integrity might be compromised by the admission of unlawfully obtained evidence emerged first in the United States, principally in the context of illegal search and seizure.[75] It is somewhat ironic that that idea has caught on in other parts of the common law world at just the time that the jurisprudence of the Supreme Court of the United States has downgraded or even abandoned it.[76]

The Principle or Principles Stated

We may begin with a statement of Justice Traynor in the Californian case of *People* v. *Cahan*:[77]

> When . . . the very purpose of an illegal search and seizure is to get evidence to introduce at a trial, the success of the lawless venture depends entirely on the court's lending its aid by

[73] *Ibid.*, paras. 4.118 and 4.119.

[74] See *Miranda* v. *Arizona*, 384 US 436 (1966) (for confessions) and *Mapp* v. *Ohio*, 367 US 643 (1961) (for search and seizure). For the recent Supreme Court jurisprudence on these doctrines, see, Ch. 12, text between nn. 3 and 94 below.

[75] See, in particular, the dissenting opinions of Justices Holmes and Brandeis in *Olmstead* v. *US*, 227 US 438 (1928), at 469 and 471, respectively. This was a phone-tapping case. See also *Elkins* v. *US*, 364 US 206 (1960), at 222–3; *Mapp* v. *Ohio*, 367 US 643 (1961), at 659–60; *Terry* v. *Ohio*, 392 US 1 (1968), at 12–13.

[76] See, e.g., *US* v. *Peltier*, 422 US 531 (1975), at 536–9; *US* v. *Janis*, 428 US 433 (1976), at 459; *Stone* v. *Powell*, 428 US 465 (1976), at 485–6 and 498–9; *Illinois* v. *Gates*, 462 US 213 (1983), at 259; *US* v. *Leon*, 468 US 897 (1984), at 921. The modern view seems to be that the principle of judicial integrity is subordinate to, or even subsumed by, the disciplinary principle (or deterrence rationale). For a recent example, see *Arizona* v. *Evans*, 514 US 1 (1995).

[77] 282 P. 2d. 905 (1955), at 912.

allowing the evidence to be introduced. It is no answer to say that a distinction should be drawn between the government acting as law enforcer and the gatherer of evidence and the government acting as a judge. . . . Out of regard for its own dignity as an agency of justice and custodian of liberty the court should not have a hand in such a 'dirty business'. . . . It is morally incongruous for the state to flout constitutional rights and at the same time demand that its citizens observe the law.

We should observe immediately two features of the principle here stated. First, it is clearly a matter of moral imperative; it is not right to punish breach of the law by the accused while condoning its breach by the police. Secondly, it is the court which must apply its own standards of propriety and decency in this respect. We may describe this as 'court-centred integrity'.

A rather different flavour is conveyed by the following words from the famous dissenting opinion of Justice Brandeis in *Olmstead* v. *United States*: '[i]f the government becomes a lawbreaker, it breeds contempt for law; it invites every man to become a law unto himself; it invites anarchy.'[78] Here, the matter seems to be made one of predicted consequences. Will admission of the evidence in question tend to increase the amount of lawbreaking? Furthermore, our attention is directed to the likely reaction of the general public, rather than to the court's own standards. An appropriate description of this variation of the integrity principle might be 'public conduct integrity'.

Yet a third variation is provided by asking the question whether or not the administration of justice would be brought into disrepute by the admission of the evidence. Viewed as a matter of moral imperative, addressed to the court itself, this variation seems to add nothing to court-centred integrity. If judges do soil their hands by becoming parties to a 'dirty business', then they render the system they operate disreputable at the same time as compromising their own integrity. However, if attention is focused upon predicted public reaction, the idea shares something in common with public conduct integrity, yet bears a rather different tinge. Instead of engaging in a utilitarian cost/benefit analysis in terms of future criminality, the court must seek to gauge how the public will respond in its attitude to the criminal legal system. Will it lose respect for the administration of justice? This would seem to be a matter of attitude rather than conduct, so we may call it 'public attitude integrity'.

We should note two important differences between matters concerning the moral scruple of the court and those of public reaction. The validity of the moral point is independent of factual considerations or practical consequences. Were the general public to be of the opinion that it is entirely reasonable to allow evidence gathered by the use of torture to be admitted at the trial of its victim, the judges would not thereby be relieved of their moral responsibility to exclude it.[79] Presumably, even if public contempt for the judiciary should result from them taking such a lily-livered stance on torture, the judges should persist in their

[78] 277 US 438 (1928), at 485.

[79] Of course, judges living in such a society might well, themselves, see no moral problem in admitting the evidence.

moral stance. The situation is quite different with the two public reaction models. So, if there are grounds for believing that contempt for law is bred by the sight of patently guilty people escaping conviction on the basis that reliable real evidence has been obtained unlawfully, the judge has good reason for allowing such evidence to be called. This has been accepted in some of the Supreme Court jurisprudence. Thus, in *Stone* v. *Powell*, Justice Powell, delivering the opinion of the Court, said: '[w]hile courts, of course, must ever be concerned with preserving the integrity of the judicial process, this concern has limited force as a justification for the exclusion of highly probative evidence'.[80] The point has been put more vividly by Judge Wilkey, extra-judicially, as follows: 'the exclusion of valid, probative, undeniably truthful evidence undermines the reputation of and destroys the respect for the entire judicial system'.[81] Presumably, if one of the public reaction models is to be applied, the judge should ask himself the question whether exclusion in the particular case would be more likely to increase than decrease lawbreaking, or, as the case may be, would be more likely to enhance rather than reduce the reputation of the administration of justice.

A second point is that, if it is court-centred integrity which inspires action, an issue which must arise is whether or not every failure to comply with the rules during the course of investigation can be said to compromise the integrity of the courts. Where a provision of some fundamental document such as the US Constitution or the Canadian Charter of Rights and Freedoms has been breached, the call for exclusion would seem to be more compelling than where, as must be the case in England, only some rule of the ordinary law has been breached. Put shortly, at what point does moral scruple properly obtrude?

JUDICIAL INTEGRITY IN ENGLISH LAW

The Canadian Charter of Rights and Freedoms, enacted in the 1980s, gives explicit recognition to the judicial integrity principle in its disrepute form:

> Where . . . a court concludes that evidence was obtained in a manner that infringed or denied any rights or freedoms guaranteed by this Charter, the evidence shall be excluded if it is established that, having regard to all the circumstances, the admission of it in the proceedings would bring the administration of justice into disrepute.

It is clear from the considerable amount of authority relating to this provision, section 24(2), that the Supreme Court of Canada is taking a positive, interventionist stance, sympathetic to the call for exclusion.[82] In addition, recent authority suggests that the Australian courts' discretionary power to exclude

[80] 428 US 465 (1976), at 485.

[81] (1978–9) 62 *Judicature* 215, at 223. See also Kaplan (1974) 26 *Stan. L Rev.* 1027, at 1035–6.

[82] See, in particular, the leading case of *Collins* [1987] 1 SCR 265. For comment, see Delisle (1987) 56 *CR (3d)* 216; Mirfield (1987–8) 30 *Crim.LQ* 434; Paciocco (1989–90) 32 *Crim.LQ* 326. A most influential article which preceded *Collins* is Morisette (1984) 29 *McGill LJ* 521. Recent cases in which the court has ruled in favour of exclusion include *Mellenthin* [1992] 3 SCR 615; *Bartle* [1994] 3 SCR 173 *Cobham* [1994] 3 SCR 360; *Burlingham* [1995] 2 SCR 206.

confessional and other evidence for public policy reasons is best explained in terms of the need to prevent judicial disrepute.[83]

In England too, the judicial integrity principle has, very recently, come to have a role to play in the common law. Here, however, that place is, at least for the present, not in the law concerned with the exclusion of evidence, but in that concerned with the staying of proceedings on the ground of abuse of the process of the court. First, in *R.* v. *Horseferry Road Magistrates' Court, ex p. Bennett*,[84] the House of Lords stayed proceedings because the accused had been brought into the country in breach of both international law and the law of another state, as well as in disregard of the available extradition process. Lord Bridge spoke of 'respect for the rule of law' as the motivating consideration.[85] Lord Lowry also referred to the rule of law, but went on to say that what it demanded was 'that the court should not have to make available its process and thereby endorse . . . unworthy conduct when it is proved against the executive or its agents, however humble in rank'.[86] Earlier, in words rather bringing to mind those of Justice Traynor quoted earlier in this section,[87] he said that to try the accused would offend 'the court's sense of justice and propriety'.[88] It will be observed that Lord Lowry's language suggests that he had the court-centred variety of judicial integrity in mind.

More recently, in *Latif and Shahzad*,[89] the House acknowledged that the judicial integrity principle is capable of demanding a stay where there has been entrapment of the accused, though it concluded that no stay was called for on the particular facts. The speech of Lord Steyn, which had the support of all their Lordships, merits extensive quotation:[90]

> If the court always refuses to stay such proceedings, the perception will be that the court condones criminal conduct and malpractice by law enforcement agencies. That would undermine public confidence in the criminal justice system and bring it into disrepute. On the other hand, if the court were always to stay proceedings in such cases, it would incur the reproach that it is failing to protect the public from serious crime. The weaknesses of both extreme positions leaves [*sic*] only one principled solution. The court has discretion: it has to perform a balancing exercise. . . . Weighing countervailing considerations of policy and justice, it is for the judge in the exercise of his discretion to decide whether there has been an abuse of process, which amounts to an affront to the public conscience and requires the criminal proceedings to be stayed. . . . [P]roceedings may be stayed in the exercise of the judge's discretion not only where a fair trial is impossible but also where it would be contrary to the public interest in the integrity of the criminal justice system that a trial should take place. . . . [I]t is possible to say that in a case such as the present the judge must weigh in the balance the public interest in ensuring that those that are charged with

[83] The case usually cited as the source of this doctrine is *Bunning* v. *Cross* (1978) 141 CLR 54. The views of Zuckerman—see *The Principles of Criminal Evidence* (1989), 354–6—and Dennis—see [1989] *CLP* 21, at n. 61—that this power flows from the judicial integrity principle had the support of the majority of the High Court in *Ridgeway* (1995) 129 ALR 41—see 48–9 (*per* Mason CJ, Deane and Dawson JJ) and 89–91 (*per* McHugh J). Cf. Pattenden (1980) 29 *ICLQ* 664, at 672 and 678. The *Bunning* v. *Cross* discretionary power is considered in detail, at Ch. 12, text to nn. 236–266 below.

[84] [1994] 1 AC 42.

[85] *Ibid.* 67.

[86] *Ibid.* 77.

[87] See, text to n. 77 above.

[88] [1994] 1 AC 42, at 74.

[89] [1996] 1 WLR 104.

[90] See *ibid.* 112–13.

grave crimes should be tried and the competing public interest in not conveying the impression that the court will adopt the approach that the end justifies any means.

Three features of Lord Steyn's analysis are immediately apparent. First, it is not for him a moral issue for the scruple of the court, but an issue of public confidence in the integrity of the system. Secondly, as under the Canadian Charter, it is public attitude, not public conduct, which is relevant, for 'disrepute' is clearly a key word. Thirdly, Lord Steyn acknowledges that the principle has two faces to it, for disrepute can flow no less from the guilty escaping conviction than from the judiciary putting up with or condoning the unlawful action of law enforcement agencies.

It seems very likely that these recent judicial developments were significantly influenced by the growing body of English academic opinion which favours some version or other of the integrity principle. Two writers cited by Lord Steyn himself have argued that, where the burden of the accused's argument is that he was entrapped into committing the offence, the granting of a stay will, in the appropriate case, be a better judicial response than the exclusion of evidence.[91]

Other commentators have presented a more general argument, one not restricted to the particular case of entrapment. They have, indeed, relied upon the idea that decisions whether or not to exclude evidence should be informed by some principle of judicial integrity. Foremost among these commentators are Zuckerman and Dennis. Zuckerman prefers the phrase 'principle of legitimacy', but it is clear that there is no substantial difference between this and the integrity principle.[92] His most detailed description of what he has in mind is to be found in the following claim:[93]

The criminal trial has a special moral dimension. It is concerned with the determination of moral blame, which may in turn justify the infliction of suffering and humiliation on an individual, as well as of legal liability. The willingness of the public to accept the authority of the criminal court as a dispenser of punishment depends on the extent to which the public believes in the moral legitimacy of the system. The morality or fairness of a system of adjudication hinges on many factors. . . . Amongst these must be numbered a publicly acceptable judicial attitude towards breaches of the law. A judicial community that is seen to condone, or even encourage, violations of the law can hardly demand compliance with its own edicts.

Though the last few words may seem to smack of public conduct integrity the rest of this statement, taken together with what Zuckerman says elsewhere in his writings, clearly points to public attitude integrity. Yet it is important to appreciate that the issue has a moral dimension and is not merely one of prudence. The judge acts for moral reasons, though not ones stemming from his own conscience. It is clear that Zuckerman, like Lord Steyn, embraces the idea that what is called for is a balancing operation, in which the case for admission of the evidence in question will flow from its likely value in promoting rectitude of decisions.[94]

[91] Roser (1993) 67 *ALJ* 722; Choo [1995] Crim.LR 864. See also Choo's *Abuse of Process and Judicial Stays of Criminal Proceedings* (1993), ch. 6.

[92] See, n. 83 above, 350 and n. 23.

[93] *Ibid.* 344.

[94] See, in particular, *ibid.* 350–60.

Dennis's argument seems to be to broadly similar effect. He prefers to use the phrase, 'the moral authority of the verdict' and he states expressly that the rationale he supports is not the same as the judicial integrity principle, though he does also accept that it has certain similarities with that principle.[95] His point seems to be that his favoured rationale is capable of explaining not just the exclusionary rules and powers with which this book is concerned, but also every other exclusionary principle of the law of evidence.[96] At all events, he argues that the moral authority of the verdict is to be distinguished from its factual authority as a matter of rectitude of decisions. He gives the example of torture as a gross violation of the suspect's right to respect and dignity, and goes on to say:[97]

> Such a violation destroys the moral authority of the verdict. This is because a verdict which is derived from a disregard for the core principle of criminal law is self-contradictory. It cannot function as an expressive message that the criminal law incorporates values which it is necessary to uphold while appearing to be based itself on a deliberate flouting of those values. This must inevitably lead to a loss of respect both for the trial process and for the criminal law itself.

In the present context, this argument would seem to have an impact essentially the same as the judicial integrity principle in its public attitude form. Certainly, Dennis, no less than Zuckerman, is concerned with rectitude of decisions as part-and-parcel of the principle which he espouses. Thus, he says that '[a] judgment that the defendant did commit the offence should, presumptively, result in a conviction. It would tend to undermine the aims of the criminal law if those judged to have broken its terms in fact were not convicted'.[98] However, truth-finding is an instrumental value, a means by which a legitimate (or authoritative) verdict is secured, for 'it is the legitimacy of the verdict which is the ultimate goal'.[99]

Testing the Principles

Finally, it seems appropriate to ask how the application of the various principles which have been considered is properly affected by some common potential features of the cases which come before the courts.

Cogency of Evidence

We may begin by considering what significance the cogency of the evidence obtained has for the issue of exclusion. Obviously, the more cogent the evidence, the greater will be its probative value, and so the reliability principle must call more strongly for inclusion as cogency increases. Impact on the *nemo debet* and protective principles would seem to be equally straightforward. Both focus upon

[95] See n. 83 above, at 34. Dennis develops his theory, in the specific context of the privilege against self-incrimination in [1995] *Camb. LJ* 342.

[96] See [1989] *CLP* 21, n. 61. [97] *Ibid.* 37. [98] *Ibid.* [99] *Ibid.* 38.

what was done to the accused rather than upon what, if anything, resulted. That said, having regard to Ashworth's view that the strength of response should be proportionate to the degree of disadvantage,[100] it might even be argued that the protective principle has greater reason to apply as the evidence obtained increases in cogency.

Rather more needs to be said about the disciplinary principle. Though it might be argued that one should not seek to deter the police from acquiring cogent evidence of crime, this reflects not application of the principle but a possible extraneous constraint upon it, dictated by a desire to see the guilty convicted. In other words, we may conclude that it is not worth seeking to deter in the future where the cost would be high, in the present case, in terms of loss of cogent evidence. It might be different if the potential cogency of the evidence were to be something apparent to the officer at the time of prospective transgression of a rule. Though one can envisage circumstances in which cogency might be predictable at that stage, this is most unlikely to be so in the vast majority of cases. Thus, to factor cogency into the equation would inevitably be to blunt the disciplinary message.

Finally, if we turn to the judicial integrity principle, much seems to turn upon which version of that principle one is considering. In the court-centred version, the essence of the objection is to the court joining hands, so to speak, with the officer who conducted himself as he did. It follows that the key time, at which the principle bites, is the time of the unlawful or improper investigative step. With either public reaction version, by contrast, the reaction which the courts have in mind is to the decision made *at trial* whether or not to exclude the evidence. It will quickly be apparent that cogency is properly a matter which informs a judicial decision predicated upon public reaction, for the spectacle of the guilty going free (because cogent evidence is excluded) is quite capable of having a negative effect upon their perception of the criminal justice system. It seems to be clearly otherwise with court-centred integrity. The acceptability of conduct cannot be changed merely by chance consequences, though it is, of course, entirely consistent with instrumental moral theories that one should factor the *predicted* consequences into the equation. The problem for that kind of moral theory is that, as has already been observed, it seems that the cogency of the evidence (if any) acquired is most unlikely to be predictable at the time of the conduct in question. One might possibly treat cogency as relevant in those few cases where it was predictable.

Heinousness of Breach

Not all breaches of the rules governing investigation of crime are equally heinous. A breach may be serious or trivial; it may be deliberate or accidental; it may be committed in bad or in good faith. Taking the reliability principle first, the seriousness of the breach may well be significant. For example, a suspect denied

[100] See text at n. 57 above.

legal advice may be denied it for a short or a long period of time. Particularly if that suspect were to be vulnerable in some way, perhaps because mentally handicapped, we might reasonably suppose that the danger of unreliability would increase in accordance with the length of the period of denial. Of course, what we are concerned with here is a tendency, not an inevitable effect. The other elements of heinousness, which might be summarized in terms of the guiltiness of the investigating officer's mind, would seem, in general, to be irrelevant to unreliability. This is because they would not usually form part of the suspect's conscious experience. However, awareness of the guiltiness of the officer's mind might occasionally be an element of the interaction. One can imagine, in these circumstances, that there might be an increased prospect of an unreliable confession because of the suspect's sense of just how far the police might go to prise one from him.

With the *nemo debet* principle, we must distinguish the maxim itself from the various rules governing the conduct of investigations which are capable of being regarded as acting in support of it. The test is whether or not the item of conduct in question was a sufficiently unacceptable way of persuading the suspect to self-incrimination for there to be a call for exclusion. So, once it has been determined that the suspect's right has been breached, nothing would seem to turn either on the level of seriousness of that breach or the guiltiness of the minds of those in breach. It is otherwise with rules supporting the main right itself. If we again take the right to legal advice as an example, there seems no reason why the seriousness of the breach of that right, or the fact that it was committed deliberately or in bad faith, should not be relevant factors as regards filling out the open texture of the governing principle, for these matters go to the unacceptability of the conduct.

So far as the protective principle is concerned, we should recall that it is remedial, rather than substantive, in nature. Hence, it is capable of providing remedial support for rights other than that not to be compelled to incriminate oneself. Where the focus is on particular rights in the investigative process, and not on the self-incrimination right itself, it can be cogently argued that the seriousness of the breach, or its deliberateness, or the fact that it was committed in bad faith are nothing to the point. One's rights are no less damnified by the blundering police officer than by the malevolent one.[101] In Ashworth's words: '[o]n a protective principle, the central question is whether the defendant was disadvantaged: the damage may be the same whether the breach was intentional or not, and perhaps even whether it was "technical" or not'.[102]

We may contrast this with the position so far as the disciplinary principle is concerned, for it has as its goal the deterrence of unacceptable police conduct. It is easy to see that, as the seriousness of the breach increases, the case for deterrence becomes stronger. The degree of guiltiness of mind of the officer in question seems, at first blush, to be inevitably relevant in the same way. This would lead

[101] Cardozo J once (famously) said of the exclusionary rule: '[t]he criminal is to go free because the constable has blundered'—see *People* v. *Defore*, 150 NE 585 (1926), at 587.

[102] N. 55 above, 123. See also Birch [1989] Crim.LR 95, at 103–4.

one to say that an accidental breach, even if negligent, would not be such as to call for discipline. Here, the blunder of the officer ought not to result in exclusion. However, this would be to place a surprising premium upon the ignorance of the particular officer and, perhaps more importantly, upon the failure of more senior officers or the police service as a whole to ensure that he be thoroughly trained in his duties.[103] The most balanced view may well be that, *ceteris paribus*, there is more reason to use the exclusion of evidence as the vehicle for discipline where malevolence was present than where ignorance or mistake was. Ignorance and mistake may often be driven out by the provision of information or, where appropriate, censure. Malevolence, by contrast, is unlikely to respond to such tactics, but is more likely, if the empirical basis for the principle is sound, to respond to the sanction of exclusion.

There can be no doubt that the heinousness factors are relevant to the application of the judicial integrity principle. There is a clear moral distinction between the mistaken or ignorant officer and the one who deliberately flouts the law, though there may be great difficulty in drawing that line in hard cases. This applies no less where the principle is concerned with public reaction than where it is court-centred, for the public is surely able to draw that distinction and will find it relevant to what it thinks of action taken by the court. It would seem no less plain that the seriousness of the breach will be a factor tending towards exclusion, for it must be worse to condone more serious or significant breaches than to condone other breaches. It might even be argued that the judicial integrity principle does not come into play at all unless there is an element of deliberate flouting of the law in the official conduct at issue, though this seems an unnecessary qualification.[104]

Seriousness of the Offence

At first blush, it may seem reasonable to suppose that, as the seriousness of the offence at issue becomes greater, so the call for exclusion of evidence becomes less persuasive. Put bluntly, the stakes for society are higher in a murder case than in a criminal damage one. In fact, this view is over-simplistic.

It must be remembered that the reliability principle is also an *un*reliability principle. The point here is that, though it is more important to convict the murderer than the person guilty of criminal damage, it is no less important, and arguably more important, to acquit the innocent person of the former than of the latter. It ought to follow that seriousness of the offence is either a neutral factor or, possibly, one tending towards exclusion.

With both the *nemo debet* principle and the protective one, there is a strong argument that no account should be taken of the seriousness of the offence. Each

[103] A point made by Kaplan (1974) 26 *Stan. L Rev*. 1027, at 1044. See also Zuckerman, n. 83 above, 355.

[104] Dennis seems to think that there should be such a qualification—see the passage quoted at n. 97 above.

has, as its natural focus, the official conduct which brought about the acquisition of the incriminating evidence. Both the right which the former principle acknowledges and the rights for which the latter principle may be enlisted to provide support are granted to the suspect[105] as such, and not because he is suspected of a crime of a particular level of seriousness.

Similar considerations may be thought to apply in the case of the disciplinary principle, but there may be a little more to it. It will always be the case that, at the time they are investigating, the police know something of the nature of the matters at hand. This will entail them having an idea of the seriousness of the crime which may have been committed. It does not follow that they will be able, at that stage, accurately to classify the crime in legal terms, let alone that the crime eventually charged will coincide with their knowledge or belief when they were taking the relevant investigative steps. For example, they may have had rape firmly in mind, yet the eventual charge might well be indecent assault. The important point is that the disciplinary message is capable of being tailored to the perceived seriousness of the matters at hand as they are being investigated. There is an important difference, then, between perceptions of seriousness, which are likely to be reasonably accurate, and predictions of cogency of evidence, which are likely to be no more than hunches at best. This has, indeed, led to suggestions being made in the United States that there should be a 'serious cases' exception to the exclusionary rule dictated by *Mapp* v. *Ohio*.[106] Thus, one writer who regards that rule as justifiable only in terms of a deterrent rationale has argued that it should not apply to treason, espionage, murder, armed robbery, or kidnapping by organized groups (unless the Fourth Amendment breach were to be sufficiently shocking).[107] Another possibility is that the court balance the comparative reprehensibility of the officer's breach and the accused's crime before deciding whether or not to exclude the evidence. Both proposals have been attacked by Kamisar, the former on the basis that no shortlist of the most serious crimes would, in practice, be kept short, the latter on the basis that the deterrent message would be substantially blunted.[108] The question, then, as so often with the disciplinary principle, boils down to the predicted effect upon actual police behaviour.

Equally difficult is the significance of the seriousness of the offence for the judicial integrity principle. As with cogency of the evidence, the court-centred version might seem bound to take no account of it, but this is not necessarily so. If, as suggested above, we think of the question as being whether or not the court can decently join hands with the officer at the time of his conduct, the answer may be that it can because the officer *was* right to do what he did, given his own

[105] Or, occasionally, to persons not, at the relevant point, suspects—e.g. juveniles, the mentally disordered, and the mentally handicapped enjoy the right to have an 'appropriate adult' present at an interview even before they have become suspects—see the *Code of Practice for the Detention, Treatment and Questioning of Persons by Police Officers* (Code C), Apr. 1995, para. 11.14.

[106] 367 US 643 (1961).

[107] See Kaplan, n. 103 above, 1046. This argument was accepted by Justice Cameron in *State* v. *Bolt*, 689 P 2d. 519 (1984), at 530, though he would add to the list 'such crimes as rape or arson'.

[108] See (1987–8) 86 *Mich. L Rev.* 1.

knowledge or belief about the seriousness of the offence. To take an extreme example, there might be incontrovertible evidence in the officer's hands of the commission of multiple killings and the circumstances might demonstrate a need to act very quickly if the perpetrator was to be caught, with the result that that officer honestly decided that there was no time for respect for the legalities. A judge might, consistently with a tenable moral position, treat the seriousness of the offences as relevant to his conclusion that even rather gross breaches of the accused's rights might be excused,[109] though he would, in doing so, have implicity rejected or marginalized the idea that the ends do not justify the means. Therefore, much turns here on the particular moral theory which is espoused.

The public attitude or conduct versions of the principle would seem appropriately, to adopt a rather Janus-like view of the seriousness of the offence. As Zuckerman has succinctly put it:[110]

> On the one hand, the more serious the offence, the more difficult it is to justify exclusion and thereby risk acquittal of a guilty and possibly dangerous person. On the other hand, the more serious the consequences of conviction the higher should be the moral rectitude of the means by which it is achieved.

Complicating matters even further is the need to decide through which prism public reaction is to be viewed. Does every citizen, no matter how miserable his own morality, get a vote, so to speak? Or do we view matters from the perspective of the reasonable citizen with a responsible and thoughtful character? Or do we see things from the point of view of the judge himself, albeit a judge taking proper account of community values?[111]

[109] It is appreciated that the urgency of the situation is also a factor in the moral equation. However, seriousness is relevant in that, had the offences been trivial, the breaches might not have been excused, even though, in terms of urgency, the situation would be the same.

[110] N. 83 above, 356.

[111] Each possibility seems to find support in the Canadian case law and academic commentary on exclusion, under s. 24(2) of the Charter of Rights and Freedoms 1982, to avoid bringing the administration of justice into disrepute. A detailed discussion will be found at Ch. 12, text between nn. 267 and 289 below.

3

Procedural Issues and Exclusion

Where the defence seeks to have excluded at trial evidence which was acquired in the course of investigation of an offence, whether this be by virtue of the exclusionary rule, for confessions, or the exclusionary discretion, for both confessions and non-confession evidence, various important, procedural issues are capable of arising. It will be convenient here not to separate the treatment of confession evidence from that of non-confession evidence.

Three provisions need to be kept in mind. First, there is section 76 of the Police and Criminal Evidence Act 1984, ('the 1984 Act') in respect of the confessions rule. Secondly, section 78 of that Act grants the judge discretion to exclude unfair evidence. Thirdly, section 82(3) preserves the common law discretion to exclude such evidence. Before we consider each in detail, we need to be aware of the developed position at common law.

The Developed Common Law Position

Confession Evidence—Arguments about Admissibility

Here, our principal concern is with decisions whether or not confessions are admissible in evidence. The common law drew a firm line between trial at the Crown Court and summary trial. The reason for this is easy to see. Magistrates are judges both of the law and of the facts. The questions under present consideration are legal ones, but magistrates will eventually have to decide, assuming they rule in favour of admission, whether or not the confession is true, and that is obviously an issue of fact. Indeed, having put it that way, we may observe that there is an air of artificiality about the theoretical distinction between the two tasks. To ask a magistrate to put out of mind the details of a confession which he had concluded should, in principle, be excluded is rather like asking him to tell himself not to think of pink elephants. At the Crown Court, where there is jury trial, there need be no such artificiality. The judge, sovereign over issues of law, may sensibly make rulings about exclusion of evidence in the absence of the jury, thus leaving the jury, sovereign over facts, with nothing to put out of its collective mind.

However, there is a complication in confession cases. While most issues can be settled by the judge simply after hearing legal argument, decisions about the exclusion of confessions are essentially tied up with certain factual issues. So it is likely to be the case that, if the accused alleges that his confession was beaten out of him, the police will deny that that was the case. A judge will not be in a position to decide about admissibility unless and until he has heard evidence on the issue. Therefore, the basic procedural device to be used by the judge is the 'trial within a trial' or trial on the *voir dire*.[1]

Having regard to these matters, the common law position for, respectively, Crown Court trial and summary trial, was markedly different. For the former, the procedure was helpfully set out by the Privy Council in *Ajodha* v. *The State*,[2] a case decided only a few years before the 1984 Act provisions came into force. Where defending counsel proposes to challenge the admissibility of a confession, he will inform his opponent, who will then not mention the confession in his opening speech. Usually, the giving of evidence will proceed in the normal way until the point is reached at which the prosecution would adduce evidence of the confession. However, it may be appropriate, in some cases, for the judge to hear argument before any evidence at all is heard.[3] Such a course will be taken, for example, where the prosecution could not satisfactorily open its case to the jury without referring to the confession. At whatever point the argument is heard, the exclusion issue will be decided by the judge alone, usually by trial on the *voir dire*. However, if the accused should, while testifying on the general issue (rather than on the *voir dire*), raise for the first time an issue as to the admissibility of his confession, the judge may, in the exercise of his discretion, require relevant prosecution witnesses to be recalled for further cross-examination. If he does so, he will eventually have to consider whether to direct the jury to disregard the confession evidence.

Though we have said that the issue will be tried by the judge alone, we need to be aware that this is not invariably the case. Certainly, the jury would, in general, be asked to retire while the *voir dire* is held. Indeed, it would rather seem to defeat the object of the exercise to allow them to be present. It is absolutely clear that the defence can insist upon the jury being absent, but it is unclear whether it is entitled to require the jury's presence. The authority traditionally relied upon for the proposition that it is so entitled is *Anderson*,[4] but that case is actually concerned with legal argument; no question of calling evidence arose. Nonetheless, Lord Hewart CJ seemed to have a broader principle in mind when he said, in that case, '[i]t is difficult to imagine any circumstances in which, except at the request or with the consent of the defence, a jury can possibly be asked to leave the box in order that statements may be made during their absence.'[5] In *Hendry*, the Court of Appeal sought to confine *Anderson* to its particular facts, adding: 'it is for the judge to have the final word as to whether the jury should or should not remain in

[1] The latter term will be used in general in this work, though we shall see that, in cases where a trial within a trial is required in the magistrates' court, it does not share every feature of the trial on the *voir dire* in the Crown Court.

[2] [1982] AC 204, at 223.

[3] See *Hammond* [1941] 3 All ER 318, at 320.

[4] (1929) 21 Cr.App.R 178.

[5] *Ibid.* 183.

court during submissions which are being made to him'.[6] Again, there was no question here of there being a trial on the *voir dire*, *Hendry* being concerned with a defence submission that one of the prosecution witnesses should be recalled to give further evidence.

The only authorities directly in point conflict. In *Ajodha* v. *The State*, the Privy Council relied upon *Anderson* for the proposition that the judge will normally conduct a trial on the *voir dire* about the admissibility of a confession in the absence of the jury, but that this would be subject to the right of the defence to decide otherwise.[7] Though this was no more than a *dictum*, there seems to be no obvious reason why the defence should not have a veto in such a case, given that it is the defence which has the keenest *interest* in keeping his confession from the jury. However, *Davis*[8] is Court of Appeal authority to the contrary. There, the judge had held a *voir dire* in the jury's absence over the objections of the defence. His ruling was upheld on appeal, the Court placing reliance upon *Hendry*. It seems, as a matter of precedent, that *Davis* must be regarded authoritative.

If a *voir dire* is held, the prosecution will be in a position to call evidence about the circumstances in which, as it alleges, the confession was made. There is old authority indicating either that the accused is incompetent himself to testify on the *voir dire* or that the judge has a discretion to allow him to testify.[9] Yet it is hard to see how that authority can stand against the clear words of section 1 of the Criminal Evidence Act 1898, which make the accused competent 'at every stage of the proceedings'. In practice, it seems inconceivable that a judge would seek to deny an accused access to the witness box. Attention will be given later to the restrictions placed upon prosecution cross-examination of the accused on the *voir dire*.[10]

In the context of summary trial, it is important to distinguish the question of *when* an issue of admissibility of a confession is to be decided from *how* it is to be decided. The common law set its face entirely against trials within trials,[11] though it recognized that there could be no fixed rule regarding the point during the trial upon the issue of guilt or innocence at which preliminary or incidental matters about the admissibility of evidence should be decided. It might sometimes be appropriate to settle the matter before any evidence was heard. In the case of confessions, it would usually be appropriate to wait until the conclusion of the evidence before deciding whether or not account should be taken of the confession. However, this was not an invariable rule at common law. Thus, in *ADC* v. *Chief Constable of Greater Manchester*, Robert Goff LJ said:[12]

To give a very simple and perhaps extreme example, if the only evidence before the magistrates is the evidence of a confession and nothing else, then as a matter of common justice

[6] (1988) 88 Cr.App.R 187, at 190. [7] [1982] AC 204, at 223. [8] [1990] Crim.LR 860.

[9] See, respectively, *Baldwin* (1931) 23 Cr.App.R 62 and *Cowell* [1940] 2 KB 49.

[10] See, Ch. 4, text to nn. 76–84 below.

[11] The leading case is *F* v. *Chief Constable of Kent* [1982] Crim.LR 682.

[12] Unreported, 15 Mar. 1983. The following passage is to be found in *Vel* v. *Chief Constable of North Wales* (1987) 151 JPR 510, at 513.

the magistrates ought to deal with the issue of the admissibility of that confession as a preliminary point, before the close of the prosecution case, so that the defendant can decide whether to make a submission of no case to answer.

In the earlier case of *F* v. *Chief Constable of Kent*,[13] Lord Lane CJ seems to have been of the view that a similarly early decision would be appropriate even where there *was* other evidence in the case, in order to enable the accused to decide how to conduct his own case, so far as the giving and calling of evidence was concerned. However, in the *ADC* case itself, the facts seem to have been precisely those envisaged by Lord Lane CJ, and yet the Divisional Court ruled that the magistrate's decision to settle the issue at the end of the hearing was perfectly fair.[14]

Whatever be the correct common law position on this matter, one should be aware of a difficulty to which neither Robert Goff LJ nor Lord Lane CJ alluded in those cases. A decision at the end of the prosecution case will, so far as the evidence is concerned, inevitably be one-sided, for the accused's version of events will not have been heard. It is to be noted that there is clear authority, as regards jury trial, that such an issue must be decided on the basis of the evidence, rather than on the basis of the witness statements.[15] It is difficult to accept that it is any more reasonable to base a decision on only half of the evidence than for it to have no evidential foundation at all.

Even in the Crown Court, the *voir dire* procedure will be appropriate only where the accused seeks to have excluded a confession which he admits making. If he denies having made the particular oral statement or alleges forgery by the police of a written statement attributed to him, the issue raised is a straightforward, factual one. It follows that it is an issue for the jury and that there is no need for a ruling from the judge.[16] Now, there is one English case, *Roberts*,[17] which acknowledges that, if there is no evidence fit to go to the jury that the relevant statement was made by the accused, the judge must instruct the jury not to have regard to it in reaching its verdict. It seems clear that, even so, it will not be right for the judge to conduct a trial on the *voir dire*.[18] Of course, if the judge cannot make a decision on a submission that the evidence should be excluded without first determining whether or not the accused was its author, or if in some other way, the two sorts of issue are inextricably linked, a *voir dire* will be appropriate.[19]

Confession Evidence—Arguments about Discretion

All the authority so far discussed has been concerned with situations where the defence has argued that the confession has been inadmissible under the common

[13] [1982] Crim.LR 682.

[14] The facts of and decision in the case are revealed in *Vel* v. *Chief Constable of North Wales* (1987) 151 JPR 510. See also *R.* v. *Epping and Ongar Justices, ex p. Manby* [1986] Crim.LR 555.

[15] See *Chadwick* (1934) 24 Cr.App.R 138.

[16] See, e.g., *Flemming* (1986) 86 Cr.App.R 32.

[17] [1953] 2 All ER 340, considered in detail, in Ch. 7, text to n. 3 below.

[18] The leading authority is *Ajodha* v. *The State* [1982] AC 204, at 222. See also *Flemming* (1986) 86 Cr.App.R 32 for an express ruling to this effect.

[19] See *Ajodha* v. *The State* [1982] AC 204, at 221.

law exclusionary rule. There is a distinct lack of authority on whether or not a *voir dire* should be held in the Crown Court where it has argued for exclusion as a matter of judicial discretion. And there seems to be no authority at all on how magistrates are to deal with an argument that they should, at least, decide the issue in question as a preliminary point.

The common law cases at Crown Court level demonstrate that, very often, the defence would be arguing that the confession should be excluded under the rule, but that, if not, it should be excluded as a matter of discretion.[20] In these circumstances, common sense and convenience combine to suggest that the two issues be decided at the same time, after a trial on the *voir dire*. However, there is one Central Criminal Court case in which the defence relied only upon discretion. In that case, *Stewart*,[21] Mr Recorder Hawser QC did hold a *voir dire* to settle the issue, which there turned on whether the accused's confession was so unreliable that it ought not, because more prejudicial than probative, to be revealed to the jury. Given the guiding notion that it is highly undesirable for the jury to hear evidence which it is later instructed to disregard, the course there taken seems to be abundantly reasonable. It may, therefore, be taken to represent the position at common law not only in respect of discretionary exclusion for unreliability, but also in respect of such exclusion for unfairness.

It would seem to be equally a matter of common sense that the common law procedural position at summary trial would be the same for discretionary exclusion as for exclusion under the rule. The factors which, as we have seen,[22] the magistrates should take into account in deciding at what point during the proceedings to settle the issue of admissibility will be relevant in exactly the same way where their discretionary power is invoked.

Non-confession Evidence

All the authority at common law on the holding of a trial on the *voir dire* in order to decide whether or not to exclude *non-confession evidence* relates to evidence of the results of pre-trial identification procedures. In one, briefly reported, Crown Court case,[23] the judge did hold a *voir dire* before deciding to exclude such evidence, apparently on the basis that it had been obtained unfairly. However, in two later cases in which the trial judge had taken a similar course, the Court of Appeal (Criminal Division) held that he should not have. In one of them, *Walshe*, though the Court certainly said, 'that is not a procedure which a judge at a trial ought to adopt',[24] it is unclear whether this was based upon the proposition that, even though such evidence may properly be excluded in the exercise of a discretion, the *voir dire* was the wrong vehicle for the judge's decision, or upon the notion that the judge enjoys no such discretion at common law in any event.

[20] Good examples are *Houghton and Franciosy* (1978) 68 Cr.App.R 197 and *Hudson* (1980) 72 Cr.App.R 163.

[21] (1972) 56 Cr.App.R 272.

[22] See text to nn. 11–15 above.

[23] *Leckie and Ensley* [1983] Crim.LR 543.

[24] (1980) 74 Cr.App.R 85, at 87.

However, in *Flemming*,[25] rather more help was given. There, it was clear that the defence case for exclusion was based upon the notion that the potential prejudicial effect of the evidence outweighed its probative value. It was not being argued that it ought to be excluded by reason of some unfairness in the way it had been obtained. In these circumstances, the Court's decision that no *voir dire* should be held is hardly surprising, for *Sang*[26] establishes that the discretion to exclude evidence more prejudicial than probative is a general one, available in all criminal cases and in respect of every kind of evidence. No court could face with equanimity the prospect of the widest availability of the *voir dire* procedure, involving as it does, where the judge eventually rules against exclusion, the hearing of the same evidence twice over, with the consequent lengthening of trials caused thereby. It does not *necessarily* follow that the *voir dire* procedure would be equally objectionable in a case where the accused relies upon the unfairness of the way in which the evidence was obtained as the reason for discretionary exclusion. Where no *voir dire* is held, *Flemming* suggests that the judge should settle the issue of exclusion either at the end of the prosecution case or after all the evidence has been called. It also acknowledges that there may be exceptional cases where the written statements make the matter so clear that an earlier ruling is appropriate.

Reconsidering Exclusion Issues

It may sometimes happen that evidence given during the trial of the general issue causes the judge to have second thoughts about the voluntariness of a confession he has previously ruled admissible. *Watson* decides[27] that, in an appropriate case, the judge may act upon such second thoughts by changing his decision on its admissibility. The Court of Appeal stressed that only in 'very rare and unusual cases' would further evidence persuading the judge to change his decision emerge. The courses open to the judge in such cases are to direct the jury to disregard the confession, to direct them to acquit should there be no other sufficient evidence against the accused, or to order a new trial. A new trial should be ordered only if the judge considers there to be a real risk that, in spite of a warning to disregard the inadmissible evidence, the jury will be so influenced by it that they will convict. The influence here of the understandable general reluctance to order new trials is unfortunate. The reason the admissibility issue is normally decided in the absence of the jury is a fear of prejudice to the accused flowing from the supposed inability of many jurors, even under strong judicial direction, to put inadmissible confession evidence out of their minds. This risk of prejudice will be no less present in the unusual circumstances predicated in *Watson*.[28]

Presumably, this power to reconsider is not restricted to the situation where a *voir dire* has been held. So, if, in a non-confession case, the judge had made a

[25] (1986) 86 Cr.App.R 32. [26] [1980] AC 402. [27] (1980) 70 Cr.App.R 273.

[28] *Cornelius* (1936) 55 CLR 235, at 249, suggests that the Australian courts are more willing to act to prevent this kind of prejudice.

formal ruling in favour of admission of the evidences at the close of the prosecution case, it is possible, though very unlikely, that evidence given as part of the defence case might make him change his mind. It has certainly been held in the Northern Irish case of *Murphy*[29] that the power of reconsideration applies no less to exclusion as a matter of discretion than to exclusion by rule, and no doubt was cast upon that holding in *Watson* itself.

The Police and Criminal Evidence Act 1984

Exclusion under Section 76

The relevant part of section 76(2) of the 1984 Act states:

> If, in any proceedings where the prosecution proposes to give in evidence a confession . . ., it is represented to the court that the confession was or may have been obtained [in a way which would render it inadmissible], the court shall not allow the confession to be given in evidence except in so far as the prosecution proves to the court . . . that the confession . . . was not obtained [in such a way].

We shall see that these words have more than one radical effect upon the position at common law, but there are a few preliminary points to be made. First, the key to tripping the procedure embraced by section 76(2) is a representation from the defence that the confession is inadmissible. What seems clearly to be envisaged is a formal submission to the court, and it has been held that cross-examination of prosecution witnesses the effect of which is that the confession was obtained in breach of section 76(2) does not count as a representation.[30] Secondly, once such a representation is made, the issue of admissibility must be decided before any evidence is given about the confession. Thirdly, since the prosecution must *prove* that the confession was not obtained in a way which renders it inadmissible, it is quite clear that the court must hear evidence on that issue before deciding it.

An important departure from the common law is that magistrates, no less than the Crown Court judge, must hold a trial within a trial where the relevant representation is made. The words of the subsection makes it plain that it applies 'in any proceedings'. Having confirmed in *R.* v. *Liverpool Juvenile Court, ex p. R*[31] that that is indeed the case, the Divisional Court went on to adapt the Crown Court *voir dire* procedure to work more conveniently before magistrates.[32] So it would not be necessary to call twice the prosecution evidence about the obtaining of the confession. Of course, in the case of the accused, he might very well have things to say, later in the trial of the issue, over and above that which it was necessary or relevant for him to say at the trial within a trial. Given that the

[29] [1965] NI 130.

[30] See *R.* v. *Liverpool Juvenile Court, ex p. R* [1988] QB 1, at 10–11.

[31] *Ibid.*

[32] The various adaptations in question make it inappropriate to refer to the procedure as a trial on the *voir dire*, since that term connotes an *entirely separate* enquiry into the issue in question. The broader term, 'trial within a trial', is to be preferred, and it will be used here.

magistrates do not have to re-hear prosecution evidence about the confession, they do not need to announce their decision immediately after the trial within a trial is concluded, though *Ex p. R* lays down that it must be announced no later than at the end of the prosecution case.

The Divisional Court in *Ex p. R* expressly stated that it was not laying down any guidance as regards trial at the Crown Court. This must be taken to mean that the adaptations for the magistrates would not apply in the Crown Court. Therefore, it must be necessary to hold a *voir dire* at that Court once a representation has been made.[33]

For completeness, it should be mentioned that it was held in *R. v. Oxford Justices, ex p. Berry*[34] that section 76 applied no less to committal proceedings than to trial proceedings. Though the good sense of conducting, in committal proceedings, an enquiry about the admissibility of a confession was doubted in that case, the words 'in any proceedings' were decisive.[35] Though *Ex p. Berry* did not expressly state that the appropriate way of conducting the enquiry was by hearing evidence at a trial within a trial, that would seem to be the inescapable conclusion. However, now that Part II of Schedule 1 of the Criminal Procedure and Investigations Act 1996 has been brought into effect[36]—*Ex p. Berry* is no longer good law. Paragraph 25 thereof inserts a new subsection (9) into section 76 of the 1984 Act which expressly disapplies section 76(2) in the case of committal proceedings. It follows that no question of excluding a confession is now capable of arising in proceedings of that kind.

Exclusion under Section 78

Section 78(1) provides:

> In any proceedings the court may refuse to allow evidence on which the prosecution proposes to rely to be given if it appears to the court that . . . the admission of the evidence would have such an adverse effect on the fairness of the proceedings that the court ought not to admit it.

The formulation differs slightly from that in section 76(2), in referring to the giving of evidence on which the prosecution proposes to rely, rather than to the prosecution proposing to give a confession in evidence. Thus, the prosecution would propose to *give* a confession in evidence once for all at the time it first sought to adduce it, but might propose to *rely* on it much later on. Still, in both cases, the result of the court acceding to the defence submission will be a refusal to allow evidence 'to be given'. So as a matter of ordinary language it ought to follow that,

[33] There is first instance support for this proposition—see *Millard* [1987] Crim.LR 196. There is explicit, though *obiter*, Court of Appeal authority to the same effect—see *Davis* [1990] Crim.LR 860—and this seems to have been assumed to be the case in *Sat-Bhambra* (1988) 88 Cr.App.R 55.

[34] [1988] QB 507.

[35] They are equally capable of comprehending extradition proceedings—see *Re Walters* [1987] Crim.LR 577.

[36] See SI 1997, No 683, which brought Sched.1 into effect on 1 April 1997.

under section 78(1) no less than under section 76(2), a decision on exclusion must be taken no later than the point at which first reference is made to the confession or other evidence, i.e. before it is given.

In fact, the authority on this matter is in serious disorder. It seems to say, in effect, that the same words have a different result according to whether the trial is at the Crown Court or the magistrates' court, and according to whether the evidence in question is confession or non-confession evidence.

Starting with confession evidence in the Crown Court, *Manji*[37] favours the ordinary language interpretation. There, the defence relied only upon section 78 in seeking to persuade the trial judge to exclude the accused's confession. The Court of Appeal held that the judge had been wrong to refuse to hold a *voir dire*. Though the issue was an essentially factual one, namely whether or not a caution had been given, that Court was clear that the correct procedure was to render its decision about exclusion before the confession was first adduced in evidence.

No reference was made in *Manji* to the earlier, non-confession case of *Beveridge*,[38] where the evidence in question was the product of an identification parade. The report fails to give full details of the defence's complaint, though it seems to have included the fact that there had been six persons, not the recommended minimum of eight, at the parade. It may be surmised that the case for exclusion was that, because of breaches of the identification code, the evidence was unreliable, or more prejudicial than probative. It will be recalled that the common law authority was quite strongly against both the holding of a *voir dire* and the making of a decision whether to exclude or not, unusual cases apart, at a point before the evidence in question was adduced. *Beveridge* largely follows the common law on the first point, but seems to depart from it on the second. In the words of McCowan J:[39]

> it is apparent to this Court that a trial judge must consider the depositions and statements and the submissions of counsel when a point is taken on an identification parade. There may be occasions when the trial judge will think it desirable to hold a trial within a trial in order to determine what his course of action should be. Such occasions, in the view of this Court, will be rare.

Though the effect of this passage is not absolutely clear, it can be taken as saying that the decision whether or not to exclude *must* be made before the evidence in question is first adduced, though, rare cases apart, this should be done on the papers rather than on the basis of a *voir dire*. The later, briefly reported case of *Martin and Nicholls*[40] seems to confirm that the holding of a *voir dire* should indeed be very rare. Nonetheless, it is right to add that there are certainly two cases in which the trial judge had resorted to the *voir dire* procedure and in which

[37] [1990] Crim.LR 512. See also *Dutton*, 11 Nov. 1988 (transcript through LEXIS); *Ryan* [1992] Crim.LR 187.

[38] (1987) 85 Cr.App.R 255.

[39] *Ibid*. 258.

[40] [1994] Crim.LR 218. See also *Harwood* [1989] Crim.LR 285.

the Court of Appeal offered no adverse comment upon the course taken.[41] In neither of them was reference made to *Beveridge* or *Martin and Nicholls.*

When we turn to the authorities concerned with summary trial, we find that even with regard to confession evidence, the notion that the exclusion issue *must* be settled before the evidence is adduced has been rejected. In the leading case, *Vel* v. *Chief Constable of North Wales*, the Divisional Court concluded that 'there is . . . no right on the part of the defendant in a magistrates' court to have the question of the admissibility of the evidence in question determined under s. 78 in advance of that evidence being given'.[42] The Court gave two reasons for the conclusion. First, the decision under section 78 is discretionary, while that under section 76 is rule-governed. Secondly, it said that there is no burden of proof on the prosecution to disprove unfairness under section 78, whereas there is such a burden under section 76. Neither reason is persuasive. The difference in the juridical nature of the two types of decision seems far less significant than the danger of a jury placing reliance upon evidence eventually excluded, yet the Divisional Court's point is indifferent as between the two modes of trial. It seems better for summary procedure to be tugged by that in the Crown Court. Certainly, no similar point on the significance of discretion was taken in *Manji.* The second reason was given without any discussion of the law about burden and standard of proof as regards confessions alleged to be inadmissible, nor to the admittedly slight authority relating to burden and standard in discretionary decisions.[43] All in all, it is extremely difficult to see how the same words, in section 78, can have one meaning for magistrates, but another for the Crown Court.

In any event, the Divisional Court in *Vel* went on to say that magistrates should proceed as they had before the Act, so that the pre-Act decisions continue correctly to state the law. Therefore, according to the Court:[44]

> In some cases [magistrates' courts] should deal with an application to exclude evidence when it arises. In other cases they may leave the decision until the end of the hearing. It is impossible to lay down a general rule, other than that the object should always be to secure a trial which is fair and just to both sides.

The effect of this would seem to be to endorse the idea of a *power* to deal with, as a preliminary point in appropriate cases, the question whether or not the confession should be excluded. There is an unreported confession case[45] which seems to contemplate not merely the taking of the point as a preliminary one but the hearing of evidence at a trial within a trial, in order to decide it, in such cases.

[41] *Kitchen* [1994] Crim.LR 684 (transcript through LEXIS) and *Cooke* [1995] 1 Cr.App.R 318.

[42] (1987) 151 JPR 510, at 514. *Vel* was followed in *Halawa* v. *FACT* [1995] 1 Cr.App.R 21, at 34.

[43] See text to nn. 67–81 below. Interestingly, in *Manji* itself, the Court of Appeal said that it was the judge's task to make a finding whether or not the prosecution had *proved* that a caution had been given.

[44] (1987) 151 JPR 510, at 515. The pre-Act decisions are *F* v. *Chief Constable of Kent* [1982] Crim.LR 682 and *ADC* v. *Chief Constable of Greater Manchester*, unreported, 15 Mar. 1983, both of which are considered at text to nn. 11–15 above.

[45] *Carlisle* v. *DPP*, 19 Nov. 1987, discussed in Gibson (1988) 152 JPN 228.

There is also a case about exclusion of non-confession evidence in the magistrates' court, namely *DPP* v. *British Telecommunications plc*.[46] The accused company was charged with the absolute offence of using on a road a trailer with a defective braking system. After a road accident, their vehicle had been examined on behalf of the prosecution with a view to establishing the condition of its brakes. No defence representative was present, yet the effect of the examination was to prevent any future examination revealing whether or not they were defective. The defence argued that admission of the inspector's evidence that the brakes were defective would have an adverse effect on the fairness of the proceedings. In effect, everything turned on this point, for, if it were rejected, the defence was hardly in a position to challenge that evidence. The justices decided the section 78(1) issue as a preliminary one without hearing evidence from the inspector or anyone else. The Divisional Court held that they had been wrong to do so. In so holding, the Court seems, in effect, to have rejected the device which *Beveridge*[47] accepted in the case of Crown Court trials, namely a decision based upon the papers and upon legal argument. Nor did the Court have a trial within a trial in mind as an alternative; the proper course would have been to hear the prosecution evidence and then to decide, at the close of its case, upon its proper weight.[48]

Finally, so far as section 78(1) is concerned, in *R.* v. *King's Lynn Justices, ex p. Holland*,[49] the Divisional Court considered the power of magistrates to exclude evidence in respect of committal to the Crown Court. Relying on *Ex p. Berry*,[50] the Court held that section 78(1) applied, in principle, to committal proceedings. However, it applied in a very much attenuated form. Paragraph 26 of Part II of Schedule 1 of the Criminal Procedure and Investigations Act 1996 has overturned *Ex p. Holland* on this point.[51] It adds a new subsection (3) to section 78 of the 1984 Act expressly disapplying that section in the case of committal proceedings.

Reconsideration and Deferral of Exclusion Issues

It will be recalled that *Watson*,[52] for rule cases, and *Murphy*,[53] for discretion cases, establish that the court has power to reconsider its earlier decision in favour of admission of a confession in evidence.[54] Because the wording of both section 76(2) and section 78(1) seems to treat the court's initial ruling as a once-and-for-all decision, it would seem to follow that in neither case is reconsideration now possible. Under section 76(2), once the confession is in evidence, it cannot be said that the prosecution is *proposing* to give it in evidence, while, under section 78(1), the court's power is to refuse to allow evidence *to be given*.

In *Sat-Bhambra*, the Court of Appeal confirmed that *Watson* (on section 76(2)) has indeed bitten the dust, and it went on to add that the effect of section 78(1) is

[46] (1991) 155 JPR 869. [47] (1987) 85 Cr.App.R 255, considered at text to nn. 38–41 above.
[48] See (1991) 155 JPR 869, at 873. [49] [1993] 1 WLR 324.
[50] [1988] QB 507, considered at text to nn. 34–6 above.
[51] See SI 1997, No 683, which brought Sched. I into effect on 1 April 1997.
[52] (1980) 70 Cr.App.R 273. [53] [1965] NI 130. [54] See text to nn. 27–9 above.

the same, so far as discretionary exclusion is concerned.[55] Although its correctness has been confirmed by the later case of *Dutton*,[56] this second point is troublesome. The logic is that, because the exclusion issue *must* be decided before the evidence is adduced, the power of reconsideration has disappeared. Yet, as we have seen, at least in the case of summary trial, section 78(1) has been interpreted as imposing no such duty on the court.[57] It ought to follow that the court, in such cases, retains the power of reconsideration, the *dicta* in *Sat-Bhambra* and in *Dutton* being inapplicable.

The apparent inflexibility flowing from sections 76(2) and 78(1) has not appealed to the judiciary. Consequently, in *Sat-Bhambra* itself, the Court went on to hold that the judge or magistrate is not powerless in either situation. Rather, section 82(3), by preserving the common law power of discretionary exclusion, also preserves in substance the *Watson/Murphy* principle.[58]

Another radical effect of the two subsections may, like the last one, be more apparent than real. *Ajodha* v. *The State*[59] confirmed the well-established common law freedom of the defence to decide to challenge the confession during the trial of the general issue, rather than, as will be much more usual, at a trial on the *voir dire*. There may be good tactical reasons for such a course; in particular, defence counsel might wish to deny the police witnesses a 'dummy run' outside the jury's hearing in relation to their account of the circumstances in which the confession was obtained. Counsel might then wish to submit, at a later stage, once that evidence and, perhaps, that of the accused had been adduced, that the jury should be directed to disregard the confession or even to acquit the accused.

On the face of it, sections 76(2) and 78(1) both have the effect of depriving the defence of this deferral option, and for precisely the reason that they seem to deny the *Watson/Murphy* principle. Yet in *R.* v. *Liverpool Juvenile Court, ex p. R*,[60] Russell LJ expressed the view that, under section 76(2) at least, the option remained, his reasoning being that, when exercising it, the defence would avoid making any representation that the confession was inadmissible.[61] However, this is only a partial solution, for one must then ask what *positive* power the defence has to challenge the confession at a later stage. Section 76(3) allows the judge, of his own motion, to require the prosecution to prove the admissibility of the confession, but this subsection too refers to the prosecution proposing to give the confession in evidence. Furthermore, section 76(1) seems designed to forestall recourse to any common law doctrine of challenge, for it says that a confession

[55] (1988) 88 Cr.App.R 55, at 62.

[56] 11 Nov. 1988 (transcript through LEXIS). See also *Hassan* [1995] Crim.LR 404.

[57] See the discussion in the text to nn. 42–8 above. It is possible that the same may, in due course, be applied to trial on indictment.

[58] (1988) 88 Cr.App.R 55, at 62.

[59] [1982] AC 204, at 223.

[60] [1988] QB 1, at 10. This aspect of *Ajodha* was referred to expressly in *Raghip, Silcott and Braithwaite*, unreported, 5 Dec. 1991, without any indication being given that it has failed to survive enactment of s. 76 of the 1984 Act.

[61] Though the case is directly concerned with summary trial, if Russell LJ's reasoning is valid, it must apply equally to Crown Court trial.

may be given in evidence 'in so far as it is relevant to any matter in issue in the proceedings and is not excluded by the court in pursuance of this section'. It seems to follow that the exclusionary rule proper is restricted, so far as its availability is concerned, to the time before any evidence of the confession has been given. As Lord Lane CJ said in *Sat-Bhambra*, '[i]f a defendant wishes under section 76 to exclude a confession, the time to make his submission to that effect is before the confession is put in evidence and not afterwards.'[62]

The day may, once again, be saved for the defence lawyer by section 82(3). It might reasonably be thought unfair for the prosecution to be allowed to rely upon a confession obtained by oppression, while the adducing of a confession rendered unreliable by anything said or done to the accused might be thought unfair in allowing the trier of fact to consider evidence more prejudicial than probative. Whether or not judges will, in fact, be prepared to use section 82(3) to get around these limitations of section 76 is another matter. Used to allow a judicial re-think about admissibility, section 82(3) empowers the judge or magistrate, but used to allow unorthodox defence tactics, it gives power to the accused.

There is a briefly reported case concerned with the equivalent problem under section 78(1). *Harwood*[63] appears to say that the defence tactic of allowing the evidence to be called, then seeking a ruling from the judge at some later stage, is impermissible. The Court of Appeal doubted that the judge would ever be entitled to withdraw such evidence from the jury or to direct it to acquit in these circumstances. Of course, if the section 82(3) argument works, so far as section 76(2) is concerned, it ought to be equally capable of preserving the power of discretionary exclusion after the adducing of the evidence.

It is not necessarily the case that the judge or magistrate will change his mind in favour of exclusion; he may decide that an initial decision to exclude was wrong. The latter situation will, perhaps, be rare, but there is one Court of Appeal case to the effect that reconsideration in this direction is, in principle, permissible. That case, *Allen*,[64] was itself concerned with discretionary exclusion, but the same notion should be no less capable of applying to the exclusionary rule. Here, of course, the wording of section 76(2) and of section 78(1) creates no problem because, in the premises, the evidence in question will not have been given when the change of mind occurs.

Sections 76 and 78 Relied Upon in the Alternative

We have seen that there are significant differences between sections 76 and 78 in procedural terms. In particular, so far as summary trial is concerned, it seems clear that, if the defence challenge to a confession is mounted under section 76 the court is obliged to conduct a trial within a trial, yet that if it is mounted under section 78 it is, perhaps exceptional cases apart, obliged not to conduct one. Therefore, it might appear that magistrates who are faced with a challenge to a

62 (1988) 88 Cr.App.R 55, at 62. 63 [1989] Crim.LR 285. 64 [1992] Crim.LR 297.

confession under both sections in the alternative must split that challenge, holding a trial within a trial only on the section 76 element. Good sense surely tells against any such course, and, indeed, there is clear Divisional Court authority in support of the proposition that both issues should be settled at a trial within a trial.[65]

Exclusion under Section 82(3)

We have already seen that section 82(3) may have, as one of its practical functions, the preservation of a number of important procedural rules of the common law. That subsection provides:

> Nothing in this part of this Act shall prejudice any power of a court to exclude evidence (whether by preventing questions from being put or otherwise) at its discretion.

There will be cases in which, in substantive terms, little will be lost by the defence if it seeks to have evidence excluded under section 82(3), rather than under section 76 or 78. So it could, in principle, be argued that, should the defence eschew reliance on both of these sections, section 82(3) ought to carry with it the full procedural régime defined by common law. However, it seems unlikely that a court would be willing to countenance the making of minor procedural distinctions between, in effect, the section 78(1) and section 82(3) powers.

The Judicial Power under Section 76(3)

Reference has already been made to the power of the judge or magistrate, of his own motion, to require the prosecution to prove that the accused's confession was not obtained by oppression or in circumstances rendering it likely to be unreliable. Though it is possible that the subsection might be used for other purposes, it is probable that its most significant purpose is to enable the judge or magistrate to protect the unrepresented accused.[66]

Burden and Standard of Proof

There is one other matter which is also procedural and which may conveniently be discussed as a general issue, arising no less in section 78 cases than section 76 ones. What are the respective obligations, if any, of the prosecution and defence with regard to making out the case for or against exclusion of confession or non-confession evidence?

Here it is important to distinguish purely factual matters from matters of judgement and value. Thus, if an accused alleges that he confessed because threatened with violence and the police deny making any such threats, the judge

[65] See *Halawa* v. *FACT* [1995] 1 Cr.App.R 21, at 33.

[66] As suggested, e.g., by Andrew and Hirst, *Criminal Evidence* (2nd. edn., 1992), at para. 19.22.

will have to decide, first, whether or not they were made, and then, if he concludes that they were, whether or not they constitute, in law, oppressive conduct. The burden and standard of proof are relevant only to the former issue; it makes no sense to say that it has to be proved that the threats in question amounted in law to oppression.

Of course, where factual issues are left to a *jury* to decide, the law usually requires the prosecution to prove them beyond reasonable doubt. No such *general* proposition applies in respect of the decision of the *judge* on a fact constituting a condition precedent to the admissibility of some evidential item.

The Exclusionary Rule for Confessions

Taking first the case where the admissibility of a confession under section 76 is in issue, the express statutory wording makes the position absolutely clear. Subsection (2) requires the prosecution to prove the factual elements in question beyond reasonable doubt. And where the judge invokes subsection (3) in order to test the admissibility of the confession, again it is stated that the prosecution bears the burden of proof. Though that subsection makes no specific mention of the standard of proof, it is inconceivable that it differs from that under subsection (2).

The position under section 76 accords with that of the English common law.[67] It should briefly be noted that other common law systems vary as to the appropriate standard, though all place the burden upon the prosecution. Both Canada and New Zealand favour proof beyond reasonable doubt,[68] while Australia finds proof on the balance of probabilities sufficient.[69] In the United States, most state jurisdictions, as well as the federal jurisdiction, endorse the preponderance of evidence standard (equivalent to that of the balance of probabilities), though a minority of state jurisdictions favour the higher standard.[70] As a matter of US constitutional jurisprudence, there is a requirement that state jurisdictions impose *at least* the preponderance of evidence standard upon the prosecution.[71]

A question never expressly raised in the English cases is whether or not the defence bears a burden of adducing evidence of the factual elements, though the pre-Act case of *Steel*[72] provides limited inferential support for the view that it did not do so at common law. Section 76 seems to provide us with a clear answer under the statutory law. All that is required of the defence is that it *represent* to the court that the accused's confession was obtained in one of the forbidden

[67] See *Sartori* [1961] Crim.LR 397; *McLintock* [1962] Crim.LR 549; *Cave* [1963] Crim.LR 371; *Ping Lin* [1976] AC 574; *Angeli* [1979] 1 WLR 26; *Wong Kam-ming* [1980] AC 247; *McIlkenny* v. *Chief Constable of the West Midlands* [1980] QB 283; and *Hunter* v. *Chief Constable of the West Midlands* [1982] AC 529.

[68] The leading cases are, respectively, *Pickett* (1975) 31 CRNS 239 and *McCuin* [1982] 1 NZLR 13.

[69] See, in particular, *Wendo* (1963) 109 CLR 559, at 562 (*per* Dixon CJ) and at 572–3 (*per* Taylor and Owen JJ).

[70] The relevant authorities are collected together in *Wigmore on Evidence*, 1997 Supplement by Arthur Best, 303–7.

[71] See *Lego* v. *Twomey*, 404 US 477 (1972).

[72] (1981) 73 Cr.App.R 173, at 188.

ways. Any such representation gives rise to a duty in the court not to allow the confession to be adduced in evidence unless and until the prosecution proves it not to have been so obtained. Thus, no evidential threshold need be crossed. However, as was noted earlier it is established that an *express* representation is required; a suggestion to a witness in cross-examination (or, presumably, examination-in-chief) will not be sufficient.[73]

THE EXCLUSIONARY DISCRETION

There is no authority at appeal court level on the burden and standard of proof in respect of the discretionary exclusion of evidence which is more prejudicial than probative or which has been unfairly obtained. In the first instance decision in *Westlake*,[74] Hodgson J did clearly hold that the prosecution had to satisfy him so that he was sure that there had been no breach of the then-applicable Judges' Rules and Administrative Directions. Yet, in the Australian cases, *Lee*[75] and *Wendo*,[76] it was held that the defence bore a burden of proving the relevant factual matters on a balance of probabilities, the reason given in the former case being, '[t]he discretion rule represents an exception to a rule of law, and we think that it is for the accused to bring himself within the exception'.[77]

So far as the statutory discretion is concerned, there is, once again, no clear authority on burden and standard. In *Vel* v. *Chief Constable of North Wales*,[78] the Divisional Court seems to have accepted counsel's argument that 'there is no burden on the Crown to disprove unfairness under s. 78', though this was no more than a step on the way to dealing with another point. Presumably, if there is no burden on the Crown, there must be one on the defence to prove the factual elements of its case for exclusion. In *Manji*,[79] on the other hand, the Court of Appeal held, in a case concerned only with exclusion under section 78, that '[i]t was [the trial judge's] task to make a finding as to whether the prosecution had proved that a caution had been given'.[80] One can, therefore, sympathize with Stuart-Smith LJ's remark in *Anderson* that 'it is not entirely clear where the burden lies so far as section 78 is concerned'.[81]

In principle, there seems much to be said for the view that the burden ought to be on the prosecution and to be one beyond reasonable doubt. If there is a concern to ensure that the prosecution has the opportunity of presenting evidence to negative the defence case, that concern may be met, quite adequately, by imposing a burden of adducing evidence on the defence, something which both the common law and section 78(1) itself leave the courts free to do. There is a pressing argument for consistency with section 76, in that it is very common for the defence to rely upon both that section and section 78(1). For example, the same

[73] See *R.* v. *Liverpool Juvenile Court, ex p. R* [1988] QB 1, at 10–11.
[74] [1979] Crim.LR 652. [75] (1950) 82 CLR 133. [76] (1963) 109 CLR 559.
[77] (1950) 82 CLR 133, at 152–3. [78] (1987) 151 JPR 510, at 514.
[79] [1990] Crim.LR 512. [80] See LEXIS transcript for the precise quotation.
[81] [1993] Crim.LR 447. See LEXIS transcript for the precise quotation.

alleged item of conduct may be said both to amount to oppression and to be capable of rendering the proceedings unfair. It would be most unsatisfactory were the judge able to find the conduct in question to have taken place as regards oppression, yet not as regards unfairness. That would be a distinct possibility if the burden under section 78(1) were to be on the defence, and a bare possibility even if the burden were on the prosecution, but on a balance of probabilities. Set against that pressing argument, it may be said that, given that express words were used in section 76 but not section 78, it may be taken that Parliament intended different results. However, it is to be noted that section 78 was a very late addition to what became the Act, and it must be very doubtful that the distinction between the two sections was deliberate.

4

Confessions—Preliminary Issues

It will be convenient to begin by setting out the core exclusionary rule for confessions. Section 76(2) of the Police and Criminal Evidence Act 1984 ('the 1984 Act') provides:

> If, in any proceedings where the prosecution proposes to give in evidence a confession made by an accused person, it is represented to the court that the confession was or may have been obtained—
>
> (a) by oppression of the person who made it; or
> (b) in consequence of anything said or done which was likely, in the circumstances existing at the time, to render unreliable any confession which might be made by him in consequence thereof,
>
> the court shall not allow the confession to be given in evidence against him except in so far as the prosecution proves to the court beyond reasonable doubt that the confession (notwithstanding that it may be true) was not obtained as aforesaid.

It will be seen that there are two heads to the exclusionary rule, an oppression head and an unreliability head. For purposes of exposition here, the word 'voluntariness' and the expression 'voluntariness rule' will sometimes be used to comprehend the content of both heads.

Functions of Judge and Jury

It is the judicial function to decide all questions of admissibility relating to a confession, the jury function to determine whether or not the confession is true. The same division of function applies, in principle, to magistrates, though they fulfil each function in turn. Of course, the jury may also have to decide the proper meaning and effect of the confession, which may, aptly construed, be a full admission of guilt, or something less than that. In its fact-finding role, the jury is to be assisted by appropriate judicial directions and advice.

One logical consequence of the judge's sovereignty over issues of admissibility is section 76(3) of the 1984 Act, which provides:

> In any proceedings where the prosecution proposes to give in evidence a confession made by an accused person, the court may of its own motion require the prosecution, as a condition of allowing it to do so, to prove that the confession was not obtained as mentioned in subsection (2) above.

Thus, the judge is free to 'trump' the defence where the defence has not taken the admissibility point. This is a rather unlikely outcome, except, perhaps, in cases of accused persons not legally represented. It follows that subsection (3) has particular significance for summary trials.

It would seem quite clear, in principle, that the voluntariness of the confession, as opposed to its truthfulness, is not an issue for the trier of fact. Of course, evidence of the circumstances in which the confession was made may go to the former issue as well as to the latter. Hence, it is open to the accused to cross-examine before the jury witnesses who gave evidence on the *voir dire*.[1] Equally, the accused himself is entitled to give evidence before them about the circumstances in which the confession came to be made. It by no means follows, as the Court of Criminal Appeal held in *Bass*,[2] that the jury should be directed by the judge that, if not themselves satisfied that the confession was made voluntarily, they should disregard it. There seems to be no good reason for the accused to have two bites of the cherry in relation to the issue of admissibility. Fortunately, the law does not now seem to be as stated in *Bass*. There are five pre-Act decisions, two in the Privy Council and three in the Court of Appeal,[3] which expressly or impliedly reject the *Bass* view. Their effect is that the jury should be directed to consider the evidence of the circumstances in which the confession[4] was made in deciding upon the weight and value to be attached to that confession. In other words, the jury may perfectly properly convict on the basis of a confession they believe to have been acquired by, say, oppression, as long as they believe it to be true. None of this powerful authority has been called into question in any reported decision under the 1984 Act,[5] and it seems clear that the law, in this respect, remains unaltered.

The Meaning of 'Confession'

Section 76(2) and (3) are both predicated upon the item of evidence in question being a 'confession'. Section 82(1) defines that term to *include* 'any statement wholly or partly adverse to the person who made it . . . whether made in words or otherwise'. It is to be noted that this definition is not, on the face of it at least, exclusive. The two key phrases are 'wholly or partly adverse' and 'made in words

[1] See *Murray* [1951] 1 KB 391.

[2] See [1953] 1 QB 680, at 684–5. A similar view was taken in a number of cases in the late 1950s and early 1960s, on which see MacKenna [1967] Crim.LR 336.

[3] *Chan Wei Keung* [1967] 2 AC 160; *Ragho Prasad* [1981] 1 WLR 469; *Burgess* [1968] 2 QB 112; *Ovenell* [1969] 1 QB 17; *McCarthy* (1980) 70 Cr.App.R 270. See also *Ajodha* v. *State* [1982] AC 204, at 221 (*per* Lord Bridge) for a *dictum* to similar effect. An argument that the statement of the law to be found in *McCarthy*, at 272, supported the *Bass* view was rejected in *Ragho Prasad* [1981] 1 WLR 469, at 473.

[4] See also the Australian cases of *Basto* (1954) 91 CLR 628 and *MacPherson* (1981) 37 ALR 81, at 88, to similar effect.

[5] Wolchover and Heaton-Armstrong, *Confession Evidence* (1996), at para. 4.157, refer to the unreported case of *Brown* (1990), and suggest that it restores the rule in *Bass*. It is difficult to believe that, if *Brown* is authority for that proposition, it will be followed.

or otherwise'. Before considering their significance, however, we need to be aware of the position so far as judicial confessions are concerned.

Judicial Confessions

It is established that both a plea of guilty[6] and an informal admission made in earlier judicial proceedings[7] are, *prima facie*, admissible in later proceedings.[8] Where a plea of guilty has been withdrawn, the power of the court to exclude evidence more prejudicial than probative has been acknowledged to be of great significance. Indeed, it was said in *Rimmer* that the occasions on which such evidence would be admitted would be rare.[9] So, where the plea has been withdrawn because the legal elements of the offence were initially misunderstood, as, for example, where a person charged with handling stolen goods did not realize that he could not be guilty merely by virtue of having been in possession of goods which were, in fact, stolen, the probative value of the plea will be low, yet its prejudicial potential great. Nonetheless, there will be some cases in which the probative value of the plea is sufficient to allow evidence of it to be adduced.[10] The law shows no equivalent tenderness to the accused so far as informal admissions in earlier judicial proceedings are concerned. For example, inculpatory statements at an abortive earlier trial for the same offence are freely admissible,[11] though, in principle, the probative value/prejudicial effect discretion is available.

With regard to all judicial confessions, the voluntariness rule in section 76(2) is potentially applicable. However, given that any such confession will have been made in open court before a judge, it is most unlikely that either head of the rule will apply in fact.[12]

A number of statutes provide for the examination of citizens under the compulsion of punishment for failure to answer satisfactorily. There are significant difficulties, in some of the examples, with regard to the admissibility of statements made under that kind of compulsion, but in this work such issues are more conveniently dealt with as part of the treatment of the accused's right to silence or privilege against self-incrimination, so the reader should consult that part of the book.[13]

Admissions Falling Short of Full Confessions

As we have seen, section 82(1) specifically includes within the definition statements which are 'partly adverse' statements. It was pointed out in *Sat-Bhambra*[14] that this phrase was no doubt included in order to make it clear that the holding in *Customs and Excise Commissioners* v. *Harz and Power*[15] is good law under the

[6] *Rimmer* [1972] 1 WLR 268.
[7] *McGregor* [1968] 1 QB 371.
[8] See, generally, Pattenden (1983) 32 ICLQ 812.
[9] See [1972] 1 WLR 268, at 272.
[10] See, e.g., *Hetherington* [1972] Crim.LR 703.
[11] *McGregor* [1968] 1 QB 371, at 377.
[12] See n. 8 above, at 828, for suggestions about circumstances in which the rule might apply.
[13] See Ch. 9, text to nn. 8–52 below.
[14] (1988) 88 Cr.App.R 55, at 61.
[15] [1967] 1 AC 760.

Act. The House of Lords decided, in *Harz and Power*, that no distinction was to be drawn between full confessions of guilt and admissions falling short thereof. In Lord Reid's words, '[i]n similar circumstances one man induced by a threat makes a full confession and another induced by the same threat makes one or more incriminating admissions. Unless the law is to be reduced to a mere collection of unrelated rules, I see no distinction between these cases.'[16] For these purposes, it is equally wrong to seek to draw a more limited distinction between an acknowledgment in express words of the truth of some essential part of the guilty fact charged, on the one hand, and an acknowledgment of some subordinate fact, not directly indicative of guilt, on the other. Such a distinction was favoured by Wigmore,[17] but has little to commend it. For example, it would lead to the conclusion that the accused's admission that he believed particular goods to be stolen would constitute a confession, while an admission that he bought them in a public house at an absurdly low price would not. Though this intermediate possibility was not explicitly canvassed in *Harz and Power*, it is clear that at least some of the incriminating statements which the prosecution sought to adduce in that case could not be said to amount to admissions of facts in issue.[18] The same seems to be true of the post-Act case of *Smith*.[19]

Statements on Their Face Exculpatory

Statements which are, on their face, exculpatory are rather more problematical. There are several reasons for this. First, the prosecution will have no reason to seek to adduce evidence of the accused's apparently exculpatory statements unless they have inculpatory value at trial. For example, the accused's denial that he was present at the scene of an offence of violence will have such value when, at trial, he admits presence but denies participation. It follows that, if the exculpatory statement in question was brought about by, say, oppressive behaviour of the police, its admission in evidence at trial would allow the prosecution an advantage it would not have gained had a confession or partial admission followed such behaviour.

Secondly, there is a widely held doctrinal view that truly exculpatory statements cannot amount to confessions because they are not caught by the hearsay rule.[20] Where the prosecution seeks to adduce a confession or admission, it relies upon the truth of that confession or admission, but where the statement is *ex facie* exculpatory, it places no such reliance.[21] This view is not, however, universally held.[22] As a matter of history, it is not clear whether the rule making confessions

[16] [1967] 1 AC 818. [17] See *Evidence* (3rd edn., 1940), iii, § 821.

[18] See [1967] 1 AC 760, at 772–3.

[19] [1994] 1 WLR 1396. The Court of Appeal was simply satisfied that the statements in question were adverse to the accused.

[20] Leading modern English proponents of this view are *Cross and Tapper on Evidence* (8th edn. 1995)—see 676–8—and Andrews and Hirst, *Criminal Evidence* (2nd edn. 1992), para. 19.04. An ingenious variant of this view is put forward by Smith [1995] Crim.LR 280.

[21] See *Mawaz Khan* [1967] 1 AC 454.

[22] See, e.g., Elliott and Wakefield [1979] Crim.LR 428.

prima facie admissible grew up as an exception to the hearsay rule or developed separately from it. Certainly, there are indications of an incipient exclusionary rule for confessions at quite an early stage in the history of the law of evidence,[23] perhaps as early as the first part of the seventeenth century.

As a matter of principle, the argument for intimate connection with the hearsay rule would seem to depend upon the propositions, first, that confessions, as statements against interest, are, unlike other statements made outside court, likely to be reliable, and, secondly, that it is only when a confession is made in circumstances which call its reliability into question that there is any reason to exclude it. The second proposition is extremely vulnerable, whatever may or may not be the merits of the first.[24] There are reasons other than fear of unreliability for excluding confessions. We have seen that the so-called protective and disciplinary principles, particularly the former, have attracted support.[25] An entirely tenable view of the oppression head of the exclusionary rule is that its concern is not the danger of unreliability, but the need to protect the accused from being subjected to unacceptable behaviour designed to persuade him to confess. It may cogently be argued that the protective principle lets the exclusionary rule out of the umbrella of hearsay, so that there is no reason for the law here to take its cue from the hearsay rule. If so, the important point is that the accused is no less in need of protection in respect of his apparently exculpatory statements acquired in breach of his rights, where used to inculpatory effect, than in respect of his *ex facie* inculpatory ones.

Thirdly, a more functional argument has been put forward. It is said to be implausible that a suspect faced with overreaching police conduct or otherwise subjected to pressure to confess 'will falsely tell [the police] what [they] do not want to hear, namely a denial'.[26] One doubts that this claim makes sufficient allowance for the variability of human reaction to pressure. Though it will usually be clear that the police are seeking a confession and nothing else, a given suspect may hope that a particular exculpatory answer will divert the police from the immediate pressure. For example, the putting forward of an alibi might be expected to lead the police to check its veracity, so terminating the interview for the time being. Nor does it seem reasonable to suppose that the suspect will always respond to pressure in an entirely rational way. In *Wattam*,[27] the accused, a murder suspect, had offered to the police in quick succession three contradictory versions of an alibi. At trial, he admitted that he had been staying near the scene of the murder at the time of its commission and gave an explanation of why he had failed to tell the police.

A fourth problem is that the line between statements inculpatory when made and those exculpatory at that time is not an easy one to draw, while, if it is

[23] Some of the relevant materials are collected in Mirfield, *Confessions* (1985), at 42–50.

[24] Modern experience suggests that the first proposition may itself be doubtful—see Ch. 12, text to nn. 140–90 above.

[25] See Ch. 2, text to nn. 55–74 above.

[26] *Cross on Evidence* (7th edn., 1990), 609. The argument is not put forward in the 8th edn., 1995.

[27] (1952) 36 Cr.App.R 72.

necessary to consider whether or not a statement is hearsay before considering the application of section 76, a further element of complexity is added. The line-drawing problem has agitated the Canadian courts very much more than the English ones. In the leading Canadian case, *Piché*,[28] there was an informative division of opinion in the Manitoba Court of Appeal about whether the accused's statement to the police was inculpatory or exculpatory at the time it was made. The accused was charged with the murder by shooting of her common-law husband. In a detailed statement to the police, she had said that she had left him asleep in their home at 1.50 a.m. on the night in question. She had gone on to refer generally to her husband's harsh treatment of her and, more specifically, to his conduct that night; he had accused her of infidelity and 'given her hell'. Finally, she had revealed that she knew something about his guns—the shot which had killed him had been fired from one—and that she knew how to load them. All three elements of her statement were capable of being helpful to the prosecution. They revealed opportunity, for she had been at the house during the period when, as other evidence showed, her husband must have died. His reported behaviour towards her, not least on the night in question, demonstrated that she had a motive, while what she had said about the guns suggested that she was quite capable of using one to kill him. For those reasons, Freedman JA (dissenting) took the view that her statement was inculpatory. Monnin JA answered the first point by saying that it was only the other evidence adduced at trial which fixed the time of death, so her remarks about the time she had left the house were not inculpatory when made. As regards his alleged behaviour, this gave her no less of a motive simply to leave the house than to kill him. Though Monnin JA said nothing about her knowledge of the guns, he must have concluded that this too was not inculpatory.

It is difficult to say which of the two views in *Piché* is to be preferred. If one were to stick to the notion that what has been said counts as an admission only if it is an acknowledgement *in express words* of some *essential part of the guilty fact charged*, Piché would not be regarded as having confessed. Yet we have seen that English law seems to have set its face against the notion that the matter stated must be an essential part of the guilty fact.[29] Furthermore, once one abandons the express words requirement, thereby opening up the issue of the adversity of statements to implication and inference, one gets into the morass of difficulty associated with so-called implied assertions in the law of hearsay. A majority of the Supreme Court of Canada seems to have had these various difficulties firmly in focus when deciding that it was better not to seek to draw the relevant line at all. In the words of Hall J:[30]

> the time is opportune for this Court to say that the admission in evidence of all statements made by an accused . . ., whether inculpatory or exculpatory, is governed by the same rule

[28] [1970] 1 CCC 257 (Manitoba Court of Appeal); (1970) 11 DLR(3d) 700 (Supreme Court of Canada).

[29] See text between nn. 14 and 19 above.

[30] (1970) 11 DLR(3d) 700, at 709–10.

and thus put to an end the continuing controversy and necessary evaluation by trial Judges of every such statement which the Crown proposes to use in chief or on cross-examination as being either inculpatory or exculpatory.

Though *Wattam*[31] seemed to provide at least inferential support for the proposition that the English common law was in line with Canadian law on this point, the weight of authority on the statutory law indicates that statements which were exculpatory when made are not caught by section 76. However, that authority is much less clear about the line which divides what is caught from what is not. The two leading cases are *Sat-Bhambra*[32] and *Park*,[33] but, before we deal with them, mention should be made of one contrary case.

In *Ismail*,[34] the Court of Appeal seems to have endorsed the view that the oppression head of the exclusionary rule was applicable to an interview relating to three complaints of indecent assault, during which the accused made no admissions. In that interview, he had denied knowing the person who eventually became his co-accused, had denied having gone to the complainants' house, and had claimed that he had been with his fiancée at the time of the assaults. By the time of trial, he had withdrawn both the denials and the claim. Plainly, the earlier statements were adverse as he stood in the witness box, but had not been adverse or inculpatory, either on their face or as a matter of what Ismail intended, when made. Though the prosecution seems to have conceded that the contents of the interview had been rendered inadmissible by police oppression, no comment was offered by the court indicating that that concession had been wrongly made.

The present issue had been first addressed in *Sat-Bhambra*,[35] though that case itself was eventually decided on another ground. The Court of Appeal 'inclined to the view that purely exculpatory statements are not within the meaning of section 82(1)',[36] its reasons being that:[37]

> [t]he words of the section do seem prima facie to be speaking of statements adverse on the face of them. The section is aimed at excluding confessions obtained by words or deeds likely to render them unreliable, *i.e.* admissions or partial admissions contrary to the interests of the defendant and welcome to the interrogator. They can hardly have been aimed at statements containing nothing which the interrogator wished the defendant to say and nothing apparently adverse to the defendant's interests.

Specific reliance is placed here upon the notion that unreliability is the only concern of section 76, a notion which can easily be challenged by reference to other authority, for example the statement of Lord Griffiths in *Lam Chi-Ming*, which is referred to a little later in this Chapter.[38] However, even putting that to one side, it is to be noted that *Sat-Bhambra* offers us two possible glosses upon the words 'wholly or partly adverse' in section 82(1). The first requires adversity to be present on the face of the statement or that it contain something apparently adverse

[31] (1952) 36 Cr.App.R 72. [32] (1988) 88 Cr.App.R 55.
[33] (1993) 99 Cr.App.R 270. See also *Jelen and Katz* (1989) 90 Cr.App.R 456.
[34] [1990] Crim.LR 109, transcript through LEXIS. [35] (1988) 88 Cr.App.R 55.
[36] *Ibid.* 61 (*per* Lord Lane CJ). [37] *Ibid.*
[38] [1991] 2 AC 212, at 220—see text at n. 49 below.

to the accused's interests. The second is that, to be relevantly adverse, it must contain something which the interrogator wished the accused to say. In fact, these two glosses will not always point in the same direction. For example, Piché's statement that she left the victim at 1.50 a.m. sleeping at home would seem to carry no adversity on its face, yet, if the police knew, when they interviewed her, roughly the timeframe in which the victim had died, it might well have been welcome to them, though obviously not as welcome as a full confession to murder.

Nonetheless, in *Park*,[39] a case which *does* seem to be binding authority in favour of the view that section 82(1) does not comprehend statements which were exculpatory when made, it was said that 'some assistance can be gained'[40] from the words of Lord Lane CJ in *Sat-Bhambra* which are quoted above. The court in *Park* then went on to offer a rather different gloss upon section 82(1), for it endorsed a statement contained in *Archbold* that 'section 82(1) was not aimed at statements which the maker intended to be exculpatory and which were exculpatory on their face, but which could later be shown to be false or inconsistent with the maker's evidence on oath'.[41] Three points should be made about this formulation. First, it is put in terms of exculpation, rather than the absence of adversity. Secondly, the intention of the maker of the statement becomes relevant. Thirdly, it seems that the statement must be exculpatory *both* on its face *and* in intention in order to be outside the subsection. It is clear that the effect of what the accused said and his intention may diverge. Thus, if we vary the facts of *Piché* such that the police are aware of the time of the victim's death and tell Piché that he died between certain times, we would find a statement that she had left him sleeping in the house at a time within the relevant limits to be inculpatory on its face, by demonstrating opportunity, yet exculpatory in intention, by virtue of the claim that the victim was alive when Piché last saw him.

It may be concluded that the distinction between partly adverse statements and those not adverse at all is far from clear. Of course, there will be many cases where the statement in question is on its face neither adverse nor inculpatory, where it was not intended to be inculpatory and where its content was not at all welcome to the police. But there will certainly be others where no such concordance is to be found. So either the test will have to be refined by the courts or a different tack altogether will have to be taken, perhaps by the House of Lords.

Where *Sat-Bhambra* and *Park* do prevent the defence seeking to have the accused's statement excluded under section 76(2), it may have recourse instead to section 78(1). Under the subsection, the court has power to exclude any 'evidence on which the prosecution proposes to rely' because of its anticipated adverse effect on the fairness of the proceedings. That evidence need not be confessional in nature, as was expressly recognized in *Park* itself.[42]

[39] (1993) 99 Cr.App.R 270. See also *Sander*, unreported, 1 Mar. 1996. [40] *Ibid*. 274.

[41] See now Archbold, *Criminal Pleading, Evidence and Practice*, 1997 edn., i, para. 15–341.

[42] (1993) 99 Cr.App.R 270, at 275. See also *Okafor* [1994] 3 All ER 741, at 747; *Kerawalla* [1991] Crim.LR 451.

CONDUCT

Conduct is clearly capable of being the functional equivalent of an oral or written statement. So while one suspect might respond to a question asking him if he had committed a given offence by replying, 'Yes', another might simply nod the head. Equally, one suspect might describe in words where the police would find the deceased's body, while another might take the police there and point it out. The words of section 82(1), in stating that a confession includes any statement, 'whether made in words or otherwise', must encompass the person who nods the head or takes the police to the body.

Though there was Scottish authority confirming that conduct equivalent to a statement was caught by the Scots exclusionary rule,[43] only the old case of *Jenkins*[44] was capable of supporting the same proposition in English law and, even then, not unequivocally. There is no authority yet concerned directly with this aspect of section 82(1), but there is a post-Act Hong Kong case in the Privy Council with strong persuasive value. In *Liu Shu-Ling*,[45] the accused, having made a full oral confession to the murder of a woman by strangulation, acceded to a police request to participate in a re-enactment of his crime. With a policewoman playing the part of the deceased, he was able to demonstrate by his actions (which were video-recorded) how he had carried out the killing. The Privy Council could see no reason for distinguishing those facts from a situation where the accused, in the course of confessing orally, might break into a physical representation of some point or other, which situation it was clear would amount to the giving of a confession. It pointed out that many illiterate people might find it easier to demonstrate an action, rather than attempt to describe it in words. It should be added that there are strong *dicta* in the later Hong Kong Privy Council case of *Lam Chi-Ming*[46] to the same effect as *Liu Shu-Ling*.

Less clear is the limit of the inclusion of conduct within the régime of confessions. The nod of the head, the taking to the body, and the re-enactment of the crime all involve assertive conduct equivalent to words. In each case, the accused must have intended, by his conduct, to assert some guilty fact. Many other kinds of conduct may be potentially inculpatory, yet without there being present that intention to assert guilt. Two obvious examples are flight and tears. One inference we may feel able to draw from the fact that the suspect, when confronted, ran away or burst into tears is that he did so from a consciousness of guilt. Yet, it seems unlikely that he *intended*, by his flight or tears, to indicate his guilt.

Whether or not apparently non-assertive conduct of the kind exemplified by tears and flight should be encompassed by the exclusionary rule is rather a similar issue to whether or not words on their face exculpatory should be encompassed. Once again, strict adherence to the notion that a confession is a kind of (admissible) hearsay will probably lead to a conclusion that tears and flight do

[43] *Chalmers* v. *Lord Advocate* [1954] JC 56. See also *Beere* [1965] Qd. SR 370.
[44] (1822) Russ. & Ry. 492. [45] [1989] AC 270. [46] [1991] 2 AC 212.

not count as confessional, though the precise ambit of the hearsay rule is again problematical here.[47] Furthermore, if the reliability principle is paramount, it is hard to conceive of an argument for bringing tears and flight within the confessions rule. For example, when a suspect responds to oppressive police conduct by bursting into tears, it is hardly likely that those tears are false ones. They may, of course, be unreliable in the sense that they do not, in fact, flow from a consciousness of guilt, but rather, say, from simple fear. However, this reliability problems is one of interpretation of the meaning of tears, and it is no more likely to arise where unlawful pressure has been brought to bear upon the suspect than where it has not. The same would appear to apply to flight.

The protective and disciplinary principles both suggest that the régime for confessions *should* apply. Oppressive conduct leading to tears or flight is no less objectionable than that which leads to a verbal admission, and the suspect is potentially disadvantaged in both situations. It is noteworthy that there is judicial endorsement, in the specific context of confessions through conduct, of the protective and disciplinary principles. Thus, in *Lam Chi-Ming*, Lord Griffiths, following the earlier statement of Lord Hailsham in *Wong Kam-Ming*,[48] said:[49]

> Their Lordships are of the view that the more recent English cases established that the rejection of an improperly obtained confession is not dependent only upon possible unreliability but also upon the principle that a man cannot be compelled to incriminate himself and upon the importance that attaches in a civilised society to proper behaviour by the police towards those in their custody.

However, there are three obvious problems with an expansive view of confessions by conduct. First, it is well-established that the confessions régime proper does not apply to the giving of fingerprints or of certain body samples, for example breath or blood, in response to oppressive police conduct, though it is right to add that evidence acquired in this way may be excluded as a matter of judicial discretion.[50] So, once again, a line needs to be drawn. It would seem that this particular line does not pose the greatest difficulty, for the cases of tears and flight differ significantly from those of fingerprints and body samples. The tears and flight, if relied upon at all as evidence of guilt, are the functional equivalents of oral statements which demonstrate a consciousness of guilt. That cannot be said of the fingerprints or body samples. And in those cases, any inference of guilt is drawn not from the conduct itself (giving the fingerprints or body sample) but from its product (the fingerprint or body sample).

The second problem is that, as we have already seen, the weight of authority with regard to statements on their face exculpatory suggests that they are outwith the exclusionary rule, and it might, therefore, be thought strange to take a more expansive view of confessions in the case of conduct. The answer to this point may be that conduct such as tears and flight is, if inculpatory at all, inculpatory at the time, so that the analogy with words exculpatory on their face is inexact.

[47] Especially after *Kearley* [1992] 2 AC 228.
[48] [1980] AC 247, at 261.
[49] [1991] 2 AC 212, at 220.
[50] See, now, s. 78 of the 1984 Act.

Finally, the very wording of section 82(1) presents a problem. It refers, it will be recalled, to statements 'made in words or otherwise'. It is not easy to see how it can be said that the distraught suspect *makes* a statement in tears. The effect, then, of the subsection may well be to allow the exclusionary rule to encompass only conduct intended to be assertive of some fact.

STATEMENT SHOWING MODE OF SPEECH, WRITING, OR EXPRESSION

Just as conduct may sometimes be equivalent to words, so may words be equivalent to conduct. In some cases, the substantive content of speech or text may not matter, but rather the manner in which it is spoken, written, or expressed. For example, the accused's tape-recorded words may show him to have a strong regional accent or a stammer. Such modes of speech may be relevant to the issue of guilt or innocence because, say, the complainant has testified that her attacker had such an accent or stammer. So, once more, the question must be whether the manner in which a statement is made or expressed is caught by the definition in section 82(1).

The well-known case of *Voisin*[51] is authority at common law on the present point. The trunk of a murdered woman, together with a piece of paper bearing the words, 'Bladie Belgiam', had been found in a parcel. Voisin, without first being cautioned, had been asked to write out the words 'Bloody Belgian'. He agreed, but in fact wrote 'Bladie Belgiam'. The Court of Criminal Appeal held that the piece of paper upon which the words were written was admissible in evidence, the exclusionary rule being inapplicable because Voisin's decision to write down those words had not been induced by any threat or promise. Implicitly, it reasoned that the piece of paper was confessional, for, had it been otherwise, the presence or absence of a threat or promise would have been irrelevant. However, Lush J expressed in argument another view:[52]

> There is a difference between the admissibility of a statement and the admissibility of handwriting. A statement may be made under such circumstances that the true facts are not brought out, but it cannot make any difference to the admissibility of handwriting whether it is written voluntarily or under the compulsion of threats.

Once again, if one has solely the problem of unreliability in view, there seems to be no reason why a case with facts like those of *Voisin* should be encompassed by the exclusionary rule.

Yet Lush J did not deliver a separate judgment in *Voisin*, so it must be taken that the common law of confessions did encompass cases like it. If so, the 1984 Act may well have changed the law. For these purposes, one must distinguish a case, like *Voisin* itself, where no acknowledgment of guilt or any guilty fact is contained in the words used from a case where there is such an acknowledgment. Thus, had Voisin made a written statement that, 'I killed that bladie Belgiam', it would contain both incriminating elements. Section 76 appears to separate out those two elements. According to section 76(4):

[51] [1918] 1 KB 531. [52] *Ibid.* 533.

The fact that a confession is wholly or partly excluded in pursuance of this section shall not affect the admissibility in evidence—

(a) ...
(b) where the confession is relevant as showing that the accused speaks, writes or expresses himself in a particular way, of so much of the confession as is necessary to show that he does so.

In the case, just posited, with facts departing slightly from *Voisin*, it would seem that, had the statement been obtained by oppression, the prosecution would, nonetheless, be entitled to use the 'Bladie Belgiam' part of it. Appropriate editing would do the trick, However, section 76(4)(b) does not seem to cover the actual facts of *Voisin*, for the sole relevance of the words written down was to show that he expressed himself in a particular way. Hence, there seems to be no impermissible part caught by the rest of section 76, with the result that section 76(4)(b) is not needed in order to save the manner of expression element.[53] This must be because Voisin's words would not count as a statement for the purposes of section 82(1). For completeness, it is right to add that the discretion, under either section 78(1) or 82(3), would be available to the judge, in an appropriate case with facts similar to *Voisin*, for both apply to 'evidence' and are not restricted to 'confessions'.

'Mixed' Statements

We have seen that it is a matter of some importance and difficulty whether or not an *ex facie* exculpatory statement of the accused counts as a 'confession' for the purposes of section 82(1) of the 1984 Act where the prosecution seeks to use it for its inculpatory effect against him. A connected issue, conveniently dealt with as another preliminary matter, arises where the accused *himself* wishes to rely upon something exculpatory which he said to the police during the course of his interrogation.

Where the accused's statement to the police was wholly exculpatory, the hearsay rule dictates that it cannot be used by the accused himself as evidence of its truth. However, there is clear authority to the effect that such a statement, if made when taxed with incriminating facts, is admissible in evidence to show his attitude at the time when he made it, and, indeed, it seems to be the general practice of the prosecution to adduce such evidence during the presentation of its own case,[54] so no question of rebutting an allegation of recent fabrication will have arisen. This would seem to constitute a mysterious and anomalous exception to the rule against narrative.[55]

[53] The contrary view which I expressed in *Confessions*, n. 23 above, 91–2, I now believe to be wrong.

[54] The leading case is *Pearce* (1979) 69 Cr.App.R 365. See also *Storey* (1968) 52 Cr.App.R 334; *Donaldson* (1976) 64 Cr.App.R 59; *McCarthy* (1980) 71 Cr.App.R 142; *Tooke* (1989) 90 Cr.App.R 417. For earlier authority, see Gooderson [1968] *Camb. LJ* 64, at 66–70. See also *Phipson on Evidence* (14th edn., 1990), para. 12–63.

[55] *Phipson ibid.*, describes it as anomalous. See also *Cross and Tapper*, n. 20 above, 307. Gooderson, n. 54 above, 68–70 takes a more favourable view.

A rather different situation arises where the statement in question is partly inculpatory and partly exculpatory. May the prosecution adduce the inculpatory parts alone, or is the accused entitled to insist that the exculpatory ones are also brought out?[56]

Again, we need to refine the question. One must first be clear about the *extent* of any admission made by the accused. So, if he said in a handling case,'I admit I had possession of the goods, but I had no idea that they were stolen', the full statement would show that he was making a partial admission only. The part which denies *mens rea* has, at least potentially, a double significance, for it may also be regarded as *positive* evidence of lack of *mens rea*. Of course, delimitation of the extent of the confession made will not always be straightforward, but the prosecution must inevitably be required to put before the trier of fact all the material needed for carrying out that task. This must be the point which James LJ had in mind when he said in *Donaldson*:[57]

> When the Crown adduce a statement relied upon as an admission, it is for the jury to consider the whole statement including any passages that contain qualifications or explanations favourable to the defendant, that bear upon the passages relied upon by the prosecution as an admission, and it is for the jury to decide whether the statement viewed as a whole constitutes an admission. To this extent the statement may be said to be evidence of the facts stated therein.

Though put in terms of *whether or not* the statement constitutes an admission, rather than in terms, also, of precisely *what* the statement does admit, the overall effect is clear.

Until quite recently, there was a clash in the authorities about whether or not the proper evidential significance of the exculpatory parts of such 'mixed' statements went beyond delimitation of the inculpatory parts.[58] On one view, the hearsay rule entailed that, considered positively, the exculpatory parts had no evidential force. If so, the accused's denial of guilty knowledge in the case of handling suggested above would not be evidence of its truth, and, logically, the trier of fact would have to be told that that was the case. On the other view, it was better for the law to make an exception here to the strict application of the hearsay rule. Directions to use evidence for some purposes, but not for others, are always difficult to follow and, sometimes, unfathomable.

The latter argument was supported judicially on more than one occasion, and it has now been endorsed by the House of Lords in *Sharp*.[59] In the result, *Sharp*

[56] For a recent, helpful treatment, see Birch [1997] Crim.LR 416. But cf. *Western* v. *DPP* [1997] 1 Cr.App.R 474.

[57] (1977) 64 Cr.App.R. 59, at 65.

[58] The leading cases were: *McGregor* [1968] 1 QB 371; *Storey* (1968) 52 Cr.App.R 334; *Sparrow* [1973] 1 WLR 488; *Barbery* (1975) 62 Cr.App.R 248; *Donaldson* (1977) 64 Cr.App.R 59; *Pearce* (1979) 69 Cr.App.R 365; *McCarthy* (1980) 71 Cr.App.R 142; *Newsome* (1980) 71 Cr.App.R 325; *Duncan* (1981) 73 Cr.App.R 359; *Leung Kam-Kwok* (1984) 81 Cr.App.R 83; *Hamand* (1985) 82 Cr.App.R 65.

[59] [1988] 1 WLR 7, at 15. For earlier authority, see, e.g., *Sparrow* [1973] 1 WLR 488, at 492 (*per* Lawton LJ) and *Duncan* (1981) 73 Cr.App.R 359, at 364 (*per* Lord Lane CJ). See also Elliott and Wakefield, n. 22 above.

decides that the exculpatory parts of 'mixed' statements adduced by the prosecution are fully admissible in evidence. The House expressed its wholehearted agreement with the following statement of Lord Lane CJ in *Duncan*:[60]

> it seems to us that the simplest, and, therefore, the method most likely to produce a just result, is for the jury to be told that the whole statement, both the incriminating parts and the excuses or explanations, must be considered by them in deciding where the truth lies. It is, to say the least, not helpful to try to explain to the jury that the exculpatory parts of the statement are something less than evidence of the facts they state.

There are a number of subsidiary points to which reference should be made. First, it may be appropriate for the trial judge rather to detract from the force of his comment that the exculpatory parts are evidence in the case, by drawing a distinction between the likely weight of the incriminating and self-serving parts. Again, the House of Lords in *Sharp* endorsed what Lord Lane CJ had said in *Duncan*, namely that:[61]

> where appropriate, as it usually will be, the judge may, and should, point out that the incriminating parts are likely to be true (otherwise why say them?), whereas the excuses do not have the same weight. Nor is there any reason why, again where appropriate, the judge should not comment in relation to the exculpatory remarks upon the election of the accused not to give evidence.

So the accused who does not testify is in a double bind, so far as his exculpatory remarks are concerned; they are weak because they favour him and weaker still because he does not support them by giving direct evidence.

Though both *Duncan* and *Sharp* were concerned with written statements signed by the accused, it was decided in *Polin*[62] that the principle which they establish is no less applicable to a series of questions (from the police) and answers (from the accused).

A third point is that the courts have not been troubled by the wording of section 76(1) of the 1984 Act, even though it might be thought capable of changing the law. That subsection permits the accused's confession to be given in evidence 'against him'. It could be argued that the exculpatory parts are not given in evidence against him where the prosecution is not seeking to rely upon their inconsistency with the defence he now raises, but, rather, the defence is seeking to have the whole thing put before the jury. One answer is that section 76 is concerned only with the confessional aspects and that it is the common law which lets in the exculpatory parts for the accused. A second is, of course, that, as we have seen, post-Act authority tells us that exculpatory statements are not confessions at all. In any event, there is now clear authority that the common law remains unchanged. In *Aziz*, the House of Lords declined an invitation to overturn *Sharp* and, indeed, gave that case a ringing affirmation, expressly stating that it did recognize an exception to the hearsay rule.[63]

[60] (1981) 73 Cr.App.R 359, at 365.

[61] *Ibid*. See also *Donaldson* (1977) 64 Cr.App.R 59, at 65.

[62] [1991] Crim.LR 293.

[63] [1996] 1 AC 41, at 48–50. See also *Polin* [1991] Crim.LR 293; *Grayson* [1993] Crim.LR 864; *Lobban* v. *R.* [1995] 1 WLR 877, at 883; *Western* v. *DPP* [1997] 1 Cr.App.R 474.

CONFESSIONS OF THIRD PARTIES

We may next collect together a number of points about the use of confessions of third parties as evidence either for or against the accused. The element which binds together these points is that it is the hearsay rule and exceptions to it which provide the essential evidential basis for the impermissibility or permissibility of any such use. We need to distinguish between confessions made by third parties who are on trial with the accused and those made by third parties who are not.

CONFESSIONS OF NON-ACCUSED THIRD PARTIES

Where a non-accused third party's statement solely exculpates the accused, it is plainly hearsay and not caught by any exception to the hearsay rule. It is, it follows, inadmissible in evidence. Furthermore, it is well established that a third party's statement inculpating himself in the crime with which the accused is charged is equally inadmissible for the latter, notwithstanding that, as a statement against interest, it might be thought to carry with it a presumption of reliability.[64] As a matter of logic, then, the defence cannot 'piggy back' that part of a third party's statement which exculpates the accused on to the part which inculpates the third party. There is no possibility of a doctrine equivalent to that approved in *Sharp*, and, indeed, there is Court of Appeal authority ruling out any such doctrine.[65]

CONFESSIONS OF CO-ACCUSED EXCULPATING THE ACCUSED

Plainly, the out-of-court statement of a co-accused exculpating the accused is no less caught by the hearsay rule than the equivalent statement of any other person. More difficult is the case where, on its face, it simply inculpates the co-accused but where its effect is to exculpate the accused. For example, it may be that only one of them could have committed the offence or that, purely by virtue of strengthening the case against the co-accused, it tends to weaken that against the accused. Of course, if it does inculpate the co-accused, the prosecution will itself have reason enough to seek to have it brought in evidence as a confession, and, once in evidence, it may redound to the benefit of the accused. Problems arise where, for some reason, the prosecution does not seek to rely upon it or where it does so seek but is prevented by reason of it being excluded, whether by rule or discretion, by the judge.

There are two separate problems here. If the accused may call evidence of the co-accused's confession when the prosecution may not, protection of the co-accused's interests will be undermined. In this respect, it is but one aspect of a wider issue, that is the extent to which the purposes of the exclusionary rule and

[64] See *Turner* (1975) 61 Cr.App.R 67; *Blastland* [1986] AC 41; *Callan* (1993) 98 Cr.App.R 467.

[65] *Campbell* [1995] 1 Cr.App.R 522; *Rogers* [1995] 1 Cr.App.R 374.

discretion may be sacrificed in order to cater for the interests of other accused persons. Once the rule and discretion have themselves been examined in detail, this wider issue will be addressed in Chapter 8.

The other problem arises when the confession is not excludable, whether under section 76, section 78, or section 82(3), but the prosecution does not rely upon it. There is authority that, nonetheless, the accused may not rely upon it, because of the hearsay rule. That authority flows from *Beckford and Daley*,[66] where the prosecution case was that all three co-accused had been involved in a murder, but that it had been neither Beckford nor Daley, but the third co-accused, Correia, who had inflicted the fatal knife wound. In order to attenuate the strength of the case against himself, Daley sought to adduce evidence of Correia's confession that he had carried out the stabbing. The Court of Appeal held that the law of hearsay prevented Daley doing so. It considered that the rule which prevents an accused from adducing evidence of a third party's confession should apply equally to his co-accused's. In fact, the analogy is inexact, for the accused can, at least in theory, compel the third party to give direct evidence, yet certainly cannot compel his co-accused. The decision has been widely criticized, both for that reason and because it appears to fly in the face of the express words of section 76(1), which state that an accused's confession 'may be given in evidence against him' as long as it is relevant and not excluded under the remainder of that section.[67]

Beckford and Daley was a case where the prosecution *had* sought to adduce evidence of the confession in question. The judge had excluded it, so far as it was concerned, under section 78(1). It was applied, in *Marviadi and Ghanchi*,[68] to a situation where the evidence had been adduced by the exculpated accused himself. The statement in question in that case was one alleged by Marviadi to have been made to him by Ghanchi, in which she had admitted that she had killed the person with whose murder both of them were charged, but had told him that this had happened in the course of her resisting rape. So the statement in question was a 'mixed' one in the *Sharp* sense, admitting the killing, but suggesting that she had a defence to murder. Marviadi sought to rely upon it both as evidence of its truth and as explaining his admitted action in helping Ghanchi to dispose of the body, but the Court of Appeal held, because of *Beckford and Daley*, that it could be relied upon only for the latter (non-hearsay) purpose.

Both of the aforementioned cases were distinguished by the same Court in *Campbell and Williams*.[69] In that case, there had been three accused. The third, Barratt, had been permitted to call evidence of a tape-recording made by her father of a conversation in which the accused Campbell had made damaging admissions which supported Barratt's defence at trial. As one might expect, the

[66] [1991] Crim.LR 833. But see now *Myers*, 24 July 1997, which overrules *Beckford and Daley* on the hearsay point.

[67] See, e.g., Archbold, *Criminal Pleading, Evidence and Practice* (1995 edn.), i, § 11–14; Birch [1991] Crim.LR 833, at 834–5; Mirfield (1992) 108 *LQR* 34. The s. 76(1) point is dealt with in greater detail at Ch. 8, text between nn. 29 and 32 below.

[68] [1992] Crim.LR 733. [69] [1993] Crim.LR 448.

prosecution had never had access to the recording. No question of excluding Campbell's admissions under the voluntariness rule or exclusionary discretion arose; only the hearsay point was taken by Campbell. The court held the contents of the tape admissible precisely because they inculpated Campbell. It followed that they might be used as evidence for Barratt as well as against Campbell. In effect, it refused to apply the hearsay reasoning employed in *Beckford and Daley*, preferring to regard that case as based upon the notion that the exclusion of the confession as against Correia under section 78(1) should not be undermined by allowing it to be adduced by Daley. It distinguished *Marviadi and Ghanchi* on two grounds. First, it said that the truth of what Ghanchi had allegedly said to Marviadi, rather than that it had actually been said, added nothing so far as Marviadi's defence was concerned. In other words, there was no additional probative value in its truthfulness, so no call for it to be used for that purpose. Rather less convincing was the court's second ground of distinction, namely that Ghanchi's statement was wholly self-serving, rather than being partly confessional.

In *Myers*,[70] the Court of Appeal expressed its preference for the position taken in *Campbell and Williams*, though it refused to accept the explanation offered in that case of the decision in *Beckford and Daley*. Given the clash of authority, it is not surprising that the court granted leave to appeal. The point of law of general public importance certified by it brings together both the hearsay issue and the issue of whether or not the accused may call evidence of a confession of his co-accused which has been excluded as against the prosecution under section 76(2), section 78(1), or section 82(3).

Confessions of Co-accused Inculpating the Accused

In principle, the position with regard to out-of-court statements of a co-accused which inculpate the accused is straightforward, though there are some difficulties of detail. Such statements are, because of the hearsay rule, inadmissible as evidence of their truth.[71] There is an obvious practical difficulty where the co-accused's statement includes a confession of his own guilt, for example if it says that the accused and he committed the offence together. The traditional response of the law is for the statement to be left unedited, but for the judge to direct the jury that it is evidence only against the co-accused and not against the accused.[72] Quite recently, intially at first instance but now in the Court of Appeal, it has come to be recognized that the trial judge has a discretion to require the statement to be edited, such as to remove the prejudicial references to the accused, before it

[70] [1996] 2 Cr.App.R 335. The House of Lords has now upheld the court of Appeal on the hearsay point—see *Myers*, 24 July 1997.

[71] See, e.g., *Rudd* (1948) 32 Cr.App.R 138; *Gunewardene* (1951) 35 Cr.App.R 80; *Rhodes* (1960) 44 Cr.App.R 23. It is, of course, different where the statement in question is relevant otherwise than as evidence of its truth—see *Mawaz Khan* [1967] 1 AC 454.

[72] See, e.g., *Gunewardene*, *Rhodes*, n. 71 above. Indeed, it seems that the direction is now so standard that a specimen one has been drawn up by the Judicial Studies Board and approved by the Lord Chief Justice—see *Jefferson* [1994] 1 All ER 270, at 284.

is put to the jury.[73] This would seem to be clearly right in principle, since the excision may well be achieved without cost in terms of legitimate probative force in other respects and will remove the danger that the jury will, in fact, rely on the statement as against the accused even though told not to do so. However, it is conceivable that the editing will result in other evidential costs, for it may either increase or decrease the strength of the statement as inculpating the co-accused himself.[74] Standard doctrine tells us that, as between the prosecution and the accused, the judge must balance the probative value to the former of leaving the statement as it is against the prejudicial effect on the latter of doing so. But where the battle is between accused and co-accused, the Privy Council case of *Lobban* v. *R.* indicates that this kind of balancing is not appropriate, the co-accused being entitled to insist on the jury seeing his statement in its entirety.[75] The statement there was a mixed one in the *Sharp* sense. The parts admissible under the hearsay exception as exculpating the co-accused also had the effect of inculpating Lobban. It is clear from the judgment that the discretion will be equally unavailable where editing would increase the level of inculpation of the co-accused, rather than remove an exculpatory element.

Questioning the Accused on the *Voir Dire*

The issue on the *voir dire* or, in the case of summary trial, at a trial within that trial, will be the admissibility of the confession or, where discretionary exclusion is sought, whether or not it is fair to admit it in evidence. Therefore, the fundamental test to be met by all questions asked of witnesses at such a proceeding is that they are relevant to that issue. A recurring problem which has arisen in that context, and which has never been conclusively resolved, is if it is ever permissible for a testifying accused to be asked whether or not his confession is true. Though, at least initially, this must be a question of relevance, we will see that there are also important issues of legal policy in play.

In *Hammond*,[76] the Court of Criminal Appeal held that the prosecution was entitled to ask such a question of an accused who alleged that his confession to murder had been beaten out of him. It is unclear whether the court considered the question relevant directly to the voluntariness issue or solely to the accused's credibility; there are indications both ways. An argument that truth or falsity is relevant to credibility is palpably unsound.[77] If the accused denies that his confession is true, it takes things no further as far as his credibility is concerned, for it is the essence of his case that the police persuaded him to tell lies. If, surprisingly, he admits its truth, this suggests (if anything) that he is also telling the truth

[73] The first instance cases are *Rogers and Tarran* [1971] Crim.LR 413; *Silcott* [1987] Crim.LR 765; *Mathias* [1989] Crim.LR 64. The Court of Appeal case is *Jefferson* [1994] 1 All ER 270, at 285.

[74] They are helpfully discussed in *Gunewardene* (1951) 35 Cr.App.R 80, at 92; *Jefferson* [1994] 1 All ER 270, at 285.

[75] [1995] 1 WLR 877.

[76] [1941] 3 All ER 318.

[77] See, e.g., Smith [1979] Crim.LR 169.

about how the police treated him. The unsoundness of this credibility-based argument persuaded a majority of the Privy Council in *Wong Kam-ming*[78] to conclude that *Hammond* was wrongly decided and that the law of Hong Kong required that questions of the truth of the confession must never be put to the accused by the prosecution on the *voir dire*.

Lord Hailsham dissented in *Wong Kam-ming* on the ground that, in some cases, questions about the truth or falsity of the confession might go *directly* to the issue of voluntariness. Questions of relevance of this kind could not be decided *a priori*. Thus, he suggested, if a man accused of murder alleges that he confessed in consequence of some relatively trivial inducement, the admitted truthfulness of that confession tends to suggest that the allegation is unfounded. Underlying this example and his Lordship's other examples is the assumption that, without pressure from the police, guilty men are more likely than innocent men to confess. Yet, if we take this assumption to be sound, it would seem reasonable for prosecuting counsel to make a practice of asking routinely each accused about the truth of his confession, a practice which Lord Hailsham himself deprecated.[79] It must follow that Lord Hailsham required more than bare relevance before the question would be permissible; it must have enhanced probative value.

It is at this point that the matter of legal policy comes into the picture. In *Hammond* itself, the Court stressed that the admission of the truthfulness of the confession could not be determinative of the issue being tried on the *voir dire*. That is, of course, correct, for a confession beaten out of a guilty suspect is clearly inadmissible. The problem is that, if the accused in such a case is imprudently frank, it must be exceptionally difficult for the judge to use his admission only in the way indicated by the probability-based reasoning. The trial judge in *Hammond* had it from the accused's own mouth that he was guilty of murder. Though it is a commonplace that judges must sometimes place their legal skills in the way of their desire that the guilty should be convicted, the difficulty of performing that task could hardly be greater than it was in *Hammond*, so it may be better for judges not to be thus tested. The difficulty would be even greater for magistrates in an equivalent case, for they might find themselves in a position where they were required to acquit someone who had confessed guilt in front of them. This suggests that English courts should reject *Hammond* and embrace *Wong Kam-ming* as regards the present issue.

The 1984 Act says nothing specific about that issue, though it does, importantly, reiterate the point that the voluntariness and the truthfulness of a confession are not the same thing. Section 76(2) states that the prosecution must prove 'that the confession (notwithstanding that it may be true) was not obtained [in breach of the subsection]'. Despite this useful provision, the danger of voluntariness and truthfulness being elided must be accentuated by the fact that the rule has, as one of its bases for exclusion, the unreliability of the confession. Now that

[78] [1980] AC 247.

[79] In *Wong Kam-ming* itself, the Privy Council was told that it was common practice for prosecuting counsel to ask that question of the accused—see [1980] AC 247, at 256.

the test of admissibility is whether or not *any* confession which the accused *might* have made in the circumstances existing at the time would be likely to be unreliable,[80] it would be particularly tempting to regard the truthfulness of this accused's actual confession as an overwhelmingly important element in that analysis, and yet a single sample provides no sensible basis for assessment of the probabilities. Though there is no binding authority on the point, all the *dicta* at appeal level, since the Act came into force, appear to favour the views of the majority in *Wong Kam-ming*.[81]

Very occasionally, it may be the accused who wishes to admit, on the *voir dire*, that he is guilty of an offence with which he is charged and to which he confessed to the police. This may have been, though it is not entirely clear, the case in *Brophy*.[82] Brophy faced forty-eight counts of serious terrorist offences, including murder, but also one count of being a member of the IRA. He had certainly confessed to the forty-eight counts and, possibly, also to the forty-ninth. He challenged the admissibility of his confessions on the basis that they had been obtained from him by unlawful interrogation techniques. Giving evidence on the *voir dire*, he had admitted in chief being a member of the IRA. His reason for doing this was that a member of that organization was more likely to be subjected by the police to unlawful interrogation, or so the defence submitted. The House of Lords held, though not as a matter of *ratio decidendi*, that Brophy's evidence on the *voir dire* was relevant to the issue of admissibility of his confessions. One can certainly see, here, the kind of enhanced probative value which impressed Lord Hailsham in *Wong Kam-ming*. Furthermore, the accused himself was clearly prepared to run the risk of prejudice on this minor count, for the sake of gaining a substantial advantage on the much more serious ones. It may well be this second factor which explains why the *per se* rule which was applied by the majority in *Wong Kam-ming* against the prosecution does not seem to apply against the defence.

In *Brophy*, the House went on to raise a broader issue in relation to defence questioning of the accused on the *voir dire*. According to Lord Fraser:[83]

> Where . . . evidence is given at the voir dire by an accused person in answer to questions by his counsel, and without objection by counsel for the Crown, his evidence ought . . . to be treated as relevant to the issue at the voir dire, unless it is clearly and obviously irrelevant.

If this *dictum* is correct, it allows the accused a very considerable latitude. It seems that what was described earlier as 'bare relevance' will suffice. In the result, defence counsel would be free to adduce evidence from his client of the falsity of his confession, as a routine matter. For completeness, it is right to add that it is hard to see how the accused could be refused an equivalent dispensation as regards cross-examination of prosecution witnesses on the *voir dire*.[84]

[80] The statutory unreliability head is considered in detail at Ch. 5, text to nn. 52–126 below.

[81] See *R.* v. *Liverpool Juvenile Court, ex p. R* [1988] QB 1, at 8; *Davis* [1990] Crim.LR 860; *Cox* [1991] Crim.LR 276.

[82] [1982] AC 476. [83] *Ibid.* 481.

[84] Lord Hailsham adverted to this very point in *Wong Kam-ming* [1980] AC 247, at 262.

EVIDENTIAL USE OF THE ACCUSED'S STATEMENTS ON THE *VOIR DIRE*

Even if *Wong Kam-ming* correctly states English law so far as cross-examination of the accused on the *voir dire* is concerned, there will still be cases where the prosecution will see advantage in seeking to adduce evidence of what he there said, or, if he testifies on the general issue, in cross-examining him about it with a view to showing inconsistency. And, of course, the effect of *Brophy* seems to be that there may be material from the defence's examination-in-chief of the accused which has potential evidential value for the prosecution at the trial of the general issue.

The Privy Council decided unanimously in *Wong Kam-ming*[85] that, for the purposes of Hong Kong law, there were very significant restrictions upon the freedom of the prosecution to put the accused's answers on the *voir dire* to evidential use. They undoubtedly intended the same restrictions to apply for the purposes of the English common law. First, the prosecution may not itself call evidence of anything said by the accused, and this restriction applies whether or not the extra-judicial confession which he was challenging was eventually ruled inadmissible. In *Brophy*,[86] the House of Lords affirmed that *Wong Kam-ming* correctly states English law in this respect, as a matter of *ratio decidendi* so far as inadmissible confessions are concerned, and as a matter of *obiter dicta* in the case of admissible ones. Secondly, if the accused elects to testify at the trial of the general issue, he may be cross-examined about what he said on the *voir dire*, in order to show inconsistency with his present testimony, only if his extra-judicial confession was, following that *voir dire*, ruled admissible. This issue did not arise in *Brophy*. To make it clear, all these restrictions apply as a matter of law; it is not a matter of the judge having discretion to disallow the adducing of evidence or the cross-examination.[87]

Two legal developments since *Brophy* must now be considered. First, it may cogently be argued that the effect of section 76(1) of the 1984 Act is to overturn all the ruled-based restrictions laid down in that case and in *Wong Kam-ming*, so far as evidential use of the accused's testimony on the *voir dire* is concerned. The argument is a technical one.[88] The definition of 'confession' in section 82(1) is not restricted to those made extra-judicially. It follows that, if the material from the accused's mouth, when one has regard to the other definitional elements of the word in section 82(1), counts as a confession, the fact that it arose in court does not prevent it being caught by section 76(1). Yet section 76(1) renders the confession of an accused person admissible against him unless excluded by virtue of the rest of that section. Since there is, presumably, no question of oppression or unreliability affecting the accused's confession on the *voir dire*, it appears to be

[85] [1980] AC 247. [86] [1982] AC 476.

[87] See *Wong Kam-ming* [1980] AC 247, at 258 and 259 (*per* Lord Edmund-Davies) and *Brophy* [1982] AC 476, at 483 (*per* Lord Fraser).

[88] It is best put by *Cross and Tapper*, n. 20 above, 186–8.

admissible against him, whether directly adduced by the prosecution or put to him in cross-examination on the general issue, and whether the original extra-judicial confession has been ruled admissible or inadmissible.

It is scarcely credible that Parliament intended thus to get rid of the important holdings in *Wong Kam-ming* and *Brophy*. No new general policy on this issue can be said to emerge from the 1984 Act, and one would have expected such a change to be effected by express words rather than by implication. There would also be one particularly strange consequence of the change. The *voir dire* testimony which is alleged to be inconsistent with the testimony on the general issue may itself be exculpatory, rather than inculpatory, in nature. If so, and, as *Sat-Bhambra*[89] and *Park*[90] tell us,[91] statements wholly exculpatory when made do not amount to confessions, then *Wong Kam-ming* would seem to continue to apply to prevent cross-examination about such statements, assuming that the underlying extra-judicial confession has been ruled inadmissible. Whether that statement is, on its face, inculpatory or exculpatory, the prosecution's purpose in seeking to cross-examine the accused about it will be precisely the same, yet, if anything, there seems *more* reason to restrict the prosecution where the statement is inculpatory than where it is exculpatory.

Because the legal policy contained in *Wong Kam-ming* and *Brophy* seems quite unaffected by the 1984 Act, it has been suggested that section 82(3) might, once again, be called in aid to protect that policy.[92] We have seen that, in both cases, discretionary protection for the accused was thought to be insufficient, yet, if the literal interpretation argument holds sway, it may be that the courts will embrace it in order to preserve the policy. No decision on the point has, so far, emerged.

The second legal development may prove much more of a threat to the *Wong Kam-ming/Brophy* policy. There seem to be three different, though overlapping, reasons given in those cases for the restrictions they announce. In *Wong Kam-ming*, Lord Edmund-Davies, in explaining why the prosecution could not itself call evidence of the accused's admission on the *voir dire* even where the underlying confession was admissible, reasoned that 'it is preferable to maintain a clear distinction between the issue of voluntariness, which is alone relevant to the voir dire, and the issue of guilt falling to be decided in the main trial'.[93] This rather suggests that the two trials should not impinge at all on each other, because concerned with different issues, or, as it may be put, that the trial on the *voir dire* should be hermetically sealed. The problem with this line of reasoning is that it lies uneasily with the Privy Council's view that the prosecution should be able to *cross-examine* the accused about his *voir dire* testimony where the underlying confession has been ruled admissible.

Lord Hailsham's reasoning in the same case was rather different, but no less hard to square with his overall view of the law. In his view, these special

[89] (1988) 88 Cr.App.R 55. [90] (1993) 99 Cr.App.R 270.
[91] See the discussion in the text to nn. 35–42 above.
[92] See *Cross and Tapper*, n. 20 above, 186. [93] [1980] AC 247, at 258.

restrictive rules were designed to support and sustain the basic exclusionary rule for extra-judicial confessions. As he put it:[94]

It is therefore of very great importance that the courts should continue to insist that before extra-judicial statements can be admitted in evidence the prosecution must be made to prove beyond reasonable doubt that the statement was not obtained in a manner which should be reprobated and was therefore in the truest sense voluntary. For this reason it is necessary that the defendant should be able and feel free either by his own testimony or by other means to challenge the voluntary character of the tendered statement. If, as happened in the instant appeal, the prosecution were to be permitted to introduce into the trial the evidence of the defendant given in the course of the *voir dire* when the statement to which it relates has been excluded whether in order to supplement the evidence otherwise available as part of the prosecution case, or by way of cross-examination of the defendant, the important principles of public policy to which I have referred would certainly become eroded, possibly even to vanishing point.

It will be plain that this reasoning legitimates only a *justified* challenge to the confession in question. So, as Lord Hailsham went on to say, once the judge has ruled that confession admissible, this policy is exhausted, and cross-examination of the accused about what he said on the *voir dire* is permissible. What he left unexplained was why the same reasoning did not equally apply to the calling of direct evidence by the prosecution of what the accused had there said.

A third line of reasoning emerges from the speech of Lord Fraser in *Brophy*. Directly concerned as he was, only with the calling of evidence by the prosecution itself, he relied upon the accused's right to silence as the basis for prohibiting it. In his words, the accused is 'virtually compelled to give evidence at the voir dire, and if his evidence were admissible at the substantive trial, the result might be a significant impairment of his so-called "right to silence" at the trial'.[95] That this argument is different again is shown by the fact that it has nothing to say about cross-examination of the accused who does (freely) elect to testify at the trial of the general issue.

Now these three strands of reasoning are, by no means, kept separate by their Lordships in the two leading cases. Thus, Lord Edmund-Davies, before expressing his own view that the *voir dire* proceedings should be, as they have been described here, hermetically sealed, seemed to endorse earlier Commonwealth authority which justified the inability of the prosecution to call evidence of the accused's earlier testimony in terms of his right to silence as regards the general issue of guilt. Furthermore, when Lord Edmund-Davies came to deal with *cross-examination* of the accused about his *voir dire* testimony, he relied upon an analogy with *Treacy*[96] in distinguishing cases where the underlying confession was inadmissible from those where it was admissible. One should not undermine the voluntariness rule by allowing the prosecution to reap advantage from the accused's *justified* challenge on the *voir dire*. In other words, Lord Edmund-Davies was having

[94] *Ibid*. 261. [95] [1982] AC 476, at 481.

[96] [1944] 2 All ER 229. The case is considered in detail in Ch. 8, text to nn. 15–24 below.

recourse to the line of reasoning endorsed by Lord Hailsham. Similarly, in *Brophy*, Lord Fraser, having expressed his argument in terms of the accused's right to silence, then went on to refer to an accused being 'obliged to give evidence at the voir dire, in order to contest a confession extracted by improper means'.[97]

The best way of reconciling these diverse lines of argument may be as follows. The *voir dire* cannot be hermetically sealed, as the exception for cross-examination when the underlying confession is ruled admissible amply demonstrates.[98] But if the other two lines may be pressed at the same time, they are capable of explaining the current state of the law, for the right to silence prevents all adducing of evidence by the prosecution, while the notion of justified challenge prevents any evidential use at all of the accused's *voir dire* testimony where the underlying confession has eventually been ruled inadmissible. Only cross-examination in the case where it has been ruled *admissible* is, in consequence, permitted, for it is condemned by neither policy.

A matter to be considered in detail later in the present work is the accused's so-called right to silence in relation to pre-trial interrogation. But the common law also granted him a right to silence *at trial*. Thus, the prosecution was statutorily prohibited from commenting on any failure of his to testify,[99] while the judge's freedom to comment upon such failure was limited. In particular, he was required to direct the jury that the accused was under no obligation to testify and that they must not assume, from the fact that he had not testified, that he was guilty.[100] Schedule 11 of the Criminal Justice and Public Order Act 1994 removes the prohibition on prosecution comment, while section 35(3) of that Act allows the court or jury the freedom, in general, to 'draw such inferences as appear proper from the failure of the accused to give evidence'. By necessary implication, it must now be permissible for the judge to direct the jury that they may draw such 'proper inferences'. We are not concerned, here, with the details of these recently-enacted changes,[101] but we are concerned with their possible impact upon the rulings in *Wong Kam-ming* and *Brophy*.

To the extent that it is no longer plausible to argue that the accused enjoys a right to silence at trial, the line of reasoning about his *voir dire* testimony which relies upon that right would seem, to say the least, vulnerable. Once the stage has been reached at which the accused may testify, section 35 of the 1994 Act seems to say that, though he cannot be compelled to testify, he really should do so. If, then, that line of reasoning falls, it may be that the element of the two decisions which prevents the prosecution from itself adducing evidence of the accused's statements on the *voir dire*, even if it survived section 76(1) of the 1984 Act, cannot survive section 35 of the 1994 Act. The important difference between the destructive

[97] [1982] AC 476, at 482.

[98] There is post-Act authority inconsistent with the notion of hermetic sealing—see *Tyrer* (1989) 90 Cr.App.R 446, at 449–50.

[99] Criminal Evidence Act 1898, s. 1(b).

[100] There are many cases, the leading ones being *Bathurst* [1968] 2 QB 99 and *Martinez-Tobon* [1994] 1 WLR 388.

[101] A little more is said about these changes in Ch. 9, text to nn. 97–108 below.

potential of section 76(1) and that of section 35 is clear. Benevolent use of the judicial discretion under section 82(3) might preserve the rule under another guise, but section 35 tends to destroy the very purpose of the rule, so that discretion could hardly be prayed in aid.

It may be said that any closing-off of the right to silence strand of reasoning will push the other two strands to the fore. The argument in terms of hermetically sealing the *voir dire*, as we have already observed, always proved too much and is, therefore, unlikely to re-emerge. Lord Hailsham's reasoning in *Wong Kam-ming* has rather more to be said for it. If the restrictions on prosecution use of the accused's testimony on the *voir dire* are to be justified as supporting and sustaining the basic exclusionary rule for involuntary confessions, only the prohibition upon the adducing of evidence of such testimony where the underlying confession has been ruled admissible would be lifted.

It must be admitted that, though resort to Lord Hailsham's reasoning would create a coherent explanation of a narrower curb upon the prosecution, it has been the right to silence reasoning which has been most commonly relied upon by commentators in explaining the aspect of *Wong Kam-ming* and *Brophy* concerned with evidence called by the prosecution, whether those commentators be for or against the law there laid down.[102] It seems right to conclude that the current status of *all* the *Wong Kam-ming*/*Brophy* restrictions upon prosecution use of the accused's testimony on the *voir dire* is extremely doubtful. The 1984 Act casts a technical doubt upon them, but the 1994 Act casts one of very real substance.

[102] See, e.g., *Cross and Tapper*, n. 20 above, 186; Smith, n. 77 above, 169; Murphy [1979] Crim.LR 364, at 366–7; Pattenden, n. 8 above, 818–21. The points made in the text are dealt with in rather more detail in Mirfield [1995] Crim.LR 612, at 617–24.

5

Confessions—The Exclusionary Rule

Before embarking upon discussion of the statutory exclusionary rule for confessions, to be found in section 76(2) of the Police and Criminal Evidence Act 1984, we should briefly examine what may be called the mature exclusionary rule at common law.

The Common Law Rule

The mature, pre-1984, exclusionary rule was conveniently stated in principle (e) of the Judges' Rules 1964, as follows:

> It is a fundamental condition of the admissibility in evidence against any person, equally of any oral answer given by that person to a question put by a police officer and of any statement made by that person, that it shall have been voluntary, in the sense that it has not been obtained from him by fear of prejudice or hope of advantage, exercised or held out by a person in authority, or by oppression.

This statement was largely derived from Lord Sumner's formulation in *Ibrahim*.[1] It is to be noted that, while principle (e) refers to 'fear of prejudice or hope of advantage', these heads of the exclusionary rule were more commonly known, respectively, as the threat and the promise head. The sole major departure which principle (e) made from Lord Sumner's formulation was the inclusion of statements obtained 'by oppression' in the category of involuntary statements. This change was the product of the final twenty years or so of the common law rule. The initial source of the change was a *dictum* of Lord Parker CJ in his *ex tempore* judgment in *Callis* v. *Gunn*, suggesting that statements obtained 'in an oppressive manner' were inadmissible.[2] The existence of the oppression head of the exclusionary rule was clearly recognized at Court of Appeal level in *Prager*,[3] though the actual confession in that case was not found proved to have been obtained by oppressive conduct on the part of the police. In 1980, that court, in *Hudson*,[4] put the matter beyond argument. One of the two *rationes decidendi* of that case is

[1] [1914] AC 599, at 609. [2] [1964] 1 QB 495, at 501. [3] [1972] 1 WLR 260.
[4] (1980) 72 Cr.App.R 163.

contained in the following words of Waller LJ: '[i]n our view these questions and answers and this voluntary statement should not have been admitted in evidence because the circumstances were such that the prosecution did not show that oppression played no part in their production.'[5]

The Statutory Rule

Section 76(2) of the Police and Criminal Evidence Act 1984 ('the 1984 Act') provides:

> If, in any proceedings where the prosecution proposes to give in evidence a confession made by an accused person, it is represented to the court that the confession was or may have been obtained—
>
> (a) by oppression of the person who made it; or
>
> (b) in consequence of anything said or done which was likely, in the circumstances existing at the time, to render unreliable any confession which might be made by him in consequence thereof,
>
> the court shall not allow the confession to be given in evidence against him except in so far as the prosecution proves to the court beyond reasonable doubt that the confession (notwithstanding that it may be true) was not obtained as aforesaid.

Briefly put, the oppression head of the common law rule remains, though, as we shall see, its substantive content may have changed. But there has ceased to be any magic in the fear of prejudice or hope of advantage. That threat or promise element of the old rule is replaced by an unreliability head which requires the court to look directly into the issue of whether or not any confession which the accused might have made in the prevailing circumstances was likely to be rendered unreliable. We shall deal, in turn, with the two statutory heads.

Oppression

Section 76(8) of the 1984 Act states that ' "oppression" includes torture, inhuman or degrading treatment, and the use or threat of violence (whether or not amounting to torture)'. The natural interpretation of that provision is that it enlarges 'oppression' to include torture, etc., rather than that it *means* and includes torture, etc.[6] In other words, the definition 'indicates an extension of the ordinary meaning, which continues to apply in appropriate cases'.[7] Though none of the post-Act cases explicitly confirms that that is indeed the case, the courts have shown themselves entirely willing to entertain arguments that a confession was obtained by oppression, even though no question of torture, etc., has arisen. In

[5] *Ibid*. 169–70.

[6] See *Dilworth* v. *Commissioner of Stamps* [1899] AC 99, at 105–6 (*per* Lord Watson).

[7] Cross, *Statutory Interpretation* (3rd edn. 1995, ed. Bell and Engle), 119.

Fulling,[8] which is the leading case, the Court of Appeal clearly considered itself free to fashion a general definition of 'oppression' without making any reference to section 76(8), so it is entirely clear that that subsection is to be interpreted naturally.

The Definition Given in *Fulling*

The court in *Fulling* considered itself no more constrained by the common law than by section 76(8). Because the Act was a codifying one, the principles laid down by Lord Herschell in *Bank of England* v. *Vagliano Brothers* were applicable:[9]

> I think the proper course is in the first instance to examine the language of the statute and to ask what is its natural meaning, uninfluenced by any considerations derived from the previous state of the law, and not to start with inquiring how the law previously stood, and then, assuming that it was probably intended to leave it unaltered, to see if the words of the enactment will bear an interpretation in conformity with this view.

It followed that the court was not bound by some rather loose statements, in two of the early cases, about what constituted 'oppression'. Thus, in *Priestley*, Sachs J had said that the word 'imports something which tends to sap, and has sapped, that free will which must exist before a confession is voluntary'.[10] In *Prager*,[11] the Court of Appeal endorsed not only this statement, but also that of Lord MacDermott, delivered extra-judicially to the Bentham Club in 1968. He had described 'oppressive questioning' as 'questioning which by its nature, duration or other attendant circumstances (including the fact of custody) excites hopes (such as the hope of release) or fears, or so affects the mind of the suspect that his will crumbles and he speaks when otherwise he would have stayed silent'.[12] Both these statements share the same difficulty, namely a tendency to focus attention on the collapse of the suspect's free will, rather than on the conduct which led to that collapse. So even Lord MacDermott's description, despite paying some attention to police conduct, also seems to allow it to be argued that the mere combination of questioning and custody led to the crumbling of the suspect's will not to speak.

In fact, notwithstanding these statements, there was no common law case in which a definition or description such as the two just mentioned was actually applied by an appeal court in ruling that the particular confession under consideration had been obtained by oppression. Rather, courts were concerned very much with police behaviour. Was it unlawful or, at least, improper? If unlawful, was it in blatant disregard of applicable law, or merely a technical breach? Was any unlawfulness or impropriety deliberate or merely accidental? A much better indication of the true legal import of the oppression head of the exclusionary rule may be gleaned from the facts of and decision in *Hudson*.[13]

[8] [1987] QB 426. [9] [1891] AC 107, at 144–5. [10] (1965) 51 Cr.App.R 1n., at 1.
[11] [1972] 1 WLR 260, at 266. [12] See (1968) 21 CLP 1, at 10.
[13] (1980) 72 Cr.App.R 163. See also *Prager* [1972] 1 WLR 260 (for the actual decision); *Steel* (1981) 73 Cr.App.R 173; *Dodd* (1981) 74 Cr.App.R 50; *Gowan* [1982] Crim.LR 821; *Mackintosh* (1982) 76 Cr.App.R 177.

Hudson, a 59-year-old planning officer with no convictions, was suspected of having received corrupt payments in return for planning favours. He was arrested at home at 6.30 a.m. on a Sunday and taken to the police station. There he remained for four and a half days. He was locked up each night and treated throughout as an ordinary prisoner. His personal effects were taken from him. He was in the close custody of police officers for some fifty hours and questioned for about half of that time. Questioning sessions lasted for about two and a quarter hours. A total of roughly 700 questions was put to him. There was no suggestion that he had been denied adequate sleep, rest, or food. Faced with all this, Hudson made some incriminating remarks on the second day, then a full confession after 105 hours in custody. Waller LJ assessed these facts as follows:[14]

> The feeling of captivity starting with the police officers at 6.30 a.m. arriving at his house and arresting him; the fact that he was taken from home at Farnham to Chelsea police station; the experience of being a prisoner in a police cell; the 25 hours of questioning; and the fact that he was always accompanied by a police officer except when in his cell and was in custody out of his cell a total of 50 hours. All of this with a man of 59 who had never been in any trouble before would inevitably provide a strong inference of oppression.

One might suppose that this would be quite enough. However, for the court, it was the fact that the police had failed to comply with the rules governing the arrest, treatment, and questioning of suspects which made the strong inference 'almost irresistible'. His arrest was 'probably unlawful', an incorrect reason for it having been given. His detention beyond forty-eight hours was, according to the court's view of the then-applicable law,[15] certainly unlawful. Finally, the police had breached principle (d) of the Judges' Rules by failing to charge him as soon as they had enough evidence to do so. The court concluded that the prosecution had failed to prove that oppression had played no part in the production of Hudson's incriminatory statements. Clearly, though Hudson's own likely reaction to his treatment, given his personal characteristics, was of importance in deciding whether or not he had been subjected to oppression, it was the characterization of the various aspects of the conduct of the police which was the central element in that decision.

At all events, Lord Lane CJ, who delivered the judgment of the court in *Fulling*, having rejected the statements of Sachs J and Lord MacDermott, turned to the *Oxford English Dictionary* and its third stated definition of 'oppression'. It is now,[16] as it was then: '[e]xercise of authority or power in a burdensome, harsh, or wrongful manner; unjust or cruel treatment of subjects, inferiors, etc.; the imposition of unreasonable or unjust burdens'. He went on to refer to one of the quotations given under the relevant definition, namely: '[t]here is not a word in our

[14] (1980) 72 Cr.App.R 163, at 169.

[15] S. 38(4) of the Magistrates' Courts Act 1952 required a person taken into custody to be brought before magistrates 'as soon as practicable'.

[16] 2nd edn., 1989.

language which expresses more detestable wickedness than oppression'. It is significant that Lord Lane CJ selected a quotation which takes oppression to be something extremely grave, for more than one of the other quotations which follow the definition does not have the same flavour. The court presumably intended the definition to be interpreted in the light of the quotation, for it must be said that the definition itself is not confined to such extremely grave misconduct. Thus, neither the exercise of authority in a burdensome or wrongful manner, nor the imposition of unreasonable burdens, really seems like an example of the most detestably wicked conduct.

Indeed, the application of the law to the facts in *Fulling* tends to demonstrate the restrictiveness of its view of oppression. Fulling's complaint was that she had been persuaded by a very unfair police tactic to confess to the offence of which she stood accused. She alleged that the police had told her that her lover, who was also implicated in the offence in question, had been having an affair for three years with a woman who was, there and then, in the next cell to Fulling. Her evidence was that this information had distressed her greatly, such that she could not stand being in the cells any longer and had agreed to make a statement in order to get out of the police station. Though the police had denied using any such tactic, the trial judge made his ruling that there had been no oppression on the assumption that Fulling's evidence was correct. The Court of Appeal upheld that ruling, though without explaining why such behaviour could not constitute oppression. One might well have supposed that it would be perfectly legitimate to describe that behaviour as involving the imposition upon Fulling of an unreasonable burden, yet one could hardly account it detestably wicked conduct.

Two other significant points emerge from *Fulling*. First, the court relied upon the proposition that the new unreliability head of the exclusionary rule would prove wider than the old common law head, which concerned itself only with fear of prejudice and hope of advantage. It would be wide enough to cover some of the circumstances embraced by what it described as 'the artificially wide' definition of oppression approved in *Prager*.[17] Of course, if, as has been argued here, the common law was, in fact, very much narrower than that definition suggested, *Fulling* may properly be taken not to restrict significantly the pre-Act conception of oppression. The second point is that the court approved of the trial judge's view that the pressure brought to bear by the conduct in question must go above and beyond that which is inherent in police custody. It went on to say that it found it 'hard to envisage any circumstances in which such oppression would not entail some impropriety on the part of the interrogator'. We shall see that this notion of impropriety, so important in the common law cases, has proved to be no less important in the cases under the Act.[18]

[17] [1987] QB 426, at 432, confining *Prager* [1972] 1 WLR 260.

[18] [1987] QB 426, at 432. This statement was quoted with approval by the Court of Appeal in *Smith* [1994] 1 WLR 1396, at 1406.

The Elements of Oppression

When I wrote the predecessor to the present work, before the 1984 Act was in force, I suggested that there were four points of particular interest about the pre-Act cases on oppression. Since the themes there identified rather repeat themselves in the cases under the Act, I take the liberty of quoting parts of the relevant passage. So my words then were:[19]

> First, the Court of Appeal has set at a very high level the point at which custodial interrogation becomes oppressive. . . . Secondly, emphasis has been placed upon the physical and temporal circumstances of the interrogation rather than the manner in which it was conducted or its content. Thirdly, the personal characteristics of the particular suspect have been of great importance. . . . Finally, and probably most importantly, the courts have attributed great significance to the presence of elements of unlawfulness in the treatment of the suspect and, where present, to their number and seriousness.

We shall consider these points afresh, in the context of the post-Act authority, though not in the same order as in the passage just quoted.

A High Level Concept

We have seen that the notion that, to be oppressive, the conduct in question must be extremely grave was a central feature of *Fulling*. The later cases do seem to tread the same path, the only exception being one Crown Court case.[20] The line taken consistently in the Court of Appeal is illustrated well by *Emmerson*.[21] The interview in question, concerned with suspected theft by Emmerson from his employers, had lasted only twenty-five minutes. Most of it had been very low-key, but, at one point, an officer did raise his voice and use bad language. The trial judge considered the officer's behaviour rude and discourteous. The Court of Appeal fully supported his view that this behaviour fell well short of being oppressive, specifically confirming the judge's opinion that 'to exclude this evidence would be to give oppression a completely false meaning'.[22] Equally, in *Paris, Abdullahi and Miller*,[23] a case to be considered in detail shortly, the Court of Appeal's decision to overturn the judge's ruling that Miller's confession was admissible was accompanied by remarks clearly demonstrating its view that the police behaviour had been gravely improper. Each member of the court had been 'horrified' by what he had heard, the officers had not so much been questioning Miller as telling him what to say, and there had been 'menace' in the delivery of questions by one of the officers.[24] The court felt able to remark that,[25] '[s]hort of physical violence, it is hard to conceive of a more hostile and intimidating approach by officers to a suspect'.

[19] Mirfield, *Confessions* (1985), 106. [20] *Beales* [1991] Crim.LR 118.
[21] (1990) 92 Cr.App.R 284. [22] *Ibid*. 287. [23] (1992) 97 Cr.App.R 99.
[24] *Ibid*. 103. [25] *Ibid*.

The Fact and Degree of Unlawfulness or Impropriety

The Code of Practice for the Detention, Treatment and Questioning of Persons by Police Officers (Code C), which was issued under powers conferred by section 66 of the 1984 Act and which, in its present edition, came into effect on 1 April 1995, is a long, detailed document governing police interrogation of suspects. It runs to over forty pages, and breach of any one or more of its provisions is something properly taken into account by trial courts when deciding whether or not to exclude a confession in the exercise of the discretion which they enjoy under section 78(1) and under section 82(3) of that Act, an issue which will be dealt with in due course.[26] But, for present purposes, we need to be aware that such breach has relevance also for the issue of oppression. Though Code C is most obviously relevant to that issue, other codes issued under the Act may also impinge upon it. In addition to all those codes, the 1984 Act itself grants certain rights to suspects and places certain duties upon the police. One must also bear in mind that other statutes may apply, in a similar way, to regulate police conduct and that there are doctrines of the common law which may be relevant.

In the result, the interplay between the criminal suspect and the police is highly regulated by these different kinds of rule, even more so than before the Act. We have already seen, from *Hudson*,[27] how important at common law was the issue of unlawfulness of police conduct. We have also seen that the leading post-Act case, *Fulling*,[28] goes so far as to say that it is hard to envisage situations in which there could be oppression without police impropriety. However, there is little authority addressing the effect of unlawfulness on oppression under section 76(2)(a), probably by reason of the fact that exclusion under section 78(1) has turned out to be a much more popular way of dealing with unlawfulness and impropriety in the process of interrogation.

The leading case in which the trial judge's decision on the issue of oppression was overturned is *Paris, Abdullahi and Miller*.[29] There, Miller, one of those later charged with the murder of a Cardiff prostitute, had been interviewed for a total of thirteen hours over a period of five days. For a considerable period of time, he denied both presence at and participation in the murder. Then he admitted being present but continued to deny participation. There appear to have been well over 300 denials of involvement. Finally, almost at the end of the five days, he made some equivocal admissions. Though the Court of Appeal referred to no breaches, either of Code C itself or of any other rule, by the police officers, it had absolutely no doubt that Miller's admissions had been made in consequence of oppression. The reason for its view was that the officers had questioned Miller in a hostile and intimidating way; they had bullied and hectored him. Indeed, the officers were not really questioning at all, 'so much as shouting at him what they wanted him

[26] See Ch. 6, text between nn. 91 and 101 below.
[27] (1980) 72 Cr.App.R 163, discussed in the text to nn. 13–15 above.
[28] [1987] QB 426, discussed in the text to nn. 16–18 above.
[29] (1992) 97 Cr.App.R 99.

to say'.[30] Under this pressure, he had broken down, eventually being prepared to say whatever they wanted him to say. Though there were other elements of the conduct of the police in that case, to which we shall return, and though Miller was, by reason of his limited mental capacity, particularly vulnerable, there is no doubt that it was the manner of interrogation which persuaded the court that there had been oppression. Yet no rule deals with this matter. The police are nowhere told that they must not question in a hostile and intimidating way, or solely in order to persuade the bullied suspect to mouth formal acceptance of the police view of the facts. So if the police questioning in *Paris et al.* is to be called improper, it must be because standards are imposed by judges from the outside. In any event, that questioning was clearly not unlawful.

Just as there may be oppression without unlawfulness, so unlawfulness does not, of itself, entail oppression. One of the phrases in the *Fulling* catalogue is 'exercise of authority or power in a wrongful manner'. In *Parker*,[31] the Court of Appeal explained that this phrase was to be interpreted in the context of the words and phrases accompanying it, in particular 'burdensome', 'harsh', and 'unjust or cruel treatment'. On the other hand, where there have been a large number of breaches, especially where they were or may have been deliberate, the argument that the conduct was oppressive will be very much strengthened. An early example is the Crown Court case, *Davison*,[32] where, in excluding the confession under section 76(2)(a), the trial judge emphasized that both elements were present. Similarly, in *Ismail*,[33] the Court of Appeal stressed the cumulative effect of various breaches of the Act and the Code, and referred to the need not to condone flouting of their provisions.

It may be proper, finally, to refer to *Miller*,[34] a case which, though the pre-Act law applied to it, was heard in the Court of Appeal after section 76(2)(a) came into force. The accused, who was a paranoid schizophrenic, was initially interviewed several times about the murder of his girlfriend, but stoutly denied his guilt. Then a detective inspector who knew about Miller's mental illness interviewed him. He began by asking Miller about his religious beliefs, then related them to death and, more specifically, to the girlfriend's death. The psychiatric evidence was that this questioning triggered off a schizophrenic episode, as an aspect of which he confessed to the murder. Certainly, as the trial judge remarked, Miller's ensuing answers to questions, and the written statement he later made, appeared to be factual statements interspersed with delusionary material. There were obvious problems about the reliability of his answers and statement[35] but the court also considered whether or not there had been oppressive conduct by the police. It concluded that there had not. There being, apparently, no finding that the questions had been put in the way they had *in order to* produce the schizophrenic episode, there had been no 'obviously wicked

[30] *Ibid.* 103. [31] [1995] Crim. LR 233. [32] [1988] Crim. LR 443.
[33] [1990] Crim. LR 109. [34] [1986] 1 WLR 1191.
[35] An aspect of this feature of the case is considered in Ch. 6, text to nn. 44–52 below.

conduct'. Had the episode been brought about deliberately, the court could not see how the confession could possibly have been given in evidence. In other words, here, the impropriety of police conduct would lie in the very intentionality of the way in which it would have led to the delusionary remarks.

It seems right to conclude that unlawfulness, particularly where involving breach of important duties and where exhibiting itself in several respects, remains a very significant factor. In addition, the presence or absence of a degree of intentionality, as far as any such unlawfulness is concerned, is a central element. However, it is not only the breach of specific rules laid down for the conduct of interrogation with which the courts are concerned; other standards of proper behaviour may be imposed upon the interrogator.

Emphasis upon the Physical and Temporal Circumstances

It will be plain that *Paris, Abdullahi and Miller*,[36] as so far explained, seems to be firm authority against the proposition that the courts are concerned only with the physical and temporal circumstances of the interview, rather than also with the manner in which it was conducted or its content. The Court emphasized the latter aspect of the case by quoting in full a short passage from one of the tapes of the interviews in which about twenty questions and answers largely entailed nothing more than contradiction, being of the 'Yes, you did. No, I didn't' type. It went on to refer to elements of trickery and bluffing assertion in the questioning, so far as the strength of the other evidence against Miller and the weakness of his own story were concerned. It pointed out that the police officers had persistently suggested that he had been under the influence of drugs, so that he could have no clear recollection of whether or not he had been present. All these matters, too, concerned the manner and content of the interviews. The only other matter stressed by the court was that there was evidence that Miller was on the borderline of mental handicap, having an IQ of seventy-five, a mental age of 11 and a reading age of 8. Even without this feature, the court said, 'the tenor and length' of the interviews would have been such as to render them oppressive and likely to result in an unreliable confession.[37] Miller's low intelligence merely strengthened the inference of oppression and unreliability.

Paris et al. was distinguished in *L*,[38] but in a way which leaves the essence of the earlier decision unaffected. There, a man suspected of a number of offences of incest with and indecent assault upon his daughter was interviewed twice on the same day, in each case for about one and a half hours, eventually confessing to a number of the alleged offences. Though some of the questioning was hostile, even aggressive, there was nothing to suggest that it was at all on a similar scale to that in *Paris et al.* There is no indication that the Court of Appeal in *L* wished to cast any doubt upon the correctness of the emphasis in *Paris et al.* upon the manner of the questioning. The appellant in *L* had, in any event, not relied upon

36 (1992) 97 Cr.App.R 99. 37 See *ibid.* 105.
38 [1994] Crim.LR 839 (transcript through LEXIS).

the oppression head of the exclusionary rule. Even as to the unreliability head, upon which reliance was placed (as it had in *Paris et al.*), the court said that it was a matter of degree, where there is aggressive and hostile questioning, at what point the threshold of unreliability is crossed. In distinguishing *Paris et al.*, the court referred to two points in particular. The interviews themselves, in *L*, had not been of excessive length, and the accused was a middle-aged man of sufficient resilience to withstand questions of the nature asked. We may remark that nothing in *L* challenges the proposition that, where the manner and content of the questions asked has had the effect of brainwashing a suspect into repeating back to the police facts which they had asserted many times to him, there was indeed oppression.[39]

Personal Characteristics of the Suspect

There was ample authority at common law to establish that what might be oppressive conduct as regards one person would not be as regards another. Potentially aggravating factors would be the youth or old age of the suspect, his low or subnormal intelligence, and the absence of a criminal record. On the other hand, a middle-aged person, of average intelligence or above, who might be described as 'a dedicated mature professional criminal'[40] or as 'a dangerous criminal'[41] should expect to be subjected to vigorous, long, and repeated questioning, without its necessarily amounting to oppression.

We have already seen that *Paris, Abdullahi and Miller*[42] and *L*[43] pay regard to the age and intellectual make-up of the accused. Just as criminal experience may tell against the accused, so may experience gained by other means. For example, in *Seelig and Spens*,[44] the Court of Appeal expressly approved the trial judge's view that experienced and sophisticated merchant bankers might properly be taken to be robust and knowledgeable enough to be capable of standing their ground when asked questions about their business affairs by inspectors appointed under the companies legislation.

TORTURE, ETC.

The partial definition of 'oppression' in section 76(8) to include torture, inhuman or degrading treatment, and the use or threat of violence does not appear, in any respect, to have undergone judicial interpretation. This is despite the fact that each of these concepts, except the use or threat of violence, has been taken from Article 3 of the European Convention on Human Rights.

'Torture' has, since the 1984 Act came into force, become directly part of the English criminal law, by virtue of section 134 of the Criminal Justice Act 1988. It is capable of being committed only by or, in effect, on behalf of 'a public

[39] See (1992) 97 Cr.App.R 99, at 105. [40] *Gowan* [1982] Crim.LR 821.
[41] *Mackintosh* (1982) 76 Cr.App.R 177. See also *Dodd* (1981) 74 Cr.App.R 50.
[42] (1992) 97 Cr.App.R 99. [43] [1994] Crim.LR 839. [44] [1992] 1 WLR 148.

official or person acting in an official capacity'. Though the Act does not define these terms, there can be no doubt that the police are caught thereby. The substance of the offence is the *intentional* infliction of *severe* pain or suffering. The pain or suffering in question may be either physical or mental. Here, the combination of the act or omission being criminally unlawful, of the crime thereby committed being a grave one (punishable by imprisonment for life), and of the requirement of intentionality would inevitably ensure that there would be oppression under *Fulling* in any event.

It would seem that 'the use or threat of violence' must be intended to connote more than the merest unlawful touching which would constitute battery under the criminal law. Since violence or the threat of it amounts *per se* to oppression, it seems inconceivable that anything less than a substantial application of force is denoted. Furthermore, it may well be that violence will take on its flavour from the content of the new crime of torture. Section 76(8) refers to 'the use or threat of violence (whether or not amounting to torture)', so it seems reasonable to suppose, for example, that intentionality will also be required here.

In the leading case concerned with 'inhuman treatment' under the European Convention, the European Commission on Human Rights stated that the phrase covers at least such treatment as deliberately causes severe mental or physical suffering.[45] It will be apparent that the kind of treatment covered seems to be virtually identical to that covered by the new English crime of torture.[46]

The European Commission on Human Rights has defined treatment of an individual as being degrading 'if it grossly humiliates him before others or drives him to act against his will and conscience'.[47] The notion of an accused having been grossly humiliated before others might possibly arise, at least where a legal representative or some other third party was present during the relevant interview. Indeed, not the least remarkable feature of *Paris, Abdullahi and Miller* was that much of Miller's 'travesty of an interview'[48] had been attended by a solicitor, who must undoubtedly have witnessed Miller crying and sobbing for extended periods thereof. Had the arguments in terms of oppression and unreliability failed, it might persuasively have been proposed that Miller had been subjected to degrading treatment in the first sense. So far as being driven to act against one's will and conscience is concerned, this would seem a less eligible candidate for endorsement. The expression rather smacks of the statement of Sachs J in *Priestley* that oppression imports something which tends to sap and has sapped the free will of the suspect.[49] It will be recalled that that statement, together with a similar, extra-judicial one of Lord MacDermott, was expressly rejected in *Fulling*,[50] so far as concerns the

[45] *Denmark et al.* v. *Greece* (1969) 12 Yearbook of the ECHR, 186 ('The Greek Case').

[46] In another case, it was accepted, both by the Commission and by the Court, that torture may be regarded as an aggravated form of inhuman treatment—see *Ireland* v. *UK* (5310/71) Report: 25 Jan. 1976 (Commission) and (1979–80) 2 EHRR 25 (Court).

[47] *Denmark et al.* v. *Greece* (1969) 12 Yearbook, 186.

[48] (1992) 97 Cr.App.R 99, at 104.

[49] See (1965) 51 Cr.App.R 1n., at 1.

[50] [1987] QB 426, considered in the text to nn. 9–12 above.

post-Act meaning of oppression. It hardly seems likely that it would have any greater appeal to the courts under the different guise of degrading treatment.

Between 1973 and 1991, the law of Northern Ireland rendered a confession to a scheduled terrorist offence inadmissible if obtained by subjecting the suspect 'to torture or to inhuman or degrading treatment in order to induce him to make it'. By section 11(2) of the Northern Ireland (Emergency Provisions) Act 1991, the categories of cases capable of leading to inadmissibility have been enlarged to include 'any violence or threat of violence (whether or not amounting to torture)'. In other words, the terrorist provision for Northern Ireland is now expressed in precisely equivalent terms to section 76(8) of the English statute. Whether or not, if English courts are eventually faced with an argument that a confession was obtained by oppression of one of the types specified in section 76(8), they will look to the Northern Irish cases for assistance is unclear. They may regard terrorist cases as inherently different. They may also stress that the Northern Irish provision specifically requires that the suspect must have been subjected to the torture, etc., *in order to* induce him to make a statement, pointing out that there has never been a requirement of purpose in English law. On the other hand, they may take on board the view adopted, with some consistency, in the cases concerned with this aspect of the emergency legislation, that it is only the *deliberate* infliction of the relevant type or level of suffering, which is forbidden.[51] They would, as we have seen, find other explicit support for a requirement of intentionality in section 134 of the Criminal Justice Act 1988, in the case of torture, and in the jurisprudence of the European Convention, in the case of inhuman treatment.

Unreliability

The oppression head of the exclusionary rule at common law was, as we have already seen,[52] a late addition to the well-established threat or promise head. So far as the threat or promise head is concerned, the history of the law of confessions shows that, by the close of the nineteenth century, it had become inflexible and technical.[53] Judges were extremely reluctant to attempt to measure the significance of a given threat or promise, as regards the likelihood of it rendering unreliable the confession made by the particular accused. In the words of Russell: 'the law cannot measure the force of the influence used, or decide upon its effect upon the mind of the prisoner'.[54] Indeed, we shall see that there was a line of authority,[55] before *Ping Lin*[56] finally ruled it incorrect, which indicated that it was

[51] See *McCormick* [1977] NI 105; *Milne* [1978] NI 110; *McGrath* [1980] NI 91; *Culbert* [1982] NI 90.

[52] See the text to nn. 1–5 above.

[53] A full account of the history of this head of the rule is to be found in Mirfield, n. 19 above, Ch. 2.

[54] *On Crimes and Misdemeanors* (5th edn. 1877), iii, 441–2.

[55] *Cleary* (1963) 48 Cr.App.R 116; *Northam* (1967) 52 Cr.App.R 97; *Zaveckas* [1970] 1 All ER 413. See also *Richards* (1967) 51 Cr.App.R 266.

[56] [1976] AC 574.

not even necessary that the inducement had had any effect at all on the accused's decision to confess.

The divorce of the voluntariness rule from its perceived purpose, namely the exclusion of unreliable confessions, was thought by many who were themselves unimpressed by the merits of a technical rule capable of quick and straightforward application to be unacceptable. More specifically, the Criminal Law Revision Committee recommended, in 1972, the reform of the rule to place the issue of unreliability firmly within its compass.[57] Its own formulation would have rendered a confession inadmissible if made 'in consequence of any threat or inducement of a sort likely, in the circumstances existing at the time, to render unreliable any confession which might be made by him in consequence thereof'. However, a more radical line was taken when the present law was created in 1984. Section 76(2)(b) of the Act dispenses altogether with the requirement that the source of unreliability must be a threat or inducement (promise). Instead, anything said or done will suffice to trigger the other elements of the rule. So, a confession is inadmissible if made 'in consequence of anything said or done which was likely, in the circumstances existing at the time, to render unreliable any confession which might be made by him in consequence thereof'. We shall deal with the issue of causation later, but we shall consider now the various elements of the test introduced by section 76(2)(b).

Anything Said or Done

There is no rule, as there was at common law, restricting this head of the exclusionary rule to the activities of 'persons in authority'.[58] However, in practice, the cases are almost invariably concerned with police investigations or, if not, with investigations carried out by officials with similar positions or duties. Three questions immediately arise. Will anything at all which has been said or done suffice? May the thing said or done have been said or done by anyone at all, including the accused himself? Thirdly, what if the complaint is of a *failure* to say or do something, for example failure to give a caution?

The key element of the first question is whether or not routine matters in the police investigative process are capable of counting. Even before the accused is questioned, a number of things will have been said or done to him. He may well have been arrested; he will have been brought to the police station; he may have had his belongings taken from him and been placed in a cell, before being taken to the interview room. It is entirely conceivable that these various experiences of the exercise of police power might induce, particularly in inexperienced, young, or vulnerable people, a state of mind in which they might confess unreliably. And, certainly, the very experience of being questioned on police territory might have a similar effect.

[57] See its 11th Report, *Evidence (General)*, June 1972, Cmnd. 4991, para. 57.

[58] A fuller discussion is to be found in Ch. 8, text to nn. 5–14 below.

There is no clearly authoritative decision on this point. In *Goldenberg*,[59] it had been the accused himself who had asked to speak to the police. Yet once they were in his company, the police had invited him to tell them what he wanted to. It seems that the defence placed no reliance on the mere holding of the interview, nor on the stated willingness of the police to listen to the accused, as being things said or done by them, so the present issue was not squarely faced. It was faced, but not settled, in *Crampton*.[60] The accused, who was suspected of conspiracy to supply heroin, was himself a drug addict. At the time of the interview, here called by the police themselves, he was undergoing withdrawal symptoms. The Court of Appeal was prepared to uphold the judge's decision to admit his confession, on the basis that, even if the holding of the interview was something done by the police, it was not such, on the particular facts, as to create a risk of unreliability. However, the Court did venture the view that:[61]

> it is in fact doubtful whether the mere holding of an interview at a time when the appellant is withdrawing from the symptoms of heroin addiction is something which is done within the meaning of section 76(2). . . . The reason why we say it is doubtful is because the words of the subsection seem to postulate some words spoken by the police or acts done by them which were likely to induce unreliable confessions.

What appears to be being argued is that the words or acts must have an *inherent* tendency to lead to unreliable confessions. If so, a throwback to the old common law rule is, in a way, being proposed, for one might well say that a threat or promise has just that inherent tendency, and without any reference to the characteristics of the particular accused.[62] The change made in 1984 would then entail only a widening to cover words and conduct, *other than* threats and promises, which are also inherently likely to result in unreliable confessions.

Section 76(2)(b) clearly cannot be limited in its impact to things said or done by the police or by some other investigator, for that would be to reintroduce a 'person in authority' requirement. In *Harvey*,[63] Farquharson J, at first instance, excluded a confession to murder because not satisfied that it had not been obtained as a result of the accused hearing her lover's confession to that same murder. The evidence was that Harvey might have confessed in a child-like attempt to protect her lover by herself taking the blame. In *Souter*,[64] a serving soldier suspected of rape was to be interviewed by a military policeman. An officer in Souter's own military unit, who was present only as an observer, addressed certain remarks to Souter before the interview began. He told him to stop crying, to be a soldier, and to be a man. He said that he was there to help. There must have been other remarks, but the officer was unable, at trial, to recall them. After some ten or fifteen minutes, Souter confessed. The officer had no authority over the investigation or prosecution of the offence, yet the Court of Appeal

[59] (1988) 88 Cr.App.R 285. [60] (1990) 92 Cr.App.R 369. [61] *Ibid*. 372.

[62] In *Phillips* (1987) 86 Cr.App.R 18, the Court of Appeal even used the old language of 'inducement', rather than the words 'anything said or done'.

[63] [1988] Crim.LR 241. [64] [1995] Crim.LR 729 (transcript through LEXIS).

overturned the decision of the General Court Martial that section 76(2)(b) did not render the confession inadmissible. It is right to add that, in doing so, that Court made no reference to any issue there might be as to the things said having been said by a third party. Nonetheless, it would seem clear that, in principle, the words or actions of *any* third party should be capable of counting as 'anything said or done' for the purposes of section 76(2)(b).

There is authority to the effect that section 76(2)(b) does not extend to things said or done by the accused himself. Thus, in *Goldenberg*,[65] counsel for the appellant argued that his client had confessed (unreliably) because he wanted bail in order to enable himself to obtain drugs to feed his heroin addiction. The Court of Appeal rejected that argument because it considered the words 'anything said or done' to be properly 'limited to something external to the person making the confession'.[66] It rather muddied the waters by saying that the thing said or done must be something likely to influence the accused, and, by implication, that things said or done by an accused to himself are *per se* incapable of causing him to confess.[67] It is difficult to see why this must be the case; it might be thought to depend upon the nature of the thing said or done. Still, though the reasoning would seem to be faulty, *Goldenberg* does establish the proposition that self-induced confessions are not caught by section 76(2)(b).

The words 'anything said or done' suggest positive acts or statements, rather than the omission to say or do something. However, the Act itself and the codes create a number of duties which the police must carry out. Many of the things prescribed are intended to assist in ensuring the reliability of any confession made. It would be most strange if, for example, a failure to provide a solicitor when asked to do so, a failure to caution, or a failure to allow breaks in questioning for rest and refreshment were to be incapable of being taken into account as regards a claim for exclusion under section 76(2)(b). In some cases, an omission may be re-interpreted as an act of commission. Thus, questioning without allowing a break may be thought of as questioning for too long a period. But such a re-interpretation will not always be convincing, so there is much to be said for regarding the words of section 76(2)(b) as capable of applying to things not done or words not spoken.

Such authority as there is tends to support the wide interpretation just suggested. In *Doolan*[68] all but one of the breaches of Code C seem to have been by omission. The accused had neither been cautioned nor reminded of an earlier caution. No contemporaneous record had been made, nor had the note made later been shown to him. There was no record of a reason for not recording contemporaneously, nor of the times of interview. Though the Court of Appeal eventually applied the proviso, it held that the evidence of the accused's confession ought to have been excluded under section 76(2)(b). In doing so, it relied solely upon the breaches by omission, though it did not indicate explicitly that such breaches, without any positive words or acts, would suffice.[69] In three later cases,

[65] (1988) 88 Cr.App.R 285. [66] *Ibid*. 290. [67] *Ibid*. [68] [1988] Crim.LR 747.
[69] See LEXIS transcript.

the same court had no difficulty in regarding failure to comply with Code C provisions as a significant factor, indeed the dominant factor, so far as exclusion under section 76(2)(b) was concerned.[70]

More recently, in *Menard*,[71] a rather different view seems to have emerged. The accused, who was in custody, had asked to speak 'off the record' to the investigating officers. It seems that all that they did was to allow him to speak to them. The prosecution did not seek to adduce evidence of what the accused had said at that meeting, but did rely upon a confession made at a later interview. The defence sought to persuade the court that the confession should have been excluded, not because of anything which had happened at the later interview but because the officers had, it said, improperly allowed him to give them information at the earlier meeting. Apparently, it was argued that the word 'done' in section 76(2)(b) encompassed 'a failure to do anything, any conduct positive or passive, by way of commission or omission'.[72] This was an unpromising argument, given that it was not at all clear what failure on the part of the officers might have led to the later confession, nor how it might have tended to render it unreliable. Still the court seemed to endorse the trial judge's view that more than mere omissions are needed before there can be said to be encouragement (of a confession) and that there can be no causal link between inactivity and any confession.[73] It is difficult to believe that such general propositions would stand up to scrutiny in a case involving clear *breaches* by omission, where the overall issue was specifically addressed

Relevance of Police Impropriety

It is established that it is unnecessary that the things said or done be improperly said or done. A very early *dictum* of Lord Lane CJ, in the leading case of *Fulling*, states: '[w]hat, however, is abundantly clear is that a confession may be invalidated under section 76(2)(b) where there is no suspicion of impropriety'.[74] That *dictum* does not seem to have been expressly challenged or even doubted in any of the succeeding cases. Moreover, in a later decision at first instance, a confession was excluded under section 76(2)(b) where there was not even a hint of impropriety.[75] However, there is an apparently contrary dictum in *Brine*,[76] where Russell LJ said: '[t]hat section 76(2) is primarily concerned with misconduct [by the police] there can be no doubt'.[77] Though his Lordship *might* there be taken to have had subsection (2)(a), as well as (2)(b), in mind, it is right to add that the appellant placed no reliance at all upon oppression and that the court referred only to the unreliability head of the rule. Still the passage is probably best explained by the fact that breaches of the Act and/or Codes will be present in the vast majority of cases where section 76(2)(b) is relied upon, precisely because very many of their provisions are designed to ensure reliability.

[70] *Delaney* (1988) 88 Cr.App.R 388; *Chung* (1990) 92 Cr.Ap.R 314; *Joseph* [1993] Crim.LR 206.
[71] [1995] 1 Cr.App.R 306. [72] *Ibid.* 312. [73] *Ibid.* [74] [1987] QB 426, at 432.
[75] *Harvey* [1988] Crim.LR 241. [76] [1992] Crim.LR 122. [77] See LEXIS transcript.

Sometimes there may be a breach of one of the code provisions, but without it being appropriate to say that there was police impropriety or misconduct. The leading case is *DPP* v. *Blake*.[78] The accused, a juvenile aged 16, had been arrested in respect of an offence of arson. In such cases, Code C then required (and still requires) an 'appropriate adult' to be present at any police interview.[79] The essence of the idea of an 'appropriate adult' is an independent adult third party capable of advising the juvenile, of observing whether or not the interview is being conducted properly and fairly, and of facilitating communication between interviewer and interviewee.[80] In the ordinary case, the police will naturally look to a parent or guardian as the obvious person to do that job. Code C defines 'appropriate adult' to include such a parent or guardian, but also a social worker, or, failing either of those categories, another responsible adult who is neither a police officer nor a police employee.[81] In *Blake*, the accused made it clear from the start that she did not want her father, from whom she was estranged, to be involved in any way; indeed, she initially refused to give the police his name and address. She told the police that she wished her social worker to be present at the interview. They contacted the emergency duty social worker, who told them that, in accordance with departmental policy, a social worker would attend only if no parent could be found or both refused to attend. So, finally, the accused revealed her father's name and address, and, in due course, he did attend. She remained adamant that she placed no reliance upon him, even refusing to reply to his question whether she was 'all right'.

The importance of these details is that they demonstrate, first, that her father was hardly in a position to carry out the responsibilities assigned to the 'appropriate adult', and, secondly, that the police were in something of a cleft stick. (It seems that the accused was also estranged from her mother.) The magistrates excluded her confession under section 76(2)(b), relying, *inter alia*, on their view that no 'appropriate adult' had been present at the interview. For the Divisional Court, that particular matter was crucial to its decision to uphold the magistrates' ruling. An estranged parent did not come 'within the spirit' of the Code, for there was no empathy between such a parent and the child.[82] Though the court clearly had sympathy for the police, in their predicament, not least because the Code failed to make any specific provision for such a case, it emphasized that the object of having an 'appropriate adult' present would not necessarily be achieved in *Blake*. We may, then, say either that the breach of the Code was merely technical, without the slightest police impropriety or misconduct, or that there was no breach at all, the spirit of the relevant provisions being distinguishable from the express duties imposed thereby. Of course, *Blake* was also a case where any breach was by omission rather than commission. The very firm message it delivers is that, where code provisions are relevant to an argument for exclusion under section 76(2)(b), it is their point or purpose in promoting the

[78] (1988) 89 Cr.App.R 179.
[79] See now Code C, para. 11.14A.
[80] See now *ibid.*, para. 11.16.
[81] *Ibid.*, para. 1.7.
[82] See (1988) 89 Cr.App.R 179, at 186 and 187.

reliability of confessions, not their status as rules for the governance of police conduct as such, which must be preserved.[83]

An additional point is that it is certainly not crucial, and may not even be relevant, whether or not the breach of any code provision was deliberate. There may be cases where the deliberate nature of the breach will itself cast a cloud over the sincerity of the police evidence and, therefore, lead the court to have a strong reason for doubting the reliability of the confession.[84] Yet code provisions may be breached quite innocently, but cast grave doubt upon reliability, as *Blake* itself may be taken to show. In *Barry*,[85] Lloyd LJ explicitly said that the question in that case did not 'depend upon showing that the breach of the Code was flagrant or cynical or even deliberate'.[86]

Very much along the same lines, it has been stressed in a number of appeals that the mere fact of breach of some Act or code provision will not, of itself, be sufficient to lead to exclusion. As Lord Lane CJ said in *Delaney*:[87]

> the mere fact that there has been a breach of the Codes of Practice does not of itself mean that evidence has to be rejected. It is no part of the duty of the court to rule a statement inadmissible simply in order to punish the police for failure to observe the Codes of Practice.

That passage was cited with approval in *Maguire*[88] and in *Chung*.[89] The trial court must go on to consider, quite properly, whether or not the other elements defined by section 76(2)(b) are present. The point was, perhaps, best put by Auld J in *DPP* v. *Blake*, as follows: 'the Code of Practice and [its] provisions . . . are simply matters to be taken into account, albeit important matters; but they are not necessarily conclusive either way in the particular circumstances of a case, and they are not the only matters to be taken into account'.[90]

The Circumstances Existing at the Time

Subsection (2)(b) requires the court to ask itself whether any confession which might be made *by this accused* in consequence of the thing said or done would be likely to be unreliable. Therefore the accused's personal characteristics are inevitably a relevant matter. Yet the courts seem prepared also to regard such characteristics as circumstances existing at the time. Thus, in *Everett*,[91] the Court of Appeal held that the condition of the accused, who had a mental age of 8, was a relevant circumstance. Other personal characteristics, whether of a similar (presumably) permanent kind or of a more temporary nature, are no less appropriate for consideration. So the very low IQ of an accused, placing him or her on the borderline of subnormality or mental handicap, was a relevant circumstance

[83] *N.B.* also the interesting Crown Court decision in *Morse et al.* [1991] Crim.LR 196.
[84] See, e.g., *Delaney* (1988) 88 Cr.App.R 338, at 341.
[85] (1991) 95 Cr.App.R 384. [86] *Ibid.* 390. [87] (1988) 88 Cr.App.R 338, at 342.
[88] (1989) 90 Cr.App.R 115.
[89] (1990) 92 Cr.App.R 314. See also *Barry* (1991) 95 Cr.App.R 384.
[90] (1988) 89 Cr.App.R 179, at 186. [91] [1988] Crim.LR 826.

in both *Paris, Abdullahi and Miller*[92] and *McGovern*.[93] In the latter case, the accused was six months pregnant at the time and had been vomiting in her cells before being interviewed. In describing these as matters forming the 'background' upon which the submission of unreliability was made, the court presumably had the statutory 'circumstances existing at the time' in mind. Characteristics or conditions which might properly be regarded as having been self-inflicted are no less capable of being part of the picture. For example, in *Crampton*,[94] though the court concluded that the accused's confession had not been rendered unreliable, despite the fact that he had been suffering from withdrawal symptoms when he had made it, it certainly did not say that the effect of these symptoms upon his fitness to be interviewed was irrelevant.

Sometimes, the personal characteristics or particular condition of the accused will tell in favour of admission of the confession evidence. If he is middle-aged and experienced, rather than young and impressionable, if he demonstrates a degree of resilience in the face of questioning, rather than breaking down, these too will be circumstances existing at the time.[95]

Of course, this is by no means an exhaustive list of what may count as such a circumstance, for it would seem that anything outside the accused which is capable of affecting his response to questions such that they are rendered more likely to be unreliable is equally capable of so counting. So, for example, the particular physical conditions of the environment in which he is placed may, without there being any question of a code breach, adversely affect his truth-telling capacity. Moreover, the accused's personal circumstances may be such as to influence the effect of the thing said or done upon the reliability of the confession. An offer of bail will, other things being equal, be more enticing to a parent anxious to return home to look after small children than to a person without any such commitment.

One important issue, so far as all the various kinds of circumstance existing at the time are concerned, is what, if any, significance is to be attributed to the absence of police knowledge or understanding of the circumstance in question. In principle, it ought, for the purposes of section 76(2)(b), to have no significance. The circumstances to be taken into account are those which may affect the confession made in consequence of the thing said or done. They will, very often, be personal characteristics or circumstances of a specific kind, and quite out of the control of the police themselves. While there may be *some* value in an interpretation of 'anything said or done' as restricted to particular categories of acts or words dictated by general rules, which rules may, therefore, be breached, there would seem to be no equivalent argument with regard to the very subject-specific matters with which we are presently concerned.

In fact, there is very clear Court of Appeal authority supporting the position argued for here. In *Everett*,[96] Watkins LJ said:

It is clear from [section 76(2)(b)] that what a judge has specially to have regard to in con-

[92] (1992) 97 Cr.App.R 99. [93] (1990) 92 Cr.App.R 28. [94] (1990) 92 Cr.App.R 369.
[95] See, e.g., *L* [1994] Crim.LR 839. [96] [1988] Crim.LR 826 (transcript through LEXIS).

sidering whether the prosecution has discharged the burden there cast upon it, are the circumstances which obviously include the mental condition of a suspect which existed at the time when the confession or confessions came into being. In regarding those circumstances we entertain no doubt at all that the test to be applied is an objective one. So it was not what the police officers here thought, if they gave any thought to it at all, about the mental condition of the person they were asking questions of which was material, but, as was subsequently ascertained from doctors, what the mental condition of the appellant actually was.

Of course, it will still be for the trial court, on the *voir dire*, to decide whether or not it accepts the medical or other evidence given which seeks to establish the particular element of vulnerability, so far as the accused is concerned, but the crucial point is that it makes no difference that the police can say, perhaps quite justifiably, that they had no idea that that element was present.

Crampton[97] seems at first glance to be inconsistent with *Everett* on this point. There, the circumstance was the accused's state of drug withdrawal at the time he was first interviewed. Stuart-Smith LJ said: '[w]hether or not someone who is a drug addict is fit to be interviewed, in the sense that his answers can be relied upon as being truthful, is a matter for judgment of those present at the time'.[98] The police themselves, who must have known that he was an addict—the case itself was concerned with conspiracy to supply controlled drugs—had asked him, before each interview, if he was 'feeling all right'. He had replied that he was. A clear confession emerged at the first interview, but Crampton was seen by a doctor only two or three hours later, before a second interview. That doctor testified at trial that, in his opinion, Crampton was then fit to be interviewed and, seemingly, that, *a fortiori*, he would have been fit at the time of the first interview, for the withdrawal symptoms would have been less severe. This enabled the Court of Appeal to conclude that, had the doctor examined Crampton before the first interview, he would have certified him fit to be interviewed. It went on to add:[99]

It is then for the judge at the trial within the trial to decide whether the assessment of those present at the time was correct. The mere fact that someone is withdrawing, and may have a motive for making a confession, does not mean the confession is necessarily unreliable.

It was properly for the police, *at the time*, to make a decision about whether or not Crampton was fit to be interviewed, but that matter of judgement was always, in a sense, provisional, for the trial court would need to determine whether he really was fit. It would, in any event, have to go on to decide what effect, if any, his condition would have had upon the reliability of his confession. We may conclude that, properly construed, *Crampton* is entirely consistent with *Everett*, which can safely be taken correctly to state the law.

Likely to Render Unreliable

The prosecution must prove that the thing said or done was unlikely to render the accused's confession unreliable. So, as well as having to decide the ordinary issue

[97] (1990) 92 Cr.App.R 369. [98] *Ibid*. 373. [99] *Ibid*. 374.

of causation, namely whether or not the thing in question caused the accused to confess,[100] there may also arise the rather different issue of what effect there might be expected to be upon its reliability.

There are hints, in some of the cases, of the courts thinking in pre-Act terms, namely that a confession brought about by an inducement must be assumed to be unreliable. In the early case of *Phillips*,[101] the Court of Appeal, having decided that the prosecution had failed to disprove the allegation that the police had offered the accused the inducement of having some of the offences alleged against him taken into consideration rather than specifically charging him with them, seems, without more ado, to have come to the conclusion that his confession had not been proved to be reliable.[102] Evidence of a similar kind of reasoning, though not in explicit form, seems to be detectable in *DPP* v. *Blake*.[103]

Reasoning of that kind would undermine one of the major purposes of section 76(2)(b), namely to allow the judge to consider whether or not the police conduct in question had in fact a tendency to render the confession unreliable. Two, more carefully considered, Court of Appeal judgments show that the old, technical rule has indeed gone. In *Crampton*,[104] the accused was suffering from drug withdrawal symptoms when he confessed. Nonetheless, the court endorsed the trial judge's conclusion that the confession was admissible because, even assuming that things done by the accused to himself came within the ambit of section 76(2)(b), they had not resulted in that confession being unreliable. The evidence in the case, from Crampton's own mouth, failed to demonstrate any motivation to lie in order to be released from custody and acquire drugs. Even stronger on this point is *Howden-Simpson*.[105] The case was rather similar to *Phillips* in that the record showed that the police had told the accused that, if he did not confess, the result would be the bringing of a large number of charges, rather than two specimen ones. The trial judge expressly rejected the argument that the holding out of this inducement should lead to automatic exclusion of Howden-Simpson's resulting confession; indeed, he decided that it had not been rendered unreliable by the inducement. The Court of Appeal confirmed the correctness of his approach, going on to uphold his decision on the facts, so far as exclusion under section 76(2)(b) was concerned.

It is right to add that, just as a court may be convinced that a threat, even one as serious as that in *Howden-Simpson*, has not rendered the confession unreliable, it may *fail* to be convinced that something said or done which is relatively innocuous on the face of it, and certainly no threat or promise, has not led to unreliability. For example, in *Waters*[106] the Court of Appeal held that, where the police officer's question, asked in breach of a Code C provision, was simply

[100] On which, see the sect. on causation, below. [101] (1987) 86 Cr.App.R 18.

[102] Support for the view that that was how the Court reasoned is lent by its treatment of the common law cases of *Richards* (1967) 51 Cr.App.R 266, and *Northam* (1968) 52 Cr.App.R 97.

[103] (1988) 89 Cr.App.R 179. [104] (1990) 92 Cr.App.R 369.

[105] [1991] Crim.LR 49 (transcript through LEXIS).

[106] [1989] Crim.LR 62 (transcript through LEXIS).

whether the accused had changed his mind and now decided to confess, the judge should have ruled the accused's affirmative answer inadmissible. The court's ruling, which has been castigated as 'almost over-indulgent',[107] seems to have turned on the likely confused state of the accused's mind, for he had, immediately before the officer asked his question, said that he maintained his earlier denial but wished to change the statement containing that denial.

A second aspect of this element of section 76(2)(b) is demonstrated by *Moss*.[108] We shall see in Chapter 10 that section 77 of the Act provides special protection at trial for mentally handicapped accused persons who have confessed while being interviewed in the absence of any 'independent person' (i.e. non-police adult). A warning of the special need for caution before convicting in reliance on such a confession must be given by the judge to the jury, there being an analogous provision for summary trial. There is a clear danger of courts being diverted by this provision from their duty to exclude altogether confessions of the mentally handicapped in appropriate cases. In a trial on indictment, why not simply leave it to the jury, properly warned under section 77, to decide whether or not reliance can safely be placed on the confession? The trial judge in *Moss* seems to have succumbed to this temptation. His decision to admit the confession in evidence was overturned on appeal because the Court of Appeal thought it unsafe to allow it to go before the jury.

It might be thought that judicial lack of confidence in the accuracy of the record of the interrogation process would hardly impinge upon the present issue. If a confession was made, its reliability or unreliability would appear to be a quality separate from whether or not it was recorded accurately. However, this has not been the approach taken by the courts. There is quite a long line of Court of Appeal cases affirming that breaches of code provisions designed to ensure that the record placed before the court by the prosecution is an accurate one are quite capable of having significance in this respect.[109] Typically, in these cases the police have failed, without good reason, to make a contemporaneous record of the interview, or to make a record as soon as practicable after the interview, or, in either case, have failed to show the record to the accused in order to enable him to sign it as correct or to indicate the respects in which he considers it inaccurate, or there has been some combination of such breaches.[110]

The basis upon which breaches of the present kind are significant was explained well by Lord Lane CJ in *Delaney*, as follows:[111]

> By failing to make a contemporaneous note, or indeed any note, as soon as practicable, the officers deprived the court of what was, in all likelihood, the most cogent evidence as to what did indeed happen during these interviews and what did induce the appellant to confess. . . . [T]he judge and the prosecution were *pro tanto* disabled by the omission of the

[107] See Wolchover and Heaton-Armstrong, *Confession Evidence* (1996) at para. 4–065.

[108] (1990) 91 Cr.App.R 371.

[109] The leading cases are *Doolan* [1988] Crim.LR 747; *Delaney* (1988) 88 Cr.App.R 338; *Chung* (1990) 92 Cr.App.R 314; *Barry* (1991) 95 Cr.App.R 384; *Joseph* [1993] Crim.LR 206.

[110] See Code C, para. 11, for the relevant provisions.

[111] (1988) 88 Cr.App.R 338, at 341–2.

officers to act in accordance with the Codes of Practice, disabled from having the full knowledge upon which the judge could base his decision.

He went on to point out that the practical, though indirect, effect of these omissions is to make it harder for the prosecution to prove beyond reasonable doubt that nothing said or done by the police was such as to be likely to have rendered unreliable the confessions in question.[112] It must be said that the *Delaney* principle does provide the police with a strong additional reason for following the book with regard to their recording practices. The advent of tape-recording as a standard feature of the interview room will probably serve merely to shift the emphasis from Code C to Code E, the *Code of Practice on Tape Recording of Interviews with Suspects*.

The *Delaney* principle has been applied even to cases where the accused denies making the confession in question.[113] This is rather difficult, for, if the accused is right, there is no confession which the prosecution might be disabled from proving admissible. And the question whether he is right or wrong is, classically, a question of fact for the jury, not one of admissibility for the judge. The following explanation is suggested. If the accused's defence were, most unusually, to be that he did not confess, but that, if he did do so, it was because of something said or done which rendered the confession unreliable, the judge would, on the basis of a defence representation under section 76(2) be bound to hold a *voir dire* to determine the admissibility of the putative confession.[114] But if, as appears to have been the situation in both cases where this point arose, the accused's sole factual defence were to be that he did not confess, can he still, in effect, put the prosecution to proof under section 76(2)? The key provision is, in fact, section 76(1), which enables the prosecution to call evidence of the accused's confession as long as relevant and not excluded by virtue of the rest of that section. It refers to 'a confession made', not to 'a confession allegedly made', yet it surely cannot be a condition of the prosecution being permitted to adduce it that they show that it *actually was made*, for this would, equally, be to usurp the jury function. Therefore, the words in question have to be interpreted as though they were 'a confession allegedly made'. There can then be no difficulty in interpreting the same words in section 76(2) in the same way. It follows that, in the situation posited, the defence is representing only that the confession *alleged* by the prosecution to have been made 'was or may have been obtained' such as to be inadmissible. In other words, the 'confession' may perfectly well be, at this stage, merely putative. If so, there is no logical difficulty with allowing the defence to say, on the one hand, that it was not made, but, on the other, that the prosecution must prove it to be admissible.

[112] In *Souter* [1995] Crim.LR 729, the absence of a complete record of things said and done by a third party may well have been taken by the Court of Appeal to have a similar effect upon questions of causation.

[113] *Doolan* [1988] Crim.LR 747; *Joseph* [1993] Crim.LR 206. And see Birch's comments at [1988] Crim.LR 748 and [1993] Crim.LR 207–8, respectively.

[114] The problem here is not unlike that of disputed authorship of a confession statement, where the accused alleges that he was compelled to sign a document written by the police—see *Ajodha* v. *The State* [1982] AC 204—where a *voir dire* must equally be held.

Any Confession Which Might be Made by Him

The criterion of unreliability of the challenged confession is defined by section 76(2)(b) not in terms of its *actual* probative value. This is shown, most clearly, by the words of subsection (2) which say that the prosecution must prove 'that the confession (notwithstanding that it may be true)' was not obtained by oppression or in a way which renders it unreliable. The very best evidence of its actual probative value would be that which showed it to be true, yet the words in parenthesis rule that out as the criterion of reliability. The crucial words in section 76(2)(b) are 'any confession which might be made by him in consequence' of the thing said or done. So, the question to be asked is about a *hypothetical* confession made by *this* accused.

The source of this unusual test is the Eleventh Report of the Criminal Law Revision Committee. Its reason for eschewing a test simply in terms of actual reliability, though not expressed, was almost certainly that it did not want the same issue to be decided, first by the judge, then by the jury. Were it so, the jury would be, in a sense, a court of appeal from the judge. So it settled on a test of admissibility broadly similar to that applicable in certain other Commonwealth jurisdictions,[115] the essence of which it described as follows:[116]

> The essential feature of this test is that it applies not to the confession which the accused in fact made but to any confession which he might have made in consequence of the threat or inducement. On this scheme the judge should imagine that he was present at the interrogation and heard the threat or inducement. In the light of all the evidence given he will consider whether, at the point when the threat was uttered or the inducement offered, any confession which the accused might make as a result of it would be likely to be unreliable.

Except for the fact that the Committee, as will be recalled, was making a recommendation less radical than that eventually enacted in section 76(2)(b), so far as the (police) conduct tripping the test was concerned, limiting it to threats or inducements, this statement seems exactly to reflect the law, as now laid down by the courts, under the 1984 Act.

In *Cox*,[117] the trial judge faced a situation in which the accused himself had, on the *voir dire*, admitted the truthfulness of the confession which the defence alleged to be unreliable. He ruled it admissible because he could not find it unreliable, in any shape or form, when it had been repeated before him by a man who, in his view, had clearly been telling the truth. His ruling was overturned on appeal, Lord Lane CJ giving the following reason:[118]

[115] In New Zealand (see Evidence Act 1908, s. 20 (as amended)), in Victoria (see Victorian Evidence Act 1958, s. 149) and in the Australian Capital Territory (see Evidence Ordinance 1971, s. 68(2)).

[116] 11th Report, n. 57 above, para. 65.

[117] [1991] Crim.LR 276 (transcript through LEXIS).

[118] This passage was cited with approval by the Court of Appeal in *Kenny* [1994] Crim.LR 284 (transcript through LEXIS).

It seems to us that the true question was not whether the confession was unreliable or untrue, so much as whether the confession, true or not, was obtained in consequence of anything done which was likely to render any confession unreliable, the burden being on the prosecution to prove beyond reasonable doubt that it was not so obtained.

No stronger example of a determination to separate the issue of admissibility from that of truth could be imagined. There are statements to similar effect in several earlier cases.[119] In one of them, *Barry*, Lloyd LJ specifically said that the test is 'hypothetical since it relates not to *the* confession but to *any* confession'.[120] It should not, however, be thought that the test is objective, for the question to be asked is about any confession by *this* accused. As previous discussion in this work has indicated, the court must pay full regard to the personal characteristics and circumstances of the particular accused at the time he confessed. It is not to imagine some ordinary or average accused being interviewed in the same way and under the same conditions as was this accused, and then ask itself about the hypothetical reliability of that accused's confession.

There would seem to be two problems with the unreliability test so clearly laid down in *Cox*, one of principle and one of practice. If the judge were to be required to exclude the particular confession where not satisfied of its actual reliability, he would guard against the possibility of the jury, in fact, placing reliance upon it in convicting the accused. Such a purpose is entirely consistent with, for example, the general discretion to exclude evidence more prejudicial than probative[121] and with the special rule of exclusion in similar fact cases which has the same organising idea.[122] (It is, of course, much harder to make sense of that purpose in the context of summary trial.) Equally, there would seem to be good reason to exclude confessions brought about by police conduct which has a general tendency to render them unreliable. The police, it may be supposed, will learn not to engage in conduct of the kind in question. Yet, the test in section 76(2)(b) would seem to fall, unhappily, between these two distinguishable purposes. One may, as in *Cox*, be required by that test to reject evidence which the jury could rely upon entirely safely. On the other side, it is unclear what *generalizable* lesson the police will learn from exclusion of a confession because this accused, with his own individual characteristics, quirks even, and specific circumstances, might have confessed unreliably. It may overstate the point to say that the lesson to learn is that the next time they interview Cherie McGovern[123] at a time when she is pregnant and has been vomiting, they should allow her to have a solicitor present and should make a proper record of what is said, but at the very least it may be said that the subjectivity of the test tends to blunt any purpose in terms of regulating future police conduct.

In the long run, it is the practical problem which may be more likely to prove

[119] *Tyrer* (1989) 90 Cr.App.R 446, at 449–50; *McGovern* (1990) 92 Cr.App.R 228, at 234; *Crampton* (1990) 92 Cr.App.R 369, at 372; *Barry* (1991) 95 Cr.App.R 384, at 389.

[120] (1991) 95 Cr.App.R 384, at 389 (emphasis in original).

[121] *Sang* [1980] AC 402.

[122] *DPP* v. *P* [1991] 2 AC 447.

[123] See *McGovern* (1990) 92 Cr.App.R 228, considered in the text to n. 93 above.

its downfall. Where the judge is confident about the actual reliability of the confession, perhaps because the accuracy of some part of it is confirmed by other evidence of an unchallengeable kind, such as the finding of the murder weapon where the accused had said it would be found, or, as in *Cox* because its truthfulness has been affirmed by the accused himself in the witness box, the idea of excluding it will be very unappealing. Thus, in *McGovern*,[124] the accused was alleged to have participated in a particularly brutal murder. Though it is not clear from the report how it came to be admitted by the defence that her confession was true, it was known, at least when the case went to appeal, that the defence challenged only its voluntariness, and not its accuracy. Farquharson LJ put the point succinctly:[125]

> Whether it is a satisfactory consequence that a confession which was admitted to be a true account of the appellant's participation in this wicked and terrible killing should be excluded because of the breaches of the Act and perhaps the Code of Conduct is, no doubt, a matter for debate, but we are satisfied that is the effect in law.

There are indications in other cases of sympathy with the predicament faced by the trial judge in a situation where he knows the confession is true, as well as of a reluctance to accept as sensible the conclusion to which the wording of section 76(2)(b) leads.[126] Today's intimations of judicial dissatisfaction may be the precursor of tomorrow's legislative changes.

Causation

In discussing the substantive heads of exclusion, reference has often been made to confessions having been 'obtained' or 'caused' by oppression, or having been made 'in consequence of' or 'as a result of' things said or done. The problem of causation in relation to the two heads of exclusion warrants, then, separate discussion. In the case of the oppression head, there is but one issue, namely whether or not the confession was obtained *by* oppression (of the person who made it). In other words, did the conduct of the police or other interrogator, assuming it to amount to oppression, cause, in the relevant sense, the confession to be made? However, there is a double question in the case of the unreliability head. Was the confession obtained *in consequence of* the thing said or done? If it was so obtained, was it likely to *render* unreliable any confession which the accused might make? This second element has been considered already.[127] The question which remains, in respect of both heads, is the nature of the causal link required between the item of conduct (usually police conduct) and the confession.

Some nineteenth century judges not only refused to ask whether a given inducement had rendered the confession unreliable but also refused to ask if it

[124] (1990) 92 Cr.App.R 228. [125] *Ibid*. 235.
[126] See *Cox* [1991] Crim.LR 276; *Kenny* [1994] Crim.LR 284 (transcripts through LEXIS).
[127] See text to nn. 100–14 above.

had even caused it to be made; it sufficed that an inducement had been held out.[128] A tension developed in the more modern authorities between that view and the view that the inducement must both have been held out and in fact caused the confession to be made.[129] The important decision in *Ping Lin*[130] made it clear that the latter view was correct. The accused, being interviewed about the presence of heroin in his flat, had initially maintained that he was merely a user. He said that, if allowed to go free, he would give the police information about an important supplier. They rebuffed the approach and he then confessed to being a supplier in a small way. He continued to offer information in return for favourable treatment. One police officer then told him that judges always bear in mind, when sentencing offenders, help given to the police. Ping Lin went into more detail about the heroin in his flat and gave them the supplier's name. There was no problem with the brief, initial confession, but the House of Lords had to decide whether or not the more detailed one was admissible. The majority ruled it admissible on the basis that it was a mere amplification of the initial one. It could not be said that the statement about judicial sentencing attitudes had in fact caused Ping Lin to admit his guilt. Lord Hailsham said: 'what excludes evidence is a chain of causation resulting from words or conduct on the part of the person in authority . . . giving rise to a decision by the accused actuated by fear of prejudice or hope of reward'.[131] Lord Morris, who founded his own view that the second confession was admissible upon his acceptance of the argument that the police officer's statement was not an inducement, also indicated agreement with the majority with regard to the causation requirement.[132]

It is probable that the causation test for both statutory heads of exclusion is the same, even though section 76(2)(a) simply uses the word 'by' to denote the causal link, while section 76(2)(b) uses the term 'in consequence of'. Nonetheless, it may well be, as a practical matter, that courts will be less likely to find there to be no such link in oppression cases than in unreliability ones. In this respect, it is noteworthy that none of the reported post-Act cases raising issues of causation under section 76 is concerned with the oppression head. Given the very restrictive view of the nature of oppression taken in *Fulling*,[133] a view which certainly seems to have been accepted in the later cases, it will rarely be possible for it credibly to be argued that the oppressive conduct in question did not cause the confession. If we take the case of *Paris, Abdullahi and Miller*,[134] it was so clear that Miller had broken down under the strain of the police's persistent hectoring and bullying questioning that there was no room for an argument that, say, it had been the voice of Miller's conscience which had been the real or substantial reason for his

[128] For an account, see Mirfield, n. 19 above, 60–7.

[129] For the former view, see e.g. *Cleary* (1963) 48 Cr.App.R 116; *Northam* (1967) 52 Cr.App.R 97; *Zaveckas* [1970] 1 All ER 413; and, perhaps, *Richards* (1967) 51 Cr.App.R 266. For the latter view, see e.g. *Smith* [1959] 2 QB 35; *Joyce* [1957] 3 All ER 623; *Sparks* [1964] AC 964; *Williams* (1968) 52 Cr.App.R 439.

[130] [1976] AC 574. [131] *Ibid*. 601. [132] *Ibid*. 597 and 595, respectively.

[133] [1987] QB 426.

[134] (1992) 97 Cr.App.R 99. The case is discussed in the text to nn. 29–30 above.

confession. Where the court finds that the accused was subjected to torture, the use or threat of violence, or inhuman or degrading treatment, it seems likely that similar considerations will apply, especially if there is held to be a requirement that the interrogator intentionally or deliberately inflicted the relevant type or level of suffering on the accused.

The decision of the Privy Council in *Burut* v. *Public Prosecutor*[135] does provide an example of that unusual situation in which there is a problem of causation in an oppression case. The accused, suspected of a firearms offence—capitally punishable in Brunei—were, in accordance with a 'special procedure' for such cases, manacled and hooded during some of their interviews. However, they made their confessions, not during those interviews, but during other ones at which they had not been manacled or hooded. The Privy Council held that the aura of oppression had persisted beyond the 'special procedure' interviews because of the implied threat that the procedure might be used again. In doing so, it noted that the gaps between the carrying out of the 'special procedure' and the making of the confession were relatively short.

The unreliability head is, undoubtedly, more difficult. The only case in which extended consideration has been given to the causation requirement was the pre-Act inducement case of *Rennie*.[136] Yet even here the obvious questions were not discussed. Is it enough (in the post-Act context) that the thing said or done contributed to the accused's decision to confess? Or must it be a substantial or main cause, or even the sole cause? Should the court ask itself whether or not he would have confessed but for the thing said or done?

The accused in *Rennie* was suspected of conspiring with other members of his family to use dud cheques to obtain goods and cash. His sister (Jacqueline) had already admitted her involvement, and the police also suspected that his mother and, perhaps, an adopted sister were involved. It was put to him that the whole thing had been a joint family operation and he replied, 'No, don't bring the rest of the family into this, I admit it was my fault. I persuaded Jacqueline to get involved.' Later, when admitting he had sold all the property acquired to friends, he showed a concern that they be not brought into the matter either. The trial judge decided that, despite Rennie's obvious concern about his family and friends, it had been the strength of the case against him which had persuaded him to confess. The *ratio* of the Court of Appeal's judgment affirming his decision seems to have been that it had not been shown that he had wrongly assessed the evidence or had failed to apply the correct principle.

Lord Lane CJ took the opportunity of delivering some important and influential remarks in *Rennie*. So far as the *general* test of causation was concerned, he recommended the judge not to embark upon 'any refined analysis of the concept of causation'[137] in instructing juries. Rather, 'he should understand the principle and the spirit behind [the exclusionary rule], and apply his common sense; and, we would add, he should remind himself that "voluntary" in ordinary parlance

[135] [1995] 2 AC 579. [136] [1982] 1 WLR 64. [137] *Ibid*. 70.

means "of one's own free will" '.[138] The final reminder may be thought less helpful now that it is clearly established that even the oppression head is not concerned with free will or voluntariness, at least in any meaningful sense. In add-ition, it is not entirely clear how common sense really assists here. So is it more common-sensical to require the thing said or done to be the sole cause, or the dominant cause, or what? An earlier passage from Lord Lane CJ's judgment may provide the troubled trial judge or magistrate with more assistance. His words were:[139]

> Very few confessions are inspired solely by remorse. Often the motives of an accused person are mixed and include hope that an early admission may lead to an earlier release or a lighter sentence. If it were the law that the mere presence of such a motive, even if prompted by something said or done by a person in authority, led inexorably to the exclusion of a confession, nearly every confession would be rendered inadmissible. That is not the law. In some cases the hope may be self-generated. If so, it is irrelevant, even if it provides the dominant motive for making the confession. In such a case the confession will not have been obtained by anything said or done by a person in authority. More commonly the presence of such a hope will, in part at least, owe its origin to something said or done by such a person. There can be few prisoners who are being firmly but fairly questioned in a police station to whom it does not occur that they might be able to bring both their interrogation and their detention to an earlier end by confession.

Yet we are still not told what the position is if the hope in question *does* owe its origin to something said or done by the police, but was only one factor in the accused's decision to confess.

In *Crampton*,[140] Stuart-Smith LJ was prepared to assume, though his own opinion was to the contrary, that the mere holding of an interview by the police at a time when the suspect was suffering from drug withdrawal symptoms was a 'thing done' for the purposes of section 76(2)(b). In reaching the conclusion that the holding of the interview had not caused Crampton to confess, his Lordship relied upon the passage from Lord Lane CJ's judgment just quoted. It would seem that, even if his main motive for confessing was to get out of the police station in order to obtain drugs, that motive was wholly self-generated. The police had not, in any way, created or encouraged it.

The Court of Appeal has felt able in other cases to conclude that, though things said or done by the police were entirely capable of causing a confession to be made unreliably, they had not in fact done so. Most strikingly, the officers in *Weeks*[141] had implied, in the course of their questioning, that the accused would be kept in custody until he told them what they wanted to hear. Only sixteen minutes later he had confessed to possession of cannabis. However, he continued to deny the further allegation that he had supplied the drug to others. It had been this determination to maintain a denial, together with the facts that he came across as an astute young man and that he had previously been interviewed at a police station, which had persuaded the trial judge that it had not been the

[138] [1982] 1 WLR 70. [139] [1982] 1 WLR 69.
[140] (1990) 92 Cr.App.R 369. [141] [1995] Crim.LR 52.

inducement that had caused him to confess. The main point here was, presumably, that his limited confession to possession would hardly be what he would suppose the police would 'want to hear'. A rather similar case is *Alladice*.[142] There, the accused had been improperly denied access to his solicitor. No doubt the burden of the defence argument on causation was that, had he been allowed to consult the solicitor, he would not have confessed. However, like Weeks, he was aware of the ways of the world. He had refused to answer some of the questions put to him. On the *voir dire*, he had said that he felt well able to cope with the interviews, that he was aware of his rights and that he wanted a solicitor present to act as a check on police conduct during the interview. So, affirming the judge, the Court of Appeal concluded that the presence of a solicitor would not have increased the likelihood of his exercising his right to silence.

In *Barry*,[143] though there were a number of other improprieties in the conduct of the police, the real gravamen of the defence case for exclusion was that, on a number of occasions, they had given him to understand that it might do him some good if he were to help them with their inquiries. He had been asked to assist them to recover a false company seal and had been told that they would put a letter before the judge encouraging the granting to him of bail, if he were to give them details of another person involved in the conspiracy. The trial judge had ruled the confession admissible because the inducements held out did not contain any express offers about making a statement. The Court of Appeal thought this approach altogether too narrow. Once the prosecution had held out the carrot of bail in return for his assistance, he might take it that a confession would help him to get it. The Court, having said that causation was 'a question of fact to be approached in a common sense way',[144] so echoing Lord Lane CJ's approach in *Rennie*, went on:[145]

> we find it impossible to hold that the appellant's decision to make a clean breast of it, contrary to all the advice he was receiving from his solicitors and counsel, may not have been influenced by his desire for bail and his belief that he would be likely, or more likely, to get bail if he made a full confession.

It will be noted that the court referred to his decision being 'influenced' by his desire and belief. Of course, that belief had been encouraged by the police. So, though these remarks may be of no lasting significance, they do seem to regard Barry's decision to confess as caused by the thing said or done even though it was not the dominant, let alone sole, reason for that decision.

Subsequent Confessions

A particular aspect of the problem of causation is appropriately dealt with here. It is quite common for confessional material to be forthcoming at more than one

[142] (1988) 87 Cr.App.R 380. See also *Tyrer* (1989) 90 Cr.App.R 446.
[143] (1991) 95 Cr.App.R 384. [144] *Ibid*. 389. [145] *Ibid*.

interview. Therefore, it is quite possible that police conduct which, as regards one interview, renders a resulting confession inadmissible will not re-occur at a second or subsequent interview. The question then arising is whether or not exclusion of any later confession under section 76, or perhaps in exercise of discretion, is the appropriate judicial response.[146]

If the oppression, or thing said or done, which caused the initial confession to be made remains directly operative at the time of the later confession, the relevant head of the exclusionary rule will apply straightforwardly. So if an offer of bail for a statement has not been unequivocally withdrawn by the police between the initial and later interview, it makes obvious sense to say that it remains causally operative. The post-Act case of *Conway*[147] may well be an example of just such continuing causation. Of course, the shorter the period of time between the first and second interviews, the stronger will be the inference that the oppression or thing said or done remains an operative cause. Where there has been a series of interviews, with only short gaps between them, all but the last affected by various improprieties or breaches tending towards unreliability, it will be extremely hard to convince the court that a confession obtained at a final, quite properly conducted, interview should be ruled admissible.[148]

However, later interviews may also be said to be tainted, in a more indirect way, by improper earlier ones. Put colloquially, 'the cat may be out of the bag' by the time the police have cleaned up their act. Thus, in *Glaves*,[149] there had been improper questioning of a juvenile at the first interview, such that section 76(2)(b) required his confession to be excluded. The trial judge had taken the view that the baleful or malign influence of that questioning no longer existed when the juvenile was again interviewed eight days later. Given that no criticism was made of the second interview, he allowed a confession there made to go to the jury. The Court of Appeal overturned his decision, on the basis that there was a continuing blight flowing from the first interview. It stressed that he had not had legal advice between the two interviews (though a legal representative had, in fact, been present at both). It seems to follow that only the conveying of information to the suspect that the first confession might be inadmissible would be capable of attenuating the taint or, using the earlier metaphor, putting the cat back in the bag.

The point just made seems to have been expressly endorsed by the Court of Appeal in *McGovern*.[150] Once again, the second interview itself had been conducted entirely properly, and nothing there said or done appeared to put the reliability of the accused's second confession in jeopardy. Yet, as the court pointed out, 'when an accused person has made a series of admissions as to his or her

[146] This issue is considered in detail by Mirfield [1996] Crim.LR 554.

[147] [1994] Crim.LR 838.

[148] See, e.g., *Ismail* [1990] Crim.LR 109 (transcript through LEXIS). See also *Burut* v. *Public Prosecutor* [1995] 2 AC 579, considered in the text to n. 135 above.

[149] [1993] Crim.LR 685 (transcript through LEXIS).

[150] (1990) 92 Cr.App.R 228.

complicity in a crime at a first interview, the very fact that those admissions have been made are [*sic*] likely to have an effect upon her during the course of the second interview'.[151] Her second confession was, therefore, tainted. Moreover, the court stressed that one crucial defect of the first interview was that the accused had been unlawfully denied a solicitor. The solicitor who had attended the second interview had not been told about that. The court pointed out that, if the solicitor had been told, 'she would have realised immediately that the first confession was suspect and in all probability would not have allowed the second interview to have taken place'.[152] Again, it seems, the cat must be returned to the bag, though here it is envisaged that it will not have a chance to re-emerge therefrom.

If this principle of indirect causative effect really is now part of the law, it would seem that there may have been a departure from the position at common law. In the leading pre-Act case of *Smith*,[153] a case which, rather surprisingly, has not been cited in any of the post-Act cases, the accused's first confession had been excluded because made shortly after a threat had issued from the regimental sergeant major who had charge of his company. That threat was that the whole company would remain on parade until whoever had been guilty of an offence involving a stabbing were to own up. The incident had taken place at night, and the parade followed it immediately. Next morning, the accused was interviewed by another officer. After referring to the incident and to the accused's confession the night before, that officer sought and was given confirmation of the confession. The Courts Martial Appeal Court ruled the second confession admissible, on the basis that 'the effect of the threat or the inducement was spent'.[154] This was obviously the case in the sense that it was no longer being made or held out. However, it surely continued to have indirect effects of the kind found to be unacceptable in *Glaves* and *McGovern*, not least because the officer had, in asking the accused if he had done the stabbing, placed specific reliance upon the first confession.

It might be thought possible to explain *Glaves* and *McGovern*, consistently with *Smith*, by reference to the court's discretion under section 78(1) of the 1984 Act to exclude evidence because of its prospective adverse effect on the fairness of the trial. One can see the validity of an argument that, even though the original conduct had ceased to have any direct effect, it would be unfair, at trial, to make the accused suffer the disadvantage of having used against him a second confession which had been obtained from him at a time when he would have assumed that he was already condemned out of his own mouth. However, in both *Glaves* and *McGovern*, the Court of Appeal made it absolutely clear that the second confession was to be excluded under section 76. It does not at all follow that section 78(1) has no significance, so far as successive confessions are concerned. Indeed this seems to have been the eventual basis for exclusion in *Ismail*.[155] There, a

[151] *Ibid.* 234. [152] *Ibid.* [153] [1959] 2 QB 35. [154] *Ibid.* 41.
[155] [1990] Crim.LR 109 (transcript through LEXIS).

whole raft of breaches of the Act and Code C had occurred during the first five interviews. Only the sixth and last had been conducted properly. The Court of Appeal concluded that its contents should also have been excluded at trial, for to say that all which had gone before could be left out of account:[156]

> would be to condone the flouting of the provisions which are designed to guard against purported confessions which are not genuine. The admission in evidence of [various interviews, including the final one would] cumulatively have such an adverse effect on the possibility of a fair trial in this case that this Court concludes that they should have been excluded.

[156] See LEXIS transcript (*per* Leonard J).

6

Discretionary Exclusion of Confessions and Other Evidence— General Principles

The Common Law Discretion

The Rule of Admissibility

Though the authority on the point is surprisingly sparse, there can be no doubt at all that it was and is a general rule of the common law that the admissibility in law of evidence is not affected by the way in which it was obtained. The special rule of inadmissibility for confessions in terms (at common law) of threats, promises, and oppression was an exception to that general rule.

There is a well-known, rather robust statement of Crompton J in *Leatham*[1] that '[i]t matters not how you get [evidence]; if you steal it even, it would be admissible in evidence.' In the more specific situation where incriminating evidence had been found upon the accused following an illegal search, Mellor J said, 'I think it would be a dangerous obstacle to the administration of justice if we were to hold because evidence was obtained by illegal means it could not be used against a party charged with an offence.'[2] In effect, the common law regarded as paramount the reliability principle, so far as non-confession evidence was concerned, taking no account of any need to discipline the police or to protect suspects.

The point was reiterated in the important decision of the Privy Council in *Kuruma* v. *The Queen*,[3] yet the very facts of the case demonstrate that the reliability of non-confession evidence may sometimes be affected by the unlawfulness of its obtaining. The tendency is to assume that, particularly in the case of real evidence, the mode of acquisition is irrelevant to its reliability. Superficially, this assumption is true; it is what it says it is. However, we often depend upon oral evidence for details of its provenance. Thus a person illegally searched may say that nothing was found in his possession and that the police are simply lying when they say that they found upon him the drugs which they now produce in court. Usually, this will come down to a question of who is believed by the trier

[1] (1861) 8 Cox CC 498, at 501. [2] *Jones* v. *Owen* (1870) 34 JP 759, at 760.
[3] [1955] AC 197, at 203–4. See also *Jeffrey* v. *Black* [1978] QB 490.

of fact, a difficulty which may equally be faced where the search itself was utterly lawful. Sometimes, though, as in *Kuruma* itself, there may be a connection between the illegality and the allegation that evidence had been 'planted'. The relevant regulation, under Kenyan emergency legislation, allowed the police to exercise stop and search powers, but only if the officer involved was of a rank of assistant inspector or above. Kuruma had been searched by officers below that rank. They claimed that they had found ammunition in his possession, but he flatly denied that allegation. It seems highly likely that the requirement of rank was designed to ensure that the officer would not 'plant' evidence. Hence, there would seem to have been a strong argument for exclusion of the ammunition evidence even in terms of unreliability. Nonetheless, the Privy Council ruled the evidence in question admissible, thus affirming the traditional view of the law.

A fortiori, the rule of inclusion applied both in the case of improprieties short of unlawfulness and in that of unfairness in the manner of obtaining the evidence. A good example is *Callis* v. *Gunn*.[4] In that case, the police had obtained fingerprints from the accused without having told him that he could refuse to provide them or that they might be used in evidence against him. There was clearly no unlawfulness, for the rules requiring an accused to be cautioned applied strictly only in respect of prospective statements by him. Any unfairness present was to be taken into account only as a matter of discretion. There are several other authorities at common law which are to similar effect.[5]

That the rule of inclusion for non-confession evidence has survived the enactment of the Police and Criminal Evidence Act 1984 ('the 1984 Act') has been categorically confirmed by Lord Nolan in *Khan*.[6] In the vast majority of post-Act cases, it will simply have been thought too obviously applicable to require reiteration.

For completeness, it is to be mentioned that it is part and parcel of a number of offences that some element of official unlawfulness was absent. Thus, a police officer is obstructed or assaulted in the execution of his duty only if he was acting lawfully at the relevant time.[7] Equally, for a person to be guilty of failure to provide a breath specimen under the drink/driving legislation, the police request to him to provide one must itself have been lawful. Therefore, if the officer in question was trespassing on the person's property at the time of the request, the latter commits no offence by refusing it.[8]

In addition, legislation may specifically provide that evidence obtained unlawfully in some way shall be inadmissible. Most notably, section 9(1) of the

[4] [1964] 1 QB 495.

[5] See, e.g., *Palfrey and Sadler* [1970] 1 WLR 416; *Beet* (1977) 66 Cr.App.R 188. *Stewart* [1970] 1 WLR 907 and *Keeton* (1970) 54 Cr.App.R 267 are to similar effect, but are complicated by the fact that, in both cases, the evidence in question seems to have amounted to a confession, though one clearly admissible under the then-applicable law because it had not been made to a 'person in authority'.

[6] See [1996] 3 WLR 162, at 171. See also *Fox* [1986] AC 281; *Apicella* (1985) 82 Cr.App.R 295.

[7] The point is well-established. A good recent example is *Riley* v. *DPP* (1989) 91 Cr.App.R 14.

[8] *Morris* v. *Beardmore* [1981] AC 446; *Fox* v. *Chief Constable of Gwent* [1985] 1 WLR 33. The actual decision in *Morris* v. *Beardmore* has been overturned by a specific statutory provision (now the Road Traffic Act 1988, s. 6(6)) permitting police entry, in certain circumstances, to require a specimen, but the general principle survives, as *Fox* shows.

Interception of Communications Act 1985 forbids the adducing of evidence tending to suggest that section 1 of that Act, which makes it, in general, an offence to intercept communications by post or through a telecommunications system, has been breached.[9]

The Discretion before *Sang*

Towards the end of the last century, courts began to assert a power to exclude confessions and admissions on the basis that they had been obtained by questioning the accused while in custody.[10] It became accepted that exclusion was a discretionary matter.[11] There were undoubted difficulties in reconciling some of the cases, so that there was a need for clear guidance to be given to the police. This was provided by the King's Bench judges in 1912, in the form of four Rules, to which five more were added in 1918. These Judges' Rules were revised and replaced in 1964, the new set being preceded by a preamble stating certain basic principles and accompanied by Administrative Directions from the Home Office. The 1964 Rules and Directions remained in effect until superseded by codes of practice made under the 1984 Act, in particular Code C, which is concerned with the detention, treatment, and questioning of suspects by the police.

The discretion, as regards confessions, grew out of a judicial desire to oversee police questioning. Its basis was that there were certain things which ought not to be done to suspects by the police. A broad view of fairness in the police station became, by virtue of the Judges' Rules, a more specific set of guidelines for the police. One could easily speak of *breach* of those guidelines and regard any such breach as an impropriety. Yet there was another aspect of fairness in relation to confessions obtained by the police. Police conduct involving neither a threat nor a promise towards the suspect might still be such as to call the reliability of a resulting confession into question. It came to be argued that the discretion to exclude confessions might properly be exercised to ensure fairness at trial, as well as to promote fairness in the police station. It is doubtful that these two elements of fairness were kept clearly separate in the judicial mind. Thus, in *Voisin*, A. T. Lawrence J said:[12]

> the mere fact that a statement is made in answer to a question put by a police officer is not in itself sufficient to make the statement inadmissible in law. It may be, and often is, a ground for the judge in his discretion excluding the evidence; but he should do so only if he thinks the statement was not a voluntary one . . . or was an unguarded answer made under circumstances that rendered it unreliable, or unfair for some reason to be allowed in evidence against the prisoner.

Over the years, the two elements have became more distinct, so that there is, in

[9] See *Preston* [1994] 2 AC 130 and *Effik and Mitchell* [1995] 1 AC 309, for detailed treatment of these provisions. See also Ch. 7, n. 299 below.

[10] See, in particular, *Gavin* (1885) 15 Cox CC 656; *Miller* (1895) 18 Cox CC 54; *Histed* (1898) 19 Cox CC 16. For more detailed treatment see P. Mirfield, *Confessions* (1985), 58–9.

[11] See, in particular, *Knight and Thayre* (1905) 20 Cox CC 711, at 713 (*per* Channell J).

[12] [1918] 1 KB 531, at 539.

the modern law, both an unfairness and an unreliability head of the exclusionary discretion for confessions.

So what was and is the position where the evidence in question is not confessional? There is an entirely general, now very well-established doctrine of the common law that evidence which cannot safely be left to the jury to take a view of its value should, as a matter of discretion, be excluded. That discretion is usually put in terms which make it applicable where the prejudicial effect of the evidence in question outweighs its probative value. Though the early case with which the doctrine is most closely associated, *Christie*,[13] was concerned with whether or not the trial judge should have allowed evidence of the accused's reaction to an accusation put to him by the complainant to go to the jury as, in effect, an admission of guilt, most of the cases are concerned either with evidence of the accused's bad character falling outside the rule of exclusion for similar fact evidence[14] or with prosecution cross-examination about his bad character of an accused who has lost his shield under section 1(f) of the Criminal Evidence Act 1898.[15] Nonetheless, *Sang*[16] firmly establishes, as we shall see,[17] that the doctrine in question, because it is a general one, is no less capable of applying to non-confession evidence obtained by the police.

However, the common law also recognizes a different kind of discretion specific to non-confession evidence which has been so obtained. No hint of a power of this kind seems to have emerged until certain, perhaps unguarded, remarks were made by Lord Goddard in the Privy Council in *Kuruma*.[18] Having first affirmed the vitality of the principle that the admissibility of evidence is independent of the manner of its obtaining, he went on to refer to the discretion of the judge to disallow evidence if the strict rules of admissibility 'would operate unfairly against an accused'.[19] In support, he cited two cases, both of which were concerned with the discretion in terms of probative value and prejudicial effect,[20] yet gave as an example a situation which seemed to involve unfair treatment, rather than the prospect of an unfair trial. In his words, '[i]f, for instance, some admission of some piece of evidence, e.g., a document, had been obtained from a defendant by a trick, no doubt the judge might properly rule it out.'[21] Rather surprisingly, he then went on to explain a series of Scottish cases which undoubtedly are concerned with a doctrine of fairness to the accused and which dictate the exclusion of evidence obtained unlawfully or irregularly (unless such unlawfulness or irregularity can be excused)[22] as though they stood for the contrary proposition that Scottish courts are equally unconcerned with how the evidence was obtained.

[13] [1914] AC 545. See 559 (*per* Lord Moulton) and 564–5 (*per* Lord Reading). For the history of the doctrine, see R. Pattenden, *The Judge, Discretion and the Criminal Trial* (1982), 63 ff.

[14] *Noor Mohamed* v. *The King* [1949] AC 182, at 192 (*per* Lord du Parcq); *Harris* v. *DPP* [1952] AC 694, at 707 (*per* Viscount Simon).

[15] *Selvey* v. *DPP* [1970] AC 304.

[16] [1980] AC 402.

[17] See text to nn. 33–50 below.

[18] [1955] AC 197.

[19] *Ibid.*, 204.

[20] *Noor Mohamed* v. *The King* [1949] AC 182; *Harris* v. *DPP* [1952] AC 694.

[21] [1955] AC 197, at 204.

[22] The two leading cases are *Lawrie* v. *Muir* [1950] JC 19 and *H. M. Advocate* v. *Turnbull* [1951] JC 96. The Scottish doctrine is considered in detail in Ch. 10, text to nn. 195–213 below. See also [1969] JR 55.

At all events, Lord Goddard's *dictum* bore fruit in a series of later cases. It became clear that his own example of unfairness, namely trickery, was not something which would necessarily make it right to exercise the discretion in favour of exclusion. In *Murphy*,[23] a Courts Martial Appeal Court case, Lord MacDermott CJ pointed out that detection by deception was a well-used police method which might need to be resorted to on occasions to enforce law and order and to protect the public safety.[24] A more complete description of the nature of police conduct giving rise to the discretion was given by Lord Parker CJ in *Callis* v. *Gunn*: '[t]hat discretion, as I understand it, would certainly be exercised by excluding the evidence if there was any suggestion of it having been obtained oppressively, by false representations, by a trick, by threats, by bribes, anything of that sort.'[25] Given that his Lordship had earlier described the exclusionary rule for confessions as encompassing cases where the confession had been obtained by oppression, as well as those where it had resulted from some threat or promise, it seems that he had in mind a discretion for non-confession evidence which would be similar in its effects to the exclusionary rule for confessions.

In *King* v. *The Queen*,[26] the Privy Council rather poured cold water on the idea of an extended, specific list of types of police conduct deemed to constitute unfair treatment, preferring instead to say that unfairness was not susceptible of close definition and to use the much vaguer phrase, 'conduct of which the Crown ought not to take advantage'.[27] Yet this kind of approach and of formulation did not appeal to the English courts in later cases. Thus, in *Jeffrey* v. *Black*, Lord Widgery CJ offered a list of conduct which included trickery and oppression, though he did go on to refer to the police simply having been unfair or having behaved in a morally reprehensible way.[28]

Significantly, the line of authority concerned with discretionary exclusion of non-confession evidence which began with *Kuruma* was applied to confession evidence in two Court of Appeal cases decided in 1978 and 1980 respectively. According to Lawton LJ in the first of them, *Houghton and Franciosy*, '[e]vidence would operate unfairly against an accused if it had been obtained in an oppressive manner by force or against the wishes of an accused person . . . or by a trick . . . or by conduct of which the Crown ought not to take advantage.'[29] In the later case, *Hudson*, the Court of Appeal was content to confirm the correctness of Lawton LJ's statement.[30]

In only the very last of the cases to which reference has so far been made was the trial judge's decision to allow the evidence in question to be adduced overturned. And, even in *Hudson*, the Court of Appeal thought that the confession should have been excluded, in any event, under the exclusionary rule as having been obtained by oppression. However, there are two pre-Act cases

[23] [1965] NILR 138, at 147.
[24] This point was supported by the Privy Council in *King* v. *The Queen* [1969] 1 AC 304, at 318–19.
[25] [1964] 1 QB 495, at 502. [26] [1969] 1 AC 304.
[27] *Ibid*. 319. See, also, *Keeton* (1970) 54 Cr.App.R 267. [28] [1978] QB 490, at 498.
[29] (1978) 68 Cr.App.R 197, at 206. [30] (1980) 72 Cr.App.R 163, at 170.

about non-confession evidence in which it was held, as a matter of *ratio decidendi*, that the judge ought to have excluded the evidence in question as having been unfairly obtained. The two cases, *Court* and *Payne*,[31] had essentially similar facts. In each, the police had persuaded the accused, who had been arrested for driving a car whilst unfit through drink, to agree to being medically examined by a doctor. The method of persuasion was that the accused had been told that the examination would be solely to see if he was suffering from any illness or physical disability and that the doctor would *not* give any opinion about fitness to drive. However, at trial, the relevant doctor was permitted to testify that the accused had been under the influence of drink to such an extent that he had been unfit to drive. In each case, the Court of Criminal Appeal held that this evidence should have been excluded and allowed the accused's appeal. At first glance, it might seem that there had been trickery on the part of the police; they had misled the accused into agreeing to the examination and, thereby, into creating evidence against himself. In fact, there had been no intention to deceive, for what Court and Payne had been told *did* reflect police policy at the time. There had simply been a change of policy between the date of the examination and that of the trial. In a way, what the Court of Criminal Appeal was saying was that the police could not be permitted to go back on their promise, for that would be unfair.[32] The effect of the two decisions is not unlike that of promissory estoppel in the law of contract.

The Effect of *Sang*

The House of Lords in *Sang*[33] was asked to settle a point of public importance in the following terms:

> Does a trial judge have a discretion to refuse to allow evidence—being evidence other than evidence of admission—to be given in any circumstances in which such evidence is relevant and of more than minimal probative value?

It may properly be said that the House was faced with an extremely difficult question, both in terms of reconciling the earlier cases and of formulating a statement of the law for future ones.

It is to be noted that the question put to the House asked, in effect, about both the unreliability discretion and the unfairness one. As regards the former, the precise terms of the test were put in issue. Those terms were uncertain in two respects. First, some formulations of the discretion made it applicable only where the evidence in question was of minimal or trifling probative value,[34] while others

[31] See [1962] Crim.LR 697 and [1963] 1 WLR 637, respectively.

[32] An analogous post-1984 Act case is *Nathaniel* [1995] 2 Cr.App.R 565, which is considered, in the text to nn. 118–20 below.

[33] [1980] AC 402.

[34] See, e.g., *Christie* [1914] AC 545, at 560 (*per* Lord Moulton) and at 564 (*per* Lord Reading); *Noor Mohamed* v. *The King* [1949] AC 182, at 192 (*per* Lord du Parcq); *Harris* v. *DPP* [1952] AC 694, at 707 (*per* Viscount Simon); *DPP* v. *Boardman* [1975] AC 421, at 463 (*per* Lord Salmon).

left open the possibility of exclusion where the true probative value, though significant, was outweighed by the high level of anticipated prejudicial effect.[35] Secondly, there was doubt whether the difference in weight between prejudicial effect and probative value must be large or substantial, as some formulations suggested,[36] or whether any difference in weight, no matter how small, would suffice.[37] In the only fully reported English case before *Sang* in which the unreliability discretion had been relied upon to exclude confession evidence, Mr Recorder Hawser QC had referred to: 'the court's general discretion to exclude evidence the probative value of which is so small that it would not be fair to the accused, or in the interests of justice, to allow it to be placed before the jury'.[38] He went on to refer to defence counsel's contention that 'the probative value of any admissions made by the defendant is small, if not minimal, whereas their prejudicial effect would necessarily be substantial'.[39]

The first of these issues is certainly settled unequivocally by *Sang*, though there is room for a little more doubt about the second. All of the House's remarks about both the unreliability and unfairness elements of the discretion were *obiter dicta*, the case being directly concerned with whether or not the unfairness element was available at all in the case of evidence acquired by an *agent provocateur*. Yet they were undoubtedly intended to be, and have in later cases been taken as being, authoritative. In the view of all of their Lordships, the unreliability element was not restricted to cases where the evidence in question was of minimal or trifling probative value. Indeed, Lord Fraser expressly rejected the strand of authority which suggested that it was.[40] On the other hand, his Lordship did take the view that the discretion could be exercised only where 'the prejudicial value of the evidence would *greatly* exceed its probative value' (emphasis added).[41] No other member imposed such a qualification, though, equally, no other expressly addressed this second issue. The answer given by the House to the relevant part of the certified question, an answer to which all of their Lordships gave their assent, simply refers to 'a discretion to refuse to admit evidence if . . . its prejudicial effect outweighs its probative value'.[42] The absence from this formulation of the word 'greatly' before 'outweighs' is to be noted, for it probably means that the issue is settled against Lord Fraser.[43]

[35] See, e.g., *Christie* [1914] AC 545, at 559 (*per* Lord Moulton); *DPP* v. *Boardman* [1975] AC 421, at 453 (*per* Lord Hailsham).

[36] See, e.g., *Christie* [1914] AC 545, at 564 (*per* Lord Reading); *Noor Mohamed* v. *The King* [1949] AC 182, at 192 (*per* Lord du Parcq); *Jenkins* (1945) 31 Cr.App.R 1, at 14 (*per* Singleton J); *DPP* v. *Boardman* [1975] AC 421, at 463 (*per* Lord Salmon).

[37] See, e.g., *Christie* [1914] AC 545, at 559 (*per* Lord Moulton); *Harris* v. *DPP* [1952] AC 694, at 707 (*per* Viscount Simon); *Cook* [1959] 2 QB 340, at 346 (*per* Devlin J); *Selvey* v. *DPP* [1970] AC 304, at 346 (*per* Lord Hodson); *DPP* v. *Boardman* [1975] AC 421, at 453 (*per* Lord Hailsham).

[38] See *Stewart* (1972) 56 Cr.App.R 272, at 276. [39] *Ibid.* [40] [1980] AC 402, at 446–7.

[41] *Ibid.* 447. [42] *Ibid.* 437.

[43] See also *Miller* [1986] 1 WLR 1191, at 1199. In Canada, the Supreme Court, in *Wray* (1970) 11 DLR (3d) 673, took an entirely different view, holding that the evidence must *both* have trifling probative value *and* be gravely prejudicial.

One additional issue, with regard to the unreliability element, is almost certainly settled by *Sang*.[44] As regards confession evidence, there were *dicta* in *Isequilla*[45] which might be taken to indicate that the discretion is available only in the case of a person who was mentally ill or mentally handicapped at the time at which he confessed. This would be an unsatisfactory limitation upon the discretion since there seems no reason why particular, temporary emotional instability should not, in extreme circumstances, render a confession wholly unreliable. Two first instance cases decided after *Isequilla* suggest that a wider view of the discretion is appropriate. In one, the trial judge excluded a confession made at a time when the accused may well have been suffering from mental confusion brought about by administration of a dose of Pethidin.[46] In the other, a diabetic may well have been suffering from a hypoglycæmic attack when he confessed; again, the confession was excluded.[47]

Though the certified question in *Sang* specifically excluded confession evidence from its ambit, it seems clear that all members of the House were agreed that particular examples of use of the discretion to exclude evidence more prejudicial than probative were no more than examples. As Lord Diplock put it, '[a] trial judge in a criminal case has always a discretion to refuse to admit evidence if in his opinion its prejudicial effect outweighs its probative value.'[48] In the later case of *Miller*,[49] the Court of Appeal, having considered the *dicta* in *Isequilla*, went on to state that the common law discretion applied where the confession 'came from a mind which at the time was possibly irrational [so that] what the defendant said may have been the product of delusion and hallucinations'.[50] It follows that the discretion is a general one; its availability in confession cases cannot be limited to cases of mental illness or handicap, nor even to those cases together with cases where some physical illness or disability has effects upon the mental state, nor does the temporariness of the irrationality matter.

With regard to the unfairness element, it is much harder to discern the House's precise ruling. The problem is that, though all members of the House approved the formulation which was stated by Lord Diplock and which had originally been formulated by Viscount Dilhorne, the actual speeches of their Lordships add significant glosses thereto which are inconsistent with each other. The agreed formulation states:[51]

> Save with regard to admissions and confessions and generally with regard to evidence obtained from the accused after commission of the offence, he has no discretion to refuse to admit relevant admissible evidence on the ground that it was obtained by improper or unfair means. The court is not concerned with how it was obtained.

[44] For a fuller account of the authorities on this issue, see Mirfield, n. 10 above, 160–3.

[45] [1975] 1 WLR 716, at 722–3.

[46] *Davis* [1979] Crim.LR 167.

[47] *Powell* [1980] Crim.LR 39.

[48] [1980] AC 402, at 437. See also Viscount Dilhorne (at 438), Lord Salmon (at 445), Lord Fraser (at 446–7), and Lord Scarman (at 452).

[49] [1986] 1 WLR 1191.

[50] *Ibid.* 1200, affirming the earlier unreported decision in *Marchant*, 27 Nov. 1981.

[51] [1980] AC 402, at 437.

On the face of it, the distinction to be drawn is between evidence obtained from the accused and after the offence, on the one hand, and all other evidence, on the other. It would be perfectly consistent with the literal meaning of those words that the judge would have discretion to exclude evidence of possession by the accused of stolen goods, at his trial for stealing them, where that evidence had been obtained by an unlawful search of the accused's person.

Yet it is absolutely clear that neither Lord Diplock nor Viscount Dilhorne regarded the discretion as being available to the judge in the case of an unlawful search, though not at all clear whether or not the rest of their Lordships agreed with them. Lord Diplock's speech at least has the virtue of clarity. In his view, the general judicial duty is to ensure the accused a fair trial. A fair trial is not put in jeopardy by admitting evidence which has been obtained in an unfair way. So exclusion of confession evidence at common law represents an exception to the principle that the judge's sole responsibility to the accused is to ensure him a fair trial. That exception must, in modern times, be regarded as based upon the maxim *nemo debet prodere se ipsum*—nobody can be required to be his own betrayer. Where the evidence is something other than a confession, the discretion to exclude is capable of coming into play only by analogy with the special régime for confessions. In Lord Diplock's own words, the discretion is one to exclude only 'evidence tantamount to a self-incriminating admission which was obtained from the defendant, after the offence had been committed, by means which would justify a judge in excluding an actual confession which had the like self-incriminating effect'.[52] This analysis has the considerable advantage of explaining all the previous decisions, though certainly not the reasoning employed. Only in *Court* and *Payne* was it held that non-confession evidence should have been excluded by the trial judge. In both cases, there was a promise which would have led, had it brought forth a confession rather than the observations of a doctor, to the exclusion of that confession under the common law exclusionary rule. Lord Diplock did not explicitly restrict the analogy to that with the exclusionary rule for confessions, so it is reasonable to assume that his view was that it extended also to the exclusionary discretion therefor.

Though Lord Diplock's scheme seems to work intellectually, and perhaps even historically, it presents three major difficulties. First, as we have seen, some of the cases concerned with discretionary exclusion of confessions themselves relied upon the line of cases about exclusion of non-confession evidence, so there is a degree of circularity present. Flowing from this point is a second one. Lord Diplock's analysis does nothing to address, let alone deal with, the uncertainties of the various conflicting descriptions of the scope of the discretion which have been given in the leading cases, whether concerned with confessions or not. Thirdly, not everyone would think satisfactory a law which gave the judge discretion to exclude evidence which the accused had been tricked into producing for the police but not one to exclude it where forced from him by their violence.

[52] *Ibid.* 436.

Though Viscount Dilhorne may be taken to agree with Lord Diplock's gloss on the overall formulation, there are indications that he would have preferred to deny the existence of any unfairness discretion at all for non-confession evidence. Unlike Lord Diplock, he expressed doubts about the correctness of the decision in *Payne*.[53] He said that the remarks of Lord Parker CJ in *Callis* v. *Gunn*[54] and those of Lord Widgery CJ in *Jeffrey* v. *Black*[55] were incorrect, though he did not reject those of Lord Goddard in *Kuruma*[56] affirming the propriety of the judge ruling out evidence obtained by a trick.

Whilst Lord Diplock considered that unfairly obtained evidence might properly be excluded even though its admission would not have jeopardized the accused's right to a fair trial, Lords Salmon, Fraser, and Scarman considered that the reason for its exclusion was precisely that it did put that right in jeopardy. It is clear that each of them must have had in mind a wider view of the right to a fair trial, such that the very use at trial of unfairly or improperly obtained evidence was inconsistent with it; the set piece in court should not be viewed in isolation. Lord Salmon indicated that both the exclusionary rule for confessions and the discretion to exclude evidence for unfairness flow from that basic right, but refused to close the categories of case flowing from it.[57] Nor was Lord Fraser willing to seek to reconcile or explain the various *dicta* from the earlier cases, though he did say that he regarded the discretion as applicable no less where the evidence had been obtained from premises occupied by the accused than where obtained from his person. He added that judges should exercise their discretion in accordance with their own views of what is 'unfair, oppressive or morally reprehensible'.[58] Lord Scarman, agreeing with Lord Diplock about the principle behind exclusion, put it in terms of the maxim *nemo tenetur se ipsum prodere* (equivalent to *nemo debet prodere se ipsum*), but, disagreeing with Lord Diplock, thought it an aspect of trial fairness.[59] He was not prepared to exclude the possibility, mentioned by three successive Lords Chief Justice, that evidence obtained by deception, or a trick, may be excluded.

In general, it has been Lord Diplock's analysis which has dominated the later decisions about the unfairness discretion at common law. Thus, in *Trump*,[60] the Court of Appeal expressly adopted the idea of an analogy to confessions. That was a drink/driving case where a blood sample had been obtained by the threat of imprisonment, fine, and disqualification for failure to provide it. In another drink/driving case, *Fox*,[61] the appellant's argument, by the time the case reached the House of Lords, was that evidence of the contents of a specimen of breath taken from him at the police station should have been excluded since he was, at the time, under unlawful arrest. In the leading speech, Lord Fraser noted that the appellant had not been tricked, nor had the police behaved oppressively towards him.[62]

[53] [1980] AC 440. [54] For which, see the text to n. 25 above.
[55] Referred to in the text to n. 28 above. [56] For which, see the text to n. 21 above.
[57] See [1980] AC 402, at 445. [58] *Ibid*. 450. [59] *Ibid*. 455–6.
[60] (1979) 70 Cr.App.R 300. [61] [1986] AC 281.
[62] See also *Gull* v. *Scarborough* [1987] RTR 261n.

Though the analogy to confessions was not relied upon expressly, it seems to lie firmly behind Lord Fraser's reasoning. A case tending the other way is *Adams*.[63] There, the Court of Appeal, having decided that the real evidence at issue in that case had been acquired in consequence of an illegal search of the accused's premises, went on to consider the possibility of exclusion under *Sang*. Though, curiously, the court referred to the absence of oppression as being significant, thereby suggesting an acceptance of the need for an analogy with confession evidence, it failed to take the simpler point that the accused had not, in any way, been compelled to produce evidence against himself. Had it taken that point, it would presumably have said that the discretion was simply not available, rather than that this was not a case where it would have been correct to exercise it in favour of exclusion. Finally, in *Apicella*,[64] the Court of Appeal quoted both the agreed formulation in *Sang* and Lord Diplock's apparently narrower gloss upon it. The court did not say whether or not it took the latter to be as authoritative as the former, simply noting that both statements were *obiter dicta*. It went on to add that, on the facts of that particular case, there was no question of the intended use of a body sample provided by the accused as evidence against him threatening the fairness of his trial, even though he was taken to have submitted rather than consented to having that sample taken from him. It is quite clear that the court favoured a narrow scope for the discretion, though not clear that it would be the same as that dictated by the Diplock gloss.

On balance, it seems right to conclude that the unfairness discretion at common law is reasoned in the way suggested by Lord Diplock in *Sang*. The most obvious restriction imposed by that reasoning is that evidence acquired by an unlawful search of the accused's person or premises may not be excluded unless, in addition to that element of unlawfulness, the accused had been persuaded to produce evidence for the police. The key element is, then, that the will of the accused has been engaged, for only if it has can he have been so persuaded. Once one has such a case, the second question arises, namely whether or not the evidence in question would have been excluded, as a matter either of law or discretion, had it been a confession. There are two subsidiary points. First, it seems likely that Lord Fraser's view that the discretion applies no less where the evidence has been obtained from the accused's premises than from his person is correct. So if, in response to a threat of violence, he were to tell the police that they would find the murder weapon in a particular cupboard (rather than in his pocket), it would be absurd for the discretion to be unavailable, assuming always that his will had been engaged. Indeed, it ought not to matter from where the evidence comes, whether his person, his property, or someone else's person or property, if the maxim *nemo debet prodere se ipsum* is the key. A second point, reiterated by Lord Diplock in *Morris* v. *Beardmore*, is that the evidence in question must be 'evidence subsequently obtained from the accused himself relating to an offence *that has already been committed by him*'.[65] So where the evidence in question is of conduct itself constituting the offence charged, like that in *Sang*

[63] [1980] QB 575. [64] (1985) 82 Cr.App.R 295.

[65] [1981] AC 446, at 454 (emphasis in original).

itself, no discretion is available. One should be clear that this may mean that it will be unavailable where the accused was already in the course of committing a continuing offence. For example, a person who responded to a threat of violence by surrendering drugs from his person might be prevented from arguing for their exclusion, for he would have been, at the time of the threat, still committing the offence of unlawful possession. It is not easy to see why this should be the case. It is possible that a distinction might, therefore, be drawn between continuing offences and ones not yet embarked upon, so that the discretion would be available in the case of the former but not the latter.

It will be clear that, at least for Lord Diplock, the principle lying behind the unfairness discretion was the protective principle, manifesting itself in support of the *nemo debet* maxim.[66] Lord Scarman seems to have been of a similar view, though this kind of protection was, for him, an element of the accused's fair trial right. Lord Diplock was strongly of the opinion that this discretion did not flow from any judicial duty or power to discipline the police. In his words, '[i]t is no part of a judge's function to exercise disciplinary powers over the police or prosecution as respects the way in which evidence to be used at the trial is obtained by them.'[67]

The Effect of the 1984 Act

The common law discretion to exclude evidence, whether in the form of a confession or otherwise, is expressly preserved by section 82(3) of the 1984 Act, which provides: '[n]othing in this part of this Act shall prejudice any power of a court to exclude evidence . . . at its discretion.' It follows that both the unreliability and unfairness elements of the discretion are capable of applying no less today than before the Act.[68]

The Discretion under Section 78(1) of the 1984 Act

Parliament was not content simply to leave the common law in place, so far as discretionary exclusion was concerned. After amendments which would have substantially altered the common law had been proposed in the House of Lords, the Government finally offered, as a substitute for those amendments, a subclause which eventually became section 78(1) of the 1984 Act.[69] According to that subsection:

[66] See the discussion, in Ch. 2, text between nn. 38 and 59 above.

[67] [1980] AC 402, at 436. Cf. *Trump* (1979) 70 Cr.App.R 300, at 304, where Eveleigh LJ stated that there might be some cases where exclusion for disciplinary purposes could be justified.

[68] Confirmation of this point, if it be needed, can be found in *Matto* v. *Wolverhampton Crown Court* [1987] RTR 337, *O'Leary* (1988) 87 Cr.App.R 387, *Christou and Wright* [1992] QB 979 and *Smurthwaite and Gill* [1994] 1 All ER 898. S. 82(3) seems almost never to be relied upon by the defence *instead of*, as opposed to in addition to, s. 78(1). For a rare example, see *Marshall*, *The Times*, 28 Dec. 1992 (transcript through LEXIS).

[69] This is not the place to rehearse the sequence of events which led to the enactment of s. 78(1).

In any proceedings the court may refuse to allow evidence on which the prosecution proposes to rely to be given if it appears to the court that, having regard to all the circumstances, including the circumstances in which the evidence was obtained, the admission of the evidence would have such an adverse effect on the fairness of the proceedings that the court ought not to admit it.

Though the words used fail, on their face, to support a restriction of the power granted such that it is available only in respect of non-confession evidence, it might have been argued that, given the significant changes to the exclusionary rule for confessions brought about by section 76 of the Act, that power should be taken not to extend to confessions. However, in two early cases, the Court of Appeal overturned the trial judge's decision not to exclude confession evidence and relied upon section 78(1) in doing so.[70] And, indeed, the majority of the large number of cases concerned with exclusion under section 78(1) decided since those early cases involve confessions.

The subsection clearly encompasses a discretion based upon unreliability. It is obvious that the admission in evidence of material more prejudicial than probative would have 'an adverse effect on the fairness of the proceedings'. There are many instances of the unreliability head being the ground for exclusion under section 78(1), but the most substantial category of case which clearly demonstrates its application is that concerned with identification evidence gathered before trial. We shall see later that very many of the cases in this category are directly concerned with whether or not such evidence is sufficiently reliable for it safely to be left to the jury.

The unfairness head might seem to present rather more of a difficulty. It is the unfairness of the 'proceedings' which counts, and 'proceedings' is defined in section 82(1) in such a way that it clearly refers to the *adjudicative* part of the criminal process, the result being that it must be broadly equivalent to 'trial'. It follows that one needs to explain how the unlawful, improper, or unfair treatment of the accused by the police or others is capable of putting at risk the fairness of the set piece in the criminal court. The difficulty is compounded by the fact that, as we have seen, the House of Lords in *Sang*[71] divided on the very issue of whether or not exclusion of unfairly obtained evidence could be justified by reference to the accused's right to a fair trial. The wording of section 78(1) resulted, in theory, in the translation of that problem into the present context. In fact, the courts have rarely troubled themselves with the theory, yet there is a vast number of cases which either apply or assume the application of section 78(1) where the essence of the accused's complaint is the manner in which he was treated by the police. We shall have occasion, later in this Chapter, to return to those cases which *do* examine the theory.[72]

For an account, see M. Zander, *The Police and Criminal Evidence Act 1984* (2nd edn., 1990), 199–200.

[70] See *Mason* [1988] 1 WLR 139; *Samuel* [1988] QB 615.

[71] [1980] AC 402, discussed, in the text to nn. 33–67 above.

[72] See the text between nn. 114 and 132 below.

Juridical Nature of Discretionary Exclusion

The very notion of excluding, as a matter of discretion, evidence admissible as a matter of law is not the easiest to understand. Judicial usage quite often refers to evidence excluded in the exercise of a discretion as being inadmissible, yet, strictly, such usage is inaccurate. Of course, where the defence seeks to have a confession excluded, it may well rely upon both the exclusionary rule and the exclusionary discretion, but only the discretion is available in respect of non-confession evidence.

The combined availability of the rule and the discretion led to confusion in a number of pre-Act cases about confessions. At times, judges described the exclusionary rule in a way which suggested that the decision whether or not the police conduct which had brought about the confession constituted a threat, a promise, or oppression was a discretionary one.[73] At other times, they appeared to be saying that the unfairness discretion was available only where the conduct complained of had rendered the confession involuntary.[74] The post-Act cases have the great merit of avoiding both of these errors. The true distinction between the rule and the discretion is clear enough. Though there does not seem to be an analysis of that distinction to be found in any of the post-Act cases, its bare bones have emerged.[75]

The distinction will be briefly described here. Once the judge has found the facts where, say, oppression is alleged, he must take a view on whether or not they do constitute oppressive conduct. He may also have to decide whether or not any such conduct caused the accused to confess. These are matters of judgment and have a rather open texture. On appeal from the judge's decision, the higher court must equally be prepared to exercise its judgment in these matters. Should its judgment differ from that of the trial judge, it has no option but to substitute its own for his. So if he has found the police conduct not to be oppressive and the Court of Appeal disagrees, it must overturn his decision and thus, other things being equal, rule the confession inadmissible. The same does not apply where discretionary power under section 78(1) or section 82(3) is invoked. From the point of view of the trial judge, the exercise is no different. So, for example, he will have to reach a judgment on whether or not admission of the evidence would so adversely affect the fairness of the proceedings that it ought not to be admitted. What he certainly is not at liberty to decide is that, though its admission would so

[73] See, e.g., *Prager* [1972] 1 WLR 260, at 267 (*per* Edmund-Davies LJ); *Conway* v. *Hotten* [1976] 2 All ER 213, at 217–18 (*per* Watkins J); *Mackintosh* (1982) 76 Cr.App.R 177, at 181 (*per* Lawton LJ). An example of the same error obtruding in a post-Act case may be *Hartley* v. *DPP*, 16 Oct. 1995 (transcript through LEXIS).

[74] See, e.g., *Prager* [1972] 1 WLR 260, at 266 (*per* Edmund-Davies LJ); *Greaves* v. *D and P* (1980) 71 Cr.App.R 232, at 236 (*per* Donaldson LJ); *Lemsatef* [1977] 1 WLR 812, at 817 (*per* Lawton LJ). For a fuller treatment of both errors, see Mirfield, n. 10 above 133–6.

[75] *Delaney* (1988) 88 Cr.App.R 338; *Maguire* (1989) 90 Cr.App.R 115; *Matthews, Dennison and Voss* (1989) 91 Cr.App.R 43; *Crampton* (1990) 92 Cr.App.R 369; *Effik and Mitchell* (1992) 95 Cr.App.R 427.

adversely affect fairness that it ought not to be admitted, nonetheless, because he has discretion, he will allow it to be given in evidence. For him at least, the words 'may refuse' in section 78(1) mean 'must refuse', once he has decided that there would be the relevant unfairness.[76] However, the responsibility of the Court of Appeal is different from that which applies in the case of the rule. It is to allow the trial judge a certain element of leeway so far as his judgment is concerned. Thus, it is entirely coherent for the higher court to say that it *would* regard the admission in evidence of the material in question as rendering the proceedings unfair and *would* itself have excluded that material, yet at the same time, for it to uphold the judge's decision.

So what degree of leeway is to be allowed to the trial judge? When should the Court of Appeal intervene to overturn him? It is now established that the limits of proper appeal court tolerance are the same as or similar to those propounded in *Associated Provincial Picture Houses Ltd* v. *Wednesbury Corporation*[77] in respect of powers exercised by administrative agencies under statutory provisions. No reported pre-Act case seems to have placed any reliance upon the *Wednesbury* ruling, though in *Conway* v. *Hotten*[78] Watkins J employed language redolent of the formulation laid down in that very well-known case. Since the 1984 Act came into force, the courts have been rather more forthcoming on the point. In *O'Leary*, May LJ accepted counsel's invitation to rule that the boundaries of discretion were set by the *Wednesbury* canons of unreasonableness.[79] In the important case of *Christou and Wright*, the Court of Appeal relied upon *O'Leary* in pointing out that the judge's exercise of discretion, 'could only be impugned if it was unreasonable according to *Wednesbury* principles'.[80]

Much the most sophisticated analysis of this point is to be found in the unreported case of *Middlebrook and Caygill*.[81] Laws J, delivering the judgment of the Court of Appeal, began by doubting that the public law rule deriving from *Wednesbury* was properly applicable to a court of appeal, as opposed to a court of review. Nonetheless, he went on to indicate that it would be right for the appeal court to intervene where the judge's decision had been wholly unreasonable. He said that:

> it is an exercise of judgment carried out by the judge in the light of all the circumstances known to him in the immediacy of the trial. Since that is its nature, it is a task or function whose discharge by the trial judge will not readily be interfered with in this court. If, of course, the material in the case discloses a state of affairs in which a reasonable judge must have concluded that the admission of the evidence would produce unfairness, this court will set aside a ruling which goes the other way. We think that this is what is meant by the references to *Wednesbury* in the cases.

[76] A point made by Laws J in *Middlebrook and Caygill*, 18 Feb. 1994 (transcript through LEXIS).
[77] [1948] 1 KB 223. [78] [1976] 2 All ER 213, at 217–18.
[79] (1988) 87 Cr.App.R 387, at 391.
[80] [1992] QB 979, at 989. See also *Khan* [1993] Crim.LR 54 (transcript through LEXIS).
[81] 18 Feb. 1994 (transcript through LEXIS). And see *Khan et al.* [1997] Crim.LR 508.

The notion that a decision which no reasonable judge could make is to be set aside is, in fact, capable of covering a great deal of the ground. It is itself recognized in *Wednesbury* as one of the bases for overturning an exercise of discretion. The others are that the decision has been made for an improper purpose, or that the decision-maker has taken into account irrelevant considerations or failed to take into account relevant ones. No doubt, what Laws J, himself an expert upon judicial review of administrative action, was wary of was the danger that the Criminal Division of the Court of Appeal might become embroiled in the difficulties of the continually developing case law of that kind of judicial review. Still, it would seem that, in principle, the other established heads of judicial control over abuse of discretion should be capable of applying to the discretionary decisions of criminal trial judges. The possibility that the judge might act for an improper purpose seems hardly a real one. However, judicial resort to irrelevant considerations, or failure to resort to relevant ones, cannot be discounted. Indeed, in the important case of *Mason*,[82] the Court of Appeal allowed the appeal precisely because, in exercising his discretion, the trial judge had 'omitted a vital factor from his consideration'.[83] There was no reference to the decision having been wholly unreasonable, and, on the particular facts of that case, any such reference would have misdescribed the Court's reasoning.[84] More recently, in *Weerdesteyn*,[85] that Court took a similar view where the trial judge had failed to take into consideration that the police had breached a specific provision of Code C concerned with ensuring the accuracy of the record.

Another recent development is of some considerable potential significance, so far as application of the *Wednesbury* principles is concerned. In two briefly reported Court of Appeal cases which, for some reason, are unavailable on LEXIS,[86] the view seems to have been taken that the trial judge was under a duty to give reasons for his decision to exercise his discretion against excluding the evidence. Should these *dicta* hold good, it seems obvious that there will be greater opportunity for the overturning of trial court decisions, both because, if no reasons are given, the appeal court will need to exercise the discretion afresh and because its view of any reasons actually given may be that they are bad ones, in the sense of not being properly related to the purposes of section 78(1).

Where the trial judge has wholly failed to exercise his discretion, whether under section 78(1) or under section 82(3), it will be the task of the Court of Appeal to exercise it in his stead. There are numerous authorities illustrating this point,[87] but it will serve to refer to one here. In *Parris*, the judge had concluded that, because there had been no breaches by the police of either the provisions of

[82] [1988] 1 WLR 139. See also *Samuel* [1988] QB 615. [83] *Ibid*. 144.

[84] For more detailed treatment of *Mason*, see the text to nn. 105–6 and Ch. 7, n. 130, below.

[85] [1995] 1 Cr.App.R 405. See also *Wright* [1994] Crim.LR 55; *Quinn* [1990] Crim.LR 581.

[86] *Allen* [1995] Crim.LR 643; *Smith* [1995] Crim.LR 658.

[87] Examples are *Matto* v. *Wolverhampton Crown Court* [1987] RTR 337; *Mason* [1988] 1 WLR 139; *Samuel* [1988] QB 615; *Delaney* (1989) 88 Cr.App.R 338; *Gall* (1989) 90 Cr.App.R 64; *Beycan and Gokan* [1990] Crim.LR 185; *Kerawalla* [1991] Crim.LR 451; *Oliphant* [1992] Crim.LR 40; *Raphaie* [1996] Crim.LR 812.

the 1984 Act or those of Code C, there was no discretion for him to exercise. Since the Court of Appeal disagreed with him on the issue of breach, its task was 'to put ourselves as far as possible in the position of the Judge and, on the basis that there was indeed a breach which had to be taken into account, to decide whether the learned judge should have ruled the evidence . . . as inadmissible'.[88]

THE CATEGORIES OF UNFAIRNESS

The investigative powers of the police are both the creatures of, and regulated by, the law. There is, of course, a police discipline code,[89] to which all officers are subject. The matters with which it deals, though often of great public significance, are clearly internal to the police. The general law of the land regulates police powers in three distinct ways. First, the common law continues to govern some aspects of their conduct. For example, the doctrine requiring certain information to be given to persons arrested or searched was established by *Christie* v. *Leachinsky*,[90] though it now has statutory force. *Christie* would seem to be quite capable, because it is clearly based upon a general principle that citizens should be informed of what coercive powers are being used against them and of the reason why, of generating equivalent requirements in respect of newly-created police powers. Furthermore, the general law, applicable to all citizens, may prove significant in some cases. It was undoubtedly a very significant factor in the decision in *Matto* v. *Wolverhampton Crown Court*[91] that, at the time when the police had required the accused to provide them with a sample of breath, the officers were knowingly trespassing upon the accused's land. Secondly, statutory provisions now impinge very extensively indeed upon the exercise of investigative powers. The most wide-ranging statute is the 1984 Act, but there are many others. Thirdly, there are the codes of practice made under the Act. At present, there are five such codes, regulating the exercise of powers of stop and search (Code A), the exercise of powers to search premises and seize property found therein (Code B), the detention, treatment, and questioning of members of the public (Code C), the identification of alleged offenders (Code D), and the tape-recording of interviews (Code E).

The study of any group of cases in which the defence has sought to have evidence excluded under section 78 will reveal that, in the vast majority of them, the defence was able to allege breach of some duty owed by the police either under statute or, even more commonly, by virtue of some provision of one of the codes of practice. Very often, a number of separate breaches will be alleged. Though this is not a book about the substantive content of police powers and duties,

[88] (1988) 89 Cr.App.R 68, at 72.

[89] Police (Discipline) Regulations 1985 (as amended). Police Act 1996, s. 50(3) makes provision for the introduction of a new set of Regulations to replace the 1985 ones.

[90] [1947] AC 573. See also *Brazil* v. *Chief Constable of Surrey* [1983] 1 WLR 1155.

[91] [1987] RTR 337.

there will often be occasion to make reference to specific statutory or code provisions.

It is very important to be aware of the precise relevance to the argument of the various codes of practice, whether that argument for exclusion be put in terms of section 76, section 78, or section 82(3). There are two separate issues. May the court take into account, when exercising its exclusionary duties and powers, the content of any relevant part of the codes? Secondly, may one describe the police, in an appropriate case, as being in breach of some rule contained within a code? Though both questions would be simply answered in the affirmative in the case of statutory duties, the answers are more complex in the case of the codes.

First, it is specifically provided by section 67(11) of the 1984 Act that:

> In all criminal and civil proceedings any such code shall be admissible in evidence, and if any provision of such a code appears to the court or tribunal conducting the proceedings to be relevant to any question arising in the proceedings it shall be taken into account in determining that question.

So it seems that every part of every code is admissible, but that only a 'provision' of a code shall be taken into account in determining any question arising to which it is relevant. Now, the form in which the codes are drafted is such that there may be as many as three different elements. There are, in all of them, numbered paragraphs, many of which are drafted in duty-imposing or power-conferring form. Some of them also have annexes, in differently numbered paragraphs, to which reference is made in the main part and which, again in many cases, impose duties or confer powers. Finally, there are what sub-headings in the codes describe as 'Notes for Guidance'. Their clear purpose is to provide guidance to police officers with regard to the exercise of their duties and powers. However, in so doing, they often seem to qualify, limit, or even extend those duties and powers.

A good example of the problem is provided by the relationship between paragraph 6.9 and Note for Guidance 6D of Code C.[92] The former says that a solicitor representing a suspect being questioned may be required to leave the interview only if 'his conduct is such that the investigating officer is unable properly to put questions to the suspect'. Note 6D tells the officer, *inter alia*, that a solicitor 'may intervene in order to seek clarification or to challenge an improper question to his client or the manner in which it is put, or to advise his client not to reply to particular questions, or if he wishes to give his client further legal advice'. Clearly, the Note spells out, partially at least, the boundaries of proper conduct. Indeed, it goes on to tell the officer that paragraph 6.9 will apply only if 'the solicitor's approach or conduct prevents or unreasonably obstructs proper questions being put to the suspect or his response being recorded'. These are words which, to an extent, repeat those of paragraph 6.9, yet also add the telling word 'unreasonably' before 'obstructs'. The professional duties of the police and the solicitor are in clear opposition here. There is obviously considerable scope for disagreement

[92] See, also, para. 6.12.

about the propriety of questions. In those circumstances, it would surely be right to expect the police officer to have regard to Note 6D and for the courts to take it into account in deciding whether or not the power to eject a solicitor had been properly exercised in a given case.

The problem which arises is that each of the codes contains, in one of the numbered paragraphs within its main body, a provision that '[t]he notes for guidance included are not provisions of this code, but are guidance to police officers and others about its application and interpretation.' In the codes with annexes, the same numbered paragraph goes on to state that '[p]rovisions in the annexes . . . are provisions of this code'. When we look back at the wording of section 67(11), we find that it is only 'provisions' of codes which are to be taken into account in determining questions to which they are relevant. Does it then follow that notes for guidance may not be so taken into account? A strict interpretation would suggest that it does, leaving the notes admissible, yet never capable of being considered, a remarkable conclusion given the importance of the content of some of them, for example Note 6D itself.

There is no reported case in which the problem just identified has been dealt with expressly, though there are several in which notes for guidance have been mentioned, and some in which a note has undoubtedly been relied upon. Several of the cases in question[93] are concerned with the definition of 'interview' in Code C. This was and is a vital matter, for very many police duties are, as we shall see later in this book,[94] predicated upon the fact that a suspect is being interviewed. At the time when the 'interview' cases were decided, the definition in question was to be found only in a note for guidance (Note 11A), though, following revisions of Code C effective from 1 April 1995, it is now contained in an ordinary provision (paragraph 11.1A) of the Code proper. Two examples of reliance upon this Note may be given. In *Menard*,[95] police officers acceded to the accused's request to be allowed to volunteer information to them. The meeting which followed was, the Court of Appeal held, not an interview, the reason being that Note 11A began by describing an interview as the *questioning* of a person. In *Weerdesteyn*,[96] the same Court decided that, because the accused had been questioned 'regarding his involvement or suggested involvement in a criminal offence or offences', it followed that he had been interviewed for the purposes of Note 11A. Certainly, in both these cases, Note 11A was not merely taken into account; it was relied upon.

Now it is possible that Note 11A was exceptional, for paragraph 11.1 specifically stated, '[f]or the definition of an interview, see Note 11A', and this might be thought to have had the effect of incorporating it into Code C proper.[97] There is at least one example in the present issue of Code C of this kind of reference to a

[93] *Williams* (1992) 156 JPR 776; *Cox* (1992) 96 Cr.App.R 464; *Oransaye* [1993] Crim.LR 772 (transcript through LEXIS); *Menard* [1995] 1 Cr.App.R 306; *Weerdesteyn* [1995] 1 Cr.App.R 405.

[94] See Ch. 7, text to nn. 14–39 below.

[95] [1995] 1 Cr.App.R 306.

[96] [1995] 1 Cr.App.R 405.

[97] This was, indeed, suggested in *Cox* (1992) 96 Cr.App.R 464, at 470.

note being made.[98] However, the standard mode of reference is by placing the details of the note in square brackets, for example, '[see Note 6F]' in paragraph 6.13. This might be thought simply to be a convenient way of drawing the officer's attention to the appropriate guidance without involving incorporation by reference.

In yet other cases, there is no reference at all to the note in the main part of the Code. A good example is the very significant Note 11B, which states:

> It is important to bear in mind that, although juveniles or people who are mentally disordered or mentally handicapped are often capable of providing reliable evidence, they may, without knowing or wishing to do so, be particularly prone in certain circumstances to provide information which is unreliable, misleading or self-incriminating. Special care should therefore always be exercised in questioning such a person, and the appropriate adult should be involved, if there is any doubt about a person's age, mental state or capacity. Because of the risk of unreliable evidence it is also important to obtain corroboration of any facts admitted wherever possible.

One can easily imagine a lawyer representing an accused from one of these vulnerable groups seeking from a police officer an explanation of why, in that case, he had failed to involve an 'appropriate adult' or to look for corroborative evidence. Note 11B might well be a crucial plank in the defence argument or, indeed, in the officer's rebuttal thereof.

There are two cases in which notes not referred to at all in the main body of any code were undoubtedly relied upon by the court. Though one was decided under section 76(2)(b), the other shows that the position must be the same for discretionary exclusion. *DPP* v. *Blake*,[99] the rule case, dealt with Note 13C of the original issue of Code C. That note gave important information about the role of the 'appropriate adult', who must, except in very limited circumstances, be present at the interview of a juvenile. It was precisely because Note 13C demonstrated that the appropriate adult was not to act simply as an observer, but also as an adviser to the juvenile, as an overseer of the fairness of the conduct of the interview, and as a facilitator of communication between the parties, that the Divisional Court concluded that the accused's father, from whom she was estranged, could not be regarded as an appropriate adult for the purposes of her interview. In *Oliphant*,[100] one of the bases upon which the appellant sought to have the trial judge's decision not to exclude his confession overturned was that the police had repeatedly asserted to him their belief in his guilt and, as a result, had failed to enable him to offer his own explanation of the facts. The judge, for his part, had gathered from Note 12A of the original Code C that it was not a permissible purpose of the questioning of a suspect to persuade him to confess, rather than to allow him to give an explanation. The Court of Appeal pointed out that Note 12A actually said: '[t]he purpose of any interview is to obtain from the person

[98] See Code C, para. 13.1, referring to Note 3D.
[99] (1988) 89 Cr.App.R 179. For detailed consideration, see Ch. 10, text to nn. 25–6 and 36–40 above.
[100] [1992] Crim.LR 40 (transcript through LEXIS).

concerned his explanation of the facts, and not necessarily to obtain an admission.' In its view, the effect of the note was to require the police to listen to the suspect's story, but not to disallow them from seeking to obtain admissions. Thus, the Court of Appeal, no less than the trial judge, was clearly relying upon that note to assist it in deciding what the code permitted and required. It must be added that neither the Divisional Court in *DPP* v. *Blake* nor the Court of Appeal in *Oliphant* had its attention drawn to the difficulties of interpretation with which we are presently concerned.

It may be concluded that, given that Note 11A was a rather special case, it is not yet clearly settled that notes for guidance not incorporated into the main body of a code may be relied upon by a court in deciding whether or not to exclude evidence. Yet the answer that they cannot be relied upon, an answer apparently dictated by a strict interpretation of the materials, would be a peculiar one. If guidance to which officers are expected to refer and upon which they may properly rely were not similarly available to the court, there would be an obvious possibility that the view of the court might depart from the plain words of a note. There is one way of escaping from such an unsatisfactory conclusion. It is arguable that, because section 67(11) uses the word 'shall', the court is *required* to take relevant provisions of a code into account but is *at liberty* to take notes into account where they are relevant. For completeness, it should be added that a similar argument would have to be deployed in the case of explanatory circulars issued by the Home Office in respect of various code provisions.

Let it be assumed that the courts do eventually decide expressly that the notes may be taken into account when they exercise their duties and powers of exclusion. We may now turn to the question of breach. The existing section 67(8), which is to be repealed when Schedule 9, Part II, of the Police Act 1996 is brought into effect, states that a police officer shall, as a general rule, 'be liable to disciplinary proceedings for a failure to comply with any provision of a code', while section 67(10) (which will remain) makes it clear that a failure to comply with a provision does not of itself render him liable to criminal proceedings. It would seem to follow that notes for guidance, since not themselves 'provisions', are incapable of being breached (or not complied with). And indeed, though the language of the notes varies considerably, the most obvious words to denote a duty, 'must' and 'shall', are generally not used. Rather, the word 'should' is relatively common. This linguistic usage may be thought strongly to support the argument in terms of literal interpretation. However, it has been argued by Wolchover and Heaton-Armstrong that, even if the points just made are sound, no real difficulty is created because it must be intended that code provisions should be interpreted in accordance with any relevant notes. Consequently, where police conduct has departed from some standard set by a note, there will have been breach of the provision in question.[101] Though this does satisfactorily remove the problem so far as the great majority of notes are concerned, there are some which are, in a

[101] See Wolchover and Heaton-Armstrong, *Confession Evidence* (1996), para. 2–022.

sense, free-standing, as for example that part of Note 11B of Code C, referred to a little earlier, which states that it is important for officers to obtain, wherever possible, corroboration of any facts admitted by a juvenile or by a mentally ill or handicapped person. It does seem likely that an officer is entitled to treat such advice as merely precatory.

Even though the statutory provisions and the codes together constitute a very substantial amount of material governing police investigations, there is no doubt that, under section 78(1) no less than at common law, there is a residual discretion to exclude despite the absence of breach of statute or code. In *Voisin*,[102] A. T. Lawrence J assumed that the common law discretion was a general one, while Lord Devlin, referring specifically to the Judges' Rules, put the position succinctly as follows: '[i]t must never be forgotten that the Judges' Rules were made for the guidance of the police and not for the circumscription of the judicial power.'[103]

We shall see in the chapter which follows that there is a large number of cases dealing with trickery or entrapment by the police. In very many of those cases, the courts have exhibited a robust view of what the suspect is entitled to expect of the police. A striking example is *Bailey*,[104] where the investigating officers had engineered an opportunity for the two suspects to have a conversation with each other in a 'bugged' cell. They had done this by telling them that an unco-operative custody officer had required that they be locked up together. The Court of Appeal, in dismissing the appeal, pointed out that nobody had interviewed them; they had simply been given the opportunity of speaking to each other in an incriminatory way. Where appeal courts have felt it right to overturn a first-instance decision to admit evidence acquired by trickery or entrapment, the reason seems to have been that the police had sought to evade or render nugatory protections for suspects provided by statute or one of the codes. The leading example is *Mason*,[105] where the police had lied not only to the accused but also to his solicitor, in saying that the accused's fingerprints had been found on a fragment of glass which had formed part of a fire bomb. Though it is possible that the Court of Appeal might have been prepared to overturn the judge's decision to admit evidence of incriminatory remarks made in consequence of that lie even if it had been told only to the accused, it is more probable that the key point for that court was that the solicitor had been misled. If a suspect has a right to legal advice, it would tend to subvert that right were the police to be able to feed the solicitor untruthful information. Examples of courts taking a less restricted view of the significance of trickery seem to be confined to first instance cases, so far as decisions to exclude are concerned.[106] The more important point for present purposes is, perhaps, that there is no indication in any of the cases concerned with

[102] [1918] 1 KB 531, at 539–40.

[103] *The Criminal Prosecution in England* (1960), 39.

[104] [1993] 3 All ER 513.

[105] [1988] 1 WLR 139. See, also, *Bryce* [1992] 4 All ER 567. And cf. *Thompson* [1995] 2 Cr.App.R 589, at 599.

[106] Examples are *H* [1987] Crim.LR 47 and *Woodall et al.* [1989] Crim.LR 288.

trickery or entrapment that, simply because no rule has been breached or would be subverted if the evidence were to be admitted, the unfairness discretion is unavailable. Where the basis suggested for exclusion is that the evidence is more prejudicial than probative, it would seem even more obvious that the discretion cannot be circumscribed by a notion of unlawful police behaviour.

THE THEORY OF SECTION 78 UNFAIRNESS

Section 78(1) refers, as we have seen, to the admission of evidence having an adverse effect on the fairness *of the proceedings*. Yet in case after case in the appeal courts since the 1984 Act came into effect, the gravamen of the argument for exclusion has been that the conduct of the investigating agency (usually the police) towards the accused was unlawful, improper, or, in some way, unfair. How, then, can it be said that what has gone on pre-trial is capable of adversely affecting the fairness of the trial itself?

One should begin by noting that in only very few cases has there been any real attempt to answer that key question. Usually, courts have satisfied themselves with assessing the pre-trial conduct in question in terms of the general law, the codes of practice, and notions of unfairness, then going on to take as read that conduct fulfilling certain criteria of 'unfairness' must endanger the fairness of the proceedings. Only rarely has a court sought to make explicit the nature of the link between the two. At least Lord Diplock's formulation in *Sang* of the unfairness discretion[107] had the merit of explaining the exclusion of non-confession evidence at common law as being an *exception* to the general principle that the courts are concerned only with the fairness of the trial proper.

THE UNRELIABILITY DISCRETION

Before turning to the cases which do contain some analysis of the key question, we may briefly refer to the situation where the reliability of the evidence, whether it be confessional or otherwise, is brought into doubt. Here, the ordinary discretion in terms of excess of prejudicial effect over probative weight may be recruited under section 78. In those cases where section 78 has been relied upon in this respect, there is nothing to indicate that the new provision adds anything to or subtracts anything from the common law, which is itself preserved by section 82(3). Thus, for the theoretical perspective, the reader is referred back to the earlier discussion of the common law discretion.[108] Whichever section be relied upon, there is no problem at all in seeing that the exclusion of the evidence will have as its rationale the preservation of the fairness of the trial itself.

There are four points about the unreliability discretion which are best dealt with in this Chapter. First, many of the provisions of the various codes of practice

[107] See text to nn. 33–67 above. [108] See text to nn. 13–17 and 34–47 above.

are undoubtedly designed to ensure the reliability of evidence gathered by the police or other investigating authority. This may itself be taken in two different senses. Thus, for example, the special rules applicable to the questioning of children and the mentally handicapped are designed, at least principally, to ensure that a resulting confession may properly be relied upon by the trier of fact. Their breach, whether deliberate or not, may put reliability in question. The second sense in which code provisions seek to ensure reliability of the material before the court is by virtue of the fact that a number of the Code C provisions and all those of Code E (the tape-recording code) concern themselves with the accuracy of the record. Here, breach, particularly where deliberate, will cast a cloud over the integrity of that record, as presented by the police.

The second point is that, where provisions designed to ensure reliability have been breached, the court sometimes seems to have in mind that version of the disciplinary principle which has as its aim the discouragement of police practices conducive to unreliability.[109] Here, the courts have felt able to acknowledge a disciplinary purpose for exclusion, even though it is not easy to see how one prevents the present proceedings from being unfair by deterring future police misconduct. In the best post-Act example, *Canale*,[110] the police had deliberately and cynically breached the general rule requiring that interviews at police stations be recorded contemporaneously. In consequence, they had also breached a number of subsidiary rules about the record. This was done for no better reason than that the officers thought it the 'best way' of conducting the interview. The Court of Appeal, in a mood of sternness not often exhibited in its attitude to police misconduct, overturned the trial judge's decision to allow the police to give evidence of the alleged content of the interviews in question. Though, of course, the accuracy of that particular record was gravely in doubt, the language of the court demonstrates that it was most anxious to direct and influence future police practice. In a later case involving breaches of the recording requirements which were, in any event, far less gross, the court refused even to contemplate the possibility of exclusion where these breaches related to a third party suspect rather than to the accused himself.[111]

A third point is that issues of unreliability and more general unfairness may, of course, arise in the same case. So the accused may, for example, allege breach both of the rules about the recording of statements and of rules granting him access to a lawyer. There are a number of cases where the Court of Appeal has found to be present breaches of both kinds.[112] This may well lead to the appeal being successful under section 76(2)(b) of the 1984 Act, but, in principle, the two disparate elements of code breach may combine in a way which leads to the conclusion that the judge should have excluded the evidence in question under section 78(1).

[109] See the discussion at p. 13. [110] (1989) 91 Cr.App.R 1.

[111] See *Roberts* [1997] 1 Cr.App.R 217.

[112] See, e.g., *Walsh* (1989) 91 Cr.App.R 161; *McGovern* (1990) 92 Cr.App.R 228; *Chung* (1990) 92 Cr.App.R 314.

The final point, a rather surprising one of considerable potential importance, is established by *Bailey*.[113] That case holds that the trial judge, in deciding whether or not the accused's confession is so unreliable that it ought to be excluded under section 78(1), may properly take into account the accused's previous convictions for similar offences, even though they would, because of similar fact rules, be inadmissible at the trial of the general issue. There is, said the Court of Appeal, nothing in section 78 to suggest that Parliament intended to confine the judge, when having regard to all the circumstances, to facts admissible at the main trial. Furthermore, the Court took the positive view that a confession is more likely to be reliable where the confessor has no convictions for similar offences. Presumably, the judge is to be trusted not to give those convictions undue weight in his assessment of reliability. It ought to follow that there can be no objection at all to the judge taking account of the other (admissible) evidence in the case implicating the accused. Yet where, as in the premises, the confession is one which, given its provenance and the circumstances of its obtaining, is of doubtful reliability, it seems strange indeed for the judge to satisfy himself of its actual reliability by a reflection that the other evidence in the case demonstrates the accused's guilt. It might be thought much safer to have such a case decided solely on the basis of the evidence extraneous to the confession.

The Unfairness Discretion

The idea of unfair conduct of the police towards the suspect is easy enough to grasp, though its vagueness renders it extremely difficult to define and delineate. The problem of relating the way in which the suspect was treated to the fairness of the proceedings once he is accused in court is much less tractable. It will be convenient to deal with it under four headings. Once that has been done, we shall refer to a factor which does not feature in the equation.

Inequality of Access to Evidence

One relatively straightforward situation may be dealt with first. As we have seen, defects in the record may well be such that admission of evidence will be more prejudicial than probative, but they may also produce potential unfairness in a rather different way. Say that the accused, though he admits that he was interviewed in the police station, will allege that the police record of the interview is inaccurate. Before Code E introduced a general duty to tape-record interviews, it was Code C which alone contained provisions relating to how the police should go about ensuring that the record presented to the court was an accurate one. Where the police have breached the provision requiring the record to be made contemporaneously and have then gone on to breach the one requiring the suspect to be given the opportunity of reading the interview record and signing it as correct or indicating the respects in which he considers it to be inaccurate[114]—a

[113] [1995] 2 Cr.App.R 262.

[114] See, respectively, Code C, paras. 11.5(c) and 11.10.

not uncommon occurrence in the reported cases—the accused would labour under a substantial disadvantage at trial if the record were to be admitted in evidence, probably many months later. He would be able to do no more than say that what the police wrote down near the event was inaccurate, for he would not, of course, have made his own record, yet the police would be in a position to refresh their memories from the defective record. In other words, the situation would involve unequal access to evidence, making availability of the discretion to exclude in order to prevent such inequality wholly explicable. This aspect of trial unfairness was expressly recognized in *Keenan*.[115] Now that there is a duty to tape-record an interview with a person who has been cautioned and is suspected of having committed an indictable offence or one triable either way, it is reasonable to expect the situation just described to be a rather rare one. However, it is entirely conceivable that equivalent situations may arise under Code E itself. For example, paragraph 4.14 thereof requires the accused to be offered the opportunity of clarifying anything he has said or of adding anything he may wish. One may envisage an accused arguing that a failure of the police to allow him such an opportunity prevented him from explaining in a way more favourable to himself some incriminating statement made at an earlier stage.

The more general problem of unequal access to evidence has been addressed in two cases which deserve greater attention than they have received. In *Quinn*,[116] one police officer had been present at the 1975 murder (by shooting) of another officer. Quinn, who was suspected of the murder, was, some three or four months later, on trial in Dublin for another offence. The surviving officer was taken there and, without Quinn or his lawyers having any prior knowledge of what was to happen, that officer was taken into court and identified Quinn as the murderer. For reasons which it is not necessary to go into here, Quinn was not brought to trial until 1988. The issue at trial and in the Court of Appeal was whether or not the identification evidence should have been excluded under section 78(1). The defence attack upon that evidence had two elements. First, because Quinn had not known in advance what was going to happen, he had been denied the opportunity of agreeing to the more satisfactory alternative of an identification parade. He had also been denied the opportunity of consulting a solicitor and of observing and recording the precise circumstances of the 'dock identification'. Secondly, because not told until after the event that the officer had identified him, he had had no timely and proper opportunity to make a record even *reasonably* contemporaneously with what had happened in the Dublin court, nor to make his own investigations about the murder and into where he might have been at the time. Nonetheless, the Court of Appeal upheld the trial judge's decision to allow the evidence to be called, arguing that the *actual* disadvantage to Quinn in making out his defence had been slight and that the evidence did not, in any event, stand alone. The case's more general significance is that Lord Lane CJ did explicitly recognize that the unequal access

[115] (1989) 90 Cr.App.R 1, at 13.

[116] [1990] Crim.LR 581 (transcript through LEXIS).

argument provided a legitimate ground for invoking section 78(1). In his words:

normally proceedings are fair if a jury hears all the relevant evidence which either side wishes to place before it, but proceedings may become unfair if, for example, one side is allowed to adduce relevant evidence which, for one reason or another, the other side cannot properly challenge or meet, or where there has been an abuse of process, e.g. because evidence has been obtained in deliberate breach of procedures laid down in an official code of practice.

A rather more mundane example of the relevance of the inability of the defence to challenge or meet evidence sought to be adduced against it is provided by *DPP* v. *British Telecommunications plc*.[117] The case concerned an accident in which a trailer owned by British Telecommunications had gone out of control, the eventual result having been the death of a person in another vehicle. The substance of the construction and use charge against the company was that its trailer had had a defective braking system. After the accident, an authorized vehicle examiner had examined that system and would say that it was indeed defective. However, the effect of his examination had been, as was accepted on all sides, so to alter a part or parts of the system as to disable a defence expert from carrying out any similar examination. The magistrates, relying upon section 78(1), had refused to allow the examiner to give his evidence. Though the Divisional Court did recognize the force of the defence's argument, it seems to have been of the view that no question of exclusion arose. Rather, that argument went to weight. Yet, as Otton J pointed out, it would have been prudent for the police to have informed the owner that the examination was about to take place and to have allowed a representative of the owner to be present to make his own observations. Therefore it is surprising that the discretion should be regarded as not available at all. A better explanation of the actual result may well be that the magistrates should not have made their decision to exclude 'on the papers', but should have allowed the evidence to be given *de bene esse* and cross-examination to take place, before deciding whether or not to exclude it.

Breach of Promise as to Use

Another way in which the circumstances of the obtaining of the evidence are properly such as to raise issues of trial unfairness is illustrated by *Nathaniel*.[118] The accused had originally been suspected of raping two Danish females. In accordance with the applicable procedure under the 1984 Act, he was asked to provide a blood sample in order for a DNA profile to be prepared. That procedure entailed, *inter alia*, him being made certain promises before he provided the sample. He was told that it was required in respect of the present case, that it

[117] (1991) 155 JPR 869. There is additional discussion of this case in Ch. 3, text to n. 46 above. See, also, *DPP* v. *Snook* [1993] Crim.LR 883.

[118] [1995] 2 Cr.App.R 565.

would be destroyed if he was eventually cleared of those rapes, and that any refusal to allow a sample to be taken might result in inferences being drawn against him at trial. Though he was later acquitted of the two offences, the DNA profiles were not destroyed. In due course, forensic scientists matched those profiles with other profiles made up from semen taken from the victim of a quite different offence of rape. The trial judge permitted the prosecution to adduce that evidence at Nathaniel's trial for that offence and a connected offence of robbery. In overturning his conviction, the court ruled that it ought not to have been admitted. Lord Taylor CJ emphasized that not only had there been breach of the statutory rule requiring destruction of such samples, but that the accused 'had in effect been misled into consenting to give the blood sample by statements and promises which were not honoured'.[119] The point here is that the promises included the implicit one that the profiles would *not* be adduced at any trial other than that for the rapes of the two Danish females. In other words, that promise related specifically to use of that evidence at trial. It is not clear whether the breach of the statutory duty to destroy, without any promise to the accused, would have sufficed to demand exclusion.

Nathaniel is a striking case, for, though the court refused to speculate about the cogency of the DNA evidence, it is reasonable to suppose that it pointed unequivocally at the accused, who, on conviction, had been sentenced to eleven years in prison. The common law cases of *Court* and *Payne*[120] were not cited to the court, but they seem to be precisely in point, not least because we may assume that the officers making the relevant promises had no reason to believe that the samples would not be destroyed as required by the Act. The principle re-affirmed by the case will remain equally valid even after the coming into force of section 57(3) of the Criminal Justice and Public Order Act 1994, which *expressly* renders inadmissible information derived from a sample which ought to have been destroyed.

Nathaniel is to be contrasted with *McDonald*.[121] The accused, having been arrested for murder, was examined by a psychiatrist for the purpose of determining his fitness to plead, whether or not he might be suffering from diminished responsibility, and his mental state in general. During the proper course of the examination, the accused was asked about a letter to the victim's parents in which he had expressed remorse but had asked them to understand how he had felt to be in the presence of someone (their son) who had been having sexual intercourse with his wife. He told the psychiatrist that he had given that explanation because he had to make up some reason for his behaviour. The Court of Appeal upheld the trial judge's decision to allow the prosecution to adduce evidence from the psychiatrist of that remark in order to rebut McDonald's defence of provocation. In doing so, it stressed that the psychiatrist had not asked the question for some purpose extraneous to his proper one, that there had been no

[119] See *ibid*. 571. [120] These cases are considered in the text to nn. 31–2 above.
[121] [1991] Crim.LR 122 (transcript through LEXIS).

oppression or inducement, and that no confidentiality privilege attaches to communications between doctor and patient. It did not accept as decisive counsel's argument that there was an aura of trust and confidence involved which encouraged the patient to a frankness which he would not otherwise display. The Court referred to *Payne*, but seems to have thought it distinguishable on the basis that no promise had been made to McDonald by the psychiatrist that anything he said would not be used adversely to him outside the context of relevance to his mental state. That which one may assume or expect is not, then, to be equated with that which one has been promised. It does seem that, whether the evidence obtained by the promise is confessional (as in *McDonald*) or non-confessional (as in *Nathaniel*), it is the need to provide remedial support for the *nemo debet* principle which is central to judicial reasoning.

Judicial Fiat

It is possible to relate the suspect's treatment to the fairness of the proceedings simply by judicial fiat. For example, section 58 of the 1984 Act grants the suspect a right to legal advice where he has been arrested and is held in custody at a police station. In *Samuel*, Hodgson J described this as 'one of the most important and fundamental rights of a citizen'.[122] Though in that case the Court of Appeal refused to lay down guidelines on the exercise of the discretion under section 78(1), it went on to overturn the trial judge's decision to allow to be adduced a confession acquired in breach of that fundamental right. In other words, in some undisclosed way, fair trial would be prejudiced by prosecution use of such evidence.

No similar status has been accorded to any of the other rights bestowed upon suspects by the 1984 Act or by the codes made thereunder. For example, section 56 of the Act grants a person arrested and being held in custody a right to have some other person, nominated by him, informed of his arrest and of where he is being held. This is generally known as the right not to be held incommunicado, though the nomenclature is rather inaccurate, given the very limited and specific nature of the right. The cases concerned with breach of this provision or of the equivalent one in paragraph 5 of Code C do not treat this right in a way similar to the right to legal advice. The issue is, however, rather an empty one for, in practice, a police decision to hold the suspect incommunicado almost invariably entails a decision to deny him legal advice. So, though breach of the narrow section 56 right could be combined with compliance with section 58, the authorities, at least at appeal level, do not deal with that possibility. In any event, the notion of describing as 'fundamental' the right to have someone told about one's arrest and whereabouts seems a rather unlikely one.

Some more helpful, general guidance is to be found in *Walsh*, where, picking up a phrase which seems to have been used first by Bingham LJ in *Absolam*,[123] Saville J said that:[124]

[122] [1988] QB 615, at 630. See, also, *Beycan* [1990] Crim.LR 185.
[123] (1988) 88 Cr.App.R 332, at 337. See, also, *Keenan* (1989) 90 Cr.App.R 1, at 13.
[124] (1989) 91 Cr.App.R 161, at 163.

> if there are significant and substantial breaches of section 58 or the provisions of [Code C], then prima facie at least the standards of fairness set by Parliament have not been met. So far as a defendant is concerned, it seems . . . to follow that to admit evidence against him which has been obtained in circumstances where these standards have not been met, cannot but have an adverse effect on the fairness of the proceedings.

He went on to point out that, even if the trial judge found there to be such an adverse effect, he would still have to decide whether or not justice required the evidence to be excluded.

The key phrase from Saville J's judgment is indeed 'significant and substantial breaches', a phrase often referred to and relied upon in later cases.[125] Regard is presumably to be had to the importance of the provision breached, to the relative seriousness or triviality of the breach, to whether or not the breach was deliberate and/or committed in bad faith,[126] and to the number of breaches where there has been more than one. This is, quite clearly, a rather open-textured idea, extending a considerable degree of freedom both to the trial judge in deciding whether or not to exclude and to the appeal court in deciding whether or not to overturn his ruling. Furthermore, Saville J made no attempt to explain why such significant and substantial breaches should, even *prima facie*, entail that the standard of fairness *of the proceedings* has not been met. Once again, the matter seems to be one of judicial fiat.

The Decision in Keenan

We turn then, at last, to the only thoroughgoing attempt, at least in a reported case, to relate the code breaches to the trial proceedings. In *Keenan*,[127] Hodgson J considered a variety of situations in which the prosecution wished to call confession evidence, but in which that evidence had been acquired in breach of an Act or code provision. We have already referred to the point he made about unequal access to evidence. However, in addition, he pointed out that an accused who would not have given evidence were his confession to have been excluded would be prejudiced at trial if tactically forced to testify in order to rebut the content of that confession. Furthermore, an accused with a criminal record alleging that the police evidence had been concocted would, in so testifying, lose his shield against cross-examination about that record. As Hodgson J himself remarked, calculations in relation to those kinds of trial prejudice are problematical, for the judge may well have to make his decision whether or not to exclude at a time when he does not and cannot know the accused's intentions with regard to testifying on his own behalf and may not have full details of what he will say about the confession evidence with which he is faced. It may be that he would have testified anyway, while the argument about loss of the shield is contingent upon his particular character and antecedents. If that is so, all that the judge will be able to conclude

[125] See, e.g., *Dunford* (1990) 91 Cr.App.R 150; *Quinn* [1990] Crim.LR 581; *McGovern* (1990) 92 Cr.App.R 228; *Kerawalla* [1991] Crim.LR 451; *Oliphant* [1992] Crim.LR 40; *Raghip, Silcott and Braithwaite*, *The Times*, 9 Dec. 1991.

[126] On which, see text to nn. 133–43 below.

[127] (1989) 90 Cr.App.R 1.

is that the accused *may* end up being disadvantaged in one way or another and that that (incalculable) risk cannot properly be taken. However, once one boils it down to that, one is bound to note that *any* improperly or unfairly obtained evidence is entirely capable of placing the accused at a disadvantage. It seems to follow that there will always be an argument, in terms of trial unfairness, for excluding such evidence. But we are then back to where we started, asking ourselves when we should regard the breach or breaches as so significant and substantial that we cannot allow the risk of disadvantage to be taken.

No Recourse to Disciplining the Police

It is rather easier to make a negative statement about the unfairness discretion. A series of post-Act cases clearly confirms that the position stated by Lord Diplock in *Sang*[128] with regard to the common law discretion applies equally to the section 78(1) discretion. It is inappropriate to use the discretionary power in order to discipline the police, or, in other words, to discourage them from future illegality. Here, the argument favouring discretion tailored to that purpose is that the conduct should, because itself unacceptable (as well as unlawful), be discouraged. It is not, as is the version of the disciplinary principle which bolsters the unreliability principle, concerned to drive out conduct with a tendency to lead to unreliable evidence. Rather, officers ought not to behave towards suspects in given ways because those modes of behaviour are not to be tolerated in a civilized society. So, for example, it would be possible to justify exclusion of evidence acquired in breach of the police duty to allow the suspect access to a lawyer on the basis that exclusion will lead to officers in like situations in future complying with that duty.

A collection of *obiter dicta* in the Court of Appeal rejects this kind of discipline or deterrence. In *Mason*, Watkins LJ remarked that the court was 'not the place to discipline the police'.[129] In *Oliphant*, Woolf LJ specifically refused to endorse criticism, from counsel for the appellant, of the trial judge for 'saying that it was not his job to educate or discipline police officers'.[130] Similarly, Lord Taylor CJ, in *Christou and Wright*, quoted Lord Diplock's words in *Sang* without disapproval.[131] Finally, in *Hughes*, a case itself concerned with the conduct of customs officers, Lord Taylor CJ gave direct support to the tenor of Lord Diplock's position, saying: '[i]t has been said more than once in this court that the object of a judge in considering the application of section 78 is not to discipline or punish police officers or customs officers for breaches of the code.'[132]

It must be said that the wording of section 78(1) is exceptionally hard to tease into any disciplinary rationale. Whatever else the 'fairness of the proceedings' idea may connote, it surely does connote that the focus of the issue is *these* proceedings, and not the further conduct of the police or other investigating agency.

[128] [1980] AC 402, at 436. His words are quoted in the text to n. 67 above.
[129] [1988] 1 WLR 139, at 144C. [130] [1992] Crim.LR 40 (transcript through LEXIS).
[131] [1992] QB 979, at 987. [132] [1994] 1 WLR 876, at 879.

Deliberate and Bad Faith Breaches

We have already seen that the impropriety of police conduct, particularly where some applicable rule has been breached deliberately, is a central element in the concept of 'oppression' under section 76(2)(a), but that this does not apply to 'unreliability' under section 76(2)(b).[133] Properly regarded, the law relating to section 78(1) largely mirrors that treatment. So where the argument for exclusion is put in terms of the unfairness of police conduct, the very fact that there have been breaches regarded as significant and substantial is, as *Walsh* dictates,[134] of considerable importance. Also of importance is whether or not those breaches were deliberate or in bad faith. By contrast, neither of those factors will, in general, be at the forefront of the argument for exclusion where it is put in terms of unreliability.

The deliberateness of the breach or bad faith of the police is often the *central* concern where the unfairness of conduct is relied upon. For example, in *Matto* v. *Wolverhampton Crown Court*,[135] the sole ground upon which it was sought to have excluded evidence that a sample of breath taken from the accused was over the prescribed limit was that, at the time an earlier sample had been taken from him, the police had been knowingly trespassing on his land. It was this element of police bad faith which was the crucial factor, for the Divisional Court, in allowing Matto's appeal. In *Alladice*,[136] a case concerned with police denial of legal advice to a suspect, the Court of Appeal provided a more detailed explanation of the significance of bad faith. It said:[137]

> If the police have acted in bad faith, the court will have little difficulty in ruling any confession inadmissible under section 78. . . . If the police, albeit in good faith, have nevertheless fallen foul of section 58, it is still necessary for the court to decide whether to admit the evidence would adversely affect the fairness of the proceedings and would do so to such an extent that the confession ought to be excluded.

In *Walsh*, Saville J related the presence or absence of bad faith directly to the 'substantial and significant breach' test. He said, 'although bad faith may make substantial or significant that which might not otherwise be so, the contrary does not follow. Breaches which are in themselves significant and substantial are not rendered otherwise by the good faith of the officers concerned'.[138] Overall, we may observe that the way in which impropriety, misconduct, bad faith, and deliberateness are relevant to the exercise of the section 78 discretion illustrates, yet again, that, whatever the statute itself may say, it is the unfairness of the pre-trial police conduct which is really the issue where the unfairness element of that discretion is invoked.

It is clear that the unreliability element of the section 78 discretion may appropriately be exercised in favour of exclusion even where there is no hint of

[133] See Ch. 5, text to nn. 19–35 and 74–90 above. [134] See text to nn. 123–6 above.
[135] [1987] RTR 337. [136] (1988) 87 Cr.App.R 380. [137] *Ibid*. 386.
[138] (1989) 91 Cr.App.R 161, at 163.

impropriety.[139] Even where some code provision has been breached, that breach may not have been such as to result in unreliability. For example, in *Brine*,[140] the police had breached a number of the Code C provisions concerned with breaks from questioning and with refreshment of the suspect during those breaks. However, it was the (unchallenged) evidence that Brine was, at the time he confessed, suffering from a form of paranoid psychosis which would render him likely to make untruthful admissions which led the Court of Appeal to the view that his confession should never have gone to the jury. The code breaches do not seem to have played any part in his paranoid psychotic episode. It was, no doubt, with this kind of situation in mind, that Russell LJ remarked that 'section 78 embraces circumstances which may or may not involve improper conduct on the part of the police authority'.[141] Equally, where there has been a breach, the fact that it was deliberate or in bad faith will not, in a majority of cases, be significant. Though there does not seem to be any case stating explicitly that the presence of either of those factors made no difference to the argument for exclusion for unreliability,[142] it is, in principle, difficult to see how the state of mind with which the police officer acts can *directly* affect the probative value of the evidence obtained. Though we shall see in the next chapter[143] that the deliberateness of the breach or bad faith of the police is sometimes a relevant factor, we shall also see that, in those circumstances, it operates either *indirectly* or for reasons outside the confines of the particular case.

Fairness to Both Sides

It has often been emphasized that the trial court should, in assessing whether or not admission of the evidence would have an adverse effect on the proceedings, take account of the interests of the prosecution as well as those of the defence.[144] The cases making this point proceed more by assertion than explanation. In general, what judges seem to have in mind is that the conviction of the guilty is the relevant prosecution interest. Indeed, it was put in those specific terms by Lord Scarman in *Sang*,[145] in a passage later endorsed by Lord Taylor CJ in *Smurthwaite and Gill*.[146] In that way, the prosecution represents an element of the public interest. Of course, where this is what courts have in mind, the factor arises only where the unfairness element of the section 78 discretion is invoked. There can be no public interest in adducing unreliable evidence against the accused which has more potential for prejudice than for proof.

[139] See, e.g., *O'Leary* (1988) 87 Cr.App.R 387; *Clarke* [1989] Crim.LR 892.

[140] [1992] Crim.LR 122 (transcript through LEXIS).

[141] See LEXIS transcript of *Brine*.

[142] *Quinn* [1990] Crim.LR 581 (transcript through LEXIS) gets close to distinguishing the unfairness and unreliability aspects of s. 78 in this respect.

[143] See Ch. 7, text to nn. 42–7 and nn. 213–17 below.

[144] See, e.g., *Hughes* [1988] Crim.LR 519; *Walsh* (1989) 91 Cr.App.R 161, at 163; *Quinn* [1990] Crim.LR 581; *Oliphant* [1992] Crim.LR 40; *Smurthwaite and Gill* [1994] 1 All ER 898, at 902–3; *Middlebrook and Caygill*, unreported, 18. Feb. 1994; *Cooke* [1995] 1 Cr.App.R 318, at 328. Relevant transcripts through LEXIS.

[145] [1980] AC 402, at 456.

[146] [1994] 1 All ER 898, at 902–3.

Trial courts have been given no guidance on *how* they are to balance the interests of fairness to the accused against those of fairness to the prosecution. In other common law jurisdictions, it has come to be recognized that there may be more to discretionary exclusion of confessional and other evidence than the private interest of the accused in not being subjected to unlawful, improper, or unfair treatment by the police.[147] Thus, as it was succinctly put in the Australian case of *Bunning* v. *Cross*, what is involved is:[148]

> no simple question of ensuring fairness to an accused but instead the weighing against each other of two competing requirements of public policy, thereby seeking to resolve the apparent conflict between the desirable goal of bringing to conviction the wrongdoer and the undesirable effect of curial approval, or even encouragement, being given to the unlawful conduct of those whose task it is to enforce the law.

In that case, the High Court went on give five guidelines on when the discretion should and should not be exercised. First, was the illegality intentional or reckless, rather than merely negligent? Secondly, how cogent is the evidence in question? Thirdly, how easy would it have been for the police to comply with the law? Fourthly, the more serious the offence, the more tolerant of unlawfulness the court should be. Finally, where it is legislation which has not been complied with, is that legislation drafted in a way which demonstrates a desire narrowly to restrict the police in the exercise of their powers?

Some of the factors described by these guidelines have certainly been relied upon in some of the English cases under section 78(1) and have probably featured in the reasoning in other cases without being articulated. As we have just seen, the first guideline, relating to the culpability of those in breach, has figured explicitly and prominently in the reasoning of appeal courts. Moreover, in one recent case, the Court of Appeal made express reference to the fact that the cogency of the evidence in question was high,[149] while in another that Court adverted to the seriousness of the offence with which the accused was charged.[150] However, it would be wrong to suppose that English courts are moving towards an approach like that of *Bunning* v. *Cross*, not least because such an approach is very hard to square with the wording of section 78(1) itself. That subsection has as its explicit purpose the avoidance of *unfairness* in relation to the (*present*) *proceedings*. Just as this purpose, as has already been pointed out, seems inconsistent with the disciplinary principle, so it seems also to clash with the *balancing* of public interests in the way supported by *Bunning* v. *Cross*. Furthermore, the central concern of that case is with lawbreaking (on both sides) and not with unfairness.[151] Therefore, allusions in English cases to the interests of the prosecution or the public should

[147] The jurisdictions in question are Australia and Canada. In the one, the analysis is a creature of the common law (Australia), in the other, of the Canadian Charter of Rights and Freedoms.

[148] (1978) 141 CLR 54, at 74 (*per* Stephen and Aickin JJ). See, also, in particular *Ireland* (1970) 126 CLR 321 and *Cleland* (1982) 43 ALR 619. Detailed consideration is given to the *Bunning* v. *Cross* line of authority in Ch. 12, text to nn. 236–66 below.

[149] *Cooke* [1995] 1 Cr.App.R 318, at 328.

[150] *Latif and Shahzad* [1995] 1 Cr.App.R 270, at 278.

[151] See Ch. 12, text to nn. 236–45 and between nn. 251 and 254 below.

probably be taken only as a reminder to trial courts that they should eschew a radically civil libertarian approach to exclusion and not as anything else.

WIDER THAN *SANG*

There were indications in some of the early section 78(1) cases that that subsection did no more than re-state the common law power of the judges.[152] This was never a terribly persuasive view, given the existence of section 82(3), and it is now clear that the statutory discretion is significantly wider than the common law one. There are five points to be made here in that respect.

The first, and much the most important, point is that it is now established that the boundaries of the unfairness element of the discretion—we are not concerned here with the unreliability element—are not set by the self-incrimination rationale. There is now no need to show, in the case of non-confession evidence, that there is some analogy with the principles concerning exclusion of confessions. This point is put beyond doubt by *Smurthwaite and Gill*,[153] a case concerned with entrapment. Detailed discussion of the case will be found in the next chapter. It suffices here to point out that the Court of Appeal emphasized that, as regards section 78(1), the courts should not 'strain for an interpretation which either re-asserts or alters the pre-existing law',[154] and went on to acknowledge that it will be right for the trial court to exclude evidence obtained by entrapment, or by the use of an *agent provocateur*, or otherwise by a trick, as long as the adverse effect described by the statute would be present were it to be admitted. This was, of course, precisely the proposition rejected by the House of Lords in *Sang*, so far as the common law discretion was concerned.

A second point is incidental to the first. *Sang* restricted discretionary exclusion to evidence obtained *after* the offence. Yet the *agent provocateur* or entrapper may very well have significant information to give about things said or done by the accused before the offence itself was committed or, if a continuing offence, began to be committed. It follows that, under section 78(1), there is no need for the evidence to have been obtained after the offence.

The third point is, perhaps, entailed by the first. On one view of *Sang*, it was only if the evidence had been obtained from the accused's person that the common law discretion was available. It is not at all clear why such a restriction should be proposed even where the sole rationale for the discretion was, as a majority of their Lordships accepted, the self-incrimination one. Why should the accused's will have been engaged any the less where the evidence was eventually obtained from his surroundings or his house, rather than from his person? Now that self-incrimination is certainly not the key, there is no reason at all for there to be artificial constraints upon from whom or from where the evidence must have come. We shall see in the next chapter[155] that identification evidence

[152] see *Matto* v. *Wolverhampton Crown Court* [1987] RTR 337, at 346; *Mason* [1988] 1 WLR 139, at 144.

[153] [1994] 1 All ER 898.

[154] *Ibid.* 902.

[155] See Ch. 7, text to nn. 195–203 below.

acquired in breach of a provision of Code D may, in some circumstances, properly be excluded in exercise of the unfairness element of the discretion, rather than simply because that evidence is not sufficiently reliable to go before the jury. Obviously, there will then be no question of the evidence being acquired *from* the accused or his surroundings, or his home.

Fourthly, what about unlawful searches of the accused's person or his property? It was part and parcel of Lord Diplock's reasoning in *Sang* that, because no question of self-incrimination arose in such cases, the common law discretion was unavailable. In that respect, *Jeffrey* v. *Black*[156] correctly stated the law. There is no binding appeal court authority on the position under section 78(1), yet there is no real practical doubt that, here too, the statutory discretion diverges from the common law one. Apart from one, briefly reported, Crown Court decision to exclude evidence of the finding of drugs on the accused's person during the course of an unlawful search,[157] there was, until quite recently, no decision at appeal level squarely raising the point. But in two cases decided in 1993 and a further one in 1996, the Court of Appeal has recognized that the discretion is available, even though no question of self-incrimination arose in any of them.[158] It is right to add that in none of those cases was it held, on the facts, that the discretion ought to have been exercised in favour of exclusion. More extended consideration will be given to unlawful search cases in the next chapter.

A final point is that one should not see a well-known *dictum* of Lord Taylor CJ in *Christou and Wright* as detracting from any of the four points just made. He said: '[the trial judge] held that the criteria of unfairness are the same whether [he] is exercising his discretion at common law or under the statute. We agree. What is unfair cannot sensibly be subject to different standards depending on the source of the discretion to exclude it.'[159] His Lordship had, immediately before that passage, alluded to the point that the statutory discretion might be wider than the common law one. What he must have had in mind was that, whatever the difference in the cases to which the discretion applied, it should operate according to the same principles. Given that, as we have already seen, the principles in question can hardly be said to have been clearly identified in the post-Act cases, the *dictum* should not create any difficulty in future in situations in which no question of self-incrimination arises.

Causation

Rather like section 76(2)(b), section 78(1) is capable of raising two distinct issues of causation.[160] Section 76(2)(b) requires both that the confession was made in

156 [1978] QB 490. 157 *Fennelley* [1989] Crim.LR 142.

158 See *Wright* [1994] Crim.LR 55 (transcript through LEXIS); *Hughes* [1994] 1 WLR 876; *McCarthy* [1996] Crim.LR 818. But cf. *Khan et al.* [1997] Crim.LR 508, in which none of the three seems to have been cited.

159 [1992] QB 979, at 988.

160 See Ch. 5, text to nn. 100–14 and 127–45 for discussion of the two issues as regards s. 76(2)(b).

consequence of the thing said or done *and* that any confession which the accused might have thus made would be likely to be rendered unreliable thereby. As regards section 78(1), where a confession or other evidence is said to be so unreliable that its admission in evidence would be more prejudicial than probative, often no real question of causation will arise. There is no requirement that its unreliability flow from any particular source, nor even that it was created or discovered as a result of any particular type of conduct. However, it should be added that, where there is some rule, whether in a code or otherwise, which has been breached, issues of causation may arise. For example, in *Ryan*,[161] investigating officers had, in breach of Code D, themselves been involved in an attempt to identify the offender by means of a confrontation. The Court of Appeal was persuaded that the identifying witness's recognition of the accused as the offender had not, in fact, been contaminated as a result of the breach. It relied upon the fact that the process of confrontation had been overseen by the accused's solicitor, the purpose of whose presence was to ensure that the procedure was carried out in a way fair to his client.

Where it is said that the fairness of the proceedings is imperilled other than by virtue of the unreliability of the evidence, the manner of its obtaining is inevitably a crucial element. So a court may well have to ask itself if the accused confessed or revealed the whereabouts of, say, real evidence as a result of some police breach of the rules. Furthermore, even if it be satisfied of the establishment of that causal link, the court may still have to ask itself whether or not the pre-trial gathering of the evidence in question impinged upon the fairness of the trial itself. This second question, central to the very theory of section 78(1), has been dealt with earlier in this chapter.[162] However, the first question—was the accused actually caused *pre-trial* prejudice by the conduct of the police?—needs to be considered now.

In the leading case of *Alladice*,[163] a case which also deals with causation under section 76(2)(b),[164] the Court held that the accused had not been prejudiced, for the purposes of section 78(1), by an improper delay in allowing him access to a solicitor. He had shown himself, by his conduct and demeanour when questioned without his solicitor, well able to cope with the interview and to refuse to answer questions where he thought that to be in his best interest; therefore, the presence of a solicitor would have added nothing.[165] There is a danger of courts applying *Alladice* rather more widely than seems to have been intended. Thus, there was no evidence in *Oliphant*[166] that the accused was of an especially robust character, well able to look after himself without need for the support of legal advice. Yet the trial judge felt able to conclude that, where the accused had, part way through an interview, requested a solicitor and the police had failed, in breach of paragraph 6.3 of the original Code C,[167] then to terminate that interview, there had

[161] [1992] Crim.LR 187. [162] See text to nn.114–59 above. [163] (1988) 87 Cr.App.R 380.

[164] See Ch. 5, text to n. 141 above.

[165] See, also, *Dunford* (1990) 91 Cr.App.R 150, to similar effect. [166] [1992] Crim.LR 40.

[167] Para. 6.6 of the present Code C.

been no prejudice. The judge's reason for taking that view was that the accused had wanted to make admissions. The Court of Appeal found this approach satisfactory, notwithstanding that there seems to have been nothing to indicate that the accused was keen to confess, other than the bare fact that he had confessed. A rather similar case is *Anderson*,[168] though, there at least, the police had responded to overtures from the accused to be allowed to speak to them. By way of contrast, the detail of a case may sometimes demonstrate that the presence of a solicitor *would*, very probably, have made a difference. Thus, in *Parris*,[169] the Court of Appeal attributed considerable significant to the fact that, when the solicitor did eventually arrive, the accused had declined to answer police questions.

In the recent case of *Roberts*,[170] the Court of Appeal considered a rather different but important causation issue. The police had breached certain Code C contemporaneous recording requirements in respect not of Roberts himself, but of his fellow suspect, one Connolly. Roberts had later made incriminating remarks whilst in a cell with Connolly, which remarks had been surreptitiously recorded. Though it is not entirely clear on what basis counsel for Roberts argued that his client had been adversely affected by the breaches, the court made it quite clear that it was no part of the purpose of the Code C recording requirements to protect suspects other than the one being interviewed and that there was, in consequence, no causal link between those breaches and Roberts's subsequent incriminating statements.

Subsequent Confessions

We have already had occasion to consider the law relating to the exclusion of a later confession where an initial confession has been ruled inadmissible under section 76.[171] What, then, if the initial confession has been excluded under section 78(1)? The first point to make is that, if the elements which led to exclusion of the first confession continue to act or be present so far as the second is concerned, it will be right also to exclude that one. Even if the later interview has been conducted entirely properly, things said or done in the earlier one may still be operative on the accused's mind.[172] However, it is not clear whether the law goes further than this, dictating that, where the accused has been (unfairly) caused to let the cat out of the bag, that in itself casts doubt on the fairness of admitting in evidence the later confession. It will be remembered that *Glaves* and *McGovern*[173] indicate that, in a section 76(2) case, the initial taint must be positively removed by the police in order for the confession not to be excluded. In relation to exclusion under section 78(1), the authorities appear to be in conflict.

[168] [1993] Crim.LR 447. [169] (1988) 89 Cr.App.R 68.
[170] *Roberts* [1997] 1 Cr.App.R 217. [171] See Ch. 5, text to nn. 146–56 above.
[172] See *Gillard and Barrett* (1990) 92 Cr.App.R 61; *Conway* [1994] Crim.LR 838.
[173] *Glaves* [1993] Crim.LR 685; *McGovern* (1990) 92 Cr.App.R 228.

Though *Canale*[174] seems, at first glance, to favour the *Glaves/McGovern* view, on closer inspection it turns out to be equivocal. There, police accounts of initial interviews in which Canale had made admissions were to be excluded because, quite deliberately, the police had not made a contemporaneous record of them and had committed a number of consequential breaches of Code C. Two later interviews were recorded contemporaneously, with no other breach being present, yet the Court of Appeal held that these were also to be excluded. Had the issue been whether or not Canale had made the initial admissions, the original taint would have ceased to be directly operative, and the issue of the indirect, 'cat-out-of-the-bag' effect might have been squarely raised. In fact, the issue was whether or not those admissions, which he accepted he had made, had been made because of a police trick. Therefore, the non-recording of the initial interviews disabled the court from deciding what was leading him to make further admissions at the later interviews. Hence, the original taint remained directly operative.

In two later cases, the line taken is hard to reconcile with that suggested, for section 76 cases, by *Glaves* and *McGovern*. *Gillard and Barrett*[175] was decided after *McGovern*, but before *Glaves*, though *McGovern* was not referred to in that case. The Court of Appeal rightly pointed out that there can be no universal rule that, whenever earlier interviews are excluded for code breaches, later interviews must also be excluded. It distinguished *Canale* on the ground suggested in the preceding paragraph, but seems not to have grasped the 'cat-out-of-the-bag' argument which was being put to it by counsel for the appellants. It appears from the report that in the case of neither appellant was legal advice taken after the various excluded interviews but before the final one the contents of which were admitted in evidence, and also that no legal adviser was present during those final interviews. It is hard to believe that either of them was aware that the slate against them might well be clean.

The Divisional Court relied largely upon *Gillard and Barrett* as the basis for its ruling in *Yeoman* v. *DPP*.[176] The indirect taint point was strongly relied upon by counsel, yet the court concluded that the magistrates could not be said to have exercised their discretion wrongly in allowing to be adduced the contents of the final interview. Again, there is no suggestion that the accused had been made aware of the vulnerability of the earlier interviews before the final one took place, though Taylor LJ did emphasize that the solicitor had been present at that interview. It seems that the actual decision in *Yeoman* was also much influenced by the fact that his first confession seems to have been entirely spontaneous, the sole breach being a failure to record it immediately. No doubt, many courts would have thought that breach to be insufficient reason for excluding it.

A view more consonant with *Glaves* and *McGovern* seems to have been taken in a more recent decision of the Court of Appeal in which reference was made to

[174] (1989) 91 Cr.App.R 1. [175] (1990) 92 Cr.App.R 61.
[176] [1991] Crim.LR 917 (transcript through LEXIS).

all the leading authorities. The case in question, *Neil*,[177] has not been fully reported and appears not to be available on LEXIS. The court, overturning the trial judge's decision, explained that the appellant would have considered himself bound by the earlier confession, the circumstances of the second interview being insufficient to provide him with a 'safe and confident opportunity of withdrawing the admissions'.[178] It should also be pointed out that, in *Wood*,[179] the argument for excluding the second of two confessions was put in terms both of section 76 and section 78. Though, rather surprisingly, the court referred only to the section 78 authorities, it seems clear that it thought that, in principle, the position ought to be the same under either section. That must surely be correct. The difference between the two is that the prosecution may well find it less easy to prove that the *direct* taint had been dissipated where oppression or something said or done tending to unreliability led to exclusion of the earlier confession than where unfairness led to it.[180] The position as regards indirect taint would seem to be identical. As in *Neil*, the court in *Wood* spoke very much more in terms suggestive of the *Glaves/McGovern* line of approach to such indirect taint. The case itself was an extreme one in that, though the accused had seen his solicitor for twenty minutes between the first and second interviews, his mental incapacity was such that he would have been in no position to instruct the solicitor about what had led him, at the earlier interview, to confess. Therefore, the trial judge had been wrong to admit the contents of the second interview in evidence. However, the court did suggest that the opportunity for full discussion with a solicitor was of great importance in the case of someone of normal intellect and capacity, no doubt because of the opportunity given for the slate to be cleaned.

The authorities about subsequent confessions under section 78, no less than those under section 76, are of very great importance. It is a commonplace for suspects to be interviewed more than once, and not uncommon for later interviews to avoid the sins of earlier ones. A clear decision, with full discussion of all the relevant authorities under both sections, whether in the Court of Appeal or the House of Lords, would be of great practical, as well as doctrinal, value.

Cases Where the Questioning Code (Code C) is Inapplicable

Though breach of a code of practice is not a necessary feature of exclusion under section 78(1), it is a very common feature. Furthermore, it has been breach of the questioning code (Code C) which has been most often in issue. In a number of cases, it has been argued by the prosecution that, despite the apparent technical applicability of that Code, it ought to be treated as not in fact applicable. In most of these cases, the basis for the argument has been that, if the police or other investigating authority had to comply with some given provision of the Code,

[177] [1994] Crim.LR 441. [178] *Ibid.* [179] [1994] Crim.LR 222 (transcript through LEXIS).
[180] A point expressly recognized in *Wood*, *ibid.*

they would be improperly frustrated in carrying out entirely reasonable criminal investigation activities. However, before those cases are dealt with, reference must first be made to a point of a rather different kind.

In *Parchment*,[181] the accused had, by his violent conduct, disrupted an interview. The two police officers then terminated the interview and had him returned to his cell. Though they recorded the fact of and, it appears, reason for that termination, the accused was never shown the record of the interview, nor asked to sign it as correct or indicate inaccuracies. The Court of Appeal held that this did not entail a breach of paragraph 12.12 of the original Code C, for that paragraph was to be taken to apply only to a normal interview which proceeded in a co-operative spirit between the parties. Here, the accused had manifested his wish not to carry the interview through to its ordinary conclusion, with all that that entailed. Presumably, the same notion is capable of applying no less to the other provisions of Code C, or indeed of the other codes, where the accused's conduct has, in some respect, got in the way of their normal application by the police. What is not made clear is why Parchment's behaviour properly led to paragraph 12.12 being inapplicable, rather than being merely delayed in its application until he had calmed down.

Where police officers are involved in undercover operations which require, for their success, that the suspect does not recognize their status, it would be absurd for Code C to apply automatically and with full force. Thus, in *Christou and Wright*,[182] the police had set up a sham business buying and selling jewellery. They hoped to catch, and did catch, a number of 'customers' who had either stolen or dishonestly handled the goods they offered for sale. The various transactions were surreptitiously recorded on both audio- and video-tape, but the officers operating the sham did not, for obvious reasons, caution would-be vendors. The officers had certainly put questions to some of those against whom charges were later brought after they had become suspects, and paragraph 10.1. of the then-governing issue of Code C therefore seemed, on the face of it, to require a caution to have been given. However, the Court of Appeal held that paragraph 10.1 did not apply. Like many other code provisions, it was 'intended to protect suspects who are vulnerable to abuse or pressure from police officers or who may believe themselves to be so'.[183] Yet, the accused in this case, like the other 'victims' of the sham, were on equal terms with the undercover officers, who were not themselves acting as police officers. So the Code was not intended to apply, and did not do so.[184]

Christou and Wright indicates that the police must not exploit this implied exception to the applicability of Code C in order simply to circumvent its provisions.[185] This caveat was applied by the Court of Appeal in *Bryce*.[186] Following a tip-off, an officer had contacted Bryce about a stolen car. They had agreed a price

[181] [1991] Crim.LR 626. [182] [1992] QB 979. [183] *Ibid.* 991.
[184] See, also, *MacLean and Kosten* [1993] Crim.LR 687; *Edwards* [1997] Crim.LR 348.
[185] Affirmed by *Smurthwaite and Gill* [1994] 1 All ER 898 to be a point of importance.
[186] [1992] 4 All ER 567. See, also, *Gibbons*, unreported, 29 June 1993.

in a conversation which clearly demonstrated that it was indeed stolen. Later, they met to complete the transaction, at which time Bryce was arrested. On two occasions, the undercover agent had asked how long ago it had been stolen, and Bryce had replied that it had been taken two or three days earlier. It was these two pre-arrest questions which the court found to have a tendency to circumvent Code C. The mere fact of Bryce having possession of a car which he had agreed to sell at an absurdly low price was enough for the purposes of the undercover operation. The police had gone too far in trying to gather direct evidence of guilty knowledge. In *Christou and Wright*, by contrast, though questions had been asked of the 'customers', their purpose was to confirm to them that the business in question was a real one. Moreover, in *Bryce*, there was no contemporaneous record of the exchanges, the police version of which the defence hotly disputed.

That the line between cases which do and do not entail circumvention of code provisions is likely to prove difficult to draw in practice is demonstrated by *Lin, Hung and Tsui*.[187] An informer had provided the police with information which carried the suspicion that the accused were trying to cash a particular cheque. The informer and an undercover officer met the accused in order to gather information about a more general conspiracy to cash stolen cheques. To preserve their pose as fellow conspirators, they needed to have certain conversations with the accused about the particular cheque. The Court of Appeal took the view that, though the result was that evidence was obtained about the specific offence, their broader purpose had been such that there had been no attempt to evade the Code C protections. Given that the accused were eventually charged with the substantive handling offence as well as the conspiracy, it seems that everything turned upon the intentions of the police. Those intentions may not always be easy to discern.

It may be unsafe to assume that the equal terms idea emerging from *Christou and Wright* is the only one capable of leading the courts to regard some code provision as being inapplicable. A common scenario is that in which customs officers who have found drugs in the possession of a traveller wish to allow him to continue on his way with the drugs in case he should contact someone else involved in the illegal importation. Where drugs are found in the traveller's presence or in other circumstances in which it comes to his notice that the officers know what he is carrying, they can proceed only with his co-operation.[188] However, where they have been found following a search of luggage which has been separated from him, they may be able to proceed in a surreptitious way. In such a case, the parties will clearly not be on equal terms, yet the pull of the argument that the police be allowed to proceed in this way is obvious. In *Okafor*,[189] the Court of Appeal, having noted that, in this situation, there was no analogy with *Christou and Wright* because there was no equality of terms, went on to conclude that 'where a customs officer has reason to suspect that an offence has been committed, he must either avoid asking questions in relation to the offence or he must

[187] [1995] Crim.LR 817 (transcript through LEXIS).

[188] An example is *Weerdesteyn* [1995] 1 Cr.App.R 405.

[189] [1994] 3 All ER 741.

follow the provisions of the code and administer a caution'.[190] Though the court eventually applied the proviso, it employed this reasoning in ruling that the trial judge ought to have excluded evidence of a conversation in which the officers had asked him where he had got hold of some snail stew that they had found in his luggage. They had already found packages of cocaine within the stew, though they did not reveal their discovery to him. It may be significant that the court went on to point out that the customs officers could have achieved their extraneous purpose had they talked to Okafor about anything but the snail stew, had they then released him in the hope that he would lead them to others, and had they finally asked questions about the stew only after arresting and cautioning him. One wonders if appeal courts will take a similarly robust view where customs officers have sought to achieve dual purposes and where, as might well be the case, they would have been unable to pursue other possible offenders without asking questions which might produce incriminatory answers.

In any event, both in this situation and in others which have not yet received judicial attention, one should beware of overestimating the significance of a code being applicable or of its provisions having been breached, in this kind of case. It remains for the judge to decide whether or not fairness of the proceedings would be so severely prejudiced by admission of the evidence obtained that it ought, in justice, to be excluded. If, as we have seen to be the case,[191] fairness to both sides is to be taken into account, it may surely be argued that the public interest in conviction of the guilty applies no less to the third-party offenders than to the person being questioned himself. Moreover, a breach carried out with a desirable, extraneous, public purpose in mind might be thought far less heinous than one directly and deliberately contrary to the point or purpose of the Code, and with no other redeeming feature.

Abuse of the Process of the Court

There is one further matter which, though it is not itself directly concerned with the discretionary exclusion of evidence, is best dealt with in this Chapter. We saw, in Chapter 2, that English law has recently come to recognize that, in exercise of its inherent power to prevent abuse of its own process, a court may stay criminal proceedings against an accused on the basis that he was unlawfully entrapped into committing the offence in question. The case which establishes that proposition, *Latif and Shahzad*,[192] also establishes very clearly, as we have already seen,[193] that the principle underpinning that power is the judicial integrity

[190] [1994] 3 All ER 741, 747. [191] See text to nn. 144–51 above.

[192] [1996] 1 WLR 104. Cf. *Ridgeway* (1995) 129 ALR 41, in which the High Court of Australia held, by majority, that a stay was not the proper remedy for entrapment. For the Law Commission's views about the possible ways of dealing with problems of entrapment, see Law Com. No 83, 28 July 1977, para. 5.1–5.54.

[193] See Ch. 2, text to nn. 84–91 above.

principle in its public attitude form. The resulting overlap between discretionary exclusion of evidence under section 78(1) and the power to halt proceedings is undoubtedly considerable.[194] Indeed, in *Latif and Shahzad* itself, counsel for Shahzad conceded that, if his submissions on abuse of process failed, so must his argument based upon section 78(1). This was a surprising concession for two reasons. First, as will have become clear in the course of this Chapter, and consistently with the wording of the subsection, there seems to be no judicial inclination to embrace the judicial integrity principle as a guide in exercising the statutory discretion. Secondly, the effect of a stay is, potentially at least, significantly more drastic than is that of exclusion of evidence. There may be other evidence in the case which is untainted by the unlawful entrapment and which may be sufficient to convict the accused. Therefore it seems likely that, in future cases, those representing appellants will seek to persuade judges to disengage their statutory discretion from their common law power.

In *Latif and Shahzad*, Shahzad had agreed with Honi, who was an undercover informer employed by the US Drugs Enforcement Administration, a scheme for the exportation of twenty kilograms of heroin from Pakistan and its importation into Great Britain. The British customs and excise service having become involved, one of its officers, in admitted breach of the criminal law in one respect and assumed breach in another, brought the heroin into England. Honi coaxed Shahzad into coming to England to take delivery of the drugs. Eventually, Shahzad took possession of some packages which he believed to contain the drugs in question, though they did, in fact, contain only a powdered bedtime drink. Shahzad and his accomplice, Latif, were charged with both an offence relating to the importation itself (under section 170(2) of the Customs and Excise Management Act 1979) and one of attempting to be knowingly concerned in dealing with unlawfully imported drugs (under section 1(1) of the Criminal Attempts Act 1981).

By the time the case reached the House of Lords, Shahzad's case was based upon two propositions, namely that Honi had encouraged him to commit an offence which he would not otherwise have committed and that the customs officer had himself committed the importation offences. The House affirmed that the abuse of process power was available even though no question arose of the fairness of Shahzad's trial having been put in jeopardy and maintained that the power might be exercised in support of broader policies relating to the integrity of the criminal justice system. In the words of Lord Steyn:[195]

> Weighing countervailing considerations of policy and justice, it is for the judge in the exercise of his discretion to decide whether there has been an abuse of process, which amounts to an affront to the public conscience and requires the criminal proceedings to be stayed. . . . [T]he judge must weigh in the balance the public interest in ensuring that those that are charged with grave crimes should be tried and the competing public interest in not conveying the impression that the court will adopt the approach that the end justifies any means.

[194] As Lord Steyn pointed out—see [1996] 1 WLR 104, at 109.

[195] *Ibid*. 112–13.

The House ruled that the judge's decision that no stay should be ordered was not unreasonable. It stressed that Shahzad was no newcomer to the heroin trade and that he had taken the initiative in organizing the importation. (We shall see, in Chapter 7,[196] that, where the section 78(1) discretion is invoked by the accused, the absence of an element of 'crime creation' and the presence of predisposition in the accused to commit the relevant kind of offence are both factors which tend towards admission of the evidence in question.) So far as the criminal unlawfulness of the customs officer's conduct was concerned—and he must, inevitably, have been aided and abetted by his superiors—it was a venial breach of the law compared with that of Shahzad. His conduct was 'not so unworthy or shameful that it was an affront to the public conscience to allow the prosecution to proceed'.[197]

Though it may be somewhat early to speculate about the potential breadth of applicability of the abuse of process power, a note of caution may properly be entered even at this stage. Now that police pre-trial activity, as well as that of the prosecuting authorities, falls within the ambit of the power, defence counsel may seek to invoke it in relation to a range of such activity which has no relation with entrapment, but simply entails unlawfulness or unfairness in the gathering of evidence. It is to be remembered that the result of a finding of abuse of process will be the staying of the proceedings. If we imagine that a confession has been obtained by some overreaching police misconduct, it would seem likely that the court would wish to address that misconduct by reference to a straightforward application of the exclusionary rule or discretion. Of course, where there is little or no other evidence in the case, exclusion will have the same practical effect as a stay, but the theoretical basis for court action will remain quite different. Any application of the judicial integrity principle in such a case would be through use of analogical reasoning, with *Latif and Shahzad* providing the analogy.

It is noteworthy that in *Khan*,[198] a case decided by the House of Lords only shortly after *Latif and Shahzad*, their Lordships made no reference to their earlier decision, even though, if analogies are to be drawn, *Khan* might have seemed an obvious case in which to draw one. There, the Crown accepted that, without certain tape-recorded evidence of a conversation with others in which Khan had made damaging admissions with regard to drugs offences involving heroin, there would have been no case for him to answer. Those recordings had been obtained by surveillance activity in relation to the house of a third party which involved trespass and, at least arguably, criminal damage to property. Counsel for Khan apparently placed little reliance upon these matters of illegality in the House of Lords. Instead, he placed the accused's alleged right of privacy at the centre of his argument. In essence, this was to press for exclusion on the basis of the protective

[196] See Ch. 7, text to nn. 227–58 below. [197] See [1996] 1 WLR 104, at 113.

[198] [1996] 3 WLR 162. The case is considered in detail in Ch. 7, text to nn. 298–304 and Ch. 11, text to nn. 59–66 below.

principle. Clearly, were the judicial integrity principle thought relevant, one might well be able to argue that the unlawfulness of the police behaviour, albeit directed against a third party, was something which would count against admission of the evidence in question,[199] though the public interest in convicting those guilty of serious drugs offences might, of course, be thought to tell decisively the other way.

[199] Another leading case concerned with staying proceedings for abuse of process, *R.* v. *Horseferry Road Magistrates' Court, ex p. Bennett* [1994] 1 AC 42. was cited in argument.

7

Discretionary Exclusion of Confessions and Other Evidence—Specific Cases

In this Chapter, we shall examine the authorities concerned with exclusion under section 78(1) of the Police and Criminal Evidence Act 1984 ('the 1984 Act') according to five different categories.[1] We shall begin by examining the impact of the various provisions of Codes C and E which are concerned with ensuring the accuracy of the record made by the police of their questioning of and other discussions with the accused. Next we shall look at the treatment by courts of some of the various other 'rights' granted to suspects by Code C and in particular their treatment of the right to legal advice. After that, attention will be given to the provisions of Code D in respect of formal identification procedures used by the police during the pre-trial period. We shall move on to the developing law, outside the terms of any of the codes, dealing with trickery and entrapment. Finally, we shall look at the effect upon the power to exclude of the unlawfulness of a search, of whatever kind, carried out by the police. To some extent, discussion of cases where the operative reason for an argument for exclusion is in terms of breach of some provision or provisions of a code will necessitate quite detailed treatment of those provisions. However, the central concern will remain the significance of those provisions for the exercise of the discretion to exclude.

The Accuracy of the Record

In a little over a decade, the significance of legal constraints upon the way in which the police present evidence of what they allege to have been said by the suspect (now the accused) to them when interviewed has changed very radically. Writing in 1985, I ventured the view that what I described as the 'confession issue'—whether or not the suspect did confess, or did confess in the way

[1] A sixth category, or perhaps collection of categories, concerned with vulnerable suspects (children, the mentally ill, and the mentally handicapped) is more conveniently dealt with in a separate chapter—see Ch. 10, below.

alleged—was left largely alone by the law.[2] The impact of rules of admissibility was limited, according to *Roberts*,[3] to the need to exclude where no reasonable jury could base a conclusion that the accused did confess upon the evidence available. *Roberts* itself was a striking case, for the prosecution faced the embarrassing task of explaining how someone shown by uncontradicted evidence to have been deaf and dumb since birth could have managed to make the statements attributed to him. In addition, until 1 January 1986, the taking of written statements was governed by Rule IV of the Judges' Rules 1964. However, there was no equivalent provision in respect of oral statements allegedly made by the suspect and recorded by the police. In practice, the interviewing officers, relying on a *dictum* of Byrne J in *Bass*,[4] would usually collaborate after the interview in preparing an agreed joint note of its content. Each would write down that account in his own notebook, then by, in theory at least, refreshing his memory at trial, give his evidence directly from that notebook. Accusations from the defence that the accused had been 'verballed'—i.e. that the police had made up an incriminating response—were commonplace, and, given the circumstances, impossible to confirm or refute in a definitive way. It was not common for the police to make a contemporaneous written recording of the interview, though the practice was beginning to be more widely used even before 1986.[5]

By virtue of Code C, officers are now under various duties to make an accurate record of all interviews with suspects and, where practicable, a contemporaneous record thereof. Even more significantly, Code E creates a general duty to tape-record interviews with cautioned suspects in any case where the offence being investigated is triable only on indictment or is triable either way. As we shall see, there is a large number of cases concerned with the Code C provisions, though, at present, only one reported case concerned with a Code E provision. It would seem very likely that the way in which the courts have dealt with confessions obtained in breach of Code C provisions will be taken to have strong suggestive force for the treatment of breaches of Code E.

Breaches of the Questioning Code

The leading cases concerned with breaches of the parts of the questioning code (Code C)[6] which seek to promote accurate records of exchanges between the police and the suspect have very much concentrated on what may be described as the 'anti-verballing provisions'. These provisions have twice been altered from their original form, the first changes taking effect in April 1991, the second in April 1995. We may broadly describe the present content of the provisions in question as follows. The police have a duty to make an accurate record of each

[2] Mirfield, *Confessions* (1985), 1. [3] (1953) 37 Cr.App.R 86, at 94.
[4] [1953] 1 QB 680, at 686.
[5] A point made by Wolchover and Heaton-Armstrong, *Confession Evidence* (1996), para. 3.003.
[6] For a stimulating discussion of a number of the problems relating to Code C, see Fenwick [1993] Crim.LR 174.

interview with a suspect.[7] That record must be made contemporaneously unless this would be impracticable or would interfere with the conduct of the interview.[8] If not made contemporaneously, it must be made as soon as practicable after completion of the interview, and the reason for not making it contemporaneously must be recorded in the police officer's pocket book.[9] Certain other details relating to the interview, such as the time at which it began and ended and the names of those present, must also be recorded.[10] In order to minimize the number of occasions on which the accuracy of the record is challenged in court, the suspect must, again unless it be impracticable, be given the opportunity of reading the note made by the police and of signing it as correct or indicating the respects in which he considers it inaccurate.[11]

A key word in all of these provisions, and indeed in the equivalent provisions of the tape-recording code (Code E), is the word 'interview'. All of the Code C duties so far described are, like the general duty to tape-record under Code E, predicated upon the exchange between the parties counting as an interview.[12] However, a feature of the way in which Code C has developed, as changes have been made to it, is that it has come to apply, though in a more limited way, to other exchanges between the parties. So in its 1995 form it provides, in paragraph 11.13, that a written record must be made of any comments of the suspect, including unsolicited ones, as long as they may be relevant to the offence. This record, like that of an interview, must be shown to the suspect for him to sign as correct or indicate inaccuracies. Furthermore, where an interview is carried out in a police station of a suspect who is alleged to have made significant statements or maintained some significant silence before his arrival at the station, those statements or that silence must be put to him at the beginning of the interview, in order that he may confirm or deny making them or maintaining it, and that he may add anything else he chooses.[13]

Meaning of 'Interview'

The original Code C contained no definition of the word 'interview'. It was decided in *Absolam*[14] that it was not necessary that the exchange between the police and the suspect had been arranged specifically to allow questions to be put by them to him about the relevant offence. There, the custody officer, in the course of drawing up an inventory of Absolam's possessions, said to him, 'And now put the drugs on the table'. Remarkably, Absolam did just that. The custody officer then asked him a series of questions the answers to which established that he had been selling packages of drugs that day. Bingham LJ said:[15]

> It is of course plain that this was not in any formal sense a conventional interview, but equally in our judgment it is plain that it was an interview within the purview of the Code,

[7] Para. 11.5(a). [8] Para. 11.5(c). [9] Paras. 11.7 and 11.9, respectively.

[10] See paras. 11.5(b) and 11.8. [11] Para. 11.10.

[12] As are a number of other duties laid down by Code C, e.g. the duty to ensure that an 'appropriate adult' is present at the interview of one of the vulnerable categories of suspect—see para. 11.14 and n. 1, above.

[13] Para. 11.2A. [14] (1988) 88 Cr.App.R 332. [15] *Ibid.* 336.

in that it was a series of questions directed by the police to a suspect with a view to obtaining admissions on which proceedings could be founded.

So where the police purpose is to obtain admissions the exchange will undoubtedly constitute an interview.[16] It was held in *Sparks*[17] that, even where the particular officer does not have the obtaining of an admission as his purpose, the exchange will count as an interview where any reasonable officer would have realized that the question he was putting might result in the acquisition of evidence against the suspect. In *Sparks* itself, the officer, who was an acquaintance of the suspect, had said that his purpose in speaking to him had been to find out what was happening and to provide him with reassurance, yet their conversation was certainly about the offences which eventually became the subject of the charges.

After a period from 1991 to 1995 during which Code C did contain a definition of 'interview', but only in a note for guidance (Note 11A of the 1991 issue of the Code), one is now to be found in a provision of the Code itself. Paragraph 11.1A (repeating the crucial words of Note 11A) defines it, in general terms, as 'the questioning of a person regarding his involvement or suspected involvement in a criminal offence of offences'. In the leading case dealing with Note 11A, *Cox*,[18] the Court of Appeal both applied Bingham LJ's definition in *Absolam* and cited *Sparks* with approval. It ought to follow that both cases still state good law.[19] Furthermore, it should not matter that the exchange in question was a brief one. Indeed, in two cases concerned with the original Code C, it was held that one question and answer amounted to an interview.[20]

Two other situations present greater difficulty, namely that where the police claim that their purpose was to allow the accused an opportunity of giving an innocent explanation and that where it was the suspect who initiated the exchange. Note for Guidance 12A in the original Code C stated, '[t]he purpose of any interview is to obtain from the person concerned his explanation of the facts, and not necessarily to obtain an admission.' This might have been thought to provide inferential support for the view that the first situation does entail an interview, yet the Court of Appeal decided the contrary in *Maguire*, Otton J saying, 'the Code does not prevent a police officer from asking questions at or near the scene of a suspected crime to elicit an explanation which if true or accepted would exculpate the suspect'.[21] The case is difficult both as to this statement of the law and as to its application to the facts. In *Hunt*,[22] Steyn LJ pointed out that:

[16] Other cases under the original Code C which follow *Absolam* are *Goddard* [1994] Crim.LR 46 and *Rowe* [1994] Crim.LR 837.

[17] [1991] Crim.LR 128.

[18] (1992) 96 Cr.App.R 464.

[19] *Oransaye* [1993] Crim.LR 772 (transcript through LEXIS), a case arising under the 1991 issue of the Code, involved facts strikingly similar to those of *Absolam* and may provide inferential support for the view expressed in the text, given that the result was the same as in *Absolam*.

[20] See *Hunt* [1992] Crim.LR 582; *Ward* (1993) 98 Cr.App.R 337. See also *Manji* [1990] Crim.LR 512 (three questions and answers).

[21] (1989) 90 Cr.App.R 115, at 119.

[22] [1992] Crim.LR 582 (transcript through LEXIS).

[i]f it were to be held that an exchange of questions and answers between a police officer and a person in custody is not an interview, if the police officer can say he was, in the time-honoured phrase, trying to eliminate the suspect from enquiries, that would drive a juggernaut through the policy of [the 1984 Act] and the Codes.

It followed that *Maguire* could not be authority for such an extreme proposition and that 'that decision may have turned on its own very special facts'. At most, the case can be authoritative only with regard to questions asked at or very near the scene shortly after the event. In *Hunt* itself, the relevant (single) question was asked during the journey to the police station in a patrol car, so not at or near the scene. It was, the officer claimed, asked 'out of curiosity', a claim which the Court of Appeal viewed with some scepticism. The court held that Hunt had indeed been interviewed.

What Otton J may have had in mind is the need not to frustrate the police in making very preliminary investigations on the spot. In the later case of *Weekes*, Farquharson LJ pointed out that it would be absurd to count as an interview a situation in which 'a police officer is in the street seeking information and trying to establish whether there are grounds for arresting a suspect'.[23] The line drawn seems to be between questions about suspicious behaviour and those put to someone the officer reasonably suspects has committed an offence.[24] Yet, in *Maguire*, one of the exchanges between the officer and Maguire had taken place after he had been cautioned and arrested. It is, therefore, hard to accept that the officer's purpose, at that stage, could have been to give the suspect an opportunity to exculpate himself. It may be added that, on the rather similar facts of *Weekes* itself (where the accused had also been both cautioned and arrested), though it quoted the relevant passage from *Maguire* without expressing disapproval, the Court of Appeal eventually decided that an interview had taken place.[25]

The court went on to offer a rather different way of drawing the line between interviews and other exchanges. The question to be asked was: '[i]s the nature, length, sequence and place where the enquiries takes [*sic*] place such that the person questioned is entitled to the protection of the provisions of the Code concerning interviews?'[26] There is an obvious element of circularity here, though one can see the point of asking whether or not the stage has been reached at which the various protections are appropriately to be granted. Of course, this would, in theory, render it possible for a given exchange to be considered an interview for the purposes of some protections but not others. An alternative would be to take a very broad view of 'interview', in the knowledge that breach of a code provision by no means automatically leads to exclusion. Qualitative assessments of the sort contemplated in *Weekes* may best inform the discretionary decision.

Where the suspect instigated the meeting and then volunteered information without being prompted by police questions, there can be no question of an interview having taken place. The reason for this was given by Evans LJ in

[23] (1992) 97 Cr.App.R 222, at 226–7.
[24] See also *Marsh* [1991] Crim.LR 455.
[25] See also *Goddard* [1994] Crim.LR 46.
[26] (1992) 97 Cr.App.R 222, at 227.

Menard; the definition in the Code of 'interview' is such that it necessarily involves questioning.[27] More difficult is the situation in which, though the suspect may be said to have made the running, some questions were put to him by the police. Rather different views were expressed in two cases concerned with the original issue of the Code. In *Matthews*, Morland J said, '[n]ormally any discussion or talk between a suspect or prisoner and a police officer about an alleged crime will amount to an "interview", whether instigated by the suspect, or prisoner or a police officer.'[28] In that case, the officer's contribution to the exchange seems to have been limited to cautioning Matthews and to acceding to her request that he make no record. Still, that exchange was held to constitute an 'interview'. By contrast, a distinctly more active role had been assumed by the police in *Younis and Ahmed*.[29] At one point, Younis had said that Ahmed had asked him to collect heroin on Ahmed's behalf and that he (Younis) had agreed to do so. An officer had then asked him what he would have done with the heroin. Given that the offence suspected was that Younis had been knowingly concerned in the importation of heroin, it would seem clear that this did involve discussion between the two of them about an alleged crime, yet the Court of Appeal held that the judge had been entitled to conclude that no interview had taken place. This clash of authority is most regrettable, particularly having regard to the significance of this issue for the accuracy of the record.

It has already been noted that *Sparks*[30] decides that the purpose of the exchange in the mind of the officer is not necessarily decisive as to whether or not it constitutes an interview. A slightly different twist has been given to that argument by the later cases of *Hunt*[31] and *Cox*.[32] While *Sparks* pays attention to what would be going through the mind of the reasonable officer, these two cases stress the importance of the potential impact of the exchange upon the suspect. Steyn LJ said in *Hunt*, '[t]he intentions of the police officer are no doubt part of the contextual scene which a court should consider, but so is the potential impact on the person in custody who is being questioned.'[33] *Cox* makes clear that greater emphasis is to be placed upon the effect of the questions on the suspect than upon what lay in the questioner's mind.[34]

It should be noted that paragraph 11.1A of the 1995 issue of Code C places a very important limitation on the meaning of 'interview'. It does this by restricting the word to questioning which is required to be carried out under caution. Paragraph 10.1 imposes a duty to caution only in respect of a person whom there are grounds to suspect of an offence, i.e. a suspect, and, even then, only where questions are to be put to him regarding his involvement or suspected involvement in that offence. It goes on to state that, therefore, he need not be cautioned if questions are put for *other* purposes, several of which are given as examples. Some of the examples are straightforward enough—questions to establish identity or the

[27] See [1995] 1 Cr.App.R 306, at 315. [28] (1989) 91 Cr.App.R 43, at 48.
[29] [1990] Crim.LR 425 (transcript through LEXIS). [30] [1991] Crim.LR 128.
[31] [1992] Crim.LR 582 (transcript through LEXIS). [32] (1992) 96 Cr.App.R 464.
[33] See LEXIS transcript. [34] See (1992) 96 Cr.App.R 464, at 472.

ownership of a vehicle, for instance—but one, namely questions in furtherance of the proper and effective conduct of a search, may prove more difficult.[35]

The necessary basis for any search will be that the officer has reasonable grounds for suspecting that the person to be searched has in his possession stolen or prohibited articles or dangerous drugs. Hence, the proper and effective conducting of such a search will very often entail the officer seeking to establish, before searching, whether or not his initial suspicions are justified. For example, in *Park*,[36] following a routine traffic stop, the police officers began to suspect that Park's car contained stolen goods and, indeed, that the car itself may have been stolen. There followed quite a long conversation, one of the clear purposes of which was to establish, by questioning Park, who it was that owned the various items in the car. But, as Park produced an unlikely set of replies, for example that he was unsure of the make of electrical equipment which he claimed to be his, the officer, not unnaturally, probed his story, concluding by asking him where he had been all day. Only after that final question had been put and answered was a caution administered. In the view of the Court of Appeal, what had begun as an inquiry had become an interview, though 'only just'. Now it is to be noted that *Park* was decided under the first (1985) issue of Code C. It is unlikely that the later parts of the conversation in question would, under the present issue of the Code, still be on that side of the line.[37] For one thing, the court accepted the judge's conclusion that the caution had not been given too late. If so, it would undoubtedly not now count as an interview. Even if a more realistic view were to be taken of the officer's growing suspicions, such that a caution ought to have been administered earlier, the close connection between the fact of possession of stolen goods and the commission of the offence of handling such goods or that of theft leaves the line extremely vague. Thus, can it not be argued that a proper question in pursuance of the search would be 'Did you steal these goods?', in that a positive response would establish that the goods in his possession were stolen. Yet, at the same time, the answer would certainly appear to the suspect to be one concerning his involvement or suspected involvement in an offence.

There is an additional reason why this may well turn out to be a point of some considerable importance under the presently-governing issue of Code C. In addition to the recording requirements to which reference has already been made, the Code places, by paragraph 11.1, a general duty on the police not to interview a suspect, except at a police station, once a decision has been taken to arrest him. No such decision was taken in *Park* until after the conversation, but this may very well not be the case. Thus, in *Khan*,[38] an arrested suspect was taken in turn to two

[35] Under the 1991 issue of Code C, Note for Guidance 11A excluded such questions from the definition of 'interview', but directly and not by reference to whether or not there was a need for a caution.

[36] (1993) 99 Cr.App.R 270.

[37] The same would seem to be true *a fortiori* of *Langiert* [1991] Crim.LR 777 (transcript through LEXIS), where the questions about goods found during a search seem to have been strictly limited to finding out whether or not they belonged to the suspect.

[38] [1993] Crim.LR 54 (transcript through LEXIS).

flats and questioned intermittently while the searches were going on. Though, on its own facts, the Court of Appeal concluded that some of the questions asked had gone beyond what was necessary in order to carry out the search effectively and involved asking Khan about the circumstances in which they suspected him to have committed the offence, the overlap suggested here between search questions and questions about guilt may be such as to enable the police to delay taking arrested suspects to the police station. As was pointed out in *Khan* itself, many of the Code C procedural rights are predicated upon the suspect's arrival at and detention in a police station. In particular, the suspect's right to be informed of his entitlement to consult a lawyer arises only on his arrival at the police station or other authorized place of detention. We shall see, later in this Chapter,[39] that the special provision for search following arrest must not be used by the police as a way of depriving the suspect of those procedural rights.

The Discretion in Cases of Interview Breach

Most of the cases concerning breach of the Code provisions which seek to ensure the accuracy of the record conform to a pattern. Typically, the police will have failed to make a contemporaneous note, even though it was practicable to do so, will have failed to endorse the custody record with a reason for not making such a note, and will, once they have made a note after the event, have failed to show it to the suspect for his comments. Of course, there were numerous variations upon this theme even under the original Code C, but changes effected to that Code, to some of which reference has already been made, open up more varied opportunities for breach.

What factors have influenced the appeal courts' view of the exercise of the discretion in such cases? In the leading case, *Canale*, Lord Lane CJ said:[40]

> the importance of the rules relating to contemporaneous noting of interviews can scarcely be over-emphasised. The object is twofold: not merely to ensure, so far as possible, that the suspect's remarks are accurately recorded and that he has an opportunity when he goes through the contemporaneous record afterwards of checking each answer and initialling each answer, but likewise it is a protection for the police, to ensure, so far as possible, that it cannot be suggested that they induced the suspect to confess by improper approaches or improper promises. If the contemporaneous note is not made, then each of those two laudable objects is apt to be stultified.

The first object, ensuring that the court has before it an account of the interview which neither side will challenge, is a realistic one, though use of tape-recording is an even better assurance of unchallengeability. The second object is incapable of being completely achieved, for the record offered in court can never be one which contains details of *all* exchanges between the police and the accused. Nonetheless, apparent police sloppiness with regard to recording may sometimes seem to take on an element of deviousness, so that the court may have a hunch that the police are covering up their own misconduct, whether during the course

[39] See text to nn. 185–6 below. [40] (1989) 91 Cr.App.R 1, at 5.

of the interview which does appear on the record or of some other, wholly unrecorded, exchange between the parties.[41] In such a case, police bad faith or deliberate disregard of the rules casts a shadow over the integrity of their investigation as a whole, suggesting, albeit indirectly, the unreliability of the formal record put before the court.

It may be partly because of a hunch of the kind just mentioned that the flagrancy of the breach will be a factor favouring exclusion, particularly where, as in *Canale* itself, that breach was also deliberate.[42] But there is reason to believe that the courts sometimes have in mind, when excluding evidence found in a record prepared in deliberate breach of the rules, future police interrogations. Though Lord Lane CJ said in *Delaney* that it was not part of the court's role to punish the police for failure to observe code provisions,[43] we should remember that the disciplinary lesson may serve, as here, the cause of promoting the reliability of future confessions to be adduced in court.[44] In *Canale*, there is an unmistakable whiff of that kind of discipline in the air. However, courts may hope that a disciplinary lesson may sometimes drive out ignorance as well as malice. Thus, in *Keenan*,[45] Hodgson J described as 'appalling' the admitted ignorance, on the part of the testifying officers, of a number of important provisions of Code C. Moreover, even where there is no general lesson to be learned for the future, the mistake of an inexperienced officer acting in good faith may still be such as to require exclusion of the evidence in question.[46] On the other hand, where the breach was a highly technical one which caused no actual prejudice of any kind to the accused, it will be regarded as neither significant nor substantial, so that exclusion will not be at all appropriate.[47]

An appeal court is much more likely to overturn a trial judge's decision to allow evidence to be admitted where the inadequately recorded confession comes accompanied by fully and properly recorded interviews at which the accused either denied his involvement or maintained silence. There are several examples in the authorities,[48] but the most instructive is *Scott*.[49] There, the accused was alleged to have made a highly incriminating remark during a break between two tape-recorded interviews at which he had made no admissions. It seems to have been this feature which was the prime reason for the Court of Appeal's decision to overturn that of the trial judge to allow the prosecution to adduce evidence of the remark. Presumably, the reason this factor is important is that the content of the surrounding interviews itself casts doubt upon the

[41] A point made, also by Lord Lane CJ, in *Delaney* (1988) 88 Cr.App.R 338, at 342.

[42] See also *ibid.*; *Chung* (1990) 92 Cr.App.R 314; *Weerdesteyn* [1995] 1 Cr.App.R 405.

[43] (1988) 88 Cr.App.R 338, at 341.

[44] See the general discussion at p. 13.

[45] (1989) 90 Cr.App.R 1. *Canale* and *Keenan* were both distinguished in *Roberts* [1997] 1 Cr.App.R 217, where the accused sought to take advantage of breaches of Code C in respect of a third party. The Court of Appeal stated that it was no part of the purpose of the Codes to 'protect another suspect'.

[46] A good example is *Sparks* [1991] Crim.LR 128.

[47] *RSPCA* v. *Eager* [1995] Crim.LR 59.

[48] See, e.g., *Chung* (1990) 92 Cr.App.R 314; *Joseph* [1993] Crim.LR 206.

[49] [1991] Crim.LR 56.

accuracy or truthfulness of the record of the incriminating remark put by the police before the court.

A venial failure to record an interview contemporaneously may be wholly cured or, at least, significantly reduced in its impact if the police put to the suspect their later-recorded note of his alleged admission or confession while the details of the interview remain fresh in his memory. Paragraph 11.10 of the 1995 issue of Code C does indeed place the police under a duty, unless it be impracticable, to show the suspect the note they have drawn up of that interview, so that he may read it and sign it as correct or indicate inaccuracies.[50] Failure to comply with that paragraph will compound the earlier failure to record, for reasons well put by Hobhouse LJ in *Weerdesteyn*:[51]

> What happened in the present case was that at the very earliest he did not know that he had said anything significant during [the] conversation or that the prosecution were in any way relying upon anything that he might or might not have said in the conversation until at least two-and-a-half months later. When it came to the trial all that he could say is [*sic*] that he had no recollection of the conversation at all; that is not surprising. So that was the result which was produced by this failure to observe the provisions of the Code.

Paragraph 11.10 says nothing about how quickly it should be shown to the suspect, nor does it refer at all to the presence of a lawyer when it is so shown. Nonetheless, in two cases in the Court of Appeal, it has been held that delay in showing the note to the suspect and failure to alert a solicitor, already present advising him, of the existence of any such note are both factors favouring exercise of the discretion in favour of exclusion. These factors would seem to be of particular importance where the note has been composed before the conducting of any formal interview in the police station, yet in neither case had the police shown it to the suspect or his solicitor (if present) nor referred to its existence. Thus, in *Chung*,[52] the admissions allegedly made at an earlier interview carried out while the accused's house was being searched were the sole evidence against him. The Court of Appeal found the failure of the police to alert either the accused or his solicitor to the content of the note 'quite astonishing'.[53] This failure was a significant factor in the court's decision to overturn the trial judge's ruling that those admissions could be given in evidence. In the similar case of *Cox*,[54] the Court offered guidance to first instance courts on this very point, as follows:[55]

> (1) If such a note has, for whatever reason, not been shown to the suspect prior to the arrival of his solicitor, fairness, both to the suspect and to the police themselves, requires that it be shown to him in the presence of his solicitor.

[50] Para. 12.12 of the original issue of Code C, though to the same essential effect, applied only if the suspect was still at the police station at the time the record was completed. More importantly, it was held in *Brezeanu and Francis* [1989] Crim.LR 650 that the duty arose only in respect of interviews which had themselves taken place in the police station. (See also *Beycan and Gokan* [1990] Crim.LR 185; *Francis and Findlay* [1992] Crim.LR 372.) There is no such limitation in the present para. 11.10.

[51] [1995] 1 Cr.App.R 405, at 410.

[52] (1990) 92 Cr.App.R 314.

[53] *Ibid*. 322.

[54] (1992) 96 Cr.App.R 464.

[55] *Ibid*. 476 (*per* McCullough J).

(2) If such a note has been shown to the suspect before the arrival of the solicitor, fairness to both sides requires that the solicitor be informed of the fact when he arrives.

(3) Where the court concludes that the police have acted less than fairly, the chance that the evidence of the conversation noted will be excluded will be materially increased.

We may conclude this section by referring to two factors which have been held to tell against exclusion. First, where, though the interview was not recorded contemporaneously and the note of it was not shown promptly to the accused and his legal adviser, the adviser was present during the course of that interview, that will be a factor favouring admission in evidence of its contents. Three reasons were given in *Dunn*[56] for this. The legal adviser would be able to intervene in the conversation before the relevant answers were given. The mere presence of a legal adviser would tend to inhibit the police from fabrication. Finally, the legal adviser could testify at trial to the contents of the conversation in question. The validity of these points may be challenged, for they assume that the legal adviser will be someone professionally competent and experienced enough to be able properly to perform the tasks in question.[57] As we shall see later in this Chapter, the empirical evidence suggests that the legal adviser in question will rarely be a solicitor;[58] indeed, in *Dunn* itself, the adviser was a solicitor's clerk.

Though section 78(1) is concerned with evidence in general, and not solely with confessions, the absence of anything directly incriminatory in the police record of the relevant interview will count against exclusion. For example, in *Park*,[59] the prosecution sought to make use of an interview, as containing previous inconsistent statements, for the purposes of impeaching the accused. The absence of directly incriminatory material is relevant to the accuracy of the record in that officers minded to misrepresent what the accused had said would hardly be likely to put into his mouth material of such restricted and contingent value.

Tape-recording

Though there are a handful of post-Act cases concerned with the conditions of admissibility in evidence of tape-recordings of police interviews and transcripts thereof, there is a surprising paucity of authority on the provisions of the *Code of Practice on Tape Recording of Interviews with Suspects*. This Code, Code E, was initially issued in July 1988, but an amended version was issued in April 1995. A number of the more recent cases reveal that interviews were tape-recorded, and, indeed, appeal courts have relied upon the contents of recordings in making their decisions as to admission of confessions and other material in evidence, having regard to the provisions of sections 76 and 78 of the 1984 Act.[60] Yet LEXIS searches carried out in July 1997 revealed only one case in which an appeal court

[56] (1990) 91 Cr.App.R 237.

[57] See Hodgson [1992] Crim.LR 854, at 860–1.

[58] See text to nn. 156–7 below.

[59] (1993) 99 Cr.App.R 270.

[60] The best example is *Paris, Abdullahi and Miller* (1992) 97 Cr.App.R 99, discussed in Ch. 5, text to nn. 29–30 and 36–7 above.

found that a Code E provision had been breached and, even there, the breach was described as a technical one.[61]

There are several opportunities for breach which are broadly equivalent to those which have been so often litigated under Code C. As has already been mentioned, it is only when an 'interview' has taken place that the duty to make a taped record arises.[62] That duty applies in respect of any interview at a police station about an indictable offence, including an offence triable either way, as long as the person in question has been cautioned (or, presumably, ought to have been cautioned).[63] To seek to ensure that incriminatory statements or silences occurring before the tape-recorder was switched on are authoritatively placed on the record, the officer must put to the suspect any significant statement or silence so occurring and must ask him whether he confirms or denies it and whether he wishes to add anything.[64] There are, of course, numerous other provisions designed to establish the place and time of and participants in the taped interview, as well as to ensure the integrity and security of the tape.

Several legal issues have arisen about the adducing of tape-recorded evidence or of transcripts thereof in court, as well as about the preparation by the police and adducing in court of summaries of the taped record. Though they do not relate to the core content of this Chapter, they are most conveniently dealt with at this point.

Admission of the Taped Record Itself

Starting with the original taped record, it is established by *Maqsud Ali*[65] that there is no objection in principle to its admission in evidence. It should be admissible, according to that case, 'provided that the accuracy of the recording can be proved and voices properly identified; provided also that the evidence is relevant and otherwise admissible'.[66] Neither of the first two requirements will present any practical problem, at least in the case of recordings made in the controlled environment of the police station. The officers who conducted the interview will be in a position both to identify the voices on the tape and to vouch for the accuracy of the record.[67] In those circumstances, it will be only if there is evidence of tampering, or, at least, evidence that breaches have taken place of provisions of Code E which are designed to ensure the security of the tape, that the issue of the accuracy of the tape as a record will be at all likely to arise. It may be that, if the defence does challenge the authenticity of the tape, the prosecution will be required to prove that fact on a balance of probabilities, though the authorities are not at all clear on the point, perhaps because of the difficulty of separating questions of authenticity from those of originality—i.e. has this tape been shown to be the original?[68] Two textbooks argue that it should be enough for the prosecution to satisfy an evidential burden, with the need to show only

[61] See *Blackwell et al.* [1995] 2 Cr.App.R 625. [62] See Code E, para. 3.1.
[63] *Ibid.*, para. 3.1(a). [64] *Ibid.*, para. 4.3B. [65] [1966] 1 QB 688. [66] *Ibid.* 701.
[67] See *Rampling* [1987] Crim.LR 823.
[68] See *Stevenson* [1971] 1 WLR 1; *Robson* [1972] 1 WLR 651.

prima facie evidence of authenticity,[69] and one of the cases seems to lend support to this proposition.[70]

The issue might be a more pressing one if tape-recording of exchanges outside the police station were to become more common, for it would be more difficult to provide a copper-bottomed guarantee of their security. In this respect, it is to be noted that paragraph 11.1 of Code C contains a general requirement that interviews with suspects whom the police have decided to arrest should not be conducted outside the station. Though, as we have seen,[71] there is some scope for argument that a given exchange does not amount to an interview, paragraph 11.1 does provide significant discouragement of the use of hand-held tape-recorders.[72]

The statement in *Maqsud Ali* also refers to the need for the tape-recorded evidence to be relevant and otherwise admissible. Since that evidence is direct evidence of the words pronounced at the interview, no hearsay problem arises as regards what was actually said, any more than it would if a human being related what had been said. Of course, to the extent that the words are adduced as evidence of their truth, the hearsay rule does come into play, but the exception to that rule for admissions and confessions will apply. As far as the other rules of inadmissibility are concerned, appropriate editing of the original tape will ensure that the trier of fact does not hear anything it ought not to hear.[73] For obvious reasons, the prosecution and defence will need to co-operate over any such editing, though in a Crown Court case, the judge may have to be involved in the question if no agreement can be reached between the parties. Detailed provisions for such editing and, more generally, for the agreeing of a record or a transcript of the interview are contained in a Practice Direction issued by Lord Lane CJ in 1989.[74]

In cases where editing is necessary, there will be no question of it being the original tape which is adduced in evidence. Either a transcript, excluding the inadmissible or irrelevant material, will have been prepared, or, though this is less likely given that editing will tend to make it obvious that material has been excluded, a re-recorded copy tape will be presented to the court. There would be no question of the 'best evidence' rule preventing either of these methods being used, for they would each provide the court with the best available evidence, having regard to other applicable rules.

Admission of the Transcript with the Taped Record

There may be other reasons why the parties wish to adduce evidence of the content of the interview otherwise than through the playing of the original tape.

[69] See *Cross and Tapper on Evidence* (8th edn., 1995), 190; Blackstone's *Criminal Practice* (1997 edn.), para. F.8.42.

[70] *Robson* [1972] 1 WLR 651, at 654 (*per* Shaw J).

[71] See text to nn. 14–39 above.

[72] A discouragement regretted by Wolchover and Heaton-Armstrong (1991) 91 *Police Review* 751. See also *Royal Commission on Criminal Justice*, Research Study No 22 (1993) (by Moston and Stephenson), at 42–4.

[73] See, e.g., *Riaz and Burke* (1991) 94 Cr.App.R 339, at 342.

[74] *Practice Direction (Crime): Tape Recording: Police Interviews* [1989] 1 WLR 631.

Before dealing with those reasons, we must refer to the more straightforward case where a party seeks to have put before the trier of fact a transcript of the tape *in addition to* the tape itself. The post-Act English authorities[75] establish three propositions clearly. First, there is no objection to use of the transcript as an aid to interpretation of the contents of the tape. Secondly, the matter is one for the discretion of the judge, as an administrative matter, and is not dependent upon the consent of either prosecution or defence. Thirdly, and most importantly, where transcripts are used in this way, they do not themselves constitute evidence in the case. Rather, they amount to a device to assist the trier of fact, in the same way as does a schedule. This point was expressed well by the High Court of Australia in *Butera* v. *DPP for the State of Victoria*:[76]

> The jury should be instructed that the purpose of admitting a transcript is not to provide independent evidence of the conversation but so as to aid them in understanding what conversation is recorded on the tape, and that they cannot use the transcript as a substitute for the tape if they are not satisfied that the transcript correctly sets out what they heard on the tape.

This view of the proper use of the transcript seems entirely tenable, in practice no less than in theory, where the quality of the original recording is high, as when an interview has been routinely recorded at a police station. However, where the very reason for allowing the trier of fact to have access to the transcript is that parts of the tape are very hard to decipher, it would seem to be unrealistic to argue that the transcript is merely a device to help it.[77] This is a very likely eventuality in the case of surreptitiously recorded conversations. Where the words used are in a foreign language, and the transcription comes accompanied by a translation, it seems even clearer that what is written down must amount, in reality, to evidence in the case. However, at least in the case of transcription of recordings which are hard to decipher, there is Court of Appeal authority confirming the correctness of the notion that it is not itself evidence in the case.[78] In any event, the judge should be mindful of the possibility of prejudice to the accused if the transcript is made available to the jury, and should, presumably, exercise his discretion against making it available in such circumstances.[79]

Admission of the Transcript Alone

Might it be possible to avoid the problems created where both the tape and the transcript are adduced by offering *only* the transcript in evidence? Two objections might be taken to use of a full transcript in this way, a hearsay objection and

[75] *Rampling* [1987] Crim.LR 823; *Moley*, unreported, 20 July 1994; *Taylor, Tharme and Holness*, unreported, 31 March 1995 (all transcripts through LEXIS).

[76] (1987) 164 CLR 180, at 188 (*per* Mason CJ, Brennan and Deane JJ). The Court of Appeal in *Taylor, Tharme and Holness*, n. 75 above, expressed its agreement with this statement.

[77] A point made forcefully by Dawson J (dissenting) in *Butera*, n. 76 above, at 197.

[78] See *Taylor, Tharme and Holness*, unreported, 31 March 1995 (transcript through LEXIS).

[79] *Robson* [1972] 1 WLR 651, at 656; *Moley*, unreported, 20 July 1994 (transcript through LEXIS).

a 'best evidence' one. The former objection has, itself, two elements. First, does the transcript constitute an accurate record of what is on the tape? This can be dealt with easily enough by calling the person who transcribed the contents of the tape to give direct evidence of the accuracy of the transcription.[80] Secondly, does the transcript constitute an accurate record of what was actually said at the interview? Here, though there is no case directly in point, the bulk of authority on an analogous issue concerned with identification evidence would indicate that one may, in effect, add together the officer's evidence that the tape accurately records the interview and the transcriber's evidence that the transcript accurately reflects the tape, in order to allow the (non-hearsay) conclusion that the transcript contains an accurate record of the interview.[81]

The 'best evidence' principle has as its most important, perhaps its only, manifestation in the modern law the rule requiring that, in general, the contents of a document must be proved by the production of the original. Does the documentary originals rule apply to tape-recordings? There are two first instance decisions early in the 1970s which say that it does.[82] In addition, according to *Archbold*, the Court of Appeal in the second of those cases affirmed the trial judge's view.[83] However, the more recent case of *Kajala* v. *Noble*[84] is Divisional Court authority casting the greatest doubt upon the correctness of those rulings. That case itself was concerned with a copy of an original video-recording. Ackner LJ said of the documentary originals rule: 'In our judgment, the old rule is limited and confined to written documents in the strict sense of the term, and has no relevance to tapes or films.'[85] Unfortunately, the Divisional Court did not refer to the authorities concerned with audio-recordings, so it might be argued that a line is to be drawn between such recordings (caught by the rule) and video-recordings (outside it). Such a distinction would have no merit. As long as there is satisfactory evidence of the accuracy of the transcript or (where used) the copy tape, there is everything to be said, where the original would yield no extra relevant material, for allowing evidence of the interview to be given entirely from the (full) transcript or copy.

In any event, this issue may now be moot, for section 27 of the Criminal Justice Act 1988 provides for proof of an admissible statement in a document: '(whether or not that document is still in existence) by the production of a copy of that document . . . authenticated in such manner as the court may approve'.[86] The effect of

[80] This will be unnecessary where the transcript is used as a device to assist the jury, rather than as evidence. There, the officer may, where he has checked the transcript, produce it at trial even though he did not make it—see *Rampling* [1987] Crim.LR 823.

[81] See *Burke and Kelly* (1847) 2 Cox CC 295; *Grew* v. *Cubitt* [1951] 2 TLR 205; *Jones* v. *Metcalfe* [1967] 1 WLR 1286; *Osbourne and Virtue* [1973] QB 678. See also Libling [1977] *Crim.LR* 268. But cf. *McLean* (1967) 52 Cr.App.R 80, which seems to be favoured by *Cross and Tapper*, n. 69 above, at 586–7.

[82] *Stevenson* [1971] 1 WLR 1; *Robson* [1972] 1 WLR 651.

[83] Archbold, *Criminal Pleading, Evidence and Practice*, (1997 edn.) para. 4.290, referring to *Robson*, unreported, June 1973.

[84] (1982) 75 Cr.App.R 149. [85] *Ibid.* 152.

[86] It is possible that s. 27 is restricted in its effects to statements rendered admissible by ss. 23 and 24 of the 1988 Act itself and so would not apply to the situation dealt with in the text. However, there

Schedule 2, paragraph 5, of that Act is that, for these purposes, the word 'document' *does* include a tape-recording and the word 'copy' includes a transcript. Clearly, the statement itself (on the tape) is admissible, and it would seem to be for the court to decide how a transcript of the tape should be authenticated. There is no reason why the evidence of the transcriber should not, for these purposes, suffice.

We may conclude that, whether because the 'best evidence' rules does not apply, or because the 1988 Act derogates from it, there is, in principle, no difficulty with use of a transcript in substitution for the original recording, as long as properly authenticated. Yet it will be wise for the prosecution to proceed by agreement with the defence. This is certainly what is envisaged by the 1989 Practice Direction. There is a danger, if it proceeds otherwise, that the defence will seek to challenge at trial the accuracy of the transcript; a dispute of this kind would necessarily have to be resolved by reference to the original tape. Or the defence might argue that the tape itself adds something significant to the transcript, as where the tone of voice of one of the participants is relevant.[87] In *Rampling*,[88] the Court of Appeal laid down guidance on, *inter alia*, the relevance of the accused's consent to use of the transcript alone. It said that the accused is 'entitled, if he or she so requires, to have the tape, or any part of it, played to the jury'.[89] This almost certainly means that only if consent has been withheld pre-trial is there an absolute right to have the tape played, for the court will surely want to be given a satisfactory reason for a change of mind on the part of the defence arising at trial.[90]

Admission of a Précis or Summary

Finally, may a précis or summary, i.e. a condensed or abbreviated written account, be adduced by the prosecution in substitution for the original tape or a full transcript of its contents? Certainly, it was a crucial element of the Government's intention in setting up the tape-recording scheme that tapes would rarely need to be played, full transcripts rarely need to be prepared. The 1988 issue of Code E, in paragraph 5, very clearly envisaged the interviewing officers preparing a summary of the interview (the 'interview record'[91]). Note for Guidance 5B to that paragraph stated that '[t]he record shall comprise a balanced account of the interview including points in mitigation and/or defence made by the suspect. Where an admission is made the question as well as the answer containing the admission shall be recorded verbatim in the record.' In addition, Home Office Circular 76/1988 told the police that:[92]

is a significant body of opinion that it is of general application—see, e.g., *Blackstone's Criminal Practice*, n. 69 above, para. F. 8.2; Andrews and Hirst, *Criminal Evidence* (2nd. edn., 1992), paras. 11.24 and 19.01; Keane, *The Modern Law of Evidence* (4th edn., 1996), 200. Even if it is not of general application, it may be that it applies to all evidence admissible by way of some exception to the hearsay rule, including the exception for confessions—see May, *Criminal Evidence* (3rd edn., 1995), para. 3.12. *Archbold*, n. 83 above, para. 9.100, simply says that it should not be considered to be applicable where the document is being tendered as real evidence.

[87] See *Emmerson* (1990) 92 Cr.App.R 284; *Riaz and Burke* (1991) 94 Cr.App.R 339.

[88] [1987] Crim.LR 823 (transcript through LEXIS).

[89] See LEXIS transcript.

[90] See *Riaz and Burke* (1991) 94 Cr.App.R 339, at 342.

[91] See para. 5.3.

[92] Issued on 17 Aug. 1988—see para. 23.

[t]he successful introduction of tape recording depends on the provision by the police of an adequate written record of the contents of an interview which is acceptable to the crown prosecutor and the defence—so as to keep to a minimum the need for the tape to be listened to or for a full transcript to be provided.

The April 1995 issue is silent on these matters, but Home Office Circular 26/1995[93] provides the police with national guidelines on the preparation of records of interviews which are clearly designed to promote the confidence of everyone, including the parties, in their accuracy.

There is no doubt at all that use of interview records of this kind in this way is now a regular feature of the criminal trial process. The point was adverted to by Lord Lane CJ in *Riaz and Burke*, as follows:[94]

The tape itself . . . is the primary exhibit, although as a matter of convenience and also speed, the prosecution usually arrange, with the consent of the defence, for a condensed or abbreviated transcript of the contents of the tape to be provided for the use of the court and the jury. Of course either side, or the jury themselves, may ask for the tape itself to be played during the currency of the trial. If the request is a reasonable one, the judge no doubt will almost always accede to it.

In *Aitken*,[95] the defence had not disputed the content of the summary prepared by the police. That summary was admitted at trial, the tapes themselves not being produced in evidence. Later, the jury asked to hear the tapes, and the issue for the Court of Appeal was whether or not the trial judge had been right to allow them, over defence objections, to do so. There is not the slightest hint in the case that, had the jury not made its request, something would have gone amiss at trial. It may be added that there is plenty of empirical evidence that the police predominantly prepare summaries instead of organizing the preparation of full transcripts.[96] The basis upon which the summary is admitted in evidence must be that the defence accepts that it accurately reflects what transpired at interview, though, of course, it does not necessarily accept that the substance of what was there said is true. Both *Riaz and Burke* and *Aitken* make it clear that the defence's consent to use of the summary in substitution for the tape must be obtained. It does not follow that the defence is wise to give its consent, for, as we shall shortly see, there is also empirical evidence which suggests that police summaries of the interview record are often inaccurate, sometimes grossly so.

Ancillary Matters

We must complete the present section by dealing with two ancillary matters about use in court of tape-recordings. Where prosecution and defence have agreed before trial to proceed on the basis of a transcript or summary, one or

[93] Made under Code E, Note for Guidance 5A.

[94] (1991) 94 Cr.App.R 339, at 342. See also *Emmerson* (1990) 92 Cr.App.R 284, at 286–7 (*per* Lloyd LJ).

[95] (1991) 94 Cr.App.R 85.

[96] See Baldwin and Bedward [1991] Crim.LR 671 and *Royal Commission on Criminal Justice*, Research Study No 2, 1992 (by Baldwin).

other may seek to persuade the judge, at some stage before the conclusion of his summing-up, that the tape itself, or part of it, should be heard. In the alternative, the jury may ask for it to be played. Subject to the judge's discretion, having heard counsel, to refuse the request where injustice might be done to the accused, there is no objection to it being granted. These rules apply whether or not the tape itself has already been made an exhibit in the case.[97]

More difficult is the case where counsel or the jury makes the request after conclusion of the judge's summing-up, either immediately before the jury retires to consider its verdict or during the course of that retirement. Where the tape has not been made an exhibit, there would seem to be no question of it being played to the jury once they have retired, for no new evidence can then be heard.[98] Before they retire, it seems that, very exceptionally, fresh evidence may be called, but only on the application of the defence.[99] Where it *has* been made an exhibit, because, technically, no question of calling fresh evidence arises, the judge enjoys greater freedom. There seems to be no distinction here between cases where the jury has and where it has not already retired. Where, as in *Riaz and Burke*,[100] the jury has heard evidence of the contents of the interview by means of a full transcript, the jury is entitled to hear the tape itself. On the other hand, where, as in *Hagan*,[101] the transcript has, as a matter of fairness to the accused, been edited in order to remove inadmissible, irrelevant or prejudicial material, it would clearly defeat the object of the exercise to allow the jury to listen to the unedited tape. Both decisions stress that, in any event, any playing-back of the tape should, as a general rule, take place in open court and not in the retiring room.

There does not appear to be any authority concerning the situation where one of the parties asks for the tape to be played. One may suppose that, at such an extremely late stage, the judge will require a great deal of convincing that there are grounds for such an application. Nor does there seem to be any authority concerned with a situation in which the jury has, up to the point of retirement, heard only a summary of the interview. Plainly, if the tape can be played back in these circumstances, the requirement that this take place in open court will equally apply. However, one can foresee such a great potential for clashes between the content of the summary and of the tape, with the attendant risk of jury confusion, that a court might well shy away from allowing the tape to be played at all.

A slightly different situation arises where the tape, or part of it, *has* been played in open court during the ordinary course of the evidence. There are, again, two issues here. May the jury hear the tape again after the judge's summing-up? If they may, should it be played in open court or in the retiring room? Regarding the first issue, *Emmerson*[102] points out that there are three distinct possibilities. Where the whole of the tape has been played in open court, the jury should, if either side or

[97] *Aitken* (1991) 94 Cr.App.R 85. See also *Sinclair and Peters* (1993) 157 JPR 161.

[98] *Browne* (1943) 29 Cr.App.R 106; *Owen* [1952] 2 QB 362; *Davis* (1975) 62 Cr.App.R 194. But cf. the apparently contrary *dictum* of Lord Taylor CJ in *Rawlings* [1995] 2 Cr.App.R 222, at 227E.

[99] *Sanderson* [1953] 1 WLR 392.

[100] (1991) 94 Cr.App.R 339.

[101] [1997] 1 Cr.App.R 464.

[102] (1990) 92 Cr.App.R 284.

they themselves wish, be able to hear it again. If only part has been played, but the jury has a transcript of the whole tape, then they may hear the whole tape. Finally, if only part has been played and the jury has no transcript, the tape must be edited to ensure that they hear only what has been given in evidence. In the same case, Lloyd LJ expressed the view that the better course, where the jury is to re-hear a passage which has already been played in open court, is to allow it to be played to them again in the retiring room. Certainly, there could be no objection to that course if one could be sure that nothing new would be disclosed to the jury, but Lord Lane CJ, in *Riaz and Burke*, expressed a fear that material which the jury should not hear might be inadvertently left on the tape. Therefore, in Lord Lane CJ's view, there should, for safety, be a presumption in favour of reassembling the court for the tape to be played back. Support for that view was given by Leggatt LJ in *Tonge*, though he added that there would be an exception where 'it would be more convenient for them to hear in their room a tape which they have heard before in open court, of which there is an agreed transcript, and which does not contain inadmissible passages'.[103] It is noteworthy that, apart from the reference to the need for there to be an agreed transcript, the passage is consistent with the tenor of Lloyd LJ's remark in *Emmerson*.

Other Elements of the Formal Record

For completeness, it is necessary to refer briefly to the remaining possible elements of the formal record of the accused's interactions with the police. Before the advent of routine tape-recording of interviews inside the police station, it was the accused's own written statement of confession which might be expected to provide the most cogent evidence of his guilt. Annex D to Code C makes detailed provision for the making of such written statements. There are a number of duties imposed upon the police by that Annex, in particular in relation to the situation where it is a police officer who actually writes out the statement at the accused's dictation, which might have been expected to lead to allegations of breach coming before the courts. In fact, this does not seem to have been the case, at least as a matter of such importance as to surface in reported decisions at appeal level. It may be reasonably safe to assume that this element of the recording process is operating in a relatively smooth and straightforward way.

Where the accused's written statement is exhibited at trial, the ordinary rules relating to documentary evidence apply. The reader should refer to general works upon the law of evidence for treatment of those rules.

In certain circumstances, a record of an interview with the accused which was prepared by the police themselves may become the accused's own statement and may be exhibited by the prosecution as such. Thus in *Todd*,[104] a verbatim, contemporaneous record had been prepared in that way and then signed by the accused. The Court of Appeal had no doubt that he had, by his signature, made

[103] See (1993) 157 JPR 1137, at 1142. [104] (1980) 72 Cr.App.R 299.

it his own. It would seem necessarily to follow that the position is the same where the account to which the accused added his signature was non-verbatim but contemporaneous, or even a summary compiled afterwards. There are several provisions in Code C which require the police to give the suspect the opportunity of verifying by his signature that their record of an exchange with him is accurate. Though these provisions are of far less practical significance now that there is routine tape-recording of interviews, the principle laid down in *Todd* remains capable of applying to signed records of such exchanges.

Dicta in *Fenlon*[105] indicate that the suspect may be taken to have adopted the record as his own otherwise than by signing it. This might result where the suspect either had himself read the police account or had had it read over to him and had then orally acknowledged it as correct. Though these *dicta* are, no doubt, sound as a matter of principle, it seems most unlikely that they will be applied to questioning governed by Code C, for it will be extremely difficult for the police to explain why someone invited to confirm the accuracy of the police account unequivocally by signing it might refuse to do so, yet, at the same time confirm it orally.

Defects of the Formal Record

Though it is not a primary concern of this work to deal with empirical data about how the 1984 Act and the codes made thereunder operate in practice, it would be wrong to fail to advert to it at points where it has a particular pertinency, one of which has now been reached.

The Completeness of the Record

It is clearly impossible for there to be a taped or written record of all exchanges and transactions between the police and the suspect, both inside and outside the police station. By virtue of paragraph 11.3 of the original (1985) issue of Code C, the duty to make a contemporaneous (non-mechanical) record of an interview applied only to those conducted at the police station. There was much concern during the early days of that Code and, indeed, of the tape-recording scheme itself that off-the-record questioning might be taking place. Considerable empirical evidence that it was taking place on a substantial scale began to emerge.[106] Changes to Code C, first effected in 1991 and re-affirmed in 1995, impose duties which are clearly designed to attenuate the problem. Their combined effect is that an accurate written record must be made of each interview with a *suspect*; that the record must, exceptional cases apart, be made contemporaneously; and that a written record must be made of any *comments* made by a suspect, even unsolicited ones, where they might be relevant to the suspected offence.[107] In

[105] (1980) 71 Cr.App.R 307.

[106] See, e.g. McConville and Morrell [1983] Crim.LR 158 (itself concerned with the Scottish experience); Dixon, Bottomley, Coleman, Gill, and Wall (1990) 1 *Policing and Society* 115, at 133–5; Wolchover and Heaton-Armstrong [1991] Crim.LR 232, at 242.

[107] See, in particular, paras. 11.1, 11.5, and 11.13 of the 1995 issue. For the meaning of 'interview', see text to nn. 14–39 above.

addition, there is a general duty not to interview an *arrested* suspect except at a police station so that, once an arrest has been made, it will be almost inevitable that the police must make a contemporaneous record. It will be appreciated that only in the case of a non-suspect is there no recording requirement at all.

However, so far as tape-recording is concerned, the provisions of Code E are very much more relaxed. The effect of paragraph 3.1 is that a taped record is required only where a *suspect* is *interviewed* at a *police station*. This clearly allows considerable scope for both exchanges (i.e. non-interviews) at the police station and interviews outside it to be conducted off-tape.

A study carried out for the Royal Commission on Criminal Justice by Moston and Stephenson[108] sought to find out the extent to which suspects were being interviewed, or being questioned without being interviewed, outside the police station. The data came from questionnaires completed by the officers involved. The researchers offered them definitions of interviewing and of questioning derived from the then-applicable Note for Guidance 11A. Though, in these circumstances, it could not be claimed that the line between the two was watertight, the researchers found that 8 per cent of suspects had been interviewed and some 31 per cent questioned. As many as three-quarters of the interviewed suspects were reported to have made an admission of some kind. No equivalent figure is available as regards the questioned suspects, for the police were not asked to say if any confession or admission had come from them. An important finding was that there was a marked correlation between the fact that there had been an interview or other exchange outside the police station and the outcome of a later interview at the station. There was a significantly greater likelihood of an admission being made at the formal interview where there had been an exchange with the police before arrival there. Though Moston and Stephenson acknowledge that there may be explanations of these findings other than that earlier encounters tend to be used to soften up the suspect for later ones, they do go on to say, '[t]he taped interview represents only a partial picture of a suspect's exchanges with police officers and could be a stage-managed, and sanitized version of police interviewing procedures taken as a whole'.[109]

It seems likely that paragraph 11.2A of Code C, introduced in April 1995, is designed to attenuate the problem identified by Moston and Stephenson. It provides:

> At the beginning of an interview carried out in a police station, the interviewing officer, after cautioning the suspect, shall put to him any significant statement or silence which occurred before his arrival at the police station, and shall ask him whether he confirms or denies that earlier statement or silence and whether he wishes to add anything.

Clearly, then, the suspect must be given early warning of incriminating remarks (or non-remarks) which he allegedly made before arrival at the station. And, his response to any such allegation will form part of the taped record.

[108] Research Study No 22 (1993). [109] *Ibid*. 43.

It is noteworthy that paragraph 11.2A does not apply to exchanges *inside* the police station not amounting to interviews. There is some empirical evidence that softening-up may take place in the station no less than outside it. McConville was able to video-tape a number of exchanges which did not appear at all on the formal taped record of the interrogation.[110] Some of these video-tapes showed that deals were struck or pressure put on the suspect which, had they been known about at trial, would have been very likely to have resulted in exclusion of any resulting confessions to be found on the formal record. It is unnecessary to go into detail here, but Moston and Stephenson's reference to the taped interview as capable of being a sanitized version of an earlier exchange seems entirely apt.

It is worth adding that courts have sometimes been made aware that there have been unrecorded exchanges between the parties which have resulted in incriminating remarks from the suspect. A good example is *Williams*.[111] The police had spent a full hour making a 'social visit' to Williams in his cell. In the course of that visit, he discussed with the officers the possibility of pleading guilty, yet no record was made of it. Rather, at a formal interview which followed immediately, he gave the officers a detailed confession. This was recorded. The Court of Appeal deprecated the paying of such 'social visits' to persons in custody, but went on to uphold the trial judge's decision to allow the confession to be given in evidence. Paragraph 11.13 of Code C, which did not apply at the time the facts of *Williams* arose, would now require a written record to be made and shown to the suspect. However, it may be asked whether the police really have an incentive to make such a record where they have all they need on tape. They are perfectly at liberty, in fact though not in law, to say that he made no comments relevant to the offence. Even if paragraph 11.2A were to be extended to significant statements and silences in the police station, the same would apply.

The Accuracy of Prepared Summaries

The other major issue raised by the empirical evidence is the extent to which reliance can properly be placed upon the accuracy of the summary of the taped record which is usually prepared by the police for use in the proceedings. Two separate surveys, concerning three different police areas, suggest that, in as many as half of the cases, the summary 'cannot be considered a fair reflection of what the suspect said in the interview room'.[112] Though these surveys were necessarily impressionistic, the researchers involved give a number of examples which appear strongly to support their case. Common sense reflection suggests that it would be surprising if there were not a significant tendency to inaccuracy. Police officers have no training, formal or otherwise, in the complex literary and intellectual process of précis. Moreover, they cannot look at or listen to the

[110] [1992] Crim.LR 532. [111] (1992) 156 JPR 776. See also *Purcell* [1992] Crim.LR 806.

[112] See *Royal Commission on Criminal Justice*, Research Study No 2 (1992) (Baldwin). The other survey's findings are reported by Baldwin and Bedward [1991] Crim.LR 671.

record neutrally. Where a suspect has, or is believed by the officers to have, confessed, he will be regarded by them as a guilty person. Baldwin puts it well, as follows:[113]

> The inherent difficulties of preparing an accurate précis are compounded by the need to exercise sound judgment about what can be left out without distortion, and, the more summaries that one examines, the more convinced one becomes that police officers suffer from an understandable, and probably ineradicable, tendency to view matters through a prosecution prism. The compilation of summaries is not a neutral fact-gathering exercise but one that depends on intuitive judgment. In consequence, the scope for conscious and unconscious bias (not to mention more subtle attempts at distortion) is infinite.

As we have seen, the use of summaries has been encouraged not only by the original Code E, but also by a circular issued by the Home Office in 1988[114] and by a statement of Lord Lane CJ in *Riaz and Burke*.[115] Yet savings in terms of cost and convenience may well be outbalanced by losses in terms of accuracy. It is not surprising that, when presented with a neat summary which they have no specific reason to believe to be inaccurate, lawyers for both sides are disinclined to compare it with the taped record. The defence lawyer, in particular, may assume that it will suffice to ask his client whether or not the summary is accurate. As Baldwin has pointed out, '[i]t is unrealistic to expect a suspect, perhaps weeks after the event, to be able to confirm that the summary is accurate, still less to be able to identify any omissions or to appreciate the legal significance of what was said at the time.'[116] He suggests that the only satisfactory solution is for lawyers to use the summary only after having played the tape itself.

The Code C Rights

Putting the various provisions about recording of interviews to one side, there are to be found in Code C—the Code concerned with detention, treatment, and questioning of persons by the police—a number of procedural rights which are granted to suspects. Some of them, for example the right to legal advice and the right not to be held incommunicado, also have a statutory aspect, i.e. they are granted by the Police and Criminal Evidence Act 1984. It is proposed to concentrate here upon those two rights, together with the right to be cautioned at appropriate points in the investigation and that not to be detained unlawfully. In most cases where reliance is placed upon a failure to accord the suspect a Code C right, the argument for exclusion will go to the unfairness element of the section 78 discretion. However, this will not necessarily be the case. For example, refusal to allow a mentally handicapped suspect to have legal advice may cause

[113] Research Study No 2, n. 112 above, 22.
[114] HO Circular 76/1988. See also later Circulars, 39/1991, 21/1992 and 26/1995.
[115] (1991) 94 Cr.App.R 339, at 342, quoted at n. 94 above.
[116] Research Study No 2, n. 112 above, 22, n. 23.

the court to have real doubts about the reliability of the confession made by that suspect.[117]

Right to Legal Advice

Principle (c) of the preamble to the Judges' Rules 1964 stated that 'every person at any stage of an investigation should be able to communicate and to consult privately with a solicitor'. Yet even in a case demonstrating the most egregious breach of that provision, the Court of Appeal refused to overturn the trial judge's decision to admit in evidence the confession in question.[118] The same court has taken an entirely different view of the right to legal advice granted by section 58 of the 1984 Act and by section 6 of Code C. In the first appeal case relating to this issue which was fully reported, *Samuel*, Hodgson J described the appellant as having been 'denied improperly one of the most important and fundamental rights of a citizen'.[119] The Court went on to quash the appellant's conviction for robbery, an offence in respect of which the trial judge had imposed a ten-year prison sentence. Hodgson J's description of the right has often been referred to in later cases, and without a hint of disapproval.[120] It follows that trial courts have been given every encouragement to treat as a matter of great seriousness a failure to accord that right to the suspect.

Varieties of Breach

It is important to realize that there exist a variety of possible ways in which the right to legal advice may be breached. Most of the early cases, and some of the more recent ones, involve an out-and-out refusal by the police to allow the suspect to consult a lawyer. Refusal may have been based upon a fear that the lawyer might, whether deliberately or inadvertently, alert other persons involved in the offence under investigation[121] or upon a more general police decision that the suspect should not be allowed contact with any outsider.[122] Sometimes the basis for police refusal is not made clear in the case.[123] Refusal to allow legal advice is to be distinguished from failure to allow it. Sometimes, it has been a misunderstanding or lack of communication between various officers

[117] See, e.g., *McGovern* (1990) 92 Cr.App.R 228, itself a case concerned with exclusion under s. 76(2)(b).

[118] *Lemsatef* [1977] 1 WLR 812. To similar effect is the first instance case, *Elliott* [1977] Crim.LR 551. It is to be noted that a rather more robust view was taken in three other first instance cases, namely *Allen* [1977] Crim.LR 163, *Trickett* [1981] Crim.LR 331, and *Marsh* [1985] Crim.LR 47.

[119] [1988] QB 615, at 630.

[120] See, e.g., *Gokan and Beycan* [1990] Crim.LR 185 (transcript through LEXIS); *McGovern* (1990) 92 Cr.App.R 228; *Chung* (1990) 92 Cr.App.R 314; *Oliphant* [1992] Crim.LR 40 (transcript through LEXIS).

[121] See, e.g., *Samuel* [1988] QB 615; *Alladice* (1988) 87 Cr.App.R 380; *Kerawalla* [1991] Crim.LR 451.

[122] See, e.g., *Parris* (1988) 89 Cr.App.R 68; *Francis and Findlay* [1992] Crim.LR 372.

[123] As in *Walsh* (1989) 91 Cr.App.R 161; *Dunford* (1990) 91 Cr.App.R 150; *McGovern* (1990) 92 Cr.App.R 228.

or an oversight by them which has resulted in no legal adviser being called in,[124] even though no officer ever took a conscious decision to bring about that result. Not surprisingly, courts take a dimmer view of an improper refusal than of a negligent failure.

Code C contains various provisions requiring the police to inform the suspect of his right of access to legal advice.[125] In a number of cases, there has been a failure to comply with one or more of those provisions.[126] In one of them, *Gokan and Beycan*, Bingham LJ rejected the argument that failure to inform a suspect of the right was less serious than a denial of that right.[127]

Problems have arisen where it has been the legal adviser who has attempted to make contact with the suspect, rather than the other way around. It is quite clear that an adviser has no right to see a potential client; the right is that of the suspect to take advice. However, it is not uncommon for relatives or friends of the suspect to contact a solicitor and to ask him, in turn, to contact the suspect. In consequence, the solicitor may then go to the police station or make a telephone call to it. In the former case, paragraph 6.15 of Code C proper and paragraph 3 of Annex B thereto make it clear that the police are under a duty to alert the suspect to the solicitor's arrival and to ask him whether or not he wishes to see that solicitor. This applies even where the suspect has previously declined legal advice. A breach of these provisions might well make it appropriate for the confession to be excluded.[128]

None of these provisions applies, on the face of it, to telephone calls from lawyers. That was exactly what had happened in *Chahal*,[129] yet the Court of Appeal envisaged the possibility of excluding a confession where the police had failed to alert the suspect to the call. On the particular facts, that court was clear that the accused really had not wanted to see a solicitor and that he was not a person of weak intellect or other disadvantage who might not fully appreciate the circumstances in which he found himself. It is hard to justify a distinction between personal calls and electronic ones, so that the *dicta* in *Chahal* may be expected to bear fruit in the future, either on the basis that there has been a breach of the spirit of Code C or that a court is quite at liberty to exclude even in the absence of any specific code breach. It may be added that it was probably just that kind of purposive view of the right to legal advice which led the Court of Appeal in *Mason*[130] to rule that the fact that lies had been told by the police to the accused's solicitor as well as to the accused himself, lies which, on any view,

[124] Examples are *Hughes* [1988] Crim.LR 519; *Chung* (1990) 92 Cr.App.R 314; *Anderson* [1993] Crim.LR 447.

[125] See, in particular, paras. 3.1, 3.2, 6.1, 6.3, 11.2, and 15.3.

[126] *Absolam* (1988) 88 Cr.App.R 332; *Gokan and Beycan* [1990] Crim.LR 185; *Kerawalla* [1991] Crim.LR 451; *Sanusi* [1992] Crim.LR 43; *Franklin*, unreported, 16 June 1994.

[127] [1990] Crim.LR 185 (transcript through LEXIS).

[128] As in *Franklin*, unreported, 16 June 1994 (transcript through LEXIS).

[129] [1992] Crim.LR 124 (transcript through LEXIS).

[130] [1988] 1 WLR 139, discussed in detail at Ch. 6, text at n. 105 above and this Chap., text to nn. 268–74 below.

tended to subvert the latter's right to legal advice, was something which the judge should have taken into account in deciding how to exercise his discretion.

Significant and Substantial Breaches

Though the notion that, where breaches can be described as 'significant and substantial', there is a presumption in favour of exclusion is, as we have seen,[131] applicable generally, it originated in cases where those breaches related to the right to legal advice. In the leading case of *Walsh*,[132] there were breaches of the recording provisions of Code C as well as those concerned with the right to legal advice, yet the Court of Appeal clearly seems to have had the latter at the front of its mind when it indicated that, *prima facie*, evidence acquired by such serious breaches should be excluded. In *Sanusi*,[133] the same court based its decision, to overturn that of the trial judge to allow the evidence in question to be given, firmly and clearly on the failure of the investigating officers—in that case, customs officers—properly to inform Sanusi of his right to legal advice. Woolf LJ, in *Oliphant*,[134] referred to the 'respectable history' of the 'significant and substantial' breach formula, 'in relation to challenges to the admissibility of evidence on the basis of non-access to legal advice'. He went on to say: '[i]t is quite clear that the failure of a defendant to receive legal advice when he is entitled to receive that legal advice amounts to a serious inroad on his rights.'[135]

In cases where the *Walsh* formula is satisfied, it seems that it will be only where the breaches have resulted in no actual detriment to the accused that the evidence is properly to be admitted.[136] We shall consider the special problem of causation in this context once we have dealt with the significance of the degree of culpability of the officers who have breached the suspect's right to legal advice.

Culpability and Bad Faith

To have one's rights transgressed deliberately or in bad faith may be thought to make the transgression materially worse. The cases acknowledge that that is so, but also that the breaches may be sufficiently significant and substantial even though neither of those factors is present.[137] The emphasis on their importance does vary from case to case. However, the following statement of Stuart-Smith LJ in *Anderson* is probably fairly representative:[138]

> [W]hat the judge had to look at . . . was the degree of culpability on the part of the police. Was this something which they did deliberately or in flagrant dereliction of their duty, such as deliberately or recklessly disregarding the appellant's rights? If that was not so, was the breach a significant and substantial one, having regard to the consequences for the appellant?

[131] See Ch. 6, text to nn. 122–6 above. [132] (1989) 91 Cr.App.R 161.
[133] [1992] Crim.LR 43 (transcript through LEXIS).
[134] [1992] Crim.LR 40 (transcript through LEXIS).
[135] See transcript.
[136] See *Dunford* (1990) 91 Cr.App.R 150; *Oliphant* [1992] Crim.LR 40.
[137] *Alladice* (1988) 87 Cr.App.R 380; *Walsh* (1989) 91 Cr.App.R 161; *Kerawalla* [1991] Crim.LR 451.
[138] [1993] Crim.LR 447 (transcript through LEXIS).

Causation

In all but one of the reported cases at appeal level in which an issue of causation has arisen, the question has been whether or not the accused would have been equally likely to confess had he been legally advised. The exception is *McGovern*.[139] Though the decision in that case was based upon section 76(2)(b) of the 1984 Act, the Court of Appeal did say that the confession must equally have been excluded under section 78. McGovern was a woman with an IQ of 73 and a mental age of 10. She was six months pregnant, had been vomiting in her cell before the interview took place, and had wept heavily during the interview. The court had no doubt that any solicitor would, in these circumstances, have stopped the police from putting questions to her, precisely because no reliance at all could properly be placed on any answers she might give.

In each of the other cases, whether the appeal court has overturned or upheld the judge, the argument has been about the likely effect of a legal adviser's presence upon the suspect's willingness to give incriminating answers.[140] In two, the Court of Appeal seems to have contented itself with saying that, in the final analysis, the suspect did genuinely consent to going ahead with or continuing the interview without the legal adviser being present.[141] This was reason enough not to overturn the judge's decision that the confession evidence should be admitted. It must be added that, in both cases, the argument that the suspect really did consent rather lacked conviction on the facts.

Alladice[142] is representative of the other type of case. The Court of Appeal has shown itself willing to take into account how robust a defender of his right to silence the given accused appears to have been. Alladice himself had said at trial, imprudently as it turned out, that he understood the caution and that he was well aware of his rights. He had, indeed, exercised his right to silence on several occasions during the course of the interview. The court concluded that the advice of a solicitor would have added nothing to the accused's own knowledge of his rights, so that no detriment had resulted from the absence of a solicitor. Commenting on the case of *Dunford*,[143] in which precisely the same kind of reasoning was employed, Hodgson has argued that it confuses knowledge that one is entitled to remain silent with knowing how to exercise that right and understanding its significance.[144] This point has considerable force. At all events, the decision went the other way in three cases. In two, a lawyer did eventually attend and, when he did attend, the suspect maintained silence.[145] In the third, the breach had been failure to tell the suspect about the right. Once that breach was remedied, he told the

[139] (1990) 92 Cr.App.R 228.

[140] The cases are *Samuel* [1988] QB 615; *Alladice* (1988) 87 Cr.App.R 380; *Hughes* [1988] Crim.LR 519; *Parris* (1988) 89 Cr.App.R 68; *Walsh* (1989) 91 Cr.App.R 161; *Dunford* (1990) 91 Cr.App.R 150; *Oliphant* [1992] Crim.LR 40; *Sanusi* [1992] Crim.LR 43.

[141] *Hughes* and *Oliphant*, both n. 140 above.

[142] (1988) 87 Cr.App.R 380.

[143] (1990) 91 Cr.App.R 150.

[144] [1992] Crim.LR 854, at 859.

[145] *Parris* (1988) 89 Cr.App.R 68; *Walsh* (1989) 91 Cr.App.R 161.

police that he would not answer any further questions until a lawyer did attend.[146]

There has been speculation about the possible effect of the changes made by sections 34, 36, and 37 of the Criminal Justice and Public Order Act 1994 to the pre-trial right of silence in the face of police questioning.[147] Though the effect of those sections is merely to attenuate the right, there is little doubt that, where they do apply, they render maintenance of silence a less eligible option. May it be said, therefore, that the importance to the suspect of having someone present to advise him about whether or not he should refuse to answer questions is in consequence reduced?[148] A counter-argument is that, whatever may be the effect on how often silence will be maintained, the decision whether or not to speak has been rendered even more important than it was before the legislative changes.[149] An unadvised and unwise refusal to answer may now be almost as detrimental to the suspect as making a confession. Furthermore, presence of a solicitor will continue to be crucial to the interests of someone who, like the accused in *McGovern*, may, without advice, confess quite unreliably,[150] while it is to be remembered that there is clear authority indicating that another responsibility of the solicitor is to seek to ensure the accuracy of the record.[151]

In principle, it is clear that a breach which has been remedied before the accused says anything incriminating will not be such as to result in exclusion.[152] So if a suspect has not been told of his right to legal advice before a first interview at which he said nothing to his detriment, but is then told about it before a second interview at which he does say something to his detriment, there will be no reason to exclude. However, the courts will be alert to ensure that the breach really was cured. Thus, in *Gokan and Beycan*,[153] the police question which was alleged to have put right the breach was 'Are you happy to be interviewed in the normal way we conduct these interviews without a solicitor, friend, or representative?' Particularly having regard to the fact that the suspect in question was a Turkish Cypriot who would not be alive to the shades of meaning of the English language, this question amounted to a discouragement to him from asking for a solicitor, because it suggested that asking for one was something out of step with ordinary practice.

Breath Test Cases

Paragraph 11.1A of Code C confirms the decision of the Divisional Court in *DPP* v. *Billington*[154] that post-arrest breath test procedures carried out under what is now section 7 of the Road Traffic Act 1988 do not amount to interviews for the purposes of that Code. The effect of this is that the police are perfectly at liberty to

[146] *Sanusi* [1992] Crim.LR 43 (transcript through LEXIS).
[147] The pre-trial right to silence is considered in detail in Ch. 9 of this work.
[148] See Fenwick [1995] Crim.LR 132. [149] See Roberts [1995] Crim.LR 483.
[150] A point made by Fenwick, n. 148 above, 135–6.
[151] *Parris* (1988) 89 Cr.App.R 68; *Dunford* (1990) 91 Cr.App.R 150.
[152] See, e.g. *Francis and Findlay* [1992] Crim.LR 372.
[153] [1990] Crim.LR 185 (transcript through LEXIS). [154] [1988] RTR 231.

carry out the procedures without first allowing the arrested suspect to take legal advice. However, it was held in *Hudson* v. *DPP*[155] that, where the police had misled the arrested suspect into believing that he *was* entitled to consult a solicitor before providing breath specimens for analysis, the section 78 discretion was available, in principle, to exclude evidence of that person's refusal to provide them.

Adequacy of Legal Advice

It is again appropriate to turn briefly to some empirical findings, this time in relation to the nature and quality of the legal advice made available to suspects at police stations. Plainly, if the right to legal advice is to be described as fundamental, it is necessary that a high level of professional skill be found in those who provide it.

A number of research surveys have been carried out to discover in what percentage of cases the legal advice is given by fully-qualified solicitors and in what percentage by others. Though the findings vary somewhat, the conclusion of Bridges and Hodgson that, on balance, probably between two-fifths and one-half of all attendances at police stations are by personnel who are not fully qualified[156] seems to be representative.[157] Some of these non-solicitor personnel will be persons training to become solicitors, while some will be ex-police officers employed by firms of solicitors. These findings are hardly surprising in view of the unattractiveness of advisory work at police stations in both financial and other terms. During the daytime, solicitors are likely to be engaged in more lucrative work, while at night they will not be in the least keen to go out. It is noteworthy that the suspect who asks for a duty solicitor is more likely actually to get a qualified adviser.

One might suppose that a trainee's lack of experience would place him very much at a disadvantage as regards the police, as well as entailing him having insufficient professional knowledge to be able to give the best advice. Equally, it might be expected that many ex-police officers would not easily be able to turn themselves, so to speak, from gamekeeper to poacher. In fact, the research evidence uniformly supports the proposition that the standard of advice given is, in general terms, low. This is not the place to deal in any detail with the various findings supporting this conclusion, but a few may be mentioned. Consultations before the police interview tend to be brief; McConville and Hodgson found that

155 [1992] RTR 27.

156 [1995] Crim.LR 101, at 104.

157 The leading surveys are Sanders *et al.*, *Advice and Assistance at Police Stations and the 24 Hour Duty Solicitor Scheme*, Lord Chancellor's Department, November 1989; Brown *et al.*, *Changing the Code: Police Detention under the Revised P.A.C.E. Codes of Practice*, Home Office Research Study No 129, 1992; Baldwin, *The Role of Legal Representatives at the Police Station*, Research Study No 3 for the Royal Commission on Criminal Justice, 1992; McConville and Hodgson, *Custodial Legal Advice and the Right to Silence*, Research Study No 16 for the Royal Commission, 1993. See also Dixon *et al.* (1990) 1 *Policing and Society* 123; McConville *et al.*, *Standing Accused: The Organisation and Practices of Criminal Defence Lawyers in Britain* (1994). For a much more exhaustive survey of the empirical studies about the nature and quality of legal advice than is offered here, see Wolchover and Heaton-Armstrong, n. 5 above, paras. 2–341 to 2–386.

in 50 per cent of cases the consultation took ten minutes or less and that there were even some cases where there was no consultation at all.[158] Their admittedly impressionistic view was that in only about 27 per cent of cases did the adviser have a *thorough* knowledge of the case pre-interview. In a significant number of cases, the adviser did not attend the interview itself.[159] Even when the adviser does attend, he will, in a substantial majority of cases, be merely a passive observer who does not interrupt at all the flow of questions.[160] Indeed, Baldwin found that it was almost as likely that the adviser who did interrupt would do so as a third interrogator as that the interruption would be to support the suspect's interests.[161] Overall, the evidence bears out Baldwin's own conclusion that:[162]

> [w]hile it would not be accurate to say that most lawyers describe their role as being to facilitate police questioning, they certainly do not see it in the opposite terms. Most lawyers view themselves more as neutral referees, ready to intervene without hesitation if questioning gets out of hand, rather than assuming an adversary stance from the outset.

Steps were taken in the mid-1990s to attempt to remedy the situation just described. The Royal Commission on Criminal Justice was troubled by the findings of its own commissioned research, which it described as 'disturbing'.[163] Five of its own recommendations were concerned with the quality of advice.[164] One of them, Recommendation 68, said, '[i]n the longer term, the training, education, supervision and monitoring of all legal advisers who operate at police stations should be thoroughly reviewed.' Two steps have already been taken in this respect. Before the Royal Commission reported, the requirement that legal advisers undertaking this kind of work should be formally accredited applied only to those who participated in the duty solicitor scheme. In consequence of action taken jointly by the Law Society and the Legal Aid Board in 1994, there is now an accreditation system applicable outside that scheme, though one which, rather strangely, does not extend to qualified or trainee solicitors. The other step, taken by the Law Society alone, was the publication of a police station 'skills' package. It remains to be seen, of course, what difference, if any, these, and any other steps which may be taken, will have upon the quality of advice to suspects.[165]

Right Not to be Held Incommunicado

Though section 5 of Code C is headed 'Right not to be held incommunicado', the right actually granted by both that section and section 56(1) of the 1984 Act itself

158 N. 157 above, 53–4.

159 *Ibid*. 65.

160 Brown *et al.*, n. 157 above, 87, suggest that this may happen in 43% of cases.

161 N. 157 above, 28.

162 *Ibid*. 49–50. Not everyone accepts that the assumption of an adversarial role by the adviser from the outset is in the suspect's best interests—see Roberts [1993] Crim.LR 368. But cf. Baldwin [1993] Crim.LR 371.

163 See their *Report*, July 1993, ch. 3, para. 59.

164 Recommendations 65–69, at 193–4.

165 For a candid assessment of both the extension of the accreditation system and of the 'skills' package (Shepherd, *Becoming Skilled: A Resource Book* (1994)) see Bridges and Hodgson [1995] Crim.LR 102, at 106–12.

is the rather narrower one of an arrested person held in custody to have someone named by him told of the fact of his arrest and where he is being detained.[166] Viewed as such, the right is wholly separate from that to legal advice. However, in a number of the reported cases at appeal level, the police have made a decision to hold a suspect incommunicado, that is not to allow him to speak to or otherwise contact any outsider.[167] Of course, the consequence of any such decision will be to deny the suspect the opportunity of taking legal advice, as well as that of having a person notified of his arrest and whereabouts. In three of the cases in question,[168] it was denial of legal advice which was the sole matter of complaint, so nothing of interest was said about the section 56(1) right. In the fourth,[169] the request had been both to see a named solicitor and to have a named friend informed. Neither request was met. It is not clear whether counsel relied, at the appeal stage, upon both refusals as breaches, or upon only the refusal to allow him to see the solicitor. In any event, the breach, if indeed it was a breach, of section 56(1) played no part in the Court of Appeal's reasoning.

The only reported case which involved a police decision to deny a suspect the opportunity to make contact with a named person but not to deny him access to legal advice would seem to be *Chahal*.[170] The accused had asked for his son to be informed of his detention, but delay had been authorized in accordance with what was then, and still is, paragraph 1 of Annex B to Code C. It does not seem to have been argued that the delay was improper. However, when the embargo on notification was later lifted, Chahal was not told of that decision. Consequently, it must have been the case that what was then paragraph 3 of Annex B (now paragraph 4) was not complied with. It required (and paragraph 4 still does require) the suspect to be told when the grounds for delay have ceased to apply and for him then to be asked, as soon as practicable, whether or not he would like a named person to be notified of his whereabouts. Nonetheless, whether because the police did eventually notify the son or because the family had, in some other way, got to know about Chahal's detention, family members did take steps to have a solicitor contact him. The core of the appeal concerned the failure of the police to inform Chahal that a solicitor had been trying to reach him. It was dismissed on the basis that he had shown, throughout the period of his detention, that he did not want to see a solicitor and that he was someone of sufficient maturity and experience to be able to make that decision for himself. Thus, even in *Chahal*, the issue came down to the precise nature of the suspect's right to legal advice, and the significance of the breach of paragraph 3 of Annex B was neither argued nor considered.

It may be concluded that the right in question cannot, in any way, be properly considered 'fundamental'. One may speculate that breach of the right itself, or of

[166] This right, like the right to legal advice, is backed up by various duties to inform the suspect of its existence and applicability, and to record formally decisions made about it—see, in particular, Code C, paras. 3.1(i) and 5.8 and Annex B to Code C, para. 4.

[167] See, e.g., *Parris* (1988) 89 Cr.App.R 68; *Dunford* (1990) 91 Cr.App.R 150; *Chung* (1990) 92 Cr.App.R 314; *Francis and Findlay* [1992] Crim.LR 372.

[168] *Parris, Dunford*, and *Francis and Findlay*, all n. 167 above.

[169] *Chung*, n. 167 above.

[170] [1992] Crim.LR 124 (transcript through LEXIS).

the various rights to be given information and have decisions recorded which back up the main right, is not likely often to result in exclusion of a confession under the section 78(1) discretion. It may be difficult for the accused to get on its feet an argument that breach led him to confess or to confess unreliably. Yet one can certainly not rule out that possibility. For example, a parent concerned that a child should know about his or her whereabouts might be able to show that the breach did have an effect in one way or the other.

Other Rights

This Chapter is not intended to provide an encyclopædic coverage of the many other rights granted to suspects by the 1984 Act and/or Code C. However, we shall briefly consider two rights which were of some importance as regards exercise of the discretion at common law, before the 1984 Act came into effect.

The Right to be Cautioned

The Judges' Rules 1964 were principally concerned with the requirement that a suspect be informed about his right to silence before some further step could be taken by the police. There are now three major points at which, according to Code C, a person must be cautioned. A person who has not been cautioned before arrest must be cautioned on arrest.[171] A person whom there are grounds to suspect of committing an offence must be cautioned before any questions are put to him regarding his involvement or suspected involvement in that offence, as long as his answers or silence in response may be given in evidence in a prosecution.[172] A detained person must be cautioned again when he is charged or informed that he may be prosecuted.[173]

There is one, rather surprising, case in which it was held that a failure to caution a suspect before interviewing him was a breach properly to be taken into account in deciding whether or not to exclude a confession under section 76(2)(b) of the 1984 Act.[174] As one commentator has observed, it would seem that failure to caution is somewhat unlikely to give rise to a confession being unreliable. Rather, the caution served, at least before enactment of sections 34, 36 and 37 of the Criminal Justice and Public Order Act 1994, to remind the suspect of his right not to speak at all.[175]

The argument that admission of evidence resulting from a failure to caution would have an adverse effect on the fairness of proceedings has been raised in sev-

[171] See para. 10.3. [172] See para. 10.1.

[173] See para. 16.2. There are several other subsidiary points for caution. So where there is a break in questioning, the officer must ensure, before it re-starts, that the suspect is aware that he remains under caution—see para. 10.5. Where, after charge, the police wish to put further questions of the limited kind permitted by para. 16.5 of Code C, that same para. requires them to administer the appropriate caution before doing so. Para. 10.5B deals with the special caution to be administered to a suspect if adverse inferences are to be capable of being drawn under ss. 36 and 37 of the Criminal Justice and Public Order Act 1994.

[174] *Doolan* [1988] Crim.LR 747. [175] Birch [1988] Crim.LR 748.

eral cases at appeal level, but has not yet persuaded an appeal court to overturn a trial court decision not to exclude. In two cases concerned with the need to caution before questioning, the Court of Appeal concluded that, on the facts, the duty to caution had not arisen at the relevant time.[176] In two other cases, that court held that any breach of the duty to caution had not resulted in any prejudice to the accused. Thus, in *Oni*,[177] the accused had been cautioned about a suspected offence of possession of a cannabis cigarette. Then, only a few minutes later, the police found a very large quantity of heroin and some money in a bag which had been in Oni's possession. Even though that discovery clearly gave them reasonable grounds for suspecting him of the offence of possession of a Class A drug with intent to supply, rather than merely possession *simpliciter* of a Class B drug, no further caution was administered. The Court of Appeal thought 'unrealistic' the suggestion that there had been a breach, but that, even if there had been one, there was no evidence of prejudice to Oni, who, after all, had very recently been cautioned about the lesser offence.[178]

In *Pall*, the Court of Appeal ventured the view that 'the absence of a caution in most circumstances is bound to be significant'.[179] This is of some importance, for it will be recalled that one ingredient of the analysis in section 78 cases is whether or not the breach was 'significant and substantial'.[180] Absent the special circumstance in which the suspect has already (and very recently) been cautioned in respect of some other offence, it is hard to see how a failure to caution at all, as opposed to some imprecision in the caution actually given, could be other than a substantial breach. However, it remains to be seen whether or not, now that the right to silence in the police station has been attenuated by sections 34, 36, and 37 of the Criminal Justice and Public Order Act 1994, failure to caution at some relevant point will still be regarded as significant. The issue is really the one which we have already seen arises with respect to the right to legal advice.[181] Though the right to silence is attenuated, the importance of the decision whether or not to speak is greater than ever, precisely because of the adverse inferences which are capable of being drawn from silence.

The Right Not to be Detained Unlawfully

Before the 1984 Act and Code C became law, the judges had attributed considerable significance to the notion that, in the words of section 43(4) of the Magistrates' Courts Act 1980, a person taken into custody must be brought before a magistrates' court 'as soon as practicable'.[182] The changes effected in 1984 resulted in this rule applying only to persons who have been *charged* and are held

[176] *Purcell* [1992] Crim.LR 806; *Shah* [1994] Crim.LR 125.

[177] [1992] Crim.LR 183 (transcript through LEXIS).

[178] A similar case is *Pall* (1992) 156 JPR 424. [179] *Ibid*. 431 (*per* Glidewell LJ).

[180] See *Walsh* (1989) 91 Cr.App.R 161, at 163, considered at Ch. 6, text to nn. 124–6 above.

[181] See text to nn. 147–51 above.

[182] Good examples are *Hudson* (1980) 72 Cr.App.R 163; *Re Sherman and Apps* (1980) 72 Cr.App.R 266.

in detention. The *uncharged* suspect's position is now governed by section 37 and sections 39 to 45 of the 1984 Act. Though this is not the place for an extended consideration of those sections, their effect is that, if magistrates are willing to issue a warrant of further detention and then to extend it, an arrested person may lawfully be kept in custody without charge for up to ninety-six hours. The police themselves may keep such a person in custody, without reference to the magistrates, for no more than thirty-six hours.

There appears to be only one reported case at appeal level concerned with discretion to exclude evidence obtained while the police were (unlawfully) detaining the uncharged suspect beyond a relevant period, as defined by those sections of the 1984 Act. In that case, *Taylor*,[183] the evidence which the defence had sought to have excluded was evidence that the accused had been identified by the complainant as her assailant at a confrontation at Wembley Police Station. The Court of Appeal held that, even assuming that the keeping of Taylor in custody to attend that confrontation had been unlawful under section 42(4) of the 1984 Act because it had begun after the end of a maximum permitted period of detention, there had been no resulting unfairness. The reason for exceeding the period in question was that the police had, more than once, attempted without success to arrange an identification parade. This purpose had been a laudable one, and the confrontation evidence finally acquired resulted from an entirely fairly conducted procedure.[184] A more promising defence argument that unlawful detention had prejudiced the accused might be mounted where detention has been deliberately continued well beyond legal limits in order to prise a confession from the accused. Still, in such circumstances, the argument might perhaps be phrased in terms of oppression, rather than unfairness.

A more restrictive and interventionist approach has been taken by the Court of Appeal in the rather different situation of unlawful detention which arises where the police have delayed taking the accused to the police station with due despatch. Thus, section 30(1) of the 1984 Act provides for a general duty to take an arrested person, as soon as practicable after arrest, to a police station. Many of the suspect's protections are predicated upon arrival at the station, so that the police might seek to get around relevant code provisions by keeping him away therefrom. In *Khan*,[185] the Court of Appeal did not overturn the judge on the particular facts, but it did say that the police must not seek to use periods of detention outside the station which were themselves permissible for some other purpose—there the conducting of a search—in order to circumvent code provisions by interviewing the suspect. If they did so use them, an exercise of the unfairness discretion in favour of exclusion would be appropriate. In *Raphaie*,[186]

[183] [1991] Crim.LR 541 (transcript through LEXIS).

[184] See also *Hansen*, unreported, 5 July 1990, stating that, while breaches of ss. 40 and 42 must never be countenanced, the trial judge had been right to conclude that no prejudice had flowed from breach in that case.

[185] [1993] Crim.LR 54 (transcript through LEXIS). See also *Keane* [1992] Crim.LR 306.

[186] [1996] Crim.LR 812.

the same court applied the *dicta* in *Khan* and overturned the trial judge's exercise of his discretion because there had been precisely that kind of abuse.

Identification Procedures

Because of the known infirmities of eye-witness identification evidence, the law has developed a set of rules for the guidance of trial courts in cases where such evidence is disputed.[187] Whether or not direct, informal evidence is available, the investigating authority, usually the police, may well wish to carry out some formal, pre-trial, identification procedure. Furthermore, the suspect or accused may himself wish one to be carried out, so that it may be very much in the public interest that it be carried out. The *Code of Practice for the Identification of Persons by Police Officers* (Code D) lays down rules governing these procedures. Where a pre-trial identification has been carried out in breach of the rules in question, the danger which may well arise will be that the resulting evidence is unreliable. Hence, the argument for exclusion of that evidence under section 78(1) (or, for that matter, section 82(3)) will be that it cannot safely be left to the trier of fact to assess its weight. However, sometimes it will be not that a procedure has been carried out improperly which is relied upon, but that it was not carried out at all, though it should have been. Where the accused has been denied the opportunity of taking part in an identification parade or other identification procedure, it may be argued that the weight of some other, less satisfactory, identification evidence is adversely affected,[188] or, more strongly, that it should be excluded.[189] A third possibility is that, even though the Code is, for some reason, inapplicable or, though applicable, has not been breached, it may still be the case that the evidence acquired by the police is so unreliable that it ought to be excluded.

Though these various aspects of the discretion to exclude in the present context will be the principal focus of this section, it will be necessary to consider some of the specific provisions of Code D in a little detail in order to inform the discussion.

We will first consider the position where the police have failed to carry out some identification procedure when, in the view of the court, it ought to have been carried out.

Failure to Carry Out an Identification Procedure

The Hierarchy of Procedures

Code D distinguishes between two situations in which the need for some pre-trial identification process may be present. In a case where either the identity of the

[187] The leading case is *Turnbull* [1977] QB 224.

[188] *Graham* [1994] Crim.LR 212.

[189] *Nagah* (1990) 92 Cr.App.R 344.

suspect is not known to the police or, if it is known, the suspect is unavailable to take part in any formal identification procedure, the police may show to the potential identifying witness photographs, photofits, identikits, or similar pictures.[190] Of course, none of these methods requires the co-operation or even presence of a suspect. However, where there is a suspect who is both known to the police and available to them, none of those methods may be used. Rather, the police, if they are to seek a formal identification, must have recourse to one of four alternative procedures, the identification parade, the group identification, the video-film identification, or the confrontation.

Paragraph 2 of Code D establishes a hierarchy as between the four alternative procedures. Starting at the bottom, resort may be had to a confrontation between suspect and witness only if no other procedure is practicable.[191] The other three procedures are clearly ranked, as a matter of preference, in the descending order—identification parade, group identification, and video-film identification. However, this is no more than a matter of preference, so that the police are left with a considerable degree of discretion as to which to use in the particular case.[192] More specifically, there is no requirement that a procedure higher up this hierarchy of three must be impracticable before one further down may be used.

The Relevance of a Dispute about Identification

Paragraph 2.1 of Code D lays down that, where the suspect's identity is known and he is available, the police are bound, in a case involving 'disputed identification evidence', to use one or other of the four formal identification procedures to which reference has just been made. Furthermore, according to paragraph 2.3: '[w]henever a suspect disputes an identification, an identification parade shall be held if the suspect consents unless paragraphs 2.4 or 2.7 or 2.10 apply [*sic*]. A parade may also be held if the officer in charge of the investigation considers that it would be useful and the suspect consents.' Paragraph 2.4 exempts the police from the duty laid down by paragraph 2.3 where it would be impracticable to assemble sufficient people resembling the suspect to make a parade fair. Paragraph 2.7, *inter alia*, grants the police discretion to hold a group identification where considered to be more satisfactory than a parade, while paragraph 2.10 grants discretion to conduct a video-film identification where the police consider it the most satisfactory course of action. The overall effect would seem to be that, subject to the practicability point in paragraph 2.4, there is a duty to resort to one or other of the three preferred procedures whenever there is a dispute about identification and the suspect consents, for the police could hardly argue that they were entitled to prefer a group or video-film identification to a parade, yet then not to go on to conduct the one or the other.

[190] See para. 2.18 and Note for Guidance 2E. See also *Kitchen* [1994] Crim.LR 684.
[191] See para. 2.13.
[192] See paras. 2.3, 2.7, and 2.10.

It is clearly of some importance, then, so far as the various duties imposed by paragraph 2 are concerned, whether or not there is a dispute about an identification. Both *Rutherford and Palmer* and *Montgomery*[193] were concerned with the phrase 'disputed identification evidence', which, in the issue of Code D in force before April 1995, was to be found in both paragraph 2.1 and paragraph 2.3, but which, in the present issue, is to be found only in paragraph 2.1. In the former case, it was held that the duty applied even where an identification dispute was not already in existence, as long as one might reasonably be anticipated, as, for example, where a witness had indicated that he or she would be able to identify the offender or there was a reasonable prospect of him or her doing so. According to *Montgomery*, it is otherwise where there is no reasonable possibility that the witness in question will be able to make an identification. Though, as we have seen, paragraph 2.3 now employs the phrase '[w]henever a suspect disputes an identification', it seems reasonable to suppose that these cases will be taken to state good law here too. Of course, the police remain at liberty to hold a parade or use one of the other formal procedures, where they consider it useful to do so, even in a case where there is no dispute and none is anticipated.

Powell v. *DPP*[194] establishes that the police cannot avoid compliance with the duties laid down in paragraph 2 on the basis that the other evidence in the case points so unequivocally to the accused's guilt that there can be no 'real' dispute about the identification evidence, as, for example, where the accused has confessed his guilt.

Effects of Breach

The issue of Code D in force before April 1995 placed a duty upon the police in certain circumstances to hold a parade. One of the applicable circumstances was that the suspect had asked that a parade be held.[195] The point or purpose of this duty seems clear enough, and was described very well by Hutchison J in *Conway*, as follows:[196]

> the failure to accede to the defendant's request for an identification parade effectively deprived him of the opportunity of properly putting to the test the crucial issue of whether or not witnesses knew him. Had they failed at such a parade to identify him, the case would inevitably have collapsed. Conversely, had they identified him, their evidence that he was the assailant would have been immensely strengthened.

In that case, the police had twice been asked by the defence to hold a parade, yet had not done so, the result being that the only evidence available upon the crucial

[193] See (1993) 98 Cr.App.R 191 and [1996] Crim.LR 507, respectively. See also *Hope, Limburn and Bleasdale* [1994] Crim.LR 118.

[194] [1992] RTR 270.

[195] The spirit of that duty, as opposed to its letter, was preserved by the Court of Appeal in *Graham* [1994] Crim.LR 212. It decided that, where the only reason that the suspect had failed to request a parade was his understanding from the police that they had, for themselves, decided to hold one anyway, they were indeed obliged to do so.

[196] (1990) 91 Cr.App.R 143, at 147. See also *Brown* [1991] Crim.LR 368 (transcript through LEXIS); *Graham* [1994] Crim.LR 212; *Macmath* [1997] Crim.LR 586.

issue of identification was some unsatisfactory eye-witness evidence and two dock identifications. The Court of Appeal was firmly of the view that the defence case had been substantially prejudiced by the failure to hold a parade, so that either the trial judge should have stopped the case or he should have directed the jury to take the code breach into account, as well as its consequences, in deciding whether or not the prosecution had proved its case.

No question arose in *Conway* of *excluding* any of the weak identification evidence. However, it has now become clear that, in some cases, it will be right for the trial judge to exclude such evidence because the police have failed in their duty to hold an identification parade. The leading cases are *Nagah* and *Johnson*.[197]

In *Nagah*,[198] the suspect was asked if he would stand on a parade and said that he would. Yet no parade was held, the police preferring to release him from custody in the hope that the complainant would identify him in the street as he left the police station. The Court of Appeal held that the trial judge should have excluded evidence of the resulting (positive) street identification. Once the police had concluded that a parade would be useful, as they clearly had, they should not resort to a far less reliable procedure. In effect, the court deemed the police to be under a duty to hold a parade, even though the suspect had not requested one. It should be added that the court also attributed considerable significance to the fact that the police had deliberately flouted the Code.[199]

In *Johnson*,[200] rather than inviting the arrested suspect to stand on a parade, the police asked an eye-witness if a woman shown on a film from a security camera which had been operating near the scene at about the time of the offence was the offender. The eye-witness said that she was, and other evidence established that the person on the film was the accused. The police gave as their reason for using such an unsatisfactory procedure that they had not believed that the accused would be prepared to stand on a parade, given that she had refused to be interviewed by them. In the Court of Appeal's view, that was not a good reason; the police should have asked. Because of the unfairness to the accused which would flow from admitting the weak evidence it ought to have been excluded, and the trial judge's decision not to exclude it was overturned.

Though both *Nagah* and *Johnson* concerned failure to hold or to seek to hold a parade, it is to be remembered that the issue of Code D which is now in force establishes a hierarchy of three procedures, all of which are to be preferred to the kind of confrontation carried out in each of those cases. Thus, in *Johnson* itself, even if the accused *had* refused to stand on a parade, either the group identification or the video-film identification procedure, neither of which requires consent, could have been used.[201] It ought to follow that the section 78(1) discretion to

[197] (1990) 92 Cr.App.R 344 and [1996] Crim.LR 504, respectively. See also *Gaynor* [1988] Crim.LR 242; *Britton and Richards* [1989] Crim.LR 144; *Ladlow et al.* [1989] Crim.LR 219; *Brown* [1991] Crim.LR 368; *Allen* [1995] Crim.LR 643.

[198] (1990) 92 Cr.App.R 344. See also *Penny* (1991) 94 Cr.App.R 345.

[199] See text to nn. 213–17 below.

[200] [1996] Crim.LR 504.

[201] As Birch points out—see, *ibid*. 507. It is to be noted that the viewing of the security film by the

exclude weak identification evidence should be available whenever one or other of the preferred procedures has not been used, especially where the police have demonstrated their own belief in the value of one or other of them, whether by asking for the suspect's consent or otherwise. Even though a personal right in the suspect can no longer be supported, there is a clear public interest in the police using the best procedure available, and this interest, as Hutchison J pointed out in *Conway*,[202] is no less that the innocent suspect should not be identified than that the guilty one should.

It should be added that the theory behind exclusion in this context has not been explained in the cases. If one has regard to the interests of the accused, it would seem that one cannot be thinking simply in terms of evidence which is likely to have more prejudicial effect than probative value at trial. The evidence is not rendered less probative or more prejudicial by the fact that better evidence ought to have been acquired. Thus, some broader notion of fairness must be in question. Where the suspect has been denied his right to a parade, one might well say that the unfairness consists in his being deprived of the opportunity of securing evidence casting doubt on the accuracy of the evidence actually available. In a broad sense, admission of that evidence would tend to render the proceedings unfair. Of course, the suspect retains the *interest* in securing contrary evidence, even though he no longer enjoys the *right* to try to secure it. That may suffice, yet one cannot help thinking that uppermost in the judicial mind is the general public interest in the police employing the best identification procedure reasonably available to them. Their failure to employ it tempts the court to use the discretion for disciplinary purposes, in order to encourage the police to obtain the most reliable evidence possible in future cases. It has been suggested, earlier in this work, that there are other situations in which courts will countenance exercise of the section 78(1) discretion to that purpose.[203]

Impracticability

Reference has already been made, more than once, to the issue of whether or not it is practicable to carry out some given identification procedure. Thus a parade need not be held where the police consider that it would not be practicable to assemble sufficient people resembling the suspect to make the parade fair.[204] Next, paragraph 2.6 provides: '[i]f a suspect refuses or, having agreed, fails to attend an identification parade or the holding of a parade is impracticable, arrangements must if practicable be made to allow the witnesses an opportunity of seeing him in a group identification, a video identification, or a confrontation'. Thirdly, paragraph 2.13 states that a confrontation may not take place unless none of the other procedures is practicable. Other examples could be given of use of practicability as a criterion.

eye-witness did not constitute a video-film identification. That procedure entails the witness being shown film of other persons of similar appearance carrying out the same activity as the suspect.

[202] See text to n. 96 above.

[203] See Ch. 6, text to nn. 109–11 and this Ch., text to nn. 42–7 above.

[204] See para. 2.4.

Authorities under the old Code D concerned with the practicability of holding a parade established that the courts should not simply accept a police officer's statement that to hold one was impracticable. Rather, they should ensure that the officer is present in court so that his opinion can be tested, bearing in mind that the onus lies with the prosecution to prove impracticability.[205] For these purposes, impracticability is not to be equated with inconvenience. Thus, where the police had decided in a juvenile case that it was impracticable to hold a parade, partly on the basis that it was impossible to find enough juveniles for a parade during school holidays, the Divisional Court held that this was not an appropriate consideration, though it upheld the decision of the magistrates on other grounds.[206] In doing so, the court considered that an officer's opinion about practicability could be overturned only on the basis that it was perverse, or involved the application of an inflexible policy, or was one not open to the officer on the facts, or was, in some other way, unreasonable according to the ordinary canons of the *Wednesbury* doctrine.[207] Presumably, these authorities will be applied, *mutatis mutandis*, in other situations where the police invoke impracticability.

Contamination of Identification Procedures

At least as important a problem as the failure of the police to carry out appropriate identification procedures is their failure to carry them out properly. Here the basis for exclusion under section 78(1) is more straightforward. Code D contains five annexes governing the various procedures which may be employed. Between them, they regulate the process of formal pre-trial identification in considerable detail. Their purpose is both to ensure that any identification made can be relied upon and that the suspect can be confident that everything really has been carried out in a fair manner. If the evidence is clearly unreliable, then section 78(1) applies in its unreliability mode, while, if there are legitimate suspicions about fairness of procedures, it is not difficult to see that admission of the evidence would compromise the fairness of the proceedings more generally.

The danger of a witness's participation in a procedure being contaminated by information being passed to him by an officer involved in the case or by some other witness, whether deliberately or inadvertently, is a particular concern. So, for example, the officer responsible for the arrangements for and conduct of the parades, group identifications, and video-film identifications (the 'identification officer') must, according to the various applicable annexes to Code D, ensure that, before taking part, witnesses do not communicate with each other about the case or overhear any witness who has already taken part.[208] In addition, Code D

[205] *Penny* (1991) 94 Cr.App.R 345.

[206] *Tomkinson* v. *DPP* [1995] Crim.LR 60 (transcript through LEXIS).

[207] See *Associated Provincial Picture Houses Ltd* v. *Wednesbury Corporation* [1948] 1 KB 223. The applicability of that test to discretionary decisions about exclusion generally is considered in Ch. 6, text to nn. 77–88 above. See also *Gaynor* [1988] Crim.LR 242.

[208] See Annex A, para. 12; Annex B, para. 9; Annex E, para. 17.

itself contains an important provision which is applicable no less to confrontation than to the other three kinds of procedure. According to paragraph 2.2, the identification officer must be someone not involved with the investigation, and any officer who is so involved may take no part in any of those procedures.

Though here, as elsewhere when the section 78(1) discretion is relied upon, the courts have made the point that exclusion is not the automatic result of breach, even substantial breach,[209] breach of the contamination rules is very likely appropriately to lead to exclusion. For example, in *Gall*,[210] an investigating officer had brought the witness to the parade, had then looked into the room where it was being held, had spoken to the identification officer, and had finally conducted the witness into the room. At a first trial, the judge had excluded the witness's positive identification of the accused. At a second, a different judge had allowed it to be given in evidence, essentially because he did not think that the investigating officer could be said to have taken any part in the arrangements for or conduct of the parade. The Court of Appeal thought that he had indeed taken a part in its conduct and, exercising the judge's discretion for him, held that the evidence should have been excluded, on the basis that the accused would legitimately feel considerable suspicion about what had taken place.

A rather different view was taken in *Ryan*,[211] a case which was concerned with a confrontation between witness and suspect. Though more than one investigating officer had been involved in the confrontation, there was evidence that the suspect's solicitor had satisfied himself that the officer who had brought the witness to the confrontation had not spoken to him and evidence that the solicitor had been in a position to overhear anything said to that witness by the other officers. Therefore, the rather serious breaches had not *in fact* resulted in prejudice or unfairness to Ryan.[212]

This clash in the authorities, between the view that what matters is whether or not there has been actual contamination and the view that the appearance of unfairness suffices, has not been resolved in any later case.

Deliberate and Flagrant Breaches: Bad Faith

Whether the accused argues that a particular item of identification evidence comprehended by the Code should be excluded because prescribed procedures have not been carried out properly or that identification evidence of some kind or other should be excluded because the police failed to invoke one or other of the Code procedures when they ought to have done so, an important element in the case for exclusion has often been that the breach or breaches were deliberate or flagrant, or in bad faith.

[209] See, e.g., *Ryan* [1992] Crim.LR 187.
[210] (1989) 90 Cr.App.R 64. See also *Johnson* [1996] Crim.LR 504.
[211] [1992] Crim.LR 187 (transcript through LEXIS).
[212] A similar view seems to have been taken in *Quinn* [1995] 1 Cr.App.R 480 and *Khan* [1997] Crim.LR 584.

The leading case on this issue is *Nagah*,[213] a case to which reference was made earlier in this section. There, the police, despite having obtained Nagah's consent to take part in a parade, had deliberately engineered a rather unsatisfactory street identification by releasing Nagah from the police station at an appropriate moment so that he would be seen by the complainant. It was clearly an important element in the Court of Appeal's decision to overturn the judge's ruling allowing the prosecution to adduce evidence of the relevant street identification that there had been what it described as 'a complete flouting of the Code' by the police.[214] A case to similar effect with regard to contamination of procedures carried out by the police is *Finley*, where so many breaches had been committed by the police that the very fact of their number led the Court of Appeal to conclude that it was 'not easy to believe [that there had been] mere inefficiency rather than deliberate flouting of the Code'.[215] In several other cases, the same court has stressed, when deciding to uphold a judge's decision not to exclude evidence, that given code breaches did not involve bad faith or improper conduct on the part of the police.[216] For example, in *Tiplady*[217] it was held that the fact that the conduct of trading standards officers, which was in gross breach of Code D, had been carried out in good-faith ignorance of the applicability of that Code, was a relevant factor favouring admission of the evidence.

It bears repeating that, having regard to the fact that the fundamental or central reason for exercising the discretion in favour of exclusion in such cases may be supposed to be the need to ensure that the identification evidence presented to a court is sufficiently reliable for the trier of fact to consider it, there is probably an element of disciplinary purpose in the cases which stress the significance of the presence of flagrancy or bad faith. The courts will not tolerate deliberate evasion of procedures and safeguards designed to ensure a flow of reliable identification evidence to them.

Significance of the Suspect's Consent

There are a number of points in Code D where it is expressly required that some procedure or element thereof shall not be carried out without the suspect's consent. Where consent is thus required, clearly a failure to obtain it will amount to breach of the provision in question. However, a factor which has emerged in some of the cases is that the suspect and/or his lawyer have/has consented to some irregularity which took place during the process. Thus, in *Penny*,[218] it had been argued that the police ought to have held a parade, rather than organizing, as they had, a street identification. The Court of Appeal held that, even assuming that the Code had been breached in this way, it was of con-

[213] (1990) 92 Cr.App.R 344. [214] *Ibid*. 348.

[215] See [1993] Crim.LR 50 (transcript through LEXIS).

[216] *Penny* (1991) 94 Cr.App.R 345; *Rutherford and Palmer* (1993) 98 Cr.App.R 191; *Knowles* [1994] Crim.LR 217.

[217] (1995) 159 JPR 548. [218] (1991) 94 Cr.App.R 345.

siderable importance that both the accused and his solicitor had agreed that the former should take part in the street identification. Clearly, then, consent of this kind may be a factor telling against exclusion of the evidence in question. It is unclear whether or not it would have made a difference if the consent had been given without legal advice having been taken. Since the suspect is hardly likely to be aware of the duties of the police under the Code, the better view would seem to be that unadvised consent should not count as a factor against exclusion.

It is clear that the presence even of advised consent is not necessarily a decisive factor. So in *Joseph*,[219] a confrontation in the cells, immediately before the start of the accused's trial, had been organized at the behest of his counsel, no doubt in the hope that a positive identification would not ensue. In fact, two witnesses did point the finger at Joseph. The judge allowed evidence of their recognition of him to be given, relying upon the idea that, if he hoped for the best, he must accept the worst. The Court of Appeal rejected the idea that the issue of exclusion might properly be decided on this 'tit for tat' basis. In fact, no proper reliance could be placed upon the confrontation evidence in question, which should, therefore, have been excluded.

Exclusion where Code D is Inapplicable

The section 78(1) discretion is available even where the identification process has been arranged and carried out by a lay person, before the police became involved in any way.[220] Even once the police are involved, a face-to-face identification may be made in circumstances such that the Code has no call to apply. In a series of cases in which a suspect was identified at or near the scene by a witness asked by the police to say whether or not that person was the one who had carried out the crime in question, the Court of Appeal has upheld the trial judge's decision to allow evidence of that identification to be given.[221] The principle behind these decisions is that the Code is concerned with formal procedures taking place after the event but before the trial, and not with informal identification used to establish whether or not there exist grounds for arrest or otherwise not designed and organized in order to obtain evidence for use at trial.

That principle would seem to have been extended far beyond its natural limits in *Hickin et al.*[222] There, a number of men believed to have taken part in violent disorder in Blackpool had been arrested. The police then took eye-witnesses to look at those men with a view to the eye-witnesses making positive identifications. The Court of Appeal pointed out that the hierarchy of procedures under Code D is imposed only where the identity of the suspect is 'known' to the police.

[219] *Joseph* [1994] Crim.LR 48 (transcript through LEXIS).

[220] *O'Leary* (1988) 87 Cr.App.R 387.

[221] See *Oscar* [1991] Crim.LR 778; *Kelly* [1992] Crim.LR 181; *Rogers* [1993] Crim.LR 386; *Malashev* [1997] Crim.LR 587. See also *Long* [1991] Crim.LR 453.

[222] [1996] Crim.LR 584 (transcript through LEXIS). Cf *Mcmath* [1997] Crim.LR 586.

It described itself as inclining strongly to the view that these arrested persons were not 'known'. This is mystifying, not least because the court seems to have considered that the practicalities—how could the police arrange a large number of identification parades at such short notice?—meant that even Note for Guidance 2D, which says that a suspect is 'known' where there is sufficient information to justify his arrest for the offence in question, could not dissuade it from that view. Since that Note was not contained in the issue of Code D in force when the facts of *Hicklin et al.* arose, the court's remarks are, fortunately, not binding. Much the better view is that these arguments of practicality, rather than leading to a court flying in the face of clear words, should go to the question whether or not to exclude the weak, non-Code, identification evidence in the particular case. In this respect, it is to be noted that the court did eventually decide that, in the case of all but two of the accused who had been identified, the evidence should, because of a catalogue of weaknesses, be excluded in any event. It is also noteworthy that, in none of the other cases concerned with informal identifications immediately after the event, had an arrest already been made.

There are also a number of cases in which an informal identification opportunity has arisen in relation to a person who has been charged with, and is awaiting trial for, an offence. Where the identification was genuinely spontaneous, rather than having been engineered by the police,[223] it must be doubtful that Code D applies at all. For example, in *Martin and Nicholls*,[224] prosecuting counsel told the police that a parade should be conducted, but none had been by the time the two accused appeared before the magistrates at a pre-trial hearing. The two complainants, present inside the court building, then, apparently spontaneously, identified the two accused as their assailants. The Court of Appeal overturned the trial judge's decision to allow evidence of those identifications to be given, its reason being that they were made in highly unsatisfactory conditions by young witnesses—they were aged 12 and 13—a very long time after the incident in question had occurred. The brief report of the case which is available fails to reveal whether or not the court considered that Code D applied. But, given the factors that it stressed, it would seem that the evidence simply was too unreliable to be admitted in evidence in any event. In *Campbell*,[225] where there had been a similar, apparently accidental, confrontation, the court affirmed the trial judge's decision to allow the evidence to be called, apparently on the basis that, because the witness said that he had recognized the accused both as one of his assailants and as a former schoolmate, the identification suffered from no greater infirmity than would one made at a parade.

It is entirely clear that the Code does not apply at all to identification processes carried out at the behest of the police but in foreign parts. In *Quinn*,[226] a police officer who had witnessed the murder of a colleague was taken to Dublin in order

[223] Though cf. *Tiplady* (1995) 159 JPR 548, considered at text to n. 217 above.

[224] [1994] Crim.LR 218.

[225] [1996] Crim.LR 500 (transcript through LEXIS).

[226] [1996] Crim.LR 581 (transcript through LEXIS). A case to similar effect is *Konscol* [1993] Crim.LR 950 (concerned with Code C).

for him to be able to say whether or not Quinn, who was standing trial on another matter at the Special Criminal Court, was the murderer. Evidence of his positive identification was ruled admissible at Quinn's trial for that murder some thirteen years later. Though the Code was incapable of applying, the Court of Appeal, in upholding the judge's ruling, made it absolutely plain that it had to be decided whether or not what had happened in Dublin would have such an adverse effect on the fairness of the proceedings that it ought to be excluded. In the particular circumstances of that case, there was no such sufficient adverse effect for it to be right to exclude it.

Trickery and Entrapment

We must now deal with the expanding group of cases in which the argument for exclusion has not been based upon any breach of law, in particular any breach of the 1984 Act or the codes made under it. In the present section, we shall deal, therefore, with cases concerning trickery and entrapment. It has already been seen that the common law, in its mature form as explained in *Sang*,[227] drew a distinction between evidence acquired *after* commission of the offence and evidence obtained *during*, or even *before*, its commission. The discretion to exclude for unfairness was available only in the first situation. The result was that there was a crucial distinction between cases involving trickery and those involving entrapment. Where a person had, by some misrepresentation, whether express or implied, been persuaded to produce incriminating evidence against himself in relation to the offence committed, whether in the form of a confession or otherwise, the common law granted a discretion to exclude it for unfairness. No sophisticated analysis of the kinds of trick which should properly lead to exclusion had been essayed before section 78(1) of the 1984 Act became law. However, where the person had been entrapped into doing some criminal act or some act pursuant to a criminal purpose, or had been persuaded to make remarks demonstrating his criminal purpose or intention before or during commission of the offence, the discretion was, *Sang* decided, unavailable.

Some Terminology

Before we consider the post-Act law, we must deal with some important terminology. First, it is sometimes said that criminal conduct took place as a result of the activities of an *agent provocateur*. The Royal Commission on Police Powers defined an *agent provocateur* as 'a person who entices another to commit an express breach of the law which he would not otherwise have committed and then proceeds or informs against him in respect of such offence'.[228] This definition

[227] [1980] AC 402, discussed in Ch. 6, text to nn. 33–67 above.
[228] *Report*, 16 March 1929, Cmnd. 3297, at 40–1.

was, without express acknowledgement, adopted in almost identical terms by the Court of Appeal in the leading post-1984 Act case, *Smurthwaite and Gill*.[229] What is clearly in mind here is the possibility that the police themselves, or a person acting at their behest, may in effect 'create' a crime. The *prima facie* undesirability of the police engaging in such activity, particularly where actual commission of the offence would result in damage or injury to third parties, is obvious. However, we shall see that in some situations courts have had no real difficulty in coming to terms with it.

Next, we need rather to refine the definition given above, by separating cases where no offence would have been committed but for the activities of the *agent* from those where the offence would merely have been committed with a different content. The point was well made in the unreported case of *Lawrence and Nash*[230] by Leggatt LJ, as follows:[231]

> An example of an offence which would in any event have been committed is the offer by a person to sell drugs to an undercover officer in a public house mistaking him for a user. Of that supply it could fairly be said that such an offence would have been committed in any event. But where a police officer prompts others to obtain drugs for him, believing them to be suppliers, it is not apparent without more that they would in any event have supplied others.

Even this is not entirely straightforward, for the reasonableness of saying that the offence 'would have been committed anyway' may turn on the specificity with which the offence is described. So what if the supplier offered the undercover officer cannabis, but the officer said he would have only heroin? If heroin were to be supplied, would that offence have been committed anyway? It may be that it was an appreciation of the existence of problems of this kind which led Leggatt LJ to say, on behalf of the court in *Lawrence and Nash*, that he did not find the label, *agent provocateur*, at all helpful.

A further point to be stressed about the meaning of the term is that there must be an element of enticement present. So, in Leggatt LJ's first example, the undercover officer would not, in any event, be an *agent provocateur* because there is nothing to suggest that he sought to persuade the other person to supply him. *Williams* v. *DPP*[232] may provide a case-law example of the same point. In the course of a motor vehicle crime initiative, the police left an unsecure and unattended van parked in the street, which van appeared to contain a valuable load of cartons of cigarettes. Eventually, two people began to remove cartons from it and were arrested. Wright J was clear that the police had not acted as *agents provocateurs*, for they had done nothing to force, persuade, encourage, or coerce the accused into doing what they had done.[233] Farquharson LJ was less certain

[229] [1994] 1 All ER 898, at 903 (*per* Lord Taylor CJ).

[230] 14 Dec. 1993 (transcript through LEXIS). [231] See transcript.

[232] [1993] 3 All ER 365. See also *DPP* v. *Marshall and Downes* [1988] 3 All ER 683; *London Borough of Ealing* v. *Woolworths plc* [1995] Crim.LR 58.

[233] See [1993] 3 All ER 365, at 369.

about this, though he thought the question of labelling not to be of prime importance.[234] His reason for doubt may have been that the police had put temptation in the way of members of the public. It is not obviously wrong to describe what they had done as enticement. In another case, the Court of Appeal seems to have held that the accused had acted out of a sense of obligation to the other person, rather than because enticed.[235]

A second important word is the word 'entrapment'. It is often used in a very much wider sense than the phrase *agent provocateur*. Though it is common enough to use it to cover activities of the kind described by the Royal Commission, it is also capable of extending to activities taking place before or during the commission of an offence which may aid its commission or even influence the precise way in which it is carried out, but which do not 'create' the crime. This point is not always taken by the courts. For example, in *Edwards*,[236] the Court of Appeal said that, since the undercover officers had joined in a larger conspiracy which was already afoot, there could be no question of them being *agents provocateurs*, and then went on to assume, in effect, that it followed that there was equally no question of entrapment. No such view was taken in *Smurthwaite and Gill*,[237] where the two terms were carefully separated. However, the word 'entrapment', inconsistently with the understanding in *Sang*, is now sometimes used in cases which involve only the obtaining of evidence after the commission of the offence. In *Jelen and Katz*[238] and in *Bailey*,[239] incriminating remarks of accused persons had been surreptitiously recorded by, or at the instigation of, the police. The Court of Appeal felt it quite appropriate in each case to describe the conduct in question, to use the words of Auld J in the former, as involving 'an element of entrapment'.[240]

Agents Provocateurs, Entrapment, and Section 78(1)

It will be recalled that it has recently been established by the decision of the House of Lords in *Latif and Shahzad*[241] that, in an appropriate case, proceedings may be stayed for abuse of the process of the court where the accused was entrapped into committing the offence charged. But, in addition, it became established a few years before *Latif and Shahzad* that the section 78(1) discretion is, unlike the common law one preserved by section 82(3), available even in cases where the evidence was obtained before completion of the offence in question. Conflict in the earlier authorities, as regards this issue, was settled by *Smurthwaite and Gill*.[242] The Court of Appeal set out what it described as some of the factors which

[234] *Ibid*. 371.

[235] *Pattemore* [1994] Crim.LR 836.

[236] [1991] Crim.LR 45 (transcript through LEXIS).

[237] [1994] 1 All ER 898.

[238] (1989) 90 Cr.App.R 456.

[239] [1993] 3 All ER 512.

[240] (1989) 90 Cr.App.R 456, at 464. See also *Ali (Shaukat)*, *The Times*, 19 Feb. 1991.

[241] [1996] 1 WLR 104, discussed in Ch. 6, text to nn. 192–9 above.

[242] [1994] 1 All ER 898. See also *Farooq and Ramzan* [1995] Crim.LR 169; *Latif and Shahzad* [1996] 1 WLR 104. The earlier authorities, in conflict, were *Harwood* [1989] Crim.LR 285 and *Gill and*

the judge should take into account in exercising that discretion. According to Lord Taylor CJ, five such factors are:[243]

> Was the officer acting as an agent provocateur in the sense that he was enticing the defendant to commit an offence he would not otherwise have committed? What was the nature of any entrapment? Does the evidence consist of admissions to a completed offence, or does it consist of the actual commission of an offence? How active or passive was the officer's role in obtaining the evidence? Is there an unassailable record of what occurred, or is it strongly corroborated?'

He went on to add that a further consideration was whether or not the officer involved had abused his role by putting questions which ought properly to have been asked only in accordance with Code C. This particular matter has already been discussed.[244]

Something has already been said about the issue of whether or not the person in question acted as an *agent provocateur*. If he did, this will certainly be a factor pointing towards exclusion, for the result will have been the generation of crime. It should certainly not be assumed that the fact that crime has been generated will necessarily be decisive. Though the police who put temptation in the way of the public in *Williams* v. *DPP*[245] may not count as *agents provocateurs*, it is noteworthy that the Divisional Court saw nothing at all wrong with the magistrates' conclusion in that case that the evidence acquired should be admitted. Yet the effect of the police conduct was certainly that an offence was committed which would not, without their intervention, have been committed. In this respect, that case may properly be contrasted with *DPP* v. *Marshall and Downes*.[246] There, two officers had made a test purchase of liquor at a shop which was licensed to sell it only by the case. Dressed in civilian clothes, they had succeeded in buying quantities below those which were permitted. Though this particular offence—selling to the officers—would not have taken place had they been in uniform, their conduct had resulted only trivially in an extra crime being committed, for the shop would undoubtedly have been equally willing to sell similar amounts to an ordinary customer.

The second factor, concerning the nature of any entrapment, probably relates to the way in which the intervention took place, as well, perhaps, as its culpability, both in terms of public danger and otherwise. For example, a police *agent* who joined in an already existing conspiracy[247] would surely be more culpable if the conspiracy were one to cause explosions than if it were one to supply cannabis. It is right to add that to treat this kind of culpability factor as relevant

Ranuana [1989] Crim.LR 358. Another case of interest is *R.* v. *Governor of Pentonville Prison, ex p. Chinoy* [1992] 1 All ER 317.

[243] [1994] 1 All ER 898, at 903.

[244] See Ch. 6, text to nn. 181–91 above.

[245] [1993] 3 All ER 365, discussed at text to n. 232 above.

[246] [1988] 3 All ER 683. See also *Ealing London Borough Council* v. *Woolworths plc* [1995] Crim.LR 58.

[247] As in *Edwards* [1991] Crim.LR 45.

would be to add a disciplinary tinge to the discretion, here to discourage the police from activities quite plainly involving serious public danger. We shall refer to the appropriateness of this kind of disciplinary approach at the end of this part of the present section.

One may interpolate here a point about entrapment more generally. It remains the case that entrapment is not itself a defence to a criminal charge,[248] yet the effect of excluding evidence obtained by entrapment will, at least very often, be that there is no admissible evidence of commission of the offence. This was what undoubtedly persuaded the House of Lords in *Sang*[249] that the argument for discretionary power fell with defeat of the argument for a substantive defence. Though it has been convincingly demonstrated that the two issues are separable,[250] it may be supposed that courts will find themselves particularly reluctant to exclude the evidence where to exclude would mean, in effect, that the accused must inevitably be acquitted.

The third factor identified by Lord Taylor CJ is concerned with whether the evidence in question is or is not confessional. Of course, a confession necessarily relates to a completed offence, as his Lordship indicates, so there is no historical problem in that situation with applicability of the discretion. The new freedom is to exclude evidence of the actual commission of the offence. It is not at all clear which way, then, this factor is intended to point the judge, unless it be to the type of problem which has just been discussed.

The active or passive nature of the officer's role in obtaining the evidence is clearly a factor of some importance. In *Smurthwaite and Gill* itself, even though the offences charged were the solicitation of murders, the police who had become involved had had only a minimal role in planning the murders in question and had not sought to persuade, or even buoy up, the relevant accused. Equally, in *Mann and Dixon*,[251] a case which also concerned two separate offences of solicitation of murder, the role of the police had not been an active one. Indeed, on more than one occasion, the accused had been asked if he was sure that he really wanted to go through with the murder, and had affirmed that he did.

The final factor is also of considerable importance. The courts are clearly concerned that, in the absence of a record of some or all of the transactions between the parties, there may be considerable doubt whether or not the accused really did say or do what the undercover agent alleges. Once again, in *Smurthwaite and Gill* itself, there was a very full, taped record of the substantial majority of exchanges. Like all the other factors, this one is not necessarily decisive. In *Latif and*

[248] Contrast the position in the USA, where it is very widely so regarded. The defence has generated very great problems of its own, particularly as to whether one should adopt an objective or subjective approach. The former focuses on the inducements offered by the police or their agents, so is concerned with how culpable is the activity, the latter upon whether or not the accused was predisposed to commit crimes of the kind charged. The leading cases are *Sorrells* v. *US*, 287 US 435 (1932); *Sherman* v. *US*, 356 US 369 (1958); *US* v. *Russell*, 411 US 423 (1973); and *Hampton* v. *US*, 425 US 484 (1976). For a stimulating discussion, see Park (1975–6) 60 *Minn.L Rev*. 163.

[249] [1980] AC 402. [250] See, e.g., Heydon [1980] Crim.LR 129, at 131–2.

[251] (1994) 145 NLJ 254 (transcript through LEXIS).

Shahzad,[252] the undercover agent had been involved in complex arrangements for smuggling into the United Kingdom heroin worth in excess of £3 million. There is no indication that the relevant exchanges had been recorded, yet the trial judge's decision not to exclude the evidence was affirmed on appeal both in the Court of Appeal and in the House of Lords.

Two additional factors seem to have emerged in *Latif and Shahzad*. First, both courts of appeal placed some emphasis on the seriousness of the alleged offence, particularly having regard to the value of the heroin. Secondly, both pointed out that the accused Shahzad was not to be regarded as a total newcomer to the drugs scene who had been enticed into doing something he would not otherwise have contemplated. The suggestion here is not that the offence was in train anyway, but that Shahzad was *predisposed* towards commission of offences of this type. Though the specific context for the endorsement by the House of Lords of these two factors as relevant was the appellants' claim that the proceedings should be struck out as an abuse of the process of the court,[253] there is nothing at all to suggest that it did not consider these factors equally relevant with regard to the issue of admissibility of evidence. It does seem likely that the predisposition factor, in particular, will turn out to be a rather important one in practice.[254]

Is the discretion available where the person working undercover was neither himself a police officer or other official, nor working at the behest of or with the connivance of the police or other official? In *Morley and Hutton*,[255] a newspaper reporter had set up a meeting with the accused at which the reporter had been able to buy a quantity of counterfeit notes and to arrange to buy some more. The newspaper had been put on to the story by an informant. It is clear that neither the informant nor the reporter was acting at the instigation of the police, who had become involved only later. Though the Court of Appeal upheld the judge's decision to allow the evidence to be given, it clearly held the discretion to be available in principle. Indeed, counsel for the appellants had argued that it was *more* important for the discretion to be exercisable where the police had not been involved than where they had. If *Morley and Hutton* is to be taken at face value, the issue clearly is whether or not the accused had been improperly enticed into criminality. In US terms, this is a subjective approach to entrapment, for the concern is the restricted culpability of this particular accused, a matter indifferent as between official and non-official entrapment. It would be possible, as we have seen already,[256] to take an objective position, asking about the degree of culpability *of the police* (or other public authority): is this sort of criminal investigation activity to be tolerated? There are, perhaps, hints in *Mann and Dixon*[257] that the law should not concern itself with the unsolicited activities of persons who some-

[252] [1995] 1 Cr.App.R 270 (Court of Appeal); [1996] 1 WLR 104 (House of Lords).
[253] This aspect of the case is discussed, in Ch. 6, text to nn. 192–9 above.
[254] It is certainly an important factor in the US cases—see n. 248 above.
[255] [1994] Crim.LR 919 (transcript through LEXIS). See also *Smith* [1995] Crim.LR 658.
[256] See text to n. 247 above. And, for the US position, see n. 248 above.
[257] (1994) 145 NLJ 254 (transcript through LEXIS).

times act as police informers. Yet it must be said that a disciplinary approach of this kind, designed to discourage police behaviour which is unacceptable as such, has not generally been favoured by the courts[258] and that it is not easy to justify taking it by reference to the need to prevent an 'adverse effect' on 'the fairness of the proceedings'.

Unfair Gathering of Evidence

Kinds of Evidence

When we turn to the gathering of evidence after the completion of the crime, we observe that the evidence may very well be confessional in nature. Thus it may be a statement, whether by words or conduct, which is wholly or partly adverse to the accused. The reader should recall that the precise line between confessions proper, caught by section 76 of the 1984 Act, and other evidence to be found in the words or conduct of the accused is not at all clear.[259] In some of the cases concerned with the application of section 78(1) to evidence obtained after the event, it is quite clear that the evidence in question was confessional; in others it is quite clear that it was not; and in others still there is doubt. So, in *Mason*,[260] the accused had admitted preparing fire bombs and encouraging a friend to use them to damage a third party's car. On any view, this was a confession. In *Christou and Wright*,[261] concealed cameras revealed the identity of persons selling property and the nature of the property itself, which was being sold to police officers pretending to run a shady jeweller's shop. Other evidence showed the property in question to be stolen. The evidence from the camera was, very clearly, non-confessional. In *Jelen and Katz*,[262] the police organized a surreptitious recording of a conversation between one of the accused and a third party. That accused did not make any express statement of involvement in the offence, but he did make certain remarks from which his guilt could be inferred. The Court of Appeal seemed doubtful that the accused had made any confession or admission, yet it would seem that the remarks in question were confessional, for the purposes of section 82(1) of the 1984 Act, in that they constituted a 'statement wholly or partly adverse to the person who made it'.[263]

The important point to make is that the cases under section 78(1) of the 1984 Act do not take the line between confessional and other statements to have significance so far as availability of the unfairness discretion is concerned.[264] It also seems clear that the notion that the evidence in question must be 'tantamount to a self-incriminatory admission',[265] if applicable at common law, does not apply

[258] See, in particular, *Sang* [1980] AC 402, considered in detail in Ch. 6, text to nn. 33–67 above.

[259] For discussion, see ch. 4, text to nn. 14–53 above.

[260] [1988] 1 WLR 139.

[261] [1992] QB 979.

[262] (1989) 90 Cr.App.R 456.

[263] The reader may find it helpful to refer to the discussion of the meaning of 'confession' in Ch. 4, text to nn. 6–63 above.

[264] N.B. *Maclean and Kosten* [1993] Crim.LR 687 (transcript through LEXIS).

[265] *Sang* [1980] AC 402, at 436 (*per* Lord Diplock).

under section 78(1)—a point neatly illustrated by *Christou and Wright*—nor does there seem to be any reason why the evidence in question need have been obtained, in some sense, from the accused (or, perhaps, his surroundings).[266] However, it must be added that there seems to be no reported case at appeal level dealing with the statutory discretion in the present context in which the evidence had been obtained *other than* from the accused.[267]

The Grounds for Exclusion: Express Deception

The cases to be considered here are those in which the police, or persons acting on their behalf, have used some trick, deception, or subterfuge to obtain the evidence from the accused. Where there has been express deception, the courts are, it would seem, more likely to think exclusion the appropriate course. It will be recalled that in *Mason*[268] the police had lied both to the accused and to his solicitor, when saying that the accused's fingerprints had been found on fragments of glass discovered at the scene of a petrol-bombing. It was the trial judge's failure to take any account of the deception of the solicitor which led to the appeal being allowed. What remains unclear is whether or not such a blatant deception of the accused alone, which Watkins LJ described as 'bad enough',[269] would have sufficed.

Mason was distinguished in *MacLean and Kosten*.[270] There, relatives of a person who had been acting as a courier in respect of an illegal importation of cannabis which had been concealed in a car were persuaded by customs officers to tell Kosten that the courier had been injured in a car accident and was being detained in hospital. Kosten was given the name of a person who was said to be a car salvage operator, but who was, in fact, a customs officer. In telephone calls to and a meeting with that officer, Kosten made a number of incriminating remarks and told some lies, though nothing he had said was regarded as confessional in nature. Even though the deception was no less express here than in *Mason*, the Court of Appeal had no doubt that the judge had been right to allow Kosten's statements to be given in evidence. It stressed that it had been Kosten who had initiated contact with the courier's family, that he had been put under no pressure to reveal any information which might incriminate him, and that none of the exchanges were between a suspect and someone in the role of an investigating officer. As Tudor Evans J put it, 'by a ruse, they afforded him the opportunity'[271] of incriminating himself.

Much of what was said in *MacLean and Kosten* seems to echo some influential remarks of Lord Taylor CJ in *Christou and Wright*.[272] Though the latter case did not involve any expressly deceptive words, it did lead his Lordship to say that 'the trick was not applied to the appellants; they voluntarily applied themselves to the

[266] As stated in *Sang* that it must—see *ibid.* at 437.
[267] For a general discussion of the effect of s. 78(1) upon *Sang*, see Ch. 6, text to nn. 152–9 above.
[268] [1988] 1 WLR 139.
[269] *Ibid.* 144. [270] [1993] Crim.LR 687 (transcript through LEXIS).
[271] See transcript. [272] [1992] QB 979.

trick'.[273] So it seems that giving a person, by some deception, an opportunity to incriminate himself is somehow different from deceiving him into incriminating himself. The distinction is a difficult one to understand, for it could equally be said that Mason was afforded the opportunity of incriminating himself and that, in a sense, he voluntarily took that opportunity, especially since he did consult his solicitor again before making his admissions. A better line of distinction between *Mason* and *MacLean and Kosten* would seem to be that the officer who told the lie in the former case was, indeed, acting openly as an investigating officer, but that neither the relatives who lent their assistance nor the particular customs officer who spoke to Kosten had any such open role. As we have seen, this was suggested in *MacLean and Kosten* itself as one ground of distinction. It was also adverted to in *Christou and Wright*. Of course, this is to assume that deception in the course of undercover investigative operations is *properly* to be distinguished from deception in ordinary policy interrogation. If one is unpersuaded that it is a proper distinction, one may stress, as has been done elsewhere in this work, that it was the deception of the solicitor which really was the key to the decision in *Mason*, in that it undermined Mason's fundamental right to legal advice.[274]

In any event, it was clearly held in *Bailey*[275] that not every kind of express deception practised in the course of ordinary police interrogation procedures will necessarily result in exclusion. There, police who had failed to get any admissions from the two co-accused by questioning them, placed them together in a 'bugged' cell. Before doing so, in order to lull the accused into a false sense of security, the investigating officers had acted out a charade, the effect of which was that they had wanted to place the co-accused in separate cells but had been compelled by an unco-operative custody officer to put them in the same cell. This element of express deception was 'merely a detail',[276] akin to one practised in the common law case of *Stewart*.[277] Therefore, the remaining issue related to the surreptitious nature of the recording itself.

The Grounds for Exclusion: Implied Deception

There have been indications that impliedly deceptive conduct is to be distinguished from expressly deceptive words. Thus, in *DPP* v. *Marshall*,[278] police officers dressed in civilian clothes had simply failed to reveal that they were officers. Distinguishing *Mason*, Woolf LJ said:[279]

> There, however, there was an express misrepresentation and a clear deception practised and you can understand how, if a deception of this type occurs, it could have an effect on the fairness of the trial, but here it is difficult to see how the fact that the police officers did not reveal their identity could have any effect on the trial.

[273] *Ibid.* 989.

[274] For discussion of this point, see Ch. 6, text to nn. 104–6 and this Ch., text to n. 273. This was the view of *Mason* taken by the Court of Appeal in *Ali (Shaukat)*, *The Times*, 19 Feb. 1991 (transcript through LEXIS).

[275] [1993] 3 All ER 513. [276] *Ibid.* 523. [277] [1970] 1 WLR 907.

[278] [1988] 3 All ER 683. [279] *Ibid.* 685.

It is certainly the case that the courts have exhibited a considerable degree of tolerance of surreptitious tape-recording by, or at the instigation of, the police, and in a whole variety of situations. Here, of course, the deception is merely implied, in the sense that it is an ordinary assumption that private conversations will not be tape-recorded. In *Jelen and Katz*,[280] a man acting on behalf of the police had recorded Jelen's incriminating remarks. This had taken place before Jelen had been arrested or interviewed, a point which the Court of Appeal stressed in upholding the judge's decision to allow the tape-recording to be given in evidence. A similar view was taken in *Ali (Shaukat)*[281] of a recorded conversation between the accused and a number of his relatives in a police interview room, even though he had been arrested, interviewed by the police for several hours, and, indeed, charged before these events. The Court of Appeal in *Bailey*[282] could find no reason to distinguish *Ali (Shaukat)*, for a conversation between the two co-accused in that case (who had also been charged) was no different from one between an accused and his relatives. In the words of Simon Brown LJ: '[o]f course these accused at the relevant time could not properly have been subject to further police questioning. But that is not to say that they had to be protected from any opportunity to speak incriminatingly to each other if they chose to do so.'[283] This may suggest that the court will take a different view where the suspect has been charged *and* his interrogator is an agent for the police. *Christou and Wright*[284] demonstrates that far more intricate deceptive stratagems may be used by the police in order to collect evidence, without section 78(1) being properly applied to exclude it. The police set up a jewellery shop, to which they hoped and expected thieves and handlers would go in order to sell stolen jewellery. It was manned by two undercover officers who asked questions of potential vendors which a 'shady' jeweller might have been expected to ask and which might also be helpful in tracing the true owners. In addition, they behaved in other ways just as would be expected of such a jeweller. Everything that transpired was recorded. Plainly, though neither officer ever said, 'I am a "shady" jeweller, willing to handle stolen property', that was the implication of all that they said and did. In addition, the 'customers' would certainly not expect what went on to be recorded. Here, of course, no question arose of the persons who were eventually prosecuted having been arrested or interviewed before entering the shop. Indeed, they were not even suspects at that stage. Therefore, the various implied deceptions did not undermine any provisions of either the Act or Code C. Had the officers gone beyond their immediate purpose of having those in possession of stolen property hand it over, in order to enable them later to be prosecuted, and begun to question them about the circumstances in which they had acquired the property or their state of mind about it at the time or subsequently, they would have been seeking to circumvent the Code C provisions

[280] (1989) 90 Cr.App.R 456. See also *Cadette* [1995] Crim.LR 229.
[281] *The Times*, 19 Feb. 1991 (transcript through LEXIS).
[282] [1993] 3 All ER 513. See also *Roberts* [1997] 1 Cr.App.R 217.
[283] [1993] 3 All ER 513, at 522. [284] [1992] QB 979.

about police interviews, so that, by analogy with *Mason*, exclusion would have been appropriate.[285]

Unlawful Searches and Trespass

Unlawful Searches of the Person or Property

One clear message of Lord Diplock's formulation in *Sang*[286] was that the common law discretionary power of exclusion was not applicable to unlawful searches, whether of the person or of property. Unless the suspect had been *persuaded* by the police to bring forth self-incriminating evidence, the discretion was unavailable.[287] Though there is no decision at appeal level deciding, as a matter of *ratio decidendi*, that Lord Diplock's restriction does not apply to the section 78(1) power, there is a number of cases which assume that that power is, in principle, available.

Some of the cases in question are capable of being explained satisfactorily in a way which is consistent with Lord Diplock's analysis. Thus, where the accused was persuaded by oppressive police treatment to give a sample of breath in pursuance of the drink/driving procedures, the analogy to the confessions rule was such as to permit, for that reason, the court to exclude evidence brought into existence in consequence of that treatment.[288] Similar analysis is capable of explaining *Cooke*.[289] There, the accused had initially refused to provide a sample of his hair, but he was then told by the police that it would be taken from him, if necessary, by force. There was no doubt of the seriousness of their intentions, for three officers present at the accused's cell were wearing riot headgear. So the accused submitted to samples being plucked from his scalp. The Court of Appeal decided that the samples taken had been non-intimate ones which, under section 63(3) of the 1984 Act, *could* be taken without consent. Therefore, the police had not done anything unlawful. However, had the sample been an intimate one, their behaviour would have been clearly unlawful. Consequently, it would have been perfectly possible to say that the discretion would have been available because the threat of force had been oppressive. In fact, the court did not press that line of thought. Rather, it said that if it was wrong about the intimate nature of the sample, the discretion would have been available, not by reason of the analogy but because section 78(1) had granted trial courts 'a substantially wider discretion to

[285] See *Bryce* [1992] 4 All ER 567. And cf. *Lin, Hung and Tsui* [1995] Crim.LR 817; *Edwards* [1997] Crim.LR 348. For a more detailed discussion of cases where Code C may be said not to apply, see, Ch. 6, text to nn. 181–91 above.

[286] [1980] AC 402.

[287] One cannot say that this view was shared by all of their Lordships in *Sang*—see the discussion of that case in Ch. 6, text to nn. 33–67 above.

[288] See, e.g., *Matto* v. *Wolverhampton Crown Court* [1987] RTR 337; *Sharpe* v. *DPP* [1993] RTR 392.

[289] [1995] 1 Cr.App.R 318.

refuse to admit evidence improperly obtained'[290] than that available at common law. It is worth adding that the facts of *Cooke* demonstrate neatly the lack of substantial merit in the idea of restricting availability of the discretion to cases by analogy with confessions cases. If we imagine that Cooke had resisted to the end, so that actual force had had to be used, the analogy would not have been present, so that the discretion would have been unavailable. It would be hard to see any sense in that.

Two Court of Appeal cases which do raise directly the issue of the treatment of evidence obtained by unlawful search are *Wright*[291] and *Hughes*.[292] In neither case were the elements of unlawfulness considered to be of great seriousness. In the former, the sole statutory breach was a failure to enter on the accused's custody record details of a search of his premises, though there were also relatively minor breaches of the relevant code of practice (Code B). In the latter, the accused, when approached by a police officer, had attempted to swallow what turned out to be cannabis resin. By physical means, the officer had forced him to spit it out. Though, in the Court's view, there had been a number of breaches of the 'stop and search' provisions of the 1984 Act and the code of practice dealing with the same matter (Code A), principally those requiring a suspect to be provided with certain information before the search,[293] it could be said that it was hardly reasonable for the accused to complain of breaches which he had made almost inevitable by his own conduct. Yet, in cases neither of which was the most propitious for the call to recognize the availability, in principle, of the exclusionary discretion, the court cast no doubt all upon its availability.

It is of considerable interest that, in *Wright*, Beldam LJ relied upon an important passage from Lord Lane CJ's judgment in *Quinn*.[294] That passage, it will be recalled, refers to the possibility of proceedings being unfair where evidence has been obtained in deliberate breach of procedures laid down in a code of practice. Though Beldam LJ correctly pointed out that, as the weight of authority indicates, the deliberateness of the breach is not an essential element, the broader significance of the passage is that it refers to breach as such, without giving any indication that the presence of (resulting) self-incrimination is necessary.

Though, for these reasons, it does seem clear that there is considerable scope for the application of the section 78(1) to cases of unlawful search, there are some indications in recent authorities of a return to a more *Sang*-like approach. Thus, in *Stewart*,[295] entry to the accused's home had been effected in a way which entailed breach of a number of provisions of Code of Practice B (which governs searches of premises). Once inside, the officers discovered that mechanical appa-

290 *Ibid*. 328.

291 [1994] Crim.LR 55 (transcript through LEXIS). 292 [1994] 1 WLR 876.

293 See 1984 Act, s. 2(2) and (3); Code A, paras. 2.4–2.6. Is there no exigent circumstances exception, by way of implication, to some or all of those provisions?

294 [1990] Crim.LR 581 (transcript through LEXIS). The passage in question is to be found quoted at p. 135 above.

295 [1995] Crim.LR 500 (transcript through LEXIS). See also *Khan et al.* [1997] Crim.LR 508.

ratus had been used to divert both the gas and electricity supplies such as to bypass the relevant meters. The Court of Appeal held that the breaches in question could have no adverse effect upon the fairness of the proceedings. The court's reason for so holding was that the apparatus in question had been there for all to see. It made no difference whether or not those there to see it were or were not in breach of the code provisions. One commentator has described the case as 'a rather dubious precedent',[296] and rightly so. Whenever there is a lawful method of searching, it makes no difference, in this sense, whether that method or one in breach of law is used. The effect of that kind of reasoning is, in practical terms, to make the discretion unavailable. A rather similar approach to that in *Stewart* seems to have been adopted in the later case of *McCarthy*.[297]

Unlawful Surveillance

It should not be thought that it is only in cases of personal or property search that the new freedom is enjoyed. It was recognized by the Court of Appeal in *Khan*[298] that the discretion may be invoked in cases where the police have obtained evidence by the use of surveillance methods which entail unlawfulness. Khan had, with another man, been searched on his arrival in England from Pakistan. A large amount of heroin was found in his companion's possession, but Khan himself had none. Several months later, he happened to visit the house of a third party named Bashforth. Unbeknown to either Bashforth or Khan, a listening device had been installed by the police on the outside of the house. The recorded conversation between Khan, Bashforth, and two others included the admission by Khan that he had been a party to the illegal importation of heroin. This was the sole substantial evidence against him at his trial for the relevant offence. The placing of the device on Bashforth's house had undoubtedly constituted a civil trespass and, at least arguably, the offence of criminal damage.[299] However, the impropriety of the action of the police was significantly mitigated by the fact that they had complied with certain Home Office guidelines concerning surveillance in placing the device there.[300] Counsel for Khan, as well as relying upon these elements of unlawfulness in domestic terms, argued that a further reason for excluding the evidence was that it had been obtained in breach of Khan's right to privacy under Article 8 of the European Convention on Human Rights. The Court of Appeal gave short shrift to the argument that these various elements rendered the evidence inadmissible in

[296] Professor D. J. Birch—see *ibid.* 500. [297] [1996] Crim.LR 818. [298] [1995] QB 27.

[299] Rather different considerations apply where the defence argues that the unlawfulness consists in a breach of the provisions of the Interception of Communications Act 1985. Since that Act has been held not to authorize surveillance for the purposes of gathering evidence to be used in a prosecution—see *Preston* [1994] 2 AC 130—it follows that the discretion cannot come into play; the evidence in question is, in effect, inadmissible in evidence. See also *Effik and Mitchell* [1995] 1 AC 309; *Rasool and Choudhary* [1997] 2 Cr.App.R. 190.

[300] Interference with property for the purposes of surveillance of the kind carried out in *Khan* is now regulated by statute—see Police Act 1997, Pt. III.

law—a point on which it was later resoundingly endorsed by the House of Lords[301]—but had no doubt that the section 78(1) discretion to exclude was, in principle, available. On the particular facts, for reasons to be mentioned shortly, it considered that the trial judge had been right to exercise that discretion in favour of admission.

Once *Khan* did reach the House of Lords, the emphasis of counsel's argument with regard to discretionary exclusion had changed. According to Lord Nolan, counsel had placed almost exclusive reliance upon the alleged breach of Article 8, the trespass and apparent criminal damage having ceased to be fundamental to his argument.[302] The House concluded that the trial judge, who had taken account of the possible breach of Article 8, had been fully entitled to rule as he had. The European Convention aspect of the case is given detailed consideration in Chapter 11. For present purposes, it suffices to point out that the House of Lords cast no doubt upon the Court of Appeal's opinion that the section 78(1) discretion had been available to the judge.

Factors Relevant to the Exercise of the Discretion

We may now consider the factors which may be relevant to the exercise of the discretion in the present context, whether the case be one of unlawful surveillance or one of unlawful search of the person or property. Taking surveillance first, the Court of Appeal in *Khan* somewhat surprisingly thought that the factors described in *Smurthwaite and Gill* as being appropriate for consideration in cases involving *agents provocateurs* and entrapment more generally were relevant also to unlawful surveillance. However, it went on to describe the factors which made exclusion inappropriate in the particular case at hand in a way making rather more sense for the situation where the gravamen of the defence complaint is the unlawfulness of the police conduct. First, as we have noted, the police had acted in accordance with the Home Office guidelines, and not in some arbitrary and uncontrolled manner. Secondly, the elements of trespass and damage were relatively trivial. The upshot of these two factors was that the illegality in question was considered to be not one of great seriousness. Thirdly, the offence being investigated was, by contrast, itself one of great seriousness, namely the importation, on a large scale, of heroin into the United Kingdom.

An additional factor which might have been mentioned, but was not, is that the damage and trespass were done to a third party, rather than to the accused, so that they entailed no prejudice to Khan himself.[303] Had the damage and trespass

[301] [1996] 3 WLR 162, at 171. [302] See *ibid*. 172 and 175.

[303] An authority which might be thought significant in this respect is *Roberts* [1997] 1 Cr.App.R 217, considered in Ch. 6, text to n. 170 above. This is an issue of considerable importance in relation to Fourth Amendment jurisprudence in the United States. The leading cases include *Jones* v. *US*, 362 US 257 (1960); *Alderman* v. *US*, 394 US 165 (1969); *Rakas* v. *Illinois*, 439 US 128 (1978); *Rawlings* v. *Kentucky*, 448 US 98 (1980); *Minnesota* v. *Olson*, 495 US 91 (1990). For an illuminating discussion, see La Fave, *Search and Seizure* (3rd. edn., 1996), V. iv, § 11.3.

been discounted in this way, the appellant would have been left only with the complaint that the privacy of his conversations had not been respected. As we have already seen, there is ample authority at Court of Appeal level indicating that the fact that a suspect's remarks were recorded surreptitiously is most unlikely to lead to their exclusion.[304] That authority was relied upon by counsel for the Crown but was not referred to by the court. The House of Lords, of course, need not have been inhibited by the cases at the lower level, but, though it had the opportunity to decide whether or not English law recognizes a broader right of privacy, it declined to do so on the basis that, on well-established principles, any breach of such a right, if it should exist, would not render inadmissible in law evidence obtained thereby. It does not seem to have considered that this issue of *domestic* law, as opposed to that of possible breach of the Convention, was relevant so far as discretionary exclusion was concerned.

In surveillance cases, the evidence may well be confessional, or, even if not confessional, will certainly be contained in words spoken by the accused. By contrast, in cases involving unlawful search of his person or property, the evidence obtained will, in general, be real evidence of some kind or other. This distinction may well prove to have a continuing importance, though now as relevant to the proper exercise of the discretion, rather than to its availability in the first place. For example, the evidence in *Cooke*,[305] which came from a sheath of the accused's hair, was DNA evidence. It was alleged to show, beyond any reasonable doubt, that the accused had raped the complainant. Glidewell LJ pointed out that, on the assumption that the hair sample had been obtained unlawfully, the manner of its obtaining did not affect the accuracy or strength of the evidence in any way. In this respect, the evidence differed from a disputed confession, where the truth of that confession might well be itself in issue. This well-tried line of thought rather neglects the point that the rules and discretion in relation to confessions are not wholly concerned with the rooting out of unreliable examples. A better reason for the view taken in *Cooke* that the DNA evidence ought not to be excluded was that the offence itself was one of great seriousness, that the evidence was extremely cogent, that it had as great a capacity for demonstrating innocence as guilt, and that any assault upon the accused had been of a relatively trivial kind.

[304] See *Jelsen and Katz* (1989) 90 Cr.App.R 456; *Ali (Shaukat)*, *The Times*, 19 Feb. 1991; *Bailey* [1993] 3 All ER 513; *Cadette* [1995] Crim.LR 229. And see the discussion in the text to nn. 280–3 above.

[305] [1995] 1 Cr.App.R 318.

8

Confessions: Ancillary Issues Under the Exclusionary Rule and Discretion

We have dealt both with the rule for confessions and with the exclusionary discretion for confessions and other evidence. It is now appropriate to examine a number of ancillary issues, all concerned with or arising out of the law relating to confessions.

Involuntary Signature

As we have seen, where the accused says that he did confess but claims that his confession was involuntary, the exclusionary rule is explicitly prayed in aid. On the other hand, where he denies making it at all, the rule does not usually come into play. However, it was pointed out in an earlier chapter[1] that the accused may simply say that he did not confess, yet, by pointing to police breaches of the code provisions which deal with the recording of confessions, place the prosecution in the difficult position of having to prove the reliability (under section 76(2)(b) of the Police and Criminal Evidence Act 1984 ('the 1984 Act')) of a confession which is, at the *voir dire* stage, merely putative.

A rather different problem arises where the accused denies making a confession, yet admits putting his signature at the end of a written statement, but goes on to allege that he was persuaded to sign by some oppressive conduct on the part of the police. In *Ajodha* v. *The State*, the Privy Council held that, in these circumstances, the prosecution is:[2]

> relying on the signature as the acknowledgement and authentication by the accused of the statement as his own, and . . . from this it must follow that, if the voluntary character of the signature is challenged, this inevitably puts in issue the voluntary character of the statement itself.

This matter may, in principle, seem to be rather less straightforward than their Lordships suggested. Certainly, no consistent view on the point had emerged in

[1] See Ch. 5, text to nn. 113–14 above. [2] [1982] AC 204, at 220.

the authorities from Guyana and from Trinidad and Tobago which were considered in *Ajodha*.[3] It would be an entirely tenable view that, since the signature is not itself a confession, there is no challenge to the voluntariness of any confession; in other words, this situation is to be dealt with no differently from that where the accused simply says that the police invented his confession.

There does not seem to be any post-Act authority on the *Ajodha* point. If *Ajodha* is good law so far as the present position in England is concerned, it ought to apply no less to the case where the signature is attached, not to a written statement proper, but to a record made by the police of their interview with the accused.[4] Even if it is not good law, it would seem perfectly possible for the statement or record to which the accused's signature was involuntarily added to be excluded under the section 78(1) discretion, for the admission of such evidence would seem clearly to be capable of having an adverse effect on the fairness of the proceedings. Furthermore, the reliability of the putative confession may, just as in the case where it is not signed, be put in doubt by any failure on the part of the police to follow the requirement of the code provisions which seek to ensure the accuracy of the record.

No 'Person in Authority' Requirement

At common law, it was established at Court of Appeal level that the exclusionary rule applied only to confessions made to 'persons in authority'.[5] The essence of the idea of a 'person in authority' was that it comprehended persons with authority over the course of the prosecution of the accused, though not all examples of such persons could be explained in these terms.[6] The absurdity of a rule rendering admissible a confession made in response to a death threat from an outsider yet inadmissible one made in response to a statement from a police officer that it would be better to confess persuaded the Criminal Law Revision Committee to recommend abolition of the requirement.[7] Section 82(1) did, among other things, put that recommendation into effect.

It does not follow that the status or authority of the person questioning the suspect has become irrelevant. Section 67(9) of the 1984 Act provides:'[p]ersons other than police officers who are charged with the duty of investigating offences or charging offenders shall in the discharge of that duty have regard to any relevant provision of a [code of practice made under the Act].' The most obviously relevant Code of Practice is Code C, dealing with the detention, treatment, and questioning of suspects. As we have already seen, this Code impinges greatly

[3] See Lord Bridge's discussion, *ibid*. 214–20. [4] Under Code C, para. 11.10.

[5] See *Moore* (1852) 2 Den. CC 522, 169 ER 608; *Sleeman* (1853) 6 Cox CC 245; *Cleary* (1963) 48 Cr.App.R 116.

[6] See, e.g., *Upchurch* (1836) 1 Mood. 465, 168 ER 346 (the wife of a private prosecutor) and *Wilson and Marshall-Graham* [1967] 2 QB 406 (the owner of stolen goods).

[7] 11th Report, Cmnd. 4991 (1972), para. 58. See also Mirfield [1981] Crim.LR 92.

upon issues of admissibility under section 76(2) and is even more significant so far as discretionary decisions to exclude under section 78(1) are concerned. Though it is to be noted that the title of Code C restricts itself to the acts of 'police officers', it is clear that persons 'charged with the duty of investigating offences or charging offenders' must at least *have regard to* its provisions. So who are the persons covered by section 67(9), and what is the nature and significance of their obligation under that subsection?

The courts have interpreted quite widely the category of persons within the ambit of section 67(9). Where the investigator comes from some governmental or quasi-governmental agency which has responsibility for the investigation of crime, there would seem to be no problem at all. So customs officers clearly come within the terms of that subsection.[8] But not all agencies which may come across evidence of crime in the course of their duties have *investigation of crime* as their task. For example, inspectors appointed under section 432 of the Companies Act 1985 to investigate the affairs of a company and to report back to the Secretary of State have no duty to take the lead in inquiring into the commission of any criminal offences which they uncover, but only to refer them to the police.[9]

Where a public body is being considered, its powers will have the authority either of statute or of the prerogative, but where the body is private, the law of contract or the general common law will be the source of power. The courts have not restricted the ambit of section 67(9) to public bodies, preferring to say that the source of the duty, in legal terms, does not matter.[10] Hence, the emphasis is upon whether or not there exists a duty and, if there does, its content. The earliest reported case on the subsection, *Twaites and Brown*,[11] concerned commercial investigators employed by a major chain of betting shops to look into employee fraud. The Court of Appeal, perhaps impressed by the fact that the investigators were ex-policemen who followed closely the methods of their erstwhile profession, had no difficulty in regarding them as within the terms of section 67(9). It has been said that the question is one of fact in each case,[12] but also that a question of law may arise if the court has to construe some statute or other document.[13]

The significance of a decision that the person in question either is or is not a person charged with the relevant duty should not be overestimated. Oppression remains oppression whether or not the person who brings it to bear has any formal investigatory role. The same may be said of statutory unreliability, or, for that matter, conduct which is examined in terms of its effect on the fairness of the proceedings under section 78(1). The codes are, at most, relevant to these issues, so that neither the presence nor the absence of breach thereof is conclusive. Still, the defence will undoubtedly be in a better position to argue for exclusion if it can

[8] *Sanusi* [1992] Crim.LR 43.
[9] *Seelig and Spens* [1992] 1 WLR 148. See also *Smith* [1994] 1 WLR 1396.
[10] See, in particular, *Joy* v. *Federation against Copyright Theft Ltd* [1993] Crim.LR 588.
[11] (1990) 92 Cr.App.R 106.
[12] *Seelig and Spens* [1992] 1 WLR 148, at 158.
[13] *Bayliss* (1993) 98 Cr.App.R 235, at 238.

point to some provision or provisions of Code C, in particular, which were applicable but breached, for it will then have concrete information to put before the court. Whether or not there is a difference between the duty to comply with code provisions which lies upon the police and the instruction to 'have regard to them' which is imposed upon the persons caught by section 67(9) does not seem to have been discussed in the cases. Presumably, it will be much less reasonable to expect a store detective, if such person is held to be within the ambit of the sub-section,[14] to know chapter and verse than it is to expect that of a police officer. It may be supposed that the letter of those provisions will be considered less important, for the non-police investigators, than the spirit behind them.

Use of Excluded Confessions other than by the Prosecution as Part of Its Case

The straightforward situation is where the prosecution seeks to adduce the contents of the accused's confession as evidence of their truth. The hearsay rule does not prevent such use, but the special exclusionary rule for confessions or the exclusionary discretion as applied to confessions may well do so. Yet there are a number of other ways in which the prosecution itself or some co-accused may wish to use the accused's confession statement. The law as to these uses is very complex, probably because the hearsay rule itself and the special exclusionary principles for confessions both have a place in the argument. However, it is unnecessary to repeat here how the hearsay aspects of the present problem have been dealt with by the courts, for they have been given detailed treatment in Chapter 4.[15]

The issue with which we are now concerned is whether or not a confession which has been or would be excluded as against the prosecution as part of its own case may be used either by the prosecution itself or by a co-accused, at some other stage of the trial, in a way detrimental to the accused. We must begin with *Treacy*.[16] In that case, a man who was already in police custody on a murder charge was questioned by a policeman about that offence. Despite complications introduced by Treacy's state of mind at the time, it seems clear that the reason for the Court of Criminal Appeal's decision that his answers ought not to be admitted in evidence was that there had been a breach of rule 3 of the Judges' Rules 1918.[17] The court went on to decide that the document containing his answers could not be used by the prosecution for the purposes of cross-examination of Treacy as to his credit. As Humphreys J succinctly put it: '[i]f it is not admissible, nothing more ought to be heard of it, and it is quite a mistake to think that a document can be made admissible in evidence which is otherwise inadmissible

[14] Which will itself depend on the terms of the store detective's contract and the scope of his duties—see *ibid*. 239.

[15] See Ch. 4, text to nn. 64–70 above.

[16] [1944] 2 All ER 229.

[17] Strangely, there is no express mention of the Rules in Humphreys J's judgment.

simply because it is put to a person in cross-examination.'[18] Though the language here is that of admissibility and inadmissibility, it seems that, since the document was the subject of discretionary exclusion, strictly the case stands only for the proposition that a confession excluded in the exercise of the discretion cannot be used for prosecution cross-examination purposes.

Treacy has been treated in later cases[19] as authority in relation to confessions inadmissible under the exclusionary rule and, indeed, the argument of principle articulated by Humphreys J would apply *a fortiori* to inadmissible confessions. It is clear that, at common law, prosecution cross-examination which revealed either the contents of the confession or the fact that it was made[20] was impermissible in both types of case. Furthermore, the same principle applies in favour of any co-accused of the maker of the statement.[21]

Though not expressly explained in the cases, the policy behind the *Treacy* line of authority seems clear enough. Whatever be the underlying rationale for exclusion, whether it be the danger of unreliability, the need to protect the accused, or the desire to discipline the police, it will be seriously undermined if the prosecution is at liberty to cross-examine the accused about it as a previous inconsistent statement. We may lack confidence in the jury's ability to follow a direction that they must use the confession only as relevant to the accused's credit and not as itself evidence of his guilt, so 'nothing more ought to be heard of it'. There is, of course, a sacrifice in that the accused is not exposed to the need to explain why he denies doing that to which he once confessed, but this sacrifice is regarded as worth making.[22] It is right to add that not all common law jurisdictions have been persuaded. Thus, the Supreme Court of the United States held, in *Harris* v. *New York*,[23] that a confession excluded for breach of the *Miranda* rules,[24] as part of the prosecution's own case, may be used in cross-examination of the accused for purposes of impeachment.

It is a little less clear why the co-accused should necessarily be able to shelter behind the exclusion of the accused's confession. To the extent that it is excluded for unreliability or in order to discipline the police, the parasitic impermissibility of the cross-examination makes sense, but where the law is pursuing the protective principle, there seems to be no reason to protect anyone but the accused himself. The answer may be that *it is* a way of securing protection of the accused, for once the confession is in evidence, it may, in fact, be used directly against the accused.

Where the interests of the accused and co-accused are in conflict, the policy is much less clear-cut. There is now ample authority for the proposition that the

[18] [1944] 2 All ER 229, at 236.

[19] *Rice* [1963] 1 QB 857, at 868; *Wong Kam-ming* [1980] AC 247, at 258–9.

[20] For the latter point, see *Rice*, n. 19 above, at 868. [21] *Ibid.*

[22] See *Wong Kam-ming* [1980] AC 247, at 258–9. See also Ch. 4, text to nn. 96–8 above.

[23] 401 US 222 (1971). See also *Oregon* v. *Hass*, 420 US 714 (1975). Cf. *Calder* (1996) 132 DLR (4th) 577, in which the Supreme Court of Canada took a position so far as breach of a constitutional rule was concerned somewhere between *Harris* and *Treacy*.

[24] See *Miranda* v. *Arizona*, 384 US 436 (1966).

co-accused may himself cross-examine the accused about the latter's confession as a previous inconsistent statement, even though that confession has been excluded as against the prosecution.[25] The sole restriction upon the co-accused is that necessarily imposed by the requirement of relevance; the attack must tend to forward his case, rather than being merely gratuitous. It is to be observed that the freedom thus given to the co-accused entails potential prejudice to the accused.[26] Though the judge must instruct the jury to use the evidence in question only in relation to the credibility of the evidence given by the accused against the co-accused and not in support of the prosecution case against the accused,[27] one may reasonably doubt the efficacy of such an instruction. If so, it becomes abundantly clear that, for the sake of the co-accused, the accused may, in fact, be substantially and adversely affected by evidence ruled unreliable, obtained by oppressive conduct, or whatever. The interests of the co-accused in not being prevented or discouraged from defending himself are preferred to those of the accused in not having excluded evidence used against him, and no weighing of those interests in the particular case is, according to the authorities, permissible.[28]

What then where the co-accused wishes to go further and to adduce evidence of the accused's confession, not as a previous inconsistent statement, but as itself relevant to the issue of the co-accused's own guilt or innocence? There is conflicting authority on this point at Court of Appeal level. According to *Campbell and Williams*,[29] a confession excluded as against the prosecution, under either section 76 or section 78, cannot be relied upon by the co-accused. Though this point was not taken in *Beckford and Daley*,[30] it was the way that case was sought to be explained in *Campbell and Williams* itself. In the words of Hobhouse J: '[i]t is implicit in the decision in *Beckford* that a co-defendant cannot be in a better position than the prosecution in relation to the proof of an inadmissible confession as a confession.' The reference here is to an 'inadmissible' confession, yet the one in *Beckford and Daley* had been excluded by the trial judge using his section 78 discretion. So, the gist of Hobhouse J's statement is presumably that both true inadmissibility under section 76(2) and discretionary exclusion under section 78(1) are comprehended.

The source of the principle receiving support from *Campbell and Williams* must be the common law, for both section 76(2) and section 78(1) are expressly limited to denying the *prosecution* use of the accused's confession. Any such view of the law lies uncomfortably with the authority on cross-examination to show

[25] *Rowson* [1986] QB 174; *Lui Mei-Lin* [1989] AC 288.

[26] In some cases, it may be possible to avoid the prejudice by ordering separate trials—see *O'Boyle* (1990) 92 Cr.App.R 202. And separate trials may be ordered even where the exculpated accused suffers significant disadvantage thereby—see *Clare* [1995] Crim.LR 726.

[27] See *Rowson* [1986] QB 174, at 182; *Lui Mei-Lin* [1989] AC 288, at 298.

[28] This is the *general* view taken by the courts of this kind of conflict of interest between the co-accused—see, e.g., *Miller* (1952) 36 Cr.App.R 179; *Lowery* v. *The Queen* [1974] AC 85; *Murdoch* v. *Taylor* [1965] AC 574; *Reid* [1989] Crim.LR 719.

[29] [1993] Crim.LR 449 (transcript through LEXIS). See now *Myers*, 24 July 1997 (HL) and n. 32 below.

[30] [1991] Crim.LR 834 (transcript through LEXIS).

inconsistency, but also fits uneasily with the wording of section 76(1). That subsection positively permits evidence of a confession to be adduced 'against' an accused person unless excluded in pursuance of the rest of the section. There is absolutely no indication that the co-accused does not enjoy this statutory permission. Therefore, as a matter of literal interpretation, the provision would seem to allow the co-accused complete freedom to use the accused's confession against him, as long as relevant to advance his own case.[31] There is one possible answer to this point. Perhaps it may be said that the co-accused is adducing evidence in his own favour, rather than *against* the accused, and so is outside section 76 altogether. The common law would then be available to preserve the integrity of the exclusionary rule and discretion by denying the co-accused the advantage of the indirect exculpatory effect of the accused's confession in order to ensure that the trier of fact does not use it for its direct, inculpatory effect. However, it must be admitted that this explanation does not square well with the reasoning in *Campbell and Williams*, for the Court of Appeal considered that the confession was available in favour of Barratt precisely because it went against its maker, Campbell.

A quite contrary view of the law was taken by the Court of Appeal in *Myers*.[32] It was there held that the trial judge had been right to allow the appellant's co-accused to adduce evidence of the appellant's admissions in order to support the co-accused's own case, even though the prosecution had not sought to rely upon them in its case against the appellant because obtained in breach of various Code C provisions. Though it is not expressly stated, it seems very likely that this was a case where the admissions were properly to be excluded under section 78(1). This seems to make the case on all fours with *Beckford and Daley* (as explained in *Campbell and Williams*); hence the clash of authority.

The decision of the court in *Myers* to certify a point of general public importance and to grant leave to appeal presents the House of Lords with the opportunity to place the law on this issue on a sound footing. It may be that the House will be assisted in that task if it seeks to tailor the law to the principles lying behind the exclusionary rule and discretion. Where, as must necessarily be the case under section 76(2)(b), the reason for exclusion is the potential unreliability of the confession, there seems every reason for excluding it no less as against the co-accused than as against the prosecution. Why should it be any more reliable in its indirect exculpatory effect that in its direct inculpatory effect? On the other hand, where, as may be the case under section 76(2)(a), the purpose of exclusion is to protect the accused's pre-trial rights, there is an obvious conflict between that purpose and the co-accused's trial right to defend himself. No hint of such a possible difference between the various heads of the exclusionary rule and

[31] The point has been made by a number of commentators—see, e.g. Hirst [1989] Crim.LR 603; Tunkel [1991] Crim.LR 396.

[32] [1996] 2 Cr.App.R 335. Its view has now been upheld in the House of Lords—see *Myers*, 24 July 1997. There are indications, particularly in the speech of Lord Hope of Craighead, that the point made in the paragraph which follows in the present text has been taken. See also Law Com. No. 245, June 1997, paras. 8.93–8.95 and recommendation 19.

discretion has yet emerged in the cases, yet it could not be right for the law to content itself with a rough and ready compromise, not dictated by principle, which denied the co-accused all use of the accused's confession as relevant to the issue, but allowed him complete freedom to use it to attack the accused's credibility, even though it is available to the prosecution for neither purpose.

Evidence Yielded by Inadmissible Confessions

Subsections (4) and (5) of section 76 address some ancillary problems which may arise in respect of material of evidential value yielded by, though separate from, the strictly confessional aspect of the accused's statement. Reference has been made already to the situation where that statement is sought to be used as showing that the accused speaks, write, or expresses himself in a particular way,[33] but a little more needs to be added here.

Mode of Speech, Writing, or Expression

It will be recalled that, in *Voisin*,[34] the accused had been invited to write out the word, 'Bloody Belgian', but had actually written, 'Bladie Belgiam'. This was exactly the misspelling the police had found on a label attached to a parcel containing the trunk of the body of the Belgian woman with whose murder Voisin was charged. It has been argued, earlier in this work, that, because the definition of 'confession' in section 82(1) of the 1984 Act, is put in terms of a 'statement' which is wholly or partly adverse to its maker, the piece of paper upon which Voisin had written, 'Bladie Belgiam' for the police would not constitute a confession. It cannot be said that the words written *state* anything.

Where there *is* a statement from the accused, whether oral or written, as long as it is wholly or partly adverse to him, it is a confession and, therefore, is caught by section 76. Had Voisin written, 'I hate bladie Belgiams', his words would have been adverse to him at the time when written, for his misspelling of the last two would be equally incriminating. If the words written had been, 'I killed the bladie Belgiam', they would be doubly incriminating, both in what they stated and in how they stated it. Each of these statements would be comprehended by section 76(4)(b) of the Act, which states:

> The fact that a confession is wholly or party excluded in pursuance of this section shall not effect the admissibility in evidence—
>
> (a) . . .
>
> (b) where the confession is relevant as showing that the accused speaks, writes or expresses himself in a particular way, of so much of the confession as is necessary to show that he does so.

So if we imagine either statement to have been forced from Voisin by oppression,

[33] See Ch. 4, text to nn. 51–3 above. [34] [1918] 1 KB 531.

the prosecution will be able to adduce only the 'bladie Belgiam(s)' part thereof. Editing here would be quite straightforward. Much more difficult would be a case where the accused had, in making a statement admitting his guilt of the crime in question, done so with a pronounced stammer or in a thick regional accent, for the stammer might come or the accent be most pronounced in the very part of the statement where he accepted his guilt. To let the jury hear that part, because section 76(4)(b) indicates that they should, would be to put before them the inadmissible confessional element. Of course, an appropriate direction would have to be given in any event, but there might well be more prejudicial effect than probative value in the evidence in question even if accompanied by such a direction. If so, it would seem to be right for the judge to exclude the statement in question under section 78(1) as likely to have an adverse effect on the fairness of the proceedings.

Facts Discovered in Consequence of the Confession

It sometimes happens that the accused reveals something in his confession which enables the police to discover a fact which incriminates him. For example, he may say, in the course of a confession to murder, that the weapon used can be found on nearby waste ground. The weapon is then found there by the police. Now, if the weapon can be shown to be the murder weapon and if the accused's fingerprints are to be found upon it, there will be strong evidence against him, without the need for reference to how the weapon came to be found.

The argument that, if the accused's confession is inadmissible by virtue of the exclusionary rule, the facts discovered in consequence of that confession should also be inadmissible was rejected in *Warickshall*.[35] There the accused had confessed to receiving stolen goods and, in consequence of her confession, those goods were found concealed in the bed in her lodgings. It was held that evidence could be given as to where they had been found since '*a fact*, if it exist at all, must exist invariably in the same manner, whether the confession from which it derived be *in other respects* true or false'.[36] Section 76(4)(a) of the 1984 Act puts this decision into statutory form. It states that the fact that a confession is wholly or partly excluded under the section does not affect the admissibility in evidence 'of any facts discovered as a result of the confession'.

We must here consider the much-criticized case of *Barker*[37] in the light of section 76. Barker was obliquely informed by a tax inspector that he would not be prosecuted if he voluntarily disclosed certain tax frauds. He then produced two fraudulently-prepared ledgers, yet, despite the inspector's assurance, he was later prosecuted. The trial judge ruled admissible both these ledgers and certain other documents Barker had produced. The Court of Criminal Appeal reversed him. It

[35] (1783) 1 Leach CC 263, 168 ER 234.

[36] *Ibid.* 264 (emphasis in original) and 235, respectively.

[37] [1941] 2 KB 381. For criticism, see, e.g., Gotlieb (1956) 72 *LQR* 209, at 222–3 and Cowen and Carter, *Essays on the Law of Evidence* (1956), at 65–8.

accepted that evidence could be given of facts discovered in consequence of an inadmissible confession, but sought to distinguish the present case because the offer not to prosecute expressly related to the production of business books and records and that, therefore, the documents stood on precisely the same footing as an oral or written confession brought into existence as a result of such an inducement.

Barker itself is not an example of the *Warickshall* situation, for the ledgers were not discovered in consequence of any oral or written confession by Barker. However, there may seem to be an indication in the judgment of the court that the ledgers would have been equally inadmissible had Barker first confessed to the offences in question and then told the inspector where the ledgers were to be found. If so, *Barker* suggested that there was an exception to *Warickshall* whenever the facts discovered could be said to be precisely equivalent to a confession and the inducement related to those facts.

It has been argued that, since the *Warickshall* principle is clearly based upon the reliability of the facts discovered, it ought to be extended to the facts of *Barker* and that therefore, as a decision on admissibility, *Barker* is wrong.[38] Since the inducement was held out after the ledgers had come into existence, it could not have had any effect upon their reliability. Thus, there was no good reason for them to stand on the same footing as an ordinary confession. This argument would leave the earlier case of *Cason*[39] undisturbed. In that case, otherwise essentially similar to *Barker*, the documents in question were statements of the accused's capital wealth which had been drawn up after the inducement had been held out.

It will be recalled that section 82(1) defines a 'confession' as including 'any statement wholly or partly adverse to the person who made it'. Now, in both *Barker* and *Cason*, the documents would seem to have been adverse to their maker no less when made than when sought to be relied upon by the prosecution, since the fact that tax had been evaded was (presumably) discoverable from them. But would 'confessions' of this kind be within the potential scope of the exclusionary rule laid down by section 76(2)? The early part of that subsection seems to distinguish the making of a confession from its obtaining. It could be said that, in *Barker*, a confession made earlier was obtained later. However, section 76(2)(b) refers to the possible unreliability of any confession which might be *made* by the accused *in consequence of* anything said or done. Here, the word 'made' is used in a context the same as that in which 'obtained' is used elsewhere in section 76(2). It does seem that, considered as a whole, section 76(2) contemplates that the confessions to which it applies are ones made in consequence of oppression or things said or done. If that is right, a confession like that in *Barker* is now outside the scope of the exclusionary rule. It must be recognized that a consequence of this interpretation of section 76(2) is that a statement in a diary, admitting the commission of an offence and written before its maker was interrogated, would also be outside its scope. Such a result would have met with the

[38] See Gotlieb, n. 37 above, 222 and Cowen and Carter, n. 37 above, at 67–8.
[39] (1935) 14 ATC 471.

approval of Crompton J; long ago, in *Leatham*,[40] he suggested that a pre-existing, non-induced confession was properly analogous to the body of a murder victim rather than to a later, induced confession. The documents in *Cason*, however, would be within the potential scope of the exclusionary rule, though they might be found to be reliable.

If the foregoing argument is sound, the exception to *Warickshall* apparently suggested by *Barker* will have disappeared; the ledgers could no longer be regarded as the precise equivalent of a confession for the purposes of the exclusionary rule. The actual decision in *Barker* remains explicable only by reference to the exclusionary discretion based upon fairness which has been considered in the preceding two chapters.[41]

Where there is nothing on the murder weapon, like fingerprints, to connect it to the accused, a more difficult and controversial issue arises. Since the facts, namely the finding of the murder weapon in the place indicated by the accused, confirm the reliability of at least that part of his confession which deals with the whereabouts of the weapon, should that part, or indeed the whole of the confession, be admissible in evidence? Wildly divergent views on this point were taken in the eighteenth- and nineteenth-century cases.[42] Fortunately, little, if anything, would be gained by examining them here, not least because the post-Act Privy Council case of *Lam Chi-ming* v. *The Queen*[43] confirms that the common law dictated that no part of the *prima facie* inadmissible confession was rendered admissible by the discovery of the relevant (reliable) facts. Lord Griffiths pointed out that the more recent English cases establish:[44]

> that the rejection of an improperly obtained confession is not dependent only upon possible unreliability but also upon the principle that a man cannot be compelled to incriminate himself and upon the importance which attaches in a civilised society to proper behaviour by the police towards those in their custody.

The statutory provisions, as Lord Griffiths also pointed out in *Lam Chi-ming*,[45] confirm the mature common law position. The exclusionary rule in section 76(2) *prima facie* applies even to confirmed confessions, and there is nothing in the rest of section 76 to defeat that position. Furthermore, the Act rejects a rather mysterious device suggested in two nineteenth-century cases[46] and supported by a majority of the Criminal Revision Committee in 1972,[47] namely that the prosecution should be allowed to adduce evidence that the fact was discovered 'as a result' of a statement made by the accused. Section 76(5) renders prosecution evidence of this kind inadmissible, 'unless evidence of how it was dis-

[40] (1861) 8 Cox CC 498, at 501.

[41] Gotlieb, n. 37 above, at 222–3, considered this to be the best way of explaining *Barker*.

[42] See *ibid*. 211–23 for a treatment of these cases.

[43] [1991] 2 AC 212.

[44] *Ibid*. 220.

[45] *Ibid*.

[46] *Thurtell* (1824) Annual Register 4 and *Harris* (1832), cited in Joy, *The Admissibility of Confessions and the Challenge of Jurors* (1842), 83–4. *Berriman* (1854) 6 Cox CC 388, at 389, is emphatic authority the other way.

[47] 11th. Report, n. 7 above, para. 69.

covered is given by him or on his behalf'. The qualification seems to envisage the possibility of such evidence being used to challenge the credit of the accused where he has given a different version of how the facts came to be discovered. So if he keeps quiet, the device is inoperative. This seems right in principle, for 'it is wrong that the jury should be informed indirectly of something which it is thought that the interests of justice require that they should not be informed directly'.[48] Section 76(6) makes a sensible exception to the rule stated in section 76(5) for case in which the confession has been only partly excluded and in which the fact was discovered as a result of the unexcluded part.

Care will be necessary, in some cases, in deciding where the line is to be drawn between the confession itself, which is inadmissible, and the facts discovered, which are admissible. In *Lam Chi-ming* v. *The Queen*,[49] the police video-recorded the defendants directing a car to a place on the waterfront, then each of them in turn making gestures indicating where the murder weapon had been thrown. Divers had then found the weapon at that spot. The Privy Council agreed with the view of the Court of Appeal of Hong Kong that these actions and gestures were 'as much a part of the confession as were the accompanying words to the like effect'.[50]

One further issue needs to be raised in this section. It must certainly be assumed that the *Warickshall* principle applies no less to facts discovered in consequence of a confession eventually excluded as a matter of discretion than to those discovered in consequence of one excluded under section 76.[51] But what if it should be argued that evidence of the facts themselves should, in either case, be excluded under the discretionary power? There seems to be no English case directly in point,[52] but there would seem to be no good reason for distinguishing the case where non-confessional evidence is acquired with the intervention of a confession from the case where it is acquired directly. It would follow that the discretion, whether under section 78(1) or under section 82(3), would be available to the judge.

It may be argued that this conclusion is inconsistent with the plain words of section 76(4)(a) which provide that the fact that a confession is wholly or partly excluded under section 76 shall not affect the admissibility of any facts discovered as a result of the confession. The weakness of such an argument is that it fails to distinguish the question whether or not evidence is admissible from the question whether or not it ought to be admitted. Here, as elsewhere, exercise of the discretion to exclude involves refusal to allow admissible evidence to be admitted.

[48] See *ibid*. 46, n. 4 (the view of the minority).

[49] [1991] 2 AC 212.

[50] *Ibid*. 216. See also *Jenkins* (1822) Russ. & Ry. 492, 168 ER 914.

[51] It might be just possible to argue that, since s. 76(4)(b) renders the facts admissible only when the confession is excluded 'in pursuance of this section', the application of the *Warwickshall* principle to cases where confessions are excluded as a matter of discretion has been impliedly revoked. Yet the result would be so illogical—the facts being inadmissible in law though the confession is excludable only as a matter of discretion—that any such argument would almost certainly be defeated, probably by saying that s. 78 has no provision to replace the *Warwickshall* principle because it was intended to leave it untouched, for these purposes.

[52] Though reference should be made to the discussion of *Barker* [1941] 2 KB 381 earlier in this section.

9

Compelled Self-incrimination and Incriminating Silence

General Introduction

This is not a book about that aspect of the privilege against self-incrimination which entitles a person, whether suspected of crime or not, to refuse to answer questions because the answer might be capable of being used as evidence against him at some later trial. It is of considerable importance in the civil law, no less than in the criminal, but our sole concern here is with the evidential use of incriminating material at a criminal trial. The whole point of that aspect of the privilege is to prevent such material becoming available in the first place. However, there are now a number of situations in which Parliament has removed it, or has been taken by the courts to have removed it, usually in the context of some investigative purpose apparently separated and apart from the concerns of the criminal law itself. Where the law provides for the examination of the citizen under the compulsion of punishment for failure to answer satisfactorily, it is plain that there is every chance of incriminating statements being made. Then, the question for consideration becomes whether or not such statements will be available to the prosecution at some subsequent criminal trial of the citizen in question.

Equally, the law does allow for forms of compulsory gathering of non-confession evidence by the police or by others acting in an investigatory role. Here there is usually supposed to be less of a difficulty in their later use at a criminal trial. This is partly because such powers are very often given to the police with a view to their collecting incriminatory evidence for trial, rather than for some separate purpose. In addition—and this is probably why powers are granted more directly in this case—it seems clear that the aspect of the privilege against self-incrimination referred to above can have no application at all to the gathering of what is, typically, real evidence. However, if we think more broadly than about that aspect of the privilege and attend to the meaning of the Latin maxim *nemo debet prodere se ipsum*, we may conclude that the key distinction is not in terms of the nature of the evidence acquired but of whether or not the will of the person in question was engaged in bringing about its acquisition. Thus, if I am persuaded by threats of violence to allow the police to take a blood sample, I am certainly made to produce evidence against myself. It is quite otherwise if the police knock me unconscious and then extract the sample. This is not, of course, at all to say that the latter police tactic is to be preferred or that there is a better reason to exclude the sample in the first case than in the second.[1] At all events, the line between cases which do and do not entail self-incrimination is inevitably an extremely difficult one to draw in practice.[2]

Outside the area of compelled self-incrimination, but having much in common with it, is the topic of what evidential use may be made, at the criminal trial, of the accused's silence when questioned by the police. We shall see that the well-established common law idea that silence (or even a denial) in the face of accusation is capable, in some situations, of counting as an implied admission of the accuracy of that accusation has recently had added to it a statutory rule (or, actually, collection of rules) allowing adverse inferences to be drawn directly from silence in the face thereof.[3] Even more recently, Parliament has given its *imprimatur* to the drawing of such inferences, in certain circumstances, from failure to disclose adequately and properly before trial the nature and content of the accused's defence.[4] Here, if you like, the suspect/accused is faced with the prospect of disadvantage should he fail to speak up, so his refusal or failure to answer is made costly. Where a penalty is imposed upon the person who fails to comply with a requirement made under compulsory investigative powers, his refusal or failure is equally made costly. This renders the situations sufficiently analogous for treatment within the same chapter to be appropriate. Moreover, each situation has the potential to be reviewed for legality in terms of Article 6(1) of the European Convention on Human Rights, which grants the accused the right to a fair trial. In due course, we shall pay attention to the impact of Article 6(1), particularly as interpreted by the European Court of Human Rights in *Murray* v. *United Kingdom*[5] and in *Saunders* v. *United Kingdom*.[6] The former case concerns inferences direct from silence, the latter the use of compelled incriminating evidence at a criminal trial. However, these matters will be considered not in this Chapter but in Chapter 11, which gathers together the various respects in which the law of the Convention is relevant to the present study.

There is considerable interest in the history of the 'privilege against self-incrimination' or the 'right to silence', particularly on the opposite side of the Atlantic. This is no more a book about the history of those concepts than one about their application other than in relation to the use of evidence in criminal proceedings. There are many excellent historical treatments,[7] though it may

[1] A point made at p. 117 above.
[2] See Easton [1991] Crim.LR 18 for some helpful comments.
[3] See Criminal Justice and Public Order Act 1994, ss. 34, 36, and 37.
[4] See Criminal Procedure and Investigations Act 1996, s. 11.
[5] (1996) 22 EHRR 29.
[6] (1997) 23 EHRR 313.
[7] See, in particular, Wigmore (1891) 5 *Harv. LR* 71; Morgan (1949) 34 *Minn. LR* 1; Kemp (1958) 1 *William and Mary LR* 247; Levy, *Origins of the Fifth Amendment* (1968), *passim*; Langbein (1994) 92 *Mich. LR* 1047.

fairly be said that there is radical disagreement among scholars about how these concepts came to be enshrined in the Anglo–American common law.

Compulsory Examination of Suspects and Others

The Substantive Provisions

The leading case, *Scott*,[8] was concerned with compulsory examination of a bankrupt under the Bankrupt Law Consolidation Act 1849, so the willingness of Parliament to waive the idea of a privilege against self-incrimination in order to promote other public policies is of some antiquity.[9] Though there are very many other examples of powers being given to officials to examine citizens under threat of penalty, it is in the context of the commercial and corporate field that modern provisions have been most abundant. For example, under the Insolvency Act 1986, compulsory examination of both individual bankrupts and officers of insolvent companies may take place,[10] but powers are not restricted to those with the most obvious reason to be able to give an account of the financial position and of the whereabouts of any money or other property. So, under section 366(1) of that Act, not only the bankrupt but also the bankrupt's spouse or former spouse, as well as any person known or believed to have in his possession any of the bankrupt's property or to be indebted to him, and any person appearing to be able to give information about the bankrupt's dealings, affairs, or property, may be examined. Under section 235(3), the net is cast equally wide in the case of companies, catching those who took part in the company's formation and its employees. The purpose of all these provisions is clearly to protect the interests of creditors and others with a legitimate claim against the bankrupt or the insolvent company, yet the opportunity for the revelation of criminal acts by persons examined is obviously of great importance as a side-effect.

More directly concerned with criminal fraud of a serious kind is section 2(2) of the Criminal Justice Act 1987 ('the 1987 Act'). The Director of the Serious Fraud Office has power, under section 1(3), to investigate any suspected offence which he reasonably supposes to involve serious or complex fraud. Section 2(2) itself provides:

> The Director may by notice in writing require the person whose affairs are to be investigated . . . or any other person whom he has reason to believe has relevant information to attend . . . at a specified time and place and answer questions or otherwise furnish information with respect to any matters relevant to the investigation.

This is a draconian provision, not least in its wide application to persons not

[8] (1856) Dears. & B. 47, 169 ER 909.

[9] For a general treatment, see Heydon (1971) 87 *LQR* 214. See also McCormack [1993] *JBL* 425; A. T. H. Smith in *Pressing Problems in the Law: Criminal Justice and Human Rights* (ed. Birks, 1995), 75 ff.

[10] Individuals under ss. 290 and 366, company officers, etc., under ss. 133, 235, and 236.

themselves suspected but who may have useful information to give, which is designed to assist in the investigation and successful prosecution of serious fraud. The reason for its introduction, following the report of the Roskill Committee was,[11] no doubt, that the compelling of suspects and other witnesses to speak up would render the task of the prosecution less daunting in cases of complex fraud.

Their Evidential Effects

There are two questions which ought to be kept separate but are sometimes conflated.[12] The first is whether or not, on a proper interpretation, the statutory provision in question does remove the examinee's privilege. The second is, assuming that it does remove it, what evidential use can be made of the incriminating information obtained.

The first question might seem relatively easy to answer, at least in most cases. Attention to the statutory scheme as a whole will tend to show that it is not just statements by a third party incriminating the person at the centre of the investigation which are to be 'encouraged', but statements also from that person himself. It would seem to be part and parcel of the giving of information by such a person that it may well be self-incriminatory, so that the privilege will be regarded as overridden even where express words to that effect are not used.[13] It is now settled that a purposive approach of this kind is to be taken to legislation, at least where it is clear that it imposes a duty upon the examinee to answer. In the leading case, *Bishopsgate Investment Management Limited* v. *Maxwell*,[14] the Court of Appeal, after a detailed discussion of the earlier cases and of the various statutory provisions, concluded that the privilege had been impliedly but clearly excluded in respect of investigations under section 236 of the Insolvency Act 1986.[15] In doing so, that court rejected the opinion of Ferris J in *Barlow Clowes Gilt Managers Ltd (Liquidator)* v. *Mitchell*[16] that, in the absence of an express provision, the person examined was entitled to rely on the privilege.

It does not necessarily follow that incriminating statements obtained at an examination may be used against the examinee at a civil trial, let alone at a criminal one. However, here too the courts have not insisted that express words allowing its use are required. The earliest authorities, indeed, suggested that, where the statute was silent, the answers would necessarily be admissible, even at a criminal trial.[17] In the leading nineteenth-century case, Lord Campbell CJ made

[11] *The Fraud Trials Committee Report* (London, 1986).

[12] See, e.g., the judgment of Dillon LJ in *Bishopsgate Investment Management Ltd* v. *Maxwell* [1993] ch. 1, at 19–20. See also the judgment of Stuart-Smith LJ, at 40–1.

[13] Express words are sometimes used—see, e.g., Children Act 1989, s. 98(1).

[14] [1993] ch. 1.

[15] See also *In re Levitt Ltd* [1992] ch. 457 (also concerned with s. 236); *Bank of England* v. *Riley and Another* [1992] ch. 475 (concerned with s. 42 of the Banking Act 1987); *Seelig and Spens* [1992] 1 WLR 148 and *In re London United Investments plc* [1992] ch. 578 (both concerned with Companies Act 1985, s. 434(1) and (2)).

[16] Unreported, 31 July 1990.

[17] *Scott* (1856) Dears. & B. 47, 169 ER 909; *Widdop* (1872) LR 2 CCR 3; *Coote* (1873) LR 4 PC 599; *Erdheim* [1896] 2 QB 260.

the point that the maxim *nemo tenetur se ipsum accusare* 'applies to the time when the question is put, not to the use which the prosecutor seeks to make of the answer when the answer has been given'.[18] Yet the true position is now as stated by Lord Reid in *Harz and Power*:[19]

> Some statutes expressly provide that incriminating answers may be used against the person who gives them and some statutes expressly provide that they may not. Where . . . there is no such express provision the question whether such answers are admissible evidence must depend on the proper construction of the particular statute.

The answer to that question will depend upon what is the scheme and purpose of the relevant piece of legislation.[20]

In fact, modern statutory provisions do tend to spell out the admissibility of the incriminating evidence, whether in absolute or limited terms. For example, section 433 of the Insolvency Act 1986 provides that any statement made in pursuance of a requirement imposed by or under that Act 'may be used in evidence against any person making or concurring in making the statement'. Given that it is a very obvious possibility that compulsory examination may result in criminal charges being brought, there is no scope for the argument that section 433 pertains only to *civil* proceedings.[21] There is a similarly unequivocal provision in section 434(5) of the Companies Act 1985 which engaged the European Court of Human Rights in *Saunders* v. *United Kingdom*.[22]

One anomaly, created by the interaction of the insolvency provisions and those relating to serious fraud under the Criminal Justice Act 1987, deserves brief mention. As we have seen, the latter provisions are directly concerned with investigation of crime as such, whereas criminal prosecutions arising out of the former entail something of a side-effect. Section 2(8) of the 1987 Act restricts prosecution use of self-incriminating statements obtained under it, in general to cases where the accused has testified inconsistently therewith.[23] Section 2(3) allows the Director of the Serious Fraud Office to require persons, including persons other than the one under investigation, to produce specified, relevant documents. Now, given the possibility of bankruptcy or insolvency investigations going on at the same time or having gone on earlier, some responsible officer might well have obtained an incriminating statement from the party under investigation under compulsive powers given by the Insolvency Act 1986. There would seem to be nothing to prevent the Director requiring the officer in question to release that document to the Serious Fraud Office. In *Hamilton and Others* v. *Naviede*,[24] the House of Lords

[18] *Scott* (1856) Dears. & B. 47, at 59, 169 ER 909 at 914. [19] [1967] 1 AC 760, at 816.

[20] Heydon, (1971) 87 *LQR* 214, at 228–36, discusses what principles of construction should be applied by the courts.

[21] It was so held in *Kansal* [1993] QB 244, even though s. 31(1) of the Theft Act 1968 had been argued to apply to prevent use of the statement in a prosecution under that Act.

[22] (1997) 23 EHRR 313 The case is considered in Ch. 11, text to nn. 18–26 below.

[23] A statement can also be used in chief where the charge is one that the accused has made a misleading statement in his examination under the Act itself.

[24] [1995] 2 AC 75.

held that the Director was indeed at liberty to do so and that, if that were done, he would be able to use such a statement quite free of the restrictions imposed by section 2(8). In principle, subject to the precise terms of the statutory language used, the same would seem to apply to statements indicating guilt of serious fraud which have been collected under any other statutory power precluding the privilege against self-incrimination, at least where the statute in question grants full admissibility at a criminal trial. The result in *Naviede* was described by Lord Nolan as 'anomalous in the extreme',[25] but both he and the rest of their Lordships thought it flowed from the language of the 1987 Act, particularly that of section 2(3).

NON-APPLICATION OF THE ORDINARY LAWS OF CRIMINAL INVESTIGATION

Cases like *Naviede* suggest that the various compulsory examination procedures may give rise to what will seem to many to be unfairness to accused persons, if the evidence in question is inevitably to be allowed to be given against them. This reflection is bolstered by the fact that many of the protections imposed by the ordinary law and the codes of practice made under the Police and Criminal Evidence Act 1984 ('the 1984 Act') do not apply to compulsory examinations.

It will be recalled that section 67(9) of that Act provides: '[p]ersons other than police officers who are charged with the duty of investigating offenses or charging offenders shall in the discharge of that duty have regard to any relevant provision of such a code.' The key phrase is 'charged with the duty of investigating offences or charging offenders', since, if not caught by it, the person in question need have no regard to code provisions. It will be quite obvious from the text in the preceding chapters hereof that Code C, in particular, contains many crucial protections for those suspected of crime, and especially for those arrested and detained. Therefore, it is of some significance that in *Seelig and Spens* the trial judge's decision that inspectors appointed under section 432(1) of the Companies Act 1985 were not caught by section 67(9) of the 1984 Act was upheld. The Court of Appeal considered the issue one of fact, but it did quote, without adverse comment, Henry J's words in ruling on the point, which were:[26]

> [the inspectors'] obligation is to investigate the affairs of the company and to report. In the course of such investigation criminal offences will often emerge, but the fact they do so does not alter the duty of the inspectors. Their duty is to investigate the affairs of the company and to ascertain the facts; they are not conducting a trial of those investigated. It is for others to investigate any criminal offences that may be uncovered.

This will, of course, be an equally proper comment to make, *mutatis mutandis*, of the very many other statutory powers of investigation which preclude the self-incrimination privilege, including those granted by the Insolvency Act 1986. Moreover, the Court of Appeal has more recently, in *Saunders et al.*,[27] rejected the argument that, once it appeared that criminal offences have been or may have

[25] See *ibid.* 109. [26] [1992] 1 WLR 148, at 157–8. [27] [1996] 1 Cr.App.R 463.

been committed, the police should have been brought in to conduct further interviews, to which the provisions of the 1984 Act and Code C would have applied.

The practical significance of the non-applicability of section 67(9) is considerably reduced by the fact that the important Code C rights, with one exception, are granted to persons who are not merely suspects, but have been arrested or are in police detention. As far as the exception is concerned, the right to be cautioned, it would hardly be appropriate for a caution to be addressed to the examinee, in any event, since it begins by telling the suspect that he does not have to say anything, a quite inappropriate statement in the case of compelled investigative examination.[28] It should be added that the important statutory rights to have someone informed of one's arrest and to take legal advice (under sections 56 and 58, respectively, of the 1984 Act) are equally granted only to persons arrested and held in custody.

Nonetheless, it is entirely conceivable that a statutorily–empowered investigator might wish to question a person previously arrested and detained by the police and now awaiting trial on a resulting criminal charge. An analogous situation arose in *R.* v. *Director of Serious Fraud Office, ex p. Smith*.[29] In that case, following an ordinary police investigation, Smith had been charged with an offence under the Companies Act 1985. The case came to the attention of the Director of the Serious Fraud Office, who served a notice requiring Smith to attend to answer questions or otherwise furnish information, under section 2(2) of the Criminal Justice Act 1987. He sought judicial review of the Director's decision to seek to enforce compliance with that notice. The House of Lords held that that decision was entirely valid; the powers of the Director did not cease once the person in question had been charged with an offence. Furthermore, power to question the person after charge was not constrained by the very tight restrictions imposed upon the police by paragraph 16.5 of Code C in the ordinary case of criminal investigation.[30] Lord Mustill, delivering the only substantial speech, considered that the clear words of section 2(5) of the 1987 Act overrode the argument that questioning by the Director must be thus restricted. This might seem to establish a very substantial qualification to the general principle that the ability of those having responsibility for the investigation of crime to enlist the suspect himself in their quest for evidence comes to an end once the suspect is charged, at which point the prosecution phase commences. However, it has been pointed out that the conditions in which questioning by Serious Fraud Office investigators takes place are very different from those which obtain in the police station.[31] For example, the person summoned has advance notice of what

[28] A point made by Lord Mustill in *R.* v. *Director of Serious Fraud Office, ex p. Smith* [1993] AC 1, at 38.

[29] [1993] AC 1.

[30] These restrictions have the effect of forbidding questions except those necessary for prevention or limitation of harm to individuals or to the public generally, or for clearing up any ambiguity, or for giving the person charged the opportunity of commenting upon information which has come to light since charge.

[31] See Jackson (1994) 57 *MLR* 270, at 274.

is required of him and is positively encouraged to have a legal adviser present during the interview.

It seems to follow from *ex p. Smith* that a similar exception to the ordinary principle embodied in paragraph 16.5 ought equally to apply in the case of investigations not directly concerned with crime. Indeed, the situation here will be more straightforward, for paragraph 16.5 is a rule, like all the others in Code C, to which the relevant investigators need not have regard. Yet, even though that paragraph does not formally apply, authority concerned with investigations by inspectors appointed under section 432(1) of the Companies Act 1985 indicates that the trial judge might properly exclude the evidence obtained, by virtue of an exercise of his discretion to prevent unfairness to the accused (under either section 78(1) or 82(3) of the 1984 Act).[32]

Exclusion Under the Evidential Provisions of the 1984 Act

A number of judges, faced with the rather draconian effects of the various legislative provisions with which we have been concerned, have observed that information acquired under the relevant compulsive powers might properly be excludable either as a matter of rule under section 76(2) of the 1984 Act or as a matter of discretion under section 78(1) or 82(3).[33]

So far as section 76(2)(a) is concerned, the argument that a statement of confession made under statutory compulsion could properly be excluded as having been obtained by oppression seems extremely tenuous. It will be recalled that, in *Fulling*, Lord Lane CJ found it hard to envisage circumstances in which there could be oppression without some impropriety on the part of the interrogator,[34] yet the questioning bringing about the confession in the present circumstances would be statutorily mandated and not simply lacking in impropriety. The unreliability head of the exclusionary rule may, by contrast, be invoked even without impropriety,[35] so the argument for its availability in principle is a stronger one, and that argument is clearly supported by *Seelig and Spens*.[36] Notwithstanding the (assumed) regularity of the questioning process and its statutory mandate, the particular examinee might be vulnerable in such a way as to render any confession made by him statutorily unreliable. However, it should be recalled that *Crampton* may suggest that section 76(2)(b) applies only to the case of things said or done by the interrogator which have an *inherent* tendency to result in unreliable confessions.[37] In addition, it will usually be the case, at least with company insolvencies and irregularities, that the person questioned will not be especially vulnerable. If they also have the support of a legal adviser, it may be supposed

[32] *Seelig and Spens* [1992] 1 WLR 148, at first instance (*per* Henry J—see 161); *In re London United Investment plc* [1992] ch. 578, at 600 (*per* Dillon LJ).

[33] See *Seelig and Spens*, n. 32 above 154–5 (*per* Watkins LJ); *Hamilton and Others* v. *Naviede* [1995] 2 AC 75, at 107–8 (*per* Lord Browne-Wilkinson) and at 110 (*per* Lord Nolan).

[34] See [1987] QB 426, at 432. And see, Ch. 5, text to nn. 6–51 above.

[35] See *Fulling* [1987] QB 426, at 432.

[36] [1992] 1 WLR 148, at 155 and 158–60.

[37] See (1990) 92 Cr.App.R 369, at 372. And see Ch. 5, text to nn. 59–2 above.

that counsel at trial will have the gravest of difficulty in persuading the court to exclude under section 76(2)(b).

A more general point about exclusion under either head of section 76(2) is that it may simply be inconsistent with the scheme of the statute which empowers the investigators. Thus, section 434(5) of the Companies Act 1985—the governing legislation in *Seelig and Spens*—states that the evidence obtained 'may be used in evidence against' its maker. Does not this rule of admissibility logically override those of inadmissibility under section 76(2)?

As regards section 78(1) or section 82(3), the absence of any requirement that something must have been said or done will make inapplicable any argument against exclusion for unreliability based upon *Crampton*, but the other likely problems for the defence will remain. Where the defence relies upon more general considerations of trial or pre-trial unfairness, it may seek to rely upon certain *dicta* of Lords Browne-Wilkinson and Nolan in *Hamilton and Others* v. *Naviede*.[38] Both of their Lordships seem to have had in mind the potential element of unfairness flowing from their own conclusion that, in law, the prosecution might introduce, as part of its case, incriminating statements made by the accused to company liquidators and later acquired by the Serious Fraud Office. In Lord Browne-Wilkinson's words, the 'unexplained anomaly' that the prosecution might introduce these statements but not statements made directly to Serious Fraud office investigators was something which could be taken into account by the trial judge in exercising his section 78(1) power.[39] Though Lord Nolan agreed with Lord Browne-Wilkinson on this matter, he also made the telling point that '[i]t seems strange that evidence of admissions by the defendant may be excluded on these grounds, even though it was obtained in strict compliance with an express statutory power'.[40] In other words, where everything has been done in accordance with the statute, it is hard to see how exclusion of evidence could be justified other than on the basis that the whole statutory procedure was itself unfair. The thought that, though that may indeed be the case, it is hardly the place of the judge to say so was clearly in the mind of the Court of Appeal when it had referred back to it, in *Saunders et al.*,[41] the case of the Guinness accused. Still, the door seems not to be completely closed here on the section 78(1) argument, for that court also endorsed Lord Browne-Wilkinson's remarks in *Hamilton and Others* v. *Naviede*, saying, 'in considering whether the particular application of the statutory regime in a given case created any unfairness, a judge can . . ., as part

[38] [1995] 2 AC 75, at 107–8 and 110. In *R* v. *Director of Serious Fraud Office, ex p. Smith* [1993] AC 1, at 43, Lord Mustill referred to 'the power of the trial judge to ensure that the conduct of the trial is fair', but he seemed to have in mind the judge's general power to control the proceedings before him rather than the s. 78(1) or s. 82(3) discretion, for he was dealing with the possibility that the Director might seek to have the person in question interrogated during his actual trial for the offences with which he had been charged, or, in other words, with interference with the trial at hand.

[39] See [1995] 2 AC 75, at 108. [40] *Ibid.* 110.

[41] [1996] 1 Cr.App.R 463, at 478. See also Henry J at first instance in *Seelig and Spens* [1992] 1 WLR 148, at 161.

of the background setting, have in mind that under that regime there is an obligation to answer the inspectors' questions on pain of sanctions'.[42]

Compulsory Acquisitions of Non-Confessional Evidence

Preliminary Remarks

Whilst acquisition of confessions or admissions by compulsory process of law is allowable only by way of exception to the general principle forbidding compelled verbal self-incrimination, there is no equivalent principle applicable to non-confessional evidence. That does not mean that it is impossible for such evidence to be obtained in a way which raises self-incrimination issues. It will be recalled that, in *Sang*,[43] Lord Diplock considered that the *nemo debet* principle or 'right to silence' was quite capable of embracing the obtaining from the suspect, and possibly others, of non-confessional evidence. By contrast, Lord Mustill, in *R.* v. *Director of Serious Fraud Office, ex p. Smith*[44] confined the right to silence to cases where a person, whether suspected of crime or not, is questioned.[45] Now, one can clearly be made to provide evidence against oneself without being questioned, so the *nemo debet* principle itself is surely capable of embracing self-incrimination other than that flowing from questioning. Moreover, it is entirely possible for non-confessional evidence to be obtained by questioning, for example where the suspect is persuaded by interrogation to reveal the whereabouts of a murder weapon. It is difficult to find any logic in having a special concern in that case, yet not in a case where the accused was persuaded, simply by police threats of violence, to turn out his pockets, thus producing the weapon. In other words, there is much to be said for Lord Diplock's view that it is the fact of engagement of the will of the person in question which defines the proper boundaries of the self-incrimination concern.[46]

Documents Ancillary to Compulsory Examination

Where Parliament has granted power to a court or office-holder to require persons to undergo compulsory questioning, it will commonly also have granted power to compel production of documents. For example, under section 2(3) of the Criminal Justice Act 1987, the Director of the Serious Fraud Office may require production of specified documents by a person under investigation by that office or production by any other person. With three exceptions, this kind of power raises no fresh issues additional to those discussed in the previous section of this Chapter.

Though there seems to be no authority with regard to the application of

[42] [1996] 1 Cr.App.R 463, at 478.
[43] [1980] AC 402, at 436. [44] [1993] AC 1, at 30–2.
[45] See the discussion in Ch. 2, text to nn. 38–48 above.
[46] See the discussion in Ch. 2, text to n. 50 above.

section 76(2), 78(1), or 82(3) of the 1984 Act to the case of non-confessional evidence obtained under such compulsory process, the position seems clear. It has been argued elsewhere in this book that a document might, because wholly or partly adverse to the accused both when made and when relied upon by the prosecution at trial, count as a confession for the purposes of section 82(1) of the 1984 Act.[47] It follows that an adverse document obtained under compulsory process of the present kind might be regarded as confessional. However, it was also argued in the same place that the scheme of section 76(2) is such as to suggest that it encompasses only adverse statements actually made, rather than merely obtained, in consequence of oppression or a thing said or done. If that argument is sound, there is no possibility of section 76(2) applying to documents acquired compulsorily.

So far as discretionary exclusion is concerned, while documents obtained may themselves be unreliable, it is hard to see how any such unreliability could flow from the compulsory process itself. If so, no special unreliability issue would arise. Should the unfairness element of the discretion be relied upon, the prospects for exclusion seem no less remote than in the case of confessional evidence, assuming that the statutory rules have been dutifully followed.

A person might, at his compulsory examination, be asked about the existence and/or whereabouts of documents. Were any such documents to be discovered in consequence of his answers, it ought to follow that the ordinary *Warickshall* doctrine, as now put into statutory form by section 76(4)(a) of the 1984 Act, would apply. Were the answers themselves to be ruled inadmissible under section 76(2), section 76(5) would prevent any recourse to the content of those answers in order to reveal how the documents come to be discovered.[48]

Non-confessional Evidence Otherwise Acquired Compulsorily

The law may make specific provision for compelling persons to produce evidence against themselves or otherwise to co-operate in a process which enables such evidence to be taken from them. There could be no better example than the rules relating to the breath-testing of persons suspected of driving vehicles with an alcohol concentration over the prescribed limit. Section 6(4) of the Road Traffic Act 1988 makes it an offence, without reasonable excuse, to fail to provide a specimen of breath when required to do so in accordance with that section. Plainly, where a person has provided a positive specimen in those circumstances, he may very well have done so only because section 6(4) served to compel him. His will has certainly been engaged, and it makes entirely good sense to say that he has been made to produce evidence against himself, yet there is no hint whatsoever in the authorities that there is any prospect, where the police have complied fully with the laws and have not conducted themselves in a way which

[47] See Ch. 8, text to nn. 40–1 above.

[48] For the general discussion of these matters, see Ch. 8, text to nn. 35–52 above.

would have led to exclusion had a confession been obtained, of persuading the court to exclude such evidence under the unfairness discretion.

Statute may provide for effective compulsion to co-operate, not by making it an offence to refuse to do so, but by waiving the ordinary principle that persons cannot be subjected to force without their consent. The 1984 Act provides two important examples of this method of compulsion. In certain circumstances, the police do not need consent in order to obtain fingerprints (under section 61) or non-intimate samples (under section 63) from persons (who need not necessarily be themselves suspects at the time). If force needs to be used, no question of self-incrimination arises, for in no sense will the will of the person in question be engaged. However, it is entirely likely that a person threatened with force will submit to the relevant procedure. Thus, in *Cooke*,[49] as we have already seen, a suspect who had initially refused to allow hair samples to be taken from him had, when told force would be necessary, a threat made very real by the presence in his cell of three officers wearing riot headgear, eventually allowed hair to be plucked from his scalp. The sole basis upon which an argument for discretionary exclusion could be mounted was that the sample was an intimate one and, therefore, could not be taken non-consensually. If, as the Court of Appeal held, the sample was non-intimate, no question of exclusion arose.

Similarly, the 1984 Act provides[50] for a whole range of police powers to search persons or premises without the need for consent. Here, though there is no specific reference to the possibility that the citizen might consent in order to obviate the need for forcible entry or search, there is every reason for the police to seek to proceed consensually and why they might tell the citizen that they are able to enter or search without consent, if necessary. Where the citizen's consent has been thus obtained and the search would have been lawful if carried out without consent, the position would seem to be exactly the same as in *Cooke*.

Sometimes the power to compel may be, or seem to be, implicit in the general situation at the time, rather than being specifically provided for by statute. A good example is the pre-1984 Act case of *Apicella*.[51] The accused had been in prison at a time when a physician took from him a sample of body fluid, which sample was later used against him at his trial for various sexual offences. A prison officer had told him that, as a prisoner, he had to allow the sample to be taken. In fact, there was no such power of compulsion, with the result that the defence was able to argue on appeal, albeit unsuccessfully, that the sample should have been excluded in exercise of the judicial discretion. No such argument could have been mounted had the prison officer's opinion been correct.

In all the situations discussed in the present section apart from that concerning breath samples, the accused will have co-operated passively, rather than actively, in the relevant procedure. Cooke allowed a hair sample to be taken, while Apicella allowed body fluid to be extracted. Though the will of each was

[49] [1995] 1 Cr.App.R 318. See Ch. 7, text to nn. 289–90 above.

[50] In Pts. I–III.

[51] (1985) 82 Cr.App.R 295.

undoubtedly engaged, neither was persuaded or made to produce evidence against himself. It may be recalled that Lord Diplock translated *nemo debet prodere se ipsum* as 'no one can be required to be his own betrayer'.[52] Were Cooke and Apicella required to be their own betrayers? If the analogy to confessions favoured by Lord Diplock himself is pressed, it would seem that they should not be regarded as so required, for a confession can be made only actively. Yet that would mean that the *nemo debet* principle would be at issue where a person suspected of driving whilst over the prescribed limit was persuaded to *provide* a breath sample, but not where he was persuaded to allow a blood sample to be *taken*, a distinction which hardly commends itself. If that distinction is unacceptable, it should follow that the key question is simply whether or not the person's will was engaged in co-operating in the process, whether actively or passively.

Silence and Refusal as Incriminating Evidence: Introduction

It is necessary to distinguish a number of different situations in which a person refuses or fails to co-operate with those engaged in the criminal investigation process. Most obviously, a person accused of crime may refuse to answer questions put to him about that crime. If so, he may be said to invoke, in the time-honoured phrase, his 'right to silence'. However, he may equally fail to make remarks in relation to such questions without in any sense claiming the right. For example, say that an accused's defence at trial is self-defence, yet he made no mention of facts supporting that defence when the police put to him that he had assaulted the victim. There will then be a gap in the case which may properly be described as a silence, even though the accused may have spoken volubly in response to police questions. However, it is not only by refusing or failing to speak that the suspect may be unforthcoming. Instead, he may have been invited to provide fingerprints or a sample of some kind, or some other item, but have failed or refused to do so. Equally, the police may, having, on the facts, no power to compel, ask him to co-operate by allowing them to search his home or his person, and he may refuse their request.

We shall see that the common law treated rather differently the case of silence in the face of accusation and that of refusal to provide items to assist the police investigation. It treated differently again refusal to permit search, which situation may conveniently be dealt with now.

It does not seem to have been suggested that adverse evidential inferences could properly be drawn from an accused's refusal to allow search of his person or premises. This may be because, outside the well-established circumstances in which non-consensual search is specifically permitted, the rights of the citizen to be free of interferences with his person and to exclude others from his property

[52] [1980] AC 402, at 436.

are deemed so important that they must be exercisable without adverse consequences, at least at common law.[53]

Evidential Effects of Pre-Trial 'Silence'[54]

The Four Kinds of Evidential Significance

We may begin by noting that the law has, at various stages, recognized four distinct ways in which silence might be regarded as evidentially significant. Most obviously, failure to respond to an allegation might be treated as direct evidence of guilt, at least so far as the terms of the allegation went, and possibly beyond. If it be thought that a truly innocent person would speak up to rebut an allegation, the suspect's failure to do so might be regarded as showing a consciousness of guilt. The point about the extent of guilt is not without importance. Say the suspect was silent in the face of an accusation that he had been in possession of stolen goods. It could be said that he manifested guilt only as to the fact of possession, or it could be said that, since a person guilty as to that fact but innocent in the mind would have said so, his complete silence is evidence of guilt of the full crime.

The second kind of evidential significance is that silence might be treated as capable of corroborating evidence given by prosecution witnesses. If so, it would be used to support the credibility of their evidence rather than as itself direct evidence of guilt. However, where courts have contemplated this kind of use, they have had in mind 'corroboration' in the strict sense of that term understood in English law.[55] To be capable of corroborating in that sense, the evidence in question would almost certainly amount also to direct evidence of guilt.

A third way of regarding silence attends to the possibility, already mentioned, that the accused may raise at trial a defence to which he did not refer when questioned by the police—the so-called 'ambush defence'. His failure to raise that defence at the earlier stage is taken to have an adverse effect upon its credibility at trial. This is to treat the 'silence' as evidential material incapable of doing more than destroy that defence. Thus, if the defence to an alleged assault were to be self-defence, it would do nothing to assist the prosecution to prove that the accused carried out the assault with the appropriate mens rea. Moreover, it is very difficult to see how this kind of evidential use could be relied upon should the accused not testify but rely instead on his witnesses to put forward the defence. The credibility of *their* testimony could hardly be challenged by a reference to *his* failure to mention the defence earlier.

Finally, a line of cases including the leading one of *Christie*[56] establishes that even a denial of some allegation made to the face of the accused may, in certain

[53] It must be admitted that the argument in the text does not fit in at all well with the decision in *Smith* (1985) 81 Cr.App. R 286, which is considered in the text to nn. 208–9 below.

[54] The inverted commas are used because the accused may, for reasons given in the preceding sect., have been relevantly silent though he spoke volubly.

[55] See *Baskerville* [1916] 2 KB 658.

[56] [1914] AC 545.

circumstances, be capable of being treated by the jury as implied acceptance of that allegation, i.e. as an admission. Plainly, the case of silence is *a fortiori* that of a denial, and we shall see that there is authority on this kind of relevance too.

The Common Law Position (Other Than on Implied Admissions)

For reasons which will become apparent later, it will be convenient in this section to deal only with the first three kinds of evidential use to which reference has just been made. The implied admission doctrine will be given it own section.

Though the effect of enactment of sections 34, 36, and 37 of the Criminal Justice and Public Order Act 1994 ('the 1994 Act') seems to be to allow direct adverse inferences to be drawn, in some circumstances, from pre-trial silence where there were none in which they could be drawn at common law, the common law has continuing importance for two reasons. First, it is almost impossible to understand the statutory changes without knowledge of what it was that was changed. Secondly, section 34(5)(b) preserves the common law to the extent that it did permit inferences to be drawn from the silence or other reaction of the accused.[57] It follows that, even where no statutory adverse inferences is permissible, the judge will have to consider whether or not any common law inference may properly be drawn.

Apart from the exceptional statutory cases, dealt with earlier in this Chapter, in which the suspect or other citizen could lawfully be subjected to compulsory examination on pain of criminal penalty, the law has always recognized a 'right to silence' in the sense that citizens are not under any enforceable legal obligation to answer police questions. However, the common law view of the right to silence was much more positive than that. Though it never required the judge to direct the jury not to treat the accused's silence as evidence against him in any respect, nor otherwise to use it in a way adverse to him, it did significantly restrict the judge in making adverse comments about his silence.

After some early decisions had indicated that the accused's silence might be capable of corroborating the evidence of witnesses in need of corroboration,[58] this possibility was authoritatively rejected in *Littleboy*.[59] *A fortiori*, where the judge had, in effect, directed the jury that silence was direct evidence of guilt, the appeal court would find this to have been a misdirection.[60] However, in *Ryan*,[61] it was accepted that, while it was improper for the trial judge to suggest that an inference of guilt might be drawn, it would be permissible for him to remind the jury that the accused had not advanced his explanation before trial and to tell them that they might take that fact into account when assessing the weight to be given to that explanation. In *Gilbert*, the Court of Appeal (Criminal Division)

[57] See also ss. 36(6) and 37(5).

[58] See, e.g., *Cramp* (1880) 14 Cox CC 390; *Tate* [1908] 2 KB 680; *Feigenbaum* [1919] 1 KB 431.

[59] [1934] 2 KB 408, at 414. The courts found this type of direction especially objectionable where the accused had been reminded, by virtue of the caution, that he was not obliged to say anything if he did not wish to do so—see *Whitehead* [1929] 1 KB 99; *Naylor* [1933] 1 KB 685.

[60] See, e.g., *Leckey* [1944] KB 80; *Davis* (1959) 43 Cr.App.R 215; *Sullivan* (1966) 51 Cr.App.R 102.

[61] (1964) 50 Cr.App.R 144, at 148.

specifically rejected the *Ryan* direction, commenting that it could see no clear dividing line between direct adverse use and credibility adverse use, the latter being merely a more oblique variety of the former.[62]

Judicial equivocality about the common law position came to the surface in a number of cases. For example, in *Sullivan*, Salmon LJ thought that the trial judge's comment fell clearly on the wrong side of the line, yet found no unfairness in that comment. In his words, '[i]t seems pretty plain that all the members of [the] jury, if they had any common sense at all, must have been saying to themselves precisely what the learned judge said to them.'[63] Of course, one response to that reflection would be to say that the law needed to get in line with common sense, openly allowing, indeed encouraging, direct adverse inferences to be drawn.[64] Another would be that it reveals that, rather than merely disallowing unfavourable judicial comment, it should require the judge to direct the jury not to draw adverse inferences and, perhaps, to explain to them why silence might be perfectly consistent with innocence.[65]

More mysteriously, in *Gilbert* itself, having rejected the *Ryan* approach, the Court went on to say that 'it may not be a misdirection to say simply "This defence was first put forward at this trial" or words to that effect'.[66] What possible purpose could this serve other than to invite the jury, in 'a nod is as good as a wink' fashion, to take this into account when assessing the weight of the defence? Equally puzzling is the remark of Lord Parker CJ in *Davis*[67] that the judge's comment was not merely to the effect that it was 'unfortunate' that the accused had not given an answer. This is to encourage adverse comment shrouded in half-light, and should have no place in the law. It is earnestly to be hoped that, in any future case in which the common law is invoked, judicial remarks like those in *Gilbert* and *Davis* will not be relied upon.[68]

It seems right to conclude this review of the common law by pointing out that, whenever the jury did become aware of the accused's silence in the face of police questioning, it was quite capable of drawing its own conclusions therefrom, whether with or without judicial encouragement. Therefore, it is arguable that there is something to be said for a rule requiring the judge to instruct the jury, in all cases, about the possible significance of the accused's pre-trial silence. As it was put in a US Supreme Court case, itself concerned with trial silence:[69]

> How can it be said that the inferences drawn by a jury will be more detrimental to a defendant under the limiting and carefully controlling language of the instruction here involved

[62] (1977) 66 Cr.App.R 237, at 244. In *Petty and Maiden* (1991) 173 CLR 95, the Australian High Court divided on this point, some members supporting the *Ryan* approach, others its rejection in *Gilbert*.

[63] (1966) 51 Cr.App.R 102, at 105.

[64] The line apparently taken by Parliament in enacting ss. 34, 36, and 37 of the 1994 Act.

[65] See Greer (1990) 53 *MLR* 709, at 729–30.

[66] (1977) 66 Cr.App.R 237, at 244.

[67] (1959) 43 Cr.App.R 215, at 218.

[68] In *Petty and Maiden* (1991) 173 CLR 95, at 108, Brennan J firmly rejected the notion that it was legitimate for the trial judge to tell the jury that the defence was first put forward at trial. Gaudron J, at 129–30, seems to have taken a similar view.

[69] *Griffin* v. *California*, 380 US 609, at 621 (1965) (*per* Justice Stewart, with whom Justice White agreed (dissenting)).

than would result if the jury were left to roam at large with only its untutored instincts to guide it, to draw from the defendant's silence broad inferences of guilt?

THE 'RIGHT TO SILENCE' DEBATE

For almost a quarter of a century after the publication of the Eleventh Report of the Criminal Law Revision Committee,[70] it was a matter of heated national debate whether or not the common law position was satisfactory. The debate went well beyond discussion between judges, practising lawyers, and legal academics, becoming a matter of anxious political disagreement. No historical review of that debate will be attempted here,[71] but the main issues of principle and policy will be considered.[72]

The most fundamental argument in favour of allowing, at least in appropriate cases, adverse inferences to be drawn from silence is said to be the commonsense one adverted to by Salmon LJ in *Sullivan*.[73] In Bentham's famous words:[74]

> If all criminals of every class had assembled, and framed a system after their own wishes, is not this rule the very first which they would have established for their security? Innocence never takes advantage of it. Innocence claims the right of speaking, as guilt invokes the privilege of silence.

This is certainly a striking statement, and it provided the principal basis upon which, in 1972, the Criminal Law Revision Committee recommended the changes that have, very largely, now been made law by section 34 of the 1994 Act.[75] There are two comments to be made. First, Bentham himself was writing about silence *at trial*. Now it is obvious that the protections available to the accused in court are very much more extensive than those available to the suspect in the police station. The many features of the trial which do not apply in the police station include the fact that there is an impartial judge present, that the accused's innocence is presumed, that *everything* in court goes on openly and is recorded, that all of the prosecution evidence is presented in a coherent form before the accused is called upon to say anything, that his evidence (if any) is presented through the medium of questions put by his own lawyer, that he will

[70] *Evidence (General)*, June 1972, Cmnd. 4991.

[71] The earlier historical stages are particularly well described by Greer, n. 65 above, at 715–18.

[72] For 'official' opinion, see C.L.R.C., 11th Report, n. 70 above, paras. 28–52 and 108–13; Royal Commission on Criminal Procedure, *Report*, January 1981, Cmnd. 8092, paras. 4.33–4.66; *Report of Working Group on the Right of Silence*, HO, July 1989, *passim*; Royal Commission on Criminal Justice, *Report*, July 1993, Cm 2263, ch. 4, paras. 1–30 and ch. 6, paras. 57–73. There was a great deal of academic commentary, including (recently) Zuckerman (1986) 102 *LQR* 43, Galligan [1988] *CLP* 69; Zuckerman [1989] Crim.LR 855; Greer, n. 65 above; Dixon [1991] *PL* 233; Jackson [1991] Crim.LR 404; Jackson (1993) 44 *NILQ* 103; Williams (1994) 110 *LQR* 629; Jackson (1994) 57 *MLR* 270. Two valuable research studies carried out for the Royal Commission on Criminal Justice are those of Leng, Research Study No 10 (1993), and of McConville and Hodgson, Research Study No 16 (1993).

[73] (1966) 51 Cr.App.R 102, at 105—see text to nn. 63–5 above.

[74] *A Treatise on Judicial Evidence* (ed. Dumont, 1825), 241 (and see, generally, 240–5).

[75] See 11th. Report, n. 70 above, para. 31.

necessarily be legally represented, that the emphasis is placed upon allowing him to say everything he wishes which is relevant, and that the accused can be accompanied by family and friends.[76] In those circumstances, the strength of the *rational* call for the accused to make some response to the case against him is very much stronger than where the suspect is under police questioning. Secondly, Bentham's claim seems to allow of no exceptions, yet there can be no doubt that there are reasons for silence which are consistent with innocence. The Criminal Law Revision Committee itself acknowledged this point, instancing cases where the suspect might be too shocked by the accusation to respond to it, or where an exculpatory fact might reveal something embarrassing to him, or where he sought to protect a family member. Of course, the appropriate response to this point may be thought to be that a proper, controlling judicial direction would be capable of opening up to the jury any such possibility.[77]

A second argument often put forward is that the common law rule allowed 'ambush defences' to be put forward at trial, without the prosecution having had a proper opportunity to investigate the defence in question in order to be able to combat it. This does seem to have been a recurring element of the case for reform, yet it is a very strange argument indeed. What it really suggests is that the accused should be required to disclose the nature and (perhaps) details of his defence before trial, possibly some considerable period of time before trial. As we shall see, section 5 of the Criminal Procedure and Investigations Act 1996 now imposes precisely such a requirement upon the accused. Disclosure will prevent ambush of the present kind. But as an argument for attributing adverse evidential significance to the accused's silence in the police station, it really adds nothing to the standard, Benthamite argument from common sense. In other words, it is precisely because the defence was not put forward at the first opportunity that we doubt its truthfulness. It may be appropriate to add that research carried out by Leng suggests that the problem for the police and prosecution may well be not that the accused really did keep back his defence, but that the police had failed to realize that he was saying what was his defence or had brushed his exculpatory remarks to one side because interested only in admissions.[78]

A third argument, that the common law rule worked particularly in favour of hardened and experienced criminals accused of serious offences, entails an empirical claim which is hard to evaluate. The Criminal Law Revision Committee invoked this argument, though wholly without empirical support and presumably on the basis of anecdotal experience.[79] Research carried out for the Royal Commission attempted to evaluate the claim, but it was, as the Commission itself observed, equivocal in its conclusions.[80] There would seem to be no real force to this argument.

[76] For these and other points, see Kamisar, *Police Interrogation and Confessions* (1980), Essay 2.

[77] See HO Report, n. 72 above, para. 65, for a possible set of guidelines for judges.

[78] See Research Study No 10, n. 72 above, 56.

[79] See n. 70 above, para. 30.

[80] Royal Commission on Criminal Justice, July 1993, Cm 2263, *Report*, ch. 4, para. 17. See Research Study No 16, n. 72 above, para. 10.7 and Zander and Henderson, Research Study No 19 (1993).

Finally, a more complex, *quid pro quo* argument has come to be relied upon by many. Now that the suspect benefits from a whole gamut of safeguards in the police station under the 1984 Act, and in particular from the much more extensive availability of legal advice, it is said to be safer to draw adverse inferences from his silence. The argument is put in terms of a balance of fairness between the prosecution and the defence: the 1984 Act having tilted the balance in favour of the defence, attenuation of the right to silence would properly shift it back into equilibrium. In July 1987, the then Home Secretary, Mr. Hurd, re-opening the debate about the right to silence which had lain substantially dormant since the mid-1970s, placed reliance upon the balancing argument.[81] Less than a year later, in *Alladice*, Lord Lane CJ added his voice to the call for a shift back in favour of the prosecution, saying that it was 'high time' that adverse judicial comment on silence was permitted.[82] He referred specifically to the suspect's easier access to legal advice. It may be supposed that his view was that the suspect who avails himself of legal advice is much more likely to maintain silence than the one who does not. The prospect of judicial comment would push both the suspect and his lawyer back the other way. There is some empirical support for this commonly held view,[83] though one commentator has argued that the causal connection between legal advice and assertion of the right may be less strong than is sometimes assumed.[84] In any event, it may be recalled that there is certainly a good deal of research evidence to suggest that the quality of legal advice is not, in general, high and that advisers sometimes act in a way which facilitates police questioning or, if not, assumes a neutral stance.[85]

Much of the case for retention of the common law position, or even for a 'beefing up' thereof by requiring the trial judge to instruct the jury to eschew *all* adverse inferences, is contained in the responses, outlined above, to the various arguments *for* change. However, to defeat the case for change is not to create a positive case for preservation of the *status quo* as it was before the 1994 Act became law. The Royal Commission on Criminal Justice was of the view that a change would put at risk some innocent suspects, without sufficient compensation in terms of likely additional convictions of the guilty.[86] Not everyone accepts the proposition that the possibility of drawing direct adverse inferences from silence in the police station puts the innocent at risk.[87] Those who do accept it

[81] In delivering the annual Police Foundation Lecture.

[82] (1988) 87 Cr.App.R 380, at 385.

[83] See, e.g., *Report of the Working Group on the Right of Silence*, n. 72 above, App. C; Moston and Williamson, in the *Right to Silence Debate* (eds. Greer and Morgan, 1990), 38.

[84] Dixon, n. 72 above (PL), 251.

[85] See the material referred to in Ch. 7, text to nn. 156–65 above.

[86] See *Report*, n. 70 above, ch. 4, paras. 22–3. In this respect, the Commission was utterly at one with the earlier Royal Commission on Criminal Procedure in its *Report*, n. 72 above, para. 4.50.

[87] See, e.g., Zuckerman (1986) 102 *LQR* 43, at 48 and 64–5; Zuckerman, *The Principles of Criminal Evidence* (1989), 306. Much of Zuckerman's case against what he terms the privilege against self-incrimination seems to be based upon the position of the accused in court, yet is applied, without more, to the suspect in the police station. Elsewhere, he has pointed out, as has been argued in this work, that the position in the police station is quite different from that in court, for these purposes—see [1989] Crim.LR 855, n. 72 above, at 859–62.

emphasize that an innocent suspect without any of the special reasons for silence (to prevent embarrassment, to protect family members, etc.) would still, in principle, often be wise to stay silent in the face of police questioning.[88] The imbalance between police officer and suspect, even one who has a legal adviser present, remains substantial. It is a mistake to think that the police are neutral investigators, anxious simply to get the suspect's side of the story. The evidence to the contrary is overwhelming.[89] As McConville, Sanders, and Leng put it, '[i]nterrogations are best understood therefore as social encounters fashioned to *confirm* and *legitimate* a police narrative'.[90]

More particularly, the suspect typically suffers from what has been aptly described as an 'information deficit', and this even where he has had the advantage of legal advice.[91] The police reveal details of the material implicating the suspect as they choose, and often in dribs and drabs. It was put to the Home Office Working Group on the Right of Silence that the police should show more of their hand before they could reasonably expect a suspect to be forthcoming. The Group was unconvinced:[92]

> It is not possible to prescribe the techniques which the police should use in interviews, particularly when they are dealing with those suspected of complicity in serious offences. They may have to conceal how much they know from the suspect, and being forced to reveal their case could be highly damaging.

Yet the innocent suspect pressed to respond immediately to an unformulated or inadequately formulated charge, with little or no idea of what he is alleged to have done, might be very wise to keep his counsel. Indeed, McConville and Hodgson found that, in over half the cases where a lawyer advised silence, the dominant reason was the information deficit. They also found some evidence of use of silence as a bargaining chip in encouraging the police to provide more information.[93] Where the suspect elects to speak, it may be rather naïve to suppose that his tape-recorded, halting, perhaps self-contradictory replies will be taken by jurors as anything other than evidence of consciousness of guilt, yet they may in fact reflect the inadequate responses of an innocent but vulnerable person to a wholly unsatisfactory accusation, made in an environment quite alien to the ordinary juror's experience. It may be far too much to hope that a suitable, cautionary direction, even if given, would redress the balance.[94]

Apart from the foregoing argument about innocent suspects, the only other argument for the common law assumes that it is worth supporting the right or

[88] See, e.g., Greer, n. 65 above, 726–30.

[89] See, in particular, Royal Commission on Criminal Justice, Research Study No 16, n. 72 above, *passim*; Baldwin, *Video Taping Police Interviews with Suspects—an Evaluation*, Police Research Series Paper 1 (1992), 16–17; McConville, Sanders, and Leng, *The Case for the Prosecution* (1991), ch. 4.

[90] *Ibid.* 79 (emphasis in original).

[91] See McConville and Hodgson, n. 72 above, 90–3.

[92] See their *Report*, 13 July 1989, para. 91.

[93] See McConville and Hodgson, n. 72 above, 90–3.

[94] See Dennis [1995] Crim.LR 4, at 12–13. He relies strongly on McConville and Hodgson's findings.

privilege of the guilty not to speak. This argument is much more problematical. Though the idea that the state is not entitled to expect the suspect to condemn himself out of his own mouth can clearly be supported philosophically, most opinion sympathetic to such a limitation on state power would tend to be concerned with the methods which the state should be allowed to use to persuade the suspect to condemn himself. A blanket principle that the state should not be allowed to recruit the suspect would seem to suggest that police questioning of suspects should be disallowed altogether. There are probably very few who would be willing to stomach such a fundamental change to our pre-trial criminal procedure.

The Statutory Law on Pre-trial Silence

Whatever may have been the merits and demerits of the arguments for and against attenuation of the accused's right to pre-trial silence, Parliament has, in enacting sections 34, 36, and 37 of the Criminal Justice and Public Order Act 1994, very significantly attenuated it. At the same time, section 35 has attenuated the accused's right to trial silence in an analogous way. Though that provision is not directly relevant to this work, it has two features which make brief reference to it appropriate. In the first place, because of the necessary time-lag in police questioning to which sections 34, 36, and 37 are capable of applying coming before the court, the earliest authorities on the new regime concerned section 35. Secondly, there is clearly a way in which adverse inferences under the sections concerned with pre-trial silence may act doubly to the accused's disadvantage at trial. The strength of the adverse inference, if any, from failure to testify will, *inter alia*, depend upon the strength of the prosecution evidence against him. It is entirely possible that part of that evidence will relate to his pre-trial silence.

Before we get to the substantive law, it is worth addressing the question whether or not the Act has abolished the right to silence. In *Cowan et al.*, Lord Taylor CJ claimed that it is wrong to say that the right to silence *at trial* has been abolished, for section 35(4) states that the accused remains non-compellable and that he is not guilty of contempt by virtue of failing to testify.[95] A similar point could be made about the pre-trial provisions, for no question of criminal penalty for failure to answer arises. His Lordship went on to point out that significant inhibitions on the accused's decision to testify or not existed before 1994.[96] Once again, an analogous point might be made about pre-trial silence, though here the rather weaker one that there were good grounds for fear about what the jury might actually make of that silence. There is force in these arguments, yet it would be quite wrong to conclude that the 1994 Act merely tinkers with the significance of the accused's pre-trial silence. Attenuation may be all that has come about, but it is very substantial attenuation indeed.

[95] [1996] QB 373, at 378.

[96] See, in particular, *Martinez-Tobon* [1994] 1 WLR 388.

Silence at Trial (Section 35)[97]

The central provision is section 35(3), which states: 'the court or jury, in determining whether the accused is guilty of the offence charged, may draw such inferences as appear proper from the failure of the accused to give evidence or his refusal, without good cause, to answer any question'. The reference to 'proper' inferences clearly demonstrates that it will not be right for the jury to conclude that the accused is guilty, or for the judge to tell them that they may do so, simply from his failure to testify.[98] Furthermore, it will undoubtedly be necessary for the court and the jury to consider whether or not the prosecution evidence does call for an answer and, if it does, whether or not the accused is the person to give it. This was stressed both by Lord Mustill and by Lord Slynn in the Northern Irish case of *Murray* v. *DPP*,[99] which was concerned with article 4 of the Criminal Evidence (Northern Ireland) Order 1988, a provision with wording almost identical to that of section 35. It should follow that no answer will be called for from the accused where for example, the defence is one of insanity or diminished responsibility.[100] In any event, it will be only where the prosecution has made out a *prima facie* case without regard to the accused's trial silence that the possibility of adverse inference will arise. This is implicit in section 38(3), which provides that conviction on the basis of a section 35(3) inference alone is not legitimate, but is also confirmed by the speech of Lord Mustill in *Murray*.[101] In *Cowan et al.*, the Court of Appeal (Criminal Division) went further than this in deciding that the jury must be *told* not to draw any adverse inference unless themselves satisfied that the rest of the evidence raises a case to answer, so it is not purely a matter for judicial determination.[102]

Where the prosecution evidence does clear the *prima facie* case hurdle, it does not necessarily follow that, even though the accused is the person who would naturally give the explanation, adverse inference from his failure to do so will be proper. There seems much to be said for the view that the accused has no responsibility for dignifying a weak prosecution case by answering it.[103] In this respect, Lord Slynn referred to the need to respond to a 'clear prima facie case' in *Murray*.[104] However, in the unreported case of *Byrne*,[105] which was concerned with section 35 itself, Lord Taylor CJ remarked that the strength or weakness of

[97] For the law relating to the failure of the defence to call other witnesses at trial and to permissible judicial comment thereon, see *Bryant and Dickson* (1946) 31 Cr.App.R 146; *Wheeler* [1967] 1 WLR 1531; *Gallagher* [1974] 1 WLR 1204; *Wilmot* (1988) 89 Cr.App.R 341; *Couzens and Frankel* [1992] Crim.LR 822; *Weller* [1994] Crim.LR 856. See, also, the helpful discussion in Archbold, *Criminal Pleading, Evidence and Practice* (1997 edn.), paras. 4.400–4.401.

[98] The specimen direction which was suggested by the Judicial Studies Board and which was described in *Cowan et al.* [1996] QB 373, at 381, as being 'in general terms a sound guide', makes this clear.

[99] [1994] 1 WLR 1, at 5 and 11, respectively.

[100] *Bathurst* [1968] QB 99 should remain good law.

[101] [1994] 1 WLR 1, at 3–4.

[102] [1996] QB 373, at 381. See also *Lockley*, 17 Jan. 1997 (transcript through LEXIS). As Munday [1996] Crim.LR 370, at 376–7, has pointed out, this is a rather strange thing to tell a jury.

[103] The point is convincingly made by Pattenden [1995] Crim.LR 602, at 605–6.

[104] [1994] 1 WLR 1, at 11.

[105] 21 Nov. 1995 (transcript through LEXIS).

the prosecution case was not, of itself, any general ground for requiring a judge to take a particular course as regards his jury direction. His Lordship made no mention of Lord Slynn's remarks in *Murray*, so any clash between the two sets of *dicta* is probably accidental. For the reason given, it is hoped that Lord Slynn's view will prevail.[106]

Assuming that the various requirements referred to in the preceding paragraphs are fulfilled, *Cowan et al.* tells us that it is a matter for the broad discretion of the trial judge, not lightly to be interfered with by an appeal court, to decide whether or not any proper inference is capable of being drawn by the jury. He should direct them not to draw such an inference only if there is some evidential basis for so directing them or some exceptional factor in the case making it a fair course to take. Otherwise, it is for the jury to decide, as a matter of fact, whether an inference should properly be drawn.[107]

A final point about section 35 inferences is that it is clear that, in an appropriate situation, they are capable of providing direct evidence of guilt on the whole charge, and not merely of supporting some specific element of the prosecution case or of undermining some defence relied on by the accused. This too was made clear by the House of Lords in *Murray*.[108] Of course, cases may well arise where some more limited adverse inference is the only one properly to be drawn.

Pre-trial Silence—the Essential Elements (Section 34)

Before we summarize the five essential elements of the drawing of adverse inferences from pre-trial silence under section 34, we must note a preliminary point. Section 34 applies not only to police questioning, but also to questioning by others 'charged with the duty of investigating offences or charging offenders'.[109] The wording is identical to that of section 67(9) of the 1984 Act. The reader is referred to the discussion of that subsection in Chapter 8.[110]

The five essential elements, then, under section 34, are:

(i) 'such inferences as appear proper' (proper inferences);
(ii) from the accused's failure to mention, either when questioned by an officer who is trying to discover whether or by whom an offence was committed, or when charged (silence);
(iii) 'any fact relied on in his defence' in the proceedings (defence facts);
(iv) as long as the fact is one 'which in the circumstances existing at the time the accused could reasonably have been expected to mention' (reasonable expectation);
(v) and as long as he was cautioned before being questioned or charged (caution requirement).

[106] A court may be assisted to this view by reference to the jurisprudence relating to the European Convention on Human Rights—see Ch. 11, text to nn. 38–40 below.

[107] [1996] QB 373, at 380–2. See also *Napper* (1997) 161 JPR 16. Cf. Ch. 11, text to nn. 45–9 below.

[108] See also *Haw Tua Tau* v. *Public Prosecutor* [1982] AC 136, a Privy Council case about a Singaporean provision allowing adverse inferences to be drawn from silence at trial.

[109] See s. 34(4).

[110] See Ch. 8, text to nn. 5–14 above.

It will be convenient to take these elements in turn, though not in the order in which they have just been set out.

Caution Requirement

This seems to be a necessary requirement, so it follows that, if a suspect has not been cautioned when he should have been, adverse inferences simply cannot legitimately be drawn.[111] The new caution, provided for by paragraph 10.4 of Code of Practice C, states:

> you do not have to say anything. But it may harm your defence if you do not mention when questioned something which you later rely on in court. Anything you do say may be given in evidence.

It should be noted that that paragraph goes on specifically to say that minor deviations do not constitute a breach of the caution requirement, as long as the sense of the caution is preserved. So far as the sense is concerned, it must be said that, while the caution correctly informs the suspect of his legal position—he commits no offence by refusing to answer and, indeed, his refusal to answer may not, in the end, be harmful—it does so in a way which is (understandably) oblique[112] and, to the untutored mind, might seem to give with one hand only to take away with the other.[113] One issue which may emerge at some stage is what the trial judge should reasonably make of a defence claim that the accused was so confused by the caution that it was unreasonable to expect him to have mentioned the fact on which he later relies and/or that any adverse inference from his failure would not be proper. Note for Guidance 10C of Code C does say that, if it appears to the officer that the person cautioned does not understand what the caution means, he 'should go on to explain it in his own words'.

Silence

Though one puts it here in terms of silence, it is crucial to note that the section refers to the accused's 'failure to mention' facts. It follows that section 34 is capable of applying not only to the person who says 'No comment', or something equivalent, in response to the police questioning,[114] but also to those who do talk, even volubly, yet not about the defence upon which they later rely. It follows that the impact of section 34 is not confined to the deliberately obstructive suspect who, at least in the police view, sets out to frustrate the ordinary processes of the system.

[111] It will be recalled that para. 10.1 of Code C requires a 'person whom there are grounds to suspect of an offence' to be cautioned before any questions regarding his involvement in that offence are put to him.

[112] To spell things out would make the caution excessively long, complex, and legalistic.

[113] Research suggests that it is difficult to understand—see Munday [1996] Crim.LR 370, at 379.

[114] The number of suspects who say absolutely nothing at all, i.e. pronounce no words, must be minimal in the ordinary criminal case, though this does seem to be quite a common feature of cases where terrorist crime is alleged—see, e.g., *Connolly and McCartney*, 10 June 1994 (transcript through LEXIS).

Section 34(1) refers to failure to mention facts 'on being questioned under caution' and 'on being charged'. Presumably, these words should be taken literally, so that no adverse inference is permissible in relation to silence before questioning begins. This is not a point of great significance, for it is very likely that the accused will have been questioned at some time and certain that he will have been charged.

More importantly, it has been argued that the failure to confine the ambit of section 34 to interviews at the police station is regrettable in that it is likely to result in the kinds of dispute about what was and was not said, by whom, and when, which so dogged the law relating to confessions before 1984.[115] The reason for the likelihood of such a result is said to be that it is only the taking place of an *interview* which trips the Code C contemporaneous recording requirements and only the taking place of an interview *in the police station* which trips the Code E tape-recording requirement. In fact, though it would undoubtedly have been better expressly to apply section 34 only to interviews and, perhaps, only to interviews at police stations, there seems little prospect of the silence relied upon not having been silence at a police station interview. It will be recalled that an 'interview' is defined as 'the questioning of a person regarding his involvement or suspected involvement in a criminal offence . . . which, by virtue of paragraph 10.1 of Code C, is required to be carried out under caution'.[116] Paragraph 10.1 requires the police to caution '[a] person whom there are grounds to suspect of an offence', before such questions are put to him. Paragraph 10.3 requires, in general, the caution to be given on arrest. When we turn to section 34(1)(a), we find that adverse inferences may be drawn only when an accused under caution was questioned by an officer 'trying to discover whether or by whom the offence had been committed'. But if the person being questioned is himself suspected of, or has been arrested for, the offence, any question put would have to be about his alleged involvement in order for it to be at all reasonable to draw any adverse inference from his silence in response to it.[117] If so, it will, of course, amount to an interview, with all that that entails. It must be added that there is a rather limited possibility of the interview taking place outside the police station and, therefore, not requiring to be tape-recorded. It is only where the police have made a decision to arrest the suspect that the general rule that the interview must take place at the police station (under paragraph 11.1 of Code C) applies. It follows that the prosecution might legitimately rely upon the

[115] See Card and Ward, *The Criminal Justice and Public Order Act 1994* (1994), 162; Allen and Cooper (1995) 58 *MLR* 364, at 377. But cf. Wolchover and Heaton-Armstrong, *Confession Evidence* (1996), who take a position similar to that taken in the present text—see paras. 5.079–5.082.

[116] Code C, para. 11.1A. On the meaning and significance of the accused having been 'interviewed', see Ch. 7, text to nn. 12–39 above.

[117] Though it must just be possible that the silence was in the face of a question whether or not any other person was involved and that the fact relied on at trial by the accused is that some third party carried out the offence. This remote possibility seems unimportant, given that *some* of the questions will inevitably concern the accused's own involvement and that that will mean that he was being 'interviewed'.

silence of the accused, when interviewed as an unarrested yet cautioned suspect, before his arrival at the police station, even though the interview was not recorded on tape. However, even in this rather limited case, a further duty impinges upon the police. Paragraph 11.2A of Code C requires the police, at the beginning of an interview at the police station, to put to the suspect any significant statement *or silence* which occurred before his arrival there.[118] If the police fail to put to him an earlier silence, they will hardly be in a position to rely upon it at trial, while, if they do put it to him, he will have the opportunity of denying that he was silent.

Should the silence upon which the prosecution seeks to rely at trial amount to evidence obtained in breach of one or other of the recording requirements, it seems reasonable to suppose that it will have a difficult task in persuading the judge to allow an adverse inference to be drawn from it. The courts have certainly adopted a tough stance in respect of *confession* evidence of like provenance.[119] In the case of silence, the trial judge may either exclude the evidence altogether under section 78(1) of the 1984 Act[120] or instruct the jury that no adverse inference may properly be drawn.

What if the accused accepts that he was silent at interview but says that that was because he had already told the police about his defence at some earlier stage? It has been argued that the lack of a record of earlier exchanges might be problematical.[121] However, the problem seems to be one which is more apparent than real. What the accused will be arguing, in such a case, is either that he could not reasonably be expected to mention his defence a second time, or that no proper adverse inference can be drawn from his failure to do so, or both. Yet in those circumstances, is not the very least that would reasonably be expected of him that he would point out that they had already heard his account, or use words to that effect? If he has not done even this—for he could, most obviously, have repeated the exculpatory statement—it seems entirely proper for the jury to be entitled to draw an adverse inference.

Finally, there is certainly one practical problem about failure to mention facts which may well prove to create some difficulty. Even if we may be confident about the integrity of the record, we would be foolish to suppose that there will not be arguments about the correct interpretation of the accused's answers to police questions. Interviews are not conducted with precision, loose ends are left untied, and language is used in an imprecise way. It may be said that the accused alluded to the facts upon which he now relies and that he should not be made to suffer for his lack of clarity. One supposes, though section 34 says nothing on the point, that the onus will lie upon the prosecution to show that the accused really did not mention the fact in question.

[118] What about such statements or silences made *in* the police station but before interview?

[199] See, in particular, *Canale* (1989) 91 Cr.App.R 1 and, in general, Ch. 7, text to nn. 40–59 above.

[120] The impact of discretionary exclusion under s. 78(1) is considered in the text to nn. 190–7 below.

[121] See Wasik and Taylor, *Criminal Justice and Public Order Act 1994* (1995), 56–7.

Defence Facts

The key question here is what it means to say that the accused *relies on* a fact in his defence. There can be no problem in a situation where the accused or one of his witnesses gives evidence of that fact, but it is quite clear that reliance is not confined to such cases, for, as will be discussed in more detail later, the pre-trial silence is capable of being used as part of the prosecution case when the court has to decide whether or not there is a case to answer.[122] At this stage, no defence evidence can have been called. The real difficulty is whether or not there must be *evidence* of some kind which is inconsistent with the earlier silence.

The Criminal Law Revision Committee, in recommending enactment of a provision essentially similar to section 34, seems to have taken the view that the fact must be in evidence, for it said, of the words 'any fact relied on in his defence', that they 'are intended to apply to any definite statement made by a witness at the hearing and supporting the case for the defence'.[123] Now it is clearly possible for a prosecution witness to make such a statement, usually, though not necessarily, in cross-examination. However, it is to be noted that the defence must itself place *reliance* on that statement. Of interest in this respect is the Northern Irish case of *McLernon*,[124] which was concerned with article 3, paragraph 1 of the Criminal Evidence (Northern Ireland) Order 1988. The wording of that paragraph is identical to that of section 34(1). The accused had maintained silence for six days in the face of police questioning, but had then made a written statement explaining his presence at a house where firearms had been found. That statement was adduced in evidence by the prosecution and was eventually rejected by the trial judge as a contrived falsehood. At one point, the judge asked defence counsel if he relied on that statement, and, after initially maintaining that it was prosecution evidence upon which he did not rely, he finally agreed that he did so rely. This is puzzling, for, presumably, the prosecution had adduced it not for its hearsay use but as evidence of falsehood. Any reliance on it by the defence would be to exculpate the accused, and so would be an (impermissible) hearsay use.[125] Furthermore, had defence counsel stuck to his guns, article 3 could not have been invoked. *McLernon* involved a 'Diplock trial' without a jury, but, were a similar situation to arise under section 34, the defence could enjoy the double advantage of escaping adverse inference yet having the accused's statement placed before the jury.

In *McLernon* itself, Sir Brian Hutton LCJ expressly stated that one way in which article 3 might properly be invoked would be 'where defence counsel suggested a fact, which assisted the accused, to a prosecution witness in the course of cross-examination and the witness accepted it'.[126] In two other Northern Ireland Court of Appeal cases,[127] Sir Brian Hutton has indicated that, where

[122] See s. 34(2)(c). [123] 11th. Report, n. 70 above, para. 33.

[124] 1 April 1992 (transcript through LEXIS).

[125] It does not seem to have been suggested that it was a 'mixed' statement, on which see Ch. 4, text to nn. 54–63 above.

[126] See LEXIS transcript.

[127] *Devine*, 13 May 1992; *Lamont*, 14 Dec. 1992 (transcripts through LEXIS).

the defence merely probes the prosecution case, 'without suggesting a fact which the accused relied on to a prosecution witness',[128] article 3 may not be invoked. It seems that in both cases counsel had simply made the point that the facts proved by the Crown were insufficient to create a *prima facie* case. There is an important doctrinal difference between counsel suggesting a fact and a witness accepting that suggestion, for counsel does not give evidence. One commentator has argued, apparently relying upon what Sir Brian Hutton said in these two cases, that all that is necessary for the adverse inference to be drawn is for 'the defence to suggest a fact of assistance to the defence'.[129] If he is right, then article 3 does not require the fact inconsistent with silence to be *in evidence*, nor, if the same reasoning is applied, would section 34. That would be to leave the line between suggesting a fact to a prosecution witness and probing the prosecution evidence with the purpose of arguing that it establishes no *prima facie* case a rather precarious one. Defence counsel might suggest, to a person complaining that he was assaulted by the accused in a public house, that his client was merely turning around quickly in response to a summons from a third party, and thus accidentally struck the complainant. This would suggest a fact but would also be to probe the part of the prosecution case alleging *mens rea* against the accused. Indeed, it is hard to conceive of effective cross-examination of prosecution witnesses which does not involve putting alternative possibilities to them.

On the other hand, it has been suggested that the *McLernon* view has the effect of contradicting the purpose of the legislation, for, if the fact is accepted by the prosecution witness, it is no longer in issue.[130] This would not seem to be accurate. Though the prosecution would undoubtedly be embarrassed by its witness's response, it might be in just such a case that it would be most anxious to rely on the accused's failure to mention the fact as something to set against that response. And, of course, it is quite conceivable that other prosecution witnesses might have refused to accept the truth of the fact put to them by the defence.

On balance, the better view would seem to be that the fact must indeed be one which is in evidence. In addition to having been put forward by the Criminal Law Revision Committee, that view has the support of several commentators on the 1994 Act.[131]

Reasonable Expectation

Even the strongest opponents of the common law position accepted that there may, in some cases, be perfectly good reasons for maintaining silence which are consistent with innocence, so it is not surprising that section 34(1) requires that the fact be one which 'in the circumstances existing at the time the accused could reasonably have been expected to mention'. The test seems to be partly

128 The quotation is from *Devine*, as related in *Lamont*—see transcript.

129 Jackson [1995] Crim.LR 587, at 591. See also Wolchover and Heaton-Armstrong, n. 115 above, paras. 5–085 and 5–087–5–092.

130 See Wolchover and Heaton-Armstrong, n. 115 above, para. 5–088.

131 See Card and Ward, n. 115 above, 166; *Blackstone's Criminal Practice* (1997 edn.), para. F. 19.4; and possibly Pattenden, n. 103 above, 604.

subjective, in relating itself to the particular accused, but partly objective, in referring to what he could reasonably have been expected to mention. It is to be noted that the question posed is one of law, for, if it is concluded that it is not reasonable to have expected the accused to respond, no inference at all may be drawn under that section. Some general remarks will be made first, then followed by a discussion of two specific issues relating to legal advice.

We shall deal first with what may be called 'extraneous reasons'. It has already been observed that the suspect might maintain silence, for example, in order to avoid embarrassment to himself or to protect others from prosecution.[132] The defence might successfully mount an argument, in that kind of situation, that the accused could not have been expected to mention the fact in question. Presumably, for reasons given earlier with regard to the accused's reliance on facts, there would have to be an evidential foundation for such an argument, though not necessarily from the lips of the accused himself.[133] Of course, if there really was good reason this kind for silence in the police station, it might very well subsist at trial.

Two other features of the interrogation process may prove productive so far as the defence is concerned, namely the accused's *knowledge* and *understanding* at the time of silence. We have already adverted to the 'information deficit' often suffered by the suspect. Where the police are keeping their cards very close to the chest, is it reasonable to expect the suspect to show them his hand? It may be argued that the very possibility of the drawing of adverse inferences from silence renders the police station, from the suspect's point of view, a much more adversarial place.[134] A crucial aspect of adversarial natural justice is that one is given notice of the case against one before being expected to respond. That is not to say that it will be reasonable for the suspect to expect chapter and verse before responding, for example by requiring a detailed written statement of the case against him, perhaps with notice of the names of those making that case. But it is to say that it will be reasonable for the suspect to expect more than the police have traditionally provided and that the legal adviser should have that point firmly in mind. In this respect, it is worthy of note that the Home Office Working Group on the Right of Silence recommended that the trial judge should be required, by formal guidelines, to instruct the jury to take certain factors into account when assessing the veracity of the accused's defence at trial.[135] Though no such guidelines have been introduced, one of the suggested factors to be taken into account was the extent of the accused's knowledge of the case against him. Furthermore, in *Argent*[136] the Court of Appeal expressed sympathy with the information-deficit argument as a factor properly to be taken into account, though it did go on

[132] See text to nn. 76–7 above.

[133] In *Cowan et al.* [1996] QB 373, at 383, the view taken, in the case of failure to testify at trial, was that reason for that failure must appear from the evidence rather than simply from defence counsel's submissions.

[134] It is not suggested that it was a place for gentle chit-chat before the coming into effect of the 1994 Act provisions!

[135] See n. 72 above, para. 65.

[136] [1997] 2 Cr.App.R. 27, at 35. See also *Kavanagh*, 7 Feb. 1997 (transcript through LEXIS).

to say that the police may well have had reasons, in the particular case, for limiting disclosure.

The accused's understanding at the time of questioning may prove no less important. It will be abundantly clear from the rest of this book, and particularly from the immediately preceding chapter, that very many confession cases involve vulnerable suspects, whether they be young, mentally ill, or mentally handicapped. In addition, someone who falls into none of these categories may be so shocked or confused as to clam up. One might expect the judiciary to be more concerned with the plight of the identifiably vulnerable groups than of others. Probably, where shock or confusion is relied upon, the judge will leave the matter to the jury as an issue of what inference, if any, may properly be drawn. But with vulnerable groups, there is a greater likelihood that the adverse inference will be ruled out by the judge.

The first specific issue to be raised is one of very great importance. What if the suspect was firmly advised by his lawyer to remain silent and he relies, at his trial, upon that advice as justifying his silence?[137] On the one hand, it can be said that it is hardly reasonable to expect him to go against expert advice. On the other, if adverse inferences were to be impermissible, the suspect and his lawyer might then seem to have a trump card to play, arguably driving a coach and four through the legislative purpose. Though the commentators have been remarkably consistent in arguing that, in principle, the inference should be ruled out,[138] it now seems clear, as a number of those commentators themselves predicted, that English law will follow the dictates of policy rather than principle. Just as did the Northern Irish courts before them,[139] the Court of Appeal has firmly rejected such a *per se* rule in the first three cases before it to raise the point, *Condron and Condron*, *Argent* and *Roble*.[140]

In *Condron and Condron*, that court was plainly impressed by what has been described here as the 'coach and four' argument. In the words of Stuart-Smith LJ, to recognize a *per se* rule 'would render section 34 wholly nugatory, at least in any case where the defendants had a competent solicitor, since this would be the advice that such a solicitor would be bound to give'.[141] With respect, the argument is not entirely convincing. If the case against the suspect has been put to him in suitable detail by the police, if that case is, on the face of it at least, a strong one and if there is no other reason for silence, such as one of the 'extraneous' ones

[137] His case will, of course, be all the clearer if he explains his silence in that way on the taped record.

[138] See, e.g., Card and Ward, n. 115 above, para. 5.38; Wasik and Taylor, n. 121 above, 57–8; Dennis [1995] Crim.LR 4, at 16–17; Jackson, n. 129 above, at 594; Pattenden, n. 103 above, 609–10; Wolchover and Heaton-Armstrong, n. 115 above, paras. 5–131–5–147. In addition, the Royal Commission on Criminal Justice adverted to the possibility of the lawyer advising silence as being such as to be likely to frustrate any change to the common law—see n. 72 above, Ch. 4, para. 22.

[139] See *Connolly and McCartney*, 5 June 1992; *Martin*, 7 July 1992 (both transcripts through LEXIS). See also Jackson, n. 129 above.

[140] See [1997] 1 Cr.App.R 185, [1997] 2 Cr.App.R. 27 and [1997] Crim.LR 449 (transcript through LEXIS), respectively.

[141] [1997] 1 Cr.App.R 185, at 191.

referred to above or the vulnerable state of the suspect, the better advice may be that he *should* speak up. It is not to be forgotten that the jury may, *in practice*, hold silence against the accused even when offered no judicial encouragement to do so and, perhaps, even when directed not to do so. It is to be noted that it was by no means the invariable practice of legal advisers to counsel silence before section 34 came into effect, though admittedly a negative judicial direction was never required at common law.

What is very striking about *Condron and Condron* is that the facts were such as to make out a strong case for the advice there given. The two accused were heroin addicts, and their solicitor's ground for counselling silence was that they were suffering from withdrawal symptoms. Even though the police surgeon had certified them fit to be interviewed, one would suppose that, from different perspectives, reasonable people might disagree about that. Nonetheless, the court held, the fact that they had been so advised was but one factor to be taken into account by the jury in deciding whether or not the given accused could reasonably have been expected to mention the facts upon which he now relied. This kind of approach was endorsed in the later cases of *Argent* and *Roble*. In both *Condron and Condron* and *Argent*, it was emphasized that the solicitor in question had, in accordance with Law Society advice, told his client both that adverse inferences might be drawn from silence and that the decision whether or not to speak was his.

Another element of the decision in *Condron and Condron* may prove to be of the greatest importance as regards legal advice to stay silent. Not only had the accused testified that they had relied upon their solicitor's advice about their condition in maintaining silence, but also the solicitor had testified to having given them advice in those terms. The prosecution had availed itself of the opportunity of cross-examining the solicitor, albeit under some restraint imposed by the judge, so the Court of Appeal thought it proper to explore the effect of the testimony of both the accused and their solicitor upon the legal professional privilege *prima facie* attaching to those discussions. In its view, a mere statement by the accused that he had been advised not to answer questions would not entail waiver of that privilege. Having pointed out that the matter had not been fully argued before the court, Stuart-Smith LJ went on to say that, if the accused were to go further and state the basis or reason for the advice:[142]

> it may well amount to a waiver of privilege so that the accused, or if his solicitor is also called, the solicitor, can be asked whether there were any other reasons for the advice, and the nature of the advice given, so as to explore whether the advice may also have been given for tactical reasons.

The significance of the waiver point was made clear by Rose LJ in *Roble*:[143]

> The evidence must generally go further and indicate the reason for that advice, for this must be relevant when the jury are assessing the reasonableness of the conduct in remaining silent.

[142] [1997] 1 Cr.App.R 185, at 197.
[143] [1997] Crim.LR 449. See LEXIS transcript for the passage quoted.

Plainly, counsel for the accused could hardly contemplate with equanimity the opening up before the court of the interchanges between solicitor and client. He might well find himself in something of a cleft stick. Should he call the solicitor as well as the accused, he would provide the prosecution with a heaven-sent opportunity for what might prove to be devastating cross-examination. Yet should he ask the accused about the reasons but not call the solicitor, the prosecution would have plenty of ammunition for adverse comment in any event, and might even take the risk of putting the solicitor into the witness box. It is of interest that, writing before *Condron and Condron* was decided, Wolchover and Heaton-Armstrong went so far as to say that 'it is inconceivable that there should ever be any question of a defendant being required to reveal to the jury the details of legal advice received, waiving lawyer–client privilege, as the *quid pro quo* for averting an adverse inference from silence'.[144] Assuming that the early authorities are followed on this point, the courts will have enacted the inconceivable.

Another important point about legal advice was raised in the Northern Irish case of *Quinn*.[145] What if the accused asked for legal advice before he would speak to the police, but no such advice was made available? If, as seems clearly to be the case, the court has a discretion under section 78(1) of the 1984 Act to exclude silence as adverse evidence for unfairness, any breach of the suspect's right to legal advice would trip that discretion. However, in *Quinn*, because the case was one to which the emergency legislation applied, there had been no such breach. The Northern Ireland Court of Appeal held that the absence of legal advice was not such as to make it impermissible to draw inferences under article 3. However, the case was a rather peculiar one, such that both the trial judge and the Court of Appeal were satisfied that the accused had no need of legal advice before revealing the exculpatory facts upon which he relied at trial. It does not at all follow that, under section 34, it will be held irrelevant, in *all* cases, to the decision whether or not the accused could reasonably have been expected to mention the fact in question, that he asked for but was (legitimately) denied legal advice. It is even possible that it will be considered relevant that a particular suspect did not have advice, even though he did not ask for it. However, given the statutory scheme and the way in which, as we shall see shortly, the courts seem inclined to interpret it, it is very likely that, where no breach of the accused's right to advice is made out, it will be held that the judge should leave it to a (properly directed) jury to decide what, if any, adverse inference may properly be drawn, rather than rule out adverse inference altogether.[146]

The courts have given some attention, more generally, to the words, 'in the circumstances existing at the time'. According to Lord Bingham CJ in *Argent*, the phrase should not be interpreted restrictively, but rather:[147]

[144] See n. 115 above, para. 5–133. [145] 17 Sept. 1993 (transcript through LEXIS).

[146] For the possible impact of the jurisprudence relating to the European Convention on Human Rights on this issue, see Ch. 11, text to nn. 44–9 below.

[147] [1997] 2 Cr.App.R. 27, at 33. See also *Roble* [1997] Crim.LR 449.

matters such as time of day, the defendant's age, experience, mental capacity, state of health, sobriety, tiredness, knowledge, personality and legal advice are all part of the relevant circumstances; and those are only examples of things which may be relevant.

Proper Inferences

Much of what has been discussed in the immediately preceding subsection is potentially no less relevant to the issue of the inference which may properly be drawn from the accused's failure to mention the fact in question. For example, defence counsel's argument that, because of the fact that the accused was seeking to protect third parties or was suffering from an information deficit or was a vulnerable person or had received legal advice to remain silent or had not received legal advice, it was unreasonable to expect him to speak might also be presented as an argument in terms of what inference should properly be drawn by the jury.

A more difficult question is precisely what use is allowed, as a matter of law, of the accused's failure to mention the fact in question. It will be recalled that, before *Gilbert*, the common law appeared, whilst ruling out use of pre-trial silence as itself evidence of guilt or as capable of corroborating other evidence of guilt, to allow such evidence to be taken into account in assessing the weight to be attached to the explanation proferred by the accused at trial. May it then be argued that section 34 merely restores the law to its pre-*Gilbert* state (described here as 'limited force')? Or is its effect that failure to mention a fact is capable of amounting to positive evidence of guilt (described here as 'extensive force')?[148] It should be noted that, even under the limited force view, should a jury conclude that the 'facts' now relied upon have been made up by the accused, this may properly have an adverse effect on his *general* credibility.

The Eleventh Report of the Criminal Law Revision Committee is rather ambiguous on the present issue. In its opening paragraph on the issue (paragraph 28), it seems to support the limited force option, but this is inconsistent with its later recommendation (in paragraphs 40–42) that silence be capable of being used as corroboration. On balance, it seems likely that it favoured the extensive force option. The Home Office Working Party, by contrast, firmly favoured the limited force option, giving as its reason that 'once silence becomes positive evidence of guilt, the burden of proof is shifted'.[149]

Academic opinion is radically divided on the point. Andrews and Hirst,[150] Card and Ward,[151] and Pattenden[152] clearly support the extensive force view, but Blackstone,[153] May,[154] and Dennis[155] equally clearly support the limited force view. Other commentators are rather less confident about the correct answer.[156]

[148] There is little point adverting, so far as the present law is concerned, to possible use of the evidence as corroboration, now that ss.32 and 33 of the Criminal Justice and Public Order Act 1994 have abolished the remaining corroboration and corroboration warning requirements.

[149] See n. 72 above, para. 83.

[150] *Criminal Evidence* (1995 Supplement to 2nd. edn., 1992), para. 19.98D.

[151] N. 115 above, paras. 5.31–5.32.

[152] N. 103 above, at 607.

[153] N. 131 above, para. F. 19.4.

[154] *Archbold News*, 25 Feb. 1994, 7 (and see 28 Jan. 1994, 6).

[155] N. 94 above, at 15–16.

[156] See, e.g., Wasik and Taylor, n. 121 above, 53; Jackson, n. 129 above, at 595–601.

The best reason for taking the extensive force view of section 34 is that it seems to be implicit in the section itself. The most obvious use to which pre-trial silence may be put is in relation to the eventual decision of the trier of fact. However, section 34(2) expressly allows of two other significant uses. A magistrates' court may draw proper inferences from it when inquiring into the offence as examining justices.[157] A court may draw proper inferences from it in deciding whether or not there is a case to answer. Taking the latter eventuality first, plainly the only facts now relied upon by the accused would be those which emerged from the evidence of prosecution witnesses. It is a considerable stretch to argue that the accused's pre-trial silence could affect adversely the credibility of *his* witnesses, but quite beyond stretching distance to argue that it could have this effect on that of *prosecution* witnesses. It must follow that, if his pre-trial silence is to be used against him at all, it would be used either as itself direct evidence of guilt or to support the evidence of others which is adverse to him. Though it is certainly true that a case to answer cannot be made out *solely* on the basis of the accused's pre-trial silence, this simply entails there being a special rule about the *weight* of such evidence and has nothing to do with the *use* to which it may be put. The committal proceedings possibility adds nothing to the present reasoning.

A further argument in favour of the extensive force view is said to be that it is proper to draw here an analogy with the evidential use which may, by virtue of section 35, be made of failure to testify.[158] As we have already noted, *Murray* v. *DPP*[159] makes it clear that this use includes use, in an appropriate case, as positive evidence of guilt. As a matter of precedent, this argument has the weakness that the point certified for decision by the House of Lords related only to trial silence and that, though pre-trial silence points had arisen in the courts below, no comment was made upon them. Equally, the earlier Privy Council case, *Haw Tua Tau* v. *Public Prosecutor*,[160] was concerned with a provision dealing with trial silence, there under Singaporean law. Furthermore, there are two reasons why the analogy seems inexact. First, it was firmly established at common law that there *were* cases where strong judicial comment, apparently inviting the jury to take silence as evidence of the accused's consciousness of guilt would be appropriate,[161] so the putting of that position into clearer and more general terms by section 35 is hardly a radical change. Secondly, the notion that silence might go to the credibility of the accused's evidence is necessarily inapplicable in the case of the accused who does not testify.

Notwithstanding these deficiencies, the analogy with section 35 inferences impressed the Court of Appeal in *Condron and Condron*.[162] Indeed, that court

[157] Initially, it was intended that committal proceedings should be replaced by a new 'transfer for trial' procedure, and s.34(2), like s.36(2)(a) and s.37(2)(a), as originally enacted, referred thereto. However, there was a change of mind, committal proceedings have been retained, and ss.34(2)(a), 36(2)(a), and 37(2)(a) have been amended accordingly—see Criminal Procedure and Investigations Act 1996, s.44(3).

[158] See Card and Ward, n. 115 above, para. 5.32. [159] [1994] 1 WLR 1.

[160] [1982] AC 146. [161] See, most recently, *Martinez-Tobon* [1994] 1 WLR 388.

[162] [1997] 1 Cr.App.R 185. See also *Roble* [1997] Crim.LR 449.

thought that one specific element of the direction proposed by Lord Taylor CJ in *Cowan et al.* for the purposes of section 35 ought also to be given in section 34 cases. In Lord Taylor's words:[163]

If, despite any evidence relied upon to explain his silence or in the absence of any such evidence, the jury conclude the silence can only sensibly be attributed to the defendant's having no answer or none that would stand up in cross-examination, they may draw an adverse inference.

It would seem to be implicit in this formulation that an inference of the extensive kind would be capable of being the appropriate one to draw. It may be added that the Northern Irish courts have firmly embraced the extensive force view in respect of article 3 of the Criminal Evidence (Northern Ireland) Order 1988.[164] One should, of course, remember that the inference may amount to positive evidence of guilt without logically foreclosing the whole case against the accused and that an inference other than one amounting to positive evidence of guilt may well be appropriate in some cases.

One other matter should be dealt with. It is a commonplace of police interrogation of suspects that more than one interview takes place. It is perfectly possible that the suspect will mention an exculpatory fact at a second or subsequent interview which he had not mentioned at the first one. Alternatively, it may be argued that he failed to mention that fact at as early a stage of a given interview as he might. In both cases, the possibility of drawing adverse inferences clearly arises as a matter of law, yet it would seem that, as a matter of common sense, the strength of the proper inference would be less great than where the fact was not mentioned at all.

Even after all police questioning has ceased, the revelation of the fact in question after charge but before trial might seem, again as a matter of common sense, to reduce the potential weight of any adverse inference. The force of this argument was recognized by the Court of Appeal in *Condron and Condron*, where Stuart-Smith LJ pointed out that 'it is always open to an accused person who has failed to mention some important fact at interview, to communicate it to the police at any time before trial; but unless it is done promptly, it is unlikely to rebut an adverse inference which might otherwise be drawn'.[165] The message to accused persons and their lawyers is clear enough; fill any gaps in the defence to the charges brought as soon as possible after charge.

Pre-trial Silence—Procedures (Section 34)

Now that we have dealt with the five essential elements of section 34 inference, we need to consider two further issues concerning the way in which arguments between prosecution and defence on any of those elements and, indeed, on any other elements which may emerge are to be dealt with by the judge. First, how is

[163] [1996] QB 373, at 381.
[164] See, in particular, *McLernon*, 1 Apr. 1992; *Martin*, 7 July 1992 (transcripts through LEXIS).
[165] [1997] 1 Cr.App.R 185, at 197.

the responsibility for making decisions about the elements of section 34 divided between judge and jury? Secondly, according to what procedure are issues for the judge to be settled and at what stage of the trial? It must be emphasized that though the early Court of Appeal authority which must be dealt with has been concerned with those issues in the context of section 34 inferences, they may equally be expected to crop up in the context of the inferences permissible under sections 36 and 37, which sections are considered later in this Chapter. The reader should bear in mind that there is every reason to suppose that the discussion which follows is equally relevant, *mutatis mutandis*, to those sections.

The Division of Responsibility

The obvious question which arises is which issues under section 34 are for the judge to settle and which are left to the jury? The general message emerging from the early authorities in the Court of Appeal, is clear enough. Because the section seems to be concerned to allow the fact-finder to draw common-sense inferences, there is a strong presumption in favour of the jury being left, though with proper judicial guidance, to decide when to draw an inference and, if it is to draw one, what the nature of that inference should be. Lord Bingham CJ, in *Argent*,[166] was most anxious to stress that point. More particularly, first, where the question is what inference may properly be drawn, this means properness as it appears to the jury. Secondly, it is for the jury to decide whether or not any fact relied upon by the accused is one which he could reasonably have been expected to mention. Thirdly, it is a matter for the jury whether or not some fact has been relied on in his defence. Finally, it is for the jury to decide whether or not the accused actually did fail to mention that fact to the police. Though his Lordship also acknowledged that the judge must direct the jury not to draw any adverse inference where a decision to do so would be perverse, it will readily be apparent that the effect of what he is saying is to grant to the jury a very large degree of autonomy in relation to each of the last four elements of section 34, as just discussed. Nor is there any reason to suppose that his Lordship would have taken a different view with regard to the first element, namely the caution requirement.

It does not at all follow that there are no issues of law capable of arising under section 34. To stick with the caution requirement, it would surely be the judge's duty to direct the jury that, should they decide that the accused was not cautioned, they *must not* draw any adverse inference under section 34. There must be a number of similar possibilities in relation to the other elements.

The Procedure for Decision-making

In both *Condron and Condron* and *Argent*,[167] the trial judge had conducted a *voir dire* before deciding that he might properly direct the jury on the possibility of drawing adverse influences. In both, the defence placed at least partial reliance on

[166] See [1997] 2 Cr.App.R. 27, at 31–3. See also *Condron and Condron* [1997] 1 CR.App.R. *Roble* [1997] Crim.LR 449 and *Kavanagh*, 7 Feb. 1997.

[167] [1997] 1 Cr.App.R 185 and [1997] 2 Cr.App.R. 27, respectively.

the discretion to exclude evidence under section 78(1) of the 1994 Act, even though, in *Argent* at least, there seems to have been no suggestion that any code provision had been breached. Stuart-Smith LJ, in *Condron and Condron*, pointed out that challenge on the basis of code breach and challenge under the terms of section 34 should be kept separate. In relation to any defence submission simply that the jury should not be invited to draw any adverse inference, that submission should in the ordinary case be made in the absence of the jury at the conclusion of the evidence. A ruling earlier in the trial would be appropriate only where the defence argument was that it would be perverse for the jury to draw an adverse inference or that cross-examination of the accused was impermissible, and, even then, on the *voir dire* only if necessary. Lord Bingham CJ, in *Argent*, on the other hand, seems to have conceived of it being possible for section 78(1) to be invoked even where the case for ruling out the inference was based solely upon the perversity of drawing it. The point of holding a *voir dire* being that the jury should not hear evidence which the judge might later decide to exclude, it must follow that the general message of the two cases is that defence counsel is most unlikely to be able to persuade the judge to hold one and will be confined to making submissions at the conclusion of the evidence on the content of the judicial directions which ought to be given to the jury.[168]

Other Adverse Inferences from Pre-trial Silence (Sections 36 and 37)

The 1994 Act makes separate provision for two kinds of situation in which the accused failed or refused to account for certain incriminating facts. Section 36 deals with objects, substances, or marks found in his possession or at the place where he was at the time, while section 37 deals with his presence at the scene of the offence at or about the time of its commission. The essence of the two sections is that his failure or refusal, in these circumstances, to give an explanation makes it permissible to draw proper adverse inferences. It must be noted at the outset that these two sections and section 34 all stand separately from each other, with the result that the fact that an adverse inference may not be drawn under the one does not at all mean that one may not be drawn under either of the other two.

Features Common to Both Sections

There are four important elements, common to both sections, which distinguish them from section 34. First, no reliance on any fact by the accused is necessary in order for adverse inference to be permissible. In effect, it is the incriminating fact, as put to the accused, which provides the analogy to defence reliance under section 34. Secondly, as was noted by the Court of Appeal in *Roble*,[169] there is no requirement of a reasonable expectation of response from the accused. It must be assumed that it is considered reasonable *per se* to expect a person found in the relevant circumstances to respond, no matter what may be that person's particular

[168] Nothing inconsistent, in this respect, with *Condron and Condron* and *Argent* emerged in either *Roble* [1997] Crim.LR 449 or *Kavanagh*, 7 Feb. 1997.

[169] [1997] Crim.LR 449.

characteristics or state at the time. Thirdly, by virtue of sections 36(5) and 37(4), the applicability of the two sections beyond the police is extended only to officers of customs and excise, rather than to any person charged with the duty of investigating offences or charging offenders (as under section 34).

The final point is that, while section 34 requires that the accused's silence be in response to questions under caution, sections 36(1)(a) and 37(1)(a) make those sections applicable only to arrested persons. There may be some scope for the argument that no adverse inference is permissible in law if, though there was the fact of arrest, that arrest was unlawful. This is because there is authority for the proposition that an unlawful 'arrest' is not really an arrest at all, but merely the assertion of force or factual power. Thus, in *Spicer* v. *Holt*, Lord Edmund-Davies expressed the view that, when the word 'arrest' was used in a statute, it could mean 'nothing other than a valid and lawful arrest'.[170] However, in the same case, Viscount Dilhorne's view was that '[w]hether or not a person has been arrested depends not on the legality of the arrest but on whether he has been deprived of his liberty to go where he pleases'.[171] The same view prevailed in two later cases in the Court of Appeal (Criminal Division).[172] Yet in *Spicer* v. *Holt* itself, all members of the House of Lords agreed that the unlawful 'arrest' in that case did not constitute an arrest 'under section 5(5) or 8' (of the Road Traffic Act 1972). In other words, the particular statute may, as a matter of interpretation, require the arrest to have been lawful. It seems probable that such an argument would fail as regards sections 36 and 37. In *Spicer* v. *Holt*, the House stressed that the coercive power there tripped by arrest, power to take a blood or urine sample, was one which Parliament had shown it wished to confine narrowly. Under sections 36 and 37, no interference with bodily integrity beyond arrest itself is contemplated, so one might expect the courts to take Parliament not to have intended to restrict their application to lawful arrests.

Two other features are common to the two sections, namely the 'reasonable belief' criterion and the information requirement. In the case of section 36, the investigating officer must reasonably believe that the presence of the object, substance, or mark about which he asks the arrestee may be attributed to his participation in the commission of an offence.[173] Similarly, under section 37, the officer must reasonably believe that the arrestee's presence at the time and place in question may be so attributable. The information requirement is quite complex. The officer must not only tell the arrestee of his belief and request him to account for the relevant incriminating fact, but must also tell him in ordinary language what will be the effect of section 36 or 37 (as the case may be) if he fails or refuses to comply with the request.[174] A gloss upon these information requirements is provided by paragraph 10.5B of Code C. It informs the officer that he must tell the suspect, in ordinary language:

[170] [1977] AC 987, at 1005. [171] *Ibid*. 1000.

[172] *Lewis* v. *Chief Constable of South Wales* [1991] 1 All ER 206, at 210; *Dawes* v. *DPP* [1995] 1 Cr.App.R 65, at 71–2.

[173] See ss.36(1)(b) and 37(1)(b). [174] See ss.36(1)(c) and (4), and 37(1)(c) and (3).

(a) what offence he is investigating;
(b) what fact he is asking the suspect to account for;
(c) that he believes this fact to be due to the suspect's taking part in the commission of the offence in question;
(d) that a court may draw a proper inference if he fails or refuses to account for the fact about which he is being questioned;
(e) that a record is being made of the interview and that it may be given in evidence if he is brought to trial.

We may call this the 'special caution'. There is no provision, equivalent to that of paragraph 10.4 in respect of the ordinary caution, that minor deviations do not constitute breach, presumably because paragraph 10.5B does not prescribe a set form of words. Nonetheless, there will, of course, be considerable scope for defence argument that the special caution actually given failed to convey all the necessary information. Where that information is required by the Act itself to be given, it ought to follow that substantial failure in any respect would lead to it not being permissible for the jury to draw the adverse inference. That said, it is right to add that it would be only the statutory inference which would be ruled out, for sections 36(6) and 37(5) preserve the possibility of an inference at common law or, indeed, under any other statutory provision, from a failure to account for the incriminating fact.

Another important point emerges from the immediately preceding discussion. One might have supposed that sections 36 and 37 were concerned with the putting of incriminating facts to the arrestee immediately after their emergence. So the man found with the smoking gun would be asked then and there to give an explanation. Yet it seems clear that no such question can properly be put until arrival at the police station. This point has been made, at some length, with regard to section 34 silence,[175] but bears brief repetition here. The combined effect of paragraphs 10.3, 11.1A, and 11.1 of Code C is that, in order to be properly requested to give his account under sections 36 and 37, the arrestee must, very unusual cases apart, be under interview at the police station when the request is put. It follows that the various contemporaneous recording requirements will apply, something which is implicit in the duty under paragraph 10.5B(e) to tell the arrestee that a record is being made of the interview. Though something of a surprising conclusion—the red-handed are most effectively questioned when their hands are at their reddest—it does have the welcome consequence that the prospects of the special caution being delivered inadequately, incorrectly, or in a garbled fashion must be very much reduced.

Features Distinguishing the Two Sections

The obvious distinguishing feature is that the two sections deal with different possible elements of the situation following arrest, section 36 being concerned with what may be described broadly as possession of incriminating material, section 37 with presence at the scene at or about the time of the offence. Both

[175] See text to nn. 115–18 above.

sections have a potential for wide application. Section 36(1)(a) refers to objects, substance or marks (or marks on objects) which are:

(a) on his person; or
(b) in or on his clothing or footwear; or
(c) otherwise in his possession; or
(d) in any place in which he is at the time of his arrest.

Though (i)–(iii) seem straightforward, (iv) may be rather wide. Section 38(1) defines 'place' to include 'any building or part of a building, any vehicle, vessel, aircraft or hovercraft' and 'any other place whatsoever'. Plainly, buildings can be rather large, while, as Wasik and Taylor point out,[176] a football stadium would seem to constitute a place. As they go on to add, this may be less significant than would at first sight appear, for it is to be remembered that section 36 allows only proper inferences to be drawn, and nothing could properly be inferred (extraordinary cases apart) from the arrestee's failure to account for the presence of an object some 100 yards away, at the other end of the stadium. A similar comment applies to section 37, for the words of subsection (1)(a) refer to the arrestee having been found 'at a place at or about the time the offence for which he was arrested is alleged to have been committed'.[177] The words 'at or about the time' are presumably apt to place a reasonably tight time constraint on inference. Presumably, the appropriate way of dealing with these questions of degree would be through the judicial direction.

That leaves us to deal with two important limitations, of different kinds, upon the two sections. Section 36(1)(b) requires the investigating officer to specify the offence in relation to which he reasonably believes the presence of the object, substance, or mark implicates the arrestee. The rest of the subsection and subsection (2) have the combined effect of confining proper inference to proceedings against him 'for the offence so specified'. The inevitable result is that no adverse inference may permissibly be drawn as regards any *other* offence in respect of which proceedings are eventually brought.[178] One need think only of the range of possible offences which may arise from a violent assault to realize how anomalous the effects may be. What if the specified offence is one of the grievous bodily harm offences but the offence finally charged assault occasioning actual bodily harm? It may be wise for the officer, who will at least have had time to think about it, to specify a range of offences in that kind of situation, though the criterion of reasonable belief will create a restriction on his wilder speculations. Even if the offence finally charged is not one of those specified, there remains the possibility that an adverse inference may be drawn under section 34, as long as the terms of that section are met.

[176] See n. 121 above, 61–2.

[177] It may be noted that the words used do not make it clear that it is the place of the offence, not the place of the arrest, which is crucial, though the former must, presumably, have been intended.

[178] As long as an offence specified is eventually charged, it does not matter that an alternative verdict is returned, for s. 38(2) extends the meaning of 'an offence charged' to include 'any other offence of which the accused could lawfully be convicted on that charge'.

Even more restrictive is section 37, for adverse inferences there may be drawn only in respect of the offence for which the accused was arrested.[179] Obviously, the very fact that it is presence at the scene which calls for explanation naturally confines proper inference to the incident or incidents which led to the arrest. However, one can well imagine that the police might arrest the person, at the scene of a killing, for murder, yet the eventual charge be one of manslaughter. The restriction here may be expected to prove more troublesome in practice than that of section 36, for there will have been no time before arrest to consider the range of offences which may have been committed. Once again, section 34 may be available as an alternative.

It is worth noting that, with regard to both the issue of which offence or offences was or were specified and that of for which offence or offences the accused was arrested, there may be questions of law for the judge to decide. Though a conditional direction about proper adverse inferences will sometimes be appropriate, cases may certainly arise in which it would be the judge's duty to direct the jury to draw no such inference under the relevant section. For example, if, on the unchallenged evidence, the accused's arrest was for murder yet the sole charge is manslaughter, there will be no factual issue to be determined by the jury under section 37.

Evidential Use of Adverse Inferences

It seems overwhelmingly probable that it will be held to be permissible, where it is proper to draw an adverse inference, for the adversity of that inference in an appropriate case to be that it goes directly to show guilt of the offence charged. All the arguments put forward with regard to inferences under section 34 apply no less to those under sections 36 and 37. However, in addition, it is clear that the incriminating fact will, in all probability, be one which goes to advance the prosecution's own case. So, the *logical* argument for confining the use of silence to destroying, or at least reducing, the evidential force of the exculpatory material cannot apply in respect of incriminating facts under sections 36 and 37. It does not at all follow that the proper inference to be drawn will necessarily be that the accused is guilty of the offence, for pre-trial silence is not, under the 1994 Act any more than it was at common law, *as such* evidence of guilt. Everything depends upon the particular circumstances of the case.

There is one other point about evidential use which is specific to sections 36 and 37. It must not be forgotten that the incriminating fact which the accused was asked to explain will itself be circumstantial evidence of his guilt. Depending upon its probative weight in that respect, the failure of the accused to offer an explanation will be of greater or lesser value to the prosecution. For example, where the accused was indeed found with a smoking gun and leaning over the corpse, his failure to account for his possession of the gun or his presence by the corpse may

[179] Or, as long as that offence is the one charged, any other offence of which he could lawfully be convicted on that charge—see s. 38(2).

well add little to an already strong circumstantial case. But in other situations, the circumstantial evidence may be less persuasive, perhaps because pointing less clearly at the accused, and his failure to give any explanation, when an innocent one would have been easy enough to give, may be highly incriminating.

Elements Common to Sections 34, 36 and 37

Though they have been adverted to for other purposes during the preceding discussion of the pre-trial silence provisions of the 1994 Act, two elements common to all of those provisions should be dealt with in their own right.

The relevant adverse inference is capable of having legal significance at four distinct stages of the criminal process. The first is that at which a magistrates' court is 'inquiring into the offence as examining justices', presumably where it is being argued that there is insufficient evidence to go before a jury.[180] The second is that where the judge has to decide whether or not to dismiss certain charges (of serious fraud or of violent or sexual offences against children) in respect of which notice of transfer for trial has been given.[181] The third stage is where the court is asked to determine whether or not there is a case for the accused to answer.[182] Finally, there is the stage at which the court or jury has to decide the issue of guilt.[183]

At the first stage, oral evidence may not be given,[184] so the magistrates' ability to draw any adverse inference from silence is limited by the content of the prosecution statements. By contrast, at the second stage, the judge may grant an oral hearing,[185] so there may be greater scope for adverse inference and, presumably, for the judge being persuaded not to draw such an inference or to draw a less adverse once. When a no case submission is made, all the prosecution evidence will have been heard, but no defence evidence called. It should follow that, at each of the first three stages, it is much more likely that adverse inferences will properly be drawn under section 36 or 37 than under section 34. By contrast, at the final stage, with all the evidence heard, section 34 is just as likely to be applicable. The judicial task may, as we have already seen, include the giving of directions, either in absolute or conditional terms, ruling out adverse inference in appropriate cases, but must, in every case, entail advice on how the jury should approach its task, on what factors they may wish to consider, and on the nature of any adverse inferences which may be thought to arise.

There are no statutory guidelines upon which the judge may draw in directing the jury, for the Government decided not to follow the recommendation of the Home Office Working Party that they should be provided. A specimen direction suggested by the Judicial Studies Board was given the Court of Appeal's general

[180] See ss.34(2)(a), 36(2)(a), and 37(2)(a) (as amended by Criminal Procedure and Investigations Act 1996, s.44(3)).

[181] See ss.34(2)(b), 36(2)(b), and 37(2)(b).

[182] See ss.34(2)(c), 36(2)(c), and 37(2)(c).

[183] See ss. 34(2)(d), 36(2)(d), and 37(2)(d).

[184] Magistrates' Courts Act 1980, s.5A(2) and (3), as added by Sched. 1 to the Criminal Procedure and Investigations Act 1996.

[185] See Criminal Justice Act 1987, s.6(2), and Criminal Justice Act 1991, Sched. 6, para. 5(4).

approval in *Condron and Condron*.[186] The direction is not, it seems, publicly available,[187] though the court did quote what it described as the relevant part, as follows:

If he failed to mention . . . when he was questioned, decide whether, in the circumstances which existed at the time, it was a fact which he could reasonably have been expected to mention.
The law is that you may draw such inferences as appear proper from his failure to mention it at that time. You do not have to hold it against him. It is for you to decide whether it is proper to do so. Failure to mention such a fact at that time cannot, on its own, prove guilt, but depending on the circumstances, you may hold that failure against him when deciding whether he is guilty, that is, take it into account as some additional support for the prosecution's case. It is for you to decide whether it is fair to do so.

The court stressed that the usual direction on the burden and standard of proof would also be necessary and that the form of the caution was such that the jury would inevitably understand that the accused had been entitled to remain silent at interview. It also considered that the judge should go beyond the terms of the specimen direction by including an instruction to the jury to draw an adverse inference only if they should conclude that his silence was to be attributed to his having no answer or none that would stand up in cross-examination. No doubt, further refinement of the content of what the jury is to be told will emerge in later cases, together, perhaps, with full details of the direction commended by the Judicial Studies Board. Furthermore, for all one knows, there may well be similar such directions offered to trial judges in respect of inferences to be drawn under sections 36 and 37.

Section 38(3) states:

A person shall not have the proceedings against him transferred to the Crown Court for trial,[188] have a case to answer or be convicted of an offence solely on an inference drawn from such a failure or refusal as is mentioned in section 34(2), 35(3), 36(2) or 37(2).

Were common sense to be the sole guide, this provision would not have been enacted. Its effect is that there must be other evidence in the case, at the relevant stage, in order for the hurdle to be cleared, but also that a case unfit to proceed to the next stage without reference to an inference from silence may be made fit by the addition of that inference. For example, there may be no case to answer without the silence, but one to answer with it.

Two difficulties emerge from the way in which section 38(3) is drafted. First, the subsection says that the accused shall not be convicted solely on the basis of

[186] [1997] 1 Cr.App.R 185. See also *Roble* [1997] Crim.LR 449.

[187] For a general discussion of the point about these specimen directions not being generally available, see Munday [1996] Crim.LR 296.

[188] These words must be taken as if they read, 'committed for trial at the Crown Court'. The transfer for trial procedure was abandoned before it was ever given effect in law—see Criminal Procedure and Investigations Act 1996, s.44(2). That Act made a number of consequential changes to ss.34, 36, and 37 of the 1994 Act, but not to s.38(3). Presumably, this was a simple error.

an inference from silence. In the jury trial context, this is, of course, quite impossible to achieve, for the jury may reject the other evidence and rely on the accused's silence. However, it surely ought to mean that the judge is under a duty to instruct the jury, and magistrates to remind themselves, that they must not convict solely in reliance upon the silence, and, indeed, the Judicial Studies Board's specimen direction does contain an appropriate instruction. Secondly, it is not clear whether the prosecution may use more than one of the four sections about silence, but without any extraneous evidence, to clear the relevant hurdle. In other words, must there always be *some* non-silence evidence? This may be a non-issue where either or both of sections 36 and 37 form part of the mixture, for then there will necessarily be the circumstantial evidence flowing from the incriminating fact itself. However, there could arise a situation, at the close of evidence, in which the prosecution is able to rely only upon sections 34 and 35, and upon no extraneous evidence. If silence alone, albeit both at the police station and in court, cannot warrant conviction, the judge will have to instruct the jury to acquit. But if the message of section 38(3) is that no conviction on the basis of one element of silence alone is allowable, a suitable judicial direction will be the order of the day.[189]

Exclusion of Unfair Evidence of Silence

Sections 34, 36, and 37 do, at least, have the merit of ridding us of the idea, to be found most recently in *Gilbert*,[190] but also in some of the earlier cases, that silence in the police station may, in some unannounced way, cast a cloud over the defence, without being evidence in the case. Under all three sections, where the adverse inference is properly to be drawn it constitutes evidence, whether it be of entire guilt or something short of that. It necessarily follows that discretionary exclusion of that evidence under section 78(1) or 82(3) of the 1984 Act is a possibility.[191] Indeed, in the first two cases concerned with section 34 to come before the Court of Appeal, there are *dicta* firmly supporting the availability in principle of the section 78(1) discretion.[192]

Not much needs to be added here to the discussion of discretionary exclusion in Chapters 6 and 7 above. There may arise cases where a particular failure to mention a fact or other silence is unreliable, in the sense of being more prejudicial than probative. For example, a mentally handicapped suspect, provided with neither a lawyer nor an appropriate adult, may well fail to mention a fact because disorientated and confused. This will, in any event, lead naturally to the

[189] The European Convention dimension to this issue is discussed in Ch. 11, text to nn. 36–7 below.

[190] (1977) 66 Cr.App.R 237.

[191] Those who have written about the new provisions are at one in supporting the proposition in the text—see, e.g., Card and Ward, n. 115 above, 165 and 171; Blackstone, n. 131 above, para. F. 19.10; Dennis, n. 94 above, at 14–15; Pattenden, n. 103 above, at 610–11; Allen and Cooper (1995) 58 MLR 364, at 377.

[192] *Condron and Condron* [1997] 1 Cr.App.R 185; *Argent* [1997] 2 Cr.App.R. 27. Note also that s. 38(6) of the 1994 Act specifically preserves the power of the court to exclude evidence at its discretion.

conclusion that no adverse inference may properly be drawn, and it could be said that an adequate judicial direction will meet the justice of the case. However, the argument that this is a sufficiently safe course to take seems no better here than with a confession. It may be supposed that, outside this kind of circumstance, courts are likely to be wary of excluding a properly recorded 'silence' for unreliability.

However, it may be predicted that here, just as in the case of confessions, the most common argument for exclusion will be based upon breach of the various recording requirements of Codes C and E, or upon improper failure to allow the suspect to take legal advice. It seems no less important that one have confidence in the integrity of the formal record of exchanges between the police and the suspect for present purposes than in other respects. Where the prosecution relies upon failure or refusal to account for incriminating facts, but can provide no contemporaneous record, it is, for reasons adverted to earlier,[193] overwhelmingly probable that the police will have breached code provisions. Equally, where it says that a fact relied upon at trial is one which the accused failed to mention when questioned in the police car on the way to the station, police breach of those provisions is very likely to have occurred.[194] In either situation, the defence case for exclusion on the basis of the unreliability of the record and of inequality of access to evidence[195] will be a strong one.

Though, as we have already seen, it now seems most unlikely that legal advice to remain silent will be treated as a trump card, leading to the necessary ruling out of adverse inferences as a matter of law,[196] it does not at all follow that the right to take legal advice has been rendered less important by the Act. Indeed, the reverse may well be the case, for, precisely because a suspect's decision not to speak now has a potential for such adverse consequences, that decision more anxiously requires to be made under expert advice.[197] Therefore, it seems entirely possible that an accused who has been improperly denied advice will be able to show that, had he been allowed it, he would not have failed to mention facts or to give an explanation of incriminating material. If so, the defence will clearly have a case for the 'silence' to be excluded as a matter of discretion.

The Common Law Relating to Implied Admissions

Christie[198] establishes that the accused's *denial* of an accusation of crime put to him is capable of amounting in law to *acceptance* of the terms of that accusation. However, this rule is subject to the qualification that the judge should, as a matter of practice, allow evidence of the statement of accusation to be given only if it would be reasonable to draw the inference that, despite appearances to the

[193] See text to n. 175 above. [194] See text to nn. 115–18 above.
[195] On which, see Ch. 6, text to nn. 114–17 above. [196] On which, see pp. 255–6 above.
[197] See Roberts [1995] Crim.LR 483. Cf. Fenwick [1995] Crim.LR 132.
[198] [1914] AC 545.

contrary, the accused really did accept that statement, making it wholly or partly his own. Plainly, if even a denial may properly be construed as acceptance, there can be no objection of principle to treating silence in exactly the same way.[199] The *Christie* doctrine is preserved by section 34(5) of the 1994 Act, which states that that section does not 'prejudice the admissibility in evidence of the silence or other reaction of the accused in the face of anything said in his presence relating to the conduct in respect of which he is charged, in so far as evidence thereof would be admissible apart from this section'. There were two important factors restricting the application of *Christie* with regard to silence in response to police questioning. In the first place, the pre-1994 Act caution, being geared to the potential for direct use of silence as constituting consciousness of guilt, told the suspect that he did not have to say anything unless he wished to do so. It would then have been a trap to permit a *Christie* use where he had been so cautioned, and so the law firmly ruled out such use.[200] The position so far as the suspect who had not been cautioned was concerned was less clear. In *Hall* v. *R.*, Lord Diplock said that such a suspect's position was the same, for the caution 'merely serves to remind the accused of a right which he already possesses at common law'.[201] But in *Chandler* the Court of Appeal expressed its reservations about Lord Diplock's *dictum*.[202]

Secondly, whether or not the suspect had been cautioned, no *Christie* use was possible where the parties had not been on even terms at the time when the relevant accusation was put. Before section 58 of the 1984 Act instituted a right in the suspect to legal advice, it would almost inevitably have been the case that they were not on even terms, for the most obvious way in which they might be evened up would be for the suspect to have a lawyer present when questioned.[203] Even since the coming into force of section 58, it is only in a minority of cases that legal advice is taken at all, and in only some of those that the lawyer is present during questioning. Moreover, given the rigid Code C regime for interviewing suspects, those who did have a lawyer present would almost certainly have been cautioned before the interview began. Therefore, the actual decision in *Chandler* that a *Christie* use was permissible where a suspect who had not been cautioned had his solicitor present was of little practical importance.

It has generally been assumed that the common law position on implied admissions under *Christie* must simply transfer, unaltered, into the post-1994 Act world, and so be of no real significance.[204] However, it is arguable that this

[199] See *Mitchell* (1892) 17 Cox CC 503, at 508 (*per* Cave J).

[200] *Whitehead* [1929] 1 KB 99; *Charavanmuttu* (1930) 22 Cr.App.R 1; *Naylor* [1933] 1 KB 685; *Keeling* [1942] 1 All ER 507; *Hall* v. *R.* [1971] 1 WLR 298.

[201] [1971] 1 WLR 298, at 301.

[202] [1976] 1 WLR 585, at 588–9. See also *Raviraj* (1986) 85 Cr.App.R 93, at 105–6, and *Horne* [1990] Crim.LR 188.

[203] One *can* envisage other ways, e.g. where the Chief Constable of the police force was being questioned by one of his junior officers.

[204] See, e.g., Card and Ward, n. 115 above, para. 5.7; Wasik and Taylor, n. 121 above, para. 3.13; Dennis, n. 94 above, at 16. But, cf. Wolchover and Heaton-Armstrong, n. 115 above, para. 5–099, though note also *ibid.*, para. 5–125.

is to fail to take sufficient account of the revolution wrought by sections 34, 36, and 37.[205] It may be thought that, while the new general caution does tell the suspect that he does not have to say anything, it also gives him the rather clear message that this would be an unwise privilege to press.[206] At the very least, it seems much less clear than it was that to allow the *Christie* use in the case of the cautioned suspect would be to trap him. The blanket ban on that use would now seem to be insupportable. Instead, the key question should be, as it is where the police are not involved, whether or not it is a tenable proposition that the accused *actually did* accept the allegation.[207] Ironically, the point may prove particularly apposite where the parties were, because a lawyer was present, on even terms. Given the extra risks which undoubtedly attend silence, it may be very hard indeed to argue that the accused who maintained silence on advice did thereby acknowledge the truth of the allegation put to him. The proposition that he did acknowledge its truth will be much more tenable in many cases where the accused did not have the benefit of legal advice, and, more specifically, did not have a lawyer present when interviewed. This could be of some importance, for none of the limiting conditions set for direct adverse inference by section 34 would, of course, apply.

Evidential Effects of Pre-Trial Refusal to Provide Items

In *Smith*,[208] an alleged accomplice had told the police that Smith had confessed to him his guilt of a robbery. The police had grounds for suspecting that a cap found at the scene might have been worn by Smith during the robbery. It had hairs attached to it, so they wished to get hair samples from him for comparison. Smith's solicitor being present, Smith was requested to allow samples to be taken. In response to a question from the solicitor, the police revealed that the hairs with which comparison would be made had been found on an item recovered at the scene. Smith was again asked to give a sample but replied, 'in that case, no I am not'. The Court of Appeal (Criminal Division) ruled that the judge had been right to allow the jury to use evidence of that refusal as corroboration of the accomplice's evidence. It noted that there was no previous authority on the point. It refused to accept that there was any proper analogy with the suspect's right to pre-trial silence at common law. It emphasized that the parties had been on equal terms and, no less significantly, that Smith had used the words, 'in that case', before giving his negative answer. Clearly, it would have been possible to

[205] The argument is to be found, in more detail, in Mirfield [1995] Crim.LR 612, at 615–17.

[206] *Blackstone* may be thought to place too much stress on the first part of the caution, in arguing that 'the appropriate inference from failure to deny an accusation under caution is still that the suspect is relying on his right to silence'—see *Blackstone*, n. 131 above, para. F.19.3.

[207] The words of Lawton LJ, in *Chandler* [1976] 1 WLR 585, at 590, are likely to prove salutary in this respect.

[208] (1985) 81 Cr.App.R 286.

distinguish *Smith* in a later case where no lawyer had been present at the time. Furthermore, Smith seemed necessarily to be saying that it was because hairs had been found on an item at the scene that he would not provide a sample for comparison. As a matter of ordinary common sense, the exchange was highly incriminating, suggesting that Smith had something to fear, namely that his hairs would match those found at the scene. It might have been possible to take an entirely different line where the suspect had, from the start, insisted that he would not have his bodily integrity compromised by providing samples, perhaps samples more intimate than mere head hairs. Here, it might be thought much clearer that he was insisting on some sort of right.

Section 63 of the 1984 Act (as amended) now gives the police wide powers to take non-intimate samples, such as head hairs, from a suspect without his consent. However, intimate samples, as defined by section 65, may be taken only with consent, so *Smith* was capable of living on in that context in any event. In fact, section 62(10) makes specific provision for the drawing of adverse inferences from refusal to consent to the taking of intimate samples, but without the limitations, in terms of the need for the parties to be on equal terms or for the refusal to be unequivocally incriminating which *Smith* seemed to suggest.[209]

Now that sections 34, 36, and 37 are law, any force which the analogy to the 'right' to pre-trial silence may have is properly to those sections. And, indeed, section 62(10) was amended by the 1994 Act such as to make it reflect the general message of those sections. The inferences which may be drawn from refusal are those which appear proper. They may be drawn at all the various stages of the criminal process at which inferences may be drawn under sections 34, 36, and 37. The one limitation to which reference should be made is that the refusal must have been 'without good cause'. It is probably the case, given that only *proper* inferences may be drawn that many reasons for refusal (embarrassment, a strong belief in civil liberties, etc.) may appropriately be taken into account in that respect, that 'good cause' will be interpreted narrowly.[210] Keane suggests that a Jehovah's Witness would presumably have good cause for refusing to provide a blood sample and that the mental or bodily condition of the suspect might also provide good cause.[211]

A final point is that, though there is no statutory requirement that the police warn the suspect what will be the effect of section 62(10), should he choose to refuse to provide an intimate sample, paragraph 5.1 and Note for Guidance 5A of Code of Practice D make provision for an appropriate cautionary warning.[212]

[209] A possible third limitation on *Smith* was that the inference could be drawn only for corroborative purposes, though it seems unlikely that any such limitation was intended. At all events, s. 62(10) was available, from the date of its enactment, to allow the refusal to be direct evidence of guilt, and not solely corroborating evidence. When s. 32 of the Criminal Justice and Public Order Act 1994 became law, the words of s. 62(10) which referred specifically to use as corroboration were repealed.

[210] There does not seem to be any authority at present.

[211] *The Modern Law of Evidence* (4th. edn., 1996), 381.

[212] A point made by Keane, *ibid*.

Evidential Effects of Pre-Trial Non-disclosure or Defective Disclosure

Introduction

The focus of this work is the evidential effects of pre-trial investigative procedures carried out by the police or similar officials. However, an incomplete picture would be presented were nothing to be said about recent innovations as to defence disclosure after completion of those procedures but before trial of the accused.

The long-established policy of English law as regards disclosure of evidence before trial has been that though, in serious cases at least, there must be full disclosure by the prosecution of the evidence on which it proposes to rely at trial, the accused is under no such duty. Furthermore, he was under no general duty to reveal even the barest details of what his defence would be. In recent years, three limited exceptions were made to the accused's privilege not to reveal his hand. Under section 11 of the Criminal Justice Act 1967, an obligation was placed on the accused who had been committed for trial on indictment to give notice of particulars of any alibi, the sanction for non-compliance being that he would be unable to call evidence in support of his alibi without leave of the court.[213] Section 81 of the 1984 Act requires both sides to give advance notice of any expert evidence to be adduced at trial, the sanction being the same as with alibi. Finally, a detailed regime of disclosure in serious fraud cases in the lead-up to a preparatory hearing before the judge under section 7 of the Criminal Justice Act 1987 was provided for by section 9 of that Act. Here, for the first time, the sanction provided for non-compliance or inadequate compliance, whether by the prosecution or the defence, was the possibility of (proper) adverse inferences being drawn from the failure.

The Royal Commission on Criminal Justice, having rejected thoroughgoing reform to the law on pre-trial silence, suggested that a better way of discouraging 'ambush' defences would be to require the accused to reveal his defence between the dates of charge and trial.[214] At the same time, it recommended significant limitations upon the duty of the prosecution to disclose material which may, in broad terms, be described as material of assistance to, or potential assistance to, his defence.[215] Part I of the Criminal Procedure and Investigations Act 1996 effects both recommended changes,[216] though in ways of which the Royal Commission might not have wholeheartedly approved.

[213] S. 11 is repealed by Criminal Procedure and Investigations Act 1996, Sched. 5.

[214] See *Report*, n. 72 above, Ch. 6, paras. 57–73.

[215] The prosecution's duty was laid down in a series of cases culminating in *Keane* [1994] 1 WLR 746 (see also *Davis* [1993] 1 WLR 613; *Ward* [1993] 1 WLR 619; *Brown* [1995] 1 Cr.App.R 191; *Turner* [1995] 1 WLR 264; *Tatenhove and Doubtfire* [1996] 1 Cr.App.R 408; *Saunders et al.* [1996] 1 Cr.App.R 463) and in the Attorney-General's Guidelines on Disclosure (1981) 74 Cr.App.R 302.

[216] The relevant provisions have effect from 1 Apr. 1997.

THE ELEMENTS OF THE NEW DISCLOSURE REGIME

Before dealing with section 11 of the Act, which provides, in certain circumstances, for adverse inferences to be drawn against the accused, it will be necessary to set out briefly the various elements of the new disclosure regime[217]. It is to be noted that *compulsory* disclosure by the defence is limited to cases where the accused is to be tried at the Crown Court in respect of an indictable offence.[218] Once committal proceedings have taken place, the accused will have received copies of all witness statements and all other written evidence on the basis of which he was committed for trial. In the case of an offence triable either way, he may instead have received a summary of the facts and matters on which the prosecution proposes to rely at trial.[219] At some stage, almost certainly after committal, the prosecution must fulfil its duty under section 3(1) of the 1996 Act to disclose any prosecution material, not previously disclosed, which in the prosecutor's opinion—the subjective formulation of the duty is to be noted—might undermine the case for the prosecution, or to provide the accused with a statement that there is no such material. At the same time, the prosecution must, under section 4, provide what will be, in effect, a schedule of all other non-sensitive material not covered by the section 3(1) duty, such schedule having to indicate 'the nature of that material'.[220]

Once the prosecutor has complied with, or purported to comply with, section 3, the accused falls under a duty of disclosure under section 5. According to section 5(6), he must, within the prescribed period,[221] provide the court and the prosecutor with a defence statement:

(a) setting out in general terms the nature of the accused's defence,
(b) indicating the matters on which he takes issue with the prosecution, and
(c) setting out, in the case of each such matter, the reason why he takes issue with the prosecution.

Once provided with a defence statement,[222] the prosecutor has a duty of secondary disclosure under section 7. Section 7(2)(a) requires him to disclose any previously undisclosed material 'which might be reasonably expected to assist the accused's defence' as found in the defence statement or to give the accused a

[217] For detailed treatment of Part I of the 1996 Act, see, e.g., Card and Ward, *The Criminal Procedure and Investigations Act 1996* (1996), chs. 2 and 3; Ryan, Savla, and Scanlan, *A Guide to the Criminal Procedure and Investigations Act 1996* (1996), chs. 2 and 3.

[218] This is the combined effect of ss. 1(2) and 5(1)(a). A minor exception is that disclosure is also compulsory in the case of a summary offence tried at the Crown Court with an indictable offence (under Criminal Justice Act 1988, s. 40).

[219] Under Magistrates' Courts (Advance Information) Rules 1985, r. 4(1)(b).

[220] See s. 24(3). The details are contained in the Code of Practice for Criminal Investigation, paras. 6.3 and 6.9–6.11. The Code is dealt with at text to n. 224 below.

[221] This period is generally one of 14 days from the day on which the prosecution complied with or purported to comply with s. 3—see the Criminal Procedure and Investigations Act 1996 (Defence Disclosure Time Limits) Regulations 1997, reg. 2 (SI 1997, No 684).

[222] Whether under s. 5, or, as a voluntary matter, for summary trial, under s. 6.

written statement that there is no such material. Where the accused has reasonable cause to believe that section 7 has been breached, section 8 permits him to apply to the court for an order requiring prosecution disclosure.[223] Section 9 provides for a continuing prosecution duty, after all the earlier stages of disclosure have been completed, to keep under review the question whether there is prosecution material which may undermine its case or assist that of the defence and to disclose any such material.

One further element of the new statutory rules of disclosure must be mentioned. A Code of Practice for Criminal Investigation prepared by the Secretary of State under the terms of sections 23 and 25 of the Act was brought into effect on 1 April 1997, at the same time as Part I of the Act itself was activated.[224] Its purpose is to ensure that proper systems and procedures are in place in both police forces and the prosecution service to give effect to the aims of Part I. Hence, it makes provision for the proper recording and retention of information and material obtained in the course of criminal investigations. In order to promote compliance by the prosecutor with his obligations of disclosure, it requires the police to reveal to him all the information and material which they have collected. Finally, it seeks to ensure that all relevant information and material is made appropriately available to the accused.

Adverse Inferences from Faults in Disclosure

No sanction, other than the prospect of a section 8 court order, is provided with regard to prosecution breach of its disclosure duties. Indeed, section 10 lays down that failure to comply with time limits for disclosure under section 3 or 7 does not, on its own, constitute grounds for staying proceedings for abuse of process, though it goes on to state that failure may constitute such grounds if it involves such delay that the accused would not get a fair trial.

Section 11, by contrast, visits the accused with the sanction of potential adverse inference in respect of various faults in his disclosure. There are special provisions for alibis, but, as regards the generality of cases, there are four possible faults, namely failure to give a defence statement,[225] delay in giving such a statement, setting out inconsistent defences therein, and putting forward at trial a defence not disclosed therein.[226] According to section 11(3), where the section applies:

(a) the court or, with the leave of the court, any other party may make such comment as appears appropriate;
(b) the court or jury may draw such inferences as appear proper in deciding whether the accused is guilty of the offence concerned.

[223] It will be noted that there is no equivalent provision for primary disclosure by the prosecutor under s. 3.

[224] See SI 1997 No. 1033. For a helpful discusson of the draft code which formed the basis for the 1997 Code, see Card and Ward, n. 217 above, Ch. 3.

[225] This applies only in respect of compulsory disclosure.

[226] See s. 11(1) and (2).

In the case of the accused whose defence at trial is different from that set out in the defence statement, section 11(4) specifically provides that, in doing or in deciding whether to do anything under section 11(3), the court is to have regard to the extent of the difference in the defences and to whether or not there is any justification therefor. This presumably allows the judge to deny the prosecution any comment and to refuse to leave to the jury the possibility of adverse inference in cases where the departure from the accused's pre-trial position is slight or where, for example, developments since the defence statement was filed have properly changed the nature of the appropriate defence.

We should note several elements of section 11. First, the judge may, of course, have to decide whether or not it is correct to say that there was some fault in disclosure. As we have seen, section 5(6) requires the defence statement to set out the nature of the accused's defence 'in general terms' and to indicate the matters on which issue is taken with the prosecution, as well as the reasons for taking issue. There would seem to be ample scope here for argument about whether or not that subsection has been complied with. An ancillary point is that the prosecution may seek to persuade the judge that, though a piece of paper headed 'defence statement' was sent to them, it is so inadequate, in terms of section 5(6), that it cannot properly be described as a defence statement at all and that, therefore, the case is, in substance, one of failure to provide such a statement.

Secondly, from the wording of subsection (3)(b), it seems that there may be no use by the judge of any adverse inference in determining whether or not there is a case to answer, for only the jury *decides* whether not the accused *is* guilty. It does not at all follow that the disclosure fault may not be revealed to the judge and the jury until the accused himself gives or calls evidence. In the case of alibi disclosure faults, reference is made to the accused adducing evidence in the one case and to his calling a witness to give evidence in the other, so it is clear that the fault cannot be disclosed as part of the prosecution case.[227] However, where the fault is departure from a defence set out in the defence statement, the words used are 'puts forward a defence'.[228] It will be recalled that section 34(1)(a) of the 1994 Act refers to 'any fact relied on in his defence' and that it was argued that, to be capable of leading to an adverse inference, that fact must be *in evidence*.[229] It would seem harder to argue for a similar interpretation with regard to the putting forward of a defence. If defence counsel puts to a prosecution witness that the accused was defending himself against an attack from that witness, he would seem to put forward a defence, irrespective of the witness's response to that accusation. The other faults all relate to matters which are established before the trial begins—no defence statement, late statement, inconsistency therein—so one would suppose the intention to be that the prosecution will be free to adduce evidence of the fault as part of its case. Curiously, the drafting of section 11 is such as to fail to provide expressly for the adducing of evidence of the fault, but it must

[227] See s. 11(1)(e) and (f) and s. 11(2)(d) and (e).
[228] See s. 11(1)(d) and s. 11(2)(c).
[229] See text to nn. 122–31 above.

be impliedly allowed. This defect of drafting also results in there being no provision for the judge to be asked for leave for that evidence to be adduced, yet it surely cannot be the case that the prosecution may call such potentially damaging evidence without first asking for permission.[230]

If the preceding argument is sound, section 11 has an effect which the Royal Commission did not favour. It gave an example of a case where the defence to an alleged assault disclosed in the statement was one of self-defence, but where the prosecution evidence at trial failed to establish the assault. It thought it would be wrong for the prosecution to be able to resist a submission of no case to answer by reference to the content of the defence statement.[231] Yet, under section 11, the failure of the prosecution satisfactorily to establish the fact of an assault might well have been a consequence of probing cross-examination which would be very likely to have entailed putting forward the defence that there was no assault.

The third point is that section 11(5) provides that the accused is not to be convicted 'solely on an inference drawn under subsection (3)'. It was presumably intended that there must be some other, non-section 11 evidence, but it could be argued that, as drafted, subsection (5) would allow conviction solely on the basis of two or more subsection (3) inferences.

Finally, only 'proper' inferences are allowable. In the two situations where there is an inconsistency in defences put forward, the most obvious inference will be that neither defence proffered is valid. But where no defence statement was filed or one was filed late, it is difficult to follow how a proper response can be more specific than a vague sense of doubt about the defence side's sincerity. And what if the explanation given is simply that the defence solicitor forgot to file a statement or to file one in time? It must be very doubtful that these provisions really promote the accuracy of the fact-finding process in the Crown Court.

Speaker after speaker in both Houses complained about the unevenness of the playing field laid out in Part I of what was then the Bill. The point was, in essence, a simple and obvious one, though it was unconvincingly rejected by a range of government spokesmen. Lord Ackner made it three times, at the second reading, committee, and report stages.[232] The legislation imposes no duty upon the prosecution to file a statement of the principal facts upon which it relies. So how can the defence properly be expected to indicate the matters on which it takes issue with the prosecution or its reason for taking issue? The government response was to point out that the defence had the advantage of having disclosed to it all the witness statements and other written evidence.[233] While this is true, it is nothing to the point because, as any civil practitioner knows, there is a difference between pleading and evidence. In effect, it is as if the defendant in a civil action were required to file a defence without having received a statement of claim. Now it

[230] Lord Ackner drew attention to this defect at the Second Reading stage in the House of Lords—see HL Debs., vol. 567, cols. 491–2—but nothing was done about it.

[231] See *Report*, n. 72 above, ch. 6, paras. 61–62.

[232] See HL Debs., vol. 567, cols. 491 and 1458–9; vol. 568, cols. 1584–5.

[233] One example will suffice—see HL Debs., vol. 567, cols. 1460–1 (Baroness Blatch).

may be said that the accused will have been committed for trial on a charge or charges, but this is much more like a writ than a statement of claim. As Lord Ackner put it, to ask the accused to comply with his detailed duty, 'purely on the basis of a statement of the charge and the statements of witnesses is . . . asking too much and spoils the whole basis of the operation, which is to say clearly to the defendant, "This is our case. To what extent do you take issue with it?" '[234] In other words, if we are to have a system of criminal pleading rather akin to that for civil cases, we ought to do the job properly. His Lordship might have added that there is a model which could have been used, with suitable modifications, contained in section 9(4) of the Criminal Justice Act 1987 (dealing with preparatory hearings in serious fraud cases). The position would be a little less unsatisfactory if no defence statement could be required before the filing of the indictment, but no attempt was made to link defence statements to the indictment in this or any other way.

Though the battle for an even playing field was lost in Parliament, it may well re-emerge in the cases via two other routes. With some of the defence disclosure faults comprehended by section 11, there might well be room for argument that prosecution disclosure did not leave the defence in a position to tell what was the case against the accused and, therefore, to provide a definitive reply. If so, it may be said it would not be 'proper' to draw any adverse inference. For example, this might enable the defence to explain why more than one defence was put forward or why the defence at trial differed from that in the statement. The other possible route is opened up by the coming into effect, on 1 April 1997, of the Code of Practice on Criminal Investigation. Just as with the codes made under the 1984 Act, this Code is undoubtedly capable of being breached. In cases of breach, there must surely be an opportunity for the defence to argue that to allow evidential use of the fault in disclosure against the accused would have an adverse effect on the fairness of the proceedings and that, as a result, the judge, relying on section 78(1) of the 1984 Act, ought to rule out any such use.

It is right to add that there is no obvious reason why defective prosecution disclosure should not lead to an adverse inference against its case being drawn. This point was another one made repeatedly during the Parliamentary debates. It is not impossible to imagine a case where the prosecution fails to disclose material to the defence which would undermine seriously the prosecution case or provide substantial support for the accused's defence. Of course, in the premises, the defence might not find this out, at least before trial. But if it did, is there any logical reason at all why a proper adverse inference should be incapable of being drawn?

One final point about Part I of the 1996 Act deserves attention. If we take the Royal Commission's example of a defence statement of the confession and avoidance kind, as with the defence of self-defence, may the prosecution be able to argue that the statement contains a confession or admission by the accused,

[234] HL Debs., vol. 567, col. 1459.

admissible against him under section 76(1) of the 1984 Act? There seem to be two points against such an argument. First, is the defence statement 'made by an accused person', for the purposes of the subsection? It is certainly made at his instruction, but it may still be regarded as actually made by his lawyer. Secondly, in accordance with the authority concerned with the use of incriminating statements made under statutory compulsion which was discussed earlier in this Chapter,[235] one would need to interpret properly this particular statutory scheme. The intention seems to have been to allow only the indirect adverse use contemplated by section 11, and no other.

[235] See text to nn. 17–25 above. For a more detailed discussion see Sprack [1997] Crim.LR 308, at 313–15.

10

Vulnerable Suspects

Introduction

There are many causes of special vulnerability which may affect particular suspects who are interviewed by the police. For example, special problems clearly arise in the case of blind, illiterate, or deaf suspects, as well as with those who do not understand English well or at all. Equally, it will be apparent that the police often have to grapple with the issue of what steps should be taken as regards persons under the influence of drink or drugs. Code C contains a number of provisions which guide police conduct in these various categories of case. No detailed account either of those provisions or of their consideration by the courts will be given here.[1] However, it will be evident from much of what has preceded this Chapter that three conditions which lead to vulnerability have proved to be especially prominent not only in the authorities but also in the commentaries, namely juvenility, mental handicap, and mental disorder. Therefore, it seems appropriate to devote a separate chapter to them.

It will be convenient to set out first what is meant by the three terms, 'juvenile', 'mental handicap', and 'mental disorder', these being the key terms so far as the Police and Criminal Evidence Act 1984 ('the 1984 Act') and Code C are concerned. A juvenile is simply a person between the ages of 10 and 17. 'Mentally handicapped' is defined, for the purposes of section 77 of the 1984 Act, to mean, in relation to a person 'that he is in a state of arrested or incomplete development of mind which includes significant impairment of intelligence and social functioning'. There being no definition of the same term in Code C, it must be assumed that the one in section 77 applies equally in that context. Mental handicap is not to be confused with mental subnormality as gauged by IQ tests, though it seems most unlikely that a person in the severely subnormal range, i.e. with an IQ below 60, would fail to qualify as mentally handicapped, for the purposes of the above definition. Finally, 'mental disorder' is defined by Note for Guidance 1G of Code C to have the same meaning as is given to it by section 1(2) of the Mental Health Act 1983, namely: 'mental illness, arrested or incomplete development of mind, psychopathic disorder and any other disorder or disability of mind.' It will be noticed that there is something of an overlap between the two terms, for

[1] A very full account will be found in Wolchover and Heaton-Armstrong, *Confession Evidence* (1996), at paras. 2–242 to 2–265.

both include reference to 'arrested or incomplete development of mind'. It must follow that anyone who is mentally handicapped is necessarily also mentally disordered, though the reverse, of course, does not apply.[2] It may be that the arrested or incomplete development of mind which is a category of mental disorder is wider than mental handicap, for it may arise without there being any significant impairment of intelligence or social functioning.[3]

Next, we may note the various contexts in which the vulnerability of the mentally abnormal or young accused who has confessed may come to be considered. First, it is entirely possible for the mental make-up or youthfulness of the suspect to play a part in a decision whether or not a confession was obtained by oppression, for the purposes of section 76(2)(a) of the 1984 Act.[4] That which would not be oppressive for the robust adult of average intelligence may well be oppressive for the young person or mentally disordered adult. There is nothing additional usefully to be said on this point. Secondly, it is clear that these characteristics suggesting vulnerability may be highly relevant to application of the unreliability head of the exclusionary rule under section 76(2)(b) of the Act. Thirdly, where the discretion to exclude confession evidence is relied upon, it may be that the defence will argue that, even though the confession was not made unreliable in consequence of anything said or done to the young or mentally abnormal accused (with the result that section 76(2)(b) is inapplicable), it is nevertheless unreliable such that it ought to be excluded by virtue of section 78(1) or section 82(3). Fourthly, because paragraph 11.14 of Code C provides for a general requirement that '[a] juvenile or a person who is mentally disordered or mentally handicapped ... must not be interviewed or asked to provide a written statement in the absence of the appropriate adult', there is a possibility that that provision will be breached such that there is an additional reason for excluding any confession made during such a breach. Fifthly, the Court of Appeal (Criminal Division) has issued a practice note concerning the circumstances in which the case should be withdrawn from the jury because wholly dependent upon the confession of a mentally handicapped accused.[5] Finally, section 77 of the 1984 Act makes provision for a special warning to the jury in certain cases where the accused who confessed was mentally handicapped.

It must be stressed that exclusion under section 76(2), exclusion as a matter of discretion under section 78(1) or section 82(3), withdrawal of the case from the jury, and administration of a section 77 warning are quite separate and distinct legal ideas. It follows that failure to persuade the court to take the relevant action in any one of those respects does not, as such, dictate anything about the proper result in any other respect.

[2] See, e.g., Gostin, *Mental Health Services—Law and Practice* (1986), paras. 9.01 and 9.03.2; Ashton and Ward, *Mental Handicap and the Law* (1992), 17; Jones, *Mental Health Act Manual* (4th.edn., 1994), 17.

[3] As suggested by Hoggett, *Mental Health Law* (3rd.edn., 1990), 57–8. But cf. 4th edn., 1996, 39.

[4] See Ch. 5, text to nn. 40–4 above. An interesting case in this respect is *Paris, Abdullahi and Miller* (1992) 97 Cr.App.R 99.

[5] See *McKenzie (Practice Note)* [1993] 1 WLR 453.

Vulnerability and Section 76(2)(b)

It has been mentioned earlier in this work[6] that it is established that the mental handicap of the accused may properly be considered as a 'circumstance existing at the time' for the purposes of section 76(2)(b) and so may properly be taken into account in deciding whether his confession should be excluded under that subsection.[7] There seems no reason at all why this should not equally apply in the case where the person confessing was mentally disordered or a juvenile. Also, since section 76(2)(b) concerns itself with any confession which the *particular* accused might have made, the various factors of vulnerability ought also to be capable of being relevant directly to whether or not he may have confessed unreliably, rather than merely indirectly as circumstances existing at the time.[8] Indeed, permanent or long-lasting states such as these are more obviously features of the particular accused than surrounding circumstances. A temporary state, such as drunkenness or emotional upset, fits more easily into the notion of a circumstance existing at the time.

It merits reiteration here that the court is not concerned with whether or not the police actually realized that the accused was suffering from mental disorder or handicap.[9] The test is an objective one.[10] This is of some importance, for there is empirical and anecdotal evidence suggesting that the police are not themselves adept at discerning that a particular suspect is mentally disordered or handicapped,[11] though they may have a misplaced confidence in their ability so to discern.[12] It would hardly be surprising were this to be the case, for police officers have no expertise in these matters beyond that of the ordinary citizen. Furthermore, a failure to respond to obvious signs of mental handicap, for example an inability to read or write, may be explained by a failure of communication between various officers.[13]

Though none of the reported cases concerns vulnerability by virtue of being young, the test here must equally be an objective one. Of course, in practice, the police are likely in the generality of cases to appreciate easily that the person they are dealing with is a juvenile.

[6] See Ch. 5, text to nn. 91–4 above.

[7] The leading case is *Everett* [1988] Crim.LR 826 (transcript through LEXIS). See also *McGovern* (1990) 92 Cr.App.R 228; *Paris, Abdullahi and Miller* (1992) 97 Cr.App.R 99; *Ham, The Times*, 12 Dec. 1995 (transcript through LEXIS).

[8] *Delaney* (1988) 88 Cr.App.R 338 may provide inferential support for the view expressed in the text. The accused does not seem to have been mentally handicapped. However, he was educationally subnormal, with an IQ of 80, and had a tendency to quick emotional arousal. The Court of Appeal considered these to be features of the accused himself, which features made it more likely that he would have confessed unreliably, whether for the purposes of s. 76(2)(b) or of s. 78(1).

[9] See Ch. 5, text to nn. 96–9 above.

[10] *Everett* [1988] Crim.LR 826 (transcript through LEXIS). See also *Morse et al.* [1991] Crim.LR 195; *Ham, The Times*, 12 Dec. 1995 (transcript through LEXIS).

[11] See Nemitz and Bean (1994) 34 *Med. Sci. Law* 161; Palmer [1996] Crim.LR 633, at 634–5. And see Royal Commission on Criminal Justice, Research Study No 12, 1993 (by Gudjonsson *et al.*), 24–6.

[12] Nemitz and Bean, n. 11 above, 163.

[13] As in *Kenny* [1994] Crim.LR 284 (transcript through LEXIS).

VULNERABILITY AND SECTION 78

Stewart[14] amply demonstrates how the power of discretionary exclusion can be relied upon when the exclusionary rule cannot. The accused suffered both from mental illness (echolalia) and mental handicap (having a mental age of, at best, 5½). He was unable to report events with any degree of accuracy and was thus a wholly unreliable witness. It seems that he confessed his guilt to alleged offences of arson in response to the very first question put to him. Given that the effect of his echolalia was that he tended to repeat what he heard, rather to give real answers to questions put to him, it is hard to see how it could be said that he confessed *in consequence of* anything said or done by the police. It was his mental condition which was the effective or substantial cause of his confession, even though the question might be regarded as its immediate cause.

VULNERABILITY AND 'THE APPROPRIATE ADULT'

We have already seen that paragraph 11.14 of Code C, following similar provisions in earlier issues of that Code, *requires* that any person, whether or not a suspect, who is in one of the vulnerable groups, must not be interviewed in the absence of 'the appropriate adult'.[15] There is an exception to this requirement where any consequent delay in carrying out the interview would bring with it one of the three defined risks of deleterious consequences.[16] It is noteworthy, having regard to the obvious difficulties which officers may have in identifying a mental disorder or handicap, that Note for Guidance 11B indicates that the appropriate adult should be called in if there is any doubt about a person's age, mental state, or mental capacity. The message from both this Note and paragraphs 1.4 and 1.5 is that, when in doubt, they should assume the worst.

Treatment of these matters will be divided into four parts. First, we shall consider what view the courts have taken of failure to comply with paragraph 11.14. Secondly, we shall ask what makes a given adult 'appropriate', or, indeed, inappropriate. Thirdly, we shall examine briefly the purposes of the appropriate adult's presence. Finally, we shall look at some empirical research concerned with use of appropriate adults.

FAILURE TO COMPLY WITH PARAGRAPH 11.14

The authorities consistently support the proposition that the absence from the interview of the appropriate adult is a very strong factor favouring exclusion, and this applies no less where the accused was, at the time of the interview, a juvenile than where he was mentally disordered or handicapped.

There is a group of cases in the Court of Appeal concerned with failure to

[14] (1972) 56 Cr.App.R 272. [15] See, generally, Littlechild [1995] Crim.LR 540.
[16] See Code C, para. 11.1, and Annex C.

provide an appropriate adult for a mentally handicapped suspect. In each, that court overturned the trial judge's decision to allow the evidence of the confession to be called. In three, it relied upon section 76(2)(b) in doing so, in the other two upon both that subsection and section 78(1).

The earliest section 76(2)(b) case is *Everett.*[17] The accused had an IQ of 61, placing him in the bottom 2 per cent of the population and only a little above the severe subnormality level. No outsider at all had been present at his interview. The Court decided that his confession ought to have been excluded because the presence of an independent, mature adult would have enabled him to consider whether or not he should answer questions at all and would have ensured that, so far as possible, he really did understand the position in which he found himself. It is to be noted that there was no complaint from the defence that Everett had been denied access to legal advice. By contrast, in *Moss*,[18] the police had deliberately denied the accused access to a solicitor, as well as having failed to ensure that an appropriate adult was present. This may explain why the appeal was allowed even though the medical evidence, which had been accepted by the judge, suggested that he was just above the borderline of mental handicap.

In *Cox*,[19] the accused's IQ of 58 was such as to place him in the severely subnormal range and, indeed, in the bottom ½ per cent of the population. The medical evidence indicated that Cox was suggestible and likely to say that which he believed his questioners would wish to hear. Once again, no outsider was present at his interview. The trial judge found that one of the officers involved in the interviewing process must have known that Cox was suffering from some degree of mental handicap. On the *voir dire*, Cox had imprudently admitted that he was guilty of the burglary with which he was charged. The judge was led into the error of ruling his confession admissible on the basis that it was actually reliable. The court overturned the judge because he had made that error.[20] It seems to be implicit in its decision to quash the conviction that, had he applied the correct test, he ought then to have excluded it under section 76(2)(b).

So far as the argument for exclusion under section 78(1) is concerned, there is no reason why failure to provide an appropriate adult should not be an equally important factor. Indeed, there are two cases in which the trial judge's decision to admit the confession of a mentally handicapped accused made in these circumstances was overturned by the Court of Appeal, which relied upon both section 76(2)(b) and section 78(1) in doing so.[21]

As regards juveniles, there is one, briefly reported, first instance case[22] in which the judge relied upon section 78(1) in excluding the confession of a 16-year-old who had been interviewed in the absence of an appropriate adult. There seems to

[17] [1988] Crim.LR 826 (transcript through LEXIS). [18] (1990) 91 Cr.App.R 371.

[19] [1991] Crim.LR 276 (transcript through LEXIS).

[20] See also *Kenny* [1994] Crim.LR 284, where a similar error was made.

[21] *Dutton*, unreported, 11 Nov. 1988; *Ham, The Times*, 12 Dec. 1995 (both transcripts through LEXIS).

[22] *Fogah* [1989] Crim.LR 141.

have been no other element of the case lending support to an argument for exclusion on the basis of unreliability. In *Weekes*,[23] the accused, also aged 16, had been arrested shortly after a street robbery. An exchange between him and a police officer had then taken place, apparently in a police vehicle, and damaging admissions had been forthcoming. Having concluded that part of the exchange amounted to an interview, the Court of Appeal relied upon section 78(1) in overturning the trial judge's decision to allow it to be given in evidence. In doing so, though it referred to breaches of the contemporaneous recording requirements in Code C, it described as 'a matter of more importance'[24] the fact that no appropriate adult had been present.

Turning to exclusion under section 76(2)(b), mention must be made of the Divisional Court case, *DPP* v. *Blake*.[25] There the situation was somewhat different, in that an adult *had* been present, but, as we shall shortly see, the adult in question was regarded both by the magistrates and by the higher court as being inappropriate. It seems reasonable to suppose that provision of an inappropriate adult is equivalent to failure to provide anyone at all. The magistrates had excluded the accused's confession—she had been 16 when she made it—under section 76(2)(b), and the Divisional Court dismissed the prosecution's appeal.[26]

It must be added that there is, of course, no question of exclusion being automatic where no appropriate adult was present. The fundamental question remains whether or not the confession ought to be excluded because unreliable.[27] For example, in *Kenny*,[28] the psychological evidence was rather mixed. The accused had a reading age under 7, but his overall IQ was equivalent to that of the average child of 9 to 10 years. There was no medical evidence to indicate that he was particularly suggestible. The trial judge decided that, though the accused was mentally handicapped, his confession could properly be adduced before the jury. The Court of Appeal allowed Kenny's appeal because the judge had applied the wrong test as regards admissibility, but it is entirely conceivable that, had he applied the correct test, he could properly have reached the same decision. Certainly, the Court stressed the importance of looking at all the facts of the particular case:[29]

> Each individual case has, of course, its own features, and we would deprecate any attempt which sought to take the figures produced by particular intelligence tests in any case and apply them almost slavishly to another in order to define some sort of rigid and unswerving line, the crossing of which would lead automatically to the exclusion of evidence.

Similarly, in *Campbell*,[30] there had been a number of interviews, at some of which neither a solicitor nor an appropriate adult had been present. Counsel for the appellant argued that incriminatory admissions made at these interviews

[23] (1992) 97 Cr.App.R 222. [24] *Ibid.* 225. [25] [1989] 1 WLR 432.
[26] See also *Morse et al.* [1991] Crim.LR 195, a Crown Court case.
[27] See, e.g., *DPP* v. *Morris*, unreported, 8 Oct. 1990 (transcript through LEXIS).
[28] [1994] Crim.LR 284 (transcript through LEXIS). [29] See transcript.
[30] [1995] 1 Cr.App.R 522.

ought to have been excluded at trial. The Court of Appeal could see nothing 'plainly wrong' with the trial judge's view that no unreliability had been brought about because of their absence, and so upheld his decision not to exclude them under section 78(1). It may well be significant that Stuart-Smith LJ pointed out that the defence experts had not said that 'there was anything in the appellant's mental condition that made him especially vulnerable to suggestibility or to pressure in police interviews'.[31]

In *W and Another*,[32] the same court seems to have approved the trial judge's decision that, even if, contrary to his own opinion, the person provided by the police did not constitute an appropriate adult, it would not have been right to exclude the accused's confession. The judge's view of the interview at which that confession had been forthcoming was that it had been conducted fairly and properly, that it had not been over-long, and that it had not involved the accused being put under any pressure. It followed that there was no point at which it would have been necessary, or even desirable, for the accused to have sought advice or for the adult to have interrupted the interview. The court expressed its agreement with the judge's opinion about the interview. Presumably, though it did not say so expressly, it would have reached the same decision as did he about exclusion. The case is a particularly strong one in that, at the time of the interview, the accused was only 13 years of age.

Notwithstanding the last point, it would seem obvious that the presence of the adult will assume more importance as the age of the suspect decreases. Failure to procure an appropriate adult for a 10 year-old would be extremely hard to justify and ought to make exclusion of any confession made much more likely. Presumably, the personal characteristics, intelligence, and experience of the specific juvenile would also be highly relevant to the decision.

It is to be noted that in none of the cases so far dealt with in this section was any outsider at all present at the interview. What if a legal adviser was present? Though there is no doubt that the functions of the appropriate adult differ from those of the legal adviser, there is a considerable element of overlap. According to paragraph 11.16 of Code C, the purposes of the adult's presence are: 'first, to advise the person being questioned and to observe whether or not the interview is being conducted properly and fairly, and secondly, to facilitate communication with the person being interviewed'. One can certainly see that one reason for the suspect wishing to have a legal adviser present might be that he wanted there to be a third party in a position to ensure the fair and proper conducting of the interview. Of course, a lawyer with a sound knowledge of the 1984 Act and Code C ought to be in a better position to deal with any improprieties which might arise. Equally, the giving of advice to the suspect is no less a task for the lawyer than for the appropriate adult. On the other hand, the kind of advice which the two would find it proper to give ought to differ. Advice on whether or not to answer questions should, especially now that the right to silence has been attenuated by the

[31] *Ibid.* 530. [32] [1994] Crim.LR 130 (transcript through LEXIS).

Criminal Justice and Public Order Act 1994, be very much a matter for the lawyer's professional expertise.[33] Moreover, it is not at all clear that a lawyer should act so as to facilitate communication between the police and his client.

The logic of this considerable overlap is that failure to provide the suspect with an appropriate adult will, where a legal adviser was present at the interview, be less likely to provoke judicial concern about the reliability of the confession. There is now Court of Appeal authority in support of the foregoing proposition. In *Lewis*,[34] that court went so far as to suggest that the functions of legal adviser and appropriate adult were very largely the same. This would seem to overstate the overlap, and it may be important in some future case for the court to refine its idea of comparative roles. At all events, in the result, the court in *Lewis* had no doubt that, had the accused's mental handicap been raised at the trial, which, for reasons it is not necessary to go into here, it had not, the judge would have ruled his statements admissible under section 76(2)(b) and would have exercised his discretion under section 78(1) such as to allow them to be adduced.

An even stronger claim made by Watkins LJ in *Everett* is not supportable. He expressed the view that the role of the appropriate adult might itself be properly fulfilled by a solicitor. Even at the time, in 1988, the definition of 'the appropriate adult' did not lend itself easily to such a view.[35] Now Note for Guidance 1F expressly states that a solicitor who is present at the police station in that capacity may not act as an appropriate adult, while Note 1EE states that the suspect should always be given the opportunity to consult privately with a solicitor in the absence of the adult, where the latter has been called to the police station.

Meaning of 'the Appropriate Adult'

Paragraph 1.7 of Code C defines 'the appropriate adult'. It distinguishes appropriateness in respect of a juvenile from appropriateness in respect of a mentally disordered or handicapped person. In the former case, that paragraph lists, first, the parent or guardian of the juvenile (including, where he is in care, the organization having that care), secondly a social worker, and thirdly, failing either of the first two, any other responsible adult who is not a police officer or employed by the police. In the latter case, the first category is widened to include any relative of the suspect. The second category comprehends persons who have experience of dealing with the mentally disordered or handicapped, as long as not police officers or employed by the police. The third category is identical to that for juveniles.

DPP v. *Blake*[36] establishes that there is no necessary order of priority favouring the

[33] This seems to have been assumed in *Jefferson et al.* [1994] 1 All ER 270, at 287—see text to nn. 45–7 below.

[34] [1996] Crim.LR 260.

[35] Because the police would have had an obligation to consider persons who would be most unlikely to be solicitors before turning to the catch-all of any other responsible adult not a police officer or employed by the police—see Code C (1985 issue), para. 1.7.

[36] [1989] 1 WLR 432.

first category (parent, etc.) over the second. There, the policy of the relevant social services department was not to respond to requests for social workers to attend to fulfil the role, in the case of juveniles, unless either no parent or guardian could be found or the parent or guardian in question refused to attend. The Divisional Court considered this to be a policy which that department was not entitled to adopt.

The reason it would have been right, in *Blake*, for the police to ask a social worker to attend, and for one to be sent, was that the suspect, who was aged 16 at the time, had, after initially refusing even to divulge her father's name and address, made it clear, once she did reveal those details, that she was estranged from him and did not wish to see him. Nonetheless, given the social services department's policy, the police arranged for him to be present at the interview. The Divisional Court upheld the decision of the magistrates that her father could not, in the circumstances, count as an appropriate adult. As Mann LJ put it '[t]he appropriate adult cannot . . . be a person with whom the juvenile has no empathy'.[37] It is now specifically provided by Note for Guidance 1C of Code C that the estranged parent of a juvenile should not be asked to act as an appropriate adult if that juvenile expressly and specifically objects to his presence.

The principle propounded by the court in *Blake* and, in particular, by Mann LJ would seem capable of having a much wider impact. It must be strongly arguable that *any person* to whom the suspect expressly objects is *per se* inappropriate. This point seems to be recognized, in a qualified way and in a particular respect, by Note for Guidance 1E. It states that, in certain circumstances, it may be more satisfactory for the adult, in the case of a mentally disordered or handicapped person, to be someone with experience or training in the care of such persons. It goes on to say: '[b]ut if the person himself prefers a relative to a better qualified stranger or objects to a particular person as the appropriate adult, his wishes should if practicable be respected.' If we follow the 'no empathy' line of reasoning, there would seem to be some scope for extending the idea of inappropriateness beyond persons objected to explicitly by the accused. For example, in *DPP* v. *Morris*,[38] the adult present at an interview with a juvenile had been the manager of a children's home in which that juvenile resided. The magistrates had based their decision to exclude his confession partly on their finding that the manager 'showed a lack of the special care needed in questioning juveniles'.[39] In the Divisional Court, one argument for the respondent in support of the magistrates' decision was that the manager was, in effect, not an appropriate adult. It had been he who had summoned the police. He had not spoken privately to the respondent, and the respondent had been, because the manager was someone in authority over him, reluctant to take the initiative himself. The manager would be seen by the respondent as likely to be on the side of the police. Accordingly, the manager was not someone with the respondent's interest foremost in his mind, nor conscious of his duty to advise him. The Divisional Court was clearly dubious about this aspect of the magistrates' decision, describing it as

[37] *Ibid*. 440. [38] Unreported, 8 Oct. 1990 (transcript through LEXIS).
[39] See transcript.

'very near the borderline'[40] but concluded that the magistrates had not abused their discretion. It dismissed the prosecution's appeal on other grounds.

Other authorities deal not with lack of empathy but with lack of capacity. So, for example, the person who gave aid to the vulnerable suspect may himself or herself have been mentally handicapped or disordered. In *Morse et al.*,[41] a Crown Court decision, the juvenile's father had attended the relevant interviews. Evidence from a psychologist indicated that the father had an IQ of between 60 and 70, that he was virtually illiterate, and that it was probable that he was incapable of appreciating the gravity of his son's situation. The judge held that he did not count as an appropriate adult. The call for a mentally handicapped adult not to assume the role will, perhaps, be even more obvious where the vulnerable suspect himself is mentally handicapped or disordered.

Notwithstanding *Morse et al.*, the position may be that the proper issue for the court is not whether the adult in question was or was not suffering from mental handicap or disorder, but whether or not that adult was capable of fulfilling the functions of an appropriate adult. So in *W and Another*,[42] the judge had found that the mother of a 16-year-old was almost certainly psychotic at the time of the interview, and so mentally disordered. Yet because he accepted evidence of a forensic psychiatrist called by the prosecution that she was capable of fulfilling her functions, he ruled that she did count as an appropriate adult. One can certainly see that the nature of a particular mental disorder might be such as to leave that capability untarnished. In the case itself, the psychosis concerned the mother's neighbours and, arguably at least, did not prevent her thought processes working rationally with regard to her children. However, the case is somewhat complicated by the fact that there was also evidence that her IQ was only 76, placing her in the bottom 5 per cent of the population and within the range of borderline subnormality. Indeed, counsel for the appellant argued that she was mentally handicapped. The trial judge had described her as suffering from 'some intellectual deficit as a result of her chronic psychosis',[43] and the Court of Appeal could find no basis for overturning him either on this judgment or on his judgment of her overall capability. Therefore, it remains possible that, where the judge finds the adult to be mentally handicapped rather than mentally disordered, he must conclude that that person cannot be an appropriate adult.

Another kind of alleged incapacity was put to the Divisional Court in *D* v. *DPP*.[44] There, the 12-year-old suspect's father, present at the interview, had but a limited knowledge of English, having arrived in England from Vietnam only seven years before. The court noted the argument that the effect was to render him incapable of protecting fully his son's interests, but expressed no opinion on it, for it felt able to turn down the juvenile's appeal on the basis that, even without the incriminating remarks made at interview, the case against him was overwhelming.

[40] See transcript. [41] [1991] Crim.LR 195.
[42] [1994] Crim.LR 130 (transcript through LEXIS). [43] See transcript.
[44] Unreported, 21 June 1988 (transcript through LEXIS).

A third situation, dealt with by Code C itself, is that where the adult in question has some involvement or interest in the matters under investigation. Note for Guidance 1C rules inappropriate a person who is himself suspected of involvement in the offence, or is a victim or witness, or who is involved in the investigation or has already received admissions from the suspect in question.

Finally, in *Jefferson et al.*,[45] the Court of Appeal set its face against the idea that the behaviour of the adult in question during the course of the interview itself might show him to be inappropriate. One of the accused, Keogh, had been 15 when interviewed. His father, who had attended both interviews, was said by Auld J to have 'intervened robustly from time to time, sometimes joining in the questioning of his son and challenging his exculpatory account of certain incidents'.[46] The fact that the father had thus acted as a 'somewhat critical observer and participant'[47] did not render him inappropriate, for his duty to advise his son did not entail a need to counsel silence or to refrain from intervening to encourage truthfulness. Presumably, these are properly the tasks of a legal adviser. The case does, however, leave open the possibility that the behaviour of the adult at interview might, in extreme circumstances, perhaps involving violence or verbal bullying, render him inappropriate.

The Purpose of Presence of 'the Appropriate Adult'

We have already seen that paragraph 11.16 of Code C describes the purposes of the presence of the appropriate adult as being to advise the person being questioned, to observe whether or not the interview is being conducted properly and fairly, and to facilitate communication between the parties. It also requires the police to inform that adult that those are the purposes of his presence and that he is not expected to act only as an observer.

There is a range of provisions in Code C which are designed to back up the adult's fulfilment of these purposes or to assist him in acting as the more articulate hand of the vulnerable suspect as regards the various decisions which that suspect needs to make. As regards decision-making, paragraph 3.12 requires the custody officer to inform him that the appropriate adult is there to advise and assist him and that he can consult privately with the adult at any time. Information must be given by the police to the adult about the various rights of the suspect. Most importantly, perhaps, the effect of paragraphs 3.1 and 3.11 is that the adult must be alerted to the suspect's rights to have someone informed of his arrest, to take legal advice, and to consult the various codes of practice. As regards the caution, this must be administered, initially, in the adult's presence, or if not then repeated in his presence.

The appropriate adult would be unable to fulfil his purposes were he not provided with various other items of information and opportunity. Most obviously, he must be told the grounds for detention.[48] Where detention is reviewed by the

[45] [1994] 1 All ER 270. [46] *Ibid.* 286. [47] *Ibid.* 287. [48] See para. 3.9.

police, the adult must, if available, be given the chance of making representations about the need for continued detention.[49] If the suspect is charged, this is to be done in the adult's presence and a written notice of the charge given to him.[50] Finally, the adult may, in effect, overrule a decision of the suspect not to take legal advice. If he does, then the advice must be made available in the ordinary way.[51]

It may seem surprising, given the range of the duties applicable to the police as regards the appropriate adult, that none of the reported cases involves an allegation of breach of any of these back-up provisions. It is, of course, possible that this reflects a high level of police compliance with them. However, Evans, in a study for the Royal Commission on Criminal Justice carried out in the early 1990s, found no evidence in the taped records of interviews with juveniles that the appropriate adult was alerted to his role under paragraph 11.16,[52] so it is hard to believe that the back-up provisions are generally complied with.

Use of 'the Appropriate Adult'

Note for Guidance 11B specifically recognizes the reliability problems attached to the statements at interview of vulnerable suspects, then goes on to identify the steps the police should take when confronted with such a suspect. It states:

> It is important to bear in mind that, although juveniles or people who are mentally disordered or mentally handicapped are often capable of providing reliable evidence, they may, without knowing or wishing to do so, be particularly prone in certain circumstances to provide information which is unreliable, misleading or self-incriminating. Special care should therefore always be exercised in questioning such a person, and the appropriate adult should be involved if there is any doubt about a person's age, mental state or capacity. Because of the risk of unreliable evidence it is also important to obtain corroboration of any facts admitted whenever possible.

The Royal Commission on Criminal Justice accepted the proposition that vulnerable suspects are more likely than others to be unable to cope with the pressures of the environment of the police station and are particularly liable to make false confessions, a view which finds support not only in ordinary life experience but also in a body of modern psychological research.[53]

It follows that there are at least four elements for consideration. First, the police must be able to identify vulnerable suspects as such. Secondly, as Code C itself recognizes, it is important that, when there is doubt about the suspect in question, that person should be deemed to be within the relevant category.[54] Thirdly, an appropriate adult ought to be provided for each person eventually identified. Finally, the police should look for corroborative evidence.

[49] See paras. 15.1 and 15.2. [50] See paras. 16.1 and 16.3. [51] See para. 3.13.

[52] Research Study No 8, 1993, 39. See also Littlechild, n. 15 above, 541–2.

[53] Royal Commission on Criminal Justice, *Report*, July 1993, Cm 2263, ch. 3, para. 81. For the psychological research, see Gudjonsson, *The Psychology of Interrogations, Confessions and Testimony* (1992), *passim*.

[54] See Code C, paras. 1.4 and 1.5.

Regarding the first element, there is evidence that the police are not adept at recognizing signs of mental disorder or handicap. In a study carried out for the Royal Commission, Gudjonsson and others estimated that some 15 to 20 per cent of a sample of suspects satisfied the criteria, in one or other of those respects, of need for the appropriate adult, yet the police themselves identified only 4 per cent as needing such an adult.[55]

Assistance for the police in their task of identification may be provided by the police surgeon. According to Code C, paragraph 9.2, the surgeon is to be summoned by the custody officer whenever the suspect 'appears to be suffering from . . . a mental disorder' or 'fails to respond normally to questions or conversation'. In effect, the surgeon's responsibility is, first, to decide whether or not the suspect is fit to be interviewed, but, secondly, if he is fit, to decide whether or not an appropriate adult is required. There is some empirical evidence that these two decisions tend to become confused, whether by the surgeon or by the police, so that once the suspect is deemed fit to be interviewed the possibility that the appropriate adult's presence is required is ignored or forgotten.[56] Indeed in *Ham*,[57] the same error was carried over into the trial judge's reasoning.

In a study of the role of surgeons carried out by Robertson for the Royal Commission, a remarkable difference in decision-making emerged as between police forces inside and outside London. Only 1 per cent of London suspects referred to the surgeon for assessment were found unfit, as compared with 12 per cent of provincial suspects. As regards the appropriate adult, the figures were the other way, 23 per cent being judged to require one in London, but only 1 per cent outside. Robertson points out that the samples were small and confined to a few police stations in a few forces, with the result that one cannot tell whether the variation was a function of similar people being treated differently or of real differences in population. The Royal Commission itself was clearly troubled by these findings, notwithstanding their possible statistical unreliability.[58] It does seem wrong to leave this important matter of assessment in the hands of general practitioners, who may well have little or no psychiatric training.[59] It must be awareness of that problem which led the Home Office, in a circular issued in 1990, to encourage chief officers of police to arrange with their local health authorities for psychiatrists to fulfil the role of police surgeon in these cases.[60] One possible way of addressing the problem would be to create a duty psychiatrist scheme embracing all police stations. This possibility was, indeed, mooted by the Royal Commission itself.[61]

[55] Research Study No 12, n. 11 above, 25. The police seem to be much more adept at identifying the most disabled and vulnerable suspects—see *ibid.* 26. See also Palmer, n. 11 above, at 634–6.

[56] See Nemitz and Bean, n. 11 above, at 163.

[57] *The Times*, 12 Dec. 1995 (transcript through LEXIS).

[58] See n. 53 above, ch. 3, para. 89.

[59] *Ibid.*, ch. 3, para. 90.

[60] HO Circular 66/90, para. 4(iv).

[61] See n. 53 above, Ch. 3, para. 92. It may be supposed that the Home Office Working Party which was set up in Autumn 1995 to consider the role of the police surgeons will address this issue. See also Palmer, n. 11 above, 637–9.

One might suppose that the effect of what Note for Guidance 11B says about doubtful cases, together with that of other code stipulations,[62] would be to ensure that the appropriate adult was called upon to attend a significant proportion of police interviews. In fact, though most of the relevant stipulations for cases of doubt were to be found even in the original (1985) issue of Code C, there is evidence of under-use from the very beginning of the appropriate adult. We have already noted that Gudjonsson *et al.* found that mental disorder or handicap was identified in only about a quarter or a fifth of cases where it was present. In the report of a study of a much larger number of cases carried out for the Home Office by Brown, Ellis, and Larcombe, it is stated: '[t]he mentally disordered or handicapped constitute a far smaller group [than that of juveniles]—just over one per cent of all those detained at police stations in the present study were treated as such.'[63] The key phrase here may be 'treated as such', for the figure might have been expected to be very much higher were the criteria being applied in the way contemplated by Code C.

Even in cases where there has been a positive finding of mental disorder or handicap, it seems clear that the appropriate adult will not always be present at the interview. Thus, Nemitz and Bean, in a survey of a large number of police records covering the calendar year 1992, found evidence of failure to use the adult even in some cases where detained persons had been recorded as mentally disordered.[64] Brown, Ellis, and Larcombe also found that appropriate adults did not always attend. Their study was divided into two phases, during the earlier of which the original issue of Code C applied, but during the later of which the revised issue of 1991 applied. In the earlier phase, the adult had eventually attended in only 50 per cent of cases, while, in the later one, there was an 80 per cent attendance rate.[65] The fact that compliance is probably still somewhat short of being complete may be explained, at least partly, by the problems the police sometimes experience in obtaining persons who actually are suitable to act in the relevant capacity.[66] The Royal Commission itself was concerned that there might be an inadequate supply of appropriate persons, and recommended 'a comprehensive review of the role, functions, qualifications, training and availability of appropriate adults'.[67]

So far as corroboration is concerned, the broader question of corroboration of confessions is addressed in Chapter 12 of this work. In relation to the particular case of vulnerable suspects, there is no reported case in which the defence has relied upon a failure on the part of the police to follow Note for Guidance 11B in this respect. It will be recalled that there is, in any event, some doubt that notes

[62] See paras. 1.4 and 1.5 and Note for Guidance 1G.

[63] *Changing the Code: Police Detention under the Revised P.A.C.E. Codes of Practice*, HO Research Study No 129,1992, at 70.

[64] See n. 11 above, 163. A later survey carried out by Palmer found similar evidence of code breaches—see n. 11 above, 640.

[65] See n. 63 above, 78. [66] See Gudjonsson *et al.*, n. 11 above, 27.

[67] See n. 53 above, ch. 3, para. 86. It seems that such a review was put in operation early in 1994—see Littlechild, n. 15 above, 544—though the present author has been unable to trace any report resulting therefrom.

for guidance, like this one, which are not incorporated by reference into the main body of a code may be relied upon by a court in deciding whether or not to exclude evidence.[68] Furthermore, the sentence of the Note which deals with corroboration is not expressed in mandatory terms.

WITHDRAWING THE CASE FROM THE JURY

The leading case on the test to be applied to decide whether or not the accused has a case to answer is *Galbraith*.[69] The guidance given there was applied by the Court of Appeal to the specific situation of a confession by a mentally handicapped person in *McKenzie*. According to the court:[70]

> where (1) the prosecution case depends wholly upon confessions; (2) the defendant suffers from a significant degree of mental handicap; and (3) the confessions are unconvincing to a point where a jury properly directed could not properly convict upon them, then the judge, assuming he has not excluded the confessions earlier, should withdraw the case from the jury.

The court went on to mention some of the factors which might lead a judge to conclude that confessions were sufficiently unconvincing for these purposes. They might be so 'because they lack the incriminating details to be expected of a guilty and willing confessor, or because they are inconsistent with other evidence, or because they are otherwise inherently improbable'.[71]

In *Wood*,[72] the appeal was allowed on the basis that it was a case where the *McKenzie* ruling should have been applied. Either Wood himself or his cohabitee must have inflicted the fatal injuries on the latter's 4-year-old son. There was no evidence other than his confession to incriminate Wood. The Court of Appeal considered that Wood, though having an IQ above the subnormal range, did suffer from a *significant* degree of mental handicap. It stressed that his verbal memory skills were in the mental defective range, that he was very suggestible, and that he tended to assume the blame when things went wrong. Clearly, then, the trial judge, in deciding how significant is the degree of handicap of the particular accused, is to take account of particular factors which tend to suggest a much-increased tendency towards unreliability, or, indeed, factors indicating the reverse. It was probably with respect to the third element in *McKenzie* that *Wood* was an especially strong case. Wood had been adamant that he had struck a blow or blows to the young boy only on the day before his death, yet the unchallenged medical evidence showed that the fatal blow must have been delivered on the day of the death itself. In other words, his confession was inconsistent with the other evidence.

In *Bailey*,[73] the trial judge had been satisfied that the first two elements of *McKenzie* were present. Though there was some other evidence of the accused's

[68] See Ch. 6, text to nn. 92–100 above.
[69] [1981] 1 WLR 1039.
[70] [1993] 1 WLR 453, at 455 (Practice Note).
[71] *Ibid.*
[72] [1994] Crim.LR 222 (transcript through LEXIS).
[73] [1995] 2 Cr.App.R 262.

involvement in a fire which had caused the death of the occupant of a flat, there would have been no prosecution case without the confession evidence. The Court of Appeal supported the judge on this point, so it may be taken that a case may wholly *depend* upon confession evidence even where there is some other evidence. As regards the third element, the court stressed that it was the test itself which mattered, rather than the glosses placed upon it in *McKenzie*, though it did go on to refer to the lack of conflict between the confession and the known facts. It pointed out that the reliability of any confession is a question of fact and, therefore, normally a matter for the jury to decide.

It is rather difficult to predict the future of the *McKenzie* ruling. There is an inevitable tension here between a desire to preserve the jury's sovereign function and one to reduce the possibility of wrongful conviction. The Royal Commission gave the latter desire precedence. It thought that *Galbraith* itself should be reversed, so allowing the judge to stop the trial because of his opinion that 'the prosecution evidence is demonstrably unsafe or unsatisfactory or too weak to be allowed to go to the jury'.[74] On the other hand, it may be argued that a combination of all the other protections for the mentally handicapped suspect ought to obviate the need to use the power to stop a trial in all but the most extreme of cases.

Section 77 Warnings

Section 77, which was added to the Police and Criminal Evidence Bill at a very late stage, provides, in subsection (1), that where at a jury trial (a) the case against the accused depends wholly or substantially upon a confession, and (b) the court is 'satisfied' that he is mentally handicapped and that that confession was not made in the presence of an 'independent person', the judge must warn the jury that there is a 'special need for caution' before they convict the accused in reliance upon it. He must also explain to them that the need arises because of the circumstances referred to in (a) and (b). Subsection (2) makes analogous provision for summary trial.

We may begin by observing that, while Code C consistently regards the mentally handicapped, the mentally disordered, and juveniles as requiring broadly similar treatment, because they are all groups of vulnerable persons, section 77 applies only in the case of the mentally handicapped. The restriction is difficult to understand,[75] though the judge is, of course, free, in the exercise of his general obligation to sum the case up fairly, to suggest similar caution in the case of persons from the other two categories.[76] The definition of 'mental handicap' is provided by section 77(3), which, as we have already seen, seems to be applied also as regards exclusion under sections 76(2) and 78(1).

[74] *Report*, n. 53 above, ch. 4, para. 42.

[75] For more detailed treatment of this point, see Mirfield, *Confessions* (1985), 165–6.

[76] It should also be recalled that there is an element of overlap between 'mental handicap' and 'mental disorder'—see text to n. 2 above.

A key element of the decision about the section 77 warnings is whether or not the case can be said to depend 'wholly or substantially' upon a confession made in the absence of an independent adult. We have just seen that, where *McKenzie* is invoked, the requirement that the prosecution case depend wholly upon confession evidence does not entail that, for it to apply, there must be no other non-confession evidence in the case. Section 77 makes it even more likely that a warning will be required, by adding the word 'substantially'. Two recent cases give guidance on the criterion of substantiality. In *Campbell*,[77] one interview had been conducted in the presence of an independent person. His confession at that interview was, in consequence, not caught by section 77. In addition, there was some direct and some circumstantial evidence against him. Adding all the evidence in question together, the Court of Appeal felt able to say that, even if the confession evidence which was caught by section 77 were left out of account, the case against Campbell was no less strong. The court added: '[t]he test . . . must be whether the case for the Crown is substantially less strong without the confession made in the absence of the appropriate adult.'[78] The point was picked up in *Bailey*. The Court of Appeal said of the confessions caught by section 77 that '[i]t would be difficult . . ., if not impossible in many cases, to decide whether such confessions added up to most of the prosecution's case. Such confessions must simply form a substantial part of that case.'[79]

'Independent person' is defined negatively by section 77(3) to exclude 'a police officer or a person employed for, or engaged on, police purposes'. It is clear that, though there is a broad equivalence between this definition and that of 'the appropriate adult' in paragraph 1.7 of Code C, the two are not identical in their content. Strictly, it would seem, someone under the age of 18 could count as an independent person. Furthermore, it will be recalled that paragraph 1.7 contains a 'pecking order', such that the police must first seek out a relative, guardian, or other person responsible for the mentally handicapped suspect's care or custody, or someone with experience of dealing with the mentally handicapped, before turning to other responsible, non-police adults. In practice, no doubt, the police will follow the 'appropriate adult' definition, and there should be no problem with that in the overwhelming majority of cases. However, it is to be noted that the Court of Appeal has held that, in contrast to the situation where the question is whether or not an appropriate adult was present, the role of an independent person may be assumed by a solicitor.[80]

It is to be noted that there is no suggestion anywhere in section 77 that the police must have been at fault in failing to recognize the accused's mental handicap, or in failing to ensure the presence of an independent person. Indeed, the Court of Appeal in *Bailey*[81] pointed out explicitly that the police were not to be criticized for failing to recognize the mental handicap, for they had no reason to know that there was such a problem. This seems entirely right, and fits in with the

[77] [1995] 1 Cr.App.R 522. [78] *Ibid*. 535. [79] [1995] 2 Cr.App.R 262, at 283.
[80] *Lewis* [1996] Crim.LR 260. [81] [1995] 2 Cr.App.R 262, at 284.

application of the exclusionary rule and discretion in the case of the mentally handicapped.

It is also to be noted that the burden of proving both that the accused is mentally handicapped and that no independent person was present is borne by the accused, who must 'satisfy' the court in both respects. It is safe to assume that the standard of proof is on the balance of probabilities.

The required warning has four elements. The jury is to be warned of the special need for caution, then to be told that the need arises from the facts that the case wholly or substantially depends upon the relevant confession, that the accused is mentally handicapped, and that no independent person was present. In *Campbell*,[82] Stuart-Smith LJ provided a helpful gloss on the words of the statute.[83] Provided the sense is conveyed, there is no need to follow any specific form of words, though the judge will be wise to use the phrase 'special need for caution'. The judge should explain why the confession of a mentally handicapped person may be unreliable. This may best be done by referring to what is now Note for Guidance 11B[84] which:[85]

> indicates that persons who are mentally disordered or mentally handicapped may, without wishing to do so, provide information which is unreliable, misleading or self-incriminating. The explanation should be tailored to the particular evidence in the case, for example if there is evidence that the accused is particularly suggestible, prone to acquiesce, comply, or give in to pressure. The judge should go on to explain that the function of the appropriate adult[86] is designed to minimise the risk of the accused giving unreliable information by seeing that the interview is conducted properly and fairly and facilitating, if need be, communication between the police and suspect.

It has been argued that the combined effect of the authorities on exclusion of confessions of the mentally handicapped under sections 76(2) and 78(1) and the application of *Galbraith* to the specific case of such confessions in *McKenzie*[87] is that there will be few cases where there is a call for the procedure laid down by section 77 to be applied.[88] There is force in the point, for, as we have seen, there does seem to be an inclination on the part of the Court of Appeal to favour exclusion of confessions made in the absence of the appropriate adult.[89] Indeed, in *Moss*,[90] that court seemed to recognize the point in referring to only two situations in which section 77 might be invoked. First, Code C, by virtue of paragraph 11.1 and Annex C, paragraph 1, allows interviews of vulnerable suspects to go ahead without an appropriate adult in certain situations of urgency. Where the police have properly relied upon one of those situations, any confession made by

[82] [1995] 1 Cr.App.R 522, at 535–6.

[83] This gloss was approved in *Bailey* [1995] 2 Cr.App.R 262, at 283.

[84] Quoted in full at p. 292 above. [85] [1995] 1 Cr.App.R 522, at 535.

[86] It is noteworthy that here, as elsewhere in his judgment, Stuart-Smith LJ employs this phrase rather than 'independent person'.

[87] [1993] 1 WLR 453 (Practice Note), applying [1981] 1 WLR 1039.

[88] See *Blackstone's Criminal Practice* (1997 edn.), para. F. 17.22.

[89] See text to nn. 17–35 above. [90] (1990) 91 Cr.App.R 371, at 377.

a mentally handicapped accused should not be excluded, but a warning under section 77 would very properly be required. Secondly, a confession may have been obtained from the accused in one interview during a comparatively short period of custody. There, presumably, the trial judge might decide not to deny the jury the confession, but would need to give a section 77 warning. This second situation is rather doubtful for, in *Weekes*,[91] the Court of Appeal ruled in favour of exclusion in just such a case. It seems that no consideration was given to the possible application of section 77 in either the higher or the lower court.

In one briefly-reported case, the Court of Appeal allowed an appeal on the basis that no such warning was given when it should have been, even though the circumstances in which the appellant had confessed were clearly such that neither of the *Moss* situations arose.[92] However, the court did express its surprise that the confession in question had not been excluded, finding it unnecessary to decide whether or not the trial judge's ruling in this respect was sustainable, precisely because it thought it proper to overturn the conviction as returned without the relevant warning having been given. More significantly, in *Bailey*,[93] the same court turned down the appeal in respect of the judge's decision not to exclude the evidence in question, yet allowed it as regards his failure to give a section 77 warning. In that case, the police interviews at which no independent person was present had been three in number, there being a gap of some one and a half hours between the second and the third, so, again, neither *Moss* situation applied. It is noteworthy that the accused herself had attended the police station voluntarily and seems to have volunteered her first confession there. Indeed, there was no question of the police inveigling admissions out of her at any of those interviews: rather, she was making all the running. It should, at least, follow that the section 77 requirement cannot be restricted, as to its applicability, by reference to particular types of situation. Nonetheless, it is clearly and rightly seen as a back-up provision, with the issue of exclusion very much to the fore.

The Admissibility of Evidence to Establish Mental Disorder or Handicap

It is well established that evidence of the opinion of an expert witness is admissible only if likely to assist the court. In the words of Lawton LJ in *Turner*:[94]

> [a]n expert's opinion is admissible to furnish the court with scientific information which is likely to be outside the experience and knowledge of a judge or jury. If on the proven facts a judge or jury can form their own conclusions without help, then the opinion of an expert in unnecessary.

Quite clearly, where it is medical evidence of mental illness which is sought to be adduced, it will not only be desirable, but, in all probability, necessary that this

[91] (1992) 97 Cr.App.R 222.
[92] *Lamont* [1989] Crim.LR 813 (transcript through LEXIS).
[93] [1995] 2 Cr.App.R 262.
[94] [1975] QB 834, at 841.

be allowed to be given,[95] for this is certainly a matter beyond the ordinary experience of the layman. Consequently, the defence will be free to call such evidence where it seeks to challenge the credibility of the accused's confession because, it says, he suffers from such an illness.

However, it will be recalled that the term used in Code C for these purposes is not mental illness but 'mental disorder'. Though that term is defined to include mental illness, it also encompasses 'arrested or incomplete development of mind, psychopathic disorder and any other disorder or disability of mind'.[96] Therefore the question which arises is whether or not expert evidence tending to show some disorder or disability of mind short of mental illness is admissible to show the confession to be unreliable. A similar question must be asked about suggestions that the accused suffers from a mental handicap.

Before dealing with the foregoing questions, it is necessary to be aware that, properly considered, they have two distinct aspects. First, is such evidence admissible before the jury on the *voir dire*? Secondly, may it be adduced before the jury at the trial of the general issue? Since the fact of mental disorder or handicap trips special treatment under Code C and the Act itself, as well as special duties owed by the police, there may very well be a technical issue for the judge to decide in these respects. There will be no such issue for the jury, though, of course, it has to decide about actual reliability, and the presence in the accused of mental disorder or handicap may very well be relevant to that decision. A point which may also tend to suggest the placing of greater constraint on the evidence available to the jury than that available to the judge is to be found in one of the principal reasons for the *Turner* doctrine. That case points to the danger that laymen will consider expert evidence of matters within their own experience and knowledge more potent than it really is, and, therefore, be confused by it.[97] One would expect judges to consider themselves better able to avoid confusion of that kind.

In *Raghip, Silcott, and Braithwaite*,[98] the Court of Appeal did give separate consideration to the two aspects of the question, though without identifying why it might be legitimate to reach a different conclusion as regards the one than as regards the other. In fact, it ruled the evidence in question admissible in both respects. In *Ward*,[99] the same court seems to have taken *Raghip et al.* as authority for the proposition that both aspects would necessarily receive the same answer. It remains to be seen whether or not, given the important theoretical distinctions between the two aspects, some future court will hold that evidence admissible on the *voir dire* is not admissible on the general issue.

Ward itself establishes that, at least for the purposes of the general issue, 'the

[95] See the clear statements of Lord Pearce in *Toohey* [1965] AC 595, at 608–9, in a speech with which all their Lordships agreed.

[96] See Note for Guidance 1G to Code C, incorporating by reference the definition in s. 1(2) of the Mental Health Act 1983.

[97] See [1975] QB 834, at 841.

[98] *The Times*, 9 Dec. 1991.

[99] [1993] 1 WLR 619, at 690. This *dictum* was cited without disapproval in *Robinson* [1994] 3 All ER 346, at 351.

expert evidence of a psychiatrist or psychologist may properly be admitted if it is to the effect that a defendant is suffering from a condition not properly described as mental illness, but from a personality disorder so severe as properly to be categorised as mental disorder'.[100] In that case, consultant psychiatrists both for the prosecution and the defence had characterized the appellant as suffering from a mental disorder in the form of hysterical personality disorder, so they were clearly giving evidence that she was mentally disordered for Code C purposes. In addition, the court referred to the quality and force of the evidence, which did, it would seem, show the appellant's mental make-up to be beyond the range of the layman's experience. The earlier case of *Weightman*[101] was different in both these respects. The limit of the defence expert's evidence there was that the accused had an abnormal personality, described as a histrionic personality disorder. The Court of Appeal considered that the abnormality amounted to no more than that she was histrionic, theatrical, and likely to say things to draw attention to herself. These features did not place her beyond the ken of ordinary people. Furthermore, it is to be noted that no claim was made that her disorder was properly categorized as mental disorder. It must be admitted that much may turn on the willingness of the particular expert to attach the relevant label.

With regard to mental handicap, there appeared at one time to be an inclination in the courts to draw a firm line between evidence placing the accused in the mentally defective range and that placing him in the borderline subnormal range.[102] A test of this kind would probably be objectionable in any event, because based solely upon standard IQ test results, rather than upon the whole range of information which would properly have significance so far as the issue of mental handicap is concerned. But, in addition, by seeking to draw such a firm line in relation to what are inevitably matters of judgment and degree, it probably sought to tie the trial judge's hands unacceptably tightly.[103] *Raghip et al.*[104] reasserts the importance of the basic idea that what matters is whether or not the evidence is likely to assist the jury or, as the case may be, the judge, in its or his task. There, Raghip's IQ was 74, placing him firmly in the borderline subnormal range, yet he had a reading age considerably below that usually to be expected of somebody with such an IQ. In addition, the expert evidence indicated that he was abnormally suggestible. However, Raghip's manner in the witness box and his general appearance and demeanour were such as to make it impossible for the jury to divine any of this information. Therefore, the expert evidence revealing that information was admissible to assist the jury in its task.

In a later case in which the accused's performance on tests was very similar to that of Raghip but there was no indication of an unusual level of suggestibility,

[100] [1993] 1 WLR 619, at 690. [101] (1990) 92 Cr.App.R 291.

[102] See *Masih* [1986] Crim.LR 395, a case itself concerned with the accused's *mens rea*, rather than with confession evidence.

[103] For discussion, see Smith [1986] Crim.LR 395, at 396–7; Beaumont [1988] *Crim.LR* 290, at 293–4; Mackay and Colman [1991] Crim.LR 800, at 804.

[104] *The Times*, 9 Dec. 1991. And see Mirfield (1992) 108 *LQR* 528.

the Court of Appeal cast no doubt upon the decision of the trial judge to allow the relevant expert evidence to be adduced on the *voir dire*.[105] By contrast, it is clear from *Heaton*[106] that, where the accused's general IQ is in the dull normal range, even though the expert will say that the accused is very suggestible it will be extremely difficult to persuade a court that either the judge or the jury will find the expert's evidence helpful enough for it to be ruled admissible.

[105] See *Kenny* [1994] Crim.LR 284 (transcript through LEXIS).
[106] [1993] Crim.LR 593 (transcript through LEXIS).

11

The Relevance of the European Convention on Human Rights

Introduction

At various points in this text, it would have been relevant to refer to the possible significance of the various Articles of the European Convention on Human Rights for the interpretation of the English law of confessions, silence, and illegally obtained evidence. In general, the opportunity was not taken, for it was considered that the reader would find it more helpful to have gathered together in a specific chapter both points of general principle and particular points with regard to the actual and potential impact of the Convention upon the various domestic rules.

One must begin with a general proposition about the Convention, which, so far as the writer knows, has never been challenged in the English cases. The Convention, like all other international treaties which the United Kingdom has ratified but which have not been incorporated into law by Parliament, is not part of English law[1] or, for that matter, the law of any other part of the United Kingdom. This point was made specifically about the Convention itself by both Lord Denning MR and Geoffrey Lane LJ in *R.* v. *Chief Immigration Officer, Heathrow Airport, ex p. Bibi.*[2] It necessarily follows that clear and established domestic law, whether made by Parliament, the courts, or a combination of the two, cannot be struck down for incompatibility with the law relating to some Convention Article. However, as we shall shortly see, the law of the Convention, as interpreted by its institutions, may, in various ways, have significance when interpreting domestic law. Furthermore, in two important Convention cases concerned with UK prosecutions, *Murray* v. *United Kingdom*,[3] and *Saunders* v. *United Kingdom*,[4] both decided in the European Court of Human Rights, the view has been taken that the citizen's right to silence and privilege against self-incrimination 'lie at the heart'[5] of the notion of a fair procedure under Article 6 of the Convention. This very positive view of the value and importance of the right

[1] See, e.g., *J. H. Rayner (Mincing Lane) Ltd* v. *Department of Trade* [1990] 2 AC 418, at 500 (*per* Lord Oliver).

[2] [1976] 1 WLR 979, at 984 and 988, respectively.

[3] (1996) 22 EHRR 29.

[4] (1997) 23 EHRR 313.

[5] See *Murray* v. *UK* (1996) 22 EHRR 29, at 60 (para. 45).

and privilege contrasts starkly with the negative view implicit in recent Parliamentary incursions upon them, as set out in detail in Chapter 9.

The principal focus of this Chapter will be upon the significance of these developments for English law as it stands at present. However, it would be wrong to neglect to note where the law of the Convention departs substantially from English law, not least because it is possible that the potential for embarrassment brought about by English law being found wanting according to the lites of the Convention may persuade government to seek to have Parliament change it in order to render it more consonant with that of its sister jurisdiction. The Labour Government, which was elected in May 1997, has declared that it will take the much more radical step of making the Convention itself part of English domestic law, a step which would have very profound effects upon the subject-matter of the whole of this work. Nonetheless, it should not be supposed that this Chapter is intended to give an exhaustive coverage even of the Convention Articles most obviously relevant to that subject-matter.[6]

THE EFFECT IN ENGLISH LAW OF CONVENTION PROVISIONS

It is important to begin with some general propositions[7] before moving to the specific issues associated with the concerns of this work.

The first such proposition is that the Convention, like other international treaty obligations entered into by Her Majesty's Government, is available for use as an aid to the interpretation of any statute passed after it was signed. Speaking in general terms, Lord Diplock said in *Garland* v. *British Rail Engineering Ltd* that:[8]

> the words of a statute passed after the Treaty has been signed and dealing with the subject matter of the international obligation of the United Kingdom are to be construed, if they are reasonably capable of bearing such a meaning, as intended to carry out the obligation, and not to be inconsistent with it.

Speaking of the Convention itself, Lord Goff said in *Attorney-General* v. *Guardian Newspapers Ltd (No 2)*, 'I conceive it to be my duty, when I am free to do so, to interpret the law in accordance with the obligations of the Crown under this treaty'.[9] A difficulty inherent in these two statements is in determining *when* the judge is 'free to do so'. As we have already noted, it is clear that he is not free where the existing law is certain, and this applies no less to the common law than to statute. However, where the law is not certain, it is a commonplace observation that there may be different degrees of uncertainty about it. The argument in support of one interpretation may be very much stronger than that in support of

[6] The reader should refer to the general works about the Convention, e.g. Janis, Kay, and Bradley, *European Human Rights Law* (1995); Harris, O'Boyle, and Warbrick, *Law of the European Convention on Human Rights* (1995); Jacobs and White, *The European Convention on Human Rights* (2nd. edn., 1996).

[7] For a stimulating, though rather polemical, discussion of the *general* issues, see Murray Hunt, *Using Human Rights Law in English Courts* (1997).

[8] [1983] 2 AC 751, at 771. [9] [1990] 1 AC 109, at 283.

any other, yet without being conclusively so. In other cases, the arguments may seem to be very much in balance. Though judicial statements on the point are not all of a piece, there seems to be no statement unequivocally confining resort to the Convention to cases where the arguments are in balance. It seems likely that the following statement of Lord Bridge in *R.* v. *Home Secretary, ex p. Brind* is legally sound in this respect:[10]

> [I]t is already well settled that, in construing any provision in domestic legislation which is ambiguous in the sense that it is capable of a meaning which either conforms to or conflicts with the Convention the courts will presume that Parliament intended to legislate in conformity with the Convention, not in conflict with it.

Lord Bridge's statement does raise two other points which are more controversial. In the first place, it appears to suggest that the position under the Convention is to be taken into account *before* the court decides whether or not the legislation is, in the relevant sense, ambiguous. Though there is some judicial support for this view,[11] the weight of authority appears to favour the contrary view, i.e. that it is not appropriate to refer at all to the law of the Convention unless and until domestic law has been found to be ambiguous.[12] Secondly, and this point is almost certainly connected with the first one, is the judge under a duty to prefer the interpretation consistent with Convention law, or is that law merely something he is empowered to take into account in settling the ambiguity? Both Lord Goff in the *Guardian Newspapers (No 2)* case and Lord Bridge in *Brind* undoubtedly had judicial duty in mind. On the other hand, Lord Ackner, also in *Brind*, significantly stated that the Convention 'may be resorted to in order to help resolve some uncertainty or ambiguity in municipal law'.[13] Judicial opinion in other cases is no less divided.[14]

The second proposition, and one of particular importance for present purposes, concerns the potential relevance of Convention provisions to the exercise of discretion. Where the discretion in question is one to be exercised by some administrative authority, it seems to be settled that, though the decision-maker is empowered to take account of any pertinent Convention obligation, his failure to do so 'is not of itself a ground for impugning that exercise of discretion'.[15]

[10] [1991] 1 AC 696, at 747–8.

[11] See, e.g., the statement of Scarman LJ in *R.* v. *Home Secretary, ex p. Phansopkar* [1976] QB 606, at 626.

[12] See, e.g., *R.* v. *Chief Immigration Officer, Heathrow Airport, ex p. Bibi* [1976] 1 WLR 979, at 984 (*per* Lord Denning MR); *R.* v. *Home Secretary, ex p. Brind* [1991] 1 AC 696, at 760–1 (*per* Lord Ackner); *Derbyshire CC* v. *Times Newspapers Ltd* [1992] QB 770, at 812 (*per* Balcombe LJ), at 819 (*per* Ralph Gibson LJ), and at 830 (*per* Butler-Sloss LJ).

[13] [1991] 1 AC 696, at 761. See also *ibid.* 760.

[14] In favour of the duty view seem to be Scarman LJ in *R.* v. *Home Secretary, ex p. Phansopkar* [1976] QB 606, at 626; Ralph Gibson LJ and Butler-Sloss LJ in *Derbyshire CC* v. *Times Newspapers Ltd* [1992] QB 770, at 819 and 830, respectively. In favour of the power view seem to be Lord Denning MR in *R.* v. *Chief Immigration Officer, Heathrow Airport, ex p. Bibi* [1976] 1 WLR 979, at 984; Balcombe LJ in *Derbyshire CC* v. *Times Newspapers Ltd* [1992] QB 770, at 812.

[15] See *R.* v. *Ministry of Defence, ex p. Smith* [1996] QB 517, at 558 (*per* Sir Thomas Bingham MR). See, also, *per* Henry J, *ibid.* 564; R. v. *Home Secretary, ex p. Brind* [1991] 1 AC 696, at 748 (*per* Lord

However, where the discretion is one to be exercised by a judge, there are grounds at least for argument that the matter may be one of duty rather than power. In principle, the situation might seem to be analogous to that where the law is ambiguous, and there are certainly no considerations flowing from the separation of powers in support of a special degree of autonomy for the decision-maker. The authority on this point, outside the ambit of the particular concerns of this Chapter, is at best equivocal and, arguably, contradictory.[16]

The final proposition, though perhaps obvious, ought to be stated. Where provisions of the Convention are properly to be taken into account in a domestic case, the English court will have regard not simply to the bare words of that Convention but also to the relevant jurisprudence of its institutions, namely the Court and the Commission. The authorities are replete with reference to, and quotation from, decisions of those institutions. For express acknowledgement of the need for English courts to look to the Convention jurisprudence, we may rely upon the following words of Lord Taylor CJ in *Cowan et al.*, itself a case concerned with the 'right to silence' in court: '[w]e stress that decisions of the Commission and indeed those of the European Court of Human Rights itself are not binding upon this court. They are of assistance to resolve any ambiguity in our domestic law'.[17]

Compelled Self-Incrimination and Adverse Inferences from Silence

One may begin with the general point that, to the extent that there is uncertainty or ambiguity—whatever that means—in the law relating to compelled self-incrimination and to adverse inferences from silence, the effect of importing the law of the Convention will almost inevitably be to push the court towards an interpretation which favours the accused. This is because the case law of the Court and Commission, in particular the decisions in *Saunders* and *Murray*, does demonstrate a much stronger commitment to the right and privilege than does present-day English law. This is a point to be borne in mind whenever interpretation of statutory provisions is at issue. Attention here will focus upon the interpretation issues which seem to be both the most open to influence by the Convention and the most important in principle or in practice.

Bridge). Cf. the rather wide *dicta* of Sedley J in *R.* v. *Secretary of State for the Home Department, ex p. McQuillan* [1995] 4 All ER 400, at 422–3.

[16] See *Attorney-General* v. *Guardian Newspapers Ltd* [1987] 1 WLR 1248, at 1296 (*per* Lord Templeman) and at 1307 (*per* Lord Ackner); *In re W (A Minor) (Wardship: Restrictions on Publication)* [1992] 1 WLR 100, at 103 (*per* Neill LJ); *Derbyshire CC* v. *Times Newspapers Ltd* [1992] QB 770, at 812 (*per* Balcombe LJ); *Middlebrook Mushrooms Ltd* v. *TGWU* [1993] ICR 612, at 620 (*per* Neill LJ); and *Rantzen* v. *Mirror Group Newspapers Ltd* [1994] QB 670, at 690–2 (*per* Neill LJ). See also Murray Hunt, n. 7 above, 191–205.

[17] [1996] QB 373, at 382. Another example will be found in *Rantzen* v. *Mirror Group Newspapers Ltd* [1994] QB 670, at 687 (*per* Neill LJ).

Compelled Self-incrimination

The Decision in Saunders *v.* United Kingdom

Saunders had been Managing Director of Guinness Plc at a time when it made a successful takeover bid for Distillers Plc, having beaten off a bid from a third party in doing so. Inspectors were appointed under sections 432 and 442 of the Companies Act 1985 to inquire into allegations of certain irregularities, apparently fraudulent, in the way in which the takeover negotiations had been carried out. Saunders was one of the persons compulsorily questioned by the inspectors on pain of (eventual) punishment for contempt should he refuse to answer (under section 436(3) of the Act). He was questioned both before and after being charged with offences arising out of the takeover. At his trial, the judge allowed the prosecution to use the transcripts of what Saunders had said to the inspector as evidence against him, except that he excluded transcripts of the post-charge interviews. He was convicted, then sentenced to a term of imprisonment. He complained to the organs of the Convention that, because he had been deprived of his privilege against self-incrimination, the fairness of the proceedings against him had been seriously and adversely affected, such that Article 6(1) of the Convention had been breached. Though Article 6(1) provides expressly only that the accused is entitled to a fair hearing, the Court had previously held in *Funke* v. *France* that fairness, for these purposes, embraced the right of anyone charged with a criminal offence 'to remain silent and not to contribute to incriminating himself'.[18]

The Commission had concluded that the use against Saunders of the transcripts had been oppressive and had substantially impaired his ability to defend himself at trial, thereby depriving him of a fair hearing.[19] In doing so, it stressed the significance of the penalty—up to two years' imprisonment for failure to answer questions—and the fact that the incriminating material had furnished a not insignificant part of the evidence against him.

The Court confirmed the Commission's decision by sixteen votes to four, but in doing so it relied upon significantly narrower grounds than those of the Commission. First, it emphasized the point that it was the *use* made of the statements at trial which had rendered the hearing, i.e. that trial, unfair.[20] By contrast, the Commission's view was that Article 6(1) applied to 'the proceedings considered as a whole, including the way in which the prosecution obtained and used the evidence'.[21] To the common lawyer at least, the Court's view may carry more force, for the Article 6(1) right to a fair hearing is stated to apply only in the determination of a 'criminal charge', and, though it is clearly established that the notion of a person being charged with an offence has an 'autonomous meaning' in Convention jurisprudence which need not reflect domestic law,[22] it is difficult to

[18] (1993) 16 EHRR 297, at 326 (para. 44).
[19] See (1994) 18 EHRR CD 23.
[20] (1997) 23 EHRR 313, at 337 (para. 67).
[21] (1994) 18 EHRR CD 23, at 29 (para. 67).
[22] A point made by A. T. H. Smith in *Pressing Problems in the Law: Criminal Justice and Human Rights* (ed. Birks, 1995), 75 ff., at 82–3.

follow how, on any tenable view of the meaning of 'criminal charge', whether an autonomous view or not, Saunders could be regarded as so charged at the time when he appeared before the Inspectors.

Secondly, though nothing turned on this point on the actual facts of *Saunders*, the Court substantially limited the scope, in evidential terms, of Article 6(1). The Commission, consistently with the holding in the leading case of *Funke* v. *France*,[23] gave not a hint that the Article applied any less to documentary or real evidence acquired under compulsory powers than to things said by the accused in the course of the exercise of such powers. However, the Court, relying upon its understanding of the domestic law of the various states party to the Convention, stated that the right not to incriminate oneself:[24]

> does not extend to the use in criminal proceedings of material which may be obtained from the accused through the use of compulsory powers but which has an existence independent of the will of the suspect such as, *inter alia*, documents acquired pursuant to a warrant, breath, blood and urine samples and bodily tissue for the purpose of DNA testing.

The Court was, no doubt, fearful of declaring large parts of the pre-trial procedure of many contracting states to be unlawful in terms of the Convention, yet, as one of the dissenters, Judge Martens (joined by Judge Kuris), tellingly pointed out, the effect of the majority view is to overrule *Funke*.

Two other points may prove helpful to governments seeking to defend themselves before the institutions of the Convention in future cases. The Court said that 'the prosecution in a criminal case [must] seek to prove their case against the accused without resort to evidence obtained through methods of coercion or oppression in defiance of the will of the accused'.[25] Given the possible two-year prison sentence for failure to answer in *Saunders* itself, the strength of the words 'coercion', 'oppression', and 'defiance' was not significant in that case. However, it seems obvious that their strength might be of great importance if an applicant to the Commission or Court were to argue that the mere threat from the police that adverse inferences might be drawn from his silence had compelled him to confess and that, therefore, the failure of the domestic court to exclude that confession amounted to breach of Article 6(1). The English statutory law of confessions ought to turn out to be 'Convention-proof'. The Court also pointed out that it was not deciding 'whether the right not to incriminate oneself is absolute or whether infringements of it may be justified in particular circumstances'.[26]

The Impact of Saunders *v.* United Kingdom *upon English Law*

In terms of the present law to be found in the various statutory provisions allowing compulsory examination, the immediate impact of *Saunders* v. *United Kingdom* is bound to be slight, for, as was observed in Chapter 9, most modern

[23] (1993) 16 EHRR 297. In that case, the documents in question were bank statements relating to Funke's accounts.

[24] (1997) 23 EHRR 313, at 338 (para. 69).

[25] *Ibid.* 337 (para. 68).

[26] *Ibid.* 340 (para. 74).

statutes specifically state that answers given may be used in evidence against the person who gave them, and so leave no room for the Convention to resolve ambiguity or uncertainty. This was certainly true of section 434(5) of the Companies Act 1985, which was at issue in *Saunders* itself. Indeed, the Court of Appeal has now confirmed, on a reference of the case back to it by the Secretary of State, that Parliament's clear intention as demonstrated by the subsection must defeat Convention jurisprudence.[27] It follows that the European Court's own decision has significance at present only for those, now unusual, cases where the statute is silent on the matter, for it will be recalled that *Harz and Power* tells the court that the question then turns on 'a proper construction of the particular statute'.[28] It is possible that the jurisprudence of the Convention may properly be taken into account in such cases.

Statutes which grant a power to compel production of documents, ancillary to a power of compulsorily questioning, are unlikely to make specific reference to their admissibility against the person who provided them or anyone else incriminated by them. As we have seen, *Saunders* seems to indicate that, despite *Funke* v. *France*, documents of this kind are not embraced by the privilege. Still, it may be thought particularly unattractive for the law to rule that use of the accused's answers is unfair under Article 6(1), yet to find no unfairness in the use of ancillary documents. In any event, even if the institutions of the Convention should eventually decide that answers and ancillary documents *are* to be treated in the same way, there would be no impact upon domestic law, given the present legal status of the Convention, since the admissibility of such documents is firmly established under that law.

The statement in *Saunders* about non-confessional evidence would seem to be more straightforwardly applicable where evidence of that kind was obtained other than as an ancillary to compulsory questioning. It ought to follow that there is no potential for a clash between the law of the Convention and the English domestic laws which allow the non-consensual taking of blood, breath, urine, or other body samples and of fingerprints.

Adverse Inferences from Silence

The Decision in Murray *v.* United Kingdom

When the police arrived at a Belfast house on 7 January 1990, they found one L being detained therein. Murray was seen descending a flight of stairs and was arrested. The charges eventually brought against him included that of having, along with seven others, unlawfully imprisoned L. He was convicted of that offence by Hutton LCJ, sitting without a jury. L testified to the effect that Murray had been one of those involved in his imprisonment. He also testified to events just before the police had entered the house, saying that Murray had told him that the police were at the door and to go downstairs to watch television. As

27 [1996] 1 Cr.App.R 463.

28 [1967] 1 AC 760, at 816.

he spoke, Murray was pulling tape out of a cassette. The police, on searching the house, found a tangled tape, the salvageable portions of which revealed a confession by L to having agreed to act as a paid informer against the IRA. (The prosecution case was that the eight accused were IRA members bent on revenge against L.) The Northern Ireland Court of Appeal had found these various elements of direct and circumstantial evidence to constitute a formidable case against Murray, and the European Court of Human Rights was eventually to endorse that view.[29] However, in convicting Murray, the trial judge had also relied upon adverse inferences which he drew under Articles 4 and 6 of the Criminal Evidence (Northern Ireland) Order 1988. These Articles are, in all essential respects, similar to sections 35 and 37 of the Criminal Justice and Public Order Act 1994 (the 1994 Act). In other words, Hutton LCJ drew adverse inferences both from Murray's failure to account for his presence at the house and from his failure to testify. One element of Murray's case, before both the Commission and the Court, was that the drawing of those inferences had resulted in him being denied a fair hearing under Article 6(1) of the Convention and in a failure to accord him the presumption of innocence which is guaranteed by Article 6(2).

The Court held, by a majority of fourteen to five that neither Article 6(1) nor Article 6(2) had been violated in this respect.[30] Its reasons will be briefly stated.[31] It is to be noted that the Court seems to have accepted that those reasons were equally sufficient to defeat the claim that Article 6(2) had been breached as they were to defeat the claim of breach of Article 6(1).

The Court first acknowledged that 'there can be no doubt that the right to remain silent under police questioning and the privilege against self-incrimination are generally recognised international standards which lie at the heart of the notion of a fair procedure under Article 6'.[32] This did not entail an absolute right not to have adverse inferences drawn from one's silence, whether in the face of police questioning or in court, but only one to be protected from 'improper compulsion'. Various factors seem to have contributed to the Court's view that there had been no such compulsion in Murray's case. First, it was 'self-evident that it is incompatible with the immunities under consideration to base a conviction solely or mainly on the accused's silence or on a refusal to answer questions or give evidence himself'.[33] It followed that it was crucial that the weight of the other evidence against him was substantial. This made the drawing against him of adverse inferences a matter of straightforward common sense. Secondly, the provisions of the Order contained various safeguards for the suspect. These included the requirement that he be cautioned about the possibility of adverse inferences being drawn from his silence, the requirements (in effect) of the various Northern

[29] See (1996) 22 EHRR 29, at 63 (para. 54). The Murray in this case was not the same one as the appellant in *Murray* v. *DPP* [1994] 1 WLR 1.

[30] *Ibid.* 57 ff. By a majority of 12 to 7, it went on to hold that Art. 6(1) had been breached in that he had been denied access to a lawyer during the first 48 hours of his detention by the police.

[31] For detailed treatment of the case and its implications for English domestic law, see Munday [1996] Crim.LR 370, an article upon which considerable reliance is placed in what follows in the text.

[32] (1996) 22 EHRR 29, at 60 (para. 45). [33] *Ibid.* 60 (para. 47).

Irish provisions that there be material against him calling for an explanation, and the existence of a discretion in the judge as to whether or not to draw an inference. A third factor seems to have been that the trier of fact was an experienced judge who was required to explain the reason for his decision to draw inferences and for the weight he attached to them.

As regards its decision on the adverse inferences points, the Court was clearly concerned that Murray had been denied legal advice. Its reason for accepting that this did not involve improper compulsion seems to have been that Murray was no less able to maintain his silence before he took advice than after. He had, indeed, remained silent in all respects. Munday has suggested that there is a hint in this that the Court may eventually declare there to be 'an intimate link between the provision of legal advice and inferences from silence'.[34] If so, the Court would, no doubt, be more likely to find improper compulsion in the case of an unadvised person of less robust mental attitude than Murray.

Though there was no question, in *Murray*, of an adverse inference having been drawn from his failure to mention when questioned by the police a fact later relied upon at his trial (under Article 3 of the 1988 Order), it must follow from the case that precisely the same considerations would apply in that situation. Thus, sections 34 to 37 of the English Act of 1994 would all be subjected, in the Commission and the Court, to *Murray*-like analysis, now further informed by what the Court said in *Saunders*.

The Impact of Murray *upon English Law*

It will be plain from the general treatment, earlier in this work, of the adverse inference provisions of the 1994 Act[35] that there are a number of ambiguities in and uncertainties about those provisions. In accordance with the general English authority about the present relevance of Convention law to domestic law, there are a number of issues in relation to which *Murray* v. *United Kingdom* may be thought to have relevance. At each point, it will be necessary to bear in mind that that authority fails to tell us whether the judge is *empowered* or under an *obligation* to take the law of the Convention into account. The reader may find it helpful to refer back to the relevant pages in Chapter 9 when considering the points to be made here.

'Solely or Mainly'

Two obvious issues arise from the Court's proposition that a conviction should not be based solely or mainly upon adverse inferences from the various kinds of silence. First, it will be recalled that section 38(3) of the 1994 Act states that proceedings are not to be transferred to the Crown Court (which must be taken to mean that the accused must not be committed for trial at the Crown Court), that the accused is not to be regarded as having a case to answer, and that he is not to be convicted, solely on the basis of an inference drawn under section 34(2), 35(3),

[34] See n. 31 above, 379.

[35] See Ch. 9, sect. on the statutory law on pre-trial silence, above.

36(2), or 37(2). It was pointed out earlier that section 38(3) fails to make it clear whether or not the relevant hurdle[36] can be cleared on the basis of a *combination* of adverse inferences from silence, without there being any extraneous evidence.[37] Any court which took *Murray* v. *United Kingdom* into account must inevitably conclude that the hurdle could not be cleared in that way.

The second issue is not directly a matter for this work, for it concerns not pre-trial silence but silence at trial. However, when brief consideration was given earlier to trial silence,[38] we saw that there seemed to be a clash between *dicta* of Lord Slynn in *Murray* v. *DPP*[39] and of Lord Taylor CJ in *Byrne*.[40] The question dealt with by their Lordships is whether or not it is proper for the jury to draw, and for the judge to invite them to draw, adverse inferences from silence at trial where the case against the accused without that silence only just clears the *prima facie* case hurdle. *Byrne* seems to say that it is proper, but Lord Slynn referred to the need to respond to a 'clear *prima facie* case'. When it is recalled that the European Court of Human Rights placed particular emphasis, in *Murray* v. *United Kingdom*, upon the strength of the extraneous evidence, it would seem that that case pushes strongly in favour of Lord Slynn's view.

The Caution

The Court in *Murray* v. *United Kingdom* stressed not only the importance of the fact that the accused had repeatedly been cautioned but also of the fact that there was no indication that he had failed to understand the caution. As Munday has argued, there may well be an implication here that the Court would have been less inclined to find no improper compulsion in a case where there was evidence to suggest that the caution had been misunderstood.[41] He points out, and a similar argument has been put earlier in this work,[42] that the ordinary caution required by paragraph 10.4 of Code C to be given in order for a section 34 inference to be capable of being drawn is nothing if not confusing. Effect might properly be given to the message of *Murray* if judges were to tailor their directions about inferences under that section to reflect defence arguments in terms of confusion. This is a less tenable argument with respect to the much less equivocal special caution required by paragraph 10.5B of Code C to be given for the purposes of section 36 and 37 inferences.[43]

The Role of the Judge

The immediately preceding point about judicial directions leads us on to a more general issue in relation to the role of the judge. We have seen that the court regarded it as incompatible with Articles 6(1) and 6(2) to 'base a conviction

[36] Though *Murray* refers only to *conviction* solely or mainly on the basis of adverse inferences from silence, the breadth of the holding must be such that it would also encompass court decisions at earlier stages.

[37] See Ch. 9, text to n. 189 above.

[38] See Ch. 9, text to nn. 97–108 above.

[39] [1994] 1 WLR 1, at 11.

[40] 21 Nov. 1995 (transcript through LEXIS).

[41] See n. 31 above, 379–80.

[42] See Ch. 9, text to nn. 112–13 above.

[43] See Ch. 9, text to nn. 174–5 above.

solely or mainly on the accused's silence'.[44] Now it is plain, given the inscrutability of the English jury verdict (or, indeed, that of magistrates), that one simply will not be in a position to say that a conviction was not so based. It can hardly be the case that all use of adverse inferences from silence is forbidden by the Convention in English criminal cases, so it must be assumed that *Murray* suggests, by analogy, that the directions given by the judge to the jury, or the magistrates' 'self-directions', are of very great importance. The point is given particular force by the way in which the court stressed that the judge in a non-jury trial must explain his decision to draw inferences and the weight to be attached thereto.

It will be recalled that the early English cases concerned with adverse inferences from silence under sections 34 and 35 of the 1994 Act all emphasize the importance of the high degree of autonomy which the jury enjoys in drawing ordinary, common-sense inferences.[45] Thus, in *Cowan et al.*, a case concerned with silence at trial, Lord Taylor CJ said:[46]

> We wish to stress . . . that this court will not lightly interfere with a judge's exercise of discretion to direct or advise the jury as to the drawing of inferences from silence and as to the nature, extent and degree of such inferences. He is in the best position to have the feel of the case and so long as he gives the jury adequate directions of law . . . and leaves the decision to them, this court will be slow to substitute its view for his.

In *Argent*, a case concerned with silence in the police station under section 34, the message was very much the same. Speaking about the issue of whether or not the accused could reasonably have been expected to mention to the police the fact now relied upon in his defence, Lord Bingham CJ said:[47]

> This is an issue on which the judge may, and usually should, give appropriate directions. But he should ordinarily leave the issue to the jury to decide. Only rarely would it be right for the judge to direct the jury that they should, or should not, draw the appropriate inference.

There may be a way in which the judge's hands turn out to be tied a little more firmly than these statements of the present Lord Chief Justice and his immediate predecessor would suggest. Presumably, the general principle that, in exercising a discretion, the judge may have regard to the relevant provisions of the Convention ought to apply to his discretion as to how to direct the jury on possible adverse inferences, especially now that the recent case of *Khan*[48] has, as we shall shortly see,[49] confirmed the significance of Convention provisions for the exercise of the judicial discretion to exclude evidence under section 78(1) of the 1984 Act. It must be said that the statement of Lord Taylor CJ in *Cowan et al.* to which reference has just been made immediately followed the expression of his own

[44] (1996) 22 EHRR 29, at 60 (para. 47). [45] See Ch. 9, text to nn. 107–8 and n. 166 above.
[46] [1996] QB 373, at 382. [47] [1997] 2 Cr.App.R. 27, at 33.
[48] [1996] 3 WLR 162. [49] See text to nn. 59–66 below.

opinion that certain observations (which he quoted) from the Commission's decision in *Murray* v. *United Kingdom* were, because there was no ambiguity in section 35 requiring to be resolved, of no assistance. However, his Lordship does not seem to have had in mind the possibility that Convention jurisprudence might be of assistance to the trial judge in directing the jury about adverse inference. Of course, it would be one thing for English law to recognize that a trial judge may properly take that jurisprudence into account, but quite another for it to require him to do so. In any event, application of the general principle would provide defence counsel with a useful wedge to interpose the more friendly régime of the Convention.

Legal Advice

A particular application of the point just made may well be to the situation where the accused was not legally advised. So even where no 1984 Act or Code C provision about legal advice has been breached, the defence may be able to argue persuasively that the fact that the accused did not have it makes the proper direction one telling the jury not to draw any adverse inference.[50] This fits in well with the point, made more than once in this work,[51] that the changes made by sections 34, 36, and 37 of the 1994 Act make the provision of legal advice to suspects *more, not less*, important.

What of cases where the accused did take legal advice and the lawyer advised silence? We have already observed that the Court of Appeal has, in *Condron and Condron*[52] and *Argent*,[53] rejected the proposition that there is a *per se* rule against adverse inference in such cases. This the Court did without reference to *Murray* v. *United Kingdom*, a decision which was, apparently, not cited to it. Though it might be thought that this issue *was* one of uncertainty, in relation to which Convention jurisprudence might properly be prayed in aid, the rather ironic effect of the two English cases would seem to be that there is no longer an argument from uncertainty—unless the House of Lords is prepared to take a fresh look at the issue. In any event, it may be that reliance could be placed on *Murray* in support of the less radical argument that the trial judge should, in directing the jury, place especial emphasis on the significance of the legal advice given to the accused, for the purposes of their decision whether or not to draw an adverse inference.

Evidential Use of Silence

The court, in *Murray* v. *United Kingdom*, seems to have misinterpreted what Lords Mustill and Slynn said in *Murray* v. *DPP*[54] about the nature of the proper evidential use to be made of silence at trial. Though it rightly observed that

[50] It is to be remembered that Murray's application was allowed on the basis that he had been denied legal advice.

[51] Though see, in particular, Ch. 7, text to nn. 147–51 and Ch. 9, text to n. 197, above.

[52] [1997] 1 Cr.App.R 185. [53] *The Times*, 19 Dec. 1996. [54] [1994] 1 WLR 1.

'silence, in itself, cannot be regarded as an indication of guilt'[55] under the new English rules, it failed to notice that it is the silence *in itself* which cannot be so regarded. The point made in *Murray* v. *DPP* was that an inference of guilt may be drawn from silence, but only where the extraneous evidence calls for an explanation which the accused ought to be in a position to give.[56] The following statement of the court is, in consequence, accurate only if it seeks to describe the law under Article 6(1), rather than under section 35 of the 1994 Act: 'the Court deems it . . . obvious that these immunities cannot and should not prevent that the accused's silence, in situations which clearly call for an explanation from him, be taken into account *in assessing the persuasiveness of the evidence adduced by the prosecution*'.[57] This clearly envisages force being given to silence only as strengthening the prosecution's own evidence, and not as having force in its own right.

Let us assume that it does describe what the Convention permits. If so, one may then mount an argument that any ambiguity or uncertainty in sections 34, 36 and 37 as to whether or not the relevant silence may properly be used for its extensive force as positive evidence of guilt should be resolved against the extensive force view. However, if the argument relied upon earlier is correct, and the extensive force view is implicitly adopted by all three sections,[58] there is no ambiguity or uncertainty and, in consequence, no room for interpreting English law to be consistent with the law of the Convention.

Relevance to the Exercise of the Section 78(1) Discretion

The Decision in *Khan*

The facts of *Khan* have been set out elsewhere in this work,[59] and do not require repetition here. At trial, the judge had accepted that the aural surveillance of a conversation between Khan and three others, in which he had admitted his involvement in the illegal importation of heroin was, at least arguably, in breach of Khan's right of privacy under Article 8 of the Convention. But he had gone on to conclude that neither this nor any other circumstance of the case required exclusion of that admission, at Khan's trial for the importation, under section 78(1) of the Police and Criminal Evidence Act 1984. By the time the case reached the House of Lords, counsel for the appellant sought to have the judge's exercise of discretion overturned almost exclusively because of the alleged breach of Article 8.

In the Court of Appeal, Lord Taylor CJ had seemed to indicate that Article 8 was wholly irrelevant because there was no ambiguity or doubt about the state of

[55] (1996) 22 EHRR 29, at 61 (para. 48).

[56] See, in particular, the speech of Lord Slynn [1994] 1 WLR 1, at 11.

[57] (1996) 22 EHRR 29, at 60 (para. 47) (emphasis added).

[58] See Ch. 9, text to nn. 148–64 above.

[59] See Ch. 7, text between nn. 302 and 303 above.

domestic law.[60] The House of Lords was prepared to take a different tack, holding that the fact of apparent breach of a provision of the Convention was something which might be relevant to the judge's exercise of his section 78(1) discretion or power. As Lord Nolan put it:[61]

> [I]f the behaviour of the police in the particular case amounts to an apparent or probable breach of some relevant law or convention, common sense dictates that this is a consideration which may be taken into account for what it is worth. Its significance, however, will normally be determined not so much by its apparent unlawfulness or irregularity as upon its effect, taken as a whole, upon the fairness or unfairness of the proceedings.

There had been nothing wrong in the particular case with the trial judge's view that, even if there had been a breach of Article 8, it was not such as to require exclusion of the evidence.

It may prove to be a matter of considerable importance whether the judge falls under a duty to take into account apparent breaches of the Convention or is merely empowered to do so. The written submissions of the National Council for Civil Liberties to the House had, it seems, put the matter in terms of duty, and Lord Nolan remarked that the trial judge had 'substantially followed' that body's view of the law.[62] Furthermore, there are *dicta* in an earlier case at a lower level which was directly concerned with the section 78(1) discretion appearing to support the duty position.[63] Yet Lord Nolan himself—and all other members of the House agreed with him on the present point—puts the matter, on more than one occasion, very much in terms of what the trial judge *may*, rather than *must*, do. If it were to be a matter of duty, of course, a failure to take such an apparent breach of the Convention into account would amount to failure to take into account a relevant consideration, and thus an abuse of discretion. In the longer term, even if the Convention is not enacted into domestic law, it would be rather surprising if appeal courts were to leave the judge free to take no account whatsoever of an apparent breach of an international obligation.

Convention Breach and the Section 78(1) Discretion

In *Khan* itself, there had been breaches of the English civil law and, possibly, the criminal, as well as the apparent breach of Article 8. So the Convention provided support for an argument capable of being mounted in terms solely of domestic law. Indeed, Lord Nolan said generally of the Convention provisions that 'they embody so many of the familiar principles of our own law and our concept of justice'.[64] However, though not a point referred to either in the House of Lords or the Court of Appeal, it was not Khan's house against which the trespass had been committed or to which any criminal damage was done. There would seem to have been a strong argument that the only unlawfulness about which Khan

[60] [1995] QB 27, at 40. [61] [1996] 3 WLR 162, at 175. [62] *Ibid.* 173.
[63] R. v. *Governor of Pentonville Prison, ex p. Chinoy* [1992] 1 All ER 317, at 331–2.
[64] [1996] 3 WLR 162, at 174.

had standing to complain was the Convention breach, since this at least was of *his* right of privacy.

It could certainly not be said that in *Khan* the law of the Convention was clearly at odds with English law, for the House expressly refused to deal with the question whether or not English law itself recognizes a right of privacy in some form or other. But if we recall the enhanced protection given by Article 6 to the right to silence and privilege against self-incrimination, it quickly becomes apparent that the two systems of law could very easily be in opposition. Indeed, when the *Saunders* case itself was considered again by the Court of Appeal after the Commission had delivered its judgment, that court reiterated that there had been nothing at all wrong with the trial judge's original decision to allow evidence to be given of the contents of the relevant transcripts.[65] It is a necessary element of the Court of Appeal's position that there is no room here for the Convention to have an 'entrance point' into domestic law.[66] A decision to exclude admissible evidence here simply on the basis that Article 6 had been breached would be to prefer the law of the Convention to the law laid down by Parliament, and would thus be wholly unsound constitutionally, given the present status of the Convention in English law. The plain fact is that the governing policy behind provisions like section 434(5) of the Companies Act 1985 is fundamentally at odds with the principle which, the institutions of the Convention tell us, lies at the heart of Article 6(1).

We may conclude that, at present, the scope for the defence to appeal to section 78(1) as support for the rights of the citizen under the Convention is rather limited. Where the two systems march hand in hand, the Convention breach may add little to the breach of domestic law. Where they are in opposition, sound constitutional theory inevitably demands preference for English domestic law. Thus, while it may prove a source of serious embarrassment to the executive arm of government that our law accords so much less weight to the right to silence and the privilege against self incrimination than does a jurisprudence which has more obvious roots in civilian systems than in the common law, the judicial arm ought to be able to see where its duty lies.

The European Union Dimension

The conclusion offered in the preceding section was deliberately qualified by the words 'at present'—and not solely because the status of the Convention may soon be changed. There is a further European card which the defence may, in due course, be able to play.

It is now well-established that the law of the European Union recognizes that there exist certain fundamental human rights and, in doing so, has particular

[65] See *Saunders et al.* [1996] 1 Cr.App.R 463, particularly at 477–8.

[66] The phrase is A. T. H. Smith's—see n. 22 above, 84.

regard to the jurisprudence of the European Convention on Human Rights.[67] In the more specific context of the right to silence or privilege against self-incrimination, the Court of Justice in *Orkem* v. *Commission*[68] considered the impact of Article 6(1) of the Convention upon the law of the Union. At that time, before the decision in *Funke* v. *France*, it understandably concluded that that Article did not itself grant the citizen that right or privilege. Nonetheless, the Court went on to hold that the European Commission was bound not to infringe the right or privilege on the particular facts of that case. In the later case of *Otto BV* v. *Postbank*,[69] the Court refused to allow the *Orkem* principle to be invoked at the national level.

It seems entirely possible that *Funke* and the cases concerned with Article 6(1) subsequent to it, in particular *Murray* and *Saunders*, will persuade the Court of Justice, in an appropriate case, to recognize that the right or privilege *is* now a part of the fundamental human rights law of the European Union. It may be thought that that would, in itself, add force to a defence argument that, in interpreting the relevant element of the domestic law relating to confessions, or to the drawing of adverse inferences from silence, or to illegally or unfairly obtained evidence (if, despite *Saunders*, such evidence is within the ambit of the Article 6(1) protection), an English court should have particular regard to the relevant Convention jurisprudence.

However, once one takes account of the European Union dimension, it becomes clear that more radical possibilities must be contemplated. In his maiden speech in the House of Lords, Lord Bingham CJ, having pointed out the way in which Convention jurisprudence may become part of the law of the Union, went on to say, '[t]hat of course is a law which the courts in this country must apply since we are bound by Act of Parliament to do so, and that is a means by which, indirectly, convention rights find their way into domestic law.'[70] The Act in question is, as will be appreciated, the European Communities Act 1972. Though there may very well be difficult issues about whether or not a given item of Convention/Community law does actually bind English courts—issues well beyond the scope of this book—to be hammered out, the potential for the defence to argue that some provision of domestic law must be disapplied by the court as being inconsistent with Article 6(1) of the Convention will clearly be present, whatever may be the fate of government proposals to make the Convention directly applicable in English law, if and when *Funke* and its progeny are made part of the law of the Union.

[67] The leading cases in the European Court of Justice include (4/73) *Nold* v. *Commission* [1974] ECR 491; (36/75) *Rutili* v. *Minister for the Interior* [1975] ECR 1219; (64–61/84) *Cinéthèque* v. *Fédération Nationale des Cinémas Français* [1985] ECR 2605; (12/86) *Demirel* v. *Stadt Schwäbisch Gmünd* [1987] ECR 3719; (260/89) *Ellinki Radiophonia Tileorassi AE* v. *Dimotiki Etairia Pliroforissis and Sotirios Kouvelas* [1991] ECR I–2925.

[68] (374/87) [1989] ECR 3283. [69] (C–60/92) [1993] ECR I–5683.

[70] HL Debs., vol. 573, col. 1467 (3 July 1996). See also Grief [1991] *PL* 555; Murray Hunt, n. 7 above, ch. 7.

12

Alternative Approaches

Introduction

The Police and Criminal Evidence Act 1984 ('the 1984 Act') and the Criminal Justice and Public Order Act 1994 ('the 1994 Act') have changed radically the English law relating to the evidential effects of pre-trial investigation of offences by the police and analogous agencies. It is now time to cast our attention beyond existing domestic law.

In the United States, during the first part of the 1960s, through the two leading Supreme Court cases of *Mapp* v. *Ohio*[1] and *Miranda* v. *Arizona*,[2] a federal constitutional dimension to the treatment of evidence obtained by unlawful search or seizure and of confession evidence was authoritatively announced. In the years following those decisions, a differently constituted Supreme Court has diluted very substantially their strong spirit in a number of ways. During the last half-century, the Scottish courts have wavered between a strict view of the inadmissibility of confessions, based on the idea that the suspect is not to be cross-examined about his guilt, and a flexible one, stressing that it is only if there was unfairness in the obtaining of the confession that it ought to be excluded. In Australia and Canada, the courts have developed a jurisprudence for exclusion of both confession and non-confession evidence which is based upon the idea that the administration of justice must not be brought into disrepute. While in Canada the thrust for that development has been a constitutional one, arising from the enactment of the Charter of Rights and Freedoms, in Australia it has been entirely a creature of the common law.

In England itself, it has been suggested that confession evidence ought to be corroborated or, in some other way, supported by other evidence before reliance can properly be placed upon it. Alternatively, judges ought to be required to warn juries of the dangers of unreliability which sometimes attend confessions and advised of how best to deal with those dangers.

Exclusionary Rules In the United States

In *Mapp* v. *Ohio*,[3] the US Supreme Court held that an automatic exclusionary rule applied to evidence acquired in breach of the Fourth Amendment right of the

[1] 367 US 643 (1961). [2] 384 US 436 (1966). [3] 367 US 643 (1961).

citizen not to be subjected to an unlawful search or seizure. This rule had fomerly been a part only of the jurisprudence of the federal jurisdiction,[4] but was now applied, through the due process clause of the Fourteenth Amendment, to the states.[5] Just two years later, in *Miranda* v. *Arizona*,[6] the same court announced that, henceforward, in both federal and state cases, investigating officers were required to inform the suspect of certain rights which he enjoyed and then scrupulously to respect those rights. The various rights in question followed from the privilege against compelled self-incrimination contained in the Fifth Amendment, which privilege is also enjoyed in state cases by virtue of the Fourteenth Amendment.[7] A third topic, in relation to US law, which will be considered is the doctrine known as 'the fruit of the poisonous tree'.

The *Mapp* Rule

As formulated in *Mapp*, the exclusionary rule is both simple and straightforward. However venial, however lacking in bad faith may be the breach by the investigating authority, typically the police, of the Fourth Amendment rights of the citizen, evidence thereby acquired will be excluded at any later trial of that person for a criminal offence. It is the *fact* that his rights have been breached which results in *automatic* exclusion.

The Governing Principle(s)?

In *Mapp* itself, there was a failure clearly to identify the principle or principles lying behind the exclusionary rule which was announced. So Justice Clark, delivering the opinion of the court, sometimes used the language of the disciplinary principle, sometimes that of the protective principle, and sometimes that of the court-centred variant of the judicial integrity principle.[8] He pointed out that, in the previous year, the court had itself recognized that the purpose of the exclusionary rule was to deter constitutional violations by removing the incentive to commit them.[9] Only four pages later in that opinion, he stated that, having once found that the right to privacy had the Fourth Amendment as its source 'we can no longer permit that right to remain an empty promise',[10] but that, rather, it must be enforceable in the same manner as other constitutional rights. Yet in the same paragraph, completing the opinion, he remarked that the decision in *Mapp* gave to the courts 'that judicial integrity so necessary in the true administration of justice'.[11]

[4] See *Weeks* v. *US*, 232 US 283 (1914).

[5] *Wolf* v. *Colorado*, 338 US 25 (1949) was thus overruled.

[6] 384 US 436 (1966).

[7] There is a continuing dispute in the Supreme Court whether or not the *Miranda* rights are dictated by the Fifth Amendment itself. According to a majority of the modern-day Court, *Miranda* announced only a prophylactic rule designed to support the suspect's Fifth Amendment rights. This dispute is best exemplified in *Duckworth* v. *Eagan*, 492 US 195 (1989).

[8] For discussion of the various principles, see Ch. 2 above.

[9] See 367 US 643, at 656, relying on *Elkins* v. *US*, 364 US 206 (1960).

[10] *Ibid.* 660.

[11] *Ibid.*

However, it would now be difficult to argue that the governing principle is anything other than the disciplinary principle, or, as it is often known in the US cases, the deterrent rationale. Even in the face of spirited dissent from justices who favour the protective principle,[12] the clear majority of modern-day justices favours the view that it is deterrence of constitutional impropriety which lies at the heart of the rule. Nowhere is this more apparent than in the opinion of the Court, delivered by Justice White, in *US* v. *Leon*,[13] endorsing the following words of Justice Powell in *US* v. *Calandra*: '[i]n sum, the rule is a judicially created remedy designed to safeguard Fourth Amendment rights generally through its deterrent effect, rather than a personal constitutional right of the party aggrieved.'[14] For these justices, no question arises of exclusion being directly commanded by the Constitution in order to remedy a wrong. As far as the 'imperative of judicial integrity' is concerned, these justices assign it only a limited role. It is subordinate to, or even subsumed by, the deterrence rationale.[15]

Absence of Balancing—and its Attendant Problems

Had the Supreme Court embraced the protective principle in the present context, the logic of excluding evidence in all cases of breach of the Fourth Amendment rights of the individual would have been clear enough. But, once that Court settled upon deterrence as properly lying behind exclusion, the case for unreflective exclusion could not be made out. If we imagine a police officer, conscious of the requirement that he get a warrant to search premises yet fearful that evidence of a murder might be spirited away should he go through the process of getting one, we may well sympathize with his decision to enter without a warrant. Should he find the dead body or a murder weapon, and a court later conclude that he entered unlawfully, *Mapp* would require suppression of the evidence, even though the deterrence rationale might fail to support that result. We may suppose that future officers in similar circumstances would not actually be deterred from unlawful entry by the prospect of possible suppression of the evidence obtained. More radically, we may argue that it is not desirable to deter minor breaches of rights in such serious cases. If so, there must be an inevitable tension between the exclusionary rule and its rationale.

Reflections of this, or a similar, kind have led a number of American commentators to propose attenuation of *Mapp*. Two proposals will be referred to briefly here.[16] One is that *Mapp* should not apply in the case of the most serious crimes, such as treason, espionage, murder, armed robbery, or organized kidnapping, at least where the breach was not of a particularly shocking kind.[17] Another is that

[12] See, e.g., Brennan, Douglas, and Marshall JJ, dissenting, in *US* v. *Calandra*, 414 US 338, at 355 ff. (1974); Brennan and Marshall JJ, dissenting, in *US* v. *Peltier*, 422 US 531, at 552 ff. (1975); Brennan and Marshall JJ, dissenting, in *US* v. *Leon*, 468 US 897, at 936 and at 939–40 (1984).

[13] 468 US 897 (1984). [14] 414 US 338, at 349 (1974).

[15] See, e.g., *US* v. *Peltier*, 422 US 531, at 536–9 (1975); *US* v. *Janis*, 428 US 433, at 459 (1976); *Stone* v. *Powell*, 428 US 465, at 485–6 (1976); *Illinois* v. *Gates*, 462 US 213, at 259 (1983).

[16] Both are referred to in Ch. 2, text to nn. 106–8 above.

[17] See Kaplan (1974) 26 *Stan. LRev.* 1027, at 1046.

an assessment should be made of 'comparative reprehensibility'. In Justice Cameron's words in *State* v. *Bolt*, '[t]he internal logic of this test is simple—where the criminal conduct involved is more dangerous to society than the police misconduct, it does not make sense to sacrifice the criminal prosecution in order to deter the police'.[18] Of course, any such test would purchase flexibility at a considerable cost in terms of uncertainty.

It must be said that, for those who consider the costs of *Mapp* to be too great to bear but feel unable to enter the world of balancing, there will be an obvious temptation, where the stakes are high enough, to mould the substantive law of search and seizure in a way which makes it less likely to strike down police behaviour as in breach of the Fourth Amendment. This is not a place for discussion of that Amendment itself, but three cases in which it may be thought that a majority of the Supreme Court was a prey to that temptation are *New York* v. *Belton*,[19] *Illinois* v. *Gates*,[20] and *Alabama* v. *White*.[21]

Limiting the Impact of Mapp*—the Good Faith Exception*

The Supreme Court has shown no inclination to take *Mapp* beyond its obvious field of application, namely to evidence obtained by breach of the accused's constitutional rights under the Fourth Amendment which the prosecution seeks to adduce at that accused's criminal trial for an offence to which that evidence relates.[22] However, even within that field of application, it is now established that there is an exception to *Mapp* based upon the objective good faith of the officer who breached those rights. At present, that exception has been applied in only a limited class of situation, and, more specifically, has not been applied in the case of *warrantless* search or seizure by the police. It was developed in two cases argued and decided together in 1984. In one, *US* v. *Leon*,[23] it was held that suppression of evidence was not required even though the warrant which enabled the police to obtain it was itself invalid because not supported by probable cause. In the other, *Massachusetts* v. *Sheppard*,[24] a similar conclusion was reached in a case where, though there was probable cause for the issue of the warrant, it was facially defective and, consequently, invalid as issued. Thus, the exception applies to both substantive and procedural error and, as the names of the two cases suggest, applies in state no less than in federal cases.

The reasoning of the majorities in *Leon* and *Sheppard* had as its focus the deterrence rationale. Both cases involved error by the neutral magistrate. Since the police had acted in reasonable, good faith reliance upon the warrant issued by him, there was no deterrent reason for suppression in order to discourage the police from doing the same thing in future cases. So far as neutral magistrates and other judicial officers were concerned, there was no rational call for deterrence in their case. There was said to be no reason to suppose that exclusion in such cases

[18] 689 P 2d. 519, at 529 (1984). [19] 453 US 454 (1981). [20] 462 US 213 (1983).
[21] 496 US 325 (1990).
[22] See, e.g., *US* v. *Calandra*, 414 US 338 (1974); *Stone* v. *Powell*, 428 US 465 (1976).
[23] 468 US 897 (1984). [24] 468 US 981 (1984).

would have a deterrent effect upon the judicial officers themselves, for they are 'not adjuncts to the law enforcement team' and have 'no stake in the outcome of particular criminal prosecutions'.[25] Furthermore, there was no evidence to suggest an inclination in them to ignore or subvert the Fourth Amendment. It followed that attention must be concentrated solely on the likely effects of exclusion in such cases on the behaviour of police officers. The arguments that the prospect of exclusion would deter inadequate affidavits and 'magistrate shopping', as well as encouraging closer scrutiny of the form of warrants, were described as 'speculative'.

The Supreme Court referred to four situations in which exclusion *would* be appropriate, these being: (i) where the officer knew of, or was wilfully blind to, the falsity of information in his affidavit; (ii) where the magistrate had wholly abandoned his judicial role such that no reasonably well trained officer should rely on the warrant; (iii) where the affidavit was so lacking in the indicia of probable cause that official belief in its existence would be entirely unreasonable; and (iv) where the warrant was so deficient on its face that the executing officers could not reasonably assume it to be valid. It will be noted that it is the objective element which is very much to the fore in each of these exceptions except the first. Indeed, in *Leon* and *Sheppard*, the Supreme Court repeatedly stressed that the test of good faith was an objective one. This gives rise to two queries. First, are they merely examples, such that exclusion will be the appropriate course *whenever* the particular officer placed reliance on a warrant where no reasonable, well-trained officer would have done so?[26] Secondly, except in the first situation, is the actual state of mind of the officer always irrelevant?[27] One can certainly imagine a situation where the particular affidavit in support of a search warrant was not lacking in the indicia of probable cause, yet where the officer who drew it up had no genuine belief that he would find, at the premises in question, the articles described therein. He would not, then, act in subjective good faith. To refuse to apply the 'good faith' exception in such a case would be to offer a clear deterrent lesson to like-minded officers, though it must be admitted that courts might shy away from enquiries about the state of the officer's mind.[28]

The good faith exception has been taken beyond the case of the invalid warrant in two later Supreme Court decisions. In *Illinois* v. *Krull*,[29] a warrantless search of premises pursuant to a statutory power turned out to be unlawful because the statute itself was later declared to be unconstitutional. The court

[25] See 468 US 897, at 918 (1984).

[26] See, e.g., Goldstein, 62 *NYULRev*. 1173, at 1204–5 (1987).

[27] La Fave argues that this is the case—see *Search and Seizure* (3rd edn., 1996), i, 67–8.

[28] An analogy might be drawn with *Horton* v. *California*, 496 US 128 (1990), in which case the Supreme Court rejected the 'inadvertent discovery' element of the 'plain view' doctrine as announced by a plurality of the same Court in *Coolidge* v. *New Hampshire*, 403 US 443 (1971), giving as one of its reasons that 'even handed law enforcement is best achieved by the application of objective standards of conduct, rather than standards that depend upon the subjective state of mind of the officer'—see 496 US 128, at 139.

[29] 480 US 340 (1987).

applied reasoning essentially similar to that in *Leon* and *Sheppard* in deciding that the evidence thereby obtained need not be suppressed; legislators were not proper objects of deterrence. In *Arizona* v. *Evans*,[30] the arresting officer had acted in reliance on a computerized record which indicated the existence of an outstanding arrest warrant. The record was incorrect, yet the court held that evidence obtained from the accused during the course of the arrest should not be excluded. Once again, the *Leon/Sheppard* reasoning was employed, this time in respect of the absence of good reason to seek to deter clerical personnel from error.

It is conceivable that the good faith exception will eventually be extended to the ordinary case of warrantless search or seizure. This would be to apply it to a situation significantly different from any of those to which it has so far been applied. Here, there would be no third party who, it might be said, was not a proper object of deterrence, and so no insulation of the police officer from the error. In the ordinary case where the officer proceeds without a warrant, it is necessarily he who acts upon his own assessment of the situation. Furthermore, the application of the good faith exception to a case where the reason for unlawfulness was that the officer lacked probable cause would be particularly problematical. How can his grounds for action be objectively supportable when they fail to meet the relevant objective standard, that of probable cause? However, there might be other circumstances in which the clash between the Fourth Amendment itself and the proposed exception would be much less pointed. One example will suffice. Where the prosecution relies upon the consent of a person who has been searched as justification for that search, it is clear that the test for consent is based on the reasonable person's supposed belief in his ability to refuse to co-operate.[31] There would seem to be no reason, in principle, why the argument should not succeed that a reasonable, well-trained officer would have believed the person in question to be consenting, even though a reasonable person at the other end of the transaction would have thought himself not free to refuse co-operation. It remains to be seen whether or not the Supreme Court will be prepared to take this further step towards a more flexible approach to exclusion.[32]

THE *MIRANDA* RULE

Confessions at Common Law

The mature US common law exclusionary rule for confessions, applicable to the states by virtue of the due process requirement of the Fourteenth Amendment,[33]

[30] 514 US 1 (1995).

[31] See, e.g. *US* v. *Mendenhall*, 446 US 554 (1980); *Florida* v. *Royer*, 460 US 491 (1983); *Florida* v. *Bostick*, 501 US 429 (1991). Cf. *Ohio* v. *Robinette*, 117 SCt. 417 (1996).

[32] Even before *Leon* and *Sheppard* were decided, a bare majority of the Fifth Circuit Court of Appeals sitting *en banc* stated that it was prepared to apply a good faith exception whenever law enforcement officers believed reasonably and in good faith that their actions were proper—see *US* v. *Williams*, 622 F2d. 830 (1980).

[33] See *Brown* v. *Mississippi*, 297 US 278 (1936).

had many similarities with its English counterpart. Thus it ruled out confessions obtained by threats or promises.[34] However, unlike the English rule, its application was not confined to cases where threats had been made or inducements held out. The courts had to look at 'the totality of the relevant circumstances'[35] in order to decide whether or not the basic requirement for admissibility, that of voluntariness, was satisfied. That made it a much more open-textured rule than the English one, with both the advantages and disadvantages which that entails. Certainly, on one view of the Supreme Court's decision in *Blackburn* v. *Alabama*,[36] there might be involuntariness even in the absence of any police overreaching or misconduct, or indeed without there having been any official action at all in relation to the accused. In that case, the accused had been insane when he confessed. In another Supreme Court case, *Townsend* v. *Sain*,[37] a similar view was apparently taken of a drug-induced confession. In fact, in its post-*Miranda* decision, *Colorado* v. *Connelly*,[38] the Supreme Court held that neither *Blackburn* nor *Townsend* supported such a wide view of involuntariness. Rather, in order for the due process clause of the Fourteenth Amendment to come into play, there had to have been some kind of 'coercive police activity'. Therefore, where the accused had confessed spontaneously, though in a psychotic state, the exclusionary rule was inapplicable.[39]

The Decision in Miranda *Itself*

The watershed decision of the Supreme Court in *Miranda* v. *Arizona*[40] was undoubtedly inspired by the supposed inadequacy of the common law exclusionary rule to deal satisfactorily with the predicament of the suspect interrogated by the police in the coercive environment presented by the police station or some similar place or situation. It was principally concerned with the psychological pressures which might easily be placed upon the suspect by use of strategies recommended in various police interrogation manuals,[41] and that of Inbau and Reid in particular.[42] But it also suggested that 'the very fact of custodial interrogation exacts a heavy toll on individual liberty and trades on the weakness of individuals'.[43] The after-the-fact vagueness of the exclusionary rule based upon involuntariness was a feature rendering it incapable of counterbalancing either kind of psychological pressure. Therefore the Supreme Court devised and announced its own new exclusionary rule, the principal feature of which was that the police would be required, before questioning the suspect, to inform him both of his right to silence and of his right to have the advice of a lawyer. This was to apply no less to state cases than to federal ones. According to the Court, the rule flowed from

[34] See *Bram* v. *US*, 168 US 532 (1897), as approved in *Malloy* v. *Hogan*, 378 US 1 (1964).

[35] The phrase is Frankfurter J's in *Culombe* v. *Connecticut*, 367 US 568, at 606 (1961).

[36] 361 US 199 (1959). [37] 372 US 293 (1963). [38] 479 US 157 (1986).

[39] The Court pointed out that there was nothing to prevent individual states having a more extensive exclusionary rule—see *ibid*. 168.

[40] 384 US 436 (1966).

[41] Consideration is given to such strategies in Ch. 2, text to nn. 26–34 above.

[42] *Criminal Interrogation and Confessions* (1st edn., 1962). [43] 384 US 436, at 455 (1966).

the privilege against self-incrimination which is granted by the Fifth Amendment.

The broad propositions of law enunciated by the majority in *Miranda* are usefully summarized in the following passage from the opinion of the Court, delivered by Chief Justice Warren:[44]

we hold that when an individual is taken into custody or otherwise deprived of his freedom by the authorities in any significant way and is subjected to questioning, the privilege against self-incrimination is jeopardized. Procedural safeguards must be employed to protect the privilege and unless other fully effective means are adopted to notify the person of his right of silence and to assure that the exercise of the right will be scrupulously honored, the following measures are required. He must be warned prior to any questioning that he has the right to remain silent, that anything he says can be used against him in a court of law, that he has the right to the presence of an attorney, and that if he cannot afford an attorney one will be appointed for him prior to any questioning if he so desires. Opportunity to exercise these rights must be afforded to him throughout the interrogation. After such warnings have been given, and such opportunity afforded him, the individual may knowingly and intelligently waive these rights and agree to answer questions or make a statement. But unless and until such warnings and waiver are demonstrated by the prosecution at trial, no evidence obtained as a result of interrogation can be used against him.

Miranda, then, seemed in a sense to create a *per se* rule for the Fifth Amendment broadly equivalent to that applicable to Fourth Amendment breach by virtue of *Mapp*. The *Miranda* court said, on more than one occasion, that the procedural safeguards which it announced must be complied with unless other, fully effective means to the same end were adopted by the official agency in question. So it seems that, though the Fifth Amendment required effective safeguards, it did not necessarily require *these* safeguards. For that reason, as well as for other ones which it is inappropriate to go into here, the entire constitutional basis of *Miranda* has been questioned. It is one thing to say that the specific substantive content of the Fourth Amendment ought to be given remedial support, but quite another to give the Fifth Amendment some content not expressly stated therein and then to require remedial support.[45]

In any event, *Miranda* did indeed change the face of police interrogation of suspects in the United States. The Supreme Court poured strong spirit into the glass in announcing its decision. It will be argued here that the 30 years or so since *Miranda* have seen a process of dilution of that strong spirit such that its impact is now significantly reduced. The difficulties which would attend the unbending application of an exclusionary rule are repeatedly apparent in post-*Miranda* Supreme Court jurisprudence. The response of the Court to those difficulties is most instructive for the continuing discourse between those, on the one hand, who would favour simple, firm rules and, on the other, those who would favour

[44] 384 US 436, at 478–9.

[45] The majority and minority opinions in *Duckworth* v. *Eagan*, 492 US 195 (1989) contain important discussion of the proper constitutional basis for the decision in *Miranda*.

more complex, fact-dependent rules of an open texture, or even structured discretion.

The Retreat from Miranda

The content of the *Miranda* rule may be described as follows. Where a *person in custody* is to be *interrogated*, he must first be *warned of certain rights*, which rights must be *scrupulously honoured*, unless he *waives* them and, having waived them, does not later *re-assert* them. There are exceptions to *Miranda* for cases where the accused testifies at trial and his confession is put to him for *impeachment* purposes and for situations where the *public safety* is endangered. We shall consider these elements in turn.[46]

Person in Custody

Miranda referred to a person in custody or otherwise deprived of freedom in any significant way. However, there are two types of compulsory interferences with the citizen's personal freedom which may fail to qualify as significant deprival. In *Berkemer* v. *McCarty*,[47] the Supreme Court held that the *Miranda* catalogue was not implicated by a routine traffic stop. It refused to accord 'talismanic power' to the passage in *Miranda* about significant deprival of freedom. Rather, it was necessary to decide whether or not a traffic stop exerts upon the person detained pressures that impair his free exercise of the privilege against self-incrimination sufficiently to require that he be warned of his rights. This effectively re-opens the very question which the Supreme Court in *Miranda* sought to answer.

In *Berkemer* itself, the court went on to offer its view about the 'stop and frisk' of a citizen carried out by virtue of *Terry* v. *Ohio*.[48] The *Terry* 'stop and frisk' is a brief field detention carried out for investigative purposes and without arrest, and is permitted where the police officer reasonably suspects that the citizen is engaged in criminal activity. It is a procedure of considerable importance both in principle and in practice. However, according to the opinion of the court in *Berkemer*: '[t]he comparatively non-threatening character of detentions of this sort explains the absence of any suggestion in our opinions that *Terry* stops are subject to the dictates of *Miranda*.'[49] If this is correct, *Miranda* does not apply to many situations in which there is a very significant deprival of freedom. Though the *Terry* stop was originally seen as a very brief affair, it has been expanded and extended in a way which makes it capable of being highly intrusive and, in practical terms, very little different from an arrest—and arrest does undoubtedly implicate *Miranda*. However, there are indications in courts below the Supreme Court itself that, notwithstanding the *dictum* in *Berkemer*, the *Miranda* warning must be given in the case of some especially coercive *Terry* stops. A good

[46] What follows is certainly not intended as a comprehensive guide to the *Miranda* jurisprudence. The standard American works should be consulted for such a guide.

[47] 468 US 420 (1984). [48] 392 US 1 (1968). [49] 468 US 420, at 441 (1984).

example is *US* v. *Perdue*.[50] The police had discovered a marijuana growing facility out in the country. Perdue and his fiancée were seen approaching the facility in a car, but then to reverse, apparently on observing that the police were present. With weapons drawn, two officers stopped the car and ordered Perdue to lie face down on the ground. He may also have been handcuffed, and the guns were certainly kept drawn. Questions were asked of Perdue while he still lay on the ground, and he gave incriminating answers. The Tenth Circuit Court of Appeals refused to draw the bright line suggested by *Berkemer*, holding the stop to be so intrusive that *Miranda* applied. It remains to be seen whether or not this test of degree will appeal to the Supreme Court.

Interrogation

In the leading case, *Rhode Island* v. *Innis*,[51] all members of the Supreme Court bar one[52] were content with the definition of 'interrogation' offered by Justice Stewart. He said that:[53]

> the *Miranda* safeguards come into play whenever a person in custody is subjected to either express questioning or its functional equivalent. That is to say, the term 'interrogation' under *Miranda* refers not only to express questioning, but also to any words or actions on the part of the police (other than those normally attendant to arrest and custody) that the police should know are reasonably likely[54] to elicit an incriminating response from the suspect.

This test seems designed to ensure that particular police strategies with regard to the getting of information from the suspect which one could not describe as express questioning, whether because not employing the interrogative mood or otherwise, should not result in the *Miranda* protections being inapplicable. Yet the majority applied the test in such an extraordinary way that precisely the opposite result was achieved.[55]

Innis had been arrested for robbery and, on three separate occasions, advised of his *Miranda* rights. On the third occasion, he stated that he wished to speak to a lawyer. He was then taken by three officers to the police station. On the way, one officer, Gleckman, spoke to another, McKenna, about the shotgun used in the robbery (which had not been found). He pointed out that there were many handicapped children in the area and expressed the hope that none of them would find the weapon and any shells accompanying it, since injury might be the result. McKenna expressed agreement, adding that the search for the weapon should be continued. In response to this rather transparent attempt to persuade

[50] 8 F 3d. 1455 (1993). See also *US* v. *Bautista*, 684 F 2d. 1286 (1982); *US* v. *Elias*, 832 F 2d. 24 (1987); *US* v. *Smith*, 3 F 3d.1088 (1993).

[51] 446 US 291 (1980). [52] Stevens J—see n. 54, below. [53] 446 US 291, at 301–2.

[54] Stevens J preferred a formulation which would count as 'interrogation' any police conduct or statements which would appear to a reasonable person in the suspect's position to call for a response—see *ibid*. 310.

[55] In this respect, *Innis* is to be compared with the Sixth Amendment case of *Brewer* v. *Williams*, 430 US 387 (1977) (the 'Christian burial speech' case).

him to reveal the weapon's whereabouts, Innis did indeed take the officers to where it was hidden. Speaking for the majority, Justice Stewart concluded that it could not be said that the police should have known that their conversation was likely to elicit an incriminating response. The record did not show that Gleckman's remarks were intended to elicit such a response. So far as imputing knowledge was concerned, Justice Stewart stressed that there was no evidence that the officers were aware that Innis was peculiarly susceptible to an appeal to his conscience concerning the safety of handicapped children or that they knew him to be unusually disoriented or upset when arrested.

It is instructive to turn to the dissenting opinion of Justice Marshall, with whom Justice Brennan agreed. Though content with the majority's test, they had no doubt that it had been misapplied. They refused to accept that the absence of special knowledge of Innis's state of mind was decisive. An appeal of the type made by the officers would go to the conscience of any suspect, whether especially interested in children or not. It is hard to see how this argument can be wrong. It is noteworthy that the Supreme Court of Rhode Island, having ruled that the evidence in question should have been suppressed, had gone on to order a new trial and, in doing so, had remarked that most of the other evidence in the case was circumstantial.[56] One may speculate that it must have been hard for the majority of the US Supreme Court to contemplate the possible acquittal of Innis at a second trial for a murder he had undoubtedly committed.

Warning of Rights

We have seen that the person in question must be warned of three rights, namely his right to silence, his right to have a lawyer present, and his right to have that lawyer provided without cost should he be unable to afford to pay. Quite understandably, the Supreme Court has held that 'no talismanic incantation' is required in order to satisfy the strictures of *Miranda*.[57] Plainly, where the police have, in substance, warned the suspect of his rights, it ought not to matter that the terms of the warning were not as precise as might have been hoped. Yet in the very case in which the Court rejected talismanic incantations, it decided, by majority, that *Miranda* was complied with even though no mention at all had been made of the third right, i.e. that to free legal advice. In the later case of *Duckworth* v. *Eagan*,[58] a bare majority of the Court held that *Miranda* was satisfied where, having informed the suspect of all three rights, the police officer had gone on to say that the police themselves could not provide a lawyer, 'but one will be appointed for you, if you wish, if and when you go to court'. The minority, describing this as making a mockery of *Miranda*, pointed out that the officer's coda would lead the suspect to believe that a lawyer would not be provided until some indeterminate time in the future, after questioning.[59] In other words, it detracted from the force of *both* the second and third rights.

[56] See *State* v. *Innis*, 391 A 2d. 1158, at 1164 (1978).

[57] In *California* v. *Prysock*, 453 US 355, at 359 (1981).

[58] 492 US 195 (1989).

[59] See *ibid*. 215–16.

Scrupulous Honour

In *Miranda* itself, as we have already seen,[60] the Supreme Court said that the right to silence must be 'scrupulously honored'. This must be taken to embrace the right to have a lawyer present when interrogated, which is clearly designed as support for the essential right guaranteed by the Fifth Amendment. The boundaries of scrupulous honour have been set in a way which allows considerable flexibility to the police in getting a second bite at the cherry.

In *Michigan* v. *Mosley*,[61] the accused had invoked his right to silence when the police sought to question him about one of the robberies in respect of which he had been arrested. No questions about that offence were put. Later on, another officer, having addressed to him further *Miranda* warnings, sought to question him about an offence other than those for which he had been arrested. In this respect, the accused did not assert a right to silence, so the police questioned him. The Supreme Court, in ruling his resulting confession admissible, laid much stress on the fact that the police had no reason to suppose that the accused's initial invocation of his right to silence encompassed the other offence. On this view, his rights had been scrupulously honoured. However, there are also indications in the case that the police may, in certain circumstances, be permitted to re-open interrogation about the offence in respect of which silence was claimed, as long as further *Miranda* warnings have been administered. If this really is the law, it does seem hard to reconcile with the scrupulous honour idea. It must be hard enough for most suspects to assert their rights once, let alone twice, when one has regard to the coercive nature of the atmosphere which surrounds them.

With regard to the right to a lawyer, the court has adopted a *per se* rule outlawing further police approaches to the suspect. In *Edwards* v. *Arizona*, it stated that such a suspect. 'is not subject to further interrogation by the authorities until counsel has been made available to him, unless the accused himself initiates further communication, exchanges, or conversations with the police'.[62] However, the force of this decision is much reduced by the interpretation placed by the Court, in *Oregon* v. *Bradshaw*,[63] on the kind of activities on the part of the accused which will lift the *Edwards* ban on questioning. Shortly after invoking his right to counsel and while being taken to the county jail, Bradshaw enquired of a police officer, 'Well, what is going to happen to me now?' According to the plurality, this question 'evinced a willingness and a desire for a generalized discussion about the investigation'[64] and thus rendered interrogation permissible. Though the four dissenters preferred the notion that the *Edwards* test envisaged 'communication or dialogue about the subject matter of the criminal investigation',[65] they clearly thought their own gloss not essentially different from the one proposed by the plurality. It was the plurality's application of their gloss to the

[60] See the text accompanying n. 44. [61] 423 US 96 (1975).

[62] 451 US 477, at 485–6 (1981). See also *Minnick* v. *Mississippi*, 498 US 146 (1990).

[63] 462 US 1039 (1983). [64] *Ibid*. 1046–7. [65] *Ibid*. 1054.

facts which 'baffled' the minority,[66] and understandably so, for it seems obvious that the natural interpretation of Bradshaw's words was that he wished to know where he was being taken and how the criminal process against him would be taken forward.

Waiver

Two distinct issues arise, so far as waiver of *Miranda* rights is concerned. First, what is required in order to constitute waiver? Secondly, was the waiver in question made both voluntarily and knowingly?

Regarding the first issue, the court said in *Miranda*:[67]

> An express statement that the individual is willing to make a statement and does not want an attorney followed closely by a statement could constitute a waiver. But a valid waiver will not be presumed simply from the silence of the accused after warnings are given or simply from the fact that a confession was in fact eventually obtained.

In *North Carolina* v. *Butler*,[68] the court decided that there might be an implied waiver of rights. In its words:[69]

> The question is not one of form, but rather whether the defendant knowingly and voluntarily waived the rights delineated in the *Miranda* case. As was unequivocally said in *Miranda*, mere silence is not enough. That does not mean that the defendant's silence coupled with an understanding of his rights and a course of conduct indicating waiver may never support a conclusion that a defendant has waived his rights The courts must presume that a defendant did not waive his rights; the prosecution's burden is great; but in at least some cases waiver can be clearly inferred from the actions and words of the person interrogated.

In that case, the accused had been apprised of his rights and invited to sign a waiver clause. He expressed himself willing to talk to the police, but refused to sign the clause. He subsequently made incriminating remarks. Clearly, he had expressly waived his right to silence, but the court held that he had also waived his right to counsel. It is not clear what words or conduct the Court regarded as amounting to waiver of the latter right. Perhaps it sufficed that he had knowingly and willingly waived his right to silence, though it seems strange to regard express waiver of one right as effecting implied waiver of another one. There is much to be said for the minority's view that there should be an absolute requirement of express waiver; otherwise, the question of waiver will be 'shrouded in half-light..., allowing courts to construct inferences from ambiguous words and gestures'.[70]

It is noteworthy that this willingness to imply waiver is not matched by an equivalent willingness to imply assertion of *Miranda* rights. The 16-year-old suspect in *Fare* v. *Michael C*[71] had, when advised of his right to counsel, asked to have his probation officer present. The police had said that he could not be called

[66] In this respect, the case resembles *Rhode Island* v. *Innis*.
[67] 384 US 436, at 475 (1966).
[68] 441 US 369 (1979).
[69] *Ibid*. 374.
[70] *Ibid*. 378.
[71] 442 US 707 (1979).

out that evening. He then expressed himself willing to be interviewed without a lawyer. A bare majority of the Supreme Court held that a request to see a probation officer could not be considered equivalent to a request to see a lawyer. A probation officer would be without legal expertise and had a duty to the state as well as to his charge. Furthermore, the majority would not take the request, by itself, as an implied indication of unwillingness to be questioned; it did not have 'overwhelming significance'.[72] Three of the minority pointed out that a (presumably) unintelligent juvenile could not be expected to invoke the precise *Miranda* formula. He had asked for someone he trusted to be present to support him. Therefore, the rationale of *Miranda* required his request to be treated, at the very least, as indicative of a desire to remain silent until contact was made with his probation officer.[73]

The waiver of the right must, in any event, be both voluntary and knowing (or intelligent). It was held in *Colorado* v. *Connelly*[74] that the meaning of voluntariness here is the same as for the purposes of the involuntariness exclusionary rule for confessions.[75] In other words, some element of police overreaching must be present, it being insufficient that the accused was, by reason of his mental state, not acting under his own free will. Justice Stevens, dissenting on this issue, perceptively pointed out that, for the purposes of *Miranda*, once Connelly was in custody, questioning him assumed a presumptively coercive character. It followed that there should be no need for an added element of overt police pressure in order to render waiver involuntary.[76]

With regard to knowledge, *Miranda* itself contains a good deal of material suggesting that only if the suspect had a considerable amount of accurate information about the facts of his situation and the law applicable to it could his waiver be knowing, for these purposes. However, as is suggested in *McCormick on Evidence*: '[t]he Supreme Court's post-1985 cases collectively suggest that "intelligence", as used in *Miranda's* waiver criteria, involves only an understanding of the basic abstract Fifth Amendment rights of which a suspect must be informed'.[77] It suffices to mention one such case here, *Moran* v. *Burbine*.[78] There, no error had been made in the reading to Burbine of his rights, and he had expressly waived his right to counsel. However, in doing so, he was unaware that a lawyer, contacted by his sister, had been trying to reach him. There was some confusion about which officers might question him and about which offence, but, in any event, he confessed to a murder without having had the benefit of legal advice. A majority of the Court rejected his claim that the confession ought to have been suppressed at his trial. It said that, though the additional information might have been useful and might even have affected his decision to confess, it had never read the Constitution 'to require that the police supply a suspect with a flow of information to help him calibrate his self-interest in deciding whether to speak or stand by his rights'.[79] Like *Rhode Island* v. *Innis*, this too was a case in

[72] 442 US 707, at 724–5. [73] *Ibid*. 733. [74] 479 US 157 (1986).
[75] See the discussion in the text to nn. 33–9 above. [76] See 479 US 157, at 173–4.
[77] (4th. (student) edn., 1992), at 249. [78] 475 US 412 (1986). [79] *Ibid*. 423.

which it seemed entirely possible that, at a second trial with his confession excluded, Burbine would have been acquitted of murder.[80]

Re-assertion

Obviously, a suspect who has originally waived a right may later decide to insist upon it. It is absolutely clear that, once a right is effectively re-asserted, it must be scrupulously honoured in just the same way as if it had been claimed at the outset. *Davis* v. *US*[81] deals with the question of what counts as an effective re-assertion. In that case, the investigators were military personnel, for Davis was a serving member of the US Navy who was suspected of having clubbed a fellow sailor to death at a naval base. About one and a half hours into his interview, he said, 'Maybe I should talk to a lawyer'. The investigators told him that, if he did want a lawyer, the questioning would stop and then went on to ask him whether he did want one. He replied that he did not. A unanimous Supreme Court held that Davis's rights had been respected, so that there was no reason to suppress statements made after that exchange. However, the Court divided about the law applicable to the situation in *Davis*. Five Justices took the view that, in the case of an ambiguous or equivocal reference such as this one, the investigator would be free simply to continue questioning in the ordinary way. The remaining four Justices were of the opinion that, faced with that kind of reference, the investigator would be under a duty, before proceeding further, to verify whether or not the suspect meant to ask for a lawyer.

The imposition of such a duty would seem to be the very least that close attention to the spirit of *Miranda* would demand. It will be recalled that *North Carolina* v. *Butler*[82] allows waiver to be inferred from silence coupled with a course of conduct indicating waiver. Thus, *Butler* may be said to resolve ambiguity in favour of waiver. This contrasts starkly with the (effective) view of the majority in *Davis* that any such ambiguity as regards re-assertion should be resolved the other way.

Impeachment

According to *Harris* v. *New York*,[83] an incriminating statement acquired in breach of the *Miranda* rules, though inadmissible as part of the case for the prosecution, is admissible in cross-examination of the accused for the purpose of impeaching his credibility.

Harris was charged with selling heroin to an undercover policeman. The officer testified as to details of two alleged sales, and another officer testified as to the chemical analysis of the heroin. In evidence, Harris denied making the first sale and alleged that the substance he had sold on the second occasion was merely

[80] The First Circuit Court of Appeals described the confessional material as having been critical in obtaining his conviction—see *Burbine* v. *Moran*, 753 F 2d.178, at 187–8 (1985).

[81] 512 US 452 (1994). [82] 441 US 369 (1979), considered in the text to nn. 68–70 above.

[83] 401 US 222 (1971). See also *Oregon* v. *Hass*, 420 US 714 (1975) and the discussion of the position in English law in Ch. 8, text to nn. 16–28 above.

baking powder. The prosecution was permitted to put to him incriminating statements, made to the police, which partially contradicted what he had said in chief. These statements had been made before he was informed of his right to counsel. A bare majority of the Supreme Court held that, the statements being legally voluntary, the trial judge had been right to allow cross-examination. This result was dictated, the majority said, by precedent, principle, and policy. The minority convincingly demonstrated that the precedent relied upon by the majority was incapable of supporting their position,[84] but it is the arguments of principle and policy which have wider significance.

Principle was said to dictate that the *Miranda* shield should not be allowed to be used as a licence to commit perjury free from the risk of confrontation with previous inconsistent statements to impeach credibility. Yet as well as contradicting Harris's evidence-in-chief, those incriminating statements were highly relevant to the issue. It is hard to believe that a judicial warning not to take them as evidence of guilt—one had been given by the trial judge in *Harris*—would suffice to counteract their prejudicial influence.[85] Furthermore, the rule in *Harris* fetters the accused's decision whether or not to testify, for a decision to testify will inevitably lead to cross-examination about the illegally obtained statements.

As regards policy, the majority view was that sufficient deterrent effect upon police misconduct would flow from making the confession unavailable to the prosecution in chief, with the result that there was no need to make it equally unavailable in cross-examination. This is hard to accept even in its own terms, for the police must surely interpret the message from *Harris* as a mixed one which half discourages them from failing to accord suspects their rights. However, the broader significance of the majority view is that it embraces a deterrence rationale of *Miranda*, rather than one based either upon protection of the particular accused's Fifth Amendment privilege or upon some version of the judicial integrity principle.

Later Supreme Court jurisprudence exhibits a dispute about the governing principle behind *Miranda* which parallels that surrounding *Mapp*.[86] A number of Justices have endorsed the deterrence rationale of the *Miranda* rule, and have come to describe it as a prophylactic rule not commanded by the Fifth Amendment itself.[87] Others have averred that it is indeed directly mandated by that Amendment.[88] This view was well expressed by Justices Brennan and Marshall[89] as follows: '[u]nlike the exclusionary rule, which purportedly exists solely for deterrence purposes, the *Miranda* requirements . . . serve to protect "a criminal

[84] 401 US 222, at 228–9. See also Dershowitz and Ely, 80 *Yale LJ* 1198, at 1211–18 (1971).

[85] This was considered an important reason for refusing to apply *Harris* to Californian state trials in *People* v. *Disbrow*, 545 P 2d 272, at 279 and 282 (1976).

[86] On which, see the text to nn. 12–15 above.

[87] See, e.g., Rehnquist J in *Michigan* v. *Tucker*, 417 US 433, at 447–8 (1974); O'Connor J, joined by Scalia J, in *Duckworth* v. *Eagan*, 492 US 195, at 206 ff. (1989).

[88] See, e.g., Douglas, Brennan, and Marshall JJ in *Michigan* v. *Tucker*, 417 US 433, at 462 ff and 454 ff. (1974).

[89] *Duckworth* v. *Eagan*, 492 US 195, at 227 (1989).

suspect's exercise of [a] privilege which is one of the distinctive components of our criminal law" '.[90] So the true point of *Miranda* is said to be to provide remedial support for the *nemo debet* principle.

In any event, there is another important difference between the claim to exclusion under *Mapp* and the claim under *Miranda*, one to which reference was made in Chapter 2.[91] It has been put very clearly by Justice Marshall: '[b]ut *unlike* physical evidence seized from a suspect in violation of his Fourth Amendment rights, a statement taken from a suspect in violation of his *Miranda* rights is presumptively unreliable'.[92] *Miranda* itself was very much concerned to counterbalance the coercive environment of custody in order, *inter alia*, to promote the reliability of confessions. It follows that, even if discipline or deterrence does have a part to play, it may properly be that kind of discipline or deterrence which has as its goal the discouraging of police methods likely to result in unreliable confessions that is to the fore.[93]

Public Safety

In *New York* v. *Quarles*,[94] by bare majority, the Supreme Court recognized the existence of a 'public safety' exception to the requirement that *Miranda* warnings be given. The majority, again describing the *Miranda* rule as prophylactic, took the view that, where public safety was endangered, the police should *not* be discouraged from asking questions of the suspect in custody which might remove the present danger, even though those questions would otherwise come within the *Miranda* prohibition.

However, it is not the holding itself, but rather the exact nature of the exception fashioned by the majority, which is of the greatest interest. The facts of *Quarles* were hardly the most propitious for the development of such an exception. Police officers had pursued Quarles, who was suspected of rape and believed to be carrying a gun, into a convenience store. He was apprehended and handcuffed. The apprehending officer found him to be wearing an empty shoulder holster. Without giving *Miranda* warnings, he asked Quarles where the gun was and was directed to it. By the time that question was asked, other officers who initially trained their guns on Quarles had returned them to their holsters. This seemed to support the view, expressed in evidence by the arresting officer himself, that the situation was under control. Nor was it easy to see how that officer could have been concerned for the safety of ordinary members of the public. It was the middle of the night, and the store was, except for staff, deserted. It is hard to accept that there was, or was even perceived by the arresting officer to be, any immediate threat to public safety. So the majority said that the actual motivation of the officers involved did not matter, the key question being whether or not there was

[90] Citing *White* v. *Finkbeiner*, 687 F 2d. 885, at 893 (1982).
[91] See Ch. 2. text to nn. 9–11 and Ch. 6, text to nn. 1–3 above.
[92] In *Duckworth* v. *Eagan*, 492 US 195, at 226 (1989) (emphasis in original).
[93] This discipline/reliability principle is discussed at p. 13 above.
[94] 467 US 649 (1984).

some theoretical public danger, even if one lacking immediacy. As long as the gun was concealed somewhere in the supermarket, it posed a danger, for an accomplice might make use of it, or a customer or employee come upon it. It seems reasonable to suggest that, here, rather than the facts being interpreted in an unlikely way in order to fit the law (as in *Rhode Island* v. *Innis*), the law was expressed in a way which departed so far from its motivating reason as not really to reflect it at all. It is one thing to recognize the agony of the moment experienced by the police officer, but here the officers' conduct demonstrated that the agony had passed.

Conclusion

It would be hard to argue that today's Supreme Court views *Miranda* with affection and respect. We may say that it has been *confined* by reference to the absence of sufficient deterrent value in exclusion, as in *Harris* v. *New York*. It has been *outflanked* by crime control considerations, as in *Berkemer* v. *McCarty* with regard to routine traffic stops and, perhaps, *Terry* stops. In *New York* v. *Quarles*, it was *outweighed* by an express preference for another crime control value, namely public safety. Finally, it has been *evaded* by strange, even extraordinary, factual findings, as in *Rhode Island* v. *Innis* and *Oregon* v. *Bradshaw*, or by legal conclusions which make little sense, as (again) in *New York* v. *Quarles*. The lesson to be learned may be that an unbending exclusionary rule provides spirit of such a high alcoholic proof that the judiciary cannot drink it unadulterated.

The Fruit of the Poisonous Tree

The Basic Doctrine

We have seen that, in the classic situation exemplified by *Warickshall*,[95] in which the police first obtain a confession, later ruled inadmissible, then, by virtue of information provided in the confession, discover some other incriminating evidence, the general principle of English law is that the latter evidence is not inadmissible.[96] By contrast, the general principle of law in the United States is quite the reverse. Where some violation of a person's constitutional rights has led to the obtaining of primary, incriminating evidence, not only that evidence but also any derivative evidence flowing therefrom is to be suppressed. This is known as the doctrine of the 'fruit of the poisonous tree'. So, applied to *Warickshall*, it would result in the prosecution not being permitted to adduce evidence that the stolen goods to which Warickshall had referred in her confession had been found in the bed of her lodgings.

This is not the place for a comprehensive discussion of the many manifestations of the basic poisonous fruit doctrine. The three such manifestations most relevant for present purposes are, first, that which *Warickshall* itself exemplifies, i.e. the primary evidence is a confession, the derivative evidence non-confessional; secondly that in which both the primary and the derivative evidence are confessional;

[95] (1783) 1 Leach CC 263, 168 ER 234.

[96] See the discussion in Ch. 8, text to nn. 35–52 above.

and thirdly that in which, whether or not primary evidence is acquired at all, there has been a breach of a person's Fourth Amendment rights which has resulted in the police acquiring derivative evidence in the shape of a confession.

The doctrine was developed in the context of the third situation. The leading case is *Wong Sun* v. *US*.[97] There a confession was made following an unlawful arrest. In order for the chain of causation to be broken and for the confession to be admissible, despite the initial illegality, it must be the product of an 'act of free will unaffected by the initial illegality'.[98] In relation to that issue, the Supreme Court has said that '[t]he temporal proximity of the arrest and the confession, the presence of intervening circumstances . . . and, particularly, the purpose and flagrancy of the official misconduct are all relevant'.[99] The problem of causation is likely to be much less acute in the two situations where the primary evidence is a confession. Where the derivative evidence is non-confessional (the stolen goods, the murder weapon, the dead body), it is very likely that the immediate and sole cause of its discovery will indeed be the accused's confession. Otherwise, why did not the police find it for themselves? Where a second confession follows a first, the defence has the advantage of an obvious 'cat-out-of-the-bag' argument, an argument eloquently put by Justice Harlan in *Darwin* v. *Connecticut*:[100]

> A principle reason why a suspect might make a second or third confession is simply that, having already confessed once or twice, he might think he has little to lose by repetition. If a first confession is not shown to be voluntary, I do not think a later confession that is merely a direct product of the earlier one should be held to be voluntary. It would be neither conducive to good police work nor fair to a suspect, to allow the erroneous impression that he has nothing to lose to play the major role in a defendant's decision to speak a second or third time.

Exceptions and Non-exceptions

Since, in effect, the fruit is to be excluded only if it is *of* the poisonous tree, the element of causation just described is implicit in the doctrine itself. Therefore, where the taint has become so attenuated that it is not properly considered as still operative, but merely as background material, the doctrine is inapplicable. For example, in *Re RPS*,[101] the accused had, by the time he confessed a second time, already appeared in court with counsel in order to have his earlier confession suppressed, so he could not sensibly claim that the second confession was the fruit of the first. Equally, where the derivative evidence was actually obtained through an independent source free of the taint associated with the primary evidence, the fruits doctrine has no call to apply, for the derivative evidence comes from another (non-poisonous) tree.[102]

[97] 371 US 471 (1963). See also *Silverthorne Lumber Co.* v. *US*, 251 US 385 (1920).

[98] See *Brown* v. *Illinois*, 422 US 590, at 604 (1975). [99] *Ibid.* 604–5.

[100] 391 US 346, at 350–1 (1968). See generally Mirfield [1996] Crim.LR 554.

[101] 653 P 2d. 964 (1981).

[102] The 'independent source' doctrine was first recognized in *Silverthorne Lumber Co.* v. *US*, 251 US 385, at 392 (1920). A recent (dubious) application of that doctrine is *Murray* v. *US*, 487 US 533 (1988).

A genuine exception to the poisonous tree doctrine is provided by the inevitable discovery rule. It states that, where the derivative evidence would inevitably have been discovered without recourse to the primary, tainted evidence, the former is admissible. In *Nix* v. *Williams*,[103] the Supreme Court adopted and applied that rule. Williams had led the police to the dead body of his victim. An earlier Supreme Court decision had ruled that evidence of Williams's confession to the police and his leading them to the body was inadmissible because acquired in breach of his Sixth Amendment right to counsel.[104] The question for decision in *Nix* v. *Williams* was whether or not evidence of the condition of the body itself should, because of the fruits doctrine, also be ruled inadmissible. By majority, the Supreme Court held that this material was admissible since the prosecution had established, by a preponderance of the evidence, that the body would inevitably have been discovered (within another three to five hours) had not Williams directed the police to it. It seems that a search of the general area in which the body was situated had been suspended when it was learned that Williams was co-operating with the police. There does seem to be plenty of scope here for *post hoc* rationalization of the way in which the search would have proceeded, and much must depend upon the degree to which the prosecution must prove the inevitability of discovery. Indeed, the minority dissented for that very reason, Justices Brennan and Marshall proposing that clear and convincing evidence should be required.

The Special Rule for Primary Evidence Obtained in Breach of Miranda

Yet another aspect of Supreme Court disenchantment with *Miranda* is that the fruits doctrine seems to be inapplicable where the reason for exclusion of a first confession is failure to comply with the *Miranda* requirements. *Oregon* v. *Elstad*[105] establishes that that is the case where the derivative evidence is a second confession, but it may also be the case where it is non-confessional.

It is implicit in *Oregon* v. *Elstad* that the fruits doctrine applies with full force where the first confession was involuntary for purposes of the common law rule of exclusion. Why, then, does it not apply where there was a breach only of *Miranda*? Once again, the majority stressed the prophylactic nature of the *Miranda* rule, which means that compliance with its dictates is not a requirement of the Fifth Amendment itself. On that reasoning, the Court was free of the need to suppress as a matter of direct constitutional command and might consider afresh the good sense of applying the fruits doctrine. The majority concluded that no additional sound purpose would be served by excluding a second confession where it was involuntary and had itself been attended by full compliance with *Miranda*. The decision is striking for Elstad had, before he confessed the first time, not been warned at all of his rights. In other words, no more gross breach of *Miranda* could be imagined.

[103] 467 US 431 (1984).
[104] See *Brewer* v. *Williams*, 430 US 387 (1977).
[105] 470 US 298 (1985).

Justice Brennan, joined by Justice Marshall, certainly feared that the majority would equally have refused to apply the fruits doctrine in a case where the derivative evidence was physical.[106] The majority did indeed place reliance on the earlier Supreme Court case of *Michigan* v. *Tucker*,[107] a case in which the primary evidence (a confession) had been obtained in breach of *Miranda*, the derivative evidence was non-confessional, and yet the latter evidence was not suppressed.[108] However, *Michigan* v. *Tucker* is rather unusual in two respects. The breach in question had taken place before *Miranda* was decided. The view of the majority was that no reasonable deterrent purpose would be served by excluding the derivative evidence where the police had acted in good faith and in accordance with the law as it was understood to be at the time. Furthermore, the derivative evidence was the testimony of a witness whose identity was revealed in the accused's statement to the police. In those circumstances, just as in that of successive confessions, the person is 'free to exercise his own volition in deciding whether or not to make a statement to the authorities'.[109] By contrast, where physical evidence is that which is discovered, there will have been no opportunity for the exercise of such an intervening volition. However, it is right to add that Justice O'Connor, in *New York* v. *Quarles*, expressed the firm view that the fruits doctrine does not apply to physical evidence (there the gun) discovered in consequence of a confession which she herself regarded as inadmissible for breach of *Miranda*.[110]

Exclusion for Unfairness in Scotland

Introduction

In *Lawrie* v. *Muir*,[111] the High Court of Justiciary dealt with the question of admissibility of evidence obtained unlawfully or irregularly. The Court announced a rule requiring exclusion of such evidence unless the unlawfulness or irregularity could properly be excused. Its opinion in that case has been one of great influence, particularly in parts of the Commonwealth other than England and Wales. We shall have occasion to refer to it again when dealing with the relevant Commonwealth developments. However, in the course of that opinion, the court also referred to 'the discretionary principle of fairness to the accused which has been developed so fully in our law in relation to the admission in evidence of confessions or admissions by a person suspected or charged with crime'.[112] It is that principle of fairness to which attention will now be turned. In particular, we must consider a gloss upon that principle which was put forward in the very important case of *Chalmers* v. *HM Advocate*[113] which was decided by same court four years after *Lawrie* v. *Muir*.

[106] See *ibid*. 347–8. [107] 417 US 433 (1974). [108] See 470 US 298, at 309–10 (1985).
[109] *Ibid*. 309. [110] See 467 US 649, at 666–75 (1984). [111] [1950] JC 19.
[112] *Ibid*. 27. [113] [1954] JC 66.

The significance of *Chalmers* can quickly be deduced from the comment of Sheriff G. H. Gordon, himself both a distinguished judge and legal academic, that the case was taken by most Scots lawyers and police officers to have established that 'statements by a suspect in answer to police questioning were not admissible as evidence, at any rate if given in a police station, a venue which is a sinister one in the eyes of every ordinary citizen'.[114] In other words, the Scottish police were subject to a *per se* rule denying them the power in law to question suspects in custody. It will quickly be apparent that such a rule would be far more restrictive and have a much greater impact on police investigative practice than the rules governing the interrogation of suspects in England or even than the *Miranda* rule. The police really would have to find some source of evidence, sufficient to convict the accused, other than the accused's own mouth.

The Decision in *Chalmers*

In fact, as Sheriff Gordon points out, Chalmers was, at best, an ambiguous decision.[115] Its facts were as follows. Chalmers, then 16, was suspected of having robbed and killed a fellow foundry worker. He was taken to the police station (he had been questioned about the offences twice before) and interrogated. He was cautioned before interrogation began and later when he made a particular remark (by which time tears were in his eyes). He was then asked if he wished his father or a solicitor to be present, but declined and said he would make a statement. Another officer stepped forward to take it down, then cautioned him and again asked him if he wanted his father or a solicitor. Chalmers declined and then made a written statement, which was completed only thirty-five minutes after the interrogation had begun. Next, he took the police to a cornfield and directed them to a place where a purse belonging to the deceased was found. Later on the same day, in the presence of his father, Chalmers said, when cautioned and formally charged, 'I did it. He struck me'.

Though the issue arose rather indirectly, the remarks of the two members of the court who delivered substantial judgments were principally concerned with the admissibility of Chalmers's written statement.[116] All members of the court agreed that it was inadmissible. It was the Lord Justice-Clerk, Lord Thomson, who most clearly espoused the position that the reason for its inadmissibility was that it had been elicited by cross-examination. After stating categorically that evidence obtained by questioning tainted with bullying, pressure, third-degree methods, and so forth can never be admissible whatever stage police investigation has reached, he went on to equate with those methods cross-examination of

[114] See *Reshaping the Criminal Law* (ed. Glazebrook, 1978), at 330. Sheriff Gordon's excellent essay deals not only with *Chalmers*, but also with many of the other leading Scottish cases on confessions.

[115] *Ibid.* 332.

[116] The prosecution had not relied upon it at trial, but only upon his remarks when cautioned and charged.

a person under serious consideration as perpetrator of the crime. He said: '[o]nce that stage of suspicion is reached, the suspect is in the position that thereafter the only evidence admissible against him is his own voluntary statement. A voluntary statement is one given freely, not in response to pressure and inducement, and not elicited by cross-examination.'[117] This is not a statement of a rule requiring all the circumstances to be taken into account, such that the police might properly cross-examine a robust adult but not an emotional teenager like Chalmers himself. It forbids all cross-examination of persons upon whom suspicion has focused.

Before delivering these remarks, Lord Thomson had said that he entirely agreed with the opinion of Lord Justice-General Cooper. Furthermore, one of the reports of *Chalmers* describes the other three judges in the case as concurring in that opinion.[118] Unfortunately, the effect of Lord Cooper's opinion, plainly the leading one, is far from clear. There is, at one point, an indication that he, like Lord Thomson, intended to lay down a *per se* rule.[119] However, elsewhere in his opinion, his Lordship seems to be saying that the rule is one of general fairness, dependent for its applicability on the particular circumstances of the case. A factor informing the issue of fairness, and probably a very important one, would be whether or not the police had resorted to cross-examination to wrest the confession from the suspect. The following passage may reflect his position most accurately:[120]

> [W]hen the stage has been reached at which suspicion, or more than suspicion, has in [the police] view centred upon some person as the likely perpetrator of the crime, further interrogation of that person becomes very dangerous, and, if carried too far, *e.g.*, to the point of extracting a confession by what amounts to cross-examination, the evidence of that confession will almost certainly be excluded.

In any event, Lord Cooper did offer a helpful definition of cross-examination, one clearly having as its source the trial model. He spoke of the appellant having been 'confronted with police information contradictory of the statement which he had already made'.[121] This seems to suggest that the line to be drawn, and surely a difficult one to draw in practice, is between questions inviting the suspect to give his account or clarifying it once given, on the one hand, and questions challenging or contradicting that account, on the other.

It is to be noted that Chalmers had been repeatedly warned of his right to remain silent and twice asked if he wished to have his father or a lawyer present, yet Lord Cooper stated that the impropriety of the proceedings could not be cured by the giving of 'any number of formal cautions'.[122] The emphasis of Lord Thomson's opinion is clearly upon a right not to be subjected to cross-examination rather than upon one to choose not to be subjected to it. If such a high premium is to be placed upon the privilege against self-incrimination in the context of police questioning, it would seem that Lord Thomson's *per se* rule gives it far

[117] 1954 JC 66, at 82. [118] See 1954 SLT 177, at 186. [119] 1954 JC 66, at 79.
[120] *Ibid.* 78. [121] *Ibid.* 75. [122] *Ibid.* 79.

more realistic protection than does *Miranda*. A continuing problem with *Miranda* is that it is hard to see how a decision whether to waive the right not to speak made while in police custody is any less subject to the coercive pressures of such custody than is the decision to speak itself. That is why it has been argued, albeit unsuccessfully, in some of the American cases that a suspect should not be taken validly to waive his right to silence unless he does so having taken the advice of and in the presence of a lawyer.

DEVELOPMENTS SINCE *CHALMERS*

Just as *Miranda* seems to have proved too strong a drink for the Supreme Court, so the forty-odd years since *Chalmers* have seen an evisceration of the beast there given birth. There are three distinct elements of the retreat from *Chalmers*.

First, it has been consistently stressed that fairness is the proper test of admissibility, the fairness in question being that of the accused's treatment by the police.[123] Whether or not it was, in fact, fair will depend on the particular circumstances of the given case, so there is clearly no *per se* rule forbidding cross-examination.

However, is the fact that the police resorted to cross-examination a factor, indeed an important factor, as regards the issue of fairness? In *Lord Advocate's Reference (No 1 of 1983)*, the High Court rejected it even as such a factor. Lord Justice-General Emslie said:[124]

> For the avoidance of doubt I should add that where in the opinions in the decided cases the word 'interrogation' or the expression 'cross-examination' is used in discussing unfair tactics on the part of the police it is to be understood to refer only to improper forms of questioning tainted with an element of bullying or pressure designed to break the will of the suspect or to force from him a confession against his will.

It will be apparent that his Lordship seems to have had in mind police questioning very like that which would constitute oppression in English law.[125] One might, indeed, use Lord Emslie's definition as an accurate description of the police questioning which was held to be oppressive in *Paris, Abdullahi and Miller*.[126] Yet the wheel may, possibly, have turned again very recently, in a way which breathes life back into the corpse of *Chalmers*. In *Codona* v. *HM Advocate*, Lord Justice-General Hope explicitly rejected the import of his predecessor's words, as follows:[127]

[123] See, e.g., *Brown* v. *HM Advocate*, 1966 SLT 105; *Miln* v. *Cullen*, 1967 JC 21; *Jones* v. *Milne*, 1975 SLT 2; *Hartley* v. *HM Advocate*, 1979 SLT 26; *Lord Advocate's Reference (No 1 of 1983)*, 1984 SLT 337; *HM Advocate* v. *Graham*, 1991 SCCR 56; *Codona* v. *HM Advocate*, 1996 SCCR 300.

[124] 1984 SLT 337, at 340.

[125] In *Jones* v. *Milne*, 1975 SLT 2, at 5, it had been indicated that cross-examination, pressure, and deception are placed in close company.

[126] (1992) 97 Cr.App.R 99, discussed in Ch. 5, text to nn. 23–5 and 29–30 above.

[127] 1996 SCCR 300, at 321.

The police may question a suspect, but when they move into the field of cross-examination or interrogation, they move into an area of great difficulty. If the questioning is carried too far, by means of leading or repetitive questioning or by pressure in other ways in an effort to obtain from the suspect what they are seeking to obtain from him, the statement is likely to be excluded on the ground that it was extracted by unfair means. Lord Justice-General Emslie's definition of the words 'interrogation' and 'cross-examination' . . . should not be understood as implying any weakening of these important principles.

It is to be noted that Codona itself involved a 14-year-old girl, suspected of taking part in a murder, who had been questioned closely and at very great length by officers who repeatedly pressed her to change her story and admit her guilt. The eventual result was that she broke down in tears and confessed. So it may be that Lord Justice-General Emslie would also have regarded her treatment as unfair. Nonetheless, it does seem possible that the substantive law is now just the same as Lord Cooper, though not Lord Thomson, thought it to be when delivering his opinion in *Chalmers*. At all events, it seems clear that Scottish judicial opinion is somewhat divided on the point.

A second element of the retreat from the full force of *Chalmers* is that fairness has come to be regarded as bilateral. So Lord Wheatley said in *Miln* v. *Cullen*:[128]

While the law of Scotland has always very properly regarded fairness to an accused person as being an integral part of the administration of justice, fairness is not a unilateral consideration. Fairness to the public is also a legitimate consideration, and in so far as police officers in the exercise of their duties are prosecuting and protecting the public interest, it is the function of the Court to seek to provide a proper balance to secure that the rights of individuals are properly preserved, while not hamstringing the police in their investigation of crime with a series of academic vetoes which ignore the realities and practicalities of the situation and discount completely the public interest.

This bilateral principle was endorsed by Lords Avonside and Grieve in the later case of *Hartley* v. *HM Advocate*,[129] and, most recently, by Lord Justice-Clerk Ross in *Harley* v. *HM Advocate*.[130]

Perhaps the most important change of all since *Chalmers* is one to do with procedure, rather than substantive law. Lords Cooper and Thomson were at one in regarding the proper procedure for deciding the issue of admissibility as being, essentially, that which the English common law required in the case of jury trial.[131] That issue being one for the judge to decide, he should exclude the jury and rule on it in their absence. In doing so, he would hear evidence relating to the circumstances attending the making of the confession. Should he rule it inadmissible, the jury would hear nothing about it, but, should he rule the other way, it would be open to each side to call their evidence again in the jury's presence. The only matter properly to be left to the jury would be the reliability of the confession. No issue about fairness of the accused's treatment, or whether or not he had been cross-examined, would be left to them.

[128] 1967 JC 21, at 29–30.
[129] 1979 SLT 26, at 28 and 31, respectively.
[130] 1995 SCCR 595, at 604.
[131] See Ch. 3, text to nn. 1–26 above.

It is now clear that both the fairness issue and the cross-examination issue are essentially for the jury to decide. Thus, Lord Wheatley has said: 'if two possible interpretations can properly be put on the situation, one of which falls into the category of fairness and the other into the category of unfairness, the judge should leave the determination of that issue to the jury'.[132] His Lordship explained, in a later case,[133] that the judge would normally be justified in withholding the statement only if satisfied on the undisputed relevant evidence that no reasonable jury could hold that that statement had been made voluntarily and not extracted by unfair or improper means. Juries, he said, were as well equipped as judges to decide whether or not an accused had been fairly treated. Indeed, to deny juries this decision would be to usurp their function, since the question '*ex hypothesi* has become a question of fact'.[134] That being the case, it will very rarely be necessary to hold a trial within a trial. Presumably, the holding of one might still be considered appropriate where, on the papers, the treatment of the accused seems so blatantly unfair that the judge would suppose that, if the evidence came out as the papers suggested, he would necessarily have to exclude the evidence on the basis of the 'no reasonable jury' test.[135] It is not clear how else improper prejudice to the accused could be avoided.[136]

In two recent cases, the High Court has overturned trial judges' decisions to leave issues of fairness to the jury. In *Harley* v. *HM Advocate*,[137] the court expressly referred to the 'no reasonable jury' test as being the one for the judge to apply and went on to hold that the standards of fairness had been so flagrantly transgressed that no reasonable jury could regard the accused's treatment as fair. In the other, *Codona* v. *HM Advocate*,[138] that court quashed the accused's conviction because she had been unfairly treated, but without making any reference to the governing test. The circumstances of *Harley* make it rather easy to explain. For one thing, the trial judge seems to have had in mind only the nature and content of the questioning as relevant to the issue of unfairness, and to have taken no account of a rather unpleasant threat or inducement which had been held out to the accused by the police. Secondly, where the alleged unfairness does take the form of a threat or inducement, the question at hand may seem less value-laden and subjective than where it relates to a more general notion of fair treatment. If so, it may be thought that the question in *Harley* was more obviously one for the judge than for the jury.[139] However, in *Codona*, as we have already seen, the unfairness alleged related solely to the length, nature, and content of the police questioning, and the

[132] *Murphy* v. *HM Advocate*, 1975 SLT (Notes) 17, at 18.

[133] *Balloch* v. *HM Advocate*, 1977 SLT (Notes) 29, at 30.

[134] *Ibid.*

[135] In *Aiton* v. *HM Advocate*, 1987 SCCR 252, the trial judge (Lord Weir) held a trial within a trial in a case which had no such unusual feature and, at the end of it, ruled the confession admissible.

[136] In *HM Advocate* v. *Mair*, 1982 SLT 471n., Lord Hunter stressed that there might sometimes be dangers of prejudice to the accused where the 'no reasonable jury' test was not satisfied—see 472.

[137] 1995 SCCR 595.

[138] 1996 SCCR 300.

[139] This is Sheriff Gordon's view—see his commentary on *Codona* v. *HM Advocate, ibid.* 322. His view may itself be not without difficulty, for it seems to assume that there is a *per se* rule of inadmissibility in cases of inducement, yet the authorities consistently say that the overall test is always that of fairness.

trial judge had certainly left that issue squarely with the jury. It seems conceivable, therefore, that *Codona* may be the harbinger of a more judge-centred approach to questions of inadmissibility. Perhaps jury equity has had its day.

Supporting Evidence or Warning Requirements for Confessions

Introduction

Ever since the Fisher Report on the *Confait* case[140] recommended that there should, in certain circumstances, be a requirement of law that a confession be supported by other evidence, it has been a matter of anxious debate among practitioners and academics alike whether or not some kind of supporting evidence or corroboration requirement, or, alternatively, a judicial warning requirement, ought to be instituted in England.[141] Two Royal Commissions have considered the issue, namely the Royal Commission on Criminal Procedure in 1981 and the Royal Commission on Criminal Justice in 1993. The former rejected the idea that an accused should never be convicted solely on the basis of confession evidence.[142] The latter, while rejecting a corroboration or supporting evidence requirement (albeit by majority), went on to recommend a mandatory judicial warning to the jury, the terms of which will be considered later.[143] Though various recommendations of that Royal Commission have been enacted, this one has not. For completeness, it should be recalled that section 77 of the 1984 Act does require warnings to be given in the case of certain confessions made by mentally handicapped accused persons.[144]

When discussing the present issue (which will be described here as the 'supporting evidence issue'), it is important to distinguish two different problems, to deal with which it has been suggested that one ought to look for supporting evidence. Most obviously, it may be argued that there are numerous examples of accused persons being convicted on the basis of confessions to crimes which they did not commit. The Royal Commission on Criminal Justice helpfully set out four categories of false confession. So:[145]

(i) people may make confessions entirely voluntarily as a result of a morbid desire for publicity or notoriety; or to relieve feelings of guilt about a real or imagined previous transgression; or because they cannot distinguish between reality and fantasy;

[140] *Report of an Inquiry by the Hon. Sir Henry Fisher into the circumstances leading to the trial of three persons on charges arising out of the death of Maxwell Confait and the fire at 27 Doggett Road, London S.E.6* (13 Dec. 1977), HC 90. See para. 2.26.

[141] *Wheeling* (1789) 1 Leach CC 311n. establishes that there is no such requirement at common law. There are two more fully reported Irish cases to similar effect—see *Unkles* (1873) Ir. R 8 CL 50 and *Sullivan* (1887) 16 Cox CC 347.

[142] See Royal Commission on Criminal Procedure, *Report*, Jan. 1981, Cmnd. 8092, para. 4.74.

[143] Royal Commission on Criminal Justice, *Report*, July 1993, Cm 2263, ch. 4, paras. 85–87.

[144] See Ch. 10, text to nn. 75–93 above.

[145] *Report*, n. 143 above, Ch. 4, para. 32. For an excellent general account and argument in favour of a supporting evidence warning requirement, see Pattenden (1991) 107 LQR 317.

(ii) a suspect may confess from a desire to protect someone else from interrogation and prosecution;
(iii) people may see a prospect of immediate advantage from confessing (e.g. an end to questioning or release from the police station), even though the long-term consequences are far worse (the resulting confessions are termed 'coerced-compliant' confessions); and
(iv) people may be persuaded temporarily by the interrogators that they really have done the act in question (the resulting confessions are termed 'coerced-internalised' confessions).

Though the exclusionary rule and discretion ought to be capable of rooting out some of the confessions rendered false in one of these ways, it is inconceivable that, even in principle, they will be able to root out all of them.[146] Hence, for many, the proper conclusion is that an additional safeguard is required. Thus, we ought to look for material which assures us that the confession in any given case is indeed true.

In addition, it was very often an issue in confession cases, before the introduction of contemporaneous recording requirements under the 1984 Act and, later on, of the tape-recording requirement under Code of Practice E made under that Act, whether or not the accused really had confessed as alleged. Except in the case of incriminating statements allegedly made outside the police station, the latter kind of problem must be very largely a thing of the past. But this is certainly not so with the former kind of problem.

A second preliminary point is that there is a variety of possible ways in which the law could intervene in the present respect. It could dictate that conviction solely on the basis of the accused's confession is not allowable. Yet the law would also have to decide what other evidence in the case would be necessary in order to permit conviction. Should it apply the full-blown definition of corroboration which once applied to the evidence of accomplices, children, and complainants in sexual cases,[147] and which is associated with the case of *Baskerville*?[148] That case restricted potentially corroborative evidence to that which was independent of the accused and which implicated him in the crime alleged. In a sense, the corroborative evidence is required to 'shadow' the evidence to be corroborated. It is insufficient that it merely supports the credibility of the witness or the testimony in need of corroboration.[149] Alternatively, it might adopt some less strict definition of supporting evidence, perhaps like that instituted, in the case of identification evidence, by *Turnbull*.[150] The other way in which the law could intervene would be to require, not that there be supporting evidence, but that the jury be warned of the need to look for it, and, should they find none, pause with great care before convicting on the basis of the confession alone. Obviously, if the

[146] See Pattenden, n. 145 above, 322–31.
[147] No corroboration or corroboration warning is now required in any of these cases—see Criminal Justice Act 1988, s. 34, and Criminal Justice and Public Order Act 1994, ss. 32 and 33.
[148] [1916] 2 KB 658.
[149] For a general discussion of the *Baskerville* test, see Mirfield (1991) 107 LQR 450.
[150] [1977] QB 224.

solution adopted is that of the warning, precisely the same issue of what is capable of counting as supporting evidence arises as does where the solution adopted is that of a requirement.

We shall consider here, first and briefly, the Australian law laid down in *McKinney and Judge*,[151] then, at somewhat greater length, the Scottish common law position, and finally the recommendations of the Royal Commission on Criminal Justice.

Supporting Evidence in Australia

A bare majority of the High Court of Australia in *McKinney and Judge* introduced a supporting evidence warning requirement for cases where a person who was in custody is alleged to have confessed, but disputes that allegation. The requirement applies where the only, or substantially the only, basis for finding the accused's guilt proved is a confession 'the making of which is not reliably corroborated'.[152] The limitations of the application of the ruling should be made explicit. The accused must have been in custody at the time, though not necessarily at a police station. He must dispute the allegation that the confession was made at all or (presumably) that it had the substantive content alleged by the prosecution.[153] So where the accused admits that he did confess, but denies the truth of that confession, no warning is required.[154] Conversely, of course, there is no relevant corroboration if the extraneous evidence merely tends to show the confession to be true, rather than confirming that it was made.[155] The significance of this last point is much reduced by the fact that the warning is not called for unless the confession is the only, or substantially the only, evidence of guilt,[156] for, if other evidence shows the confession to be true, it must inevitably constitute evidence of guilt.

The combination of all the various limitations described above is such as to make *McKinney and Judge* of rather slight significance. It concerns itself not at all with the various categories of *false* confession to which reference has already been made.[157] Even within those limitations, the doctrine would have little impact in relation to present-day English procedures. It is absolutely clear that the support may be provided by a taped record of the making of the alleged confession. The making of such records is now a routine feature of interviews at the English police station. Of course, such an interview may go unrecorded in fact. Also, the prosecution may allege that the accused confessed or made some admission outside the context of the formal interview at the police station. It may be doubted whether the *McKinney and Judge* warning requirement, with the

[151] (1991) 171 CLR 468. [152] *Ibid.* 476.

[153] No doubt the existence of a trivial dispute about mere detail would not suffice to trip the warning.

[154] See *Butler (No 2)* (1991) 57 A Crim.R 460, at 466–7 (*per* Kearney J).

[155] See *Asfour* (1992) 60 A Crim.R 409, at 412 (*per* Hunt CJ at CL).

[156] As confirmed by *Small* (1994) 33 NSWLR 575. [157] See text to n. 145 above.

complexities of directing the jury which must inevitably attend it, and the opportunities for appeal resulting therefrom,[158] would really be worth adopting in England for such a slight gain. Another possibility would be the simple one of excluding all unrecorded confessions altogether, though this step was rejected by the Royal Commission on Criminal Justice.[159]

Corroboration in Scotland

Scottish law imposes a *general* requirement of corroboration in respect of all evidence.[160] It follows that an accused cannot be convicted solely on the basis of his own confession, however freely and voluntarily made. However, there is a danger of supposing that the requirement is far more strict than it really is, and, therefore, of over-estimating its significance as a protection of the accused against conviction on the basis of a false confession.

We may begin with the statement of the law given by Lord Justice-Clerk Thomson in *Connolly* v. *HM Advocate*. He said:[161]

> A confession of guilt—short of a formal plea of guilty— isn't enough. There must be evidence from some other source which incriminates the accused. If all that the Crown can produce is evidence—however complete and exhaustive—that a crime has been committed together with evidence, however credible, that the accused confessed to having committed it, the Crown must fail. There must be something incriminatory of the accused spoken to by someone other than the accused.

There are three important points to make about this statement. First, one needs to be aware that the notion that 'something incriminatory of the accused' must be spoken to by a witness is not at all the *Baskerville* notion that the corroborating evidence must incriminate the accused in a material particular. A good example of the difference between *Baskerville* corroboration and Scottish corroboration in this respect is provided by *Hartley* v. *HM Advocate*[162] Hartley, aged 17, had confessed to the murder of a boy, aged 5, who had been drowned in a burn. An eye-witness had seen a struggle between a big boy and a small one, but his description of the clothes the big boy had been wearing did not fit with what Hartley had been wearing. The supporting material which the prosecution *was* able to provide amounted to no more than evidence of Hartley's pre-sence at or near the scene and of his having had the opportunity to kill the small boy. It was certainly not evidence that he had taken that opportunity, yet all three members of the High Court thought it sufficient corroboration. In the words of Lord Dunpark: 'there must be evidence, independent of the accused's confession, that the accused was at the locus at or about the time

[158] For a valuable treatment of these complexities, see Ligertwood, *Australian Evidence* 2nd. edn., 1993), para. 4.19.

[159] See *Report*, n. 143 above, ch. 4, para. 50.

[160] For a stimulating recent explanation and account, see Gordon in *Justice and Crime* (ed. Hunter, 1993), at 33 ff.

[161] 1958 SLT 79, at 80. [162] 1979 SLT 26.

when the wee boy was drowned as corroboration of the accused's statement that he drowned him'.[163]

A second point arising from Lord Thomson's statement is that the suggestion that the incriminatory fact must be spoken to by 'someone other than the accused' is apt to mislead. Scotland has a special knowledge rule in relation to confessions.[164] So if, say, the accused revealed the whereabouts of the body of his victim,[165] the evidence of the police officer that he found the body where indicated by the accused would be capable of corroborating the confession. The special knowledge demonstrated by the accused would constitute the corroboration. This is plainly a case of self-corroboration, and it is misleading to say that the fact was spoken to by the police officer. He simply said where he found the body; it was the accused's confession which demonstrated his special knowledge.[166] However, at least if one could be confident that the knowledge really was 'special', one might properly say that it strongly supported the truthfulness of the confession. In fact, Scottish law has developed in such a way that one cannot be at all confident of the special quality of the knowledge. It is clear that it is unneces-sary that, at the time the accused revealed that knowledge, the police themselves did not have it.[167] Of course, this makes it entirely possible that the police, either knowingly or inadvertently, have conveyed the relevant information to the accused before he confessed.[168] Equally, it does not matter that the information was available to the public, or known in the circles in which the accused moved, before he confessed.[169] It seems that the question for the judge to decide is merely whether or not a reasonable jury could conclude that the accused's accurate knowledge was his own knowledge as one of the perpetrators of the crime.[170] The following remarks about the special knowledge rule, made, by Sheriff Gordon, are hard to gainsay:[171]

> It is, therefore, a little misleading to say that a person cannot be convicted of a crime in Scotland on the basis only of a confession made by him to the police. He can be virtually so convicted, providing only that the confession is sufficiently detailed to satisfy a jury that it is reliable, and provided that the fact that the crime was committed by someone is independently proved.

A third feature of the corroboration of confessions is revealed by *Hartley* v. *HM Advocate*.[172] Where the confession is itself unequivocal, 'little is required by way of corroboration'.[173] The reason why corroboration need satisfy only a lower standard in such a case was explained by Lord Dunpark:[174]

[163] 1979 SLT 26. [164] See, e.g., *Manuel* v. *HM Advocate* 1958 JC 41.

[165] As in *Manuel*, *ibid*., itself.

[166] The English courts have sometimes been a prey to similar fallacious reasoning—see *Willoughby* (1988) 88 Cr.App.R 91; *McInnes* (1989) 90 Cr.App.R 99; *Ensor* [1989] 1 WLR 497. See also Mirfield, n. 149 above, 454–62.

[167] *Wilson* v. *McAughey*, 1982 SCCR 398. [168] See, e.g., *Bainbridge* v. *Scott*, 1988 SLT 871.

[169] *Wilson* v. *HM Advocate*, 1987 SCCR 217.

[170] See *ibid*. 222 (*per* Lord Justice-General Emslie).

[171] See commentary on *Wilson* v. *HM Advocate*, *ibid*. 223. [172] 1979 SLT 26.

[173] *Ibid*. 31 (*per* Lord Grieve). See also at 29 (*per* Lord Avonside).

[174] *Ibid*. 33. And see *ibid*. 300 (for correction of original report).

unlike such other evidence, the confession of guilt by an accused person is prejudicial to his own interests and may, therefore, initially be assumed to be true. Accordingly, one is not then looking for extrinsic evidence which is more consistent with his guilt than with his innocence, but for extrinsic evidence which is consistent with his confession of guilt. If, therefore, a jury is satisfied that a confession of guilt was freely made and unequivocal in its terms, corroboration of that confession may be found in evidence from another source or other sources which point to the truth of the confession.

The problem with this approach is that the confession may be entirely unequivocal, may have been obtained without any unfair treatment of the accused, and yet be wholly unreliable, whether because a coerced-compliant or a coerced-internalized one, or whatever. Logically, it would seem, the corroboration requirement should be addressing concerns not foreclosed by unequivocality and admissibility. This seems to have been recognized by Lord Justice-General Hope in *Meredith* v. *Lees*.[175] He pointed out that there was no *rule* that little was required by way of corroboration in these cases. Rather, everything turned upon the circumstances of the case, and, more specifically, upon the circumstances in which the confession was made. Those circumstances 'may leave room for doubt as to whether it is true and can be relied upon'.[176] For example, though the confession is ruled admissible by the judge, the elements of the case which led the defence to argue for exclusion for unfairness may also leave ample basis for doubt about the reliability of the accused's admittedly unequivocal confession. Here, presumably, a great deal should be required by way of corroboration.[177]

We may properly conclude that there is much in the Scottish authorities to make English lawyers pause long before embracing its corroboration requirement as a panacea for dealing with the outstanding problems concerned with false confessions.

Recommendations of the Royal Commission

A majority of the Royal Commission on Criminal Justice was not persuaded by the chimerical attractions of the Scottish law, though a minority of three did favour a supporting evidence requirement broadly similar to the Scottish corroboration requirement, albeit without the special knowledge rule.[178] Their fellow Commissioners favoured a supporting evidence *warning* requirement.[179] It is clear that they had in mind something very similar to the *Turnbull* warning for identification cases.[180]

The precise terms of the warning should, they suggest, depend upon the particular circumstances of the case,[181] no set formula or incantation being

[175] 1992 SCCR 458. [176] *Ibid*. 463. [177] See Gordon, n. 160 above, 49–56.

[178] See *Report*, n. 143 above, ch. 4, para. 86. [179] See *ibid*., paras. 77 and 87.

[180] [1977] QB 224. This solution is also favoured by Pattenden—see n. 145 above, 338–9. For a less radical suggestion, see Choo [1991] Crim.LR 867, at 876–7.

[181] For all the proposals in the present para., see *Report*, n. 143 above, ch. 4. para. 77.

required.[182] Still, the judge should warn the jury that great care is needed before convicting on the basis of a confession alone and should explicitly refer to possible reasons for persons confessing falsely. In this context, the jury's attention should be drawn to any such reason which has been advanced by the defence. The judge should then direct the jury on which parts, if any, of the evidence given are capable of supporting the confession. Where there is no such evidence, the judge should tell the jury so. He should then go on to tell them of the need for caution before convicting on the basis of the unsupported confession, but explain that, having given his warning full weight, they may properly convict in its absence if satisfied of the truth of the confession.

There are several points to be made about these proposals. First, there is no provision, equivalent to that in *Turnbull*, for cases where the evidence in need of support is itself weak. This is presumably because, where a confession is weak in terms of reliability, it ought to have been excluded by the judge anyway under section 76 or 78 of the 1984 Act. Secondly, it may be thought that the jury will find judicial remarks about the grounds of unreliability relied upon by the defence in the particular case more helpful than remarks of a general kind. Thirdly, there would be no escape from the problem of *defining* supporting evidence. The Royal Commission, as we have already noted, would have defined it in the *Turnbull* sense.[183] It is not clear that transportation of the *Turnbull* doctrine into this context would be entirely appropriate. For example, one writer proposes that the repetition of the confession to some non-police person should be capable of providing support.[184] Certainly, *Turnbull* allows the identification evidence to be supported by other identification evidence, at least if high in quality,[185] but that entails no *self*-corroboration, whereas the repeated confession example would. At all events, that definition would have to be applied by the judge, to the material in the particular case, so we may suppose that fertile ground for possible appeals would be laid.[186] Finally, not everyone will be content with a direction that one should be cautious before convicting on the basis of an unsupported confession alone, but then goes on to say that the jury may properly do so. However, this argument challenges the whole basis for warning directions, including those dictated by *Turnbull*, and should probably be rejected for that reason. In any event, others will say that there is nothing irrational about instructing the jury to think hard before acting on the basis of particular kinds of evidence.[187]

It should be noted that the Royal Commission drew attention also to the possibility that the basis of challenge to the confession might be that it had not been made, or, at least, not been made as alleged by the police. In its view, the warning

[182] This is equivalent to the position in respect of identification evidence—see *Keane* (1977) 65 Cr.App.R 247, at 248.

[183] See *Report*, n. 143 above, ch. 4, 338.

[184] Pattenden, n. 145 above, 338.

[185] See *Weeder* (1980) 71 Cr.App.R 228.

[186] This was one reason why the Law Commission recommended abolition of the corroboration rules—see Law Com. No 202, Cm 1620, Sept. 1991, para. 2.9.

[187] As the Royal Commission itself argues—see *Report*, n. 143 above, ch. 4, para. 79.

should be required to be given where the (alleged) confession had not been tape-recorded.[188] Having drawn attention to this fact, the judge should go on to refer to any possible motive the person to whom the confession was allegedly made might have for fabrication. This may be thought rather problematical, for the police *always* have a *motive* for fabrication. Indeed, the minority of the High Court of Australia in *McKinney and Judge*[189] objected to the warning requirement favoured by the majority very largely because they believed that it had the effect of treating police evidence as presumptively suspect. Perhaps the Royal Commission had in mind particular motives specific to the case at hand. It is not entirely clear whether it would have wished to adopt the Australian model, requiring a warning only in cases where, in essence, the whole case against the accused depends on the confession, or would have the warning given in all cases where the confession was made as alleged. However, given the pattern of its recommendations for allegedly false confessions, one might properly assume that the Commission favoured the latter alternative.

Research carried out for the Commission suggested that, even were a corroboration requirement which took corroboration in the *Baskerville* sense to be instituted, only 5 per cent of confession cases which presently result in convictions would then result in acquittals.[190] Of course, a less strict view of supporting evidence than that embraced by *Baskerville* would be expected to reduce that percentage, while the autonomy of the jury to convict even in the absence of supporting evidence might be expected to reduce it further. So the 'cost', in terms of lost convictions, of legislating the Commission's proposals might be thought not very great. And those who favour a supporting evidence requirement would surely argue that any such 'cost' is not a real one, for all that would happen is that those who cannot safely be convicted would not be convicted.

Exclusion for Unfairness or to Defend Judicial Integrity

Naturally enough, many jurisdictions apart from the English one have struggled with the issue of whether or not evidence should be excluded where in some way or other it has been obtained illegally, improperly, or unfairly. No attempt will be made here to present a comprehensive account of the law of the jurisdictions to which reference will be made. Rather, some elements of the legal régimes in question which may be thought to have particular interest for purposes of comparison with English law will be given attention.

It will be recalled that, at least since the Privy Council's decision in *Kuruma*,[191] the English common law has recognized a judicial discretion to exclude both confessional and non-confessional evidence for unfairness.[192] Probably, after the House of Lords decided *Sang*,[193] the sole aspect of fairness with which that

[188] See *ibid.*, ch. 4, para. 77.
[189] (1991) 171 CLR 468.
[190] See (by McConville), Research Study No 13 (1993), at 84–6.
[191] [1955] AC 197.
[192] See the discussion in Ch. 6, text to nn. 10–32 above.
[193] [1980] AC 402.

discretion was concerned was the one encapsulated by the maxim *nemo debet prodere se ipsum.* Certain other jurisdictions having the common law as their source, or which are strongly influenced by it, have rejected fairness to the particular accused, whether in that narrow sense or some other, as the organizing principle in favour of the idea that what really matters is that those who enforce the law should themselves comply with it. In addition, some jurisdictions have not accepted that exclusion should be a matter only of judicial discretion, preferring instead to apply an admittedly open-textured exclusionary rule. It is particularly notable that, where the lawfulness of official conduct, instead of its fairness to the accused, has been emphasized, the courts, and now in Australia the legislature,[194] have provided guidelines in relation to the judicial decision whether or not to exclude. We shall consider each of the relevant jurisdictions in turn.

SCOTLAND

The Rule in Lawrie *v.* Muir

In *Lawrie* v. *Muir*,[195] the High Court of Justiciary expressly recognized the existence of a rule requiring the exclusion of unlawfully or irregularly obtained non-confessional evidence. In doing so, it relied upon *dicta* of Lord Justice-Clerk Aitchison in *HM Advocate* v. *McGuigan* that '[a]n irregularity in the obtaining of evidence does not necessarily make that evidence inadmissible',[196] but turned that proposition of law from a negative one to a positive one:[197]

> Irregularities require to be excused, and infringements of the formalities of the law in relation to these matters are not lightly to be condoned. Whether any given irregularity ought to be excused depends upon the nature of the irregularity and the circumstances under which it was committed.

In modern terminology, this amounts to a reverse onus exclusionary rule, for illegally or irregularly obtained evidence is to be excluded unless the prosecution can show some good reason why it should be admitted.

The rule retains its vitality almost half a century later. The point may be illustrated by two recent cases. In *Graham* v. *Orr*,[198] the High Court ruled that a search of the accused's car had been unlawful. It followed that the drugs which the officer had then found in the car had been acquired unlawfully by him. Since the prosecution had not managed to provide any good reason for excusal of the irregularity, it followed that the evidence of the finding of the drugs was inadmissible. In *Wilson* v. *Brown*,[199] stewards at a 'rave' believed the accused to have drugs in his possession. They were entitled to detain him only until the arrival of the police, yet they searched him and found drugs. Here the judge had allowed evidence of that finding to be given, because the accused had been behaving

[194] See Evidence Act (Commonwealth) 1995, s 138(3) and Evidence Act (NSW) 1995, s. 138(3).
[195] 1950 JC 19. [196] 1936 JC 16, at 18.
[197] See 1950 JC 19, at 27 (*per* Lord Justice-General Cooper). [198] 1995 SCCR 30.
[199] 1996 SCCR 470.

suspiciously and because it was prudent for the stewards to search him in case he was carrying a weapon. The High Court rejected both reasons. The first merely justified the accused's detention, not his being searched. The second was not made out on the facts, for it was clear that the stewards had never had in mind that the accused might have a weapon. Expressly applying the law as stated in *Lawrie* v. *Muir*, the High Court ruled the evidence inadmissible and quashed the conviction.

The Principle Behind the Rule

It is not easy to discern what principle lies behind the rule laid down in *Lawrie* v. *Muir*. In the case itself, Lord Justice-General Cooper said:[200]

> From the standpoint of principle it seems to me that the law must strive to reconcile two highly important interests which are liable to come into conflict—(a) the interest of the citizen to be protected from illegal or irregular invasions of his liberties by the authorities, and (b) the interest of the state to secure that evidence bearing upon the commission of crime and necessary to enable justice to be done shall not be withheld from Courts of law on any merely formal or technical ground.

Viewed without reference to what else was said in the case, this might be thought to amount to endorsement of the disciplinary principle, for the police should be discouraged from committing real and substantial breaches of the laws protecting the rights of the citizen. Alternatively, it might be thought to constitute recognition of the judicial integrity principle in one of its guises, for the courts ought not to offer 'a positive inducement to the authorities to proceed by irregular methods'.[201] And, indeed, it was certainly taken as support for either the disciplinary or the judicial integrity principle—probably the latter—in the important Australian High Court case of *Bunning* v. *Cross*,[202] a case to be considered in detail later in this section of the present Chapter.

However, the position is complicated by the following further remarks of the Lord Justice-General:[203]

> In particular, the case may bring into play the discretionary principle of fairness to the accused which has been developed so fully in our law in relation to the admission in evidence of confessions or admissions by a person suspected or charged with crime. That principle would obviously require consideration in any case in which the departure from the strict procedure had been adopted deliberately with a view to securing the admission of evidence obtained by an unfair trick.

Here, the emphasis appears to be upon what the particular accused was entitled to expect, rather than upon some forward-looking principle. The passage also seems to take us away from behaviour contrary to law and towards unfair police tactics such as trickery. Yet in their context the words may have been intended to do no more than indicate that an irregularity will be the harder to excuse or condone where some *deliberate* act of trickery was employed in failing to comply

[200] 1950 JC 19, at 26. [201] *Ibid*. 27. [202] See (1978) 141 CLR 54, at 75–6.
[203] 1950 JC 19, at 27.

with the prescribed procedure.[204] At all events, the apparent equivocality of Lord Cooper's various remarks in *Lawrie* v. *Muir* has certainly led the Privy Council on two occasions to conclude that fairness to the accused, rather than irregularity of official conduct, is the essential concern of Scots law in this area.[205]

Guidelines

The final feature of Scots law to be mentioned is that the courts have developed a number of guidelines in relation to the inclusionary element of excuse or condonation.[206] These guidelines are quite similar to those which, as we shall see, were developed by the High Court of Australia in *Bunning* v. *Cross*,[207] and are now to be found in the two sections 138(3) of the two Australian Evidence Acts of 1995. Detailed consideration will be given to guidelines of that kind when the Australian law is discussed,[208] but a brief treatment of some of the Scottish guidelines will be necessary here in order to allow comparison with the position in Ireland. First, the irregularity may be excused by the urgency or emergency of the circumstances, as where evidence may be lost if not seized immediately.[209] Secondly, the fact that the irregularity was the result of mistake or oversight, rather than having been deliberate, tends towards admission of the evidence.[210] Thirdly, the relative triviality or technicality of the breach will undoubtedly be a factor tending to excuse the irregularity.[211] Finally, in *Lawrie* v. *Muir* itself Lord Cooper intimated that the more serious the offence being investigated the less likely will be exclusion of evidence,[212] though in another case the same judge was not prepared to excuse an unlawful taking of scrapings from an accused's fingernails where the offence charged involved safebreaking with the use of explosives.[213]

IRELAND

The Exclusionary Rule for Evidence Obtained in Breach of the Constitution

In Ireland, a distinction is drawn between cases where some right granted to the citizen by the Constitution has been breached, on the one hand, and cases of otherwise unlawful action, on the other. In relation to the latter, there exists a discretion to exclude evidence, but there is no presumption in favour of exclusion, unlike in Scotland.[214] By contrast, where a constitutional right has been breached,

[204] This seems to be supported by Lord Cooper's own opinion in *Fairley* v. *Fishmongers of London* 1951 JC 14, at 24, and by that of Lord Guthrie in *HM Advocate* v. *Turnbull* 1951 JC 96, at 103–4.

[205] See *Kuruma* [1955] AC 197, at 204; *King* v. *R.* [1969] 1 AC 304, at 315–17. In *Sang* [1980] AC 402, at 447–9, Lord Fraser sought to set the record straight, though not entirely successfully.

[206] They are helpfully detailed by Heydon [1973] Crim.LR 603, at 608–10 and by Wilkinson, *The Scottish Law of Evidence* (1986), at 122.

[207] (1978) 141 CLR 54.

[208] See text to nn. 236–66 below.

[209] See, e.g., *HM Advocate* v. *Hepper* 1958 JC 39; *MacNeil* v. *HM Advocate*, 1986 SCCR 288.

[210] In this respect, one may compare *Fairley* v. *Fishmongers of London* 1951 JC 13 with *HM Advocate* v. *Turnbull* 1951 JC 96.

[211] See *M'Govern* v. *HM Advocate* 1950 JC 33, at 37.

[212] 1950 JC 19, at 27.

[213] *M'Govern* v. *HM Advocate* 1950 JC 33.

[214] *The People* v. *O'Brien* [1965] IR 142, at 160–1 (*per* Kingsmill Moore J).

a reverse onus rule applies. In the leading recent case, *The People* v. *Kenny*, Finlay CJ stated the rule as follows:[215]

> evidence obtained by invasion of the constitutional personal rights of a citizen must be excluded unless a court is satisfied that either the act constituting the breach of constitutional rights was committed unintentionally or accidentally, or is satisfied that there are extraordinary excusing circumstances which justify the admission of the evidence in its (the court's) discretion.

It will be apparent that there is considerable similarity between this rule about unconstitutionally obtained evidence and the Scots rule about all unlawfully or irregularly obtained evidence. However, there are several significant differences.

Scope of the Exclusionary Rule

After some initial doubt, it is now settled that the rule, unlike its Scots counterpart, applies no less to confessional than to non-confessional evidence.[216] A second difference is that the exclusionary element of the rule is brought into action only where the breach was deliberate and conscious, whereas the Scots rule is tripped simply by the fact of unlawfulness or irregularity. However, the importance of this point must not be overestimated. Though a majority of the Supreme Court in *The People* v. *Shaw*[217] took the view that what matters is whether the police knew that they were violating the accused's constitutional rights, and not whether their acts were themselves deliberate and conscious, this view has now been rejected authoritatively by the same court in *The People* v. *Kenny*[218] (by majority) and in *Larkin* v. *O'Dea*[219] unanimously.[220] In *Larkin* v. *O'Dea*, Finlay CJ's formulation of the law in *The People* v. *Kenny*, already cited, was endorsed. That formulation makes it clear that it is only where the *acts* of the police were unintentional or accidental that the exclusionary element of the rule is not tripped. There is, of course, a crucial difference between the two views, for the now-rejected view would disapply the rule where the police were ignorant either of the law itself or of its application to the facts. The latter, at least, might be supposed to be a not uncommon state of affairs. Finlay CJ's view, by contrast, means that the exclusionary element will almost inevitably be tripped by breach, for it is highly unlikely that the police will, say, enter the citizen's house without realizing that they are doing so. In this respect, both *Kenny* and *Larkin* v. *O'Dea* were themselves strong cases, involving as they did evidence obtained through use by the police of an invalid search warrant issued by a neutral judicial officer, i.e. a rather technical breach.

[215] [1990] 2 IR 110, at 134.

[216] A majority of the Supreme Court in *The People* v. *Shaw* [1982] IR 1 was of the view that it did not so apply, but that view has been rejected by the same court in *The People* v. *Lynch* [1982] IR 64 and in *The People* v. *Healy* [1990] 2 IR 73. See also *The People* v. *Madden* [1977] IR 336; *The People* v. *O'Loughlin* [1979] IR 85.

[217] [1982] IR 1. [218] [1990] 2 IR 110. [219] [1995] 2 ILRM 1.

[220] See also *The People* v. *Walsh* [1980] IR 294, at 317; *The People* v. *Healy* [1990] 2 IR 73; *The People* v. *Connell* [1995] 1 IR 244.

The Principle Behind the Rule

An additional point of difference from the Scottish position is that the Supreme Court seems to have based the rule upon the protective principle, and not upon discipline or judicial integrity. In *Kenny*, in a judgment with which Walsh and Hederman JJ agreed, Finlay CJ described the decision of the US Supreme Court in *US* v. *Leon*[221] as 'clearly and expressly based upon the principle of deterrence rather than the principle of absolute protection of the constitutional right concerned'[222] and went on to express a preference for the principle of absolute protection.[223] Indeed, that was why he rejected the idea that the police must have known themselves to be in breach of the accused's constitutional rights. He also said that it was the duty of the court to 'defend and vindicate such rights'.[224] It should be added that he did also point out that to embrace the absolute protection rule would be to encourage the police to consider in detail the personal constitutional rights of the citizen, and so seemed to strike a forward-looking stance, rather than a remedial one. However, it may be that his Lordship had in mind that the stringency of the protection provided for the accused in cases like *Kenny* itself would be such as to have the very welcome side-effect of promoting greater police care and respect for the constitutional rights of citizens in future. There is certainly no hint of approval of the judicial integrity principle, in whatever guise. Furthermore, in *The State (Trimbole)* v. *The Governor of Mountjoy Prison*, in a judgment with which three other members of the Supreme Court expressed their agreement, Finlay CJ referred to the court's duty 'to restore as far as possible the person . . . to the position in which he would be if his rights had not been invaded'.[225] There could be no clearer endorsement of the protective principle.

It may be added that it is now firmly established that evidence is to be excluded only if the constitutional breach *caused* it to be acquired.[226] A rigorous application of a causation requirement is much more obviously explained in terms of the backward-looking protective principle than of the disciplinary principle.[227] So far as judicial integrity is concerned, only court-centred integrity would seem consistent with a causation *requirement*, for both the public conduct and public attitude forms of the principle are forward-looking.[228]

The Inclusionary Exception

The final difference from Scots law concerns the inclusionary exception to the exclusionary rule. The authorities refer consistently to 'extraordinary excusing

[221] 468 US 897 (1984). The case is discussed in the text to nn. 22–32 above.

[222] See [1990] 2 IR 110, at 130. [223] See *ibid*. 133. [224] See *ibid*.

[225] [1985] IR 550, at 573.

[226] See *Walsh* v. *District Justice Donnacha O Buachalla and the DPP* [1991] IR 56; *The People* v. *Healy* [1990] 2 IR 73; *DPP* v. *Spratt* [1995] 1 IR 585.

[227] See the discussion in Ch. 2 text to n. 64 above.

[228] For a discussion of the various forms of the judicial integrity principle, see Ch. 2, text to n. 77 above.

circumstances'.[229] It will be recalled that the *Lawrie* v. *Muir* rule simply refers to the possibility that irregularities may be excused, though it does also say that they are 'not lightly to be condoned'.[230] There is no doubt that the Irish law creates a much higher hurdle for the prosecution than does the Scottish. In *The People* v. *O'Brien*, Walsh J gave as examples of extraordinary excusing circumstances the prospect of 'imminent destruction of vital evidence' and 'the need to rescue a victim in peril'.[231] So far as the former example is concerned, it is clear that Scots law requires neither that the prospect of loss of evidence be imminent nor that it be vital evidence. Thus, in a case where dental impressions had been unlawfully made of the accused's teeth in order to compare them with teeth marks found on the body of a murder victim, it was said to be sufficient to meet the urgency requirement that the accused might have visited the dentist or injured his teeth.[232] In another case, it sufficed to meet that requirement that documents unlawfully seized by the police 'possibly might have some bearing' on the whereabouts of money which the accused was suspected of having stolen.[233] Turning to Walsh J's rescue example, there could hardly be a more pressing need than to save someone from physical danger.[234]

Walsh J gave one other example of a situation of excuse, namely one in which the evidence had been obtained by a warrantless search incidental to and contemporaneous with a lawful arrest. This might be thought to be an example of a trivial breach. However, it must be said that the fact that the Supreme Court held, in two later cases, that it was insufficient excuse that the breach was that of a neutral judicial officer in issuing an invalid search warrant[235] rather suggests that this particular example may not be a valid one. There does not seem to have been any suggestion in the Irish cases that the seriousness of the offence under investigation is a factor relevant to the decision whether or not to exclude. So far as breaches which result from mistake or oversight are concerned, it must presumably follow from rejection of the idea that the exclusionary element is tripped only by knowing breaches of the accused's constitutional rights that the good faith of the police officer cannot be relied upon as an excusing circumstance for purposes of the inclusionary element.

Australia

Development of the Bunning *v.* Cross *Discretion*

Until the High Court of Australia decided *Bunning* v. *Cross*[236] in 1978, Australian law seemed to embrace a view of the discretion to exclude both confessional and

[229] The source of the phrase is the judgment of Walsh J in *The People* v. *O'Brien* [1965] IR 142, at 170. See also, e.g., *The People* v. *Lynch* [1982] IR 64, at 77 (*per* O'Higgins CJ); *The People* v. *Kenny* [1990] 2 IR 110, at 134 (*per* Finlay CJ).

[230] 1950 JC 19, at 27, cited in the text to nn. 195–7 above.

[231] [1965] IR 142, at 170.

[232] *Hay* v. *HM Advocate*, 1968 SLT 334.

[233] *HM Advocate* v. *McKay* 1961 JC 47, at 51.

[234] This particular circumstance was found to be present in *The People* v. *Shaw* [1982] IR 1.

[235] *The People* v. *Kenny* [1990] 2 IR 110; *Larkin* v. *O'Dea* [1995] 2 ILRM 1.

[236] (1978) 141 CLR 54.

non-confessional evidence essentially the same as that of the English common law. Either kind of evidence might be excluded on the basis that its use against the accused would be unfair to him, having regard to how it had been obtained. This was established for confessions by *McDermott*[237] and *Lee*,[238] though it seems to have been a matter of assumption, rather than clear precedent, in the case of non-confessional evidence.[239] In *Ireland*, Zelling J, sitting in the Supreme Court of South Australia, departed from his brethren in changing the emphasis from unfairness to the unlawfulness of the police conduct which led to the evidence being obtained and, in so doing, relied upon the Scottish and Irish authorities.[240] When that case reached the High Court, Barwick CJ, delivering the only substantial judgment, combined the elements of unlawfulness and unfairness in relation to the obtaining of the evidence, in the following words:[241]

> Whenever such unlawfulness or unfairness appears, the judge has a discretion to reject the evidence . . . In the exercise of it, the competing public requirements must be considered and weighed against each other. On the one hand there is the public need to bring to conviction those who commit criminal offences. On the other hand there is the public interest in the protection of the individual from unlawful and unfair treatment. Convictions obtained by the aid of unlawful or unfair acts may be obtained at too high a price. Hence the judicial discretion.

Though Barwick CJ appeared to stick to his guns in *Bunning* v. *Cross*, once again making unfairness no less than unlawfulness central to the exercise of the discretion, he also explicitly endorsed the approach of Stephen and Aickin JJ[242] which was, in fact, a significantly different one. For them, unlawfulness alone was to the fore, with unfairness playing no more than a subsidiary role:[243]

> What *Ireland* involves is no simple question of ensuring fairness to an accused but instead the weighing against each other of two competing requirements of public policy, thereby seeking to resolve the apparent conflict between the desirable goal of bringing to conviction the wrongdoer and the undesirable effect of curial approval, or even encouragement, being given to the unlawful conduct of those whose task it is to enforce the law. This being the aim of the discretionary process called for by *Ireland* it follows that it by no means takes as its central point the question of unfairness to the accused. It is, on the contrary, concerned with broader questions of high public policy, unfairness to the accused being only one factor which, if present, will play its part in the whole process of consideration.

What is now clear is that this *Bunning* v. *Cross* discretion has replaced the unfairness discretion in the case of non-confessional evidence but exists alongside that discretion in the case of confessions.[244] This is acknowledged and confirmed by the Evidence Act (Commonwealth) 1995, section 90 of which provides for the

[237] (1948) 76 CLR 501. [238] (1950) 82 CLR 133.

[239] See, e.g., the treatment of the topic in *Cross on Evidence* (2nd Australian edn., 1979), by Gobbo, Byrne, and Heydon, paras. 12.42–12.45.

[240] [1970] SASR 416, at 444–7. [241] (1970) 126 CLR 321, at 335.

[242] See (1978) 141 CLR 54, at 64–5. [243] See *ibid*. 74–5.

[244] See *Cleland* (1982) 151 CLR 1,; *Pollard* (1992) 176 CLR 177; *Foster* (1993) 113 ALR 1.

unfairness discretion for confessions only, section 138 for the *Bunning* v. *Cross* discretion for all evidence.[245]

The Principle Behind the Discretion

In *Ireland*, Barwick CJ spoke both about the need to protect the individual from unlawfulness and unfairness and the need to balance that need against the need to convict the guilty. Thus, there is some doubt about what he believed to be the organizing rationale for exclusion. For Stephen and Aickin JJ, in *Bunning* v. *Cross*, it appears to be much more clearly a matter of judicial integrity, for it is the court which must not provide approval for or encouragement of unlawful police conduct. This equivocality about the organizing principle behind the discretion may well have been removed by the High Court itself in *Ridgeway*.[246] Four members of a full court lent their support to judicial integrity, Mason CJ, Deane and Dawson JJ saying that '[t]he basis in principle of the discretion lies in the inherent or implied powers of our courts to protect the integrity of their processes'.[247] For his part, McHugh J referred to 'the public interest in ensuring that public confidence in the justice system is not undermined by the perception that the courts of law condone or encourage unlawful or improper conduct on the part of those who have the duty to enforce the law'.[248] This would appear to be support for that variation of the judicial integrity[249] principle which has been described in this work as public attitude integrity. It is less clear which variation Mason CJ, Deane and Dawson JJ would prefer, or whether indeed they would wish to box themselves in at all in that respect. For completeness, it should be added that Toohey J seemed, by contrast, to base the *Bunning* v. *Cross* discretion upon the disciplinary principle,[250] while it is not easy to discern from the judgements of Brennan J and Gaurdron J support for any particular organizing principle. The new provisions of the two Evidence Acts of 1995, the Commonwealth one and the New South Wales one, could hardly be less forthcoming. Section 138(1) of each refers to a weighing of the 'desirability' of admitting the evidence against the 'undesirability' of doing so.

Scope of the Discretion

We should note two general points about the scope of the *Bunning* v. *Cross* discretion. A majority of the High Court in *Ridgeway*[251] held that it applied to allow exclusion of evidence of the accused's guilt either of the whole crime or some element of it, in a case where the actual commission of that crime was brought about by unlawful police conduct. In other words, it was unnecessary that the evidence in question was obtained *by* unlawful conduct. On the facts of *Ridgeway*, the conduct in question had been the unlawful importation of heroin into Australia. It had been handed over to the accused in a motel room, then

245 See, also, the identical provisions of ss. 90 and 138 of the Evidence Act (NSW) 1995.

246 (1995) 129 ALR 41. 247 *Ibid.* 48. 248 *Ibid.* 89.

249 For discussion of the three variations, see Ch. 2, text to nn. 77–81 above.

250 See (1995) 129 ALR 41, at 68.

251 Gaudron and McHugh JJ dissented on the point.

lawfully seized when he was arrested. The effect of the majority view was that all evidence tending to show that the heroin had been unlawfully imported should have been suppressed at trial. Since the prosecution would then have been unable to show the accused to have had such heroin in his possession, his conviction had to be quashed. The actual result, therefore, was no different from that which would have been brought about by a stay of the action for abuse of the process of the court, and, indeed, the minority judges, Gaudron and McHugh JJ preferred an analysis directly in terms of abuse of process. Though the actual result, on the facts of *Ridgeway*, would be the same under section 138 of the Evidence Act (Commonwealth) 1995, that section does seem to alter the law as stated in that case. The discretion is available only where the evidence was obtained improperly or unlawfully or where obtained in consequence of improper or unlawful conduct. The *Ridgeway* evidence was certainly not obtained unlawfully but was surely obtained in consequence of the unlawful importation of the heroin. The focus of the majority in *Ridgeway* itself is different, for it is the way in which the commission of the crime was brought about, and not whether the unlawful actions had as a consequence the obtaining of evidence, which matters.

A second point is that there are *dicta* of Mason CJ, Deane and Dawson JJ which indicate that the discretion extends to cases involving official conduct that is not unlawful but merely improper. In effect, they saw this as a way of reconciling the references in *Ireland* to unfairness with the predominance given to unlawfulness in *Bunning* v. *Cross*. For them, the words 'improper' and 'impropriety' were preferable to 'unfair' and 'unfairness'. There is a considerable amount of support in the earlier cases for the notion that *Bunning* v. *Cross* applies to mere improprieties.[252] Mason CJ, Deane and Dawson JJ were anxious, however, to confine narrowly the idea of impropriety short of unlawfulness. Though eschewing description of a precise borderline, they did say that:[253]

> the stage of impropriety will be reached in the case of conduct which is not illegal only in cases involving a degree of harassment or manipulation which is clearly inconsistent with minimum standards of acceptable police conduct in all the circumstances, including, amongst other things, the nature and extent of any known or suspected existing or threatened criminal activity, the basis and justification of any suspicion, the difficulty of effective investigation or prevention and any imminent danger to the community.

We have already noted that section 138(1) of the Evidence Act (Commonwealth) 1995[254] makes provision for the discretion to be available in cases of impropriety as well as unlawfulness. It seems reasonable to suppose that when Australian courts come to interpret that subsection the above *dicta* in *Ridgeway* will prove to be of great importance.

[252] See, e.g., *Cleland* (1982) 151 CLR 1, at 5 (*per* Gibbs CJ), at 16 (*per* Murphy J), at 19–20 (*per* Deane J), and at 27, 34 (*per* Dawson J); *Duke* (1988) 83 ALR 650, at 653 (*per* Brennan J); *Pollard* (1992) 176 CLR 177, at 196 (*per* Brennan, Dawson, and Gaudron JJ); *Foster* (1993) 113 ALR 1, at 21 (*per* McHugh J).

[253] (1995) 129 ALR 41, at 53.

[254] As does the Evidence Act (NSW) 1995, s. 138(1).

It is instructive to consider how the English case of *Williams* v. *DPP*[255] might have fared under the *Ridgeway* view of impropriety. With no particular individual or individuals in mind, the police had left an insecure and unattended van in a busy city centre street. Inside it were cartons which appeared to contain packets of cigarettes but which were, in fact, dummies. A partly-opened shutter at the back of the van made the cartons visible to passing members of the public. Williams and his co-accused, O'Hare, were tempted by what they saw and removed various cartons. They were then arrested by officers who had been observing the van throughout. The Divisional Court held that the magistrates had been right not to exclude evidence of the actions of the accused. It may well be that the police conduct was improper in the *Ridgeway* sense. There was no existing or threatened criminal activity—in a very real sense, the police 'created' the relevant crimes. When referring to the difficulty of effective investigation or prevention, the members of the High Court probably had in mind 'victimless' crimes, a category into which the crimes in *Williams* did not, of course, fall. One may suppose that there was nothing more in the minds of the relevant officers than that crimes are, in general, hard to clear up. Plainly, there was no danger, imminent or otherwise, to the public. On the other hand, neither accused was harassed, though they were, perhaps, manipulated. Of course, were it to be concluded that the conduct, which was part of a Metropolitan Police initiative called 'Operation Rover', was improper, it would not necessarily follow that the evidence ought to be excluded, for the *Bunning* v. *Cross* balancing would still have to be carried out.

Presumptions and Onuses

Though there is authority in the High Court both for the view that, once unlawfulness (or impropriety) is shown, the presumption is in favour of exclusion[256] and for the view that the onus is on the accused to persuade the judge to reject the evidence,[257] it is probable that the correct view is that *Bunning* v. *Cross* entails no presumption or onus either way; the two elements are to be weighed against each other in all the various circumstances of the particular case. In contrast, under the new statutory law of the Commonwealth and of New South Wales, albeit that the relevant heading refers to a *discretion* to exclude, the statutory words themselves say that the evidence 'is not to be admitted unless the desirability of admitting the evidence outweighs the undesirability of admitting [it]'.[258] However, the burden placed upon the prosecution would not seem to be an onerous one, for it is, presumably, only where the weight present in the two sides of the scales is believed to be exactly in balance that the placing of that burden will be decisive. In this respect, the statutory scheme contrasts significantly with that recommended by the Law Reform Commission of Australia for adoption by the Commonwealth. Its report stated that:[259]

[255] [1993] 3 All ER 365. The case is briefly discussed at Ch. 7, text to nn. 232 and 245 above.

[256] See *Cleland* (1982) 151 CLR 1, at 16–17 (*per* Murphy J).

[257] See *ibid*. 20 (*per* Deane J).

[258] See Evidence Act (Commonwealth) 1995 and Evidence Act (NSW) 1995, both s. 138(1).

[259] *Criminal Investigation: Report No 2, An Interim Report* (1975), para. 298 (emphasis in original).

evidence obtained in contravention or in consequence of any contravention of any statutory or common law rule . . . should not be admissible . . . *unless* the court decides, in the exercise of its discretion, that the admission of such evidence would specifically and substantially benefit the public interest without unduly derogating from the rights and liberties of any individual.

Factors or Matters Governing the Discretion

So how is the judge to decide on which side the scales come down? In *Bunning* v. *Cross* itself, Stephen and Aickin JJ offered five factors which, they believed, ought to inform that decision.[260] The two Evidence Acts of 1995, in their sections 138(3), provide that there are eight matters which the court *is to* take into account,[261] but without limiting those which it *may* take into account. Four of these matters are broadly equivalent to the *Bunning* v. *Cross* factors.

Matter (e) in the statutory list is 'whether the impropriety or contravention was deliberate or reckless'. This was also a *Bunning* v. *Cross* factor. It is to be noted that it is the deliberate or reckless character of the breach itself, rather than of the acts constituting the breach, which is significant. In this respect, the Australian position contrasts with that for constitutional breaches in Ireland. It seem clear that any version of the judicial integrity principle would find a deliberate or reckless disregard more objectionable, *ceteris paribus*, than a negligent, mistaken, or innocent one.

Matter (a) is the probative value (or cogency) of the evidence. If, as has been argued earlier,[262] the chance fact that cogent evidence is obtained through the unlawfulness or impropriety can have no moral significance, it does seem that the version of judicial integrity embraced by the statute, as indeed by *Bunning* v. *Cross*, which also treated cogency as a significant factor, must be either the public attitude or public conduct one. There is a further point about probative value or cogency which emerges from *Bunning* v. *Cross*. Stephen and Aickin JJ said that cogency should not, in general, be a factor favouring admission where the breach was intentional or reckless, because, were it such a positive factor, it would 'serve to foster the quite erroneous view that if such evidence be but damning enough that will of itself suffice to atone for the illegality involved in procuring it'.[263] This seems, with respect, an excellent point, and it may be that Australian courts will feel able to cater for it in making decisions under the two statutes. It is worth adding that Stephen and Aickin JJ went on to suggest that there might be exceptional circumstances in which cogency might properly be taken into account, as where the evidence is both vital to the conviction *and* may be lost, because of its perishable or evanescent nature, unless immediately seized.[264]

[260] See (1978) 141 CLR 54, at 78–80.

[261] The reader may find it helpful to refer back to the general discussion of these issues in Ch. 2, text to nn. 100–11 above.

[262] See Ch. 2, text to nn. 100 above. [263] (1978) 141 CLR 54, at 79.

[264] It will be recalled that this is a matter taken into account in Scotland—see text to nn. 209–13 above.

This leads us naturally to matter (b), the importance of the evidence in the proceedings. In a sense, this might be thought to be logically comprehended by matter (a), referring, as it does, to probative value. Though the cogency of evidence is a given feature, its probative *value* may be thought to turn also on how much work it has to do, i.e. on what other evidence, if any, is available to prove the same fact or facts. Once again, on either forward-looking version of the judicial integrity principle, whether based upon the predicted effect on public conduct of, or the predicted public reaction to, admission or exclusion, this does appear to be a factor which logically favours admission. No direct reference was made in *Bunning* v. *Cross* to this factor, though, as we have just seen, it was made a necessary element of the 'perishable evidence' exception.

Matter (c) is rather more controversial. It refers to 'the nature of the relevant offence, cause of action or defence and the nature of the subject-matter of the proceeding'. The last clause presumably allows for the fact that the availability of the statutory discretion is *not* confined to criminal proceedings. However, the rest of the paragraph is clearly intended to embrace, *inter alia*, the seriousness, in a criminal case, of the offence with which the accused stands charged. Though it is not stated in what way the nature of the offence is significant, it may be assumed that it is intended that, as the seriousness of the offence increases, so does the strength of the case against exclusion. This was certainly how seriousness was regarded in *Bunning* v. *Cross*. However, proper attention to the principle behind exclusion again shows things to be rather more complex, at least as a matter of logic. First, though it is certainly more important, in public policy terms, to bring the wrongdoer to justice where the offence is murder than where it is theft, it is to be remembered that the rule which has been breached may itself have been designed to promote the reliability of evidence, so the very fact that it has been breached may make us less confident that the accused actually is a wrongdoer. The stakes get higher for the accused, no less than for the general public, arguably more so, as the gravity of the alleged offence increases. Secondly, if we assume that either public conduct or public attitude integrity is the governing principle, it may well be that one factor of significance to the predicted public reaction will be an expectation that the more serious are the consequences of conviction for the accused, the more punctilious should be the authorities in observing the various rights and privileges granted by law to the suspect. As has been suggested earlier, much may turn on which prism public reaction is viewed through.[265] For example, where there is a moral panic about a particular kind of offence, say child sexual abuse, the public in general may see nothing objectionable about throwing away the rule-book altogether.

Matter (d) is the gravity of the impropriety or contravention. Stephen and Aickin JJ did not take this as a factor significant on its own, but they did refer to the need to see it as a counterweight to the seriousness of the offence, and so as telling in favour of exclusion. In addition, their acknowledgement of the signifi-

[265] See Ch. 2, text to nn. 110–11 above.

cance of the intentional or reckless nature of the unlawful act or impropriety would seem to carry with it an implication that the seriousness of the breach is also significant. Certainly, any version of the judicial integrity principle must regard the relative gravity of the wrong as a factor favouring exclusion. It may be added that matter (f) imports a specific reference to the significance of the impropriety or contravention being contrary to or inconsistent with a right of the person recognised by the International Covenant on Civil and Political Rights.

Matter (g) is one not mentioned in *Bunning* v. *Cross*. Account is to be taken of 'whether any other proceeding (whether or not in a court) has been or is likely to be taken in relation to the impropriety or contravention'. This would seem to be a factor properly telling in favour of admission whichever principle, the reliability one apart, be regarded as governing. If some other remedy is in prospect, there is less of a call for remedial protection. Other remedies may be expected to deter future police misconduct. Judicial integrity, in whatever guise, must find a degree of solace in the fact that something has been or will be done about the breach.

Matter (h) is one which did emerge in *Bunning* v. *Cross*. The court is to have regard to 'the difficulty (if any) of obtaining the evidence without impropriety or contravention of an Australian law'. Stephen and Aickin JJ referred to the easiness—not the difficulty—of complying with the law. For them, a deliberate 'cutting of corners' would tell in favour of exclusion, though where breach was brought about by an understandable mistake, ease of compliance would be wholly equivocal in its impact. One is inclined to suppose that matter (h) is intended to push in the opposite direction, so that the harder it was to comply with the law, the stronger is the argument for admission of the evidence. (It is a surprising feature of the statutory 'matters' generally that there is no indication of the direction in which they point.) It is by no means obvious that this is the appropriate position, whether or not judicial integrity governs. The point was well made by Stephen and Aickin JJ, for their own fifth and final factor was 'that an examination of the legislation suggests that there was a quite deliberate intent on the part of the legislature narrowly to restrict the police in their power. . . . This last factor is, of course, one favouring rejection of the evidence'.[266] There would certainly be something strange about the condoning by the courts of police defiance of the legislative will.

Canada

Exclusion to Prevent Judicial Disrepute

Under Schedule B to the Constitution Act 1982, certain substantive rights and freedoms are laid down for Canadians in the Charter of Rights and Freedoms. Section 24(2)of the Charter states that evidence 'obtained in a manner that infringed or denied any rights or freedoms guaranteed by this Charter . . . shall be excluded if it is established that, having regard to all the circumstances, the

[266] (1978) 141 CLR 54, at 80.

admission of it in the proceedings would bring the administration of justice into disrepute'. A vast quantity of case law has already emerged in interpretation and application of that subsection. There would seem to be a considerable degree of affinity between that case law and the Australian line of authority beginning with *Bunning* v. *Cross*. For that reason, little would be gained by offering a detailed treatment of the Canandian law.[267] It will suffice here to refer to certain points of difference or difficulty.

Exclusion by Rule or by Discretion?

The words of section 24(2) may seem to indicate that there is a rule that if there is found to have been a breach of the Charter and it is established that admission of the evidence would bring the administration of justice into disrepute, the judge must exclude that evidence. Yet what is not made clear is whether a higher court is automatically to overturn the judge if it concludes, contrary to his view, that both elements are present. This is an important point, for, particularly with an open-textured test such as the judicial disrepute one, judges may, entirely reasonably, be of different opinion.

The Canadian Supreme Court has consistently averred that section 24(2) provides for a rule of exclusion, not a discretion to exclude.[268] However, there are unchallenged statements in a number of cases which grant to the trial judge a considerable degree of autonomy with regard to the issue of judicial disrepute. In the words of Lamer J in *Collins*, 'the judge will have met [the] test if the judges of the Court of Appeal will decline to interfere with his decision, even though they might have decided the matter differently, using the well-known statement that they are of the view that the decision was not unreasonable'.[269] There are similar statements in later Supreme Court cases.[270] The picture is rendered rather complicated by the fact that there is also a notion that the Supreme Court should allow a similar degree of autonomy to provincial *appellate* courts.[271] This renders it extremely difficult to know on what basis the Supreme Court is to decide whether or not to reverse the appeal court's decision to overturn the trial judge.

At all events, for reasons given by Le Dain J in *Therens*, the principle or policy of autonomy for trial judges seems to be regarded as consistent with the idea that section 24(2) imports a *rule* of exclusion:[272]

> Section 24(2) involves the application of a broad test or standard, which necessarily gives a court some latitude, but that is not, strictly speaking, a discretion. A discretion exists

[267] A helpful, recent survey is to be found in *The Canadian Charter of Rights and Freedoms* (3rd edn., 1996), edited by Beaudoin and Mendes, 19–47 to 19–59. See also *The Law of Evidence in Canada*, by Sopinka, Lederman, and Bryant (1992), 387–424.

[268] See, in particular, *Therens* [1985] 1 SCR 613, at 654 (*per* Le Dain J); *Collins* [1987] 1 SCR 265, at 275 (*per* Lamer J).

[269] [1987] 1 SCR 265, at 283.

[270] See, e.g. *Mellenthin* [1992] 3 SCR 615, at 625–6; *Borden* [1994] 3 SCR 145, at 167–8.

[271] See *Duguay* [1989] 1 SCR 93, at 98; *Greffe* [1990] 1 SCR 755, at 783; *Mellenthin* [1992] 3 SCR 615, at 625; *Borden* [1994] 3 SCR 145, at 167.

[272] [1985] 1 SCR 613, at 654.

where there is a choice to do one thing or another, not merely because what is involved is the application of a flexible standard. Under the terms of s. 24(2), where a judge concludes that the admission of evidence would bring the administration of justice into disrepute, he or she has a duty, not a discretion, to exclude the evidence.

This would seem to confuse two senses of discretion. Certainly, where, as for example in a sentencing decision, a judge is given a choice between various alternatives, that decision is discretionary and cannot be overturned simply on the basis that the appeal court would have chosen differently. However, there is another sense of discretion. It cannot be suggested that, once the judge has determined the disrepute issue, he has a choice whether or not to exclude the evidence, for it would be utterly perverse for him to say, for example, that he finds its admission *would* bring the administration of justice into disrepute, but then go on to admit it. Rather, the judge might be granted discretion in relation to his judgment whether or not disrepute would flow from admission. Then, the element of 'choice' would relate to that assessment. There is undoubtedly an important difference between an open-textured law which allows the trial judge a margin of appreciation and one which does not. It may be a matter of taste whether, where such a margin of appreciation is allowed, it is better to say that the law invokes a rule or grants a discretion.[273]

Causation

After some initial vacillation,[274] it is now settled that no strict test of causation applies to the question whether or not the evidence was 'obtained in a manner that infringed or denied' any of the guaranteed rights or freedoms. The position is as stated by a majority of the Supreme Court in *Strachan*, in a judgment delivered by Dickson CJ. Having dealt with what he described as the 'pitfalls' of causation in this area, he expressed a preference for:[275]

an approach that focuses on the entire chain of events during which the *Charter* violation occurred and the evidence was obtained. Accordingly, the first inquiry under s.24(2) would be to determine whether a *Charter* violation occurred in the course of obtaining the evidence. A temporal link between the infringement of the *Charter* and the discovery of the evidence figures prominently in this assessment, particularly where the *Charter* violation and the discovery of the evidence occur in the course of a single transaction. The presence of a temporal connection is not, however, determinative. Situations will arise where evidence, though obtained following the breach of a *Charter* right will be too remote from the violation to be 'obtained in a manner' that infringed the *Charter*. In my view, these situations should be dealt with on a case by case basis. There can be no hard and fast rule for

[273] Paciocco (1990) 32 *Crim.LQ* 326, at 350–2, expresses the view that the decision is discretionary in fact, given the autonomy allowed to the trial judge.

[274] See the judgments of, respectively, Lamer J and Le Dain J in *Therens* [1985] 1 SCR 613.

[275] [1988] 2 SCR 980, at 1005–6. Only a few months earlier in *Upston* [1988] 1 SCR 1083, a unanimous Supreme Court had appeared to endorse the view that there is a strict requirement of causation. For a detailed discussion of the issue, see Donovan (1991) 49 *UTFac.L Rev*. 233. See also Paciocco, n. 273 above, 345–50.

determining when evidence obtained following the infringement of a *Charter* right becomes too remote.

The statement is undoubtedly authoritative, for it has been applied in later Supreme Court cases.[276] Furthermore, it is now established that existence of a causal link is no more sufficient than it is necessary.[277] However, it is to be noted that Dickson CJ went on to say that the presence or absence of a causal link will be a factor to be taken into consideration when deciding whether admission of the evidence would bring the administration of justice into disrepute.[278]

It should be apparent that the Supreme Court's position on causation is inconsistent with a commitment to the protective principle, for the accused who was caused no detriment by the constitutional breach has no need of the remedy of exclusion, while the one who was caused detriment has a powerful call for that remedy. By contrast, it is entirely consistent with the disciplinary principle, for, as has been argued earlier, all that that principle requires is that the breach be *capable* of causing detriment.[279] The *Strachan* decision fits in equally well with the judicial integrity principle, in whichever guise. So far as it may be a matter of moral imperative in its court-centred form, it seems right that a sufficiently serious flouting of the law, even without the establishment of a strict causal connection to the obtaining of the evidence, should enable the court to exclude that evidence. Yet the moral call might be thought to grow weaker as the breach becomes more remote from the obtaining. As regards both the public conduct and public attitude forms of the principle, we may suppose that the public response in either respect would take account of causation, but not as a necessary element.

The Test of Judicial Disrepute

It quickly became apparent that a crucial issue for the Canadian courts was the criterion by which the disrepute of the administration of justice was to be evaluated. It could, at least, be said that section 24(2) is not concerned with the predicted effect upon the conduct of the general public, for the repute or disrepute in which the justice system is held is clearly a matter of attitude. But *whose* attitude should matter? Gibson suggested, at a very early stage, that it should be that of the general public itself which should be decisive, and that it should be assessed by reference to opinion polls.[280] Morisette, on the other hand, while not looking explicitly at the judge himself, formulated a test which tended to rule out the most uninformed and narrow-minded views of the general public.[281] His proposed test

[276] See, e.g., *Black* [1989] 2 SCR 138, at 162–3; *Bartle* [1994] 3 SCR 173, at 208–9.

[277] See *Goldhart* [1996] 2 SCR 463. *NB* La Forest J's spirited dissent.

[278] See [1988] 2 SCR 980, at 1006. See also *Bartle* [1994] 3 SCR 173, at 209.

[279] See Ch. 2, text to n. 64 above.

[280] See (1983) 61 CBR 377.

[281] It is not at all clear how far judicial and general public opinion depart from each other in this respect—see the contrasting conclusions of two separate surveys by Bryant, Gold, Stevenson, and Northrup (1990) 69 CBR 1, at 45, and (1990) 1 *SCLR (2d.)* 555, at 557.

was '[w]ould the admission of the evidence bring the administration of justice into disrepute in the eyes of a reasonable man, dispassionate and fully apprised of the circumstances of the case?'[282] It was this test which the Supreme Court endorsed in *Collins*,[283] but in a way which locates it uneasily between lay and judicial opinion. Morisette himself regarded his reasonable man test as a benevolent fiction, for he referred to the need for judges to find within themselves a basis for their own decisions and stated that judges 'are, in reality, the reasonable man'.[284] It is less clear precisely what the Supreme Court intended. Lamer J, while referring to the need for judges to find within themselves a basis for their decisions, pointedly made no mention of the claim that the judge is the reasonable man. His own words were:[285]

> It serves as a reminder to each individual judge that his discretion is grounded in community values, and, in particular, long term community values. He should not render a decision that would be unacceptable to the community when that community is not being wrought with passion or otherwise under passing stress due to current events.

This would seem to be a reminder to judges not to rely upon unduly narrow, self-indulgent attitudes, but, rather, to have regard to sound and settled public opinion, in reaching *his own* view of judicial disrepute.[286] However, more recently, in *Burlingham*,[287] Sopinka J appears to move the test back towards the reasonable man. While reiterating Lamer J's point that the judge must beware of pandering to short-term passions and stresses (panics perhaps?), he went on to add, '[t]hese long-term community values are to be assessed in terms of the views of the hypothetical, reasonable, well-informed and dispassionate person in the community'.[288] It seems plain that Canadian judges have succumbed to the temptation to steer a middle course between their own moral scruple and public opinion. This is, no doubt, understandable. Nonetheless, it would seem strange to regard the disrepute in which the administration of justice would be held as properly to be assessed by those who themselves administer it; one's reputation is a reflection of what others think of one. Yet if that is right, it is not obvious why, as a matter of principle, any constraints upon public opinion are properly to be set. The only appropriate constraints would be those resulting from the practical difficulty of deciding how the public—as though it could be regarded in this monolithic way[289]—really would respond. Thus, if, for example, Canadian citizens think that only lily-livered judges would exclude evidence against an alleged murderer or child molester, no matter how gross the constitutional breaches leading to its acquisition, they will almost certainly think more, not less, of the justice system should the particular trial judge decide to admit it. Once this particular genie is

[282] See (1984) 29 *McGill LJ* 521, at 538.
[283] [1987] 1 SCR 265, at 282. [284] See n. 282 above, 538.
[285] [1987] 1 SCR 265, at 282–3.
[286] For a powerful attack on the *Collins* position, see Paciocco, n. 273 above, 340–5.
[287] [1995] 2 SCR 206. [288] *Ibid*. 289.
[289] See Bryant, Gold, Stevenson, and Northrup (1990) 1 *SCLR (2d.)* 555, at 587.

let out of the bottle, it has the potential for rendering nugatory all rights of the suspect, whether they be granted by a constitution or by ordinary law. Quite clearly, Canadian judges are fully aware of the danger. However, the deeper lesson may be that there is not much to be said for that version of the judicial integrity principle which looks to predicted public reaction to the admission or exclusion of evidence.

Index

Lightning Source UK Ltd.
Milton Keynes UK
173928UK00006B/4/A

9 780198 262695